From the Enlightenment to Modernism
Three Centuries of German Literature

Essays for Ritchie Robertson

LEGENDA

LEGENDA is the Modern Humanities Research Association's book imprint for new research in the Humanities. Founded in 1995 by Malcolm Bowie and others within the University of Oxford, Legenda has always been a collaborative publishing enterprise, directly governed by scholars. The Modern Humanities Research Association (MHRA) joined this collaboration in 1998, became half-owner in 2004, in partnership with Maney Publishing and then Routledge, and has since 2016 been sole owner. Titles range from medieval texts to contemporary cinema and form a widely comparative view of the modern humanities, including works on Arabic, Catalan, English, French, German, Greek, Italian, Portuguese, Russian, Spanish, and Yiddish literature. Editorial boards and committees of more than 60 leading academic specialists work in collaboration with bodies such as the Society for French Studies, the British Comparative Literature Association and the Association of Hispanists of Great Britain & Ireland.

The MHRA encourages and promotes advanced study and research in the field of the modern humanities, especially modern European languages and literature, including English, and also cinema. It aims to break down the barriers between scholars working in different disciplines and to maintain the unity of humanistic scholarship. The Association fulfils this purpose through the publication of journals, bibliographies, monographs, critical editions, and the MHRA Style Guide, and by making grants in support of research. Membership is open to all who work in the Humanities, whether independent or in a University post, and the participation of younger colleagues entering the field is especially welcomed.

ALSO PUBLISHED BY THE ASSOCIATION

Critical Texts
Tudor and Stuart Translations • *New Translations* • *European Translations*
MHRA Library of Medieval Welsh Literature

MHRA Bibliographies
Publications of the Modern Humanities Research Association

The Annual Bibliography of English Language & Literature
Austrian Studies
Modern Language Review
Portuguese Studies
The Slavonic and East European Review
Working Papers in the Humanities
The Yearbook of English Studies

www.mhra.org.uk
www.legendabooks.com

EDITORIAL BOARD

Chair: Professor Jonathan Long (University of Durham)
For *Germanic Literatures*: Ritchie Robertson (University of Oxford)
For *Italian Perspectives*: Simon Gilson (University of Warwick)
For *Moving Image*: Emma Wilson (University of Cambridge)
For *Research Monographs in French Studies*:
Diana Knight (University of Nottingham)
For *Selected Essays*: Susan Harrow (University of Bristol)
For *Studies in Comparative Literature*:
Dr Emily Finer, University of St Andrews, and
Professor Wen-chin Ouyang, SOAS, London
For *Studies in Hispanic and Lusophone Cultures*:
Catherine Davies (Institute of Modern Languages Research)
For *Studies in Yiddish*: Gennady Estraikh (New York University)
For *Transcript*: Matthew Reynolds (University of Oxford)
For *Visual Culture*: Carolin Duttlinger (University of Oxford)

Managing Editor
Dr Graham Nelson
41 Wellington Square, Oxford OX1 2JF, UK

www.legendabooks.com

Ritchie Robertson,
photographed by Rajaroy Joseph Alphonse, Pixroy

From the Enlightenment to Modernism

Three Centuries of German Literature

Essays for Ritchie Robertson

EDITED BY CAROLIN DUTTLINGER,
KEVIN HILLIARD, AND CHARLIE LOUTH

LEGENDA

Modern Humanities Research Association
2021

Published by Legenda
an imprint of the Modern Humanities Research Association
Salisbury House, Station Road, Cambridge CB1 2LA

ISBN 978-1-78188-866-7 (HB)
ISBN 978-1-78188-870-4 (PB)

First published 2021

All rights reserved. No part of this publication may be reproduced or disseminated or transmitted in any form or by any means, electronic, mechanical, photocopying, recording or otherwise, or stored in any retrieval system, or otherwise used in any manner whatsoever without written permission of the copyright owner, except in accordance with the provisions of the Copyright, Designs and Patents Act 1988, or under the terms of a licence permitting restricted copying issued in the UK by the Copyright Licensing Agency Ltd, Saffron House, 6–10 Kirby Street, London EC1N 8TS, England, or in the USA by the Copyright Clearance Center, 222 Rosewood Drive, Danvers MA 01923. Application for the written permission of the copyright owner to reproduce any part of this publication must be made by email to legenda@mhra.org.uk.

Disclaimer: Statements of fact and opinion contained in this book are those of the author and not of the editors or the Modern Humanities Research Association. The publisher makes no representation, express or implied, in respect of the accuracy of the material in this book and cannot accept any legal responsibility or liability for any errors or omissions that may be made.

Trademark notice: Product or corporate names may be trademarks or registered trademarks, and are used only for identification and explanation without intent to infringe.

© Modern Humanities Research Association 2021

Copy-Editor: Dr Nigel Hope

CONTENTS

	The Authors	ix
	Introduction	1
1	'Gymnastik des Geistes': Lessing und die Aufklärung als Lebensform LAURA ANNA MACOR	7
2	'[D]er eifrigste [...] Aufklärer [...] in Trier': A Case Study in the Late Enlightenment in Germany KEVIN HILLIARD	23
3	Goethe's Problems Composing *Faust I*: A Conspectus T. J. REED	42
4	Werther's Patriotic Afterlives: The Imaginary of Self-Sacrifice in Works by Ugo Foscolo, Yu Dafu and Jiang Guangci JOHANNES D. KAMINSKI	52
5	Perpetual Incipience: Goethe and the Search for a Transcendental *Mittelpunkt* BEN HUTCHINSON	68
6	'nicht sehr in den kirchlichen Formen': Liberale Literatur und Katholizismus in Österreich nach 1848 WERNER MICHLER	86
7	Forgetting Virgil with Freud, Lear and James: A Hermeneutics of Concern and Co-creation BEN MORGAN	104
8	Body Politics in Arthur Schnitzler's *Professor Bernhardi* JUDITH BENISTON	120
9	'Glocalism': Local and Global in Richard Beer-Hofmann's *Der Tod Georgs* LEENA EILITTÄ	136
10	Churchill versus Bermann — Memory Politics and the Mahdi Uprising: Arnold Höllriegel's *Die Derwischtrommel/The Mahdi of Allah* FLORIAN KROBB	151
11	The Emancipated Woman on the Margins of German Modernism CHARLOTTE WOODFORD	166
12	Bloch, Benjamin, Brecht and *Bilderrätsel*: Reading the Signs in Weimar ANTHONY PHELAN	181

13	The Romantic Affiliations of Benjamin's 'Die Aufgabe des Übersetzers' CHARLIE LOUTH	198
14	*Verantwortung*: Paradoxes of Responsibility in Kafka's *Landarzt* Collection and Beyond CAROLIN DUTTLINGER	214
15	Quixotic Doubles: Kafka reads Cervantes BARRY MURNANE	229
16	Uncertainty, Realism and the Self in Kafka JENNIFER ANNA GOSETTI-FERENCEI	245
17	Kafka and his Recursors: The Process of Post-Holocaust Authors KIRSTIN GWYER	262
18	Stefan Zweig's Translations of French Poetry ROBERT VILAIN	279
19	Stefan Zweig und Frankreich: Sein 'drittes Leben' im Exil 1933–1942 JACQUES LE RIDER	296
20	'Auf der Flucht': The Motif of Flight in the Works of Bertolt Brecht TOM KUHN	311
21	The Impossibility of Homosexual Exile: Klaus Mann's *Der Vulkan* PETER MORGAN	319
22	Exile and Reality in Erich Auerbach's *Mimesis* STEFFAN DAVIES	333
23	'A second life': Shakespeare-Übersetzungen in der Gegenwartsliteratur KAREN LEEDER	348
	Index	363

THE AUTHORS

Judith Beniston is Associate Professor in German at University College London. She has written articles on numerous aspects of Austria's theatre culture, focusing especially on the period 1890–1945. From 2003 to 2010, she co-edited the annual journal *Austrian Studies* with Robert Vilain and has guest-edited *Cultures at War: Austria-Hungary, 1914–1918* (2013) with Deborah Holmes and *Placing Schnitzler* (2019) with Andrew Webber. She is one of the editors of *Arthur Schnitzler digital: Digitale historisch-kritische Edition (Werke 1905–1931)* and within this project is lead editor for Schnitzler's medical drama *Professor Bernhardi* (1912).

Steffan Davies is a Senior Lecturer in German at the University of Bristol. He read for a BA in History and German and an MSt in European Literatures at St John's College, Oxford, where he was a pupil of Ritchie Robertson's. His DPhil thesis, on the literary and historiographical reception of Schiller's *Wallenstein*, was published in the MHRA's Bithell Series of Dissertations in 2010. Research on the later work of Alfred Döblin, especially Döblin's last novel, *Hamlet oder Die lange Nacht nimmt ein Ende*, has led him to a new project on exile writing in the 'long' nineteenth century. The book of this project, *German Exile Literature in the Age of Nations, 1790–1955*, is under contract with Camden House. He is one of the editors of *German Life and Letters*.

Carolin Duttlinger is Professor of German Literature and Culture at the University of Oxford and a Fellow of Wadham College. She is also a co-director of the Oxford Kafka Research Centre and the editor of the Visual Culture series with Legenda. Her books include: *Kafka and Photography* (2007), *The Cambridge Introduction to Franz Kafka* (2013) and *Attention and Distraction in Modern German Literature, Thought, and Culture* (2021).

Leena Eilittä is docent of comparative literature at the University of Helsinki. She has also guest lectured at the universities in Germany and France. Her research focuses upon German modernism, world literature and intermediality. Her DPhil thesis on Franz Kafka was supervised by Ritchie Robertson between 1994 and 1997. Eilittä's publications include *Approaches to Personal Identity in Kafka's Short Fiction: Freud, Darwin, Kierkegaard* (1999), *Ingeborg Bachmann's Utopia and Disillusionment* (2008), three edited volumes on intermediality (2012, 2016, 2018) and several articles in scholarly journals.

Jennifer Anna Gosetti-Ferencei is Professor and Kurrelmeyer Chair in German and Professor in Philosophy at Johns Hopkins University. Her books include: *On Being and Becoming: An Existentialist Approach to Life* (2020); *The Life of Imagination: Revealing and Making the World* (2019); *Exotic Spaces in German Modernism* (2011);

The Ecstatic Quotidian: Phenomenological Sightings in Modern Art and Literature (2007); *Heidegger, Hölderlin, and the Subject of Poetic Language* (2004); and a book of poetry, *After the Palace Burns* (2003), which won the Paris Review Prize.

Kirstin Gwyer is Lecturer in German for Exeter, Jesus and St John's Colleges, Oxford. She is the author of *Encrypting the Past: The German-Jewish Holocaust Novel of the First Generation* (2014) and has also published on H. G. Adler, Günter Grass and W. G. Sebald, on recent Jewish literature, and on the German family novel. She is currently working on contemporary Jewish post-Holocaust literature in its intersections with postcolonial and transnational studies, post-terrorism studies, and dementia studies.

Kevin Hilliard is an Emeritus Fellow of St Peter's College, Oxford. He has held posts at Merton College, Oxford (1978–81), the University of Durham (1981–95) and the University of Oxford (1995–2017). His publications mainly cover German literature of the eighteenth century, including *Freethinkers, Libertines and 'Schwärmer': Heterodoxy in German Literature 1750–1800* (2011).

Ben Hutchinson is Professor of European Literature at the University of Kent. The author of six monographs — including, most recently, *Lateness and Modern European Literature* (2016), *Comparative Literature: A Very Short Introduction* (2018), and *The Midlife Mind* (2020) — he is a Fellow of the *Academia Europæa*, a Philip Leverhulme Prize winner, and Honorary Secretary of the *British Comparative Literature Association*. He is a regular contributor to numerous newspapers and magazines including the *Times Literary Supplement*.

Johannes D. Kaminski received his DPhil in German Studies at the University of Oxford in 2011 with a thesis supervised by Ritchie Robertson. He was a British Academy Postdoctoral Fellow at the University of Cambridge (2012–15) and a Postdoctoral Fellow at the Academia Sinica (2015–17) in Taipei, Taiwan. From 2018 to 2020 he held a Marie Curie Fellowship at the University of Vienna. He is currently based at the Institute of World Literature, Slovak Academy of Sciences. Recent articles include 'The Neo-Frontier in Contemporary Preparedness Novels' (*Journal of American Studies*, 55.1, 2020) and 'Leaving Gaia Behind: The Ethics of Space Migration in Cixin Liu's and Neil Stephenson's Science Fiction' (*World Literature Studies*, 13.2, 2021).

Florian Krobb is Professor Emeritus of German in the School of Modern Languages Literatures and Cultures at National University of Ireland Maynooth and Extraordinary Professor at the University of Stellenbosch, South Africa.

Tom Kuhn teaches German language and literature at the University of Oxford, where he is a Fellow of St Hugh's College. With David Constantine he is the editor and translator of *The Collected Poems of Bertolt Brecht* (2018). He is also the series editor of the principal English-language edition of Brecht's plays and other writings, with Bloomsbury Methuen Drama, and has numerous publications on Brecht and twentieth-century drama and exile literature, including *Brecht on Theatre* (2015), *Brecht on Art and Politics* (2015) and *Brecht and the Writer's Workshop: 'Fatzer' and Other Dramatic Projects* (2019).

Karen Leeder is a writer, translator and academic, and is Professor of Modern German Literature at New College, Oxford where she works especially on modern and contemporary poetry, GDR literature, angels and ghosts, and runs the project Mediating Modern Poetry. *The Fifth Dimension*, her essays on contemporary poetry, will appear next year. She is also a prize-winning translator of modern German literature into English, most recently: Durs Grünbein, *Porcelain: Poem on the Downfall of my City* (2020).

Jacques Le Rider is Professor (Directeur d'études) at the École Pratique des Hautes Études (Paris), Section des sciences historiques et philologiques. Recent book publications include: *Les Juifs viennois à la Belle Époque* (2013), *La Censure à l'œuvre: Freud, Kraus, Schnitzler* (2015), and *Karl Kraus: Phare et brûlot de la modernité viennoise* (2018).

Charlie Louth is Fellow of The Queen's College, University of Oxford, where he lectures in German. He is the author of *Rilke: The Life of the Work* (2020) and of *Hölderlin and the Dynamics of Translation* (1998), plus many articles on poetry from Goethe to Celan and Philippe Jaccottet. He is the co-editor of *'Eine Schwester Kafkas?' Nelly Sachs in Kontext* (2014, with Florian Strob), *A C. H. Sisson Reader* (2014, with Patrick McGuinness) and *Gravity and Grace* (2019, also with Patrick McGuinness). He has published translations of Hölderlin's *Essays and Letters* (Penguin, 2009, with Jeremy Adler) and of Rilke's *Letters to a Young Poet* and *Letter from the Young Worker* (2011), and is coming to the end of a complete edition of Hölderlin's letters in English.

Laura Anna Macor is Associate Professor of History of Philosophy at the University of Verona. She was educated at the Scuola Normale Superiore, the University of Pisa and the University of Padua. Over the years, she has carried out her research activity not only in Italy, but also in Germany and the UK, most notably at the KU Eichstätt-Ingolstadt, the Herzog August Bibliothek Wolfenbüttel and the University of Oxford. She is interested in the German Enlightenment and early Idealism, which she deals with from an interdisciplinary perspective open particularly to literature, theology and the history of language. She is the author of four scholarly monographs, including *Die Bestimmung des Menschen (1748–1800): Eine Begriffsgeschichte* (2013).

Werner Michler is Professor of Modern German Literature at the University of Salzburg (2013–present). Born in 1967 in Vienna, Austria, he studied German Philology and Philosophy at the University of Vienna, Dr. phil. 1997, habilitation 2012. Teaching and research at the universities of Vienna, Oxford, Münster, Berlin. President of the Austrian Society for German Studies (ÖGG), 1997–2020. His research areas are: history and theory of literary genres, German and Austrian Literature from the eighteenth to the twentieth century, literature and science, history and theory of translation, literary education. His publications include: *Darwinismus und Literatur: Naturwissenschaftliche und literarische Intelligenz in Österreich, 1859–1914* (1999); *Kulturen der Gattung: Poetik im Kontext, 1750–1950* (2015); *Gattungstheorie* (co-edited) (2020).

Ben Morgan is Fellow and Tutor in German at Worcester College, Associate Professor of German, and Co-Convenor of the Oxford Comparative Criticism and Translation Programme at the University of Oxford. In 2019, and 2020/21 he was also Visiting Associate Professor of German at Harvard University. He is author of *On Becoming God: Late Medieval Mysticism and the Modern Western Self* (2013), and numerous articles on modernist literature, film and philosophy in the German speaking world (Trakl, Kafka and Kierkegaard, Benjamin and Heidegger, Fritz Lang, Leni Riefenstahl, the Frankfurt School). He edited, with Carolin Duttlinger and Anthony Phelan, *Walter Benjamins Anthropologisches Denken* (2012), and with Sowon Park and Ellen Spolsky a Special Issue of *Poetics Today* on 'Situated Cognition and the Study of Culture' (2017).

Peter Morgan is Director of the European Studies Program at the University of Sydney. Recent book publications include: *Ismail Kadare: The Writer and the Dictatorship 1957–1990* and *Text, Translation, Transnationalism*. His most recent articles have appeared in *German Life and Letters, The Modern Language Review, Journal of European Studies, Thesis 11, New Left Review, AJS Review*.

Barry Murnane is Associate Professor in German at the University of Oxford, and Fellow and Tutor at St John's College. He is the author of a monograph on Kafka, *Verkehr mit Gespenstern: Gothic und Moderne bei Franz Kafka* (2008), and has published widely on Anglo-German cultural relations in the eighteenth and nineteenth centuries, including two co-edited volumes with Andrew Cusack, *Populäre Erscheinungen* (2011) and *Popular Revenants* (2012). Recently he has become increasingly interested in praxeological approaches to understanding the history of *Germanistik* in the period, including most recently co-publishing the edited volume *Literaturkritik nach 1700* (2019) and a special issue of *Publications of the English Goethe Society* on the material history of *Weltliteratur, Literature in the World* (90.1, 2021).

Anthony Phelan is Emeritus Fellow of Keble College, Oxford, where he became German tutor after many years teaching at the University of Warwick. With book publications on Heine, on Rilke, and on the intellectuals of the Weimar Republic, he has also published on Brecht, Benjamin, and their friendship, as well as on major figures of the Classic and Romantic canon.

T. J. (Jim) Reed (b. 1937) was Taylor Professor of German, University of Oxford (1988–2004) and Tutor in German at St John's College, Oxford (1963–88). He was elected a Fellow of the British Academy in 1987 and became Schiller Professor at the University of Jena in 1999. He was awarded the Gold Medal of the Goethe Gesellschaft in 1999 and the Humboldt Foundation research prize in 2001. In 2010 he received an honorary doctorate from the University of Freiburg. He has published many works on Thomas Mann, Goethe, Schiller, Heine, and the Enlightenment.

Robert Vilain is Fellow and Senior Tutor of St Hugh's College, Oxford, and Lecturer in German at Christ Church. He has published widely on German, French and Comparative Literature in the nineteenth and twentieth centuries, with a particular focus on poetry, Franco-German literary relations, Austrian literature and the inter-relations of words and music in opera and song. Authors on whom he has concentrated include Hugo von Hofmannsthal, Rainer Maria Rilke, Yvan Goll, Paul Valéry and Stefan Zweig. He has co-edited the journal *Austrian Studies*, was Germanic editor for the *Modern Language Review*, and now co-edits the book series *Studies in Modern German and Austrian Literature* for Peter Lang. From 2010 until 2021 he was Professor of German and Comparative Literature at the University of Bristol.

Charlotte Woodford is Fellow in German and Director of Studies in Modern Languages at Selwyn College, Cambridge. She completed her undergraduate studies in German and her DPhil at the University of Oxford. Her main publications include *Nuns as Historians in Early Modern Germany* (2002) and *Women, Emancipation and the German Novel 1871–1910* (2014); she also co-edited *The German Bestseller in the Late Nineteenth Century* (2012) with Benedict Schofield. She is currently working on fiction by women in late realism and literary modernism.

INTRODUCTION

Ritchie Robertson is one of the finest literary scholars of his generation, and one of the most highly regarded and prolific Germanists of the English-speaking world. His work is as remarkable for its range as for its depth. To cast an eye down his list of publications is an education in itself. It reveals a daunting and inspiring diversity of authors and topics. To cover that range as a reader is challenge enough; to have covered it as a literary historian and critic is little short of miraculous.

Readers opening one of Ritchie's books or articles know that they are in good hands. He has the gift of assimilating large bodies of material and giving a clear picture of the salient points emerging from them. In the shorter pieces, a problem or facet of a period or an author's work will be presented, put into context, and illuminatingly analysed. In the books a larger terrain will be mapped and take shape in the reader's mind. It goes without saying that one comes away knowing more than one did. What is more remarkable is that often questions have been raised one hadn't even thought of asking. Either way, one is the better for the encounter.

Added to the pleasure of learning is the sheer pleasure of *reading* what Ritchie has written. To be sure, there are articles and book chapters that require a certain amount of prior knowledge. But even there, one gets no sense that he is only interested in writing scholarly pieces for other scholars. In his books in particular, his accessible, lively style appeals as much to the lay readers as to experts. He speaks in one of his books about aiming 'to share with others' the 'enjoyment' he himself 'found in reading and exploring' the works he discusses. This is a resolution that has certainly borne fruit, as his readers will confirm.

In connection with Ritchie's concern for ordinary readers, it is worth mentioning two other areas of his work that might escape notice alongside the more academic publications. He is a frequent contributor to the *Times Literary Supplement*, with articles and often extensive reviews that not only give a lucid account of the merits of the work under review, but a magisterial survey of the field to which it belongs. The other area is his work as a translator. Anyone who has attempted literary translation knows what effort is involved and what skill is required. Rising to the challenge, Ritchie has provided the English-speaking world with fresh and elegant translations of works by Karl Philipp Moritz, E. T. A. Hoffmann, Heinrich Heine, and Franz Kafka, and here, too, has put the lay reader in his debt.

In his scholarly work Ritchie Robertson has always been happy to range across linguistic boundaries. Two of his later books deserve particular mention, for this and other reasons. *Mock-Epic Poetry from Pope to Heine* (2009) is a spirited survey of an under-explored area of the literary map. It brings together works, in English,

French and German, that have commonly been treated separately, and shows that they constitute a genre with its own coherent history. Each work and author receives fresh illumination from being juxtaposed to the others. Readers who will themselves typically be coming from one or other language specialism will have the pleasure of encountering unfamiliar authors and works. (How many Germanists even have heard of Joseph Franz Ratschky's *Melchior Striegel*?) Incidentally, or perhaps by design, the book is also a refreshing antidote to a literary historiography that privileges the serious genres and generally treats the comic ones as an afterthought.

Ritchie Robertson's most recent book again displays an astonishing geographical and linguistic range, and again it is written with the lay reader as well as the scholar in mind. *The Enlightenment: The Pursuit of Happiness 1680–1790* easily holds its own in a crowded field on the subject. The history of Enlightenment has in the past often been written as a history of philosophical thought in the period. Ritchie's book does not fall into this error. It deals on an equal footing with philosophy, science, religion, schemes of political and economic improvement, and other matters. It pays as much attention, if not more, to changes in habits of feeling as it does to rational debates. A consequence of this emphasis is that literary works feature more prominently in his history than they do in many others. And again, breadth and comprehensiveness do not come at the expense of clarity. The book is a model of organization. Fourteen chapters on distinct areas of interest are further subdivided into sections, rarely more than ten pages long, that present particular aspects. The narrative sweep is maintained, while at the same time each section gives concise information about the topic, informed by scholarship, and capped by the author's own crisp and well-founded judgements.

The book as a whole is sustained by the conviction that the Enlightenment still matters, and that it deserves, not of course uncritical monumentalization, but our sympathetic engagement. The Germans speak of the 'unvollendete Aufklärung' — of an Enlightenment that has yet to be completed and has yet to fulfil its promise. Works of the calibre of Ritchie Robertson's history themselves make a significant contribution towards that end. To quote the concluding words of the Preface:

> [T]he greatest motive for studying this subject is the awareness that the Enlightenment, though distant in time, remains vitally important. In an age that seems dominated by 'fake news', widespread credulity, xenophobia and unscrupulous demagogues, it matters more intensely than ever to hold on to reliable knowledge, to be aware of our common humanity, and to pursue the possibility of human happiness.[1]

That phrase, 'reliable knowledge', as well as the wider human context in which it is placed, might serve as a good indication of what one values in Ritchie's work. You go to it knowing you will find what you really need to strengthen and further your understanding, and you come from it equipped not just with specific knowledge on the subject at hand, but with the kind of insight you can use to refine your intellectual and literary bearings in the future. A good example would be the thought he leaves us with at the end of his Introduction to *Effi Briest*: 'It is part of Fontane's achievement to find room in a realist setting for areas of emotional life that resist the realist's analysis.' That's not just a finely observed and eminently useful comment on Fontane's novel — it opens onto the whole complexity and subtlety of realism. With wonderful concision it tells you that its limits are never easy to determine, and sends you back to the texts with a keener eye not merely for the intricacy of literary works but for that of life itself. And it's done so lightly that it feels like a discovery of your own.

This enabling aspect of Ritchie's writing can also be found in abundance in his book on Heine, which as he says of another short work on the poet, by Siegbert Prawer, is 'a much richer book than its modest format suggests'. As he also writes elsewhere, 'to understand [Heine] on the most basic level you have to learn a great deal about the early nineteenth century', yet in barely one hundred pages Ritchie contrives to impart the gist of this required knowledge, take us into the heart of Heine's work, and effectively provide the reader with a complete tool-kit for getting to grips with one of the most elusive of German poets. He manages this partly through his tone. Although his knowledge is vast, he never talks down to his readers but on the contrary seems to think of them as companions on a walking-tour, who catch sight of the things he is elucidating at just the moment he comes onto them. The sense of being accompanied by a sure-footed, curious and clear-sighted guide, who is not afraid to touch on controversial subjects but always finds the proper context in which to clarify them, is fundamental to the experience of reading Ritchie's work. The curiosity is particularly important: Ritchie has a knack for drawing attention to aspects of even familiar works that no one has considered before. He is a great noticer.

Heine was written for a general audience. Like his previous book on Kafka, it was rapidly translated into German, a clear sign of the esteem in which his writings were held from the beginning. Although his next book, *The 'Jewish Question' in German Literature 1749–1939*, must certainly count as a more academic work, covering as it does a wide range of often out-of-the-way texts, there is no discernible difference in the way it is written. Ritchie is not a stylist, if one understands by that a writer who in the balance between style and content seems to wish to give more weight to style. And yet a definite style emerges, which we could perhaps call the style of common sense, where common sense means not some low denominator of what is generally deemed to be the case, but an active faculty of judgement which distrusts received opinion and seeks out those points where independence of mind is compatible with the facts. Ritchie's writing always takes full account of other people's views, but he is not afraid of making gentle corrections, even rebukes, when that is necessary to bring our understanding of a subject back onto a productive course. And he has an extraordinary ability to integrate the opinions of other critics while remaining distinct and coherent himself. All these things are palpable in his style, which gives the impression of patiently uncovering a truth that was always available but hitherto overlooked. It is, besides, often pithy and memorable and to borrow a phrase of Donald Davie's (meant entirely positively!), has 'the reek of the human' about it.

As always with Ritchie, the dates in the title of *The 'Jewish Question'* are precisely chosen. His aim in that book was to 'understand the past on its own terms' by focusing on the period of Jewish emancipation and assimilation not from the perspective of the Holocaust, from where it inevitably looks like a tragic mistake, but from within, as a development which made sense in its time. As he says with characteristic clarity, 'to call the Holocaust tragic is to blame its victims for failing to read the signs', and this in turn is to 'abuse the hindsight that is ours only because we happen to live later'. A wariness of hindsight, which tends to conceal the past from us, is identifiable as a common thread running through all of Ritchie's work. And this is perhaps what makes him specifically a literary historian and scholar, since he values literature as a medium for discovering what things felt like, preserving a dynamic sense of what was imaginable in a particular time and place. Accordingly, *The 'Jewish Question'* takes as its chronological starting point Lessing's play *Die Juden* (1749) and as its corresponding end point Freud's *Der Mann Moses und die monotheistische Religion* (1939). That both these dates were already more prominently occupied by other events in German culture and history (1749 is the year of Goethe's birth) did not deter him. *The 'Jewish Question'* remains an essential and unique survey of a world that without it would be in danger of being lost from view.

The 'Jewish Question' was the culmination of a long preoccupation with German-Jewish writing, which began with his extensive work on Franz Kafka. Since his first monograph, *Kafka: Judaism, Politics, and Literature* (1985), Ritchie has returned to Kafka time and again — as scholar and translator, editor and reviewer. In 2008 he co-founded the Oxford Kafka Research Centre, a hub of international Kafka studies, which works in partnership with the Bodleian Library, home to the world's largest collection of Kafka's manuscripts.

As anyone who has attended a Kafka conference can testify, Kafka studies can be an antagonistic field, where (predominantly) 'alpha-male' critics battle it out in an effort to 'make their mark', displacing and discrediting 'rival' readings, and where even the apparently dry matter of how to edit Kafka has led to heated controversies. In this field, Ritchie has acted as a voice of calm and restraint. He does not read Kafka to map out his own terrain; rather, his foremost concern remains with Kafka's texts. His readings add to our appreciation of their nuance and subtlety, enabling us to see them in a new light by situating them within their wider cultural and intellectual tradition. Here, as in all his work, he takes his readers to be his equals, as is particularly apparent in his succinct but wide-ranging *Very Short Introduction*, which imparts a wealth of knowledge on the author, period and intellectual context in a mere 130 pages. He has also served Kafka studies as an editor, translator, and reviewer. The Oxford Classics translations, published under his editorship, have provided English-speaking readers with fresh and reliable versions of Kafka's principal prose texts, and he himself contributed an elegant version of Kafka's first novel, *Der Verschollene*.

Ritchie's ongoing service to the discipline also includes another vital but less glamorous aspect of scholarship, namely the hard grind of reviewing. To take one example, his 1994 *Modern Language Review* essay, 'In Search of the Historical Kafka', surveys a staggering 214 publications which range from editions and biographies to articles and monographs. And while Ritchie is generous with his praise, he certainly does not pull any punches. He is forensic in pinpointing where research 'tips over into speculation', spelling out the 'confused and derivative' nature of one study and another's 'hoary misconceptions about Prague German'. One section opens with the ominous words: 'His first example is not encouraging'. His reviews, whether written for academic journals or for the *Times Literary Supplement*, are always readable, witty and engaging.

To close, though, it seems apt to return to Ritchie's very first book, *Kafka: Judaism, Politics, and Literature*, which remains one of his best-known, a landmark in Kafka studies. In a period in which Kafka scholarship was largely shaped by (post-)structuralist, text-immanent approaches (which yielded important insights in their own right), this focus on cultural context is quite a bold, counter-cultural move, but the book brilliantly demonstrates the benefits of reading Kafka in this way. Context is not used to 'explain' the texts, to reduce their complexity, but rather to add to it, as the book explores how Kafka's evolving and often ambivalent engagement with Judaism shapes his writings in a multitude of subtle ways.

The book takes Judaism to encompass not only Jewish religion but 'Jewish culture and the sense of Jewish identity'. A third central component is 'Politics', which in the title mediates between Judaism and Literature. As the book demonstrates, Kafka's texts are political, not in a programmatic, ideological way but in the ways they reflect, and reflect on, the implications of specific historical or cultural constellations. This political dimension is particularly apparent in Kafka's final story, 'Josefine, die Sängerin oder Das Volk der Mäuse' (1924). In his reading, Ritchie draws attention to the virtual absence of Jewish historiography between the first-century Romano-Jewish historian Josephus and Leopold Zunz's nineteenth-century *Wissenschaft des Judentums*. As he argues, this lacuna is reflected in the mice's reliance on legend and their (however ambivalent) attachment to a figurehead such as Josefine. In this way, their situation is reflective of an ongoing dimension of Jewish experience, namely of life in the Diaspora, a reading which has since then become a canonical interpretation. This argument is not advanced as a simplistic template but in a nuanced and dialectical way, which brings out the text's subtlety and self-questioning irony. Kafka's final story, Ritchie remarks, is written in a 'spirit of self-effacement', for while it 'does not deny the value of art', it shows that 'its value is, and perhaps must be, something other than what the artist imagines'; ultimately, the mice, for all their fickle and shallow ways, understand art better than the artist. As he concludes, 'Kafka has taken the side of the people against the artist, and by doing so he has brought the relation between the two sides to a dialectical resolution, both inside and outside the story'.[2]

As a scholar, reviewer and translator, Ritchie Robertson embodies the characteristics he ascribes to the late Kafka. If his own scholarship is not exactly self-effacing, it is certainly modest, as it avoids the pitfalls of scholarly vanity, which uses the text as a mirror for its own reflected glory. Indeed, all his work is carried by a deep regard for — and often a palpable delight in — his texts, and by an equally deep commitment to his readers. In this, its dual loyalty to both 'the artist' and 'the people', it is a model and an inspiration — as the following essays so richly demonstrate.

Notes to the Introduction

1. Ritchie Robertson, *The Enlightenment: The Pursuit of Happiness, 1680–1790* (London: Allen Lane, 2020), p. xxii.
2. Ritchie Robertson, *Kafka: Judaism, Politics, and Literature* (Oxford: Oxford University Press, 1985), p. 283.

CHAPTER 1

'Gymnastik des Geistes': Lessing und die Aufklärung als Lebensform

Laura Anna Macor

'Gymnastik des Geistes' ist ein Ausdruck, der sich in Moses Mendelssohns Brief an Elise Reimarus vom 16. August 1783 findet und Lessings besondere Neigung zu 'Paradoxie und Widersprechen' beschreiben soll: Lessing habe sich lebenslang der Wahrheitssuche gewidmet, sei aber oft Opfer einer eigenartigen 'Laune' und übertriebenen 'Liebe zum Scharfsinn' gewesen, welche ihn dazu führten, sich jeglicher Meinung, ungeachtet ihrer platten Ungereimtheit, wenn auch nur probeweise anzunehmen; 'in der Hitze des Streits' sei ihm 'die Gymnastik des Geistes wichtiger, als die reine Wahrheit' gewesen.[1]

Mendelssohns Charakterisierung ist nur dem ersten Anschein nach von bloß biographischer Relevanz und impliziert eher eine tiefe Kenntnis von Lessings Grundüberzeugung: Der Mensch könne sich nur teil- und annäherungsweise der Wahrheit vergewissern und bedürfe dazu kontinuierlicher Versuche, die er selbständig, obwohl nicht selbstreferentiell und -bezogen anstellen soll. Bereitschaft zu (Selbst)Kritik, Einwand und Dissens gehört somit zur Grundausstattung des echten Philosophen und stellt keineswegs eine subjektive Idiosynkrasie dar, die dem Erkenntnisprozess etwa schaden könne (obwohl sie in Mendelssohns Augen zu einer solchen Idiosynkrasie bei Lessing wurde). Philosophie ist demnach eine unaufhörliche, gemeinschaftliche und letztlich polemische Nachforschung, die den vollen Einsatz fordert, Klarheit in die Vorstellungen der Beteiligten bringt und somit deren Einstellung zum Leben schlechthin von Grund auf verändert.

Aus dieser Perspektive leistet Lessing nicht nur einen Beitrag zur Philosophie der Aufklärung, sondern auch zur Philosophie überhaupt, und zwar zu deren Auffassung als Lebensform und -kunst, so wie sie das abendländische Denken seit der Antike kennt.[2] Diese seine Leistung wurde aber leider nur sporadisch wahrgenommen und wartet noch heute auf eine angemessene Würdigung, welche zur gleichen Zeit auch der oft angezweifelten Bedeutung von Lessing als Philosophen Gerechtigkeit widerfahren lassen kann. Ziel des vorliegenden Aufsatzes ist es demnach, diesem Manko abzuhelfen und eine sachgemäßere Rekonstruktion von Lessings philosophischen Verdiensten zu liefern.

Die Philosophie als Lebensform in und seit der Antike

Die besondere Art und Weise, wie die Philosophie in der Antike konzipiert und praktiziert wurde, deckt sich nur teilweise mit dem heutigen Bild und hat über die Jahrhunderte eine alles andere als lineare Rezeption erfahren. Die meisten Denker sowohl der griechischen als auch der römischen Zeit sahen die Philosophie als eine hauptsächlich praktische Wissenschaft an, deren Wert darin bestand, bei der existentiellen Lebensorientierung und alltäglichen Verhaltensweise Hilfe zu leisten. Dieser Ansicht zufolge erschöpft sich die Philosophie keineswegs in der Aufstellung bestimmter abstrakter Thesen, sondern lässt sich auch und vor allem auf das menschliche Tun und Lassen anwenden. Die Kenntnisnahme von theoretischen Lehrsätzen darf also nicht wirkungslos bleiben, sondern soll im Gegenteil handlungsanleitend sein, d.h. klare Anweisungen zur Ausübung der gewonnenen Einsichten enthalten und womöglich auch den ersten Schritt zu einer solchen Ausübung darstellen. Die Mitteilung bestimmter Grundsätze ist demnach nie bloße Erklärung, denn sie stellt zur gleichen Zeit auch die Mittel zu deren Verwirklichung zur Verfügung; analog sind Lesen und Zuhören nie bloßes Lesen und Zuhören, sondern werden zum ersten Anlass, den Lern- und Veränderungsprozess der Philosophie zu initiieren.

Sokrates kann dabei als die Gründungsfigur für eine ganze Tradition gelten und verdient deswegen, an prominenter Stelle zu erscheinen. In seiner Selbstverteidigung soll er Platon zufolge auf seine göttliche Sendung eingegangen sein sowie deren lebensnahe und -praktische Bedeutung betont haben:

> Meine Athener, ihr seid mir lieb und teuer; gehorchen aber werde ich dem Gott mehr als euch, und solange ich lebe und dazu imstande bin, werde ich gewiss nicht aufhören zu philosophieren, euch zu ermahnen und, wem immer von euch ich begegne, mit meinen gewohnten Worten Folgendes nachzuweisen: 'Mein Ausgezeichneter Mann, du bist doch ein Athener, ein Bürger der, was Kultur und Macht betrifft, führenden und berühmtesten Stadt. Schämst du dich nicht, dich nur darum zu kümmern, wie du zu so viel Einkünften wie möglich kommst, und zu Ruhm und Ehre, um Einsicht aber und um Wahrheit und um die bestmögliche Verfassung deiner Seele kümmerst und sorgst du dich nicht?'.[3]

Sokrates hat die Aufgabe erhalten, seine Mitbürger, oder besser: die Menschen überhaupt auf deren wichtigste Angelegenheiten aufmerksam zu machen und von konkurrierenden, jedoch letztendlich geringfügigen Sorgen zu entfernen. Der Endzweck des menschlichen Daseins ist dabei der Mittelpunkt, um den alle Bemühungen Sokrates' kreisen, und nicht von ungefähr stellt die Philosophie den einzigen Weg dar, diesen Endzweck zu erfüllen: 'das höchste Glück' bestehe nämlich darin, 'jeden Tag über die Tugend und über die anderen Dinge [...] zu diskutieren', für die sich Sokrates bekanntlich interessiert habe, nämlich Gerechtigkeit, Religion und Weisheit; die betreffende Verfahrensweise erschöpfe sich aber keineswegs in einem banalen, quasi irenischen Gedankenaustausch, sondern setze als unentbehrliche Bedingung voraus, dass man '[s]ich selbst und andere prüfe', denn 'das Leben ohne Prüfung' sei 'nicht lebenswert [...] für einen Menschen'.[4]

Die Wahrheitssuche, für die Sokrates plädiert, ist also weder lebensfremd (denn sie bevorzugt ethische und religiöse Themen) noch einfach (denn sie fordert Bereitschaft zur Selbstkritik und Mut zur Veränderung). Sie geht alle Menschen an, indem sie zur Aufklärung von existentiell relevanten und also universalen Fragen beiträgt. Zudem wirkt sie auf den ganzen Menschen, indem sie keineswegs auf die Entwicklung seiner theoretischen Fähigkeiten unabhängig von den sittlichen zielt, sondern beide zusammen beschäftigt und zu Mitteln einer umfassenden Verbesserung werden lässt.

> Dass aber die Überzeugung, man müsse suchen, was man nicht weiß, uns *besser macht und mannhafter und weniger träge* als der Glaube, was wir nicht wissen, das sei weder möglich zu finden noch nötig zu suchen, dafür würde ich wirklich streiten, wie ich nur kann, in Wort und Tat.[5]

Die philosophische Tätigkeit gewinnt also ihren Wert nicht nur aus dem Erkenntnisgewinn, den sie ermöglicht, sondern auch (und vor allem) aus dem allgemeinmenschlichen Vorteil, den nur sie imstande ist zu bieten. Die Wahrheitssuche macht den Menschen besser, glücklicher und tugendhafter, nicht bloß weil sie Suche nach *Wahrheit*, sondern weil sie *Suche* nach Wahrheit ist. Sie erfordert Mühe, Anstrengung und Aufopferung, und dauert das ganze Leben.

Soweit Sokrates. Die praktische Bedeutung der Philosophie blieb als Grundüberzeugung auch in der Folgezeit, ohne dass dies jedoch die Verbannung rein theoretischer und systematischer Interessen implizierte. Platon, Aristoteles und die hellenistischen Denker explizieren mehrmals den keineswegs bloß abstrakten Ertrag der Philosophie, die davon handelt, 'wie man leben soll',[6] darauf abzielt, uns 'tugendhaft' zu machen, 'da wir anders keinen Nutzen von ihr hätten',[7] 'den Geist veredelt und bildet, [...] Ordnung ins Leben' bringt, 'unser Handeln' bestimmt und 'zeigt, was man tun und lassen sollte'.[8] Bei dieser Bestimmung von Natur und Endzweck der Philosophie wird einstimmig Sokrates eine entscheidende Rolle zugesprochen, da er im Gegensatz zu den naturalistischen und wissenschaftlichen Interessen seiner Vorgänger den Menschen zum Hauptgegenstand habe werden lassen:

> Sokrates hat als erster die Philosophie vom Himmel herunter gerufen, sie in den Städten angesiedelt, sie sogar in die Häuser hineingeführt, und sie gezwungen, nach dem Leben, den Sitten und dem Guten und Schlechten zu forschen.[9]

Das Verdienst, diese lebensnahe und existentielle Auffassung rehabilitiert und zum Kennzeichen des antiken Denkens überhaupt erhoben zu haben, gebührt dem französischen Gelehrten Pierre Hadot, der ausgehend von den Untersuchungen von Paul Rabbow und seiner Frau Ilsetraut Hadot die Formel 'Philosophie als Lebensform' mit großem Erfolg eingeführt hat.[10] In Hadots Augen erstrecke sich die philosophische Lebensform 'nicht nur auf das Wissen, sondern auf die eigene Person und das Dasein', sie impliziere 'ein Fortschreiten, das unser Sein wachsen lässt und uns besser macht', und sei echte 'Bekehrung, die das ganze Leben verändert und das Wesen desjenigen verwandelt, der sie vollzieht'.[11] Die Wahl einer bestimmten Lebensweise entscheide über die Annahme einer bestimmten philosophischen Lehre und folglich über das Bekenntnis zu einer philosophischen

Schule, und nicht umgekehrt; es gehe in erster Linie um Existenz, und erst sekundär um (systematisches) Wissen. Diese Sicht finde in Sokrates ihren Hauptvertreter und habe ihre leitende Rolle ununterbrochen durch alle Phasen der Antike und Spätantike behalten.[12]

Der deutsche Forscher Christoph Horn hat sich dieser Neubestimmung sowohl der griechischen als auch der römischen Philosophie angeschlossen, hat sich jedoch keineswegs darauf beschränkt, Hadots Thesen zu wiederholen. Er hat nämlich einige wichtige Präzisierungen vorgenommen, die hauptsächlich darauf abzielen, die angebliche Allgemeingültigkeit der betreffenden Auffassung zu relativieren und dem eher theoretischen und wissenschaftlichen Ansatz von einigen prominenten Autoren wie den Vorsokratikern Gerechtigkeit widerfahren zu lassen. 'Die Charakterisierung der Philosophie als einer Lebenskunst' scheine 'primär auf Sokrates sowie auf die hellenistischen Philosophenschulen zuzutreffen', könne aber nicht ohne Weiteres 'auch darüber hinaus als triftig angenommen werden',[13] zumal Thales, Anaximander, Heraklit und Parmenides eher Prinzipienwissenschaft getrieben hätten und deswegen für das fragliche Modell nicht stehen könnten. Die praktische Ausrichtung mache also zwar einen (und gar den vorherrschenden), aber keineswegs den einzigen Grundzug antiken Denkens aus, was nicht im mindesten ihre Wichtigkeit, sondern nur ihren eventuellen Absolutheitsanspruch in Frage stelle.[14]

Trotz ihrer Uneinigkeit bezüglich der ausnahmslosen bzw. teilweisen Anwendung der existentiellen Auffassung sind sich Hadot und Horn jedoch über deren Hauptmerkmale einig: Sie orientiert sich primär am Adressaten, bevorzugt offene und dynamische Gattungen wie Monolog, Dialog und Brief, und sieht endlich geistige, d.h. weder bloß physische noch bloß spirituelle Übungen vor. Der Philosoph richtet sich an seine Mitmenschen, die er für eine besondere Lebensweise zu gewinnen versucht, und bedient sich dabei derjenigen literarischen und rhetorischen Mittel, die dem anvisierten Zweck am besten nützen, indem sie die Identifizierung oder direkte Beteiligung der Zuhörer oder Leser fördern. Dieser Prozess erfolgt über die kontinuierliche und regelmäßige Durchführung von ganz bestimmten Praktiken, die letztlich auf Eingewöhnung hinzielen. Es geht dem Philosophen dabei wie dem Athleten, denn beide brauchen Zeit, Anstrengung und Geduld, und beide dürfen nicht ihr Training unter-, geschweige denn abbrechen, es sei denn, sie sind dazu bereit, auf alles bis dahin Gewonnene zu verzichten.[15]

Eine solche lebensnahe Charakterisierung der Philosophie hat über die Jahrhunderte offensichtlich an Gültigkeit eingebüßt, und zwar zugunsten eines auf Wissenschaft, Methode und System aufbauenden Bildes. Sowohl Hadot als auch Horn gehen den möglichen Ursachen einer derart tiefgreifenden Veränderung nach und verweisen dabei insbesondere auf die Verbreitung des Christentums mit dessen Übernahme der bis dahin der Philosophie zugesprochenen existentiellen Rolle, auf die mittelalterliche Instrumentalisierung der Philosophie als *ancilla theologiae* und zuletzt auf die frühmoderne Subjektphilosophie samt deren Vorliebe für reine Erkenntnistheorie und -probleme.[16] All dies habe dazu geführt, dass das antike Paradigma marginal geworden und erst bei einigen, vereinzelt zu würdigenden Autoren wiederzufinden sei. Unter diesen späteren Vertretern erscheinen beispielsweise Petrarca, Erasmus, Montaigne, Shaftesbury und Nietzsche, aber auch der europäischen Bewegung der Aufklärung insgesamt wird eine gewisse Rolle zugesprochen, zumal das praxisorientierte Philosophieverständnis den antiintellektualistischen Trends des 18. Jahrhunderts und der eng damit zusammenhängenden Forderung nach Verbreitung des Wissens vollkommen entspreche. Deutsche Gelehrte wie Johann Georg Sulzer, Johann August Eberhard und Christoph Martin Wieland werden dabei explizit erwähnt, aber der echte Protagonist ist in diesem Fall Kant, dessen Weltbegriff und Tugendlehre in die Tradition der antiken Lebenskunst gestellt werden.[17]

Nicht einmal taucht der Name Lessings in diesem Kontext auf, und das gilt sogar für Hadots Monographie zu Goethe und der Tradition der geistigen Exerzitien, wo einige prominente Vertreter der Aufklärung und Deutschen Klassik wie Alexander Gottlieb Baumgarten, Schiller und Wilhelm von Humboldt aufgeführt werden, nicht aber Lessing.[18] Das überrascht umso mehr, als Lessing nicht nur ausdrücklich für Sokrates' Einstellung eintritt, sondern auch deren Verschwinden im folgenden Verlauf des abendländischen Denkens beklagt und wiedergutzumachen versucht. Dem soll nun unsere Aufmerksamkeit gelten.

Lessing und die Philosophie als Lebensform

Gotthold Ephraim Lessing (1729–81) stellt das akademische System seiner (aber auch unserer) Zeit und dessen Ausdifferenzierung in unterschiedlichen, gar separaten Disziplinen radikal in Frage. Er hat sich im literarischen, philologischen, theologischen und ästhetischen Feld betätigt, ohne jedoch irgendeine der möglichen betreffenden Bezeichnungen für sich in Anspruch zu nehmen: Er sei weder 'Dichter'[19] noch 'Theolog',[20] und nicht einmal 'gelehrt' habe er je werden wollen,[21] was aber nicht auf selbstbewusste Bescheidenheit, sondern eher als Ausdruck eines grundsätzlichen Unbehagens am jeweils vorausgesetzten Wissensverständnis zu bewerten ist.

Lessing selber klärt 1751 über Ursprung und Verfall der von ihm vertretenen Auffassung von Philosophie auf, und es überrascht nicht, dass er dabei auf die Antike zu sprechen kommt: 'Glückselige Zeiten' seien es gewesen, 'als der Tugendhafteste der Gelehrteste war', und 'alle Weisheit in kurzen Lebensregeln bestand', aber die Menschen seien binnen Kurzem dem Wahn anheimgefallen, ihrer 'Neubegierde' andere, wohl höhere 'Nahrung' zu geben als 'Wahrheiten, die jeder fassen, aber nicht jeder üben kann'.[22] 'Der Himmel' sei also vom 'Gegenstand ihrer Bewunderung' zum 'Feld ihrer Mutmaßungen', und die 'Zahlen' zu Vorboten eines 'Labyrinth[es] von Geheimnissen' geworden, 'die ihnen um so viel angenehmer waren, je weniger sie Verwandtschaft mit der Tugend hatten'.[23] Die Grundeinsicht, dass der 'Mensch [...] zum Tun und nicht zum Vernünfteln erschaffen' worden sei, habe sie offensichtlich nicht geleitet.[24]

Erst derjenige, der 'nach einem Ausspruche des Orakels' der 'weiseste unter den Menschen' war, habe sich bemüht, 'die Lehrbegierde von diesem verwegenen Fluge zurückzuholen',[25] und die Menschen auf ihr Inneres aufmerksam zu machen:

> Törichte Sterbliche, was über euch ist, ist nicht für euch! Kehret den Blick in euch selbst! In euch sind die unerforschten Tiefen, worinnen ihr euch mit Nutzen verlieren könnt. Hier untersucht die geheimsten Winkel. Hier lernet die Schwäche und Stärke, die verdeckten Gänge und den offenbaren Ausbruch eurer Leidenschaften! Hier richtet das Reich auf, wo ihr Untertan und König seid! Hier begreifet und beherrschet das einzige, was ihr begreifen und beherrschen sollt; euch selbst.
>
> So ermahnte Sokrates, oder vielmehr Gott durch den Sokrates.[26]

Die antike, um Sokrates als archetypische Figur kreisende Tradition steht hierbei offenkundig Pate, und nicht von ungefähr wird der 'Nutzen' der entsprechenden praktischen Einstellung im Gegensatz zum lebensfremden und fruchtlosen Ertrag der bloß wissenschaftlichen Untersuchungen explizit betont.

Sokrates' Vermächtnis sei aber leider von seinen Nachfolgern verraten worden, die seinem Beispiel nicht gefolgt seien. 'Nur wenige von seinen Jüngern' seien nämlich 'den von ihm gezeigten Weg' gegangen: 'Plato' habe 'zu träumen, und Aristoteles zu schließen' angefangen, und die beiden hätten '[d]urch eine Menge von Jahrhunderten, wo bald dieser, bald jener die Oberhand hatte, [...] die Weltweisheit auf uns' geführt.[27] Erst 'Cartesius' habe die Wahrheit vom 'Ansehen jener beiden Tyrannen' befreit, und darin bestehe 'sein vorzügliches Verdienst', aber kurz darauf hätten 'zwei Männer, die, trotz ihrer gemeinschaftlichen Eifersucht, einerlei Absicht hatten', eine neue, der sokratischen diametral entgegengesetzte Auffassung von Philosophie eingeführt: Newton und Leibniz seien der Ansicht gewesen, 'die Weltweisheit' enthalte 'noch allzuviel praktisches' und sei 'der Meßkunst zu unterwerfen', was auf der einen Seite ermöglichte, die 'verborgensten Geheimniss[e] der Natur' zu enthüllen, auf der anderen aber den ursprünglichen Kern der Philosophie in Vergessenheit geraten ließ.[28] Newtons und Leibniz' 'Schüler' seien 'jetzo' ehrlich davon überzeugt, 'auf den Namen der Weltweisen ein gar besonders Recht zu haben', zumal sie 'unerschöpflich in Entdeckung neuer Wahrheiten [...] durch wenige mit Zeichen verbundene Zahlen' seien, offenbarten damit jedoch genau ihr Miss- oder gar Unverständnis der authentischen Bedeutung der Philosophie.[29] Denn sie seien nur dazu imstande, 'den Kopf' zu 'füllen', während 'das Herz [...] leer' bleibt, und den 'Geist [...] bis in die entferntesten Himmel' zu führen, während 'das Gemüt durch seine Leidenschaften bis unter das Vieh herunter gesetzt wird'.[30]

Diese 'Geschichte der Weltweisheit in einer Nuß' ist offensichtlich eher eine Verfallsgeschichte,[31] die darauf abzielt zu zeigen, dass die Menschen ihrer Bestimmung nicht entsprochen haben, indem sie 'nur immer haben vernünfteln, niemals handeln wollen': 'Der Erkenntnis nach' mögen sie auch 'Engel' sein, 'dem Leben nach' bleiben sie aber immer 'Teufel'.[32]

Vor dem Hintergrund einer derart trüben Sachlage gewinnt das Profil des echten Philosophen kontrastiv an Kontur.

Lessing stellt sich einen 'Mann' vor, der 'die wichtigsten Verrichtungen unserer Gelehrten' als 'verächtlich' zu betrachten und 'mit einer sokratischen Stärke die lächerlichen Seiten unserer so gepriesenen Weltweisen zu entdecken wüßte', und lässt ihn genau diejenigen Aufgaben übernehmen, die der Philosoph in der Antike nach der damals vorherrschenden praktischen Auffassung zu bewältigen hatte: 'alle seine Ermahnungen und Lehren' zielten nicht auf Wissenschaft, sondern auf 'Tugend' als den einzigen Weg zum 'glückliche[n] Leben', und das erfordere Verzicht auf 'Reichtum[s]', Achtung vor 'Verdienst' und Gehorsam gegenüber der 'Stimme der Natur'.[33] Darüber hinaus bemühe sich ein solcher Mann darum, der Einsicht zum Durchbruch zu verhelfen, man solle 'dem Tode unerschrocken unter die Augen gehen', denn nur 'durch einen willigen Abtritt von diesem Schauplatze' könne man beweisen, 'daß man überzeugt sei, die Weisheit würde uns die Maske nicht ablegen heißen, wenn wir unsere Rolle nicht geendigt hätten'.[34] Es geht hier offenbar um diejenige *meditatio mortis*, die seit Platons *Phaidon* als die Hauptbeschäftigung des Philosophen gilt und in der gegenwärtigen akademischen Diskussion als eine der naheliegendsten Arten und Weisen angesehen wird, Philosophie als Lebenskunst zu verstehen und auszuüben.[35]

Lessing nimmt überdies an, dieser Mann besitze 'nichts von aller der Erkenntnis, die desto weniger nützt, je prahlender sie ist', er sei 'weder in den Geschichten, noch in den Sprachen erfahren' und 'kenne die Schönheiten und Wunder der Natur nicht weiter, als in soferne sie die sichersten Beweise von ihrem großen Schöpfer sind'; kurzum, er habe 'alles das unerforscht gelassen, wovon er, bei Toren zwar mit weniger Ehre, allein mit desto mehr Befriedigung seiner selbst', sagen könne: '*ich weiß es nicht, ich kann es nicht einsehen.*'[36] Dieser explizit anerkannten, gar selbstbewusst reklamierten Unwissenheit unbeschadet erhebe er ganz spontan 'Anspruch auf den Titel eines Weltweisen' und sei zudem 'so beherzt, ihn auch Leuten abzustreiten, welchen öffentliche Ämter das Recht dieses blendenden Beinamens gegeben haben'.[37] Sokrates' Leben und Lehre liefern hier das Modell, und dasselbe gilt leider auch für das unglückliche Los, das diesem imaginären Mann beschieden ist. Keiner unter den sogenannten 'Philosophen' sei nämlich dazu bereit, seinen Aussagen den ihnen gebührenden Wert zuzuerkennen, denn weder beherrsche er 'die ersten Gründe der Algebra' noch verfüge er über eine adäquate 'Theorie des Monds', ganz zu schweigen von seiner keineswegs verhohlenen Gleichgültigkeit gegenüber der Hypothese der 'Monaden'; das Ergebnis könne demnach nur Spott und Verachtung gegenüber dem als 'Schwärmer' und 'Narr' gebrandmarkten 'verwegene[n] Freund der Laien' sein.[38]

Vorzug der Moral gegenüber der Wissenschaft und entsprechende Umformung der Philosophie in eine praktische Disziplin bilden die Hauptinteressen dieses neuen Sokrates, der der modernen Vorliebe für ein angeblich reines und höheres, in Wirklichkeit aber nur lebensfremdes und unnützes Wissen entgegenarbeitet.

Lessing kommt 1751, also relativ früh, zu dieser Überzeugung und bleibt ihr zeitlebens treu, wie seine Beschreibung von Sokrates' Charakter und Lehre im 49. Stück der *Hamburgischen Dramaturgie* (16. Oktober 1767) beweist:

> Schöne Sentenzen und Moralen sind überhaupt gerade das, was wir von einem Philosophen, wie Sokrates, am seltensten hören; sein Lebenswandel ist die einzige Moral, die er prediget. Aber den Menschen, und uns selbst kennen; auf unsere Empfindungen aufmerksam sein; in allen die ebensten und kürzesten Wege der Natur ausforschen und lieben; jedes Ding nach seiner Absicht beurteilen: das ist es, was wir in seinem Umgange lernen.[39]

Es dürfte nunmehr kein Zweifel daran bestehen, dass Lessing nicht nur eine dezidiert praxisbezogene Auffassung der Philosophie vertritt, wie sie in der Antike eingeführt wurde, sondern auch deren späteren Untergang auf ähnliche Gründe zurückführt, wie es auch Hadot und Horn circa zwei Jahrhunderte nach ihm, und von ihm unabhängig, getan haben.[40] Nun gilt es aber der Frage nachzugehen, ob in Lessings Augen der Aufklärung in diesem Rahmen eine besondere Rolle zukommt, und ob sie also für eine derart existentiell orientierte, an menschlichen Grunderfahrungen und -problemen interessierte Einstellung in Anspruch genommen werden kann.

Lessing und die Aufklärung als Lebensform

Lessing wird zu Recht als einer der wichtigsten Verfechter der Aufklärung angesehen, die er in Schriften verschiedener Gattungen (Essays, Komödien, Dramen, Rezensionen) nicht nur mit theoretischen Argumenten unterstützt, sondern auch — was hier am meisten interessiert — ganz konkret in die Tat umsetzt und in Gang setzt. Er beschränkt sich keineswegs darauf, über Selbstdenken zu sprechen und den Kampf gegen Vorurteile und Aberglauben zu rechtfertigen, sondern setzt sich selbst für beide Themen ein, *indem* er sich als Autor zu ihnen bekennt und seine Leser auf sie aufmerksam macht. Bei ihm wird also das Nachdenken über die Aufklärung *performativ* im reinsten Sinne, da seine Erklärung nie bloße Erklärung bleibt, sondern unmittelbar zum aufklärerischen Akt wird. Indem er *über* Aufklärung und *für* sie schreibt, praktiziert Lessing Aufklärung. Diese besondere Einstellung erinnert lebhaft an das oben besprochene Philosophieverständnis von Hadot, Horn und Lessing selbst, wo Reflexion konstitutiv in Handlung mündet; nicht von ungefähr soll es im Folgenden darum gehen zu eruieren, ob diese performative Auffassung auch eine praktische ist, ob sie also entscheidend zur Bewältigung existentieller Fragen beiträgt und bei der Orientierung im alltäglichen Leben hilft, kurzum: ob eine derart konzipierte Aufklärung als Lebensform und -kunst in der antiken Bedeutung gelten kann.

Lessings Bemühungen stehen von Anfang an im Zeichen der Aufklärung, wie seine Jugendkomödien und deren Kampf gegen die damals so genannten Vorurteile 'der Sekte', 'der Völkerschaft' (in diesem Fall des Antisemitismus) und 'der Übereilung' eindeutig beweisen.[41] Im Stück *Der junge Gelehrte* (1747/1748) ironisiert der Protagonist Damis 'diesen oder jenen großen Philosophen', der 'schon einer ganzen Sekte' seinen Namen gegeben habe und dennoch von der wahren Weisheit weit entfernt sei,[42] und in den *Juden* (1749) warnt der unbekannte wie namenlose Reisende nicht nur seine Gesprächspartner, sondern auch (und vor allem) sich selbst vor 'allgemeine[n] Urteile[n] über ganze Völker',[43] sowie vor 'übereilte[n] Verdacht[en]'.[44]

Diagnose und Therapie von Vorurteilen liegen nicht nur Handlungsverlauf und philosophischer Absicht von Lessings Theaterstücken, einschließlich der Tragödien,[45] sondern auch der kritischen Arbeit als Dramaturg am Hamburger Nationaltheater zugrunde, wie Lessings Worte 1768 eindeutig bestätigen:

> Ich erinnere hier meine Leser, daß diese Blätter nichts weniger als ein dramatisches *System* enthalten sollen. Ich bin also nicht verpflichtet, alle die

Schwierigkeiten aufzulösen, die ich mache. Meine Gedanken mögen immer sich weniger zu verbinden, ja wohl gar sich zu widersprechen scheinen: wenn es denn nur Gedanken sind, bei welchen sie Stoff finden, *selbst zu denken*. Hier will ich nichts als Fermenta cognitionis ausstreuen.[46]

Vorurteil des Systems und Selbstdenken stehen hier einander gegenüber,[47] und wie schon beim *Laokoon* (1766) geht es Lessing nicht um die Errichtung und/ oder Verteidigung eines kohärenten und geschlossenen Ganzen, sondern eher um Anregung zum weiteren Nachdenken.[48] Sowohl der Verfasser als auch der Kritiker von Bühnenwerken sollen offensichtlich nicht auf die Mitteilung irgendwelcher miteinander eng zusammenhängenden, sich gar deduktiv implizierenden Ideen abzielen, sondern sich eher darum bemühen, ihre Zuschauer und Leser zu eigener Reflexion zu bewegen, egal ob das auf strikt logische oder untypisch rhapsodische Weise geschieht.

All dies bleibt Lessings Hauptsorge auch in seinen historisch-gelehrten, letztendlich esoterischen Werken, wo rein wissenschaftliche Interessen nur dem ersten Anschein nach jeden anderen Zweck absorbieren, in Wirklichkeit aber zum neuen Anlass werden, Aufklärung zu verteidigen und auszuüben. Nicht von ungefähr greift Lessing zu eindeutigen Schlagworten, wenn er damit beschäftigt ist, sein Vorhaben bei den *Rettungen* — auch den nicht explizit als solche bezeichneten — zu erklären.

In den einleitenden Absätzen der *Rettungen des Horaz* (1754) rechnet sich Lessing unter die Anzahl derer, 'die sich ein Vergnügen daraus machen, den Vorurteilen die Stirne zu bieten, und alles in seiner wahren Gestalt zu zeigen', ob 'ein vermeinter Heiliger dadurch zum Bösewichte, und ein vermeinter Bösewicht zum Heiligen' auch werden müsse.[49] Er kenne in der Tat

> keine angenehmere Beschäftigung [...], als die Namen berühmter Männer zu mustern, ihr Recht auf die Ewigkeit zu untersuchen, unverdiente Flecken ihnen abzuwischen, die falschen Verkleisterungen ihrer Schwächen aufzulösen, kurz alles das im moralischen Verstande zu tun, was derjenige, dem die Aufsicht über einen Bildersaal anvertrauet ist, physisch verrichtet.[50]

Lessings bekannte Sympathie für marginalisierte oder gar verurteilte Gelehrte geht immer wieder auf deren aufklärerischen Impetus *ante litteram* zurück, sodass die jeweilige Rehabilitierung keine bloß wissenschaftliche Leistung bleibt, sondern direkt in den Mittelpunkt der damaligen Arena führt und zum offenkundigen Plädoyer für die Werte der Aufklärung wird. Cardanus habe sich 'dem Verdachte der Atheisterei' ausgesetzt, nur weil er sich darum bemüht habe, 'selbst zu denken und gebilligten Vorurteilen die Stirne zu bieten',[51] und Berengar habe aus denselben Gründen das Schimpfwort 'Ketzer' auf sich gezogen, was aber bei näherem Hinsehen eher zu seinem Vorteil gereiche:

> Das Ding, was man Ketzer nennt, hat eine sehr gute Seite. Es ist ein Mensch, der mit seinen eigenen Augen *wenigstens* sehen *wollen*. Die Frage ist nur, ob es gute Augen gewesen, mit welchen er selbst sehen wollen. Ja, in gewissen Jahrhunderten ist der Name Ketzer die größte Empfehlung, die von einem Gelehrten auf die Nachwelt gebracht werden können.[52]

Terminologie und Gedankenwelt der Aufklärung spielen erwartungsgemäß eine zentrale Rolle auch bei Lessings theologischen Kontroversen, allen voran derjenigen mit Goeze, wo der eigene theologische Dilettantismus als Ausdruck von Unabhängigkeit und Unvoreingenommenheit gilt, denn der 'Liebhaber der Theologie' hat 'auf kein gewisses *System* schwören müssen' und ist also keineswegs dazu verpflichtet, 'eine andre Sprache, als die [s]einige, zu reden'.⁵³ Genauso wie in der *Hamburgischen Dramaturgie* werden Vorurteil des Systems und Selbstdenken diametral einander entgegengesetzt, nur dass diesmal Ersteres kein beliebiges Lehrgebäude, sondern das christliche, oder genauer: das luthersche voraussetzt,⁵⁴ und Letzteres nichtsdestoweniger nicht religionskritisch aufzufassen ist. Es entspricht in der Tat 'Luthers Geiste', 'daß man *keinen* Menschen, in der Erkenntnis der Wahrheit nach *seinem eigenen* Gutdünken fortzugehen, hindern muß', und es hieße, alle 'Lutherschen Pastores' zu ebenso vielen 'Päpste[n]' zu machen, sollten sie ihren Gläubigen 'vorschreiben können', wo sie 'aufhören sollen, in der Schrift zu forschen'.⁵⁵

Lessings Einsatz für die Sache der Aufklärung dürfte keinem Zweifel unterliegen, und ebenso wenig seine damit verbundene Überzeugung, gelehrtes Wissen gehöre nicht mit zu wahrer Aufklärung, zumal der Amateur den Vorzug der Vorurteilslosigkeit und Bereitschaft zur autonomen Untersuchung vor dem Eingeweihten habe, es sei denn, er werde darin vom herrschenden Aberglauben behindert. Aber was hat all dies mit der praktischen Auffassung der Philosophie zu tun, die Lessing anderenorts vertritt und ausdrücklich auf Sokrates zurückführt? Ist Lessings Einstellung ein zureichendes Zeichen dafür, dass Aufklärung eine existentielle Aufgabe übernimmt und den Menschen nicht nur klüger, sondern auch besser macht?

Es ist Lessing selbst, der uns dabei hilft. Im 11. Literaturbrief (1759) erklärt er die Wichtigkeit des '*eigenen Nachdenken[s]*' für die Erziehung der Jugend und vergleicht dabei die 'Sokratische Lehrart' mit 'der itzigen Methode', zumal beide durch die philosophische Tätigkeit auf Wahrheit und Vollkommenheit zielen.⁵⁶ Sowohl die Mäeutik als auch die Aufklärung schließen eine mechanische und passive Vermittlung des Wissens aus und erfordern den persönlichen Einsatz des Einzelnen, was über so etwas wie ein kontinuierliches geistiges Training erfolgt: 'Das große Geheimnis[,] die menschliche Seele durch *Übung vollkommen zu machen*', bestehe 'einzig darin, daß man sie *in steter Bemühung* erhalte, durch *eigenes Nachdenken* auf die Wahrheit zu kommen', weswegen es am meisten zu vermeiden sei, dass die 'Gemüter' eingeschläfert und die 'Neubegierde [...] frühzeitig gestillt' würden, kurzum: dass 'der Weg, durch *eignes Nachdenken* Wahrheiten zu finden, [...] auf einmal verschlossen' werde.⁵⁷

Unaufhörliche philosophische Praxis bewirkt offenbar die Verbesserung des Menschen. Der Erkenntnisprozess ist allem Anschein zum Trotz keine bloß theoretische und elitäre Angelegenheit, sondern wird zum erfolgreichen und wirkungsmächtigen Mittel der Selbstvervollkommnung, solange er, laut Lessings berühmtem Diktum in seiner *Duplik* (1778), auf sokratisch-platonische Weise Wahrheitssuche und -liebe bleibt, und in dieser Form allen zugänglich ist.

> Nicht die Wahrheit, in deren Besitz irgend ein Mensch ist, oder zu sein vermeinet, sondern die aufrichtige *Mühe*, die er angewandt hat, hinter die Wahrheit zu kommen, macht den Wert des Menschen. Denn nicht durch den Besitz, sondern durch die Nachforschung der Wahrheit erweitern sich seine Kräfte, worin allein *seine immer wachsende Vollkommenheit* bestehet. Der Besitz macht *ruhig, träge, stolz* —
>
> Wenn Gott in seiner Rechten alle Wahrheit, und in seiner Linken den einzigen *immer regen* Trieb nach Wahrheit, obschon mit dem Zusatze, mich *immer und ewig* zu irren, verschlossen hielte, und spräche zu mir: wähle! Ich fiele ihm mit Demut in seine Linke, und sagte: Vater gieb! die reine Wahrheit ist ja doch nur für dich allein![58]

Es ist nicht nur so, dass der Mensch zur Wahrheit nicht gelangen kann und sich insofern mit deren Suche begnügen muss; es ist auch und vor allem so, dass der Mensch nur über die Wahrheitsuche seiner Neigung zu Ruhe, Trägheit und Stolz entgegenarbeitet und somit vollkommener und besser wird.[59] Es geht nicht primär um Entdeckung oder Erfindung, sondern um Ausübung, oder, um eine kontrastive Wendung der theologischen Lessing-Forschung aufzugreifen: es geht keineswegs um 'Ortho-Doxie' (nicht einmal der Wahrheit), sondern im Gegenteil um 'Ortho-Praxis'.[60]

Dieser moralische und existentielle Prozess betrifft aber auf keinen Fall das isolierte Individuum, wie Lessings pädagogische Theaterauffassung und seine Appelle an die Leser in den Prosawerken eindeutig klarmachen,[61] sondern findet ausnahmslos auf gemeinschaftlicher Ebene statt, sodass alle Menschen zum gemeinsamen Wohl beitragen und wechselseitig aufeinander einwirken.

Lessings Plädoyer für den Nutzen der Polemik aus dem Jahr 1769 gehört letztendlich in diesen Kontext:

> unser itziges Publicum [...] scheinet vergessen zu wollen, daß es die *Aufklärung* so mancher wichtigen Puncte dem bloßen Widerspruche zu danken hat, und daß die Menschen noch über nichts in der Welt einig sein würden, wenn sie noch über nichts in der Welt gezankt hätten.
>
> [...]
> Aber die Wahrheit, sagt man, gewinnet dabei so selten. — So selten? Es sei, daß noch durch keinen Streit die Wahrheit ausgemacht worden: so hat dennoch die Wahrheit bei jedem Streite gewonnen. Der Streit hat den *Geist der Prüfung* genähret, hat *Vorurteil* und *Ansehen* in einer *beständigen Erschütterung* erhalten; kurz, hat die geschminkte Unwahrheit verhindert, sich an der Stelle der Wahrheit festzusetzen.[62]

Die Bemühung um immer wachsende Erkenntnis soll also kontinuierlich und kollektiv sein, und darf sich nicht mit einer idyllisch anmutenden zwischenmenschlichen Mitarbeit zufriedenstellen. Sokrates selber glich in seinen eigenen Augen sowie in denjenigen seiner Gesprächspartner störenden, gar gefährlichen Tieren — einer Bremse, einem Zitterrochen und einer Natter[63] — was auf den alles andere als leichten, angenehmen und friedlichen Verlauf der von ihm geführten Dialoge hinweist. Dasselbe gilt bei näherem Hinsehen auch für den Schriftsteller, den Dichter, den Essayisten und vor allem den Polemiker Lessing, der in der Kontroverse das beste, oder genauer: das einzig mögliche Mittel zur menschlichen

Vervollkommnung sah und nur deswegen so oft gegen übrigens erheblich heterogene Feinde ins Feld zog. Der gemeinsame Kampf um Wahrheit hat vorerst eine existentielle Bedeutung, und die Aufklärung als operative, methodische und letztendlich epochenübergreifende Bezeichnung stellt die beste Art und Weise dar, diesem praktischen Anliegen Rechnung zu tragen.

Eine der bekanntesten Formulierungen Lessings variierend könnte man also sagen: Der sich selbst und andere aufklärende Mensch ist der beste Mensch.

Schlussbetrachtungen

Lessings Auffassung der Philosophie entspricht offenkundig derjenigen Hadots und Horns und setzt nicht umsonst eine Rehabilitierung des antiken Denkens auf den Spuren Sokrates' voraus. Der Primat des Ethischen und Dialogischen liefert hierfür den Beweis. Lessings Eigentümlichkeit besteht darüber hinaus darin, dass er nicht nur die klassische Tradition als Keimzelle eines authentischen Verständnisses von Weltweisheit anerkennt, sondern auch seine eigene Zeit in diesen Prozess mit einbezieht und den für sie typischen intellektuellen Ansatz dafür fruchtbar macht. 'Aufklärung' ist dabei aber nicht bloß als historiographische und chronologische Kategorie zu begreifen, als gälte sie nur für das 18. Jahrhundert und sei erst in der Moderne erfunden worden. 'Aufklärung' ist von Lessings Gesichtspunkt aus ein im 18. Jahrhundert modisch gewordenes Wort, um einen präexistierenden Sachverhalt zum Ausdruck zu bringen, und zwar das zwischenmenschliche Streben nach Wahrheit aus Liebe für sie. In diesem Sinne macht Aufklärung eine regelrechte, damals wie zuvor und heute wie damals gültige Lebensform aus, welche dem Menschen zur Selbstentfaltung und -verbesserung verhilft und deswegen der philosophischen Praxis vor deren Resultaten den Vorrang gewährt. Es ist demnach bloß folgerichtig, dass Lessing kein Interesse an Kohärenz und Konsistenz zeigt, und sogar die Aporetik des eigenen Denkens selbstbewusst reklamiert, zumal nur diese für den kontinuierlichen und offenen Charakter seiner theoretischen Bemühungen bürgen kann. Lessings Verzicht auf jegliches System und seine konsequente Begrüßung alles Vorläufigen, Fragmentarischen und potentiell Widersprüchlichen sind also keine Zeichen einer konstitutiven Unfähigkeit zum vermeintlich echten philosophischen Denken,[64] sondern geben im Gegenteil Lessings tiefverwurzelte Veranlagung zur philosophischen Praxis kund, und zwar in der Nachfolge keines Geringeren als Sokrates selbst.

Mendelssohns hier titelgebende und anfangs zitierte, die antike athletische Metaphorik aufgreifende Klage, 'die Gymnastik des Geistes' habe Lessing weit mehr als 'die reine Wahrheit' am Herzen gelegen, trifft also vollkommen zu, nur dass dies keine subjektive Eigentümlichkeit, geschweige denn persönliche Schwäche, darstellt, sondern einer vorsätzlich durch Einübung einverleibten philosophischen Sicht entspringt. 1799 berichtet Nicolai nicht von ungefähr, Lessings 'Manier' beim 'Disputiren [...], entweder die schwächste Partei zu nehmen, oder wenn jemand das *Dafür* vortrug, sogleich mit seltnem Scharfsinne das *Dawider* aufzusuchen', entstünde 'nicht aus Liebe zum Widersprechen', sondern aus der Absicht, 'Begriffe dadurch noch heller und bestimmter zu entwickeln', und aus der Überzeugung, 'daß in spekulativen Dingen sehr oft die gefundene Wahrheit nicht so viel werth ist, als die Uebung des Geistes, wodurch man sie zu finden sucht'.[65]

Echte Aufklärung, auch falls auf bloß theoretische Angelegenheiten angewandt, ist selbst nie bloß theoretisch, sondern fördert die menschliche (Selbst-)Vervollkommnung und stellt insofern eine bewusst gewählte und praktizierte Lebensform dar. Ob das sich mit dem ansonsten anerkannten Primat der konkreten Praxis gegenüber jedweder Theorie verträgt, muss hier offenbleiben und ließe sich unter Umständen schon gegen Sokrates einwenden. Lessings Stellung innerhalb des philosophischen Kanons bedarf offensichtlich der Neubewertung.

Notes to Chapter 1

1. Moses Mendelssohn, *Gesammelte Schriften: Jubiläumsausgabe*, hrsg. v. Ismar Elbogen u.a. (Stuttgart-Bad Cannstatt: frommann-holzboog, 1972–), XIII (1977), S. 125.
2. Vgl. Pierre Hadot, *Philosophie als Lebensform: Geistige Übungen in der Antike*, übers. v. Ilsetraut Hadot und Christiane Marsch (Berlin: Gatza, 1991, franz. Originalausgabe: 1981; 2. Ausgabe: 1987); Christoph Horn, *Antike Lebenskunst: Glück und Moral von Sokrates bis zu den Neuplatonikern* (München: Beck, 1998); *Philosophie als Lebenskunst: Antike Vorbilder, moderne Perspektiven*, hrsg. v. Ernst Gerhard (Berlin: Suhrkamp, 2016).
3. Platon, *Apologie des Sokrates*, 29d–e, neu übers. und kommentiert v. Rafael Ferber (München: Beck, 2011), S. 42.
4. Ebd., 38a, S. 61.
5. Platon, *Menon*, 86b–c, hrsg. und übers. v. Theodor Ebert (Berlin und Boston: de Gruyter, 2019), S. 85 (meine Kursivierungen).
6. Platon, *Der Staat*, 352d, übers. v. Rüdiger Rufener, hrsg. v. Thomas Alexander Szlezák (Düsseldorf und Zürich: Artemis & Winkler, 2000), S. 93.
7. Aristoteles, *Die Nikomachische Ethik*, 1103b, übers. v. Olof Gigon, neu hrsg. v. Rainer Nickel (Düsseldorf: Artemis & Winckler, [2]2007), S. 59.
8. Seneca, *Briefe an Lucilius*, 16, 3, hrsg. und übers. v. Gerhard Fink (Düsseldorf: Artemis & Winkler, 2007), S. 87.
9. Cicero, *Gespräche in Tusculum*, V, 4, mit ausführlichen Anmerkungen neu hrsg. v. Olof Gigon (Düsseldorf und Zürich: Artemis & Winkler, [7]2007), S. 325.
10. Vgl. Hadot, *Philosophie als Lebensform*; Ders., *Die innere Burg: Anleitung zu einer Lektüre Marc Aurels*, übers. v. Makoto Ozaki und Beate von der Osten (Frankfurt a.M.: Eichborn, 1997, franz. Originalausgabe: 1992); Ders., *Wege zur Weisheit oder Was lehrt uns die antike Philosophie?*, übers. v. Heiko Pollmeier (Frankfurt a.M.: Eichborn, 1999, franz. Originalausgabe: 1995), wo Hadot selber Paul Rabbows Monographie *Seelenführung: Methodik der Exerzitien in der Antike* (München: Kösel-Verlag, 1954) und Ilsetraut Hadots Dissertation *Seneca und die griechisch-römische Tradition der Seelenleitung* (Berlin: de Gruyter, 1969) als bestimmende Anregungen für seine eigene Arbeit anerkennt (S. 23).
11. Hadot, *Philosophie als Lebensform*, S. 15.
12. Vgl. Hadot, *Wege zur Weisheit*, S. 39–58.
13. Horn, *Antike Lebenskunst*, S. 19.
14. Ebd., S. 19–20, 26–31.
15. Nicht von ungefähr verweilt Horn (ebd., S. 31) beim ubiquitären Vergleich der Philosophie mit der Gymnastik, der sich beispielsweise bei Platon, Porphyrios und Epiktet findet.
16. Vgl. ebd., S. 233–44; Hadot, *Wege zur Weisheit*, S. 291–96.
17. Vgl. Hadot, *Wege zur Weisheit*, S. 300–10; Horn, *Antike Lebenskunst*, S. 233–44.
18. Vgl. Pierre Hadot, *N'oublie pas de vivre: Goethe et la tradition des exercices spirituels* (Paris: Éditions Albin Michel, 2008). Hadot erwähnt zwar Lessing, wenn auch nur beiläufig, in seiner Untersuchung *Le voile d'Isis: Essai sur l'histoire de l'idée de Nature* (Paris: Gallimard, 2004), S. 190,

270, geht aber keineswegs auf dessen mögliche Bedeutung für die moderne Wiederbelebung der antiken Philosophieauffassung ein.
19. Gotthold Ephraim Lessing, *Hamburgische Dramaturgie, 101.–104. Stück* (19. April 1768), in Ders., *Werke und Briefe in 12 Bänden*, hrsg. v. Wilfried Barner u.a. (Frankfurt a.M.: Deutscher Klassiker Verlag, 1985–2003), VI (1985), S. 680 (von nun an als FA mit Band- und Seitennummer angegeben).
20. Lessing, *Axiomata, wenn es deren in dergleichen Dingen giebt* (1778), FA, IX (1993), S. 57.
21. Lessing, *Selbstbetrachtungen und Einfälle* (1770–81), FA, X (2001), S. 240.
22. Lessing, *Gedanken über die Herrnhuter* (1751), FA, I (1989), S. 936. Dieser Text wurde für lange Zeit auf das Jahr 1750 zurückgeführt, ist aber 2008 mit stichhaltigen Argumenten umdatiert worden. Vgl. Hugh Barr Nisbet, *Lessing: Eine Biographie* (München: Beck, 2008), S. 174–79; Friedrich Vollhardt, *Gotthold Ephraim Lessing: Epoche und Werk* (Göttingen: Wallstein, 2018), S. 62–63.
23. Lessing, *Gedanken über die Herrnhuter*, FA, I, S. 936–37.
24. Ebd., S. 936.
25. Ebd., S. 937.
26. Ebd.
27. Ebd.
28. Ebd., S. 938.
29. Ebd.
30. Ebd.
31. Ebd.
32. Ebd., S. 942.
33. Ebd.
34. Ebd. Auch Epiktet greift auf das Gleichnis mit dem Theater zurück, um das menschliche Leben und die dem Einzelnen aufgetragene Aufgabe zu beschreiben, vgl. Epiktet, *Handbuch der Moral*, 17, in Epiktet — Teles — Musonius, *Ausgewählte Schriften*, hrsg. und übers. v. Rainer Nickel (Zürich: Artemis & Winkler; Darmstadt: Wissenschaftliche Buchgesellschaft, 1994), S. 25–27: 'Erinnere dich, daß du ein Schauspieler in einem Drama bist; deine Rolle verdankst du dem Schauspieldirektor. Spiele sie, ob sie nun kurz oder lang ist. Wenn er verlangt, daß du einen Bettler darstellst, so spiele auch diesen angemessen; ein Gleiches gilt für einen Krüppel, einen Herrscher oder einen Durchschnittsmenschen. / Denn das allein ist deine Aufgabe: die dir zugeteilte Rolle gut zu spielen; sie auszuwählen, ist Sache eines anderen'.
35. Vgl. Platon, *Phaidon*, 68e, zweite, durchgesehene Auflage übers. und hrsg. v. Barbara Zehnpfennig (Hamburg: Meiner, 2007), S. 31: 'In der Tat, Simmias, sagte er, üben sich also die rechten Philosophierenden im Sterben, und das Tot-Sein ist ihnen von allen Menschen am wenigsten furchtbar.' Zur Bedeutung dieser Einübung in den Tod sowohl für die griechischrömische Tradition als auch für die weitere Entwicklung abendländischen Denkens siehe Horn, *Antike Lebenskunst*, S. 25, 32; Friedo Ricken, '"Ars moriendi" — Zu Ursprung und Wirkungsgeschichte der Rede von der Sterbekunst', in *Sterben: Dimensionen eines anthropologischen Grundphänomens*, hrsg. v. Franz-Josef Bormann und Gian Domenico Borasio (Berlin und New York: de Gruyter, 2012), S. 309–24.
36. Lessing, *Gedanken über die Herrnhuter*, FA, I, S. 943.
37. Ebd.
38. Ebd., S. 943–44. Zu Rousseaus erstem *Discours* als Quelle für Lessings Würdigung des Sokrates in diesem ganzen Passus siehe Nisbet, *Lessing*, S. 177–79.
39. Lessing, *Hamburgische Dramaturgie, 49. Stück* (16. Oktober 1767), FA, VI, S. 426. Zu Lessings 'Sokratismus' siehe: Ingrid Strohschneider-Kohrs, 'Gesten der ars socratica in Lessings Schriften der Spätzeit', in *Streitkultur: Strategien des Überzeugens im Werk Lessings: Referate der Internationalen Lessing-Tagung der Albert-Ludwigs-Universität Freiburg und der Lessing Society an der University of Cincinnati, Ohio/USA, vom 22. bis 24. Mai 1991 in Freiburg im Breisgau*, hrsg. v. Wolfram Mauser und Günter Saße (Tübingen: Niemeyer, 1993), S. 501–08; Jörg Robert, 'Generalisierte Empfindung: Sentenz und "sokratische Lehrart" in Lessings *Minna von Barnhelm*', in *Sentenz in der Literatur: Perspektiven auf das 18. Jahrhundert*, hrsg. v. Alice Stašková und Simon Zeisberg (Göttingen: Wallstein, 2014), S. 160–87.

40. In den *Gedanken über die Herrnhuter* ist ein einziger Unterschied festzustellen, und zwar in Bezug auf das Verhältnis zwischen Philosophie und Christentum, das bei Hadot und Horn als Konkurrenz verstanden, bei Lessing hingegen in Form einer Parallelisierung beschrieben wird, zumal laut Letzterem auch der ursprüngliche Kern des Christentums ein praktischer war und binnen Kurzem in Vergessenheit geriet, vgl. FA, I, S. 938–42.
41. Zur präzisen Definition dieser Vorurteile siehe unten, Anm. 42, 43 und 44. Zu dieser hier nur angedeuteten Klassifizierung sowie zur Typologie der tragenden Grundideen der Aufklärung insgesamt siehe: Werner Schneiders, *Aufklärung und Vorurteilskritik: Studien zur Geschichte der Vorurteilstheorie* (Stuttgart-Bad Cannstatt: frommann-holzboog, 1983); Norbert Hinske, 'Die tragenden Grundideen der deutschen Aufklärung: Versuch einer Typologie', in Raffaele Ciafardone, *Die Philosophie der deutschen Aufklärung: Texte und Darstellung*, hrsg. v. Norbert Hinske und Rainer Specht (Stuttgart: Reclam, 1990), S. 407–58; Rainer Godel, *Vorurteil — Anthropologie — Literatur: Der Vorurteilsdiskurs als Modus der Selbstaufklärung im 18. Jahrhundert* (Tübingen: Niemeyer, 2007); Derselbe, 'Vorurteil', in *Handbuch Europäische Aufklärung: Begriffe, Konzepte, Wirkung*, hrsg. v. Heinz Thoma (Stuttgart und Weimar: Metzler, 2015), S. 548–57.
42. Lessing, *Der junge Gelehrte*, II/6, FA, I, S. 184. Dabei handelt es sich im Grunde genommen um Bacons *idola theatri*, welche auf die Zugehörigkeit zu einer bestimmten philosophischen Schule zurückgehen und in der späten Aufklärung nicht nur als 'Vorurtheil[e] der Secte', sondern auch als Vorurteile 'des Lehrgebäudes' beschrieben werden, vgl. Georg Friedrich Meier, *Beyträge zu der Lehre von den Vorurtheilen des menschlichen Geschlechts: Kritische Ausgabe*, hrsg. v. Heinrich P. Delfosse, Norbert Hinske und Paola Rumore (Pisa: ETS, 2005), S. 72.
43. Lessing, *Die Juden*, 6. Auftritt, FA, I, S. 461. Kurz darauf bestimmt Meier das hier in Frage stehende Vorurteil als das '*Vorurtheil der Völkerschaft*', das jedes Mal stattfindet, 'wenn man etwas verwirft, weil es von einem gewissen Volke herstamt', vgl. Georg Friedrich Meier, *Auszug aus der Vernunftlehre*, § 170 (Halle: Gebauer, 1752), S. 47.
44. Lessing, *Die Juden*, 19. Auftritt, FA, I, S. 482. Der anonyme Reisende insistiert mit Nachdruck auf der Notwendigkeit, jegliches Urteil mit Bedacht und Geduld zu fällen, denn nur auf diese Weise sei man vor Irrtümern geschützt; zum betreffenden Vorurteil als einem der zwei menschlichen Grundvorurteile überhaupt siehe schon Christian Thomasius, *Einleitung Zu der Vernunfft-Lehre [...]. Fünfte und correctere Auflage*, 13. Hauptstück, § 38, § 41, § 44 (Halle: Salfeld, 1719), S. 196–98: 'Dannenhero sind praejudicia und *Vorurtheile* nichts anders *als falsche Meynungen, die uns von Erkäntniß der Wahrheit abführen, welche sich der Mensch ohne Ursache wahr zu seyn beredet, entweder, weil er aus Leichtgläubigkeit von andern, deren Autorität er getrauet, dessen beredet worden, oder weil er aus Ungedult und darauf erfolgter Übereilung sich dessen selbst beredet [...] das Vorurtheil des Übereilung [...] das praejudicium praecipitantia, rühret aus einer unvernünftigen Selbst-Liebe zu unserer Gemächlichkeit her, unserer Nachläßigkeit und Ungedult zu schmeicheln, und ihnen sanffte zu thun, und wird auf gleiche Weise durch eine unzeitige Scham oder Faulheit bekräfftiget.*' Zu diesem besonderen Vorurteilstyp bei dem von Lessing geschätzten Thomasius wie auch beim jungen Lessing selbst, siehe: Manfred Beetz, 'Transparent gemachte Vorurteile: Zur Analyse der *praejudicia auctoritatis et praecipitantiae* in der Frühaufklärung', *Rhetorik: Ein internationales Jahrbuch*, 3 (1983), 7–33; Ders., 'Zur Diagnose von Vorurteilen in Lessings Frühwerk', in *Gotthold Ephraim Lessing im Kulturraum Schule: Aspekte der Wirkungsgeschichte im 19. Jahrhundert*, hrsg. v. Carsten Gansel, Norman Ächtler und Birka Siwczyk (Göttingen: Vandenhoeck & Ruprecht, 2017), S. 301–22 (S. 306–07, 318–19).
45. Laut Gisbert Ter-Nedden (*Lessings Trauerspiele: Der Ursprung des modernen Dramas aus dem Geist der Kritik* (Stuttgart: Metzler, 1986)) wird die 'Übereilung' in 'Lessings Trauerspielen [...] jedenfalls geradezu zum Äquivalent für die *hybris*, den tragischen passe-partout-Fehler der attischen Tragödie' (S. 182).
46. Lessing, *Hamburgische Dramaturgie, 95. Stück* (29. März 1768), FA, VI, S. 654–55 (meine Kursivierungen).
47. Das Vorurteil des Systems wurde damals vorwiegend als mit demjenigen der Sekte oder des Lehrgebäudes identisch bewertet, vgl. oben, Anm. 42.
48. Vgl. Lessing, *Laokoon: oder über die Grenzen der Malerei und Poesie* (1766), FA, V/2 (1990), S. 15.
49. Lessing, *Rettungen des Horaz*, FA, III (2003), S. 159.

50. Ebd.
51. Lessing, *Rettung des Hier. Cardanus* (1754), FA, III, S. 198.
52. Lessing, *Berengarius Turonensis: oder Ankündigung eines wichtigen Werkes desselben, wovon in der Herzoglichen Bibliothek zu Wolfenbüttel ein Manuscript befindlich, welches bisher völlig unerkannt geblieben* (1770), FA, VII (2000), S. 15. Die optische Metaphorik wird von Lessing umgekehrt auch für die Beschreibung der Verblendung durch Vorurteile eingesetzt: In der Jugendkomödie *Der Freigeist* (V/3) wirft Theophan Adrast vor, 'alles durch das gefärbte Glas seiner vorgefaßten Meinungen' zu betrachten, und deswegen nicht in der Lage zu sein, 'richtige Blicke zu tun' (FA, I, S. 435). Für weiterführende bibliographische Angaben zu diesem Aspekt verweise ich auf Beetz, 'Zur Diagnose von Vorurteilen in Lessings Frühwerk', S. 320.
53. Lessing, *Axiomata, wenn es deren in dergleichen Dingen giebt*, FA, IX, S. 57 (meine Kursivierungen).
54. Meier identifiziert eine theologische 'Variante' des Vorurteils des Systems und spricht diesbezüglich von dem 'Vorurtheil der Glaubensähnlichkeit oder der Rechtgläubigkeit', das '[i]n der christlichen Gottesgelahrtheit aller Secten herrscht', vgl. Meier, *Beyträge zu der Lehre von den Vorurtheilen des menschlichen Geschlechts*, S. 75.
55. Lessing, *Anti-Goeze* (1778), FA, IX, S. 95–96 (die zwei letzten Kursivierungen stammen von mir). Zur Reformation als 'essential precondition for the Enlightenment' siehe nun Ritchie Robertson, *The Enlightenment: The Pursuit of Happiness 1680–1790* (London: Penguin, 2020), S. 37–38, 200–06.
56. Lessing, *Briefe, die neueste Litteratur betreffend, Eilfter Brief (25. Januar 1759)*, FA, IV (1997), S. 479, 481 (meine Kursivierung).
57. Ebd., S. 479 (meine Kursivierungen).
58. Lessing, *Eine Duplik* (1778), FA, VIII (1989), S. 510 (meine Kursivierungen).
59. Man vergleiche Lessings Worte mit denjenigen Sokrates' im *Menon* und man wird unvermittelt Einsicht in Lessings tief verwurzelten 'Sokratismus' gewinnen, vgl. oben, Anm. 5.
60. Arno Schilson, *Lessings Christentum* (Göttingen: Vandenhoeck & Ruprecht, 1980), S. 88–90.
61. Vgl. oben, Anm. 46 (der betreffende Passus ist nur der wohl bekannteste, aber keineswegs der einzige, in dem sich Lessing an seine Leser wendet und sie zum Mit- oder Weitermachen einlädt); für Lessings Dialog mit seinen Lesern oder Zuschauern und das dieser Praxis zugrundeliegende Verständnis von Aufklärung vgl. auch Laura Anna Macor, 'L'illuminismo di Lessing: non solo *Selbstdenken*', in *Traiettorie di pensiero: Prospettive storico-teoretiche di riflessione e ricerca*, hrsg. v. Davide Poggi (Verona: QuiEdit, 2020), S. 49–66.
62. Lessing, *Wie die Alten den Tod gebildet* (1769), FA, VI, S. 717 (meine Kursivierungen). Zu Lessings 'Theorie und Praxis' der Kontroverse verweise ich auf: Evelyn K. Moore, *The Passions of Rhetoric: Lessing's Theory of Argument and the German Enlightenment* (Dordrecht: Springer, 1993); Alexander Košenina und Ritchie Robertson, 'Lessing as Journalist and Controversialist', in *Lessing and the German Enlightenment*, hrsg. v. Ritchie Robertson (Oxford: Voltaire Foundation, 2013), S. 39–63.
63. Vgl. Platon, *Apologie des Sokrates*, 30e, S. 45; Ders., *Menon*, 80a, S. 18; Ders., *Symposion*, 217e–218a, übers. v. Rudolf Rufener, hrsg. v. Thomas A. Szlezák (Düsseldorf und Zürich: Artemis & Winckler, 2002), S. 137.
64. Als prominentes Beispiel für dieses (übrigens weit verbreitete) Missverständnis verweise ich auf Hugh Barr Nisbets einleitende Sätze zu seinem Aufsatz 'Lessing and Philosophy', in *A Companion to the Works of Gotthold Ephraim Lessing*, hrsg. v. Barbara Fischer und Thomas C. Fox (Rochester, NY: Camden House, 2005), 133–54: 'Lessing was not a philosopher. But philosophy is a recurrent presence in his works. Whether or not his scattered references on the subject reflect a consistent philosophical viewpoint is, however, debatable [...] few would now claim to reduce Lessing's assorted pronouncements to a unified philosophical system' (S. 133).
65. Friedrich Nicolai, *Ueber meine gelehrte Bildung, über meine Kenntniß der kritischen Philosophie und meine Schriften dieselbe betreffend, und über die Herren Kant, J. B. Erhard, und Fichte* (Berlin und Stettin: Nicolai, 1799), S. 41–42.

CHAPTER 2

'[D]er eifrigste [...] Aufklärer [...] in Trier': A Case Study in the Late Enlightenment in Germany

Kevin Hilliard

In 1829 the Director of the Königlich-Preußisches Gymnasium and Librarian of the Stadtbibliothek in Trier, Johann Hugo Wyttenbach, had his portrait painted by his brother-in-law Johann Anton Ramboux. It has an attractive *biedermeierlich* sobriety:

FIG. 2.1. Johann Anton Ramboux, Porträt von Johann Hugo Wyttenbach (1829). Stadtmuseum Simeonstift Trier-Inv. Nr:III.1595, Photo: Bernhard Matthias Lutz, Konz.

The dress and bearing of the sitter mark him out as a local notable. If we were unsure, the ribbon of the *Roter Adlerorden* (*Zweite Klasse*), modestly visible behind the arched finger, would be the decisive clue. The bound volume presents his credentials as a man of learning. The title can be made out: *Tod und Zukunft*. This *Anthologie für edle Menschen*, as it was called in the subtitle, was Wyttenbach's work, first published in 1806 and in a second edition in 1821.

So far, so worldly. But let us look again. The lettering in the top left corner gives the sitter's age:

FIG. 2.2. Johann Anton Ramboux,
Porträt von Johann Hugo Wyttenbach (1829) (detail)

In itself this might not seem important — no more important than the grey hair that is beginning to show. But take these together with the deliberate way in which the finger points to the title on the spine of the book, and a deeper significance is revealed (Figure 3).

FIG. 2.3. Johann Anton Ramboux,
Porträt von Johann Hugo Wyttenbach (1829) (detail)

Tod und Zukunft are not just any words. Whatever his actual life expectancy,[1] the 'future' that the sitter is anticipating has 'death' as its precondition. The painting, which celebrates a successful life on this earth, points forward to death and a life beyond the grave. The society portrait is also a discreet *memento mori*.

Inspection of the book itself confirms the impression. The reader is greeted by this frontispiece (Figure 4):

FIG. 2.4. *Tod und Zukunft. In einer Anthologie von Aussprüchen älterer und neuerer Dichter und Philosophen*, ed. by Johann Hugo Wyttenbach (Leipzig: Hempel, 1806). Frontispiece, engraved by Johann August Rosmäßler from a design by Veit Schnorr von Carolsfeld. Bayerische Staatsbibliothek, P.o.germ. 1649, urn:nbn:de:bvb:12-bsb10123809-3.

The motto on the title page that follows, taken from Voß, tells us that it is 'Weisheit [...], der Todten gedenken und seines | Todes auch'.[2]

A contemporary review of the work, from Catholic Germany, was not slow to see the affinity between what it proposed and the *ars moriendi* of the Jesuits:[3]

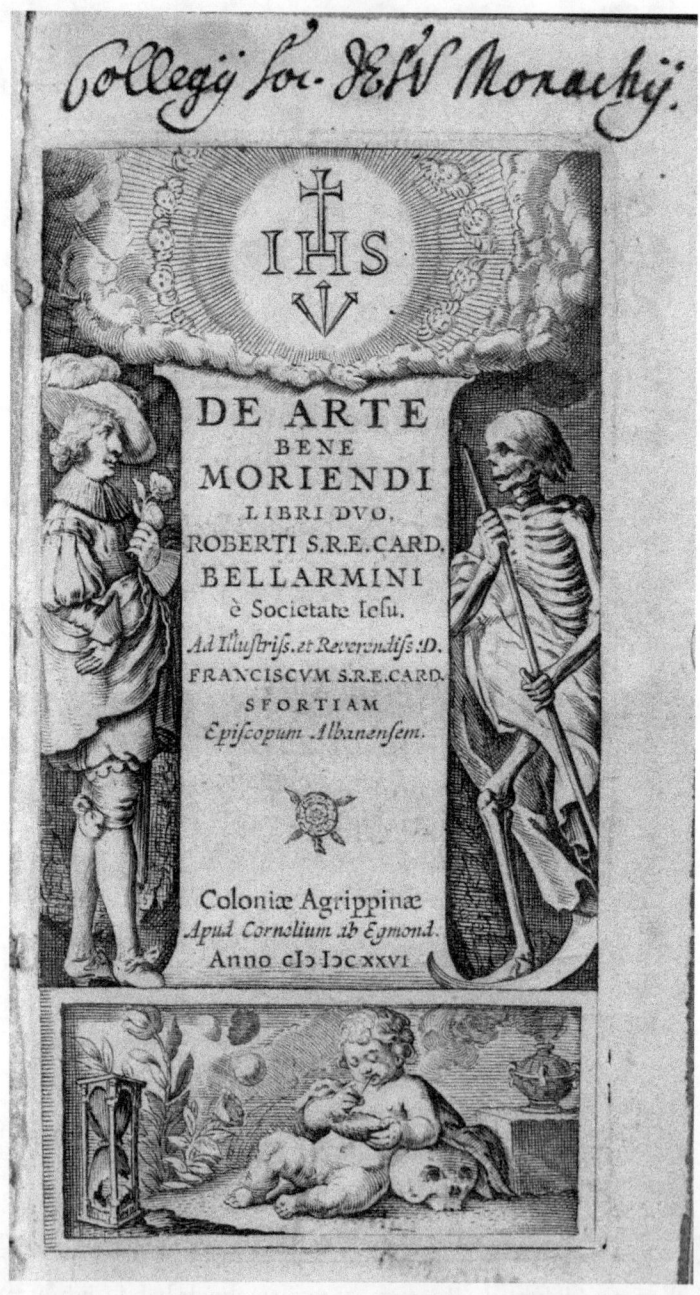

FIG. 2.5. Roberto Francesco Romolo Bellarmin, *De arte bene moriendi libri duo* (Cologne: Cornelius ab Egmont, 1626). Title page. Bayerische Staatsbibliothek, Asc. 421, urn:nbn:de:bvb:12-bsb10260028–1.

It is true that the differences are more immediately striking. Where once death was represented by a skeleton with a scythe, transience by a broken hourglass, the fragility of human life by a child's soap-bubbles, now a different iconography takes over. Wyttenbach's frontispiece is inspired by Lessing's *Wie die Alten den Tod gebildet* (1769):

> Die alten Artisten stellten den Tod nicht als Skelet [sic] vor [...] [Er] war [...] den Alten [...] ein [...] Jüngling, der in einer tiefsinnigen Stellung, den linken Fuß über den rechten geschlagen, neben einem Leichname stehet [...].[4]

A butterfly, symbolizing the soul, released from its earthly confinement, perches on the shoulder of the corpse. The heroic nudes lend death a manly beauty.[5] A prettified modern *ars moriendi* has replaced the terrors of the old.

What has not changed, however, is the conviction that there is an art to dying well, and that a manual is needed to help us master it. Wyttenbach, who had been taught by Jesuits at the seminary in Trier,[6] took away from the experience a dislike of their 'ascetische Betrachtungsbücher'.[7] But the need they addressed (or created) did not go away. *Tod und Zukunft* responds to it.

Let us dial the clock back to an earlier date — indeed an altogether different epoch. It is 10 brumaire, year VII of the French Republic (31 October 1798), and the young teacher Johann Hugo Wyttenbach is to give a speech.[8] Trier has been under French occupation since 1794. Since the beginning of 1798, it has been annexed to France, as the capital of the new Département de la Sarre (Saar-Departement).

Wyttenbach, an enthusiastic recruit to the republican regime, is one of the men of the moment. The education system is to be rebuilt from the ground up, along French lines. The French administration, impressed by 'son civisme, ses bonnes mœurs, ses talens [sic] et ses connaissances dans la philosophie critique', has nominated Wyttenbach, a private tutor for the previous ten years, to a post in the new secondary school, the École Centrale or Zentralschule.[9] The day after his speech, he will be appointed to a three-man commission to draw up proposals for the reform of the primary schools in the Departement.[10]

The occasion of the speech is a so-called 'Dekaden-Feier', marking the end of the ten-day week of the revolutionary calendar, adopted in 1792, in force since 1793, and now newly instituted in the annexed territories.[11] That Wyttenbach is giving the speech, at the very first of these ceremonial events of the new regime, is itself a mark of the confidence the new government has in him.[12] The brief is (of course) to celebrate republican values.[13] In his speech, accordingly, shortly to be published under the title 'Denkmal den Wohlthätern des Menschengeschlechts', Wyttenbach, after tracing the ascending path of human development from Osiris (!) to Benjamin Franklin, Rousseau and Kant, dwells with particular fervour on the achievements of republics ancient and modern, culminating in 1789 and the 'unvergeßlich schöne Zeiten des Ausbruchs der fränkischen Revolution'.[14]

One must assume that his listeners went away correspondingly edified. Wolfgang Hans Stein remarks that the exposition of the values of the Republic in the 'Dekadenreden' resembled that of doctrine in Christian preaching.[15] The setting in this case would have underlined the point. The 'Dekadenreden' were given in a 'Dekadentempel', which in the case of Trier was a secularized church, the Dreifaltigkeitskirche, now dedicated to a new trinity, the Republican *liberté, égalité, fraternité*. The speaker addressed his audience from the pulpit, now beribboned in the red, white and blue of the tricolour. In the crossing, in lieu of saints and martyrs, stood the freshly erected, bare-bosomed figure of the goddess of Reason.[16]

Wyttenbach knew the setting well. The erstwhile Dreifaltigkeitskirche was cheek by jowl with the old seminary,[17] in which, between 1786 and 1788, after his early schooling in Koblenz and two years of preparatory studies in theology at the university in Trier, he himself had trained for the priesthood. One of the best of his cohort ('unus ex optimis'), he had been judged 'highly suited' to his calling ('perquam idoneus').[18] In 1788, to the displeasure of his patron, who had funded his studies, he had renounced his vocation, resolving from then on to make teaching his profession.[19] Then the world changed around him. The *ancien régime* ended, the Republic began. Instead of swimming against the current, Wyttenbach was now riding the rising tide. A year after the fugitive from the priesthood stepped up to the pulpit on 10 brumaire, year VII, he would begin his career in the new Zentralschule, housed in the familiar surroundings of the seminary next door.

Republican school for seminary, temple of reason for church, republican orator and renegade seminarian for ordained priest, 'Dekadenrede' for Sunday sermon: the set of substitutions could barely be improved on as a textbook case of secularization.[20] The question is, however, whether any substitution (as opposed to eradication without replacement) does not bring with it continuity as well as change — a continuity of form, purpose, function, place in the fabric of social and individual life, in which secularization proceeds only by providing a balancing sacralization to make up for what has been abandoned. The modern *memento mori* discussed at the beginning hints at something of this kind. This will be our thread in what follows.

Wyttenbach's life and career is well documented. The *Stadtarchiv Trier* holds his voluminous personal and professional papers. There have been a number of excellent studies of the various facets of his activities.[21] I can confine myself to a few salient points.

The decisive *Bildungserlebnis* of his life was his encounter with Kant's philosophy.[22] He studied not only Kant's own writings from the moment they appeared, but also those of virtually all the major or minor Kantians of the 1780s and 1790s.[23] Like many of this group (a number of whom were theologians), what he drew from Kant's philosophy was chiefly the reassurance that the abandonment of orthodox Christianity did not entail the end of religious belief: '[D]ie Critik der Vernunft[24] [giebt] dem moralischen Menschen wieder, was sie dem bloß speculativen nahm; gründet nicht die Moralität auf Religion, sondern eine vernünftige Religion auf die Moralität.'[25] This is what, in a nutshell, Wyttenbach called Kant's 'moralischer Beweis für das Daseyn Gottes'.[26] 'Immer wieder ist spürbar', Walther Gose remarks, 'wie sehr hier Wesentliches der alten Lebenswelt dem neuen Denken in analoger Bedeutung erhalten bleiben soll.'[27] The ex-Catholic Wyttenbach was perhaps not being entirely facetious when he referred to Kant as '[der] Heilige Vater von

Königsberg';[28] and certainly not when he called his own philosophical statement of belief a 'Credo' and 'Herzens-Bekenntniß'.[29]

Another fixed point in his thinking was the notion of the *Bestimmung des Menschen*, a central idea of the *Aufklärung*.[30] Wyttenbach could not have sustained his 'rational' faith without the conviction that the world and human life had *purpose*: for it was this, above all, that needed saving from the wreckage of orthodox religion.[31] Again and again Wyttenbach appealed to this notion.[32] It assumes that human beings do not determine their own purpose, in unconditioned *Selbstbestimmung*; their purpose is determined for them, by a *Bestimmung* given them by God or nature. To this master-idea Wyttenbach assimilated Kant's own more tentative use of the language of purpose. This is what gave him licence to throw away the crutch of what Kant called 'Kirchenglaube' or 'statuarische' and 'historische Religion',[33] leaving a pure moral religion to occupy the intellectual and affective space it had vacated.

In political and constitutional questions, it was again Kant and the Kantians who gave Wyttenbach his lead.[34] It was their thought, with an admixture of natural law and Rousseau's 'general will', that informed his own republicanism.[35]

The secondary school where Wyttenbach taught, the École Centrale or Zentralschule (later renamed 'Collège'), had successively housed the Jesuit seminary, and, after the suppression of the order in 1773, the Clementinisches Seminar, where he himself had studied. Part of the same building was occupied by the Stadtbibliothek, which was formed from the collections of the former seminary and of the university, after the latter was closed down in 1798. For nearly forty years, Wyttenbach was both a teacher at the school and the city librarian (unofficially from 1799, officially from 1804).[36]

'L'univers est gouverné par les livres'.[37] True or not, this certainly reflects Wyttenbach's views. During his time, the *Stadtbibliothek* expanded considerably, successively adding the libraries of secularized monasteries and substantial private collections to its holdings.[38] After his death, his own library of around 1,500 volumes passed into the public collection.[39]

Wyttenbach's feelings for books were not solely those of a public official or private bibliophile. Instead they are part and parcel of what it meant to be an *Aufklärer*. *Aufklärung* was, among other things, a battle of and over books and reading.

The aim of the authorities in the days of the *Kurfürstentum* was to ensure that students read only permitted books, and to keep everything else out of their hands.[40] According to Kurfürst Clemens Wenzeslaus himself, it was the 'Lesung gefährlicher Bücher', among other things, that had led to the collapse of 1794.[41] His view was that the 'prétendue Aufklaerung [...] ne sert qu'à égarer le peuple et le précipiter finalement dans l'irréligion'.[42] It is not surprising that in the holdings of the seminary and university libraries works of Enlightenment thought from about 1750 onwards were weakly represented.[43] Any such literature was in any case sequestered among the *libri prohibiti*.[44]

Any young man who wished to be corrupted therefore had to look elsewhere. This explains both the size and the composition of Wyttenbach's private library, and the much larger one of his wealthier friend Johann Peter Job Hermes.[45]

It also explains the close involvement of the young Wyttenbach in the Trier *Lesegesellschaft* of 1783, which he joined in 1791, two years before it was shut down by the government; and again in the newly constituted *Lesegesellschaft* of 1799.[46] Wyttenbach acted as librarian in both societies.[47] Keeping abreast of the latest books and journals was the primary objective. The 1783 society in particular was a seed-bed of *Aufklärung* ideas and values.[48]

Their reading was the substance of the lively correspondence led by Wyttenbach with his friends Johann Christian Gecks, Ludwig Weyprecht Mohr and Hermes.[49] It was in their letters that their views coalesced around a set of *Aufklärung* convictions, prominent among them those inspired by Kant. The battle for freedom of thought was won in a *Privatöffentlichkeit* with its own channels of communication.

Wyttenbach was a teacher and a public figure. He was not content to share his thoughts only with a few chosen friends. His mission was to spread the light: to be an *Aufklärer* in the full sense of the word. In the French period, this mission coincided with the aims of the state, at least until Napoleon had himself crowned Emperor in 1804. We have already seen evidence in his public speaking. His republican sermons perhaps made the greater splash, but his ideas were more substantially embodied in the shape he gave to the school curriculum. The change of regime made Trier a laboratory of *Aufklärung* pedagogy, and Wyttenbach took full advantage of his privileged position of being in at the beginning, both as director of the secondary Zentralschule, and as a member of the small committee set up to reform the primary schools.

The manifesto for primary schooling (up to age fourteen) he published in 1799 sets forth the principles that he believed should inform education at all levels.[50] The aim is to educate future citizens of a republic. Beyond the techniques of reading, writing, etc. what counts above all is 'eine deutliche, für die Vernunft und Herz eindringliche Unterweisung in den Rechten und Pflichten des *Menschen* und des *Bürgers*':

> Die großen Wahrheiten von der Bestimmung des Menschen, seiner moralischen Vervollkommnung, der Erhaltung seiner ewig geltenden Rechte, der göttlichen Größe der Tugend, und dann von dem Zwecke des Staats, von den Rechten und Verbindlichkeiten des Staatsbürgers, rücke der Lehrer in ihrer ganzen Klarheit und Herrlichkeit vor das Auge der jungen Bürger. [...] Das allgemeine Fundament, worauf alles gestützt werde, sey [...] die unwidersprechliche Wahrheit, daß der Grund, auf welchen alle wahre Verbesserung der Welt gebaut werden muß, allein das *Gesetz der sittlichen Vernunft* seyn könne, und daß Freyheit in der Erfüllung aller Pflichten und dem vernunftmäßigen Gebrauche aller Kräfte, und Gleichheit in Rechten der Grundpfeiler seyen, worauf die gesellschaftlichen Verbindungen der Menschen errichtet seyn sollen.[51]

The Kantian foundation is unmistakable, as is the central place given to the idea of human *Bestimmung*.[52] Both are again well to the fore in a more detailed plan, published a year later.[53] Its outline of religious teaching is pure *Aufklärung*. The beauty of natural creation gives young minds an apprehension of a divine creator. This physicotheological overture, however, is only a concession to children's limited understanding.[54] As soon as possible, they must move beyond it to religious instruction proper. This takes the form of a (suitably simplified) theology based on the Kantian moral law, which in turn grounds the belief in God's existence and our hopes of immortality.[55] Christianity, scripture, revelation and historical religion are not on the curriculum.[56]

Wyttenbach's ambitions went beyond Trier and the Saar-Departement. The vehicle for his wider pedagogical aims were the anthologies he published between 1796 and 1826:

> *Aussprüche der philosophirenden Vernunft*[57] *und des reinen Herzens über die der Menschheit wichtigsten Gegenstände. Mit besonderer Rücksicht auf die kritische Philosophie. Zusammen getragen aus den Schriften älterer und neuerer Denker*, 3 vols (1796/97–1799)[58] 1032 pp.[59]

A second edition changed the title and gave the names of the editors:

> *Aussprüche des reinen Herzens und der philosophirenden Vernunft über die der Menschheit wichtigsten Gegenstände. Zusammen getragen [...] von J. H. Wyttenbach [...] und J. A. Neurohr [...]*, 3 vols (Leipzig: Roch, 1801–21) 1259 pp.[60]
>
> *Tod und Zukunft. In einer Anthologie von Aussprüchen älterer und neuerer Dichter und Philosophen* (Leipzig: Hempel, 1806; 2nd edn Leipzig: Gleditsch, 1821) 368 pp. (2nd edn 332 pp.)
>
> *Der Geist der Religion. Eine philosophische Anthologie* (Frankfurt a.M.: Mohr, 1806) 227 pp.
>
> *Urania oder die Natur in ihrer höhern Bedeutung. Ein Seitenstück zur Anthologie: Tod und Zukunft* (Leipzig: Kayser, 1823; 2nd edn 1826) 340 pp. (2nd edn 348 pp.)

The first of these was initiated by and edited together with his friend, the physician Johann Anton Neurohr, though there are reasons to suspect that Wyttenbach had the larger role, especially in the second edition.[61] The later collections were Wyttenbach's work alone.

The plan laid down in the *Aussprüche* is followed throughout the series. The body of the text, after a brief preface, is composed of shorter or longer quotations, ordered under subject headings. A list of authors and works allows readers to identify the writers who are included. As the title indicates, the *Aussprüche* were designed as a primer of 'critical' (i.e. Kantian) philosophy. With the exception of *Urania*, Kant and Kantianism remain central.

Norbert Hinske calls the *Aussprüche* one of the 'facetten-, quellen- und aufschluß-reichsten Textauswahlen der deutschen Aufklärung'.[62] They await more detailed study. A few brief observations have to suffice here.

The philosophers outweigh the poets, the moderns the ancients, the Germans those of other European nations, men the women (overwhelmingly). There is a parsimonious sprinkling of non-Europeans. Works after 1750 are more generously represented than those before. The emphasis is on uplifting and reassuring truths, on edification rather than criticism. Denominational boundaries are freely crossed; in the space of a couple of pages, Luther, Calvin and Pope Clement XIV rub shoulders with Erasmus, Spinoza, Leibniz and Rousseau.[63] A line is drawn only against atheism and materialism. The clandestine Enlightenment remains out of sight. Scepticism, cynicism and satire are banished. One would scarcely guess how much of the work of Enlightenment had consisted in clearing away tenacious errors. Only the shining truth is left standing. In the *Aussprüche*, sections on the 'Gesetz der

Sittlichkeit', 'Tugend' and 'Pflicht' tread on each other's heels. There is a section on 'Aufklärung' itself, and a substantial one on 'Bestimmung des Menschen'.[64]

Only the second volume of the *Aussprüche*'s first edition could be said to court controversy. There we find critical sections on 'Offenbahrung', 'Wunder' and 'Schwärmerey'. The section on 'Christenthum', mostly bland in what it contains, is striking in what it omits: sin, salvation, grace, redemption.[65] The second part of the volume moves on to political questions. The section on 'Revolution', unusually, presents a spectrum of opinions, from cautious advocates of evolutionary change, to outright defenders of the right to revolution, such as Georg Forster and Johann Benjamin Erhard, with Kant hedging his position in the middle.[66]

The terms of the title are carefully chosen. They articulate the notion that what modern philosophy had brought to full consciousness (in the mind) had previously been grasped intuitively (in the heart). 'Die Aussprüche des natürlichen moralischen Gefühls' were a 'verschleierte Anzeige des göttlichen Gesetzes der Sittlichkeit' revealed by philosophy (and especially critical philosophy).[67]

The phrasing is revealing. Wyttenbach takes over the metaphor of the veil from Christian hermeneutics, where it was used to characterize the opaque revelation of the Old Testament, in contrast to the full revelation of the New.[68] By extension, the same notion was applied to the better apprehensions of the pagan philosophers, discerned, not by the dim and fitful light of human reason, but by an obscure inner impulse.[69] Wyttenbach takes over the scheme, but reverses the positions. It is to philosophy that the clear understanding of truth has been vouchsafed; anything pointing in the same direction before the *Aufklärung* and Kant was an intuition dictated by the 'heart' — a rubric under which the teachings of Jesus himself were subsumed.[70]

The 'Aussprüche des reinen Herzens', then, were to the 'philosophirende Vernunft' of modern times what, under the Christian dispensation, the intimations of the prophets and philosophers had been to the manifest teaching of the gospels. Together they added up to a freshly proclaimed '*Evangelium von ewigen Wahrheiten*'.[71]

Demoted to the role of forerunner, the Christian gospel's epoch-defining power, too, was spent. The Christian era was over. A new age was dawning: 'Das kommende 7te [Jahrtausend] wird bald die Neueste Welt heißen.'[72] By a happy synchronicity, the French Republic had already started counting the days, months and years from a new year one in 1792. This was not the coincidence it might appear at first sight. For not only Kant's teaching, but the Revolution, too, was the fruit of Enlightenment. Arriving simultaneously, the two revolutions, one intellectual, the other political, but the product of ideas, went together, as related and analogous expressions of the same principle.[73] Together they inaugurated the new age. 'Von hier und heute', Wyttenbach might have said, 'geht eine neue Epoche der Weltgeschichte aus, und [ich kann] sagen, [ich bin] dabei gewesen.'[74]

For a new epoch, a new set of sacred texts. But how else to signal the substitution than to don the habit of the old? The motto to *Der Geist der Religion* puts on the mantle of St Paul:

Πάντα δοκιμάζετε, τὸ καλὸν κατέχετε.

> Prüfet Alles, das Gute behaltet.
> *Paulus*, 1. Thess. 5, 21. — [75]

A piece of compressed analogical reasoning lies behind the choice of the apostle to front the book: it is to be to the new age what the gospels were to the old. The motto itself indicates the use readers are to make of the volume, and the others in the series. This, too, is a traditional one, and appeals to intellectual and devotional habits formed in relation to Scripture. In both cases, *katechein* (*tenere*, *behalten*), 'holding fast', 'im Gedächtniß [...] verwahren, ins Herze einschließen' is the purpose:[76] new books, old practices. Best of all is when the gifts of the spirit are shared. Then reading becomes worship: '[W]o zwei oder drei versammelt sind, [...] wollen meine Anthologieen [...] seyn.'[77]

The title page of the *Aussprüche* declares that the contents have been 'zusammen getragen aus den Schriften älterer und neuerer Denker'. The variety of terms used to designate the genre of the volume and its sequels — 'Anthologie' (as just seen),[78] 'Sammlung',[79] 'Auswahl',[80] and 'Blumenlese'[81] and its Latin equivalent 'Florilegium'[82] — point to one source: the venerable practice of keeping a commonplace book to gather the 'sayings' (*apophthegmata*, *sententiae*, *dicta*, 'Aussprüche') of the wise and the 'flowers' (*anthē, flores*, 'Blumen') of the poets.[83]

Wyttenbach and his friend and co-editor Neurohr show their workings in the prefaces to the two editions of the *Aussprüche*:

> Um sich selbst in einer Übersicht das, was die edelsten, besten Menschen von jeher über das, was *wahr, gut* und *schön* gedacht, geglaubt und empfunden haben — alles, was dem Menschen wichtig ist — darzustellen, sammelten zwey Freunde aus den hinterlassenen theuren Fragmenten der vorzüglichsten Denker des Altherthums, und aus den Schätzen der Geistesthätigkeit neuerer Denker die folgenden Resultate der philosophirenden Vernunft, und Aussprüche des reinen Herzens.[84]

The next step was to publish the product of their private labours, so that others might benefit. This decision, too, was hallowed by tradition.[85] They look back to Leibniz, who looks back to the ninth-century compiler Photius (or Photios):

> Der große *Leibnitz* bestärkte uns in unserm Vorhaben. Wir erinnerten uns, daß er einmal sagte: 'Aus den Schriftstellern sollte man ausziehen, und dabey von den ältesten Zeiten anfangen, doch aber nicht Alles erzählen, sondern was zum *Unterricht des menschlichen Geschlechts* dienet, auswählen. [...] [Es] wäre [...] nöthig, aus einzelnen, und zwar den Original-Schriftstellern, Eklogen wie *Photius* zu machen, und ihr Merkwürdiges mit den Worten des Schriftstellers selbst zu sammeln.'[86]

If there was a decline in the practice in the modern period, there is no sign of it here.[87] Many kept their faith in the methods of humanist learning.[88] His series of anthologies shows that Wyttenbach remained wedded to them until well into the nineteenth century.

The very words in which he and Neurohr present their project offer the proof in practice. The art of the commonplace book was to order one's excerpts under topic headings. The self-referential topic of their prefaces and other paratexts was the value and purpose of reading and excerpting. The mottos and extracts they chose to illustrate this topic were plucked from under the relevant heading of their commonplace books. Thus the verse from St Paul discussed above; thus, too, the excerpt from Leibniz in the preface to the *Aussprüche* (taken, not from Leibniz himself, but from Herder).[89] Other commonplace books were a quarry.[90] A passage from Lucretius, quoted at the end of the preface, was a long-standing favourite:

> Möchten wir mit *Lucretius* sagen können:
> > Floriferis ut apes in saltibus omnia libant,
> > Omnia nos itidem decerpsimus aurea dicta![91]

The quotation from Horace that forms one of the mottos to the first edition of *Tod und Zukunft* — 'Inter cuncta leges, et percontabere doctos' ('amid all these affairs you will read and interrogate the philosophers')[92] — could have been found in Georg Maior's *Sententiae veterum poetarum* (1534), under the heading 'Lectio'; and in an augmented edition by Antonio Mancinelli (1551), under the heading 'Lectio bonorum authorum' [sic].[93]

One anthologist Wyttenbach and Neurohr acknowledge explicitly was Bernhard Pez, a Benedictine monk, compiler of the *Thesaurus Anecdotorum Novissimus* (1721–23), from whom they borrowed a passage from the twelfth-century writer Alanus ab Insulis (Alain de Lille).[94] We can picture Wyttenbach as the secular equivalent of Pez, as he is portrayed in the frontispiece to his great work (Figure 2.6).

The anthologist sits at his desk, open volumes propped on his knee or held up for him by obliging *putti*, so that he can copy out what he needs on the leaf in front of him.[95] His task is to extract the best from the new books flying off the printing press, 'ut prosint', 'that they may be of use', retrieve what is valuable from the old books and manuscripts that lie scattered at his feet, 'ne pereant', 'that they may not perish', and so keep the candles of learning burning, 'ut luceant', 'that they may shine brightly'. He does his work of replenishing the light by the light his work has replenished. Take away the angelic assistants and exchange the monk's habit for modern dress, and we have a perfect picture of Wyttenbach's aims and working methods (and the bookish nature of his *Aufklärung*).

The anthologies took shape, then, by a diligent habit of copying and filing under rubrics. This was well understood by reviewers: 'Die Sammler haben viele schätzbare Werke älterer und neuerer Schriftsteller durchgelesen, und Stellen daraus [...] excerpirt und unter Titel gebracht.'[96] Not everyone was impressed:

> Eine solche Art der Schriftstellerey ist nun freylich nicht eben sehr verdienstlich. Wem es nicht ganz an Einsicht und Geschmack gebricht, der darf nur mit der Feder in der Hand ruhig der Wollust des Lesens pflegen, sich zuweilen bemühen, auf besondern Blättern eine Stelle abzuschreiben, und zuletzt diese Blätter beliebig klassificiren: so ist das Produkt schon zum Abdrucke reif.[97]

This is to take a sour view of the method. The form had been engineered over centuries for the ready assimilation of ideas and their rapid reuse by readers. Rapid, but not frictionless — not in an age of critical *Selbstdenken*: '[J]enes apostolische "Prüft alles und das Beste [sic] behaltet"' was the 'Grundsatz unserer Zeiten'.[98] If the anthology itself was a receptacle (*Behältnis*), containing what the editors had

FIG. 2.6. Bernhard Pez, *Thesaurus Anecdotorum Novissimus: Seu Veterum Monumentorum, præcipuè Ecclesiasticorum, ex Germanicis potissimùm Bibliothecis adornata*. Tomus I. Augsburg and Graz: Veith, 1721. Bayerische Staatsbibliothek. 2 P.lat.c. 27–1. urn:nbn:de:bvb:12-bsb10798863–5. Engraved by Georg Wilhelm Salmusmüller. The words on the open pages and separate leaves are *lorem ipsum* filler.

'tested', the process had to be repeated by the readers.[99] It was this that Wyttenbach and Neurohr had in mind with the *Aussprüche*. The aim was to give wider currency and critical traction to the 'results' of *Aufklärung* thought.[100] A moral mission is part of the package.[101]

A more substantial criticism would be that the genre has a built-in conservative bias. As we have seen, Wyttenbach and Neurohr deliberately mixed in the new maxims of *Aufklärung* with the reassuring teachings of tradition. But in this they were only going with the grain of the form. It was in the nature of the exercise that the new was continuously added to the old without displacing it.[102] What was perhaps more insidious was that the headings under which the excerpts were filed presented a largely stable set of categories, an unquestioned framework within which all thought, new or old, had to be conducted. True, in the first edition of the *Aussprüche* 'Revolution' was added to the topic headings. But the on the whole the rubrics themselves were not revolutionary. 'Gott', 'Pflicht', 'Tugend', 'Mensch', 'Weisheit', 'Wahrheit', etc. would have found a ready place in anthologies that were many centuries old.[103] Even in the 1790s the medium may have acted as much to domesticate and contain any revolutionary energies as to release them.

The fire in any case seems to have gone out of Wyttenbach around 1805. The epoch begun so auspiciously in 1789 came to an unexpectedly rapid end. An Empire replaced the Republic.[104] The republican calendar was revoked. Restrictions on the Church were lifted. The seminary in Trier reopened.[105] Prayer books flooded the market.[106] Wyttenbach's own later anthologies beat a retreat from politics. The second edition of the *Aussprüche* took out the more incendiary headings. Kantian morality and religion remained. But the teachings of philosophy now took second place to those of the 'heart' in the title (and the reference to 'critical philosophy' was omitted altogether).

In 1814 Trier became part of Prussia. Wyttenbach made his peace with the new regime.[107] He kept his position as director of the city library and the *Gymnasium*, though there were mutterings about the liberal tendencies of the school throughout his tenure.[108] As we have seen, he was even elevated to the *Roter Adlerorden* by the Prussian king.[109] He continued to deliver speeches. His 'Schulreden' were secular sermons on the value of education and the noble ideals to which we should devote our lives. They typically ended with an uplifting quotation:

> Erinnert Euch oft der Worte des Dichters:
>
>> Nicht gab dir Gott vergebens
>> Den Geist des edlern Lebens
>> Geh' hin, und leuchte, wo er ruft.[110]

Wyttenbach would not have had far to look for the lines: they were in the *Aussprüche*, under the heading 'Aufklärung'.[111]

Notes to Chapter 2

1. On statistical average, a further eleven years (Gesis: Leibniz-Insitut für Sozialwissenschaften, Zeitreihen zur Historischen Statistik, ZA 8066, Arthur E. Imhof, Lebenserwartungen in Deutschland vom 17. bis 19. Jahrhundert, table D.3.P.m, <https://histat.gesis.org/histat/de/data/themes/1> [accessed 19 Aug. 2020]. In the event, Wyttenbach lived another nineteen.
2. Johann Heinrich Voß, 'Der Tag auf dem Lande'. In the second edition of 1821, the motto was replaced by one from Plato, *Phaedo* 81a: 'Μελέτη Θανατου' (cultivate dying) (Plato, *Euthyphro. Apology. Crito. Phaedo*, ed. and trans. by Chris Emlyn-Jones and William Preddy, Loeb Classical Library, 36 (Cambridge MA and London: Harvard University Press, 2017), p. 387).
3. *Oberdeutsche allgemeine Litteraturzeitung*, 19.2 (1806), no. 97 (16 August 1806), col. 325–30 (col. 325–26).
4. Quoted in *Tod und Zukunft: In einer Anthologie von Aussprüchen älterer und neuerer Dichter und Philosophen*, ed. by Johann Hugo Wyttenbach (Leipzig: Hempel, 1806), pp. 195–97. Cf. Gotthold Ephraim Lessing, *Wie die Alten den Tod gebildet* (Berlin: Voß, 1769), pp. 5, 10, and the vignette on the title page.
5. The review referred to above complained about the nudity of the standing figure (as n. 3, col. 330). For the second edition of 1821 a veil was added to cover the offending parts.
6. Strictly speaking, ex-Jesuits. But when the order was banned in 1773, the teachers were kept on (Franz Rudolf Reichert, 'Theologie und Priesterausbildung unter Kurfürst Clemens Wenzeslaus 1768–1798', in *Aufklärung und Tradition: Kurfürstentum und Stadt Trier im 18. Jahrhundert. Ausstellungskatalog und Dokumentation*, ed. by Gunther Franz, Ausstellungskataloge Trierer Stadtbibliotheken, 16 (Trier: Spee-Verlag, 1988), pp. 75–99 (p. 75)).
7. After *libri prohibiti*, 'Aszetik' formed the largest single group in the seminary library (Richard Laufner, 'Aufklärungsliteratur in der Jesuitenbibliothek und in der Universitätsbibliothek', in *Aufklärung und Tradition*, ed. by Franz, pp. 128–34 (p. 128)). The phrase 'ascetische Betrachtungsbücher' occurs in 'Franz Graf Spaur', in *Nekrolog auf das Jahr 1797*, ed. by Friedrich Schlichtegroll (Gotha: Perthes, 1801), I, 1–74 (pp. 3–4). The piece is attributed to Wyttenbach by Guido Groß, *Trierer Geistesleben unter dem Einfluß von Aufklärung und Romantik (1750–1850)*, Veröffentlichungen der Gesellschaft für nützliche Forschungen zu Trier (Trier: Lintz, 1956), p. 32 n. 94. The description of Wyttenbach in my title is by Groß and is taken from this work (p. 63).
8. Wolfgang Hans Stein, 'Revolutionskalender, Dekadi und Justiz im annektierten Rheinland, 1798–1801', *Francia*, 27/2 (2000), 138–75 (p. 154 n. 54).
9. Tina Klupsch, *Johann Hugo Wyttenbach: Eine historische Biographie*, Trierer historische Forschungen: Kleine Schriften, 2 (Trier: Kliomedia, 2012), pp. 138–41 ('his civic ethos, his talents and his knowledge of critical philosophy' (p. 141)).
10. Ibid., p. 145.
11. See Johann Hugo Wyttenbach, 'Ueber die Zeitrechnung der Republik und die Dekaden-Feier', *Patriotische Beiträge*, 2 vols (Trier: Hetzrodt & Schröll/Hetzrodt & Willwersch, 7ten Jahrs der fränkischen Republik [1798–99]), 1.1 (1798), 210–30.
12. Stein, 'Revolutionskalender', p. 155. The speech of 10 brumaire, year VII, was not a one-off. See 'Rede an dem Feste der Jugend, am 10. Germinal, 7. Jahres (30. März 1799)', in Wyttenbach, *Schulreden vom Jahre 1799 bis 1846* (Trier: Lintz, 1847), pp. 11–16; *Rede, gehalten von Br. Wyttenbach, Bibliothekar der Central-Schule des Saar-Departements, am 14. Julius [1801], 25 Messidor 9ten Jahres* [Trier, 1801]. 'Br.' stands for 'Bürger'.
13. Stein, 'Revolutionskalender', pp. 155–56.
14. Wyttenbach, 'Denkmal den Wohlthätern des Menschengeschlechts', *Patriotische Beiträge*, 1.1, 111–33 (p. 129).
15. Stein, 'Revolutionskalender', p. 156.
16. Jakob Marx, *Denkwürdigkeiten der Dreifaltigkeits- oder Jesuitenkirche des bischöflichen Seminars zu Trier* (Trier: Lintz, 1860), pp. 48, 51.
17. Gunther Franz, 'Trier im 18. Jahrhundert: Ein Gang zu Stätten der Bildung und Aufklärung und zu Bauten des Rokoko und des Klassizismus', in *Aufklärung und Tradition*, ed. by Franz, pp. 232–64 (pp. 248–49).

18. Klupsch, p. 34.
19. Ibid., pp. 32–36 and 46.
20. On this vast topic see Detlef Pollack, *Säkularisierung: Ein moderner Mythos?*, 2nd edn (Tübingen: Mohr Siebeck, 2012).
21. Klupsch's recent monograph provides a useful synthesis. See also: Groß, *Trierer Geistesleben*; Richard Laufner, 'Die Stadtbibliothek Trier zwischen Säkularisation und Revolution 1802–1848', in *Zur Geschichte rheinischer Stadtbibliotheken*, Sonderheft des Kurtrierischen Jahrbuchs 1980 (Trier: Stadtbibliothek, 1980), pp. 81–114; Guido Groß, 'Von der Lesegesellschaft 1783 zur trierischen Leihbibliothek 1819: Bildungsstreben des Bürgertums in Trier vom Ausgang der kurfürstlichen bis zum Beginn der preußischen Zeit', ibid., pp. 115–35; Ernst Wolfgang Orth, 'Die Einflüsse der geistigen Väter des ersten Trierer Stadtbibliothekars Johann Hugo Wyttenbach (1767 bis 1848)', ibid., pp. 136–56; Walther Gose, 'Die Kant-Rezeption im Wyttenbach-Kreis 1792–1798', in *Aufklärung und Tradition*, ed. by Franz, pp. 174–88; Wolfgang Hans Stein, 'Literarischer Republikanismus im napoleonischen Trier: Die Société littéraire (Lesegesellschaft) von 1799', *Jahrbuch für westdeutsche Landesgeschichte*, 33 (2007), 293–424.
22. Groß, *Trierer Geistesleben*, pp. 33–36; Orth, pp. 144–51; Gose; Klupsch, pp. 71–72, 84–85, 111, 118, 124–28; Hans-Ulrich Seifert, 'Kantisme, Royalisme, Républicanisme: Villers et Wyttenbach', in *Un homme, deux cultures: Charles de Villers entre France et Allemagne (1765–1815)*, ed. by Nicolas Brucker and Franziska Meier, Rencontres, 396 (Paris: Classiques Garnier, 2019), pp. 117–30.
23. His anthologies (see below) are a roll-call of the first generation of Kantians. Cf. Klupsch, pp. 127–28.
24. Under this heading Wyttenbach refers to all three of Kant's *Critiques*.
25. Wyttenbach, letter to Johann Peter Job Hermes, 18 Feb. 1795, quoted Gose, p. 186.
26. Wyttenbach, MS 'Uebersicht des Inhaltes der Hauptwerke Kants' (Jan 1785); quoted Gose, p. 180. See Kant, *Kritik der praktischen Vernunft*, Book 2, ch. 2, iv: 'Das Dasein Gottes, als ein Postulat der reinen praktischen Vernunft'. Note how a 'postulate' has become a 'proof'.
27. Gose, p. 179.
28. Quoted Groß, *Trierer Geistesleben*, p. 36.
29. Letter to Johann Peter Job Hermes, 18 Feb 1795, quoted Gose, p. 188.
30. See *Die Bestimmung des Menschen*, ed. by Norbert Hinske (Hamburg: Felix Meiner, 1999).
31. For the fear of purposelessness and the reign of chance, see 'Denkmal', p. 112. Other, associated perils are utilitarianism (Wyttenbach, '*Aristäus*, oder über Würde des Menschen und Lebensgenuß: Ein Gespräch', *Patriotische Beiträge*, 1.1, 189–210) and scepticism (Wyttenbach, 'Franz Graf Spaur', pp. 3–5).
32. For example, in his 'Credo', in the letter to Hermes, 18 Feb. 1795: 'Höchstmögliche Vervollkommnung ist des Menschen vorgestecktes Ziel; unendliches Annähern zu diesem Ziele, ist seine *Bestimmung*' (emphasis Wyttenbach) (Gose, p. 186).
33. Immanuel Kant, *Die Religion innerhalb der Grenzen der bloßen Vernunft*, 2nd edn (Königsberg: Nicolovius, 1794), pp. 145–66, 173–75, 235–46. Gose points out that this work ranked even above the *Critiques* as a point of reference for Wyttenbach and his circle (pp. 184–85).
34. Groß, *Trierer Geistesleben*, p. 32; Klupsch, pp. 111, 135–38, 167–68.
35. See his 'Versuch einer gedrängten Darstellung der vier vorzüglichsten republikanischen Verfassungen des Alterthums', *Patriotische Beiträge*, 1.2 (1799), 106–33 and 168–87 ('Urrechte des Menschengeschlechts' and '[der] allgemeine Wille' (p. 108)).
36. Laufner, 'Die Stadtbibliothek', p. 81–82. See also Franz, p. 248.
37. 'Rede in französischer Sprache am 18. Sept. 1808', in Wyttenbach, *Schulreden*, pp. 38–42; cf. Orth, p. 150. 'The universe is governed by books.'
38. Laufner, 'Die Stadtbibliothek', gives a detailed account.
39. Ibid., pp. 94–95. At one time Wyttenbach's library had contained about 2,000 volumes (Laufner, 'Aufklärungsliteratur', pp. 131–32).
40. Reichert, p. 98 (prescription to booksellers about the sale of books to seminarists, 1790).
41. Ibid., p. 79 (letter of 6 May 1795 to Johann Michael Josef von Pidoll).
42. Ibid., quoting from *Journal historique et littéraire*, 1793. 'So-called *Aufklärung* only serves to lead the common people astray and in the end to have them fall headlong into irreligion.'

43. Laufner, 'Aufklärungsliteratur', pp. 130–31.
44. Ibid., pp. 128–29. The bulk of the indexed books was made up of works by Protestant scholars and theologians.
45. Laufner, 'Die Stadtbibliothek', p. 94. Hermes's collection expanded to be over twice as large as the entire stock of the Jesuit seminary (ibid., pp. 81, 94). Together his collection and Wyttenbach's grew to match the combined numbers of the former Jesuit and university libraries (ibid., p. 81).
46. Groß, *Trierer Geistesleben*, pp. 23–28, Groß, 'Von der Lesegesellschaft', pp. 120–26; Klupsch, pp. 56–68 and 152–59; Stein, 'Literarischer Republikanismus'. Wyttenbach also belonged to semi-formal reading circles in Trier in 1793–1794 (Klupsch, pp. 68–73), and Wetzlar, where he lived from 1794 to 1798 (ibid., pp. 96–98).
47. Groß, 'Von der Lesegesellschaft', p. 124; Klupsch, p. 154.
48. This is true of Lesegesellschaften more widely. See Richard van Dülmen, *Die Gesellschaft der Aufklärer: Zur bürgerlichen Emanzipation und aufklärerischen Kultur in Deutschland* (Frankfurt a.M.: Fischer, 1986), pp. 165–71; Hilmar Tilgner, *Lesegesellschaften an Mosel und Mittelrhein im Zeitalter des aufgeklärten Absolutismus: Ein Beitrag zur Sozialgeschichte der Aufklärung im Kurfürstentum Trier*, Geschichtliche Landeskunde, 52 (Stuttgart: Franz Steiner, 2001).
49. Groß, *Trierer Geistesleben*, pp. 27–32; Klupsch pp. 109–13, 118–19, 130, 136.
50. [Wyttenbach] 'Plan einer innern Einrichtung der Primärschulen: Entworfen von der im Saardepartement für das Trierische Arrondissement angeordneten, aus den Bürgern Lelievre, Seyppel und Wyttenbach bestehenden Unterrichts-Jury', *Patriotische Beiträge*, I.2, 39–71.
51. Ibid., p. 57.
52. An appendix adds clauses on the 'Bestimmung des Weibes' (p. 58).
53. [Wyttenbach] *Handbuch für den Unterricht in den Pflichten und Rechten des Menschen und des Bürgers: Zum Gebrauche in den Primärschulen, vorzüglich in der zweiten Classe* (Trier: Hetzrodt im achten Jahre [1800]).
54. Ibid., pp. 78–81.
55. Ibid., pp. 81–84.
56. In history lessons in primary schools, similarly, the period of 'Urgeschichte' was to be studied without referring to the Old Testament as an historical source ('Plan einer innern Einrichtung der Primärschulen', p. 54).
57. The expression, coined by the Kantian Karl Leonhard Reinhold (*Briefe über die Kantische Philosophie*, 2 vols (Leipzig: Göschen, 1790–1792), I (1790), 117–18), rapidly gained wider currency.
58. Volume I was published in Leipzig and Vienna in 1796, by Rötzel; and then in identical form in Jena, in 1797, by Voigt. Volumes II and III were published by Voigt. On the circumstances, see *Oberdeutsche allgemeine Literaturzeitung*, 11.1 (1798), no. 65 (30 May 1798), col. 1028–1030 (col. 1028).
59. In further references: A1 and vol. nos (I: 1796/97 (see n. 58), II: 1798, III: 1799).
60. In further references: A2 and vol. nos (I: 1801, II: 1808, III: 1821).
61. See Klupsch, pp. 163–65. The preface to A2 II is signed by Wyttenbach alone. On Neurohr, see Guido Groß, 'Abtei und Kirche St. Matthias und die Trierer Familie Neurohr im 18. und 19. Jahrhundert', in *Neues Trierisches Jahrbuch*, 41 (2001), 113–37 (pp. 128–34).
62. Norbert Hinske, 'Einleitung. Eine antike Katechismusfrage: Zu einer Basisidee der deutschen Aufklärung', in Hinske, ed., pp. 3–6 (p. 3).
63. A2 II, 10–13.
64. Particularly in the second edition (A2 I), where it expanded from 20 to 65 pp.
65. Groß, *Trierer Geistesleben*, p. 42. The original owner of a copy of the second edition in my possession left a pencilled comment at the head of the section 'Christenthum': 'Ein meist schlechter Auszug!' The hand is that of Gotthold Emanuel Friedrich Seidel (1776–1838), a Lutheran pastor in Nuremberg, who inscribed his name on the flyleaf, with the note: 'Von meinem lieben Weib an meinem 34sten Geburtstag erhalten d. 10. März 1808'. Seidel went on to edit an anthology of his own, with a contrary tendency: *Auswahl von biblischen Sprüchen und passenden Liedern und Liederversen für den Unterricht in der christlichen Lehre* (1820). For a Catholic

riposte to Wyttenbach and Neurohr, sixty years after their work, see Christoph B. Schlüter, *Aussprüche der philosophirenden Vernunft und des gläubigen Herzens aus den Schriften des h. Augustinus* (1859).

66. See Reidar Maliks, 'Revolutionary Epigones: Kant and his Radical Followers', *History of Political Thought*, 33 (2014), 647–71.
67. A2 I, vii. Similar statements: see Gose, p. 181 n. 20; Klupsch, p. 131.
68. Cf. 2 Cor. 3. 12–18. 'Die Propheten sagten die Wahrheit, aber diese Wahrheit war mit einem Schleier bedeckt' ([Anon.] *Theologie wider die starken Geister* (Augsburg and Ingolstadt: Crätz, 1771), p. 299).
69. Jacob Brucker, *Kurtze Fragen aus der Philosophischen Historie*, 8 vols (Ulm: Bartholomäi, 1731–37), IV, 1174–76 (with reference to the opinions of Justin Martyr, and with the promptings of Socrates' *daimon* in mind). Cf. A2 I, 84, where Justin is cited.
70. A2 I, 123, 230, 590. '[Der] Mann von Nazareth' ('Denkmal', p. 129) was 'einer der vortrefflichsten Männer der Vorwelt' ('Aristäus', p. 201) — but a man *only*.
71. A1 III, iii.
72. 'Plan einer innern Einrichtung der Primärschulen' (p. 54). Wyttenbach adheres to Eusebius's ancient system of chronology, which dates the creation of the world to 5199 B.C.
73. 'Denkmal', p. 132; and almost word for word again in a letter to Charles Villers, 8 brumaire an XII (31 Oct. 1803), quoted by Seifert, 'Kantisme', pp. 123–24.
74. Johann Wolfgang Goethe, *Campagne in Frankreich 1792*, in Goethe, *Campagne in Frankreich. Belagerung von Mainz. Reiseschriften*, ed. by Klaus-Detlef Müller (Frankfurt a.M.: Deutscher Klassiker Verlag, 1994), pp. 386–572 (p. 436)). On the way to and from the battlefield of Valmy, where he supposedly uttered his famous words, Goethe spent some days in Trier. On both occasions the young Wyttenbach acted as his *cicerone* (Klupsch, pp. 125–27).
75. *Der Geist der Religion*, on the verso of the title page. The verse had previously been quoted in A2 I, 491.
76. Gottfried Büchner, *Biblische Real und Verbal Hand-Concordanz oder Exegetisch-Homiletisches Lexicon* (Jena: Fickelscher, 1746), p. 213 (lemma 'Behalten').
77. *Urania*, 1st edn, p. iv (cf. Matth. 18. 20).
78. See also the subtitle of *Tod und Zukunft*.
79. A1 I, 'Einige Worte als Vorrede' (n.p.); *Urania*, 1st edn, p. iv.
80. A1 III, iii, v.
81. A2 I, ix–x; *Tod und Zukunft*, 2nd edn, p. iii; *Urania*, 1st edn., p. iii.
82. A1 III, iii.
83. The Wyttenbach papers in the *Stadtarchiv Trier* preserve a box of 'Collectaneen' (Stadtarchiv Trier, Findbuch, NL Wyttenbach/Hs 2100), containing 'several hundred' loose notes on a variety of topics. (Information kindly supplied by Bernhard Simon, *Stadtarchiv Trier*.) Wyttenbach's original commonplace book is no doubt the proximate source for a quotation from Montaigne in the letter to Hermes, 18 Feb. 1795 (Gose, p. 188) and in A1 I, III.
84. A1 I, 'Einige Worte als Vorrede' (n.p.).
85. Ann Moss, *Printed Commonplace Books and the Structuring of Renaissance Thought* (Oxford: Oxford University Press, 1996); Gilbert Heß, 'Florilegien: Genese, Wirkungsweisen und Transformationen frühneuzeitlicher Kompilationsliteratur', in *Wissensspeicher der Frühen Neuzeit: Formen und Funktionen*, ed. by Frank Grunert and Anette Syndikus (Berlin: de Gruyter, 2015), pp. 97–138.
86. A2 I, viii–x.
87. Moss sees signs of an 'impending redundancy' in the later seventeenth century (p. 256).
88. See, for example, Christoph Meiners, *Anweisungen für Jünglinge zum eigenen Arbeiten[,] besonders zum Lesen, Excerpiren, und Schreiben* (Hanover: Helwing, 1789; 2nd edn ibid. 1791).
89. Johann Gottfried Herder, *Briefe zu Beförderung der Humanität*, ed. by Hans Dietrich Irmscher (Frankfurt a.M.: Deutscher Klassiker Verlag, 1991), pp. 346–47. Herder does not give, nor have I been able to ascertain, the source for this passage in Leibniz.
90. Cf. Heß, pp. 98, 109, 131.
91. A2 I, viii–x. Lucretius, *De rerum natura*, III. 11–12: 'As the bees in the flower-bearing glades sip from all, | We in the same way have gathered a fullness of golden sayings!' Cf. *Ioannis Stobaei*

Sententiae ex thesauris Graecorum delectae, ed. by Conrad Gesner, 3rd edn (Zurich: Froschauer, 1559), verso of the title page. The *Aussprüche* draw liberally from the early fifth-century Stobaeus (A2 I, 1–2, 55, 258, 260–61, 263, 490, 545, 576). The *Stadtbibliothek* inherited its copy from the old Jesuit seminary library. (Information kindly supplied by Dr Magdalena Palica and Dr Eva Seidenfaden, *Wissenschaftliche Bibliothek der Stadt Trier*.)

92. *Epistles* I. 96.
93. 'Reading' and 'reading of good authors'. It is relevant to the culture of commonplace books that *lectio* also means 'collecting', 'selecting', 'gathering'. Georg Maior, *Sententiae veterum poetarum, per locos communes digestae* (Magdeburg: Lotther, 1534), p. 22; Maior, *Sententiae veterum poetarum*, ed. by Antonio Mancinelli (Paris: Stephanus, 1551), p. 43. On Maior's influential anthology, see Moss, pp. 188–93.
94. A2 I, 591 (mangled there as 'Alanus ab Jesulis'). The copy of Pez's *Thesaurus* in the Wissenschaftliche Bibliothek der Stadt Trier, formerly the Stadtbibliothek, is recorded as a donation from Wyttenbach's friend Hermes. (Information: as n. 91.)
95. Specifically, what is illustrated here is the classic method of copying onto separate leaves, which will then be filed together under subject headings (as opposed to copying into a bound volume and indexing the entries). See Johann Friedrich Blumenbach, 'Ueber die vorzüglichsten Methoden Collectaneen und Excerpte zu sammeln', *Medicinische Bibliothek*, 2 (1785–86), 547–59 (pp. 549–50); Heß, pp. 100–01.
96. Review of A1 I and II, in *Allgemeine Literatur-Zeitung* (1797), no. 386, 5 Dec 1797 (col. 587).
97. Review of A1 I and II, in *Neue allgemeine deutsche Bibliothek*, 44 (1799), 329–31 (p. 330).
98. 'Hat Luther den freyen Vernunftgebrauch in der protestantischen Kirche befördert, oder gehindert?', in *Prediger-Journal für Sachsen*, 4 (1806), 396–426 (p. 396).
99. A point emphasized in the mottos by C. C. E. Schmid and Fichte to A1 I and A2 I.
100. 'Resultate der philosophirenden Vernunft': A1 I, 'Einige Worte als Vorrede', n.p.; cp. A2 I, viii.
101. Heß, pp. 102, 108.
102. See Heß, p. 123.
103. Cf. the headings in Maior (n. 3): *Deus, virtus, genus humanum, sapientia, veritas*.
104. For Wyttenbach's view of Napoleon, see Klupsch, pp. 169–71.
105. Franz, p. 249.
106. Hans-Ulrich Seifert, 'Dialektik der Abklärung — Literarische Gegenentwürfe und deutsch-französische Wechselbeziehungen unter napoleonischer Herrschaft (unter besonderer Berücksichtigung der unveröffentlichten Korrespondenz zwischen Charles de Villers und Johann Hugo Wyttenbach)', in *Unter der Trikolore. Sous le drapeau tricolore. Trier in Frankreich — Napoleon in Trier. Trèves en France — Napoléon à Trèves. 1794–1814*, ed. by Elisabeth Dühr und Christl Lehnert-Leven, 2 vols (Trier: Städtisches Museum Simeonstift Trier, 2004), I, 473–94 (p. 477).
107. Klupsch, pp. 179–82.
108. Heinz Monz, *Karl Marx: Grundlagen der Entwicklung zu Leben und Werk* (Trier: NCO-Verlag, 1973), pp. 160–78. The young Marx was a pupil at the *Gymnasium*, and is said to have been particularly devoted ('ergeben') to Wyttenbach (Monz, p. 173, quoting a letter by Heinrich Marx, Karl's father). See also Klupsch, p. 182.
109. Ibid.
110. 'Rede am 15. September 1811', in Wyttenbach, *Schulreden*, pp. 47–49 (p. 49).
111. A2 I, 474 (from Johann Heinrich Voß, 'Die Morgenheitre').

CHAPTER 3

Goethe's Problems Composing *Faust I*: A Conspectus

T. J. Reed

My title is an understatement. Goethe's *Faust* was from the start one immense compositional problem. From the work's first conception, in every separate phase — the 1770s, 1787, 1790, 1797, 1800, 1808, 1813, the 1820s — the threads were being picked up by another man with a changing aesthetic. He also had to keep clearly in view across the decades what, at any point, had already been said and what still needed to be said: every scene had connections back and implications forward. So these are not just problems *about* Goethe's *Faust*. They were Goethe's own problems in composing the work. Many of the materials in what follows will be familiar, but reviewing them in close sequence may bring home the extent and intricacy of those problems and the remarkable lack of solutions, sometimes even of any seeming concern for a solution. And we may speculate on the reasons behind these processes and responses.

Scene-sequence of *Faust I*, *Urfaust* scenes **bold**. Numbers indicate the roughly ascertainable order of composition:

23	Zueignung
24	Vorspiel auf dem Theater
25	Prolog im Himmel
1	**Nacht**
26	Vor dem Tor
27	Studierzimmer (i)
28	Studierzimmer (ii)
2	**Mephistopheles. Student** (integrated in 28)
3	**Auerbachs Keller** (versified)
21	Hexenküche
4	**Land Strase** (not used in *Faust I*)
5	**Straße (i)**
6	**Abend. Ein kleines reinliches Zimmer**
7	**Spaziergang** ('Allee' in Urfaust)
8	**Der Nachbarin Haus**
9	**Straße (ii)**
10	**Garten**
11	**Ein Gartenhäuschen**
22	Wald und Höhle

12	Gretchens Stube
13	Marthens Garten
14	Am Brunnen
15	Zwinger
16	Nacht. Straße vor Gretchens Haus
16a	Valentin's monologue
16b	Faust kills him
17	Dom
29	Walpurgisnacht
30	Walpurgisnachtstraum
18	Trüber Tag. Feld (untitled in *Urfaust*)
19	Nacht. Offen Feld
20	Kerker (versified)

Theme and Deviations

The first problem was how to accommodate this Christian morality tale of sin and damnation to Goethe's intellectual world. He had grown up in a not unduly Christian family, in an atmosphere of widening public enlightenment, and with an innate independence of mind that was to make him not just a product of the Enlightenment but its pre-eminent exemplar. As to religion, he had from very early on his own ideas of a divinity directly accessible through the natural world. His attitude to religious orthodoxy can be inferred from the monologue poem 'Prometheus'. The complaint wasn't just of Zeus' authority; it was his failure to help in situations where, as Christians piously hoped, their God would help. Zeus' failure perhaps implied another. At all events, a Faust from this poet's pen was unlikely to end up traditionally damned. It isn't even clear why Goethe had to tangle with the Faust theme in the first place.

He would pay for it with a lifetime of literary labour against the grain of the legend.

He begins conventionally enough with the discontented scholar brooding over his unrewarding life and turning to magic conjuration. But just when tradition requires the devil to appear, enter instead the Erdgeist, a powerful embodiment of nature's forces, something true to Goethe's poetic intuitions but alien to the Faust story. How would that be taken further? Then Mephistopheles belatedly turns up, not invoked, simply there, but only in a trivial role, teasing a student and playing tricks on rowdies in a tavern. Still, even that much of his presence establishes the traditional cosmogony — and in doing so creates a flat conflict with the dynamic system the Erdgeist has so excitingly described.

The Erdgeist will recur spasmodically. In an unnamed *Urfaust* scene (entitled 'Trüber Tag. Feld' in *Faust I*) Faust begs the 'große Geist' to turn Mephisto back into his original doggy form. But what did the Erdgeist have to do with Mephisto in the first place? Is this to be taken as merely Faust's conjecture, or is it the remnant of an early conception never followed through?

By the time Goethe drifts back to something like orthodoxy with a 'Prologue in Heaven' (1797), the Lord and the angels who praise his Creation plainly have no use for or even knowledge of an Erdgeist. Meanwhile Faust has addressed him once more, and again assumed he was responsible for Mephisto. With this scene, 'Wald und Höhle' (1787), Goethe is far from solving compositional problems, he is adding to them. 'Wald und Höhle' is in several ways the biggest. Except of course for Gretchen.

Gretchen is not just a problem *of* the work. For the greater part (two thirds) of those early scenes, she *becomes* the work. How and why? Sex was traditionally among the things Mephisto offered, but love was not. Gretchen is in love, an emotionally and physically convincing love: 'Mein Schoos! Gott! drängt | Sich nach ihm hin' (*Urfaust*, 1098–99).[1] Faust too is soon past the crude lust his first sight of her aroused, and moved by quite other feelings: 'Mich drangs so grade zu geniessen. | Und fühle mich in Liebestraum zerfliessen!' (*Urfaust*, 574–75).

So the love affair is launched, with its grim consequences, the whole constituting a major diversion that poses the question, not what is Gretchen doing in a Faust play, but what is Faust doing in a Gretchen tragedy. For it didn't take a legendary Faust to impregnate an innocent girl and set her on the path to infanticide.

It is well known how her story burst in among Goethe's early sketches for *Faust*. He was inspired — clearly outraged — by the trial and ceremonial execution of the infanticide Susanne Margarethe Brandt, which took place on the young lawyer's Frankfurt doorstep.[2] A cynical saying of the day — 'Sie ist die erste nicht' — especially rankled, and is put in Mephisto's mouth in (what is later called) 'Trüber Tag. Feld'. The urgency of Goethe's response is clear from the fact that he used his current work-in-progress as the first available framework. (This incidentally dates the earliest, purely Faust scenes to some time before October 1771, when the Brandt trial took place.) Goethe then committed himself fully to the deviation by completing the Gretchen tragedy, leaving the broader Faust theme suspended.

Death and Pregnancy

But there are problems within the Gretchen tragedy itself. At Faust's behest, and with his assurance that it can do no harm — he has after all studied medicine along with everything else — she drugs her mother so they can make love undisturbed. Gretchen at once conceives (by literary convention, once will serve) and her mother dies — in that same night, is the clear implication. But the simultaneity cannot last. The death is immediate; the pregnancy can only gradually come to light. There can be no morning-after scene where Gretchen cries 'Mother has died and I'm pregnant.' Nor is there any suggestion that her mother was repeatedly drugged to allow a continuing love affair — although some formulations imply there was more than a brief happiness, especially Gretchen's words in the final prison scene: 'Sie schlief damit wir uns freuten. | Es waren glückliche Zeiten!' (*Faust I*, 4572–73). Can this last encounter really be the lovers' first and only meeting since the fateful night? But against that, how could you go on making love when you've just caused your mother's death? Though against that again, in the original 'Kerker' Gretchen doesn't recall 'glückliche Zeiten' at all. In *Urfaust* she says simply 'Sie sollt schlafen daß wir könnten wachen und uns freuen beysammen'.[3] Versifying the scene, Goethe has been diverted in search of a rhyme.

Why Goethe added it to the tragedy at all is a puzzle. It wasn't a feature of the Brandt case. Pregnancy and infanticide were quite enough for tragic purposes, more intimately personal to the young woman, and a pressing social issue because a frequent fate of young women generally — 'die erste nicht' no doubt also meant 'die letzte nicht'. There was no need to load Gretchen with further guilt. There must have been other ways for the lovers to meet. The death was a decidedly melodramatic extra.

And strangely, the death then becomes virtually a blind motif. Gretchen never mourns her mother, nor even mentions her death until the final prison scene. Before then, with the gossiping girls 'Am Brunnen', all she is worried about is her own disgrace , and when she prays to the Virgin in 'Zwinger', she is in despair, again, over her lost social reputation. It takes the 'böse Geist' in 'Dom' to mention her mother's death for the first time — 'Die durch dich sich in die Pein hinüberschlief' (*Urfaust*, 1323). It can hardly be ignored at this point, since Gretchen is in the cathedral for her mother's funeral, at least according to the *Urfaust* stage direction, which reads: 'Exequien der Mutter Gretgens. *Gretgen* alle Verwandte. Amt, Orgel und Gesang'. In the same breath the Spirit taunts her with the child stirring in her womb. So with Gretchen already in advanced pregnancy, her mother is only now being buried. Adding her death to the plot has led to an implausible timeline.

But in the 1790 *Fragment* (and on into *Faust I*) a replacement stage direction for 'Dom' reads simply 'Amt, Orgel und Gesang. Gretchen unter vielem Volke'. A funeral is clearly in progress (in the background a chorus is singing the 'dies irae'), but there is no longer any explicit reference to her mother's. This is one of several occasions to ask: Did Goethe not notice a problem? Did he notice and try to mend it? Did he try to mend it but fail? Or did he notice but not care, choosing to leave things as they were?

Cutting his Losses: Faust. Ein Fragment

There was then a problem of a quite different order to which Goethe gave a radical answer: whether to go on with Faust at all. In 1790 he clearly decided not to and signalled that by publishing *Faust. Ein Fragment*.[4] Till then, only literary friends and some persons in higher society even knew about a Faust project. The first the wider public heard of it was its abandonment. The *Fragment* is sometimes talked about as if it were a staging-post towards *Faust I*. On the contrary, it was (for the time being) the end of the road. A fragment is an emergency closure, a confession of failure, at best a fire sale.

Faust. Ein Fragment[5]
Urfaust scenes again in **bold**

Nacht
Studierzimmer (249–346 = *Faust I*, 1770–1867)
Mephisto, Schüler
Auerbachs Keller
Hexenküche
Straße (i)
Abend

> Spaziergang
> Der Nachbarin Haus
> Straße (ii)
> Garten
> Ein Gartenhäuschen
> Gretchens Stube
> Marthens Garten
> Am Brunnen
> Wald und Höhle
> Zwinger
> Dom

What drove Goethe's decision? For one thing, there was a mass still to think through, and of a demanding kind, especially a major role for Mephisto and the devising of what was bound to be an unusual kind of pact. Overall there was a great gap to fill with material from the legend, if the Faust theme was to be restored to centre-stage after the intense diversion of Gretchen. Goethe's commitment to the whole project was in any case flagging. With his tastes turning classical since Italy, he no longer had an appetite for magic and Mephisto. Moreover, he was going to need time and a clear desk for his next big project, the reworking of *Wilhelm Meister*, which did indeed take till 1795/96.

How do you compose a fragment? To be consistent, everything needs to be incomplete. So Gretchen's story is cut short after 'Dom'. The social tragedy is already coming about, but the horrors of infanticide, prison and execution are not even foreshadowed. The final scenes could be cut, perhaps to Goethe's relief, for he may already have been finding, as he certainly found later, that their stark prose was intolerable (to Schiller, 5 May 1798).[6]

As for the Faust material at his disposal, this was already fragmentary enough — that had been the problem. But at least the focus on Faust could be increased to outweigh the Gretchen interest, accounting for twenty-seven pages of the *Fragment* against twenty-two. That included a good chunk of text designed to fill the 'great gap'. This material opens in mid-sentence and in the middle of a rhymed quatrain,[7] so there must have been at least a bit more. But either it was not that much, or Goethe preferred to keep it back, in the cause of fragmentariness. In the end, the balance was nevertheless tipped in Faust's favour by the seven pages of 'Hexenküche', a new scene dating from Spring 1788, written in, of all places, Rome, the gardens of the Villa Borghese. The irony at the expense of the Nordic hocus-pocus again signals Goethe's disinclination: 'Mir widerstrebt das tolle Zauberwesen!', Faust says (*Fragment*, 816).

But the most important — and problematic — text that is new in the *Fragment* was the other scene written in or soon after Italy, 'Wald und Höhle'. For one thing, it brings the Erdgeist back as the addressee of Faust's impassioned speech of gratitude — for things the Spirit precisely did *not* give him in their first encounter:

> Erhabner Geist, du gabst mir, gabst mir alles,
> Warum ich bat. Du hast mir nicht umsonst
> Dein Angesicht im Feuer zugewendet,

> Gabst mir die herrliche Natur zum Königreich,
> Kraft, sie zu fühlen, zu genießen. Nicht
> Kalt staunenden Besuch erlaubst du nur,
> Vergönnest mir, in ihre tiefe Brust,
> Wie in den Busen eines Freunds, zu schauen.
> (*Fragment*, 1890–97)

And more in the same vein. Serenity in nature, intimate access to the whole creation, profound self-understanding... It is as if Faust's high spiritual ambitions from early on had been fulfilled, and so overwhelmingly that for a while he can forget Gretchen. Yet in a bitter reflection (actually written later, but placed earlier in the text of *Faust I*) he recalls what really happened: 'Der große Geist hat mich verschmäht, | Vor mir verschließt sich die Natur' (1746–47).

Far-fetched-alternatives have been suggested to explain away the contradiction between the Erdgeist's earlier harsh rejection and these alleged benevolent revelations — for example that some quite different undetermined spirit was a later benefactor.[8] Yet the single identity is clear from the phrase 'im Feuer zugewendet', which echoes 'der Geist erscheint in der Flamme' in the stage direction to the encounter scene at *Urfaust*, 128.

Faust's serenity out among nature also largely contradicts the present action and the emotions of a love affair. The contradiction is of two kinds, depending on where 'Wald und Höhle' is located in the plot. In *Fragment*, it comes after the love-night, so Faust has strayed into the wilds leaving Gretchen behind, despite the 'wildes Feuer | Nach jenem schönen Bild' that Mephisto stokes up, and despite consciously reeling between desire, enjoyment, and fresh desire (*Fragment*, 1921–23). In the last part of the scene, a passage taken over from *Urfaust* (16b), Faust berates himself and Mephisto for destroying Gretchen's peaceful life, making her their joint victim in ways that from this standpoint can just about be made out.

But in *Faust I*, 'Wald und Höhle' comes at a point where Faust is still courting Gretchen, before her spinning-wheel monologue and her questioning of his religious belief. As yet there remains 'fast nichts mehr übrig' for Gretchen to do for him, but still the drugging of her mother, and Mephisto is still relishing her imminent fall 'Nun heute Nacht — ?' (*Faust I*, 3520, 3542). Faust's self-reproaches for destroying Gretchen's life stand as before (3345–65), but they now concern a fate he has not yet brought upon her; they have not yet made love, which means she hasn't conceived. Hence the causes of the tragedy have not yet happened, so that it still (in strict, if banal terms) need not happen at all. Although, contradiction once more, some details of their love-making — Faust's 'Was ist die Himmelsfreud' in ihren Armen? | Laß mich an ihrer Brust erwarmen! | Fühl' ich nicht immer ihre Not?' (*Faust I*, 3345–47), his reeling between desire and enjoyment, and Mephisto's admission that he has 'often' envied Faust Gretchen's breasts — these are all left standing, despite no longer fitting the case, as they did when the scene was placed after the love-making. In both locations, Faust comes out as in different degrees a callous lover. Whatever Goethe did, 'Wald und Höhle' created problems. There simply was no right place for it.

Decisions

That Goethe's resolve to leave it at that was meant to be permanent is clear from an exchange with Schiller fully four years after *Fragment* was published. Early in their friendship, Schiller asked to see any scenes that had been left out. For 'Es herrscht in diesen Szenen eine Kraft und eine Fülle des Genies, die den besten Meister unverkennbar zeigt, und ich möchte diese große und kühne Natur, die darin atmet, so weit als möglich verfolgen' (to Goethe, 29 November 1794).[9] Such admiring criticism must have been hard to resist, but Goethe was deeply averse to resuming the struggle with Faust: 'Ich wage nicht das Paket aufzuschnüren, das ihn gefangen hält. Ich könnte nicht abschreiben ohne auszuarbeiten, und dazu fühle ich mir keinen Mut.' These are not casual formulations, they all speak the same negative language — 'wage nicht', 'gefangen hält', 'keinen Mut'. There was however one positive note to ease the new friend's disappointment: 'Kann mich künftig etwas dazu vermögen, so ist es gewiß Ihre Teilnahme' (to Schiller, 2 December 1794).[10]

But that still took another three years, time Goethe spent on *Wilhelm Meister* with Schiller's intensive involvement. It was only when the plan for another journey south was blocked by Napoleon's campaign in northern Italy that Goethe, at a loose end while waiting for travel to be safe again, decided 'an meinen Faust zu gehen'. He would 'dissolve' the *Fragment* and add 'was schon fertig oder erfunden ist' — quite a bit, then. He felt the need for Schiller's help once more, asking him to think the thing through in one of his well-known sleepless nights and say what demands he would make of 'das Ganze' (to Schiller, 22 June 1797).[11]

The die is cast, the abandonment of *Faust* is reversed. These seven years had been not just any years in the long genesis of *Faust*, they were a time of deliberate abstention, even repudiation. But 1797 marks the point of no return and the start of intensive work and consultation between the friends. The central work of German literature will somehow come about.

To that end, not only must a lot more be written, but decisions must be made on what old material to keep, in what form, and where to place it. This was a much harder task than preparing the text of *Fragment*, where untidiness was to be expected. Now it is all about shaping a rounded literary work.

But at least Goethe had a relatively free hand. The public knew nothing beyond *Fragment*, so they had no expectations. Even the Weimar court had only heard those *Urfaust* readings and probably nobody, apart from Louise von Göchhausen, had read anything.

Nevertheless, Goethe's old problems still had to be confronted. One can imagine him with drafts, of vintage old and new, spread out on his desk for the task of (literally) com-posing the work. He might use, alter, add — he might even delete? Given the genetic open goal he faced, it made sense to consider that option too. What did he decide?

The Problems: Summary

GRETCHEN:

(i) Only by writing a separate new play could the whole Gretchen deviation have been removed. From early on, her fate had taken over as a joint *raison d'être* of the work, which at best could be rebalanced further towards Faust by creating scenes to fill the Great Gap with his doings.

(ii) A small alteration, conceivably meant to mask the awkward time relation of Gretchen's pregnancy to her mother's funeral, has already been noted. Yet there was no need for the death at all. Gretchen was going to have guilt enough to bear without that. The whole motif could have been deleted without causing further disturbance. It certainly didn't need to be kept just so as to display the hubris of the socially superior, educated, but crucially ignorant male: 'Würd ich sonst Liebgen dir es rathen' (*Urfaust*, 1208), words that are, perhaps deliberately, as embarrassing in substance as in style.

(iii) The major textual change in respect to Gretchen is the restoration of the final scenes, but which Goethe found so intolerable in their stark prose that he set out to veil their direct effect by versifying them (to Schiller, 5 May 1798).[12] In the event he only managed that for the very last scene, 'Kerker'.

(iv) He did however famously add a rebuttal of Mephisto's 'Sie ist gerichtet' with a 'Stimme von oben: Ist gerettet!' That fulfils the promise of 'Trüber Tag. Feld', where 'vor den Augen des Ewigen' in *Urfaust* now reads 'vor den Augen des ewig Verzeihenden' in *Faust I*. All of which still begs the question of just what there is to forgive, what Gretchen's 'guilt' consists in. She drugs and kills her mother, but on Faust's authority; and she conceives his child through love: 'Doch — alles was mich dazu trieb | Gott! war so gut! ach war so lieb!' (*Urfaust*, 1276–77). She has no tragic 'fatal flaw' other than her innocence. What follows is true to the old double standard, the man leaves the pregnant woman to disgrace and perhaps crime, and gets off scot-free. Faust was 'der erste nicht'. For the girls 'Am Brunnen' it's all just the way of the world, and an opportunity for Schadenfreude. True, Faust also ends as an outcast, but for the 'Blutschuld' of killing Gretchen's brother Valentin. (In the end he will have made a clean sweep of the whole family.)

ERDGEIST:

(i) The Erdgeist's occurrence and recurrence belong in a cosmogony that is out of sync with the one Mephisto inhabits, a problem not eased but intensified by the now added 'Prolog im Himmel'.

(ii) Faust's notion, in scenes from way back in the 1770s, that Mephisto was sent to him by the Erdgeist is likewise undone by the wager up there between the Lord and Mephisto, so it is strange to find it not just retained in its other old locations but reiterated as late as 1787 in 'Wald und Höhle'.

(iii) As to Faust's effusive gratitude for gifts the Erdgeist never gave him, there is no internal explanation. The answer can only be biographical: this is the mature post-Italy author speaking in the voice of someone whom experience has brought to an understanding of the world and himself, and who is free to express his contentment through the central character of a work which, by publishing *Fragment*, he was about to abandon anyway.

For *Faust I*, all editorial options were open, cuts would have been straightforward, even ruthless ones. Why did Goethe not simply remove the Earth Spirit's apparition and all subsequent references to him, leaving the traditional heaven-and-hell set-up, which he was busy confirming — along with the discrepancy? Surely the inconsistency of world-views was plain to see? Why did he not cut 'Wald und Höhle' and delete at a stroke Faust's misplaced harmony with nature and his unfounded thanks to the Erdgeist, simultaneously rescuing him from the charge of callousness?

An Answer?

The answer surely goes to the root of Goethe's creative genius. He was above all a poet of occasions and inspirations. The elements of the Faust complex came about at different times and in different moods, not in a continuous flow but as discrete, intense creations, already in a sense fragmentary, so many pieces within what was increasingly a complex puzzle. (He would add to it further in *Faust II* by inventing a different heaven from the one in the 'Prolog'.) They were not subject to a grand design thought out in advance. Where Schiller was an intellectually controlled, top-down creator of dramatic structures, whose help for just that reason was again keenly needed, Goethe worked concretely from the bottom up, imagining characters and their conflicts — Egmont and Alba, Iphigenie and Thoas, Tasso and Antonio — and realizing them in urgent, pithy language. They are as individually distinctive, Mephisto and the Erdgeist too, and as memorable as the highpoints of Goethe's poems. Indeed, no clear line separates drama from lyric. *Faust* may very well have begun in lyrical empathy for a legendary figure, as was the case with 'Prometheus', which symbolically had a foot in both forms — a finished poem and a fragmentary play. Once the figure is set up, once that individual voice has been heard, it is hard to have to sacrifice anything of it to an abstract principle of consistency. The creator's basic instinct is to hold on to each achieved formulation, each captured piece of human reality, his own included — or suprahuman (imagine him cutting the Erdgeist and that intense nature vision!). In crude terms, it's use it or lose it. Put more grandly, substance, quiddity — in short, poetry — take precedence over structure. There was force in Schiller's admiring recognition of 'eine Kraft und eine Fülle des Genies'. What he had seen in *Fragment* was, he knew, only 'der Torso des Herkules', there must be more. But this too would convince through its 'große und kühne Natur' rather than its formal disposition. It surely does, and can be read in that expectation.

For Goethe, all those questionable connections and dubious details were old, possibly dear, creative moments, rooted deep among the 'Bilder früher Tage' that the 'Zueignung' nostalgically celebrates (*Faust I*, 9). And they had been so familiar for so long that it may not have been easy, even for this high creative intelligence, to spot the awkward joints in the rough carpentry of his 'Sturm und Drang' period-piece.

So Goethe may simply have set his face against making cuts and corrections at all. When so much of *Faust I* had such proven poetic power, his feeling may have been, in the language of the legend, publish and be damned.[13]

Notes to Chapter 3

1. For *Urfaust* and *Faust I* I quote from Albrecht Schöne's edition: *Faust: Texte und Kommentare*, 2 vols (Frankfurt a.M.: Deutscher Klassiker Verlag, 1999). Further references are given as line-numbers in this edition, except for *Faust. Ein Fragment*. I retain the misleading but traditional title 'Urfaust' for the sketches Goethe read to the Weimar court in 1775, the text of which Erich Schmidt found in the late nineteenth century in Louise von Göchhausen's family papers. Schöne proposes the replacement title 'Frühe Fassung', but the text was never a 'version'. Better would be 'Faust. Ein Projekt', in a line continuing with 'Faust. Ein Fragment' and ending with 'Faust. Eine Tragödie'. At all events, Louise should be remembered with gratitude for her copying labours. The closeness of the published texts — the 1790 *Fragment* and *Faust I* — to her transcript shows how accurate she was.'
2. Ernst Beutler, 'Die Kindsmörderin', in *Essays um Goethe*, 7th edn (Munich: Artemis, 1980), pp. 85–98.
3. *Faust*, ed. by Schöne, I, 539.
4. In volume 7 of his 8-volume *Schriften* (Leipzig: Göschen; Vienna: Staheli, 1787–90). The public interest may not have been intense (Goethe's youthful star had declined) and the edition sold poorly, though there were also separate printings of the *Fragment*.
5. References are to the *Faust* edition by Georg Witkowski: *Goethes Faust*, 2 vols (Leiden: Brill, 1949), as Schöne leaves the *Fragment* out — a pity, given its place in the genetic story.
6. *Der Briefwechsel zwischen Schiller und Goethe*, ed. by Emil Staiger (Frankfurt a.M.: Insel, 1966), p. 68.
7. 'Und was der ganzen Menschheit zugetheilt ist, | Will ich in meinem innern Selbst genießen': *Fragment*, 249–345, which became *Faust I*, 1770–1867.
8. They are listed briefly by Albrecht Schöne in the commentary to his edition, II, 313–14 and dealt with fully by Eudo C. Mason, *Goethe's Faust: Its Genesis and Purport* (Berkeley: University of California Press, 1967), pp. 110–78. Mason authoritatively disposes of the foolish hypotheses of *Faust* scholarship.
9. *Briefwechsel*, p. 68.
10. Ibid., p. 69.
11. Ibid., p. 404.
12. Ibid., p. 624.
13. In a celebrated conversation with the historian Luden in 1806, Goethe claimed a yet wider freedom for the imagination than the plea entered above for one man's distinctive creativity: namely, that poetry by its nature cannot contain contradictions, which only exist in the real world. I discuss this implausible thesis, and adduce a contrary statement from Goethe's own pen, in the *Faust* chapter of my book *Genesis: The Making of Literary Works from Homer to Christa Wolf* (Rochester, NY: Camden House, 2020), pp. 119 and 258.

CHAPTER 4

Werther's Patriotic Afterlives: The Imaginary of Self-Sacrifice in Works by Ugo Foscolo, Yu Dafu and Jiang Guangci

Johannes D. Kaminski

The Sorrows of Young Werther (*Die Leiden des jungen Werthers*, 1774) attracted a number of notable readers. The list spans Napoleon Bonaparte, who dilated on its flaws in a famous conversation in Erfurt in 1808, Friedrich Engels, who ridiculed the protagonist as a 'schwärmerischer Tränensack',[1] and Xi Jinping, the current Chairman of the Chinese Communist Party (CCP). During a visit to the China Cultural Center in Berlin in 2009, Xi mentioned having read the novel at the age of fourteen. Amid the Cultural Revolution, when access to foreign books was reduced, he would walk thirty miles to borrow works by Goethe.[2] While Western politicians increasingly avoid boasting of their literary erudition for fear of elitism,[3] Xi's nod to Goethe is remarkable. It stands out in a reading list otherwise dominated by Russian and French realists. But was Xi speaking of the same *Werther* that his German audience had in mind? As I will elaborate in this essay, probably not.

Admittedly, there is something formulaic about Xi's *Werther* reference. Paying homage to foreign cultural heroes is a typical feature of soft power diplomacy. Indeed, Xi's sentimental literary preference clashes with the grim-faced nature of his presidency. Since declaring the 'great renaissance of the Chinese race'[4] as the ultimate ambition of his tenure, Xi has launched campaigns against dissenting intellectuals, overseen ethnic cleansing of minorities and, more than his predecessors, embraced national chauvinism as a means to centralize political power. While this authoritarian and anti-globalist trend is not limited to China, but also haunts liberal democracies, the juxtaposition of Xi's early *Werther* appreciation and his embrace of nationalism is not entirely random. It exposes a semantic dimension of *Werther* that research has largely ignored. At the onset of the twentieth century, Goethe's epistolary novel served as a template of revolution in China and was understood as a call for political transformation. In this essay, I move beyond conventional notions of *Werther.* The text is usually discussed with reference to its complicated autobiographical situation, its masterly portrait of individual pathology or, as Marxists argue, its indebtedness to a bourgeois *Innerlichkeit* that steers clear of politics. I propose an additional aspect, the novel's inclusion in literary genealogies of cultural nationalism.

My corpus belongs to the long nineteenth century and is largely divorced from German-language debates. Long before German readers discussed the text's revolutionary potential, Ugo Foscolo's *Last Letters of Jacopo Ortis* (*Ultime lettere di Jacopo Ortis*, 1802/17) adapted the tragic tale to the tumultuous pre-Risorgimento period, when Italy was divided between Austrian and Napoleonic rule. A century later, the *Werther* model emerged at the other side of the globe, in the Far East. As China struggled with its semi-colonial status and the prospect of a civil war, the country's literati embraced occidental literature and philosophy. Shakespeare, Goethe and Ibsen were seen as allies in a fight against the feudal heritage, held responsible for the country's perceived backwardness. Recalcitrant and unstable characters such as Hamlet, Werther and Nora helped articulate the transitional pains from the Neo-Confucian values of the nineteenth century to the individualism of modernity.

Werther enters these contexts as a foreign text that lends itself to transcultural grafting. Like Foscolo's novel, Yu Dafu's *Sinking* (*Chenlun*, 1922) and Jiang Guangci's *The Young Wanderer* (*Shaonian piaobozhe*, 1926) take up patterns familiar from Goethe's original and adapt them to different needs. In their respective national literary histories, these novels represent starting points of modern literature. In the wider canon of world literature, however, they only play a marginal role. English translations of Foscolo and Yu exist, but are intended for an academic audience.[5] Jiang's work has not been translated into English.

The texts' loose indebtedness to the *Werther*-model articulates itself in multiple ways: their style is epistolary and overwhelmingly subjective, they deal with unhappy love triangles, show the individual's tragic clash with the demands of a cruel society and address suicide as a radical solution for this conflict. This said, they depart significantly from the Goethean original in one aspect: they boldly move beyond the realm of personal sentiment. Here, individual tragedy is no longer seen in isolation, but placed in the wider context of socio-political struggle. Evidently, the literary genealogy proposed by this essay does not answer to Goethe's ideas about *Werther* or those of his immediate contemporaries, be it Friedrich Schiller or Madame de Staël, let alone to established narratives of literary criticism. My contextualization hopes to single out the openness of *Werther* as a text that, once divorced from its author, lends itself to vastly incompatible interpretations and adaptations. This semantic openness afforded the text an audience across the globe, including nations that struggled under the yoke of foreign occupation. Here, the protagonist's obstinate character was seen as heroic.

The Invention of a Politicized Werther

Goethe's *Werther* is separated from its patriotic revenants by the political caesura of the French Revolution. After rule by divine right and hereditary monarchy became a questionable source of political legitimacy, the nation-state emerged as a modern substitute. Benedict Anderson describes how the American and French models of revolution shaped new 'imagined realities' of the state, including institutions, flags and anthems, and made others questionable, such as dynastic empires, inherited nobilities and serfdom.[6] In the course of the nineteenth century, literature also became a key ingredient in the self-understanding of nations as naturalized entities. Amid this development, poets and artists saw themselves elevated into the role of cultural heroes.

The socio-political function of letters can vary greatly in different communities across time. Timothy J. Reiss argued that while in early England and France literature contributed to socio-political stabilization, the German, Russian, Spanish and Italian situations differed greatly. Especially at the onset of the nineteenth century in Germany, the cultural realm attained a compensatory function, making up for a nationhood that politically did not yet exist.[7] In these contexts, cultural nationalism developed *against* imperialism rather than in tandem with it; after all, 'nationalism has different effects and meanings in a peripheral nation than in a world power'.[8] The texts in question follow the German model.

Although Romance studies and comparative criticism have taken note of the threads connecting *Werther* and *Jacopo Ortis*,[9] the text remains relatively obscure outside Italy. Possibly, Goethe's muted reaction to the text is an explanation; he received a complimentary copy, but never mentioned the text.[10] Ugo Foscolo's career predates the Risorgimento, a movement that transformed Italy from a political and ethnic patchwork into a united nation-state. As the 'true initiator of Romantic literary criticism and aesthetics in Italy',[11] Foscolo was lionized by his direct successors, Giuseppe Pecchio and Giuseppe Mazzini, who attributed a quasi-religious role to literature in the process of nation-building. Foscolo's epistolary novel *Last Letter of Jacopo Ortis*, first published in 1802 and revised in 1807, transplants the *Werther* narrative into a context that goes beyond the interpretative matrix that Goethe put in place for his own text. After biting *Werther*-references already featured prominently in *Römische Elegien* (1795), the author left his most conclusive self-analysis to *Dichtung und Wahrheit* (1808–31), where he slighted *Werther* as the product of a literary fashion. Allegedly, English sentimentalism had a corrupting effect on him and his early readership.[12] Such attempts to disrupt the emphatic reception of Goethe's hero, however, bore no relevance to Foscolo's tale. The hero is not just a dejected lover and narcissist, but first and foremost a victim of power politics.

The text opens with a powerful lament:

> The sacrifice of our motherland is complete: everything is lost; whatever life is conceded to us, it will only serve us to mourn our misery and infamy. My name is on the list of the banished persons, I know it. [...] And to make things worse, we Italians ourselves wash our hands in the blood of other Italians.[13]

Jacopo finds himself caught in the geopolitical rivalry between the Hapsburg Monarchy and Napoleonic France, which occupied large parts of the Italian peninsula in 1796. Patriots like Foscolo originally greeted the French general as a liberator, but found themselves disappointed by the Treaty of Campo Formio, when the occupied Venetian Republic was handed over to Austria. Political persecution ensued, forcing public intellectuals to emigrate into the neighbouring realms, such as the Cisalpine Republic. At the novel's onset, it appears that Jacopo can ease his political frustration with two palliatives: the study of classic literature, primarily Plutarch and Petrarch, and his amorous infatuation with Teresa. Although she is already promised to Odoardo, a boring and pedantic man, they share a passionate kiss under a mulberry tree, which leaves Jacopo ecstatic. Afterwards, Teresa backtracks and warns him: 'Never can I belong to you!'[14] Gradually, he understands that her arranged marriage cannot be dissolved. Her father relies on Odoardo to avoid political persecution himself.

After this realization, Jacopo's perception of his surroundings changes. Relations between the different ranks of society appear fundamentally flawed. Like Werther before him, he loses faith in the country's elites:

> Among Italy's cultured people, I have anxiously tried to approach those who are emphatically praised as *il bel mondo*; yet everywhere I met vulgarity, among noblemen, literati and the great beauties. All of them, they are nothing but nincompoops, scoundrels and villains. All of them.[15]

Once Odoardo provokes him by applauding the Treaty of Campo Formio, Jacopo loses his temper and despairs about the lack of resistance against Austrian rule over Venice. Attempting to find solace in nature, he finds his perception altered: 'Where is her sublime beauty? [...] I only see naked rocks and precipices.'[16]

Jacopo's growing pessimism is not merely a product of narcissism. Here, the emotional breakdown has the effect of making him more susceptible to the misery of his compatriots. Fleeing from the maddening presence of his beloved, he travels a country haunted by misrule, where peasants are hanged for minor transgressions. Wherever he goes, he finds evidence for the great price his country is paying for appeasing Austria:

> So we Italians are all exiles and strangers in Italy. [...] Our harvests have enriched our oppressors; yet our lands offer neither abode nor bread to the many Italians whom the revolution has driven out from their familiar sky. Now, dying of hunger and exhaustion, they keep hearing the voice of the only, supreme friend of the destitute and the abandoned, criminality![17]

After paying a final visit to the graves of Dante, Galileo and Michelangelo, he returns to Teresa – and kills himself.

Foscolo's *Jacopo Ortis* is steeped in Wertherian references, starting with the protagonist's all-or-nothing stance towards life through to a narrative staccato that, for example, contemporary Italian *Werther*-translations failed to reproduce.[18] Given the dominance of political concerns, however, *Jacopo Ortis* is not a narrative about love primarily. The protagonist's affection for Teresa only functions as a distraction from the hero's greater pain, the loss of his motherland. Consequently, there is no organic development, as Glauco Cambon asserts: 'in *Ortis* instead, the chips are down from the start. [...] The opening clause of the novel [...] already hints at the final sacrifice.'[19] Teresa can only delay the predetermined catastrophe. In the patriotic context, Jacopo's suicide is not an admission of his failure to accommodate the practical needs of the present. The tragic end does not speak against him and in favour of an author who survived writing the text, but endows the literary protagonist with the kind of grandeur that sentimental literature lacks. In contrast to the literary wave that *Werther* set in motion across Europe, this literary figure no longer appears as a beacon of bourgeois sentimentalism, but as a righteous man who articulates justified objections against the status quo.

In German criticism, few scholars dared to evaluate Werther's suicide as a positive act. Writing after the Great War, Hermann August Korff delivered such an interpretation.[20] In moderate terms, Georg Lukács also related the novel's tragic end to the struggle of liberation. Reading the text as an analysis of the struggle between the liberal segments of the bourgeoisie and the old aristocracy, he understood Werther as an emblem of the impasse experienced by Germany's educated elite, who had little room for political participation. According to Lukács, his suicide is just another manifestation of his commitment to transgress the ethical rules of a corrupt system.[21] With few exceptions, modern criticism is less enthusiastic about his suicide and prefers to paint his death as unavoidable in terms of narrative coherence, but avoidable in a therapeutic sense.

In Foscolo's work, the celebration of self-sacrifice as an act of freedom is pervasive. Even before his epistolary novel, he staged heroic suicide in *Tieste*, a tragedy that premiered in Venice in 1795, prior to the author's banishment from the Republic. Moreover, during his years of exile in London, he ventured to translate Jacopo Ortis's literary sacrifice into political theory. Addressing the precarious role of peripheral nations facing invasion by mightier neighbours, he reiterated the trope of sacrifice – this time not of the patriot's physical life, but of personal principles. In a historical analysis of the short-lived Neapolitan Republic of 1799, Foscolo applauds the men who regarded national independence as more important than party ideologies, for example, Francesco Caracciolo, an Admiral in the Bourbon navy who became a traitor to serve the national interest.[22] Later in life, Foscolo, like Goethe, declared his disdain for his own early novel, condemning it as morally dangerous and linguistically excessive.[23] This said, his political philosophy clearly departed from his German predecessor's problematic alliance with the forces of the Ancien Régime, as W. Daniel Wilson has demonstrated in great detail.[24]

Geographical and cultural distance afforded Foscolo the liberty to treat *Werther* as a malleable text form that can be repurposed. The emphasis on political sacrifice came at the expense of the psychological tension between the protagonist and his beloved. In Goethe's original, Lotte's indecisive behaviour contributed to the protagonist's gradual loss of sanity. With the exception of the mulberry tree-scene, Teresa hardly appears as an active agent in the narrative. Jacopo's failure in love is primarily a symptom of his reduced social status. Given the pathos-laden language of *Jacopo Ortis*, it is surprising to see how well Wertherian language, the poetry of heartache, translates into patriotic lament. As the next sections will show, the libidinous dimension of the love discourse plays an important role in the context of patriotism.

Foscolo's rewriting may not have left its mark on letters outside Italy, as literary realism became the predominant style of progressive writing in the nineteenth century; a century later, however, the rewriting of Goethe's novel continued in China.

China's Semi-Colonial Status

Arguably, the plight of Italy prior to Risorgimento has some similarity to the semi-colonial situation in China. Just as in Foscolo's fragmented country, foreign aggression eroded China's sovereignty during the nineteenth century. The First Opium War (1839–42) inaugurated what today is called the 'Century of Humiliation' (*bainian guochi*). After her military defeat, China was forced to open five ports to international trade and concede settlements to France, Britain, the United States and Japan. At the turn of the century, the country's pitiful state hastened the birth of Chinese nationalism. While the Qing administration and previous dynasties never thought of their subjects as Chinese nationals, political figures such as Sun Yatsen, Liang Qichao and Kang Youwei began to promote the idea of China as a self-governing and unified nation-state – in reaction against both imperial administration and foreign interference.[25] The Qing dynasty ended in 1912, yet the succeeding administration, the Republic of China, failed to turn the country into a sovereign state. Feelings boiled over in 1919, when Wilhelmine Germany's Kiautschou Bay concession in Shandong Province was not returned to China, but awarded to Japan. The Republic's administration protested against article 156 of the Treaty of Versailles, but to little avail. At home, the student population formed the May Fourth Movement, which became a major turning point in Chinese political and cultural history. This movement shaped the consciousness of an entire generation of students and literati, notably those who established the Chinese Communist Party in 1921.

The Chinese 'Werther boom' coincided with this period of anti-imperialist struggle. Geopolitical resistance to American, Japanese and European colonialism did not stand in the way of an enthusiastic import of ideas and letters. Whereas Goethe had become an icon of national culture in Germany, *Werther* was embraced as an emblem of the struggle for liberation in China. A decade later, however, this positive judgement was revised, when orthodox Marxist classifications of bourgeois culture, including the works of Goethe, replaced such creative appropriations.

This emancipatory understanding of occidental letters at large and *Werther* in particular was the product of a complex transcultural interactions that involved not only Chinese writers and the Western literary canon, but also the mediating role of a rapidly modernizing and increasingly westernized Japan.[26] Chinese literati acquainted themselves with occidental letters during extensive stays at its universities, using the country as an entry point into literary modernity. Guo Moruo's first full translation of 1922 is indebted to this triangulated cultural transaction.[27] At the time, two aspects made Goethe's original attractive among young writers: on the one hand, its expressive literary style proved congenial to a generation that preferred vernacular style over the formulaic patterns of Classical Chinese. On the other hand, its focus on radical subjectivity served as an invitation to explore aspects of human psychology that challenged Confucian cultural norms and connected psychological nuance with the grand canvas of political fiction.

From Sexual Frustration to Patriotism

Yu Dafu produced some of the aesthetically most daring prose among May Fourth Movement letters. *Sinking*, a short story, was written in Japan in 1921. The text is steeped in intertextual references to occidental Romantic authors and even includes translations from Heinrich Heine and William Wordsworth. From the onset, the protagonist is characterized as 'the most miserable man in the world'.[28] But since the narrator's and the anonymous protagonist's voices intermix, and the text alternates between high-strung pathos and occasional fits of irony, the reader is placed in a similar position to Goethe's novel: it is difficult to tell apart delusions from legitimate complaints about being treated unfairly. After moving to Japan at the age of nineteen, the protagonist develops into a loner. He seeks solace in solitary walks in nature, where his prosaic surroundings are transformed into mythological landscapes:

> Looking around, he felt that every tree and every plant was smiling at him. Turning his gaze to the azure sky, he felt that Nature herself, timeless and eternal, was nodding to him in greeting. And after staring at the sky fixedly for a while, he seemed to see a group of little winged angels, with bows and arrows on their shoulders, dancing up in the air. He was overjoyed and could not help soliloquizing:
>
> 'This, then is your refuge. When all the philistines envy you, sneer at you, and treat you like a fool, only Nature, only this eternally bright sun and azure sky, this late summer breeze, this early autumn air still remains your friend, still remains your mother and your beloved. With this, you have no further need to join the world of the shallow and flippant. You might as well spend the rest of your life in this simple countryside, in the bosom of Nature.'[29]

As a result of his inferior position as a Chinese national in Japan, his sense of self is increasingly destabilized: 'For the Japanese look down upon Chinese just as we look down upon pigs and dogs. They call us Shinajin, "Chinamen", a term more derogatory than "knave" in Chinese.'[30] As if the locals' contempt for him at school and in everyday interactions were not enough, his awakening sex drive further aggravates the situation. He feels attracted to every female he comes across, but is unable to establish any form of interpersonal relationship. Instead, he blushes and retreats into his rented room to masturbate compulsively. After he has also severed ties with his Chinese classmates, his remaining social contact is the Japanese family where he lives. But one day, he is caught peeping at the daughter while she washes herself. In a wave of shame and guilt, he runs away, leaving the family's home for good. Now he moves into a remote hut deep in the woods, hoping to find peace in natural surroundings. Initially, the place's tranquillity soothes his tormented soul. But then, old habits reappear; this time, he eavesdrops on a couple making love out in the open. Vexed by this new stimulus, he rushes to the city's harbour and enters a *demimonde* establishment. Left alone with a pretty maid, he is immediately tongue-tied:

He wanted to look closely at her and confide in her all his troubles. But in reality he didn't even dare look her in the eye, much less talk to her. And so, like a mute, all he did was look furtively at her delicate, white hands resting upon her knees.[31]

In this awkward position, the protagonist makes a significant mental connection. The local population will always look down on him like on a pig or dog, he realizes, as long as his country of origin remains weak. He will never be able to look a Japanese girl in the eye, as long as he belongs to a bullied nation: 'O China, my China, why don't you grow strong!' Expressed while sitting next to a Japanese maid, frustrated individual male libido becomes metonymic of a national rivalry. Given the impossibility of a sudden change of his lowly status, he gets obsessed by a new idea: 'Oh, let it be, let it be, for from now on I shall care nothing about women, absolutely nothing. I will love nothing but my country, and let my country be my love.'[32] Leaving the bar, he finds himself facing a starry night over the sea. Melancholia clouds his mind. He resolves to drown himself:

After a while, he paused to look again at that bright star in the western sky, and tears poured down like a shower. [...] Drying his tears, he stood still and uttered a long sigh. Then he said, between pauses:

'O China, my China, you are the cause of my death! ... I wish you could become rich and strong soon! ... Many, many of your children are still suffering.'[33]

The open end leaves it to the reader's imagination whether he really drowns himself.

In comparative studies, scholars often emphasize the 'Wertherness' of Yu Dafu's protagonists. Jaroslav Průšek points at their shared experience of *Weltschmerz*, owing to a similar socio-political situation in both Germany around 1774 and in China in the 1920s.[34] Other scholars argue that Goethe's and Yu's protagonists are the products of a universal Romantic style that transcends geography and time.[35] Narrative and motif-related connections include solitary walks, the bookishness of their ecstasies in nature, and their shared exploration of the inner self through reading and writing, which articulates itself in a highly subjective monological style.[36] In the present essay, the odd combination of two additional aspects connect the text to the nexus of politicized Werthers: first, the protagonist's uneasy sexuality and, second, the heartfelt invocation of the motherland at the end.

In Goethe's original, sexual repression is latent, but never addressed directly. This changes in the author's self-parody in *Briefe aus der Schweiz: Erste Abteilung* (1808). Here, a sentimental traveller, loosely modelled on Werther, visits a prostitute and relishes the prospect of gazing upon a nude body. Like Yu's protagonist, he does not dare to make a move. Luckily, the girl is more accommodating than her Japanese sister, so she urges him: 'komm, mein Freund, in meine Arme, oder ich schlafe wirklich ein'.[37] In this parody, sexual frustration is a source of ridicule and hardly lends itself to the pathos of patriotism. This changes in Foscolo's work, where 'political, economic and sexual repression go together'.[38] Jacopo's celibacy is not self-inflicted, but an effect of his political ostracism. Were Teresa to dissolve her engagement, her father would be deprived of Odoardo's protection.

In Yu Dafu's prose, the case is more complicated. His libido does not attach itself to a fixed object, but jumps from giggling classmates to the soaped body of the landlord's daughter to the maid's white hands. This meandering sex drive is representative of Yu Dafu's early prose at large, which also features instances of self-harm and homosexuality, for instance in *Moving South* (*Nanqian*, 1922). What sets *Sinking* apart, however, is the forced connection between frustrated sex drive and the pangs of nationalism. This semantic complex is articulated most visibly in the lure of the maid. In the protagonist's eyes, she is not the victim of exploitation, but an envied representative of a strong nation. At first glance, his hypersexualized gaze at his surroundings seems difficult to reconcile with his political beliefs. They have a compensatory function and concern nobody but the protagonist himself. Nevertheless, Kirk Denton places the protagonist's painful patriotism in a larger context, which emerges from his 'realization that his individual identity is profoundly threatened by the collapse of the cultural whole'. Longing for his motherland, he establishes the absent cultural and national whole as the true object of his metaphysical desire: 'Suicide executed may stand either as a form of sexual union with, or a complete rejection of, the object.'[39] *Sinking* contains a contestable socio-political proposition: sexual perversion is not a question of individual psychology, but connects to the realm of geopolitics. Sexual frustration can be cured by one's motherland's patriotic rejuvenation. Would the protagonist's sorrows disappear in the moment when China becomes 'rich and strong'? In Foscolo's novel, Jacopo's situation would be radically altered by national sovereignty, for such changed circumstances would allow him to marry Teresa. The argument of Yu's text is more difficult to follow. Regardless of the nation's status, the protagonist's erratic, timid sex drive would probably – this is just a speculation – continue to jump from object to object without establishing sexual or even emotional intimacy. Yet the grand narrative of national humiliation holds the prospect of a comprehensive liberation, spanning the political and the sexual realms. During Yu's lifetime, this possibility remained a mere hypothesis.

The next section will elaborate on an aspect of Wertherian suffering that connects with politics in a less abstract manner. At the onset of the twentieth century, the era of mass mobilization offered new outlets for the frustration of alienated individuals. It turned out that pathological misfits like Werther were dormant rebels whose self-destructive drive could be repurposed to political ends.

The Battlefield as Liberation

Jiang Guangci's biography deviates considerably from those of the intellectuals who organized around the May Fourth Movement. While its most celebrated members, including Yu Dafu, moved from aestheticism towards increasingly orthodox writing, Jiang's career went the other way. Having studied at Moscow's Oriental University rather than at a Japanese institution, he returned to China as a lecturer in Marxism in 1924. His epistolary novel *The Young Wanderer* (*Shaonian Piaobozhe*, 1926) is considered the first example of proletarian revolutionary literature in China.[40]

In contrast to Werther and Jacopo Ortis, who belong to the bourgeoisie, Jiang Guangci's protagonist is of even lowlier birth than the protagonist in *Sinking*. Zhuzhong's infancy falls into the difficult period following the fall of the Qing dynasty, when the abolition of feudal privileges failed to change the living conditions of ordinary people, but saw the rise of warlords and ruthless confiscations of land. Echoing such socio-political upheavals, Zhuzhong's biography abounds with abuse. When a harvest fails and his parents cannot afford their lease, the cruel landowner simply murders them. Left on his own, the orphan seeks refuge at a Buddhist temple, where he is promptly molested by a lusting priest. After contemplating suicide for a while, he starts living on the streets and survives on handouts. Two years later, his living conditions improve. He takes up an apprenticeship at a shop and falls in love with the owner's daughter, Yumei. They develop feelings for each other, but these days of bliss are short-lived. Still in mourning, the letter writer laments in retrospective:

> I will never forget her. Not just because of her beauty or her talents, but because she was the only friend I ever had. She was the only person who ever understood me. Of course, having met a true friend in a girl in one's lifetime, that's a source of pride and a consolation in itself. But it also brought me endless sorrow, a sea of pain as deep as the ocean! Oh, my dear Weijia, the hot tears of sorrow keep streaming down my face. My soul is inscribed with a deep wound that will never stop quivering ...[41]

The tragedy begins with Yumei's engagement to Wang, the son of a land-owning bureaucrat. In protest against this arranged marriage, Yumei falls severely ill. Hoping to save her, Zhuzhong confesses their secret love to her father, who promptly reacts by sending him away with a recommendation for a placement in a distant city. Broken-hearted, Yumei dies. At a loss whom to blame for this tragedy, the young man directs his anger at the demiurge who created this unjust world: 'You devil, you ruthless thing, you creator of all the darkness in this world! Your crimes are deeper than the ocean, greater than the highest mountain, they burn hotter than fire!'[42] Failing to blame anyone in particular for his suffering, he simply endures the pain and starts a new life.

After moving to an urban centre, he learns of the heroic deeds of political activists. Under their influence, his frustration increasingly translates into concrete social analysis and a patriotic consciousness. One day, activists reproach his boss for selling Japanese merchandise. With large segments of the population calling for a boycott, a student delivers an incendiary speech:

> Aren't you Chinese? China is about to die, Chinese lives are at stake, and you are still talking about financial loss and profit? Our motherland will soon perish, we all will soon become slaves of a dead nation. If we don't rise up against it, we will share the fate of the Koreans and the Vietnamese! Sir! You are Chinese as well![43]

With Vietnam a French and Korea a Japanese colony already, the geopolitical ambitions of the world powers are targeting China next. While the shop owner, a collaborator and capitalist, remains unmoved by this speech, Zhuzhong's patriotism is awakened by this vision of gloom. From that day, his life changes. He becomes an activist himself, organizes a strike at an English-owned silk factory, is imprisoned and eventually joins the Whampoa Military Academy, a newly established institution for budding revolutionaries. After spending a lifetime at the mercy of the landowning class and opportunistic capitalists, he feels empowered by the idea of self-sacrifice for the nation. His battle cry reads:

> Having witnessed adversity and sorrow, death does not mean anything to me anymore. If I get the chance to kill a few enemies, if I can eradicate some of the vermin among humanity, then my life's goal has been achieved. My dear Weijia! I don't mean to sound like a thug, I was not born with such an unyielding mind. It's just this evil society that forces me to give my life away.[44]

Although the letter writer does not elaborate on whom he considers 'vermin', the novel suggests that the 'enemy' is composed of foreigners in the international settlements, local collaborators of the Japanese government and capitalists in general. Eventually, the narration is taken over by the recipient of Zhuzhong's letters. Intrigued by the young man's further career, an investigation brings to light his premature death. As expected, he fell on the battlefield.

In Chinese literary history, Jiang Guangci has received a mixed assessment. Irrespective of his novels' commercial success and critical acclaim, the author's unreliable political views (see below) inhibited canonization. Taken in isolation, *The Young Wanderer* makes for reliable propagandistic reading. Indeed, the novel anticipated communist literary discourse for years to come.[45] The melancholic and decadent hero of old, as portrayed in Yu Dafu's work, is replaced by a revolutionary martyr. The fateful love-triangle, the root cause of many literary suicides, is expanded by a fourth factor, revolution. Jiang Guangci summed up his creed with the formula: 'The more intense the revolution appears, the more immense the romantic heart becomes.'[46] As the 'vermin'-quote clearly indicates, this form of romanticism is not about universal values, but about the affirmation of national strength. This inaugurates a new phase of May-Fourth-inspired writing. Chinese authors were no longer satisfied by delivering imitations of occidental models and reiterations of humanist values; facing the challenges of class struggle and the prospect of war, the new generation puts forth exemplary biographies intended to strengthen the patriotic spirit among the wider population. This reorientation towards political agitation paves the way for the 'Yan'an Talks on Literature' in 1942, in which Mao Zedong, not yet Chairman of the CCP, demanded the comprehensive instrumentalization of literature and the arts for propagandistic purposes.[47]

Evidently, Zhuzhong's re-education brings with it a loss of psychological complexity. The protagonist lacks the internal contradictions that would make him a true revenant of Werther. In the cases of Werther, Jacopo and Yu's anonymous protagonist, the inner and exterior sources of suffering are entangled. Readers must evaluate the balance between imagined and legitimate grievances. As the history of *Werther* criticism demonstrates, the protagonist's anger allows for two mutually exclusive interpretations: either as legitimate protest or as a result of pathological tendencies. In contrast, Zhuzhong's case is straightforward. Once he detects the origins of life's misery, capitalism and imperialism, he joins the revolutionaries and fights oppression. The pairing of Wertherian suffering and its solution on the battlefield, however, is a pertinent postscript to Goethe's original. The letter of 25 May [1772] reads: 'Ich hatte etwas im Kopfe, davon ich euch nichts sagen wollte, bis es ausgeführt wäre, jetzt da nichts draus wird, ist's eben so gut. Ich wollte in Krieg! Das hat mir lang am Herzen gelegen.'[48] In contrast to Zhuzhong, Werther was quickly talked out of it.

Irrespective of Zhuzhong's heroic career, the mass mobilizations of the twentieth century could not ultimately absorb the spiritual losses inflicted on the modern subject – not even in Jiang Guangci's eyes. Although his blend of romanticism and revolution found many imitators, Jiang's subsequent works did not follow the optimistic model of his early novel. In *Lisa's Sorrows* (*Lisha de aiyuan*, 1929) and *The Moon Forces its Way Through the Clouds* (*Chongchu yunwei de yueliang*, 1930), his characters turned darker. In light of the failure of the communist insurgency in 1927, the ideological confidence that fed Zhuzhong's enthusiasm faded. Notably Jiang's female protagonists of the late 1930s explore the analogies between failed revolution and sexual depravity, between ideological malaise and venereal disease. This focus brought the author into conflict with party ideology. Consequently, Jiang not only lost his membership in the CCP, but also his special status in the socialist histories of modernist literature in China.[49]

With the growing power of the Chinese Communist Party, writers found it increasingly difficult to reconcile literary freedom with the ideological demands of orthodoxy. The obstinate character profiles of Yu's and Jiang's protagonists suited the revolutionary mood of the 1920s, but became increasingly problematic during the 1930s, when civil war broke out and party discipline became imperative. Suddenly, such outbursts of frustration and self-initiative were classified as petit-bourgeois anarchism that failed to connect to the masses.[50] After Werther's lachrymose protest inspired Yu's and Jiang's calls to arms, this wave of creative reception finally came to an end. Goethe's *Werther*, however, remained on reading lists up until the Cultural Revolution, when Xi Jinping, the Chinese president, read the text for the first time.

Conclusion

In a period of 150 years, Werther's frustration gradually detached itself from the unfulfilled love for a woman and transformed into the longing for national rejuvenation. The epistolary novels addressed in this essay move from bitter analyses of miserable living conditions to blunt calls to action. In Foscolo's lament about Italy's disgrace, the answers were exile and death. In Yu's elegy for China's weakness, the possibility of national rejuvenation led to an open end. Finally, Jiang's enlisted protagonist completes the semantic nexus that *Werther* set in motion in 1774.

When examining why Xi invoked *Werther* as a favourite read, it is advisable to take into account the semantic layers that attached themselves to the text after radiating beyond its immediate readership. In fact, the text complements one central ideological component of Xi's administration, the 'Century of Humiliation'.

As mouthpieces of oppressed nations, Werther's revenants, Jacopo, Yu's protagonist and Zhuzhong, underscore the urgency of a country's assertion of its rightful place in the world. Consequently, Xi's invocation of *Werther* contains a sinister note, as its literary continuations tell the story of radical will and protest against injured dignity. The text's interpretation as an example of depoliticized *Innerlichkeit* only reached China with great delay, possibly not before the Opening of China in the late 1970s. Xi's *Werther* predates this period of knowledge transfer and is still informed by Yu Dafu's and Jiang Guangci's Werthers. They want to redeem injustice, perhaps even take revenge. In this light, to mention the book title in Germany represents a Trojan Horse: what appears like an attempt at soft power diplomacy actually marks the formation of a rift, between the former aggressor and the insurgent. Political scientists and China watchers, who have pointed out the country's growing assertiveness, would not be surprised by Xi's deliberate ambiguity.[51]

Aside from the literary genealogy that connects *Werther* with Chinese modernism, the text's patriotic interpretation also has some significance for the German context. Although epistolary novels fell out of fashion during the nineteenth century, grand heroic gestures did not. The currency of liberty-minded suicide only increased in value and contributed to a mindset that would eventually culminate in the *Freikorps*-spirit in the German army in the Great War. Scholars such as Klaus Theweleit and Thomas Macho have already mapped the connection between suicidal impulse and death on the battlefield.[52] As the present essay demonstrates, the idea of patriotic suicide already lies dormant in *Werther*, at least according to its Italian and Chinese readers. This positions Goethe's text in an unexpected neighbourhood with other canonical works of German literary history that evince a complicated legacy, such as Friedrich Hölderlin's notorious poem 'Der Tod fürs Vaterland' (1800) and Richard Wagner's *Rienzi* of 1842. Like *Werther*, the latter opera boasts a list of notable admirers among statesmen and leaders.

At one point, Werther laments: 'Ach diese Lücke! Diese entsetzliche Lücke, die ich hier in meinem Busen fühle! ich denke oft! — Wenn du sie nur einmal, nur einmal an dieses Herz drücken könntest. All diese Lücke würde ausgefüllt sein.'[53] In the absence of someone to fill this void, Wertherian suffering became the gateway to ideological territories that promised healing, but ultimately wrought havoc in the twentieth century, both in Germany and in China.

Notes to Chapter 4

Acknowledgement: I am very grateful to my friend Dr Marta Cenedese (Turku Institute of Advanced Studies), who polished my muddled translations from Italian.

1. Friedrich Engels, 'Deutscher Sozialismus in Versen und Prosa', in Karl Marx and Friedrich Engels, *Werke*, 44 vols (Berlin: Dietz, 1956–68), IV (1959), 236.
2. 'Xi Jinping besucht das Chinesische Kulturzentrum Berlin', Generalkonsulat der Volksrepublik China in Frankfurt a.M., 13 October 2009, <http://frankfurt.china-consulate.org/det/sbwl/t620004.htm> (last accessed 29 September 2020).
3. The notable exception is Emmanuel Macron, the French president. See *L'Oreille tendue* (blog), 'La culture épistolaire d'Emmanuel Macron', 18 April 2017, <https://oreilletendue.com/2017/04/18/la-culture-epistolaire-demmanuel-macron/> [accessed 29 September 2020].

4. Willy Wo-Lap Lam, *Chinese Politics in the Era of Xi Jinping: Renaissance, Reform, or Retrogression?* (New York: Routledge, 2015), p. xvii.
5. See Ugo Foscolo, *Last Letters of Jacopo Ortis*, trans. by John Gordon Nichols (London: Hesperus, 2002), and Yu Dafu, *Sinking*, trans. by Joseph C. M. Lau and C. T. Hsia, in *Columbia Anthology of Modern Chinese Literature* (New York: Columbia University Press, 2007), pp. 31–55.
6. See Benedict Anderson, *Imagined Communities: Reflections on the Origin and Spread of Nationalism* (New York: Verso, 1983), p. 81.
7. Timothy J. Reiss, 'Mapping Identities: Literature, Nationalism, Colonialism', *American Literary History*, 4 (1992), 649–77 (p. 663).
8. Simon During, 'Nationalism: Literature's Other?', in *Nation and Narration*, ed. by Homi Bhabha (London: Routledge, 1990), pp. 138–54 (p. 139).
9. Romance studies and comparative literature dominate the bibliography: Ulrike Kunkel, *Intertextualität in der italienischen Frühromantik: Die Literaturbezüge in Ugo Foscolos 'Ultime lettere di Jacopo Ortis'* (Tübingen: Narr, 1994); Enzo Neppi, 'Le origini del romanzo "modern" secondo Foscolo: la "Julie", il "Werther" e ... Jacopo Ortis', *Quaderni Gargnano*, 1 (2018), 29–48; Stefan Lindinger and Maria Sgouridou, 'Looking for Love in Werther, Jacopo Ortis, and Leandros: A Comparative Analysis of Three Romantic Epistolary Novels from Germany, Italy, and Greece', *Primerjalna književnost*, 39 (2016), 91–104.
10. See Glauco Cambon, *Ugo Foscolo: Poet of Exile* (Princeton: Princeton University Press, 2014), p. 30.
11. Peter Brand and Leo Pertile, *Cambridge History of Italian Literature* (Cambridge: Cambridge University Press, 1996), p. 445.
12. This genesis is laid out in III, 13.
13. Il sacrificio della patria nostra è consumato: tutto è perduto; e la vita, se pure ne verrà concessa, non ci resterà che per piangere le nostre sciagure, e la nostra infamia. Il mio nome è nella lista di proscrizione, lo so; [...]. E noi, pur troppo, noi stessi Italiani ci laviamo le mani nel sangue degl'Italiani. (Ugo Foscolo, *Ultime Lettere di Jacopo Ortis*, in Foscolo, *Opere Scelte* (Paris: Baudry, 1837), pp. 1–141 (p. 3)) Unless indicated otherwise, translations are my own.
14. 'Non posso essere vostra mai' (Foscolo, p. 58).
15. 'Nella Italia più culta [...] ho cercato ansiosamente *il bel mondo* ch'io sentiva magnificare con tanta enfasi, ma dappertutto ho trovato volgo di nobili, volgo di letterati, volgo di belle, e tutti sciocchi, bassi, maligni; tutti' (Foscolo, p. 26).
16. 'Dov'è la sua immensa bellezza? [...] mi sembrano rupi nude e non veggo che precipizi' (Foscolo, p. 67).
17. 'Così noi tutti Italiani siamo fuorusciti e stranieri in Italia [...]. Le nostre messi hanno arricchiti i nostri dominatori; ma le nostre terre non somministrano nè tugurii nè pane a tanti Italiani che la rivoluzione ha balestrati fuori del cielo natio, e che languenti di fame e di stanchezza hanno sempre all'orecchio il solo, il supremo consigliere dell'uomo destituto da tutta la natura, il delitto!' (Foscolo, p. 88).
18. In a letter to Charlotte von Stein dated 13 December 1781, Goethe complains about Gaetano Grassi's plain Italian rendering (*Goethes Briefe und Briefe an Goethe*, ed. by Karl Robert Mandelkow and Bodo Morawe, 6 vols (Munich: C. H. Beck, 1988), I, 379).
19. Cambon, p. 55.
20. According to Korff, Werther's suicide passes judgement on the world, 'so richtet der Selbstmord Werthers gleichsam die Welt, die sich mit allen ihren Beschränkungen eines wahrhaft göttlichen Lebens nicht würdig erweist' (Hermann A. Korff, *Der Geist der Goethezeit*, 4 vols (Leipzig: Hirzel, 1923–40), I (1923), 306).
21. See Georg Lukács, 'Die Leiden des jungen Werther', in Lukács, *Goethe und seine Zeit* (Berlin: Aufbau, 1950), pp. 19–40 (p. 28).
22. See Eugenio Biagini, 'Liberty, Class and Nation-Building: Ugo Foscolo's "English" Constitutional Thought, 1816–1827', *European Journal of Political Theory*, 5 (2006), 34–49 (p. 46).
23. See Cambon, p. 64.
24. See W. Daniel Wilson, *Das Goethe-Tabu: Protest und Menschenrechte im klassischen Weimar* (Munich: Deutscher Taschenbuch Verlag, 1999), pp. 47–76.
25. See Guoqi Xu, 'Nationalism, Internationalism, and National Identity: China from 1895 to 1919',

in *Chinese Nationalism in Perspective: Historical and Recent Cases*, ed. by C. X. George Wei and Xianyuan Liu (London: Greenwood, 2001), pp. 101–20.
26. See Merle Goldman and Leo Ou-Fan Lee, *An Intellectual History of Modern China* (Cambridge: Cambridge University Press, 2002), pp. 97–141.
27. See *Shaonian Weite zhi Fannao* (*Sorrows of Young Werther*), trans. by Guo Moruo (Shanghai: Taidong chubanshe, 1922). For a linguistic analysis of this bold translation, see Johannes D. Kaminski, 'Punctuation, Exclamation and Tears: *The Sorrows of Young Werther* in Japanese and Chinese Translation (1889–1922)', *Comparative Critical Studies*, 14 (2017), 29–48.
28. Yu Dafu, 'Sinking', trans. by Joseph S. M. Lau and C. T. Hsia, in *The Columbia Anthology of Modern Chinese Literature*, ed. by Joseph S. M. Lau and Howard Goldblatt (New York: Columbia University Press, 2007), pp. 31–55 (p. 47).
29. Ibid., p. 32.
30. Ibid., pp. 51–52.
31. Ibid., p. 51.
32. Ibid., p. 52.
33. Ibid., p. 55.
34. See Jaroslav Průšek, *The Lyrical and the Epic: Studies of Modern Chinese Literature* (Bloomington, IN: Indiana University Press, 1980), p. 4.
35. See Yixue Sun, *Zhongwai langman zhuyi wenxue daoyin* (*Guide to Chinese and Foreign Romanticist Literature*) (Shanghai: Tongji Daxue chubanshe, 2002), pp. 115–19; Li Oufan, *Xiandaixing de xiangxiang: cong wan Qing dao dangxia* (*The Modern Imagination: From Late Qing to Modernism*) (Hangzhou: Zhejiang daxue, 2019), pp. 155–80.
36. Chenxi Tang, 'Reading Europe, Writing China: European Literary Tradition and Chinese Authorship in Yu Dafu's *Sinking*', *Arcadia*, 40 (2005), 153–75 (p. 164).
37. Johann Wolfgang von Goethe, *Briefe aus der Schweiz*, in Goethe, *Sämtliche Werke*, 20 vols (Munich: Hanser, 1985–98), IV.1 (1988), pp. 630–44 (p. 644).
38. Brand and Pertile, p. 417.
39. Kirk A. Denton, 'The Distant Shore: Nationalism in Yu Dafu's *Sinking*', *Chinese Literature: Essays, Articles, Reviews* (*CLEAR*), 14 (1992), 107–23 (pp. 113, 114).
40. The noun *shaonian* as a designation for late adolescence or young adulthood (rather than childhood to pre-adolescence) is an idiosyncrasy of the early 1920 and 1930s, and often found in book titles.
41. 我所以永远地不能忘却她，还不是因为她貌的美丽和才的秀绝，而是因为她是我唯一的知己，唯一的了解我的人。自然，我此生能得着一个真正的女性的知己，固然可以自豪了，固然可以自慰了；但是我也就因此抱着无涯际的悲哀，海一般深的沉痛！维嘉先生！说至此，我的悲哀的热泪不禁涔涔地流，我的刻上伤痕的心灵不禁摇摇地颤动 ... (Jiang Guangci, *Zuopin Ji* (*Works*) (Kaifeng: Henan daxue chubanshe, 2000), p. 37)
42. '你这魔鬼，你这残忍的东西，你这世界上一切黑暗的造成者啊！你的罪恶比海还深，比山岳还高，比热火还烈！' (Jiang, p. 43).
43. 你不是中国人么？中国若亡了，中国人的性命都保不住，还说什么损失，生意不生意呢？我们的祖国快要亡了，我们大家都以要做亡国奴了，倘若我们再不起来，我们要受朝鲜人和安南人的痛苦了！先生！你也是中国人啊！ (Jiang, p. 51)
44. 我几经忧患馀生，死之于我，已经不算什么一回事了。倘若我能拿着枪将敌人打死几个，将人类中的蠹贼多铲除几个，倒也了却我平生的愿望。维嘉先生！我并不是故意地怀着一腔暴徒的思想，我并不是生来就这样的倔强；只因这恶社会逼得我没有法子，一定要我的命[...] (Jiang, p. 67)
45. See Jianmei Liu, *Revolution Plus Love: Literary History, Women's Bodies, and Thematic Repetition in Twentieth Century Chinese Fiction* (Honolulu: University of Hawaii Press, 2003), p. 75.
46. Quoted in Liu, p. 77.
47. See Perry Link, *The Uses of Literature: Life in the Socialist Chinese Literary System* (Princeton: Princeton University Press, 2000), pp. 63–67.
48. Johann Wolfgang von Goethe, *Die Leiden des jungen Werthers*, in Goethe, *Sämtliche Werke*, I.2 (1987), pp. 197–299 (p. 259).
49. See David Der-wei Wang, *The Monster that is History: History, Violence, and Fictional Writing in*

    Twentieth-Century China (Berkeley, CA: University of California Press, 2004), p. 88.
50. In this respect, Jiang's and Ba Jin's literary careers have much in common. See John A. Rapp and Daniel M. Youd, 'Ba Jin as Anarchist Critic of Marxism', *Contemporary Chinese Thought*, 46 (2015), 3–21 (p. 4).
51. See Angela Poh and Mingjiang Li, 'A China in Transition: The Rhetoric and Substance of Chinese Foreign Policy under Xi Jinping', *Asian Security*, 13 (2017), 84–97; Edward Yi Yang, 'China's Strategic Narratives in Global Governance Reform under Xi Jinping', *Journal of Contemporary China*, 7 July 2020, <https://doi.org/10.1080/10670564.2020.1790904> [accessed 30 September 2020].
52. See Thomas Macho, *Das Leben nehmen* (Frankfurt a.M.: Suhrkamp, 2017), pp. 163–99; Klaus Theweleit, *Männerphantasien* (Berlin: Matthes & Seitz, 2020), pp. 83–89.
53. Goethe, *Die Leiden des jungen Werthers*, pp. 264–65.

CHAPTER 5

Perpetual Incipience: Goethe and the Search for a Transcendental *Mittelpunkt*

Ben Hutchinson

I

On 3 September 1786 at three o'clock in the morning, in the south-west German spa town of Karlsbad, a 37-year-old man crept quietly out of bed and into a waiting carriage. Bumping up and down as he went rapidly south — travelling in a post-chaise was nothing if not a rocky ride — Johann Philipp Möller felt the giddy thrill of departure. All summer long he had been planning his escape, and now, finally, here he was, hurtling south towards the Alps as fast as the roads would take him. That he had kept his plans secret only heightened the illicit pleasure; friends and enemies alike would discover what had happened to him only once he was safely on the other side of the mountains. The last thing he wanted was to be overtaken and recalled, as he had been in 1775. This time he was taking no chances. This time he would make it to Italy come what may.

It had been a difficult few years for Möller. Like many a man approaching middle age, he had become increasingly dissatisfied with his circumstances. Success had arrived early, and all too easily; his reputation thus secured, status and stability had become suffocating and repetitive. Professionally, he was stuck; personally, he was bored. Try as he might, he could not stop yearning for something new. Möller was in the throes, in short, of what we would now call a midlife crisis.

If Möller's state of mind detains us more than that of millions of people approaching middle age before and since, it is because he was, in reality, one of the greatest figures in the history of Western culture. Johann Wolfgang von Goethe's adoption of a pseudonym was not only an attempt to escape the crushing burden of fame that preceded him wherever he went; it was also an attempt to escape himself. Like Superman stepping into his phone booth, Goethe stepped into his carriage in order to become Clark Kent once again, to shake off the pressure of being the Olympian 'Goethe'. That he also pretended to be ten years younger tells us much about the motivation behind his journey to Italy. Like so many of us who find ourselves *nel mezzo del cammin di nostra vita*, he wanted to begin again.[1]

Fig. 5.1. Goethe's route through Italy. Goethe's Italian Journey, CC Search (https://search.creativecommons.org/photos/0b946453-bc4b-40c6-8d8f-cb48c89af290, accessed 15 March 2021). Creator: Zello.

Why was Goethe so desperate to get to Italy? Why now? Twice before, he had hoped to reach the other side of the Alps; in 1775 he had been recalled before he could get any further than Heidelberg, and in 1779 he had decided not to continue south from Switzerland in order to return to Weimar and his employer, Duke Karl August. Spurred on by such frustrations, Goethe's yearning for the south was given fresh impetus by the drab summer of 1786. As he notes repeatedly in the opening pages of (what would subsequently be published as) *Die italienische Reise*, by September he was in dire need of blue skies and warm air. Above all, though, he was suffering from a creative paralysis brought on by his many official duties as Privy Counsellor to the Weimar Court. Goethe, to put it in modern terms, was suffering from writer's block.

His flight south (see Fig. 5.1) constituted an attempt to revivify himself as he approached middle age. Hurrying over the Alps and down into northern Italy, Goethe noted, in the excited tone of someone setting off on holiday, that anyone coming towards him from the south would consider his breathless reaction to everything he encountered childish.[2] This moment of self-awareness captures the two main emotional impulses of the trip: a yearning for the south, and a desire to turn back the biological clock. When shortly thereafter he arrives in Venice, the sight of the gondolas immediately reminds him of a childhood game he used to play with model boats, and he enjoys 'einen langentbehrten [...] Jugendeindruck' (xv, 69). The geographical pull of the south to a northerner was also the chronological pull of childhood to middle age.

Goethe's journey may have gone down in history as 'Italian', but above all it was Roman. After two brief weeks in Venice — much of which he seemed to spend in the theatre — he hurried south to the eternal city, pausing for barely three hours in Florence. Only once he reached Rome on 1 November 1786 could he breathe out and relax; only once he reached Rome could he write to the Duke back in Weimar, safe in the knowledge that this time, at last, he had arrived at his long-anticipated destination. His desire to see the city, he writes, was 'over-ripe'. Just as in Venice, so in Rome Goethe immediately turns to a language of rejuvenation: 'Alle Träume meiner Jugend seh' ich nun lebendig' (xv, 126).

It is hard not to be carried along in his exuberant wake, so obviously thrilled is he to be in the city of his dreams. The early diary entries ooze excitement, and indeed if there is one adjective that defines them, it is 'new'. In an entry written on the day of his arrival, Goethe uses the word five times in one paragraph, sketching out his 'new thoughts' on his 'new life' in a 'new world' (xv, 135). Dante's *Vita Nuova*, the great dream of middle age, opens up tantalizingly before him. Logically enough, he rapidly starts referring to this new life as 'eine Wiedergeburt' (xv, 158); he considers the day of his arrival in Rome as 'einen zweiten Geburtstag' (xv, 158), and he wonders whether he can in fact be considered the same person, since he has been 'bis aufs innerste Knochenmark verändert' (xv, 157). Almost two months after his arrival, on 20 December 1786, he reflects at length on the nature of this transformation:

> Die Wiedergeburt, die mich von innen heraus umarbeitet, wirkt immer fort.
> Ich dachte wohl, hier was rechts zu lernen; daß ich aber so weit in die Schule

> zurück gehen, daß ich so viel verlernen, ja durchaus umlernen müßte, dachte ich nicht. Nun bin ich aber einmal überzeugt, und habe mich ganz hingegeben, und je mehr ich mich selbst verleugnen muß, desto mehr freut es mich. Ich bin wie ein Baumeister, der einen Turm aufführen wollte, und ein schlechtes Fundament gelegt hatte; er wird es noch beizeiten gewahr, und bricht gern wieder ab, was er schon aus der Erde gebracht hat, seinen Grundriß sucht er zu erweitern, zu veredeln, sich seines Grundes mehr zu versichern, und freut sich schon im voraus der gewissern Festigkeit des künftigen Baues. Gebe der Himmel, daß bei meiner Rückkehr auch die moralischen Folgen an mir zu fühlen sein möchten, die mir das Leben in einer weitern Welt gebracht hat. Ja es ist zugleich mit dem Kunstsinn der sittliche, welcher große Erneuerung leidet. (xv, 161)

The passage brings together many of the emotions Goethe felt at the time, as well as many of the reasons why he had decided, at this midpoint in his life, to throw everything up in the air. He is not only learning new things; he is also unlearning, and re-learning, old ones. The more he destroys his old self, the more he can find a new one. The image of an architect redesigning the foundations of a tower suggests Goethe's characteristic vision of reaching ever upwards — as well as his realization that in order to continue doing so, he must revisit the very fundaments of his existence. But then the passage takes a surprising twist, eliding the moral and aesthetic consequences of his midlife rebuild into a composite sense of what he *would like* this transformation to constitute — namely, a complete overhaul of his sensibility. Between 'rebirth' and 'return', Goethe was determined to emerge from his year in the sun not only with a renewed artistic, but also with a renewed *moral* sense.

A letter of five days later, written on Christmas Day 1786, provides a pithier image still for this rebirth: what joy it is, he writes, to watch a sculptor making a new mould out of plaster, as the limbs of the statue emerge from the cast to take a completely new form (xv, 162). But what shape did this new form take for Goethe? Although he had an *entrée* into any number of society addresses in Rome, he rapidly sought out the lively community of expatriate German artists and bohemians. He moved in with the painter Johann Heinrich Wilhelm Tischbein — who in due course would paint the defining portrait of the great poet at the summit of his life, reclining masterfully in front of the Italian *campagna* with the iconography of antiquity stretching out behind his two left feet (see Figure 2) — and surrounded himself with younger artists who could instruct him in Roman art. That they were younger was not accidental; Goethe was on a gap year *avant la lettre*, flirting with artists' models and living the student life. His account of this period exudes a happy, carefree *joie de vivre*, a mood that would later be captured in the erotic swoon of the *Roman Elegies* (written on his return to Weimar):

> Und belehr ich mich nicht? wenn ich des lieblichen Busens
> Formen spähe, die Hand leite die Hüften hinab.
> Dann versteh ich erst recht den Marmor, ich denk' und vergleiche,
> Sehe mit fühlendem Aug', fühle mit sehender Hand.[3]

Fig. 5.2. Goethe's two left feet. Johann Heinrich Wilhelm Tischbein, *Goethe in the Roman Campagna* (1787).

Beyond their obvious *eros*, such lines are energized by Goethe's emphasis on the aesthetics of the eye. As Ritchie Robertson notes in his *Very Short Introduction*, Goethe was nothing if not an 'Augenmensch';[4] the trip to Italy, in this regard, merely rendered explicit what had always been implicit in his aesthetic sensibility. Throughout his time in Italy, Goethe was drawn to painters and sculptors, to visual artists who enhanced not only his interest in Roman art and architecture, but also his sense of wanting to move away from being a mere scribbler of words. Overwhelmingly, his interest in Italy was visual, not verbal: as the lines quoted above suggest, he wanted to find ways of relating the touch of the hand to the vision of the eye. By the time of his second stay in Rome a year later — after having made a return trip south to Naples and Sicily, he would spend the winter of 1787 in the ancient capital — he could claim that he felt not only 'neu geboren', but also 'neu erzogen' (XV, 478).

What lay behind this re-education? Italy's status for Goethe as the very essence of the South — as the land where the lemon trees bloom, in the words famously sung by Mignon in *Wilhelm Meisters Lehrjahre* (1795) — owed much, of course, to its mild climate and *dolce vita*. But it also reflected Goethe's lifelong preoccupation with Greek and Roman art, with mythological sculptures and pagan temples, a preoccupation that was schooled in particular by his reading of the father of art history, Johann Joachim Winckelmann. Winckelmann's reflections on the 'edle Einfalt und stille Größe' of Greek sculpture, as outlined most notably in his seminal *Geschichte der Kunst des Alterthums* (1764),[5] had been famously influential in developing the aesthetic tastes of German intellectuals at the end of the eighteenth century, in particular by emphasizing the plasticity — and associated morality — of antique sculpture. Goethe had taken classes, as a young man, with Winckelmann's friend Adam Friedrich Oeser, and it was in no small measure this classicizing influence that led to him becoming an *Augenmensch*.[6] His decision to travel around Italy with one painter after another constituted a corresponding attempt to move away from the art of the mind towards that of the body — an attempt, in short, to reinvent himself not only as a man, but also as an artist. In all his artistic endeavours, in all his efforts to reinvent himself in Italy as both creator and critic, this meant that one category came to dominate his thinking: the classical.

Goethe's intense engagement with the theory and practice of classical art can be seen, at this pivotal moment in his development, as an aesthetic reflection — or perhaps deflection — of biological reality. At the midpoint of his life, the poet feels the urge 'den Mittelpunkt zu suchen, nach dem mich ein unwiderstehliches Bedürfnis hinzog' (xv, 134). Coming as it does in the very first letter he wrote on arriving in the ancient capital, this striking evocation of a transcendental *Mittelpunkt* — the midpoint of what? — suggests that for Goethe in his late thirties, all roads lead to Rome: aesthetic, emotional, psychological, physical. The term recurs, with minor variations, throughout his stay in the city: '[es] liest sich Geschichte von hier aus ganz anders als an jedem Orte der Welt [...] hier glaubt man von innen heraus zu lesen' (xv, 164), as he notes in his final diary entry of 1786. Rome functions for Goethe as the middle of world history — an echo, perhaps, of the etymology of 'Mediterranean' — as well as that of his own life.

The psychology of this new classical phase — a phase that would set the tone for the second half of Goethe's life, echoing into his subsequent friendship with Schiller and their epoch-defining cultivation of a 'classical style' when back in Weimar — pivots on his understanding of time. Perhaps the most explicit statement of Goethe's classical aesthetics in Italy occurs in December 1787, when he identifies 'was man im höchsten Sinne die Gegenwart des klassischen Bodens nennen dürfte. Ich nenne dies die sinnlich geistige Überzeugung, daß hier das Große war, ist und sein wird' (xv, 489). Aside from the conflation of body and mind so typical of Goethe's approach to ancient culture, what is notable here is his view of classical art as mediating between past, present and future — which is to say, as timeless. Yet it was precisely his *over*-awareness of time — a sentiment that we might now summarize under the term 'midlife crisis', in the sense pioneered by the psychiatrist Eliot Jaques's seminal paper of 1965[7] — that drove Goethe to Italy in the first place, and that continued to define his newly emerging sense of himself as someone seeking 'solidity': 'Ich bin nicht hier um nach meiner Art zu genießen', he claims in November 1786; 'befleißigen will ich mich der großen Gegenstände, lernen und mich ausbilden, ehe ich vierzig Jahre alt werde' (xv, 145). As he reaches middle age, then, Goethe's classical turn is a way of conferring what he calls 'ballast' or 'gravity' on his existence — a way of combating time, in short, through timelessness (xv, 178).

The works Goethe completed during this period reflect this awareness of time passing. As he settles into his second stay in Rome, a sense of struggling against time comes to characterize his way of thinking: 'jetzt, da das Alter kommt, will ich wenigstens das Erreichbare erreichen und das Tunliche tun, da ich so lange verdient und unverdient das Schicksal des Sisyphus und Tantalus erduldet habe' (xv, 378). The quintessentially Goethean verbal nouns — 'das Erreichbare', 'das Tunliche' — are positive inversions of the mythological figures that follow; in order to escape suffering like Sisyphus or being tortured like Tantalus, one must redouble one's focus on what can and cannot be achieved in the course of a single life. The two mythological characters are condemned to timelessness (always the cruellest aspect of mythological punishment); Goethe, like the rest of us, is condemned to time. 'Ich bin alt genug, und wenn ich noch etwas machen will, darf ich mich nicht säumen', he writes just a few days later. '[E]s kommt nicht aufs Denken, es kommt aufs *Machen* an' (xv, 392). In the words of Elliot Jaques's paradigmatic patient: by the time we get to the middle of life, we must do or die.

Such doing manifested itself in Goethe's renewed efforts to complete unfinished projects. As he returned to his play *Egmont* — begun several years earlier, before he had even moved to Weimar — he remarked that 'Ich fühle mich recht jung wieder, da ich das Stück schreibe' (xv, 399). This feeling notably found its way not only into the play itself, but also into the final book of Goethe's autobiography *Dichtung und Wahrheit*, which he concludes with an extract from *Egmont*:

> Wie von unsichtbaren Geistern gepeitscht, gehen die Sonnenpferde der Zeit mit unsers Schicksals leichtem Wagen durch, und uns bleibt nichts, als mutig gefaßt, die Zügel festzuhalten und bald rechts, bald links, vom Steine hier, vom Sturze da die Räder abzulenken.[8]

The middle of life becomes, in short, the basis for all of life, for the passing of time *tout court*.

While Goethe completed a number of other long-standing projects during this period — including his play on the Italian poet Tasso, which he had begun a decade earlier and which accordingly lends symbolic resonance to his pretence of being ten years younger — he also received the proofs of an eight-volume edition of his complete works up to this point. Their arrival led him, unsurprisingly, to reflect on his position at the midpoint of his life, and to divide his career into a past and a future: 'Es ist mir wirklich sonderbar zu Mute, daß diese vier zarten Bändchen, die Resultate eines halben Lebens, mich in Rom aufsuchen' (xv, 427). From this distance, and with this lapse in time, Goethe had the impression — one familiar to anyone looking back on something they wrote a long time ago — that he was no longer the person who wrote those works; the constituent elements of his art had aged and changed. Like everyone else in middle age, in other words, he was confronted with an existential version of the paradox of the philosopher's axe: if first we change our handle, and then we change our blade, are we still the same axe? Are we still the same person?

This feeling emerges, in fact, as the defining sentiment of Goethe's Italian journey. The northern traveller believed that he had come to Rome to find 'a supplement to his existence', as he noted in October 1787, yet slowly he realized that he must completely change himself and start all over again (xv, 461). This understanding of ageing as that of incessant evolution is brought out neatly by Goethe's changing responses to his 'incognito'. The poet in fact refers to his 'Halbinkognito', since he is aware — no doubt with a certain degree of satisfaction — that people only *pretend* not to know who he is (xv, 143). The great advantage of this, he claims in November 1786, is that people can no longer talk about him, and so they are forced to talk about themselves and their own projects (xv, 143). Yet six months later he encountered a Maltese aristocrat who enquired — not knowing who Goethe was, but realizing that he was German — after the hero of his youth who wrote *Werther*. Upon hearing Goethe reply that this hero was none other than he, the Maltese stranger was shocked and stuttered that he must have changed a lot; yes, replied Goethe, 'zwischen Weimar und Palermo hab' ich manche Veränderung gehabt' (xv, 260). His anonymity rumbled, Goethe is forced to confront the fact that he has aged, spiritually as well as physically.

Here as elsewhere, however, it would be a mistake to think that ageing is necessarily negative. The great lesson of Goethe's Italian journey is that one can learn to embrace the passing of time; in rediscovering his appetite for living — and in discovering a new form of classical aesthetics — the poet made a virtue of necessity, finding a 'Mittelpunkt' in both his life and his art. When we describe someone we have not seen for a long time as 'changed', we do not normally mean it as a compliment; yet continuing development, for a writer or an artist, is the one true precondition of creativity. Near the end of his life, in 1828, Goethe himself spoke of what he termed the 'wiederholte Pubertät' vouchsafed to the truly gifted: while other people are merely young or old, the genuine artist finds ways of remaining in a state of enduring adolescence.[9] The perpetual incipience that characterized Goethe's life and work may be beyond most of us — it was beyond his contemporary William Wordsworth, for instance, who produced little of note once he had finished the first version of *The Prelude* at the age of 35 — but its example can nonetheless serve us well as we grow older. How to be the same while becoming another person is the great challenge of middle age.

II

My own engagement with Goethe began, in earnest, as an undergraduate. I had been lucky enough to hear the name at school, so I was not as gauche as some of my peers with their stumbling attempts to discuss the great *Go-ether*. In fact, I felt a frisson of pride, almost of ownership, on learning that the poet came from Frankfurt, my grandmother's family having come to Britain from Frankfurt as wool merchants in the late nineteenth century. With the advent of the Great War, they had anglicized their name from *Schwan* to Swan, a pleasingly Proustian way of preserving the Jewish cadence while escaping the opprobrium of a nationalistic age. Or so it seemed, at least, to my overheated imagination.

Looking back on the works I read in my earliest years at university — and that I now teach to first- and second-year students — I am struck by how readily they map on to life as seen from the perspective of late adolescence. The *Sturm und Drang* of Goethe's love poems of the 1770s, and not least of his early novel *Die Leiden des jungen Werthers* (1774), pulses with the all-or-nothing intensity of youth; death or glory, *thanatos* or *eros*, are the only options available. Werther shoots himself not only because he cannot be with his beloved Lotte, but also because it is the sort of melodramatic gesture that corresponds to — and in a certain sense justifies — his world-view. All that matters to him is *passion*, in its etymological senses of both sentiment and suffering. There is simply too much pathos in his pathetic fallacy; the natural world reflects back to him only what he projects on to it. He has not yet learned to take existence on its own terms.

That the mature Goethe of the late 1780s was clearly embarrassed by Werther's effusiveness tells its own story. It is hardly an exaggeration to say that the whole Italian journey was conceived as an attempt to escape not only the suffocating celebrity that the novel had conferred on him, but also the cloying sentimentality of his youth. The move towards an aesthetic of objectivity, as conceptualized through Roman classicism, is nothing if not a reaction against the extreme subjectivity of his earliest work. The tone of greater distance that Goethe cultivated in the 1787 edition of the novel suggests as much; Werther's own voice (as heard through the first-person perspective of the letters that form the bulk of the text) can no longer be allowed to stand unchallenged. The excesses of the young hero Werther — and by extension of the young writer Goethe — are tamed by maturity.

Whether this is a good thing or not is, of course, a matter of taste, but there is little doubt that it reflects the standard narrative of how temperament develops over the course of a life — from passion to reason, from intensity to experience. Middle age, one might say, is supposed to temper temper. It is worth asking, however, whether this narrative corresponds to the continuing unfolding of creativity that manifests itself in the greatest artists — or whether the greatness of those artists who manage to continue creating into middle age consists precisely in finding ways to resist such a slackening of intensity, to assert what Goethe terms, in his comments to Eckermann about 'wiederholte Pubertät', the 'temporäre Verjüngung' of the truly gifted.[10] Goethe himself provides a compelling case study not only on account of his obvious artistic significance, but also because of the dramatic caesura in his life represented by the Italian journey. Rather than doing what so many of us do — continuing to drift while feeling vaguely dissatisfied — he took a decision, against no little opposition and in great secrecy, to do something about it. The path of least resistance certainly did not lead over the Alps, and yet that is the way that he went.

In Goethe's case, the development of temperament that we call maturity can be neatly illustrated by contrasting two of his best-known poems. The first, 'Prometheus', was written in the early 1770s:

Bedecke deinen Himmel Zeus
Mit Wolkendunst!
Und übe Knabengleich
Der Disteln köpft
An Eichen dich und Bergeshöhn!
Mußt mir meine Erde
Doch lassen stehn,
Und meine Hütte
Die du nicht gebaut,
Und meinen Herd
Um dessen Glut
Du mich beneidest.

Ich kenne nichts ärmers
Unter der Sonn als euch Götter.
Ihr nähret kümmerlich
Von Opfersteuern
Und Gebetshauch
Eure Majestät
Und darbtet wären
Nicht Kinder und Bettler
Hoffnungsvolle Toren.

Da ich ein Kind war
Nicht wußt wo aus wo ein,
Kehrt ich mein verirrtes Aug
Zur Sonne als wenn drüber wär
Ein Ohr zu hören meine Klage
Ein Herz wie meins
Sich des Bedrängten zu erbarmen.

Wer half mir wider
Der Titanen Übermut
Wer rettete vom Tode mich
Von Sklaverei?
Hast du's nicht alles selbst vollendet,
Heilig glühend Herz
Und glühtest jung und gut,
Betrogen, Rettungsdank
Dem Schlafenden dadroben

Ich dich ehren? Wofür?
Hast du die Schmerzen gelindert
Je des Beladenen
Hast du die Tränen gestillet
Je des Geängsteten?
Hat nicht mich zum Manne geschmiedet
Die allmächtige Zeit
Und das ewige Schicksal
Meine Herren und deine.

Wähntest etwa
Ich sollt das Leben hassen

> In Wüsten fliehn,
> Weil nicht alle Knabenmorgen
> Blütenträume reiften.
>
> Hier sitz ich, forme Menschen
> Nach meinem Bilde
> Ein Geschlecht das mir gleich sei
> Zu leiden, weinen
> Genießen und zu freuen sich
> Und dein nicht zu achten
> Wie ich![11]

Written when Goethe was in his early twenties, 'Prometheus' is typical of the *Sturm und Drang* of his youth, full-throated and fiery in its defiance of the tyrannical gods. Its very syntax and punctuation reflect this confrontational attitude, driven as it is by audacious imperatives — 'Bedecke deinen Himmel Zeus, | Mit Wolkendunst!' — and bold exclamation marks. From challenging the gods, Prometheus moves downwards to the egotistical Titan, hubristically positioning himself as rival to their divine powers of creation: 'Hier sitz ich, forme Menschen | Nach meinem Bilde'. By the end of the poem, the arrogation of power could not be clearer, as Prometheus concludes with the injunction to humanity to scorn the gods 'wie ich', the closing pronoun the very epitome of his ego. As a model of the defiant subjectivity of youth, indeed, it could hardly be more egocentric.

Only ten years later, the mature Goethe presents the relationship between man and the gods very differently:

> Wenn der uralte
> Heilige Vater
> Mit gelassener Hand
> Aus rollenden Wolken
> Segnende Blitze
> Über die Erde sä't,
> Küss' ich den letzten
> Saum seines Kleides,
> Kindliche Schauer
> Treu in der Brust.
>
> Denn mit Göttern
> Soll sich nicht messen
> Irgendein Mensch.
> Hebt er sich aufwärts,
> Und berührt
> Mit dem Scheitel die Sterne,
> Nirgends haften dann
> Die unsichern Sohlen,
> Und mit ihm spielen
> Wolken und Winde.
>
> Steht er mit festen,
> Markigen Knochen
> Auf der wohlgegründeten,

> Dauernden Erde;
> Reicht er nicht auf,
> Nur mit der Eiche
> Oder der Rebe
> Sich zu vergleichen.
>
> Was unterscheidet
> Götter von Menschen?
> Daß viele Wellen
> Vor jenen wandeln,
> Ein ewiger Strom:
> Uns hebt die Welle,
> Verschlingt die Welle,
> Und wir versinken.
>
> Ein kleiner Ring
> Begrenzt unser Leben,
> Und viele Geschlechter
> Reihen sich dauernd
> An ihres Daseins
> Unendliche Kette.[12]

First drafted in 1780, 'Grenzen der Menschheit' gently repudiates the Promethean arrogance of the earlier poem. The individual perspective has given way to that of the collective, the first-person singular to the first-person plural. Goethe now conceives of himself merely as part of the great Leibnizian 'chain of Being', albeit in terms that rewrite Leibniz's — and Arthur Lovejoy's[13] — gradation of animal entities as the succession of generations. Humans constitute only one small wave in the sea, whereas the gods see infinite numbers of waves stretching out before them. To get older is thus to realize, in true Socratic fashion, how little we know. Whereas the Promethean youth railed against the very notion of having limits, the mature poet acknowledges and celebrates them. Like Dirty Harry in the 1970s, a middle-aged man's gotta know his limitations.

The acceptance of mortality represented by this progression is surely the defining aspect of middle age. It is not only Goethe for whom the bell tolls; as we grow older, the resistance to inductive arguments about mortality that we subconsciously entertain when young — just because everyone else has aged and died, why should I? — becomes irrefutably untenable. Early middle age is the point at which the mirror becomes a *memento mori*. What purchase can literature offer on this mirror? It is not only the reader who cannot look into the same mirror twice; the writer is equally fated to view the evolution of his work from an ever-shifting perspective. If literature is like a mirror, it is because it does not, in itself, change — it is the person looking into it who changes. This is why it forms the ideal companion and therapist. Great works do not judge us or censure us, they merely listen and evolve with us as we bring our changing concerns to them. It is an oft-cited cliché that what defines the classics is their timelessness, but that is not quite right; it is their time*li*ness, their ability to reflect our ever-altering emotions, that keeps them fresh. My own encounters with Goethe — from eager undergraduate to earnest postgraduate, from stumbling lecturer to seasoned professor — have evolved with experience into something very different from their callow beginnings. The work of art may be the death mask of its conception, as Walter Benjamin famously claimed, but it is also the midwife of the reader's rebirth.[14]

What are the consequences of such a rebirth? Goethe's most explicit exploration of this question is to be found in his novel *Die Wahlverwandtschaften* (1809), the very first sentence of which draws attention to the hero's middle age: 'Eduard — so nennen wir einen reichen Baron im besten Mannesalter — Eduard hatte in seiner Baumschule die schönste Stunde eines Aprilnachmittags zugebracht'.[15] The phrasing immediately calls into question the authenticity of the cliché 'in the prime of life' (*im besten Mannesalter*), foregrounding the essential arbitrariness of how narrative constructs characters. What does it mean to be a man 'at the best age'? What shall we call such a creature? The whole story unfolds, in a sense, from this first parenthetical statement: the cliché alerts us to the inevitable temptation of the younger woman Ottilie, and of Eduard's 'chemical' attraction to her that will form the chief metaphor of the novel. Middle age — mediated via the programmatically named Mittler — becomes a kind of self-perpetuating fiction.

In Goethe's own case, this fiction emerges most vividly from the project that accompanied him for sixty years, and that would ultimately form one of the great masterpieces of world literature: *Faust* (1808/1832). From the early 1770s to the early 1830s, from youth to old age, the various incarnations of his hero preoccupied Goethe throughout his adult life; as such, when seen from the perspective of its author, *Faust* represents nothing so much as a reckoning with the existential scandal of ageing. Certainly, other works came and went, some of them directly a consequence of middle age: the erotic revivification of new-won enthusiasms in the *Römische Elegien* (1795), the emotional complications of long-term relationships in *Die Wahlverwandtschaften*. Yet no other work aged with the author in quite the same way.

When I first read *Faust*, like everyone else I thought it was a story about a deal with the devil. The relationship between Faust and Mephistopheles is, clearly, at the heart of the plot (although in Goethe's version of the legend it is, of course, not a pact but a 'wager', and one that has been anticipated — and thus ultimately forestalled — by a preliminary wager in the prologue between God and Mephistopheles). Yet as I settle ever more uncomfortably into middle age, it strikes me that the motif of the 'deal with the devil' is merely a plot device, a mechanism to enable the exploration of the real subject matter of the play: ageing.

What Faust yearns for, above all, is to be young again. Energy, innocence, enthusiasm: as the play opens, the desiccated old scholar can lay claim to none of these qualities. Having worked his way through all the principal disciplines available in the Middle Ages — from theology to jurisprudence, from philosophy to medicine — Faust still feels no wiser in the real terms of human emotion, which is why he turns to the dark arts in search of succour. He has experience; now he wants experien*ces*. Faust turns to Mephistopheles in the way that a man in a midlife crisis buys himself a new car; he seeks adventure. His tour through classical antiquity in the second part of the play — complete with the ultimate trophy mistress in the form of Helen of Troy — represents an attempt to (over-)compensate for everything he feels he missed out on when he was younger. That is why he is so confident that he will never say the fated words 'verweile doch, du bist so schön' (the words that would condemn him to an eternity of damnation); no single moment, he believes, can ever bring supreme satisfaction. It is not sex he desires so much as rejuvenation. If Mephistopheles is a pimp, he is selling time.

What is so striking for our purposes is that this is also the promise, and indeed the premise, of literature. Mephistopheles the magician is Goethe the author, rewinding the ageing process and flashing backwards and forwards as it suits him. Art enables what time disables: unfettered movement among past, present and future. In the cinema, in particular, with its essentially infinite powers of special effects, we are so used to seeing this that we barely notice it. Yet Mephistopheles has his special effects, too, whisking Faust between the centuries and conjuring up historical encounters at will. It is no coincidence that F. W. Murnau's film version of *Faust* in 1926 was one of the most expensive films ever made up to that point, exerting a decisive influence on the evolution of early, Expressionist cinema. As the years melt away from Faust's body and face, as he flies thrillingly through the skies (see figure 3), what we are seeing is not just the power of Mephistopheles to turn back time, but that of art.

FIG. 5.3. Special effects: F. W. Murnau, *Faust* (1926).

From the vantage point of middle age, however, it is not always clear how best to deploy this power. We tend to think of the middle of life as characterized by its transitional nature; if youth lives in the future tense and old age in the past, then middle age exists in the continuous present, in what Aristotle called the *akmē* of existence.[16] Yet the intermediate position this suggests is in fact illusory, since the middle-aged person *knows* youth, but can only *imagine* old age. This simple difference, obvious though it is on reflection, is in fact crucial, since it means that we give priority — in art as in life — to what has already been experienced, which is to say to the past. It is surely for this reason that the art of middle age tends to the elegy of what has been lost — Thomas Mann's *Tod in Venedig* (1912), in which the ageing artist Aschenbach lusts after the beautiful boy Tadzio, provides the paradigmatic example in German literature — rather than to the anticipation of what is to come.

The greatest artists and thinkers, however, manage to turn this tendency on its head by making middle age the basis for self-renewal. Dante's metaphysics, Montaigne's self-fashioning and Shakespeare's tragedies — to cite three of the greatest names — all make maturity out of mortality, insisting that the human condition in the middle of life is as much about believing in the future as about bemoaning the past. If Goethe belongs in this company, it is precisely because he is *not* Faust, because he manages to learn from his hero's failures. Whereas Faust cannot forgo Gretchen — thereby condemning her to her fate — Goethe comes to cultivate, in his later work, an ethic of 'renunciation' (*Entsagung*), understood as a kind of middle-aged counterpart to the all-consuming desire of his youth. Not doing things becomes a way of doing them better; self-denial becomes the basis for self-renewal.

In our age of instant gratification, such a path is not for everyone. We have to find our own way to move forward: for some this means amusing themselves, for others it means improving themselves. But we all have to move forward. It is the constant hope for something better that makes life possible; if you are in any way creative, indeed, it is what makes life tenable. Edward Said observes in his memoir *Out of Place* (1999) that he has no sense of cumulative achievement,[17] and I for my part feel the same way; my views about whatever I have achieved are constantly open to renegotiation, since I am constantly 'looking forward' to the project to come rather than backwards to the projects completed. I wouldn't like to speculate about whether the subject of the present *Festschrift* feels the same way, but his prolific rate of productivity and sheer range of interests — from works focusing on individual figures such as Kafka, Goethe, or Isaiah Berlin, to more general studies of periods or traditions such as the Enlightenment, Austrian literature, or Jewish writing — suggest something of this sense of perpetual incipience. And perpetual incipience remains, I am suggesting, the most Goethean of sentiments.

But perhaps this is, after all, the best way to live life, whether in the eighteenth or twenty-first century. Time may be an arrow — the great lesson of *Faust* is that we should not even *try* to stop it — but there is no reason why we shouldn't change its target from time to time. The mistake as we reach middle age is to think that we, or the activities to which we dedicate ourselves, are now 'set'. Maturity may be mortal, but it need not be fatal. We can always start off in a new direction, be it over the Alps or under new management. The past is a foreign country, but so is the future, and I for one want to move there. Something of this sentiment animates all productive, creative activities; we need to think that the most interesting project is the one we are working on now, since we need to think that the future will be at least as good as, if not better than, the past. As we move up the mountain of life, in short, the view narrows, but it also broadens. We may be halfway up the hill, but we are *only* halfway up the hill.

III

The second half of Goethe's hill was no less spectacular than the first. With his new, 'classical' aesthetic he undertook — and, just as importantly, completed — many an important work, including *Die Wahlverwandtschaften*, *West-östlicher Divan* (1819), *Wilhelm Meisters Wanderjahre* (1821) and, ultimately, *Faust*. The period following his return from Italy was marked by numerous new personal as well as professional projects, not least marriage to (the scandalously low-born) Christiane Vulpius and friendship with Schiller. The midlife crisis of the Italian journey gave way to the great flowering of Weimar classicism. Middle age was now maturity.

Goethe's Olympian status by this point was such that this maturity was also, more broadly, that of German culture. Throughout the eighteenth century the Germans had been plagued by an inferiority complex vis-à-vis French 'civilization', which they regarded enviously as the cradle of free thought and Enlightenment. With Goethe as their figurehead, German speakers now had a literature of international standing, as crystallized by the poet's much-mythologized meeting with Napoleon in 1808. Even if it did not yet exist as a nation — arguably *because* it did not yet exist as a nation — Germany now had a culture of its own, the pursuit of which would define much of its development in the nineteenth century.

However much he was identified with one quasi-national culture, though, what is striking about Goethe in the second half of his life is how *inter*national his interests became. In his mid-sixties he began writing love poems in the style of the Persian poet Hafiz; by the time he turned eighty he was advocating *Weltliteratur* as a model for modernity. It was not just that German culture was not enough; Europe itself could no longer hold him. The great lesson of Goethe's exemplary biography, in this as in other regards, is that middle age can — and perhaps should — be the point at which we redouble our efforts to learn new things, to continue developing ourselves 'inwardly and outwardly', as he wrote to Schiller.[18] Curiosity remains the greatest currency.

The exchange rate of this currency fluctuates, however, as we get older. The standard arc of ideology, from youthful progressivism to ageing conservatism, points to middle age as the most uncertain of life's stages. Should we turn inward to our own culture, or outward to those of others? Should we double down on what we already know, or take new risks in search of what we don't? Should we stick, in short, or should we twist? Goethe embodies this dilemma, but in a characteristically creative, productive manner. On the one hand he is the patron saint of everyone who favours taking new risks, twisting his way over the Alps to a newly revived sense of his own creativity; but on the other hand he does so, paradoxically, via a profoundly conservative turn, finding in classical antiquity the 'ballast' that he requires to anchor his new aesthetics. Goethe twists, that is to say, in order to stick.

By the time he was an old man, this double movement had become the poker tell of his style. Its most expansive example is his celebrated coinage of the term *Weltliteratur*. Talking to his amanuensis Johann Peter Eckermann in 1827, the 78-year-old poet famously claimed that 'National-Literatur will jetzt nicht viel sagen, die Epoche der Welt-Literatur ist an der Zeit und jeder muß jetzt dazu wirken, diese Epoche zu beschleunigen.'[19] His understanding of the concept is seemingly inclusive and democratic, ascribing no particular precedence to any one language or nation. Yet world literature is a pantheism with very personal gods — and for Goethe, these gods are to be found above all in antiquity.

> Aber auch bei solcher Schätzung des Ausländischen dürfen wir nicht bei etwas Besonderem haften bleiben und dieses für musterhaft ansehen wollen. Wir müssen nicht denken, das Chinesische wäre es, oder das Serbische, oder Calderon, oder die Nibelungen; sondern im Bedürfnis von etwas Musterhaftem müssen wir immer zu den alten Griechen zurückgehen, in deren Werken stets der schöne Mensch dargestellt ist.[20]

Timelessness has a time after all, then: the modern world is to be judged against the pre-determined criteria of the ancient world. *Weltliteratur* is more classical than classless.

What such a claim suggests, in other words, is that classical antiquity as he discovered it during his Italian journey — and crucially, as he *experienced* it — remained, for Goethe, the gold standard for all forms of beauty thereafter. Maturity, for him, meant not only looking beyond his native European culture, but also looking behind it (such is the essence of *Faust Part Two*, a kind of virtual-reality time machine in which the eponymous hero travels at great length through classical culture). The *Mittelpunkt* of classicism served as an anchor for the rest of Goethe's life not just because his mature style emerged during this middle period, but also because the very idea of having a midpoint became a model for his mature aesthetics, a kind of Gadamerian *Vor-urteil* that pre-determined his aesthetic tastes, no matter how much he looked beyond European culture.[21] Whether we like it or not, by the time we reach the middle of our lives we all have prejudices; whether we like it or not, by the time we reach the middle of our lives we all have a midpoint.

It is surely better, then, to be aware of our midlife prejudices, rather than to pretend that we don't have any. Self-awareness — of the kind that literature, with its blend of reason and emotion, argument and affect, is ideally placed to encourage — is the first step towards moving beyond the self. As we reach the middle of our lives, we should ask ourselves what we have taken for granted up to now, and how we might move beyond such presumptions in the second half of our time on Earth. Our lives may not be as exemplary as that of Goethe, but his questions can nonetheless be ours, too. What do we now see differently compared to twenty years ago? What projects remain incomplete, and how has our perception of them changed with the passing of time? What, in short, is the essence of our own mature aesthetics? However we answer these questions, the great lesson of Goethe's life and work — of his perpetual incipience — is that doing nothing is not an option. If to begin is to be born, to begin again and again is to be middle-aged.

Notes to Chapter 5

1. The main source for the biographical information here and elsewhere in this essay is Rüdiger Safranski, *Goethe: Life as a Work of Art*, trans. by David Dollenmayer (New York: Liveright, 2017), especially chs. 17 and 18.

2. Johann Wolfgang Goethe, *Italienische Reise*, in Goethe, *Sämtliche Werke. Briefe, Tagebücher und Gespräche*, ed. by Friedmar Apel and others, 40 vols (Frankfurt a.M.: Deutscher Klassiker Verlag, 1985–99), I. Abteilung: *Werke*, vol. xv (1993): *Italienische Reise*, ed. by Christoph Michel and Hans-Georg Drewitz, pp. 29–30. All subsequent references to Goethe are to this edition, abbreviated as FA. Further references to the *Italienische Reise* are given in brackets in the body of the text.
3. FA, I/I (1987): *Gedichte 1756–1799*, ed. by Karl Eibl, p. 405.
4. Ritchie Robertson, *Goethe: A Very Short Introduction* (Oxford: Oxford University Press, 2016), pp. 46–47.
5. The famous phrase itself was first coined by Winckelmann in his *Gedanken über die Nachahmung der griechischen Werke in der Malerei und Bildhauerkunst* (1755).
6. Goethe writes of reading Winckelmann in Rome on 3 December 1786; see *Italienische Reise* (xv, 157).
7. Elliott Jaques, 'Death and the Midlife Crisis', *International Journal of Psychoanalysis*, 46 (1965), 502–14.
8. FA, I/xiv (1986): *Aus meinem Leben. Dichtung und Wahrheit*, ed. Klaus-Detlef Müller, p. 852.
9. 'Solche Männer und ihres Gleichen [...] sind geniale Naturen, mit denen es eine eigene Bewandtnis hat; sie erleben eine *wiederholte Pubertät*, während andere Leute nur einmal jung sind.' Goethe to Eckermann, 11 March 1828, in FA II. Abteilung: *Briefe, Tagebücher und Gespräche*, vol. xii (1999): Johann Peter Eckermann, *Gespräche mit Goethe in den letzten Jahren seines Lebens*, ed. by Christoph Michel, p. 656. See also Walter Muschg, 'Wiederholte Pubertät', *Publications of the English Goethe Society*, 34 (1964), 54–84.
10. Goethe to Eckermann, 11 March 1828, FA II/xii, 656.
11. FA I/I: *Gedichte 1756–1799*, pp. 203–04.
12. 'Grenzen der Menschheit', ibid., pp. 332–33.
13. Arthur Lovejoy, *The Great Chain of Being* (Cambridge, MA: Harvard University Press, 1936).
14. Walter Benjamin, 'Die Technik des Schriftstellers in dreizehn Thesen', *Einbahnstrasse* (Berlin: Rowohlt, 1928), p. 33.
15. FA I/viii (1994): *Die Leiden des jungen Werthers. Die Wahlverwandtschaften. Kleine Prosa. Epen*, ed. Waltraud Wiethölter, pp. 269–529 (p. 271).
16. See Aristotle, *Rhetoric*, trans. by Richard Claverhouse Jebb (Cambridge: Cambridge University Press, 1909), II: XIV, p. 102.
17. Edward Said, *Out of Place* (New York: Granta, 2000), p. 8.
18. See Safranski, *Goethe*, p. 452. Cited from Goethe, *Sämtliche Werke nach Epochen seines Schaffens*, ed. Karl Richter and others, 33 vols (Munich: Hanser, 1985–98), IV.2, 515.
19. Goethe to Eckermann, 31 January 1827, FA II/xii, 225.
20. Ibid.
21. For Gadamer's value-neutral idea of 'pre-judgement', see Hans Georg Gadamer, *Wahrheit und Methode* (Tübingen: Mohr, 1960), especially pp. 270–90: ' "Vorurteil" heisst [...] durchaus nicht notwendig falsches Urteil' (p. 275).

CHAPTER 6

'nicht sehr in den kirchlichen Formen': Liberale Literatur und Katholizismus in Österreich nach 1848

Werner Michler

I

Franz Grillparzer, dessen 'Religiosität', wie er in seiner Fragment gebliebenen Autobiographie sagt, 'sich nicht sehr in den kirchlichen Formen bewegte',[1] hatte mit seiner Reserve dem Katholizismus gegenüber bei einem Romaufenthalt 1819 wenig Glück. Nicht nur erhält er aufgrund einer Verwechslung von Papst Pius VII. einen 'Spezialsegen in aller Form', er wird 'auch für einen Mangel an kirchlicher Pietät empfindlich gestraft':[2] Die Teilnahme an einer Audienz lehnt er ab, weil er den rituellen Handkuss scheut, muss aber schließlich bei anderer Gelegenheit, 'auf die Gefahr von den Schweizern zum Fenster hinausgeworfen zu werden', dem Papst den 'Fuß küssen. Alles rächt sich in dieser Welt.'[3]

Die kleine Szene von versuchter Aufsässigkeit und schließlicher Fügung in das Unvermeidliche transportiert viel von den Mentalitäten der österreichischen Intellektuellen des Spätjosephinismus.[4] Erinnert wird sie von Grillparzer in einer ganz anderen Epoche. Als er auf Aufforderung der neu gegründeten Akademie der Wissenschaften seine Autobiographie 1853 endlich niederschreibt (ohne übrigens den Text der Akademie dann auch zu übermitteln), ist längst eine neue Restaurationsphase angebrochen; das 1855 geschlossene Konkordat zwischen Österreich und dem Heiligen Stuhl wird der Kirche weitreichende Vorrechte in Bildung, Eheangelegenheiten sowie in der Stellung des Klerus einräumen — von Grillparzer mit den bissigsten Epigrammen glossiert. Diesem Konkordat war keine lange Dauer beschieden: Seine Aufkündigung durch den Staat, nach der Infallibilitätserklärung des Papstes 1870 der Sache, 1874 der Form nach, markiert in der österreichischen Geschichte des 19. Jahrhunderts einen Höhepunkt der liberalen Ära. Unter größter Beachtung der Öffentlichkeit stimmte Grillparzer (wie auch andere prägende Autoren der ersten Jahrhunderthälfte, Anastasius Grün und Friedrich Halm) 1868 im Herrenhaus für die 'Maigesetze'. (Im Austrofaschismus wurde dann 1933/34 ein neues Konkordat abgeschlossen, das im Wesentlichen noch in Geltung ist.)

An diesen auch literaturgeschichtlich relevanten Eckdaten stehen die Autorinnen und Autoren — viele weitere Namen ließen sich nennen — jedenfalls mehrheitlich nicht an der Seite der katholischen Kirche, der weithin dominierenden Konfession im Habsburgerreich.[5] Tatsächlich, resümiert Karlheinz Rossbacher für die 'Kultur der Ringstraßenzeit', scheint es, als habe es in Österreich 'keine katholische Intelligenz gegeben [...], die den Namen verdient. Bei fast allen Schriftstellern war eine mehr oder weniger kirchenkritische [...] Haltung die Regel, sie reichte vom diffusen Ressentiment bis zur programmatischen Formulierung.'[6]

Diese für sich schon bemerkenswerte Entwicklung fügt sich in eine sehr viel größere kulturelle Konfliktlage ein, vergleichbar eher mit den Verhältnissen in Frankreich und den romanischen Ländern als mit jenen in 'Deutschland'. Nach der Gegenreformation war Österreich ein weitgehend gleichförmig katholisches Land geworden, mit kleinen protestantischen, jüdischen und dann auch muslimischen Minderheiten. Die kulturelle Prägung durch die Barockkultur und die *pietas Austriaca*[7] machten Österreich zu einem Kernland der Kultur von 'Muße und Verschwendung' (Peter Hersche),[8] in einer vielsprachigen Welt, deren Hofkultur auf die Romania orientiert ist und in der größeres Gewicht auf Musik und den bildenden Künsten liegt als auf der Literatur, und hier wieder ist die Bühne dominanter als Lyrik und Prosa. Mit und nach der josephinischen Aufklärung betreten österreichische Schriftsteller und Dichter verstärkt und erkennbar die literarische Szene der in rascher Konstituierung befindlichen deutschsprachigen (Hoch-)Literatur, in deutlicher Abgrenzung von Barock und katholischer Kirche, in gespannter Nähe zum österreichischen Staat. Diese Vorentscheidungen der literarischen Intellektuellen halten lange an, bis schließlich um die Jahrhundertwende — charakteristischerweise unter dem Schlagwort der 'Barocktradition' — von einer neuen Generation wieder anders prekäre Identitätsentwürfe ins Spiel gebracht werden, bei Hugo von Hofmannsthal, Hermann Bahr, Josef Nadler und anderen, diesmal — und vielleicht in dieser Form erstmalig — unter Einbezug der katholischen Elemente. In den Katastrophen des 20. Jahrhunderts sollte auch diese Fügung bald reichlich Gelegenheit haben, sich nachhaltig zu diskreditieren.

In den 'Kulturkämpfen' des 19. Jahrhunderts stand aber auch schon mehr auf dem Spiel als ein Streit politischer Meinungen oder die Frage nach der Relevanz metaphysischer Thesen. Eine Kultur, sei es eine religiös oder eine säkular grundierte, ist kein Set von konsistenten Thesen über die Natur der Welt, sondern 'a whole way of life' (Raymond Williams)[9] und umfasst das gesamte Ensemble von leibhaften Praktiken, inkorporierten Überzeugungen, intellektuellen Gewohnheiten, das ihre Angehörigen als selbstverständlich und vorbewusst teilen. Die Ersetzung oder Überschreibung einer Kultur durch eine andere, wie das in Säkularisierungskonflikten untenommen wird, ist mithin ein komplexeres Unternehmen als ein abstrakter Kampf gegen den Aberglauben oder die Befreiung der Massen von den Mächten der Reaktion. Eine große Bandbreite an gelebten Kulturen steht hinter den *simplifications terribles* von einer alten Welt der Religion (und des Aberglaubens) und einer neuen Welt der Moderne (und der Aufklärung und der Wissenschaft); den Individuen, literarischen Figuren wie den

Zeitgenossen, ist diese Ersetzung und Überschreibung von Gesten, semantisierten Räumen, historisch erworbenen und verfestigten Habitus-, also Anschauungs- und Verhaltensformen (im Sinn Pierre Bourdieus) aufgegeben. Ausgetragen werden diese Konflikte allerdings zunächst als Konflikte zwischen Intellektuellengruppen: zwischen klerikalen und säkularen Bildungs- und Funktionseliten — als Kämpfe um Institutionen (naheliegenderweise zuerst um das Bildungswesen und andere intellektuelle Infrastrukturen) sowie als Kämpfe um Hegemonie (Antonio Gramsci), also um die Zustimmung der Nichtgebildeten und die (Um-)Modellierung von deren Habitus, als 'Moderne' oder — ebenfalls auf dem Terrain der Moderne — als 'Traditionelle'.

'Weltanschauung' ist der Begriff, mit Hilfe dessen man versucht hat, sich über diese Prozesse Klarheit zu verschaffen. Dass 'Anschauung' die wörtliche Entsprechung von 'Theorie' ist, mag bereits auf die Intellektualisierung und Dogmatisierung als eine wesentliche Austragungsform dieser Kulturkämpfe hinweisen. Die thesenhafte Zuspitzung von Überzeugungen zu 'Glaubenssätzen' (auf Seite der 'Alten' wie der 'Neuen') von 'Weltanschauungen' war selbst Kampfmittel und Ergebnis des Konflikts[10] und war daher nicht leicht als Einseitigkeit zu erkennen. Die Parallele zum Auf- und Ausbau von religiösen Dogmensystemen nach der Reformation liegt nahe und vom 19. Jahrhundert ist auch als von einem 'zweiten konfessionellen Zeitalter'[11] gesprochen worden. Die 'Konfessionalisierung' von ('katholischen', liberalen, nationalen u.a.) 'Bekenntnissen' zu gelebten, verkörperten und habituell verankerten Kulturen ist der zweite Schritt in diesem Prozess. Ein klassischer Topos ist Ernst Haeckels 1868 formulierte Gegenüberstellung einer 'übernatürlichen', mosaischen und einer 'natürlichen', evolutionistischen Schöpfungsgeschichte, 'Schöpfungshypothese' unter gleichem Recht, wissenschaftlicher Prüfung ausgesetzt zu werden — erwartungsgemäß sehr zum Schaden der ersteren.[12] Im Fall Haeckels und des 'Monismus' wird dann umgekehrt der Weg von der naturwissenschaftlichen Aufklärung zur kirchen- bzw. sektenhaften Organisationsform der 'monistischen' Bewegung zu Ende gegangen werden. Die Tendenz zur säkularistischen 'Religions-' oder 'Konfessionsbildung', die man übrigens auch am heutigen naturwissenschaftlichen Atheismus beobachten kann,[13] und die (kontrovers)theologische Fixierung, Intellektualisierung und Theologisierung von praktischen Glaubensgütern — wie die Fixierung der traditionellen vielschichtigen katholischen Marienverehrung zum Dogma von der unbefleckten Empfängnis, 1854[14] — sind Teil derselben diskursiven Verwerfung. Ob Säkularisierung tatsächlich ein unumkehrbarer historischer Großtrend ist, wird in einer Reihe von Disziplinen diskutiert; sicher scheint jedenfalls zu sein, dass Antiklerikalismus weniger als Säkularisierungserscheinung, sondern vor allem als 'Säkularisierungsprojekt'[15] zu lesen ist. Säkularisierung[16] vollzieht sich, wie auch nicht anders möglich, durchaus in von der Religion geerbten Formen: daher die Bekenntnisse, Konversionen, das Auftreten von Apostaten und Häretikern, die Hochämter, Lebensbeichten, Absolutionen, die Gebote und Verbote; aber auch die spezifischen Gottesdienste, Lebensformen, die Medienapparate, Firmung und Leichenbegängnis, Jugendweihe und Feuerbestattung, Erbauungsschriften und Unterhaltungskultur.

Säkularistische Kulturbewegungen, die an Wissenschaft, Rationalismus und Aufklärung ansetzen, haben zunächst ihre offensichtliche Grenze an dem, was Romain Rolland Sigmund Freud gegenüber als das 'ozeanische Gefühl' als der 'eigentlichen Quelle der Religiosität' bezeichnet hat, eine 'Empfindung der "Ewigkeit" [...], ein Gefühl wie von etwas Unbegrenztem, Schrankenlosem, gleichsam "Ozeanischem"'.[17] Diese Bewegungen entwickeln deshalb aus und neben der Doktrin, der 'Wissenschaft' und den aus ihr gezogenen metaphysikkritischen und metaphysischen Folgerungen, Elemente von Praktiken und Ansätze einer immer etwas intellektuell und abstrakt bleibenden forcierten 'Gefühlsstruktur' (Raymond Williams); hier bot sich, wie bemerkt, der Evolutionismus als Bindemittel und Transzendenzsurrogat an. Der Liberalismus hatte hier insgesamt schlechtere Karten als die Sozialdemokratie. Minna Kautsky lässt in ihrem sozialistischen Tendenzroman *Die Alten und die Neuen* (1885) einen finsteren und fanatischen Jesuiten den Bücherschrank eines aufgeklärten sozialistischen Salinenarbeiters perlustrieren:

> 'Darwin', murmelte er [Cölestin], und seine Augen überflogen die Zeilen, die wie glühende Lettern ihm entgegenbrannten. 'Darwin! hier ist der Schlüssel zu allem. Das ist das neue Evangelium, das sie uns entfremdet, das alles untergräbt, was bisher als Offenbarung die Welt erklärt und uns in ihr. — [...] Sie haben eine andere Poesie, einen andern Idealismus, eine andere Begeisterung — sie entgöttern alles und sezen an deren Stelle ein unerbittliches Naturgesez, die Notwendigkeit. Es ist ein furchtbares, ein äzendes Gift in alledem, das weiter frißt, weiter, weiter!' Aufstöhnend griff er nach seinem Herzen, als wäre auch ihm bereits etwas von diesem Gifte eingeimpft [...].[18]

Der Katholizismus spielte in den Kulturkämpfen des 19. Jahrhunderts die Rolle der *bête noire*, er spielte sie gut und nicht immer ungern. Die Reihe der spektakulären Absagen an die Moderne, mit der der Vatikan vor dem Hintergrund einer komplexen inneritalienischen und gesamteuropäischen Konfliktlage letztlich auf die Mobilisierung der Moderne durch die und seit der französischen Revolution reagierte, beförderte die Bildung von 'weltanschaulichen Lagern' und kulturellen Heimaten. Die Verurteilung von Irrtümern im 'Syllabus errorum'[19] etwa führte zu einer polemischen wechselseitigen Konstitution von Gegnerschaften, die in manchen Zusammenhängen bis heute spürbar sind.[20] Die forcierte und geförderte Renaissance traditioneller religiöser kultureller Formen wie der Wallfahrt und anderer Frömmigkeitspraktiken machte aus Traditionen Traditionalismus (der '"Neobarock"' des 19. Jahrhunderts zeigte sich als 'ein verstümmelter, verfremdeter, beschränkter und unfreier Barock'[21]). Zuletzt ist sehr plausibel von der 'Erfindung des Katholizismus im 19. Jahrhundert' (Hubert Wolf) gesprochen worden.

Die Literatur begleitet die Säkularisierungsprojekte, als deren ambivalente Agentur und als ihr Produkt zugleich; sie formuliert und moderiert die vielfältigen Konfliktlinien. Auf den kulturellen Formen mit ihren Narrativen, Dramatisierungen, Pathosformeln liegen damit auch die ganze Last der Modernisierung und ihre psychischen und transzendenten Folgelasten, die nicht unterschätzt werden sollten. Der Konflikt selbst erzeugt schon ein Gefühl von Leere und Unbehaustheit — Georg Lukács wird das die 'transzendentale Obdachlosigkeit' nennen — das die dominanten Fortschritts- und Konfliktdiskurse unterminiert. 'The world was void', heißt es in Byrons apokalyptischem Gedicht 'Darkness' (1816), '[s]easonless, herbless, treeless, manless, lifeless — | A lump of death — a chaos of hard clay'.[22] Die Literatur kennt das in der ersten Jahrhunderthälfte als 'Weltschmerz' und 'Zerrissenheit', in der zweiten als 'Pessimismus', eine gewisse Neigung zur Apokalyptik ist untergründig immer präsent; Symptom des tatsächlichen oder drohenden Geltungsverlusts von Institutionen und der sie tragenden Diskurse.

II

'[S]chon der Mythos ist Aufklärung, und: Aufklärung schlägt in Mythologie zurück.'[23] Eine solche Auffassung der Konstellation von 'Religion' und 'Fortschritt' hätte nicht Aufklärung und Gegenaufklärung, sondern die *Dialektik* der Aufklärung ins Zentrum zu stellen, mit der sich die historische Logik der Auseinandersetzungen im Argumentativen wie im Ästhetischen erklären lässt. Die Frage nach Terraingewinnen der 'einen' oder der 'anderen' Seite ist aber wieder nur vor dem Hintergrund der großen Auseinandersetzungen im Zeitalter expandierender kultureller und politischer Teilhabe zu denken. Insofern handelt es sich tatsächlich um einen Streit von Intellektuellengruppen um 'das Volk' und die 'Seelen', der nicht einmal, sondern immer wieder ausgefochten wird.

Selbst im Werk eines so irenisch gestimmten Autors wie Adalbert Stifter finden sich hier unterschiedliche Optionen, in Kontinuität zu josephinischen und Motiven der katholischen Aufklärung, auch Sympathien für die 'naive' Volksfrömmigkeit. Vor Konflikten mit der klerikalen Fraktion im Bildungswesen hat ihn das nicht bewahrt, auch nicht davor, vom katholischen Milieu in Deutschland nicht als ein 'Eigener' verbucht zu werden, so wie Annette von Droste-Hülshoff und Joseph von Eichendorff.[24] Stifters Literatur steht historisch, dann aber auch intentional *vor* dem Kulturkampf. Stifter, der sich als 'Mann des Maßes und der Freiheit'[25] verstand, erprobte leb- und schreibbare Positionen zwischen Liberalismus und Konservatismus, zwischen katholischer Aufklärung josephinischer Prägung und traditioneller Religiosität.[26] An mehreren Stellen in seinem umfangreichen Prosawerk finden sich regelrechte Kippbilder: so intensiv geratene Visionen der Verlassenheit, dass sie von der stets eintretenden erlösenden Wendung nur schwer aufgehoben werden — die explizit auf Byrons 'Darkness' und implizit auf Jean Pauls 'Rede des toten Christus vom Weltgebäude herab, dass kein Gott sei' rekurrierende Meditation 'Die Sonnenfinsternis am 8. July 1842'; oder die lakonische Erzählerbemerkung in 'Bergkristall', als die Kinder 'jenseits' eines Felsens wieder herabklettern wollen: 'Aber es gab kein Jenseits.'[27] Das Tremendum (im Sinn von Rudolf Otto) soll jedoch stets in das Faszinosum, eine das ganze Ich ergreifende Gewalterfahrung soll in die Gewissheit einer letztlichen Geborgenheit überführt werden. In 'Ein Gang durch die Katakomben' aus den Stadtbeschreibungen *Wien und die Wiener* ist es 'eine furchtbare, eine ungeheure Gewalt', 'der wir dahin gegeben sind, daß sie über uns verfüge — und wie riesenhaft, all unser Denken vernichtend, muß Plan und Zweck dieser Gewalt sein, daß vor ihr millionenfach ein Kunstwerk [der Mensch, W. M.] zu Grunde geht, da[s] sie selber mit solcher

Liebe baute, und zwar gleichgültig zu Grunde geht, als wäre es eben nichts!' Und doch 'durchflog mich' '[m]itten im Reiche der üppigsten Zerstörung' 'ein Funke der innigsten Unsterblichkeitsüberzeugung'.[28] Im Fall der Sonnenfinsternis ist eine 'solche moralische Gewalt [...] in diesen physischen Hergang gelegt, daß er sich unserem Herzen zum unbegreiflichen Wunder emporthürmt',[29] und auch diese Gewalt verkehrt sich am Ende in Zuversicht.

Nicht zuletzt deshalb ist die mit der Religion verbundene Perspektive die des Kindes. Die Ankunft des 'Christkindleins' ist ein

> heiteres glänzendes feierliches Ding [...], das durch das ganze Leben fortwirkt, und manchmal noch spät im Alter bei trüben schwermüthigen oder rührenden Erinnerungen gleichsam als Rükblick in die einstige Zeit mit den bunten schimmernden Fittigen durch den öden, traurigen und ausgeleerten Nachthimmel fliegt[,][30]

jenen 'ausgeleerten Nachthimmel', der die Schrecken der metaphysischen Nacht ausgemacht hatte. Nicht anders mit der Karwoche:

> Was ich auch seitdem geirrt und gesucht, wie ich gestrebt, wie ich errungen und verloren, wie ich glücklich und unglücklich war, was sich auch immer geändert: jenes tiefe, religiöse Gefühl für diese bedeutungsvollste Woche der Christenheit hat mich nicht verlassen, und immer ist mir die Charwoche die heiligste, feierlichste Zeit geblieben.[31]

Die Juxtaposition von Metaphysik und Kindlichkeit, Erhabenheit und Schönheit, Tragödie und Genre klärt die theologischen Fragen (oder gar die Frage nach der Theologie) durch den Verweis auf die Kindheit, in der diese Feste ihre unbestreitbare praxeologische Triftigkeit durch ihre Ritualität behalten. In 'Die Charwoche in Wien' ist 'die ganze Frühlingssehnsucht, in allen Wesen, besonders aber in Kinderherzen lebendig' und es ist 'diese magische Woche voll religiöser Feier und Gefühle, voll Mysterien und Geheimnisse, die mit zauberhafter Gewalt auf die jungen Herzen wirken'.[32] Kinder werden bei Stifter immer wieder den äußersten Gefahren ausgesetzt, ihre eingeschränkte Perspektive lässt sie aber '[m]it dem Starkmuthe der Unwissenheit'[33] am Weihnachtsabend über den Gletscher gehen. In der Christnacht ist es den Kindern, wie es in der 'ethnographischen' Einleitung zu *Bergkristall* heißt, 'als zögen jezt die Englein durch den Himmel, oder als kehre der heilige Christ nach Hause, welcher nunmehr bei allen Kindern gewesen ist, und jedem von ihnen ein herrliches Geschenk hinterbracht hat'.[34] Schließlich kann nach überstandenen Gefahren offenbleiben, ob nun die Kinder tatsächlich, als sie 'auf dem Berge sassen, den heiligen Christ gesehen'[35] haben. Die grammatikalische Form ist der Irrealis der Gegenwart, ein 'als ob': Das kranke Kind, heißt es in der erbaulichen Erzählung 'Die Barmherzigkeit', 1845, 'war längst schon überzeugt, und eine solche Beruhigung lag in dem Angesichtchen, als wäre Gott selber dagewesen, und hätte es gesagt; denn die Kinder glauben Alles, was die Eltern sagen'.[36] Dasselbe gilt für den Todesengel in 'Der Tod einer Jungfrau' (1847), Stifters Trostparabel auf den Tod seines Schützlings Gustav Scheibert.

Den Kindern ist auch Stifters wichtigste Pfarrerfigur, der 'Pfarrer im Kar', in 'Kalkstein' bzw. 'Der arme Wohlthäter', wie die Journalfassung noch hieß, zugeordnet. Seine eigene unter-, wenn nicht abgebrochene psychosexuelle Reifung bewahrt den Pfarrer vor jenen Anfechtungen, die sein Beruf mit sich bringt, seien sie erotischer Natur (die auffällig-unauffällig unter dem fadenscheinigen Rock getragene weiße Wäsche kann als Reinheitssymbol oder als Fetisch gedeutet werden), seien es jene der die Glaubensgewissheiten erschütternden Moderne und ihres 'öden, traurigen und ausgeleerten Nachthimmels'. Sie ermöglicht ihm, geworden oder geblieben 'wie die Kinder' (Mt 18:3), das zölibatäre Leben im Kar mit einer 'Dienerin'[37] und die demütige Gelassenheit 'eines armen Landgeistlichen'[38] dem Fortschritt gegenüber.[39]

III

Für Antonio Gramsci, Anfang der 1930er Jahre in faschistischer Gefängnishaft, machte es die Stärke der katholischen Kultur in ihrer Hegemonie aus, dass sie keinen Riss zwischen Intellektuellen und den Massen zugelassen habe. 'Die Kraft der Religion und besonders der katholischen Kirche', so Gramsci, 'bestand und besteht darin, daß sie stark die Notwendigkeit der Einheit der Doktrin bei der ganzen religiösen Masse spüren und dafür kämpfen, daß die intellektuell höher stehenden Schichten sich nicht von den niedrigeren lösen'; die katholische Kirche sei 'im Kampf für die Verhinderung der "offiziellen" Formierung zweier Religionen — einer für "Intellektuelle" und einer für die "einfachen Seelen" — immer am zähesten gewesen'.[40]

Diese Beobachtung kann als Leseanweisung für die Lebensfragen von Kulturen der Aufklärung benützt werden. So war der Josephinismus (gerade auch in Nachfolge des sehr exklusiven Jansenismus)[41] eine Kultur staatlicher Eliten, die sich mit den Mitteln des Rationalismus und der modernen Administration einer 'barocken' oder 'spätbarocken' Kultur von 'Muße und Verschwendung' gegenübergesehen haben, wie auch immer die Gewichte in den verschiedenen Phasen der maria-theresianischen Epoche verteilt gewesen sein mochten. Das paradigmatische musikdramatische Werk des Josephinismus, die *Zauberflöte* von Mozart und Schikaneder, beruht mit der ägyptisierenden Folie der Freimaurerei geradezu auf dem Gedanken zweier aparter Religionen für die Priester-Herrscher und das Volk[42] (der musikalische Plot liegt dann gerade in der — weniger imaginären als praktisch-performativen — Arbeit an der Überwindung dieses Gegensatzes). Die Jesuiten, so Gramsci, seien die 'größten Künstler' jener 'rationale[n] und richtige[n] Beziehung, die die Kirche auf ihrem Gebiet zwischen Intellektuellen und einfachen Menschen herzustellen gewußt hat' (im Text der *Zauberflöte* die 'Heuchler' und der 'Aberglaube'), während die 'Immanenzphilosophien' nicht gewusst hätten, 'wie eine ideologische Einheit zwischen unten und oben, zwischen den "einfachen Menschen" und den Intellektuellen zu schaffen ist'.[43] Ihr Problem bestehe darin, als Intellektuelle 'auf organische Weise die Intellektuellen jener Massen' zu sein, die Prinzipien und Probleme von *deren* praktischer Aktivität auszuarbeiten und zu systematisieren und im ganzen 'einen kulturellen und gesellschaftlichen Block' zu bilden (die Aufgabe einer künftigen 'Philosophie der Praxis').[44] In der Gegenreformation sei schließlich die Dialektik zwischen religiösen Massenbewegungen und der Theologie erstarrt, zumal der historische Prozess 'in seiner Gesamtheit eine zersetzende Kritik der Religionen' enthalte.[45]

Als eingreifender politischer Theoretiker stellt Gramsci die Frage auf dem Terrain der Intellektuellensoziologie, von daher auch die Unterscheidung zwischen meist der agrarischen Welt verbundenen traditionellen Intellektuellen und den organischen Intellektuellen einer Klasse. Kann man von daher zunächst verstehen, warum die liberale Literatur ein großes Interesse an der Pfarrerfigur hat und dann auch noch, wie sich zeigen wird, eine ambivalente, aber auffällige Sympathie für die katholischen Pfarrerfiguren und ihre Konflikte zeigt? Selbst in Anzengrubers Kulturkampf- und Antikonkordatsstück *Der Pfarrer von Kirchfeld* (1870) steht der Pfarrer mit dem sprechenden Namen 'Hell' einem reaktionären Aristokraten 'Graf Peter von Finsterberg' gegenüber.[46] Der Landpfarrer ist die Figur, an der verschiedene Varianten und Fügungen von 'Gebildeten' und 'Volk', Traditionalität und Aufklärung, Überzeugung und Zweifel im Prozess der Säkularisierung durchgespielt werden.

Im Folgenden soll das an einigen exponierten Texten von Autorinnen und Autoren der liberalen Ära kurz gezeigt werden. In Ferdinand von Saars 'Innocens' (1865), der ersten in der Reihe der *Novellen aus Österreich*, erzählt ein Geistlicher von einer überwundenen erotischen Anfechtung; Ludwig Anzengrubers aufsehenerregende Tendenzstücke um 1870 adressieren den Konkordatskampf und seine Einsätze umstandslos. Marie von Ebner-Eschenbachs Erzählung 'Glaubenslos?' (1893) lässt einen jungen Priester an seinem Beruf zweifeln. Peter Roseggers Roman *Das ewige Licht* (1897) ist als Tagebuchroman eines in ein abgelegenes Bergdorf versetzten Geistlichen gestaltet und extrapoliert an dieser Welt im Kleinen im Zeitraffer die historische Entwicklung der Moderne.[47] Sehr oft bildet sich in dieser Literatur der Konflikt zwischen den Kräften des Fortschritts und denen der Reaktion in der Darstellung von Protagonisten der katholischen Kirche selbst noch einmal ab (die Systemtheorie kennt das als das von Spencer Brown beschriebene *re-entry*: das 'Hineinkopieren' einer Unterscheidung in eine der unterschiedenen Seiten, zur Beobachtung der Wirkung der Unterscheidung). Die liberalen Autoren und Autorinnen privilegieren Geistlichenfiguren, die Idealisten, Zerrissene und Märtyrer zeigen; sie zeigen damit, welche innerpsychischen und sozialen Folgelasten sich mit dem 'Fortschritt', dem die Texte insgesamt, wenn auch in unterschiedlicher Form und Tragweite, ja anhängen, verbinden; sie zeigen damit 'bei den Anderen', welche Felder der Fortschritt zu bearbeiten hat, wenn er die Überschreibung einer ganzen Kultur, die sich allerdings selbst unsicher geworden ist, unternimmt.

Die Problematik von Wissenschaft/Glauben, die in den Kulturkämpfen eine Hauptrolle gespielt hat, wird auf die Seite der Religion hin verschoben. Saars Innocens liest — die Handlungszeit der Novelle sind die 1850er Jahre — 'eine zu jener Zeit vielerwähnte materialistische Schrift', und das mit Gewinn und 'vielem Vergnügen [...]; denn ich interessiere mich für jede wissenschaftliche Leistung, wiche sie auch noch so sehr von meinen eigenen Ansichten und Überzeugungen ab' (I 29–30). (Man darf hier etwa an Ludwig Büchners *Kraft und Stoff* (1855) denken, sicher keine genuine 'wissenschaftliche Leistung', sondern eine populäre Synthese des naturwissenschaftlichen Materialismus. In Ebner-Eschenbachs *Das Gemeindekind* von 1887 wird der Lehrer Habrecht über einem materialistischen Buch — Lukrez' *De rerum natura* — ertappt.) Innocens dilettiert in den Naturwissenschaften, fühlt sich zwar 'nicht berufen, die Wissenschaft durch Entdeckungen zu bereichern, oder auch nur die Zahl der schwebenden Hypothesen durch Aufstellung einer neuen zu vermehren' (I 35); sein Wissen genügt aber jedenfalls, um den Erzähler, einen Offizier, 'in die Naturwissenschaften, darin er eben so tiefe als ausgebreitete Kenntnisse besaß, einzuführen' (I 38). Innocens' Zimmer ist ein naturgeschichtliches Kabinett:

> Die Wände waren zum Teil von oben bis unten durch dichtbestellte Bücherrepositorien verdeckt; dazwischen erhoben sich hohe Glasschränke, welche naturwissenschaftliche Sammlungen zu enthalten schienen. Auf einem geräumigen Tische in der Nähe der Fenster standen und lagen chemische und physikalische Instrumente umher; ein zweiter Tisch war ganz mit Papieren und Schriften bedeckt. (I 33–34)

Bis in den Habitus ist der Priester ein Sozialaufsteiger ('der Sohn armer Landleute' (I 42)), ein Forscher 'mit erhabener, geistvollen Naturfreunden eigentümlicher Naivetät' (I 39). Der wissenschaftliche Diskurs, selbst schärferer Observanz, mag mit dem Glauben, nicht immer aber mit den Gläubigen vereinbar sein — Innocens kommt in den Verdacht, dass er seine Zeit 'mit verruchten, allen kirchlichen Dogmen hohnsprechenden Experimenten hinbringe, zu welchem Zwecke ich eine ganze Teufelsküche und die Werke aller alten und modernen Atheisten in einem Wandschranke meines Zimmers verborgen halte' (I 44). Von einem wohlmeinenden Abt auf die Zitadelle am Prager Wyschehrad versetzt, geht Innocens seinen Studien nach und darf sich am Ufer der Moldau wie Humboldt am Orinoco fühlen (I 35). Als Innocens dann den 'Mut der Entsagung' (I 68) gefunden haben wird und gegen — in der dezentesten Weise vorgetragene — Anfechtungen sein Zölibat bewahrt, reiht er sich ein in die lange Reihe jener literarischen Figuren, die den Konflikt sozialer und individueller Ansprüche durch Verzicht auf privates Glück lösen; mit Freud gesagt: als religiöser Funktionär des zivilisatorischen Triebverzichts. Dem Sohn der Fast-Geliebten Ludmilla ermöglicht Innocens 'unter meiner Anleitung eine wissenschaftliche Laufbahn' (I 69). Alle Fäden sind aufgenommen, nichts bleibt lose in dieser Erzählung; der Kulturkampf ist umgeschrieben in ein lebbares und kulturell hochgeschätztes Szenario der Bewältigung des Unbehagens in der Kultur. Der beste katholische Intellektuelle ist der, der sich im gesellschaftlichen Off auf die Seelsorge beschränkt, und die Erzählung lässt ihn das selber sagen: Am Land ist der Priester, so Innocens, ein 'wahrer Vater seiner Gemeinde, die ihn nicht als einen Heiligen über ihr, sondern als den besten und weisesten Menschen in ihrer Mitte verehrte'; in den Städten hingegen,

> '[...] [v]on den wahrhaft Gebildeten ob seiner falschen Stellung bemitleidet, von den sogenannten Aufgeklärten als Heuchler verschrien und an seinen menschlichen Schwächen und Fehlern schonungslos kontrolliert, erscheint er der Mehrzahl der Bevölkerung nur als der zufällige Träger eines gedankenlos überkommenen und ausgeübten Kultus.' Ich glaubte zu träumen. Diese Worte klangen so außerordentlich, so überraschend aus dem Munde eines katholischen Priesters, [...] daß ich in schweigende Bewunderung versank. (I 32)

Der Kooperator Leo Klinger in Ebner-Eschenbachs 'Glaubenslos?' — 'ein Mann von dreißig Jahren, ungewöhnlich groß, mit schmalen Schultern und etwas eingesunkener Brust' (G 227) — erinnert auffällig an Saars Innocens, mit langen Beinen, der schlenkernden Soutane (I 23) und dem Buch unter dem Arm. Sie scheinen auch das Zimmer zu teilen: 'Die Wände der kleinen Stube verschwanden größtenteils hinter dicht besetzten Bücherbrettern [...]. Ein den beiden Fenstern gegenüber offenstehender Schrank enthielt Erd- und Himmelsgloben, astronomische meteorologische Instrumente' (G 264). Wie bei Saar wird der Gegensatz Religion-Wissenschaft nicht zwischen 'Alten' und 'Modernen', sondern vor Ort ausgetragen. Der Konsistorialrat Pinzer, ehemals Kaplan im Dorf und jetzt in der Kirchenhierarchie aufgestiegen, erkennt in Klinger ausgerechnet in dessen Glaubenskrise einen möglichen Verbündeten und stellt ihm, nachdem der an den Menschen verzweifelte Klinger eine Strafpredigt über die Gemeinde gehalten hat, eine glänzende Karriere in Aussicht — in der neuen verhärteten 'Mauerkirche' (Friedrich Heer). Das Panorama vervollständigt der alte Pfarrer Thalberg, der in seiner Milde eine ältere Generation traditioneller Geistlicher *vor* der *ecclesia militans* der zweiten Konfessionalisierung eines Pius IX. vertritt. Klingers astronomische Bibliothek kommentiert der Konsistorialrat kundig, er ist kein Ignorant, sondern ein Stratege des Verhältnisses von 'Wissenschaft' und 'Religion':

> 'Da sind sie alle,' sprach Pinzer, auf eine lange Bücherreihe hindeutend. 'Von Kopernikus über die *Astronomia nova*, die *Philosophia naturalis*, die Kosmogonie, bis Sciaparelli. Und da steht der große Jesuit neben dem berühmten Juden. Pater Secchi neben Baruch Spinoza. Die sind mit gutem Bedacht nebeneinander gestellt worden. In *einem* Punkte hat der Jude recht: alle Wissenschaft führt zu Gott. [...] Nur weiter, also! nur vorwärts gestrebt! aber stets mit dem höchsten Ziel im Auge — dem Glauben, dem unbedingten, unerschütterlichen, zu dem Ihr Beruf Sie verpflichtet. Und wenn je ein Zweifel an der Echtheit dieses Berufes Sie erfaßt, kämpfen Sie ihn nieder.' (G 294)[48]

An der Rolle, die Klinger zugedacht ist, mit oder ohne Astronomie, besteht kein Zweifel: 'Trachten Sie, ein Eckstein unserer einzig wahren, heiligen Kirche zu werden, die allmählich die Weltherrschaft erringen und die Menschheit zum ewigen Heile führen wird' (G 295).

Neben diesen Allmachtsphantasien einer antimodernistischen pianischen Kirche sieht man die Institution freilich jenen Fehler begehen, den Gramsci als Symptom des katholischen Hegemonieverlusts gedeutet hat, die Spaltung in eine Religion für die Gebildeten und eine für die Laien. Die katholische Sakramentalienkultur des 19. Jahrhunderts bildet eine strategisch etablierte Reprise der vielfältigen sakralen Alltagspraktiken der Barockfrömmigkeit, die zur Herstellung von Loyalität im Kirchenvolk instrumentalisiert werden. Der alte Pfarrer Thalberg soll einen 'Bittgang um Regen, den die Leute abhalten wollten, untersagt' (G 292) haben. (Ein ganz ähnliches Ansinnen wird an den neu angekommenen Pfarrer Wieser bei der Überschwemmungskatastrophe in Roseggers *Ewigem Licht* herangetragen werden.) Der alte Pfarrer verteidigt sich in josephinischer Manier, es seien zwei abgebrannte Höfe wiederaufzubauen gewesen und die Leute hätten besser 'jede Stunde verwerten können zu eigenem und zu fremdem Nutzen! Und noch dazu hat mein Kooperator, der ein Astronom und ein Meteorologe ist, fast mit Bestimmtheit voraussagen können, daß es innerhalb der nächsten acht Tage ohnehin regnen wird.' 'Sie wußten, daß ein Regen zu erwarten war, und unterließen deshalb den Bittgang um Regen? Sehr gut, Hochwürden.' Pater Pinzer lächelte etwas ironisch. (G 292)

Das Gegenteil hätte man von Thalberg erwarten sollen; der Kluge soll das Ritual dann ausführen, wenn er weiß, dass sich der Erfolg nicht dem Ritual verdanken muss. Die katholische 'kirchliche Halbmagie'[49] war ohnehin heikles Terrain und ein etwas peinliches Thema der Restauration des Religiös-Wunderbaren im Katholizismus des 19. Jahrhunderts. In der Erzählung wird damit aus der 'vertrauensvollen religiösen Anheimstellung',[50] die ein solcher Bittgang sein hätte sollen, ein magisches Ritual der religiösen Manipulation der Naturkräfte — für die Uneingeweihten, aus der Wissenschaft wird Herrschaftswissen der Kleriker.[51]

Die Pfarrergeschichten von Saar und Ebner-Eschenbach enden gut, beide Protagonisten versagen sich der Welt und wirken als bescheidene Seelsorger. Auch Klingers Gewissenskampf ist am Ende von 'Glaubenslos?' 'ausgekämpft' (G 359); ihm ist zwar 'Macht gegeben über die Gemüter' (G 355), die Versuchung, gerade als Glaubensloser in den Hegemoniekampf der katholischen Kirche einzutreten, wird aber ausgeschlagen: '[T]rösten, helfen, bessern. Hier leben und sterben, ungekannt, ungenannt im bergenden Schatten, in dem allein sein ganzes Wesen sich entfalten kann. Ein stiller Hüter an einer der unzähligen Quellen, aus denen Heil und Unheil in die Welt fließt' (G 359).

Roseggers Roman *Das ewige Licht* setzt mit dem Datum 1875 ein und endet 1889; die Zäsur liegt bei 1881, nach dem Tourismus kommt die Industrie in das Hochtal. Der 'Pfarrer im Gebirge' war 'eine Lieblingsvorstellung schon des jungen Rosegger' und auch die liberale Grazer *Tagespost*, eine entscheidende Referenz für den jungen Autor, schrieb 'über das entsagungsvolle Wirken alter Leutpriester in fernen Gebirgsgegenden immer mit hoher Teilnahme und Achtung'.[52] Der 'Stadtpfarrkaplan' Wolfgang Wieser wird als Moderner, der mit progressiven Artikeln in der regionalen christlichen Presse aufgefallen ist ('Reformen' (EL 5) in Schulfrage, Zölibat, Hierarchie), nach St. Maria im Torwald versetzt, um, wie der Bischof sich ausdrückt, 'auf dem weltfernen Sprengel manches praktisch durchzuführen, was Sie hier als Schriftsteller theoretisch verlangt haben' (EL 12), um sich also unter Ausschluss der Öffentlichkeit die Hörner abzulaufen. Der Plot besteht nun weder in der glänzenden Bestätigung der Ideale noch in deren spektakulärem Scheitern, gezeigt wird vielmehr im Zeitraffer, wie die Moderne und die Globalisierung mit Eisenbahn, Tourismus, Bergbau und Industrie in das Tal einziehen und wie der Pfarrer zunehmend ratlos sozialen Makroprozessen ausgesetzt wird, die ihn obsolet machen — weil die agrarische Basis der Torwald-Gemeinden zunehmend obsolet wird, die zugezogene Arbeiterschaft den Sozialdemokraten zuläuft und in der kapitalistischen Moderne 'an die Stelle der alten lokalen und nationalen Selbstgenügsamkeit und Abgeschlossenheit' 'ein allseitiger Verkehr, eine allseitige Abhängigkeit der Nationen voneinander' tritt, die 'Bourgeoisie [...] durch die rasche Verbesserung aller Produktionsinstrumente, durch die unendlich erleichterte Kommunikation alle, auch die barbarischsten Nationen in die Zivilisation' 'reißt', 'alle chinesischen Mauern in den Grund schießt', 'das Land der Herrschaft der Stadt unterworfen' hat und 'einen bedeutenden Teil der Bevölkerung dem Idiotismus des Landlebens entrissen'[53] hat — als hätte es sich der Roman vorgesetzt, am Beispiel von St. Maria mit dieser Welt im Kleinen das *Kommunistische Manifest* zu illustrieren. Als traditioneller Intellektueller im Sinn Gramscis ist der katholische Pfarrer Wieser, auch oder vielleicht gerade als Modernist, obsolet. Seine Kirche wird im Wortsinn unterminiert, weil der Boden, auf dem sie steht, aus Spateisenstein besteht (EL 341).

Bedenkt man, wie nah eine Reihe von Wiesers Ideen an Roseggers eigenen Positionen liegt[54] und wie osmotisch die Rollen des zeitkritischen 'Heimgarten'-Beobachters, des literarischen Autors und die Rollenprojekte in seinen literarischen Texten angelegt sind, lässt sich durchaus auch hier von einer Selbstreflexion des (ex-) liberalen Intellektuellen unter den Bedingungen rasanter Modernisierung sprechen, gerade wenn die Rolle eines organischen Intellektuellen der Industriegesellschaft aus Gründen der Aufrechterhaltung einer autonomen Sprecherrolle und einer zunehmend utopischen Solidarität mit den Bergbauern keine Option ist. Dann besteht schon 'Roseggers Apokalypse [...] in der Umwandlung eines Bauernromans in einen Arbeiterroman'.[55] Der Roman über einen (katholischen) Modernisten im Strudel der (industriellen) Modernisierung bedient sich dabei selbst eines ambivalenten, manchmal manichäischen Beschreibungsinventars, das im Dienst einer (neu-)religiösen Symbolsprache steht. Der Holzarbeiter und Hirte Rolf Eschgartner, Sohn des Schmieds, urchristlich gesonnen wie einst der junge Wieser (EL 347, 349–50), pazifistisch (EL 200), mit hussitischen Sympathien (EL 277–78), eine Figur zwischen deutschem Christus, Siegfried und 'Sonnenjüngling' (EL 351), Fidus' 'Lichtgebet' vorwegnehmend, ist jene Option, die im letzten apokalyptischen Tagebucheintrag Wiesers als Hoffnung bleibt (EL 424). Wieser selbst irrt über die Berge und stirbt, 'im Angesichte einer untergehenden Welt [...] am gebrochenen Herzen' (EL 427). (Sein Vorgänger in St. Maria war über einem Gewissensfall wahnsinnig geworden.)

Auf der anderen Seite steht Luzian Stelzenbacher, von ärmlichster Herkunft, schon dem Namenssignalement nach zwischen dem Heiligen und dem Satanischen angesiedelt. Ihm wird durch Fürsorge des Pfarrers eine Ausbildung im Priesterseminar ermöglicht, er entläuft aber, weil der Geistliche 'heutzutage' 'auch im Wirtshause, auf den Straßen und in den Werkstätten' predigen müsse, der 'höllischen Ungerechtigkeit' wegen, 'die zwischen Armen und Reichen herrscht' (EL 403). Unter dem Namen 'der Weiße' macht Luzian dann als sozialdemokratischer Berufsagitator, als 'Arbeiterpfaffe' (EL 382) Karriere. Obwohl ihm ein legendärer Ruf als Redner vorauseilt, entgleitet ihm ausgerechnet eine Arbeiterversammlung im Torwald, als er nicht für Umsturz, sondern für Arbeiterbeteiligung plädiert; die Aktion endet im Tumult, die Villa des Unternehmers wird niedergebrannt, der verzweifelte Luzian quittiert den Parteidienst und will wieder Priester werden (EL 405), was ihm Wieser am Ende auszureden versucht und ihn dem Rolf anempfiehlt (EL 407). Auch Roseggers Text fügt sich durch eine dichte Kette von intertextuellen Verweisen in den literarischen Diskussionszusammenhang des Problems ein. Die Darstellung der entfesselten Proletarier erinnert nicht von ungefähr an literarische Schreckensszenarien religiöser Entgrenzung (wie in Robert Hamerlings Wiedertäufer-Epos *Der König von Sion*, 1869);[56] die umstandslose Übersetzung einer hochfliegenden Theorie in die Praxis einer unvollkommenen Welt mit katastrophalen Folgen wird im Roman auch den Sozialisten zugeschrieben, die Intellektuellen 'wissen nicht, was sie tun', wenn sie handeln. Wenn Wieser bemerkt: 'Nicht "mit Kutten ist die Sonne verhängt," sondern mit Fabriksrauch' (EL 365), zitiert er den berühmten antiklerikalen Schluss von Nikolaus Lenaus *Die Albigenser* (1842), wo eine Genealogie von den Ketzern des Mittelalters zu den Bastillestürmern konstruiert wird, 'und so weiter'. Der 'Weiße' schließlich wird der rote Luzian genannt, weil 'er grundsätzlich keine Schulden gemacht und weil er immer weiße Wäsche getragen hat' (EL 405). Zusammen mit einer Anspielung auf den gefährlichen Schulweg der Kinder im Rauhgraben, dem Wohnort seiner bettelarmen Familie (EL 84), ergibt das Hinweise auf Stifters 'armen Wohlthäter' als eine der Folien für die Figur. Wäre ein Luzian der 1840er Jahre ein armer Wohltäter geworden? Im Nachmärz ein Innocens, in der Gründerzeit ein Klinger, der, wie Luzian ohne Zölibatsqualen, mit seiner Flucht aus dem geistlichen Stand nur gespielt hätte? Auch *Das ewige Licht* diskutiert mit genuin literarischen Mitteln, welchen Ort die katholische Religion und die ihr verbundenen Intellektuellen im Diskurs und im historischen Prozess haben können; und welche, hier: zerstörerischen, 'sozialen Energien' mit ihrem möglichen Verschwinden freiwürden. Roseggers Roman sieht dem Verzweifeln des liberalen Geistlichen in der nicht-teleologischen Konstruktion des 'aufgefundenen Tagebuches' gleichsam von innen zu und lässt als Hoffnung nur eine Jahrhundertwende-typische charismatische und messianische Erneuerung des Christentums übrig, womit er sich weit von den im Innern des Einzelnen ausgefochtenen (damit latent protestantischen) liberalen Entsagungsutopien bei Stifter, Saar und Ebner-Eschenbach entfernt.

Die vollständigste Konfrontation des Christentums jedenfalls in der zeitgenössischen österreichischen Version hat Roseggers Freund und Mentor Ludwig Anzengruber, 'die Galionsfigur des liberalen Antiklerikalismus in der Literatur der Ära',[57] unternommen — nicht was die polemische Schärfe und die literarische Schematik angeht, hier waren die Antijesuitica und die antiklerikalen Zeitromane nicht zu übertreffen,[58] sondern hinsichtlich der Breite, in der Anzengruber die katholische Herausforderung der liberalen Herausforderung annimmt. Er agiert nicht so sehr als Aufklärer denn als Gegen-Gegenaufklärer, also auf dem Terrain der zweiten Konfessionalisierung.[59] Den Steinklopferhanns, 'kein Christ und kein Heid' und kein Türk'', lässt Anzengruber für die säkularistische österreichische Kulturgeschichte eine Tröstung für den Einzelnen formulieren, der die Transzendenz weggestrichen hat: 'Du g'hörst zu dem alln, und dös alls g'hört zu dir! Es kann dir nix g'schehn!'[60] 'Die Religion der Zukunft' wird die Humanität sein,[61] so der von Ludwig Feuerbach inspirierte Anzengruber, und: 'Es ist Religion, an keinen Gott zu glauben — ihn glauben, heißt ihn lästern.'[62] Das erneuerte Wallfahrtswesen, das in anderen Texten bestenfalls dezent

Erwähnung findet (G 317), wird bei Anzengruber frontal angegangen. In seinen Tendenzstücken *Der Pfarrer von Kirchfeld* und *Die Kreuzelschreiber* — das erste ein Konkordatsstück von 1870, das zweite eine Verarbeitung des Konflikts um Ignaz Döllinger, die Unfehlbarkeit des Papstes und die Altkatholiken von 1872 — bringt er mit den Wallfahrten zentrale Praktiken des pianischen Neobarock auf die Bühne. Im *Pfarrer* lässt er schon im ersten Akt einen Wallfahrerzug auf einen von den neuen Ehegesetzen ermöglichten interkonfessionellen Hochzeitszug treffen, als begegneten einander zwei Demonstrationszüge; und in den *Kreuzelschreibern* wird im letzten Akt ein parodistisch-karnevalesker Wallfahrerzug zusammengestellt, die Männer 'haben die Hüte tief ins Gesicht gedrückt und den Kopf in große Gebetbücher gesenkt, die sie mit beiden Händen vor sich halten, so, daß sie die Stöcke wie "Gewehr im Arm", nur in den verschiedensten Richtungen und Neigungswinkeln tragen', die jungen Frauen kommen 'alle sehr züchtig' daher, 'die Tücher bis zum Hals hinaufgebunden, jede trägt einen roten Regenschirm, und da sie ebenfalls große Gebetbücher ganz so wie die Männer halten, so haben sie die Schirme in allen erdenklichen Querlagen unter dem rechten oder linken Arm'.[63] Ironischerweise hat gerade Anzengruber seine von der Polemik bis zur 'ozeanischen' Alternative reichende kulturelle Konfrontationsstrategie damit bezahlt, dass er als 'Bauerndichter' in das kulturelle Gedächtnis eingegangen ist.

Notes to Chapter 6

1. Franz Grillparzer, *Selbstbiographie*, hrsg. v. Arno Dusini, Kira Kaufmann und Felix Reinstadler, Österreichs Eigensinn: Eine Bibliothek (Salzburg, Wien: Jung und Jung, 2017), S. 113.
2. Ebd., S. 118.
3. Ebd., S. 120.
4. Vgl. Ritchie Robertson, 'Poetry and Scepticism in the Wake of the Austrian Enlightenment: Blumauer, Grillparzer, Lenau', in Robertson, *Enlightenment and Religion in German and Austrian Literature* (Cambridge: Legenda, MHRA, 2017), S. 226–50; Robertson sieht Grillparzer in einer Interpretation von 'Campo vaccino' mit dem religionskritischen Aufklärer Aloys Blumauer (*Aeneis travestirt*, 1784) zusammen; vgl. auch Robertson, 'Heroes in their Underclothes: Blumauer's Travesty of the Aeneid', in Robertson, *Mock-Epic Poetry from Pope to Heine* (Oxford: Oxford University Press, 2009), S. 260–81. Zum größeren Kontext vgl. jetzt Robertson, *The Enlightenment: The Pursuit of Happiness 1680–1790* (London: Allen Lane, 2020), S. 136–98. Zum Thema s. *Catholicism and Austrian Culture*, hrsg. v. Ritchie Robertson und Judith Beniston, Austrian Studies, 10 (Edinburgh: Edinburgh University Press, 1999).
5. Vgl. als Überblick Peter Leisching, 'Die römisch-katholische Kirche in Cisleithanien', in *Die Habsburgermonarchie 1848–1918*, IV: *Die Konfessionen*, hrsg. v. Adam Wandruszka und Peter Urbanitsch (Wien: ÖAW, 1985), S. 1–247; Rupert Klieber, 'Der volkskirchliche Riese und sein Erwachen zum *Movimento Cattolico*: Katholische Kirche und Katholizismus im alten und neuen Österreich bis 1938', in *Mensch, Staat und Kirchen zwischen Alpen und Adria 1848–1938: Einblicke in Religion, Politik, Kultur und Wirtschaft einer Übergangszeit*, hrsg. v. Werner Drobesch, Reinhard Stauber und Peter G. Tropper (Klagenfurt/Celovec, Ljubljana/Laibach, Wien/Dunaj: Hermagoras/Mohorjeva 2007), S. 11–38.
6. Karlheinz Rossbacher, *Literatur und Liberalismus: Zur Kultur der Ringstraßenzeit in Wien* (Wien: Jugend & Volk 1992), S. 191; vgl. insgesamt S. 187–213 ('Literatur und Kirchenkampf'). Zum Antiklerikalismus in der Literatur vgl. ausführlich Peter Horwath, *Der Kampf gegen die religiöse Tradition: Die Kulturkampfliteratur Österreichs, 1780–1918*, German Studies in America, 28 (Bern, Frankfurt a.M., Las Vegas: Lang 1978). Die Darstellung von Jutta Osinski, *Katholizismus und*

deutsche Literatur im 19. Jahrhundert (Paderborn: Schöningh 1993) berührt die österreichische Literatur wohl auch daher nur am Rande. Die Forschungslage ist mit Ausnahme von Einzelstudien nicht gut; vgl. zuletzt Michaela Klosinski, *Zwischen Moderne und Antimoderne: Die katholische Literatur Wiens 1890–1918*, Klassische Moderne, 29 (Würzburg: Ergon, 2016). Zu den 'Kulturkämpfen' in Österreich auch Laurence Cole, 'The Counter-Reformation's Last Stand: Austria', in *Culture Wars: Secular-Catholic Conflict in Nineteenth-Century Europe*, hrsg. v. Christopher Clark und Wolfram Kaiser (Cambridge: Cambridge University Press, 2003), S. 285–312 (u.a. zum Streit um die 'Tiroler Glaubenseinheit', zum 'Bozner Lichtschießen' 1861 sowie zur Verhaftung des Bischofs Rudigier und zum Linzer Dombau).

7. Dazu klassisch Anna Coreth, *Pietas Austriaca: Österreichische Frömmigkeit im Barock*, 2. Aufl. (München, Oldenbourg, Wien: Verlag für Geschichte und Politik, 1982).
8. Peter Hersche, *Muße und Verschwendung: Europäische Gesellschaft und Kultur im Barockzeitalter*, 2 Bde (Freiburg, Basel, Wien: Herder, 2006).
9. Raymond Williams, 'Culture is Ordinary', in *Raymond Williams on Culture & Society: Essential Writings*, hrsg. v. Jim McGuigan (Los Angeles: SAGE, 2014), S. 1–18 (S. 6).
10. Vgl. im Kontext Werner Michler, *Darwinismus und Literatur: Naturwissenschaftliche und literarische Intelligenz in Österreich, 1859–1914*, Literaturgeschichte in Studien und Quellen, 2 (Wien, Köln, Weimar: Böhlau 1999).
11. Olaf Blaschke, 'Das 19. Jahrhundert: Ein Zweites Konfessionelles Zeitalter?', *Geschichte und Gesellschaft*, 26 (2000), 38–75. Zum Weiterleben Hersche, *Muße und Verschwendung*, II, 1029–78; zur Wallfahrt ('Religiöses Freizeitvergnügen'), ebd., S. 794–845; auch Kap. 'Verzauberte Welt? Bildung, Wissenschaft, Magie', ebd., S. 845–90.
12. Ernst Haeckel, *Natürliche Schöpfungsgeschichte: Gemeinverständliche Vorträge über die Entwickelungslehre* (Berlin: Reimer, 1868), S. 29; 'Schöpfungshypothese des Moses', ebd., S. 30.
13. Vgl. Terry Eagleton, *Reason, Faith and Revolution: Reflections on the God Debate*, The Terry Lecture Series (New Haven, CT; London: Yale University Press, 2009).
14. Vgl. zum Kontext Hubert Wolf, *Der Unfehlbare: Pius IX. und die Erfindung des Katholizismus im 19. Jahrhundert* (München: C. H. Beck, 2020), S. 187–219.
15. Lisa Dittrich, 'Europäischer Antiklerikalismus: Eine Suche zwischen Säkularisierung und Religionsreform', *Geschichte und Gesellschaft*, 45 (2019), 5–36 (S. 6). Die neuere internationale Forschung (im 'Interpretationsrahmen der konstruktivistisch gewendeten Säkularisierung', ebd., S. 11) resümiert Dittrich so: 'Die Säkularisierung ist nicht mehr Ausgangspunkt des Antiklerikalismus, sondern sein politisches Programm und Produkt der antiklerikalen Kämpfe' (ebd., S. 8). Evident ist auch, 'dass der Antiklerikalismus eine zusätzliche religiöse Dimension durch Formen der Sakralisierung erhielt, indem christliche und andere religiöse Semantiken übernommen, die eigenen Ideale damit parallelisiert und mit außeralltäglichem Charakter versehen wurden' (ebd., S. 35). Alltagskulturelle Aspekte des 'Catholic Revival' benennt Margaret Lavinia Anderson, 'The Limits of Secularization: On the Problem of the Catholic Revival in Nineteenth-Century Germany', *The Historical Journal*, 38 (1995), 647–70 (Klerus; Beichte und Pastoral; das Bild des Priesters; Ultramontanismus; Politik und Gemeinschaft).
16. Mit Säkularisierung seien hier jene Prozesse adressiert, in denen die — traditionelle oder restaurative — Hegemonie von Religion und religiösen Institutionen, insbesondere in Politik und Bildung, von nicht-religiös orientierten Gruppen kritisiert, bekämpft und schließlich tendenziell abgelöst wird; weder ein unumkehrbarer noch ein einsinniger oder unaufhaltsamer Prozess. Vgl. z.B. Friedrich Wilhelm Graf, *Die Wiederkehr der Götter: Religion in der modernen Kultur* (München: Beck, 2007), S. 69–101; *Säkularisierung. Grundlagentexte zur Theoriegeschichte*, hrsg. v. Christiane Frey, Uwe Hebekus und David Martyn (Berlin: Suhrkamp, 2020).
17. Sigmund Freud, *Gesammelte Werke*, hrsg. v. Anna Freud u.a. (Frankfurt a.M.: Fischer 1999), XIV, 422.
18. Minna Kautsky, *Die Alten und die Neuen*, 2 Bde (Leipzig: Reissner, 1885), I, 189.
19. Vgl. Hubert Wolf, 'Der "Syllabus errorum" (1864) oder: Sind katholische Kirche und Moderne vereinbar?', in *Kirche im 19. Jahrhundert*, hrsg. v. Manfred Weitlauff (Regensburg: Pustet 1998), S. 115–39.
20. 'Warum diese ungewöhnliche Polarisierung *in catholicis*, die weit über die Donaumonarchie

hinaus das 19. und 20. Jahrhundert prägte? [...] Mehr als die anderen Konfessionen stieg man dabei katholischerseits selbst in den Ring der Ideologien. Man überhöhte überkommene religiöse Denkmuster und Handlungsmaximen zu einer "Weltanschauung", die als theoretische Grundlage für die Mobilisierung der Basis dienen konnte'. Der 'Kulturstreit' 'bewirkte nicht zuletzt, dass es in vielen Ländern einen Katholizismus in "zwei Geschwindigkeiten" gab: ein Katholisch-Sein als Teil des kulturellen Herkommens mit vorwiegend äußerlichen Folgerungen für die Lebensgestaltung sowie einen "entschiedenen" Katholizismus, der je länger je mehr seine eigene kulturelle und politische Sprache entwickelte und die punktuelle Konfrontation mit dem "Zeitgeist" nicht scheute.' Klieber, 'Der volkskirchliche Riese', S. 12–13.

21. Hersche, *Muße und Verschwendung*, II, 1060–61.
22. Lord Byron, 'Darkness', in Byron, *The Complete Poetical Works*, hrsg. v. Jerome McGann, 7 Bde (Oxford: Clarendon Press, 1980–93), IV (1986), 42–43.
23. Max Horkheimer und Theodor W. Adorno, *Dialektik der Aufklärung: Philosophische Fragmente* (Frankfurt a.M.: Fischer, 1985), S. 5.
24. Thomas Pittrof, 'Katholizismus', in *Handbuch Literatur und Religion*, hrsg. v. Daniel Weidner (Stuttgart: Metzler, 2016), S. 76–83 (S. 79).
25. An Heckenast, 25. Mai 1848. Adalbert Stifter, *Sämtliche Werke und Briefe* (SW), hrsg. v. August Sauer u.a., 25 Bde (Prag: Gerstenberg, 1904–39), XVII (1929), 284.
26. Vgl. Markus Pahmeier, Wolfgang Braungart, 'Religion und Metaphysik', in *Stifter-Handbuch: Leben — Werk — Wirkung*, hrsg. v. Christian Begemann und Davide Giuriato (Stuttgart: Metzler, 2017), S. 279–84.
27. Adalbert Stifter, *Werke und Briefe: Historisch-kritische Gesamtausgabe* (HKG), hrsg. v. Alfred Doppler und Wolfgang Frühwald (Stuttgart: Kohlhammer 1978–), II/2, 220. In der Journalfassung hieß es: 'Aber das Jenseits, wo es nun sogleich hinabgehen sollte, war nicht da, der Wall hatte kein Jenseits.' HKG II/1, 163.
28. Stifter, HKG IX/1, 57.
29. Stifter, SW XV, 6.
30. Stifter, HKG II/2, 183–84.
31. Stifter, HKG IX/1, 247.
32. Ebd., S. 246.
33. Stifter, HKG II/2, 220.
34. Ebd., S. 184.
35. Ebd., S. 239.
36. Stifter, HKG III/1, 82.
37. Stifter, HKG II/2, 94. Die Frage des Landvermessers an den Pfarrer in der ersten Fassung, 'ob er verheirathet sei?', weist er 'roth geworden' zurück: '"Ich verheirathet? [...] ach, denken Sie nicht so etwas!"' (HKG II/1, 72).
38. HKG II/1, S. 61; HKG II/2, 65.
39. Stifter, HKG II/1, 63. Vgl. dazu Moriz Enzinger, 'Der Pfarrer im Kar', in Enzinger, *Gesammelte Aufsätze zu Adalbert Stifter* (Wien: Österreichische Verlagsanstalt, 1967), S. 163–79.
40. Antonio Gramsci, *Marxismus und Kultur: Ideologie, Alltag, Literatur*, hrsg. und übers. v. Sabine Kebir, Nachwort Giuliano Manacorda, 3. Aufl. (Hamburg: VSA, 1991), S. 78.
41. Peter Hersche, *Der Spätjansenismus in Österreich* (Wien: ÖAW, 1977).
42. Jan Assmann, *Die Zauberflöte: Oper und Mysterium* (München, Wien: Hanser, 2005).
43. Gramsci, *Marxismus und Kultur*, S. 78.
44. Ebd., S. 79.
45. Ebd., S. 78.
46. Einen guten und weitgespannten Überblick zum Thema bietet Elisabeth Hurth, *Mann Gottes: Das Priesterbild in Literatur und Medien*, Theologie und Literatur, 15 (Mainz: Matthias-Grünewald-Verlag 2003).
47. Ferdinand von Saar, 'Innocens', in Saar, *Sämtliche Werke*, hrsg. v. Jakob Minor, VII (Leipzig: Max Hesse, [1908]), pp. 13–70 (I); Marie von Ebner-Eschenbach, 'Glaubenslos? Erzählung', in Ebner-Eschenbach, *Sämtliche Werke*, IV (Berlin: Paetel [1920]), pp. 215–359 (G); Peter Rosegger, *Das ewige Licht: Erzählung aus den Schriften eines Waldpfarrers* (Leipzig: Staackmann, 1898) (EL).

48. Die Stelle erinnert an die erwähnte Büchersuche in Minna Kautskys *Die Alten und die Neuen*, einem Schlüsseltext der Darwin-Rezeption in der sozialdemokratischen Literatur. Kautsky verarbeitet hier ein realgeschichtliches Ereignis um den 'Bauernphilosophen' Konrad Deubler, das ihm zwei Jahre Festungshaft auf dem Brünner Spielberg eingetragen hat. Beide Autorinnen haben übrigens Dramen über Madame Roland verfasst, vgl. Ingrid Spörk, 'Manon Roland — "Königin der Gironde" und "Genius Frankreichs": Dramatische Bearbeitungen eines Frauenschicksals in der Französischen Revolution von Minna Kautsky und Marie von Ebner-Eschenbach', in *Minna Kautsky: Beiträge zum literarischen Werk*, hrsg. v. Stefan Riesenfellner und Ingrid Spörk, Studien zur Gesellschafts- und Kulturgeschichte, 8 (Wien: Verlag für Gesellschaftskritik, 1996), S. 79–94. Zu 'Glaubenslos?' vgl. Marie Luise Wandruszka, *Marie von Ebner-Eschenbach: Erzählerin aus politischer Leidenschaft* (Wien: Passagen 2008), S. 99–115, die Erzählung propagiere am Lernprozess Klingers ein (liberales) Konzept der '*persönliche[n] politische[n]* Beziehung' (S. 114) als Alternative zu Übermenschentum und Kollektivismus.
49. Hersche, *Muße und Verschwendung*, II, 873. Ein gewiss paradigmatisches Bild zeigen die Reaktionen auf die vielfachen Marienerscheinungen im 19. Jahrhundert, vgl. David Blackbourn, *Wenn ihr sie wieder seht, fragt wer sie sei: Marienerscheinungen in Marpingen — Aufstieg und Niedergang des deutschen Lourdes*, übers. v. Holger Fliessbach (Reinbek: Rowohlt, 1997), u.a. zur vorsichtigen und eher ratlosen Reaktion des Klerus auf eine Bewegung von unten und den drohenden Verlust der Diskursfähigkeit gegenüber Protestanten und Säkularisten (S. 324–73), zur 'katholischen Antwort' auf die Repression durch den preußischen Staat (S. 429–50) und zum 'Urteil der Liberalen' (S. 451–80).
50. Hersche, *Muße und Verschwendung*, II, 875.
51. In Roseggers *Ewigem Licht* erzählen die Mönche beim Essen heitere Priesteranekdoten, darunter die von 'jene[m] Landpfarrer', 'der die Bittprozession um Regen erst halten ließ, als der Barometer fiel' (EL 18).
52. Rudolf Latzke, *Peter Rosegger: Sein Leben und sein Schaffen. Nach den Quellen dargestellt*, 2 Bde (Graz, Köln: Böhlaus Nachfolger, 1953), II: *Der ältere und der alte Rosegger*, S. 197.
53. Karl Marx, Friedrich Engels, 'Manifest der Kommunistischen Partei', in Marx, Engels, *Werke*, 6. Aufl. (Berlin: Dietz, 1972), IV, 459–93 (S. 466).
54. Latzke, *Rosegger*, II, 198–201, insgesamt zur 'religiösen Frage' beim späten Rosegger S. 232–81. Hurth spricht von 'Roseggers liberale[m] Milieukatholizismus' (Hurth, *Mann Gottes*, S. 32).
55. Karl Wagner, *Die literarische Öffentlichkeit der Provinzliteratur: Der Volksschriftsteller Peter Rosegger*, Studien und Texte zur Sozialgeschichte der Literatur, 36 (Tübingen: Niemeyer, 1991), S. 328, zum *Ewigen Licht* S. 321–44. Wagner liest den Roman als Roseggers Auseinandersetzung mit der Sozialdemokratie.
56. Werner Hahl hat gezeigt, wie Roseggers Roman *Der Gottsucher* (1883) Hamerlings Epos und Thesen von Roseggers liberal-atheistischem Mentor Adalbert Svoboda, dem Redakteur der Grazer *Tagespost*, verarbeitet: Hahl, 'Ritualisierung der sinnlichen Erfahrung: Versuch, Versuchung und Scheitern einer Religionsstiftung in Peter Roseggers "Der Gottsucher"', in *Rosegger im Kontext*, hrsg. v. Wendelin Schmidt-Dengler und Karl Wagner (Wien, Köln, Weimar: Böhlau, 1999), S. 57–84.
57. Rossbacher, *Literatur und Liberalismus*, S. 191.
58. Horwath nennt unter den Antijesuitica der Epoche Texte von Eduard Breier, Franz Lubojatzki, Franz Julius Schneeberger und Julius Gundling, aber auch von Alfred Meissner, Moritz Hartmann und Leopold von Sacher-Masoch, die Bandbreite reicht also von der Kolportage zur engagierten Zeitliteratur (Horwath, *Kulturkampfliteratur*, S. 165–69). Vgl. Ulrike Tanzer, 'Anti-Clericalism in Literary Journalism of the Liberal Era: Ferdinand Kürnberger, Friedrich Schlögl, Daniel Spitzer and Ludwig Anzengruber', in *Catholicism and Austrian Culture*, hrsg. v. Ritchie Robertson und Judith Beniston, Austrian Studies, 10 (Edinburgh: Edinburgh University Press, 1999), S. 65–78.
59. Hurth führt Anzengruber wohl deshalb als Naturalisten (Hurth, *Priesterbild*, S. 38–42).
60. Ludwig Anzengruber, *Werke: Gesamtausgabe nach den Handschriften*, hrsg. v. Eduard Castle, 8 Bde (Leipzig: Hesse & Becker [1921]), II, 257. Zum Feuerbach-Bezug vgl. Otto Rommel, 'Die Philosophie des Steinklopferhanns', *Zeitschrift für den deutschen Unterricht*, 33 (1919), 19–25,

90–100. Zur Nachgeschichte bei Dallago, Mauthner, Mahler, Wittgenstein, Freud, Kraus und Zweig vgl. Anton Unterkircher, '"Es kann dir nix gschehn": Notizen zu einem Spruch aus Anzengrubers "Kreuzelschreibern"', *Mitteilungen aus dem Brenner-Archiv*, 24–25 (2005–06), 73–79; auch Rossbacher, *Literatur und Liberalismus*, S. 210–13. Ebner-Eschenbachs Freisinger, der nichts mehr zu verlieren hat, ist eine Art entschärfter Steinklopferhanns (G 339–40).
61. Anzengruber, *Werke*, I, 141.
62. Ludwig Anzengruber, *Gott und Welt: Aphorismen aus dem Nachlasse*, hrsg. v. Otto Rommel (Wien, Leipzig: Schroll 1920), S. 79.
63. Anzengruber, *Werke*, II, 264–65.

CHAPTER 7

Forgetting Virgil with Freud, Lear and James: A Hermeneutics of Concern and Co-creation

Ben Morgan

Tantae molis erat Romanam condere gentem
[So vast was the effort to found the race of Rome]
Aeneid 1.33[1]

Introduction

The endpoint of my argument will be a re-reading of the famous *aliquis* slip, analysed in *Zur Psychopathologie des Alltagslebens* (1904), in which a holiday acquaintance of Freud's mis-remembers the words of Dido's appeal to a future avenger in Book 4 of Virgil's *Aeneid*. The re-analysis will lead us away from salacious details of Freud's purported affair with his sister-in-law Minna Bernays c. 1900 that have been at issue in recent studies of the notorious slip, and towards a reflection on how productively to understand the sort of conversation from which the *aliquis* analysis emerges once we have left behind Freud's problematic but still influential model of the unconscious and replaced it with a revisable, empirically testable hypothesis derived from current empirical work on the sleeping psyche.[2] In the process, Freud's cultural practices become of greater interest than his explicit theorization of the mind or his self-understanding. To prepare for this re-analysis, I will first return to the context of psychology in the 1890s and to Freud's decision to establish a heuristic separation of the mind from the biological brain. In his *Principles of Psychology* (1890), William James, writing in the same intellectual world and drawing on the same authors as those to whom Freud was reacting (Hermann Helmholtz, Pierre Janet and Wilhelm Wundt), found a different way to negotiate the claims that an as yet nascent neuroscience might legitimately make with regard to analyses of the human psyche. James's approach, as we shall see, keeps mind and brain linked and, at the same time, questions the privilege of the first-person perspective even as he develops his paradigm-forming analysis of the 'stream of thought'.[3]

In this article, I shall be suggesting that the heuristic assumptions that James proposed in the 1890s have aged better than Freud's, and that they help us to a revised understanding of the ethical project of psychoanalysis as sketched by

Jonathan Lear in his philosophically oriented account of Freud's work. In Lear's view: 'psychoanalysis provides an interface in everyday life where self-consciousness and the unconscious meet'.[4] Thus:

> 'Educating oneself to the truth about oneself' is not merely a matter of learning new facts about oneself, but is rather the activity of self-consciously appropriating these wishes, effectively taking responsibility for them as one's own. It is a matter of actively integrating unfamiliar ways of thinking into self-conscious thinking. This developing 'self-knowledge' is in and of itself the active, self-conscious unifying of the psyche. (Lear, p. 18)

By contrast, the view that will be developed here will suggest a different topography of the mind, a different understanding of the role of the analytic dialogue, and will replace the ideal of integration with those of alignment, attunement and, in particular, concern. To give an advance summary that will, I hope, seem less cryptic by the end of the argument: conversations, of the sort we eavesdrop on in *Zur Psychopathologie des Alltagslebens*, can attend to and honour psychological processes, but they are not their vehicle and we, the interlocutors in that dialogue, are not their agents.

Heuristics for Thinking about Mind/Brain Interactions in the 1890s: Freud

In 1895 Freud formulated a neuron-based model of the mind, only immediately to abandon it. He hypothesized the existence of something like a synapse, or, as he called it, 'contact-barrier', which could be changed ('facilitated') by repeated activations that strengthened, or blocked and diverted, connections between neurons, thus enabling or repressing reactions. Accompanying a hand-drawn sketch showing how, rather than flowing from 'neuron a' to 'neuron b', an impulse is diverted via a 'facilitated' 'contact barrier' from 'neuron a' to 'neuron α', Freud writes:

> Stellen wir uns das Ich als ein Netz besetzter, gegeneinander gut gebahnter Neuronen vor, etwa so: So wird eine Quantität ($Q\acute{\eta}$), die von außen (Φ) her in *a* eindringt und unbeeinflußt nach dem Neuron *b* gegangen wäre, durch die Seitenbesetzung in *a* α so beeinflußt, daß sie nur einen Quotient nach *b* abgibt, eventuell gar nicht nach *b* gelangt. Wenn also ein Ich existiert, muß es psychische Primärvorgänge *hemmen*.[5]

Repression, in this thought experiment, plays out at the neuronal level; the ego's inhibition is implemented from synapse to synapse.

For Eric Kandel, who won a Nobel prize in 2000 for work on signal transduction in the nervous system, Freud's model was insightful on three counts: for its far-sighted focus on neurons; its postulation that synaptic connections were liable to alteration, that is they are 'plastic'; and its inclusion of modulating circuits of neurons which regulated the responses of other neurons.[6] Nevertheless, Freud quickly decided that this attempt to link the mind with neuronal activity was beyond the reach of scientific investigation in the 1890s. By the time of *Die Traumdeutung* (1900), the first major formulation of his meta-psychology, he was actively criticizing attempts to ground an understanding of the mind too directly in somatic processes.

The review of existing investigations of dream life in the first chapter surmises that current approaches overemphasize the role of external or bodily stimuli in the formation of dreams out of an unjustified fear that the mind might otherwise lose any grounding in physiological processes:

> Wir werden später erfahren, daß das Rätsel der Traumbildung durch die Aufdeckung einer unvermuteten psychischen Reizquelle gelöst werden kann. Vorläufig wollen wir uns über die Überschätzung der nicht aus dem Seelenleben stammenden Reize zur Traumbildung nicht verwundern. Nicht nur daß diese allein leicht aufzufinden und selbst durchs Experiment zu bestätigen sind; es entspricht auch die somatische Auffassung der Traumentstehung durchwegs der heute in der Psychiatrie herrschenden Denkrichtung. Die Herrschaft des Gehirns über den Organismus wird zwar nachdrücklichst betont, aber alles, was eine Unabhängigkeit des Seelenlebens von nachweisbaren organischen Veränderungen oder eine Spontaneität in dessen Äußerungen erweisen könnte, schreckt den Psychiater heute so, als ob dessen Anerkennung die Zeiten der Naturphilosophie und des metaphysischen Seelenwesens wiederbringen müßte. Das Mißtrauen des Psychiaters hat die Psyche gleichsam unter Kuratel gesetzt und fordert nun, daß keine ihrer Regungen ein ihr eigenes Vermögen verrate. Doch zeigt dies Benehmen von nichts anderem als von einem geringen Zutrauen in die Haltbarkeit der Kausalverkettung, die sich zwischen Leiblichem und Seelischem erstreckt. Selbst wo das Psychische sich bei der Erforschung als der primäre Anlaß eines Phänomens erkennen läßt, wird ein tieferes Eindringen die Fortsetzung des Weges bis zur organischen Begründung des Seelischen einmal zu finden wissen. Wo aber das Psychische für unsere derzeitige Erkenntnis die Endstation bedeuten müßte, da braucht es darum nicht geleugnet zu werden.[7]

Freud's position in 1900 is that the workings of the mind must in some way be governed by 'the causal chain extending between the body and the psyche'. However, explorations of the mind should not be limited by what it is currently possible to reconstruct of that connection. Psychological phenomena can and should be studied even though *c.* 1900 there is as yet no inkling of the neural correlates. Importantly, and in contrast to the position we will see in William James, Freud does not think the psychological explorations should be checked against what is currently understood about physiology. Instead, he develops his distinctive metaphorical topography of the mind that first surfaces in the developing argument of *Die Traumdeutung* in his approving comments on Gustav Theodor Fechner (1801–87). Fechner suspects

> daß auch der Schauplatz der Träume ein anderer ist als der des wachen Vorstellungslebens. [...] Was F e c h n e r mit einer solchen Umsiedlung der Seelentätigkeit meint, ist wohl nicht klar geworden [...]. Eine anatomische Deutung im Sinne der physiologischen Gehirnlokalisation oder selbst mit Bezug auf die histologische Schichtung der Hirnrinde wird man wohl auszuschließen haben. Vielleicht aber erweist sich der Gedanke einmal als sinnreich und fruchtbar, wenn man ihn auf einen seelischen Apparat bezieht, der aus mehreren hintereinander eingeschalteten Instanzen aufgebaut ist.[8]

Freud will go on to adopt this spatially imagined model of mental agencies 'set up one behind the other'. The spatially distinct 'agencies' are then each given a way of working and a set of priorities as distinct from each other as the topographical separation of agencies suggests. Moving between the spatial areas can then be conceived of as an act of translation, as we see when Freud discusses the relations between dream thoughts (located in the spatial domain of the unconscious) and dream content (available in the spatial domain of consciousness): 'Traumgedanken und Trauminhalt liegen vor uns wie zwei Darstellungen desselben Inhaltes in zwei verschiedenen Sprachen.'[9] This model underpins Freud's understanding of slips and mistakes. The agency 'behind' conscious awareness, with its distinct, spatially separated set of priorities, is constantly looking for opportunities to express forbidden content: 'Es ist ja wahrscheinlich, daß ein unterdrücktes Element allemal bestrebt ist, sich irgendwo anders zur Geltung zu bringen, diesen Erfolg aber nur dort erreicht, wo ihm geeignete Bedingungen entgegenkommen.'[10] This model makes the slip, in Freud's view, an important therapeutic tool.[11]

Freud's spatial topography is still powerfully present in recent psychoanalytic thinking, as when Jonathan Lear imagines the unconscious speaking to our conscious selves through a 'membrane', adding a histological resonance to the more neutral topography of stacked agencies first imagined by Freud (Lear, pp. 14, 16). Moreover, slips are still viewed as an integral aspect of the therapeutic dialogue.[12] Indeed the 'Freudian slip' is one of Freud's most seductive and culturally influential ideas. But as we have seen, it is in fact an awkward, historically contingent amalgam of different elements. The idea that mistakes, like dreams, can be meaningful has been combined with the spatial topography that arose as Freud developed a heuristic for dealing with the limits of neurological understanding in the 1890s, and with the notion of alien, forbidden desires for which the topographical separation of agencies supplied the metaphorical underpinning. Faced with the same problem of the limits of physiological and neurological accounts of behaviour c. 1890, William James adopted a subtly different approach, which will allow us to put the Freudian model back in its context and to re-evaluate the different elements of the amalgam.

Heuristics for Thinking about Mind/Brain Interactions in the 1890s: William James

James makes a philosophical virtue out of vagueness when it is tactfully deployed to organize what we currently know without binding us to dogmatic positions that will inhibit further discovery. For instance, the guiding hypothesis of the *Principles* is that mental and bodily life can both be understood as 'the adjustment of inner to outer relations':

> Such a formula is vagueness incarnate; but because it takes into account the fact that minds inhabit environments which act on them and on which they in turn react; because, in short, it takes mind in the midst of all its concrete relations, it is immensely more fertile than the old-fashioned 'rational psychology', which treated the soul as a detached existent, sufficient unto itself. (*Principles*, 1, 6)

Just as James links the mind to the environment with which it constantly interacts, so he unites it with the brain:

> The consciousness, which is itself an integral thing not made of parts, 'corresponds' to the entire activity of the brain, whatever that may be, at the moment. This is a way of expressing the relation of mind and brain from which I shall not depart during the remainder of the book, because it expresses the bare phenomenal fact with no hypothesis. (*Principles*, I, 177)

James's account of the mind foreshadows the 'cycle of thought' model proposed in 2018 by Nick Chater according to which, at a rate of a few cycles per second, the vast, parallel neuronal resources of our attention are applied successively to one problem after another: 'the brain works by cooperative computation across most or all of its neurons — and cooperative computation can only lock onto, and solve, one problem at a time'.[13] However, James's foreshadowing is less important than the way his 'mere empirical law of concomitance' (*Principles*, I, 177) between mind and brain, for all its vagueness, imposes on his analyses the double discipline of the precise observation of psychological phenomena and an overall account that is compatible with his broadly evolutionary and physiologically grounded grasp of the mind.

Habit plays a central role in James's account precisely because it allows the sort of ongoing, work-in-progress alignment of the physiological with the mental to which he is committed.[14] For the notion of habit is compatible with an idea of brain plasticity which allows new connections to be forged, but also explains the efficacy of established pathways: 'the whole plasticity of the brain sums itself up in two words when we call it an organ in which currents pouring in from the sense-organs make with extreme facility paths which do not easily disappear' (*Principles*, I, 107). As well as making sense at a neuronal level, habit helps to explain action at the behavioural level, both when it is working and when it is not: 'Who is there that has never wound up his watch on taking off his waistcoat in the daytime, or taken his latchkey out on arriving at the door-step of a friend' (*Principles*, I, 115). James's approach aims to integrate current thinking about the different levels of analysis in a way which is broadly compatible with an evolutionary view of creatures interacting with each other and their environment, and which, at the same time, facilitates open-mindedness and continued research, as when he is considering cases of dissociated or fragmented consciousness, noting that, although the phenomenon is not fully understood,

> a part of consciousness may sever its connections with other parts and yet continue to be. On the whole it is best to abstain from a conclusion. The science of the near future will doubtless answer this question more wisely than we can now. (*Principles*, I, 213)

Looking back at the 1890s, we can thus see two different ways of conceiving slips of the pen, of the tongue or of memory. The Jamesian approach suggests that when we are presented with mishaps, like reaching for a key at the wrong time, errors in speech (*Principles*, I, 257–58), or not quite being able to remember a name (*Principles*, I, 251–52), our approach should be guided by the rough parameters of his evolutionary model, situating meaningful mental behaviour in the wider cycles of our complex, purposive physiologically grounded interaction with our environment. Freud's model of the slip, by contrast, is private; a conflict between 'agencies' within the individual which is only very loosely integrated into an evolutionary framework because of Freud's decision heuristically to divide the mind from the brain and hence to detach mental activity from the broader situated context to which it responds and on which it has an effect.

There is a further way in which the Jamesian account is less private than its Freudian equivalent. James emphasizes the metaphysical fragility of the conscious mind, a certain lack of self-containment. In contrast, Freud, for all his presentation of the 'agency' of consciousness constantly beset by attacks from the unconscious, does not, at another level of argument, question the integrity or continuity of the territory bequeathed to consciousness by his topographical metaphors. This can be seen if we pay careful attention to the implications of his claim, in the late, summative account he set out in the *Abriß der Psychoanalyse* (1938) that: 'The real will always remain "unknowable"' [Das Reale wird immer 'unerkennbar' bleiben].[15] To claim that something is 'always' 'unknowable' is either to use a form of hyperbole, or to adopt a position beyond the predicament described, and to know it in its very unknowability. In this statement, a secure subject position survives over and beyond the vicissitudes of the ego, and is able to observe and understand its travails. One of the most attractive aspects of James's approach, and of the voice through which it is articulated, is that he tries to make the guiding assumptions of his argument, that is, the underlying metaphysics, explicit and so questionable. In this spirit, he criticizes the idea of what he calls 'the hypothetical Arch-Ego' (*Principles*, 1, 343) supposed to tie together the 'stream of thought', to be found, for instance, in the Kantian transcendental unity of apperception: an 'I think' to which all my thoughts must be attributable (*Principles*, 1, 361).

The Arch-Ego would guarantee that all the bits of our ongoing, fragile and friable experience are gathered up and unified automatically. Freud makes an unacknowledged appeal to this idea when he adopts the position from which he can securely declare that 'The real will always remain "unknowable".' In contrast, James's model of consciousness does not have the same self-assurance or automaticity. His 'stream of thought' is a work in progress which is open to error, and without guarantee. The metaphor he uses to describe his alternative position is that of a legal 'title':

> For how would it be if the Thought, the present judging Thought, instead of being in any way substantially or transcendentally identical with the former owner of the past self, merely inherited his 'title,' and thus stood as his legal representative now? (*Principles*, 1, 339)

As one cycle succeeds the next in the stream of thought, it claims the body, memory, habits and environment of its predecessor. James admits that, for all his attempt to be as clear as possible, it is not easy to formulate how this claiming might work: 'The only point that is obscure is the *act of appropriation* itself' (*Principles*, 1, 340). But the thrust of his argument is, first, that we should resist the temptation to shore up a process not yet fully understood with a metaphysical unity which functionally reproduces the theological notion of a soul, and, secondly, that we should face the vulnerability that his model suggests. James's 'stream of thought' is a unity, but a unity that might go wrong, or fall apart into dissociated fragments, get forgotten, or fail to register consciously or reappropriate aspects of its ongoing involvement in the world. Methodological parsimony allows us to go no further:

> This me is an empirical aggregate of things objectively known. The *I* which knows them [...] is a *Thought*, at each moment different from that of the last moment, but *appropriative* of the latter, together with all that the latter called its own. All the experiential facts find their hypothesis in this description, unencumbered with any hypothesis save that of the existence of passing thoughts or states of mind. (*Principles*, I, 401)

James's response to the predicament of empirical psychology in the 1890s thus differs from Freud's in a number of key aspects. The first is that he foregoes the freedom afforded to Freud by the heuristic separation of mind and brain, and insists on working with a revisable, experimentally oriented model that keeps mind and brain together, but with a minimum of dogmatic commitments — 'with no hypothesis' (*Principles*, I, 177). A second difference is that the metaphysical assumptions which will necessarily shape any enquiry are made part of the enquiry itself, and so are more easily available for questioning and revision. A third difference is that he is very aware of the contribution that the perspective of the inquirer makes to the material investigated. This is particularly true when it comes to the 'entire activity of the brain' to which the mind is understood to be correlated (*Principles*, I, 177): '*The "entire brain-process" is not a physical fact at all.* It is the appearance to an onlooking mind of a multitude of physical facts' (*Principles*, I, 178). Our enquiry will itself make particular groupings of the world show up as salient; the world is moulded by the very questions we ask of it. This might lead to a form of skepticism (Freud's 'The real will always remain "unknowable"'). But James insists we commit instead to a process of ongoing re-engagement with the world; to testing out new heuristics, rather than accepting a blanket unknowability: 'It may be a constitutional infirmity, but I can take no comfort in such devices for making a luxury of intellectual defeat. They are but spiritual chloroform. Better live on the ragged edge, better gnaw the file forever' (*Principles*, I, 179).

The comparison with James's approach to empirical psychology in the 1890s brings into focus the way in which Freud combines his topographical heuristic with the assumption of the unquestioned unity of the enquiring mind. These conceptual habits privatize experiences, cutting them off from the wider processes of interaction with the environment, as well as suggesting that the primary dynamic of the mind/brain will be one of antagonism (the conflict between the topographical zones). There is also a certain power structure built into the process of enquiry whereby the unity and self-command of the enquiring subject can never be questioned. In the lectures he delivered in Oxford in 1908 that would form the basis of *A Pluralistic Universe* (1909), James sets out a further consequence of his pragmatic and exploratory model of the mind:

> Shall we say that every complex mental fact is a separate psychic entity *succeeding upon* a lot of other psychic entities which are erroneously called its parts and

superseding them in function, but not literally being composed of them? [...] I struggled with the problem for years, covering hundreds of sheets of paper with notes and memoranda and discussions with myself over the difficulty. How can many consciousnesses be at the same time one consciousness? How can one and the same identical fact experience itself so diversely? [...] I saw that I must either forswear that 'psychology without a soul' to which my whole psychological and Kantian education had committed me [...] or else I must squarely confess the solution of the problem impossible, and then either give up my intellectualistic logic [...], or, finally, face the fact that life is logically irrational. [...] I have finally found myself compelled to give up the logic [...]. Reality, life, experience, concreteness, immediacy, use what word you will, exceeds our logic, overflows and surrounds it. [...] I myself find no good warrant for even suspecting the existence of any reality of a higher denomination than that distributed and strung-along and flowing sort of reality which we finite beings swim in. That is the sort of reality given us, and that is the sort with which logic is so incommensurable.[16]

In James's view, our concepts do not describe the world. They are tools for interacting with the 'distributed and strung-along and flowing sort of reality' of which we are ourselves an active part. This interaction can be better or worse; that is to say it will always have a normative aspect, and James's pluralistic and open-minded model is structured to facilitate conversations about the sort of interactions we might prefer: 'Compromise and mediation are inseparable from the pluralistic philosophy. Only monistic dogmatism can say of any of its hypotheses, "It is either that or nothing; take it or leave it just as it stands".'[17]

We are now in a position to turn to the *aliquis* slip recorded in *Zur Psychopathologie des Alltagslebens*. How do the slip and its analysis appear if we relinquish the mind-only spatial topography that structures Freud's account and prepares for his assertion that he has isolated 'die Störung eines Gedankens durch einen aus dem Verdrängten kommenden inneren Widerspruch'?[18] If we re-describe the event from a more Jamesian point of view, what else emerges?

Forgetting Virgil in 1900

Freud presents the context of the *aliquis* slip in the following terms:

Im letzten Sommer erneuerte ich — wiederum auf der Ferienreise — die Bekanntschaft eines jungen Mannes von akademischer Bildung, der, wie ich bald merkte, mit einigen meiner psychologischen Publikationen vertraut war. Wir waren im Gespräch — ich weiß nicht mehr wie — auf die soziale Lage des Volksstammes gekommen, dem wir beide angehören, und er, der Ehrgeizige, erging sich in Bedauern darüber, daß seine Generation, wie er sich äußerte, zur Verkümmerung bestimmt sei, ihre Talente nicht entwickeln und ihre Bedürfnisse nicht befriedigen könne. Er schloß seine leidenschaftlich bewegte Rede mit dem bekannten Vergilschen Vers, in dem die unglückliche Dido ihre Rache an Aeneas der Nachwelt überträgt: *Exoriare* ...[19]

As she kills herself, Dido calls upon a figure as yet unknown, who from the perspective of Virgil and his readers *c.* 19 BCE is the Carthaginian Hannibal: 'Out of my grave let an avenger arise' [*exoriare, aliquis nostris ex ossibus ultor*].²⁰ Freud's unfortunate interlocutor garbles his Latin in two ways: he forgets the word *aliquis*, and he also simplifies the word order, producing something like a literal translation from German back into Latin: 'let there arise from our bones [the/an] avenger', or: *exoriare ex nostris ossibus ultor.*²¹

The mistake offers Freud the opportunity to demonstrate his interpretative skills on 'eine nervengesunde fremde Person', rather than on himself, as had been the case in the opening example of the *Psychopathologie* and also in *Die Traumdeutung*, the paradigm analysis of which was Freud's dream of Irma's injection.²² When asked to focus on the forgotten word *aliquis*, the interlocutor divides it into two portions as *a-liquis*, and Freud, following a train of associations about liquid, saints, miracles and blood, deduces, to the consternation of his interlocutor, that he is anxiously awaiting the period of a female partner, which turns out indeed to be the case: 'Ich hoffe, Sie nehmen diese Gedanken, wenn ich sie wirklich gehabt habe, nicht für Ernst. Ich will Ihnen dafür gestehen, daß die Dame Italienerin ist, in deren Gesellschaft ich auch Neapel besucht habe.'²³

Freud uses the technique of free association to elicit from his interlocutor the material that reveals the unconscious worry pushing for expression. However, more recent, empirical work on the attrition of a second language (such as, in this example, Latin learned at school) approaches the matter in a different way, studying for instance, the interdependence between the forgetting of lexis and insecurities of syntax (Freud's interlocutor cannot find a word, but also muddles the word order); and also studying which vocabulary we lose: of possible hypotheses neither 'first in, last out' nor 'best learned, last out' seems to fit the data, which instead suggest that lexical loss is random.²⁴ These more recent investigations look at the attrition of second languages in the wider contexts of the scaffolding of linguistic competence by the everyday environment and of the frequency with which we use the language. They are compatible with the Jamesian attention to purposive interactions in an environment, structured by habit and expectation. This is not to say that Freud's interlocutor was not also concerned about the possible pregnancy of a woman with whom he had slept, only that the relation between this worry and the forgetting of Virgil needs to be reformulated.

In Jonathan Lear's account of psychoanalysis, the single most important aspect is Freud's so-called 'fundamental rule' of free association, which is both a therapeutic method and an ethical standard: 'The analysand tries to speak his mind, and he is everywhere *confronted* with interruptions of hitherto unconscious thinking' (Lear, p. 8). If we abandon the spatial topography of the mind, which structures the way this 'confrontation' is conceived in the first place, what remains, to redeploy a term of Lear's, is a 'peculiar conversation'.²⁵ This conversation lends itself to empirical study of the sort James imagines, and might even be 'manualized', as Falk Leichsenring and Christiane Steinert have recently suggested, that is to say structured according to protocols that have been tested in randomized controlled trials.²⁶ Three aspects of Leichsenring's and Steinert's protocol are of special interest when considering Freud's analyses in the *Psychopathologie*. First, the conversation should be conducted face to face (which is true of the exchanges in the social situations recorded in the *Psychopathologie* if not of Freud's own therapeutic practice); secondly, the level of interpretative and supportive intervention by the therapist 'depends on the patient's capacity and needs' (another feature likely to arise in a well-mannered social situation, if not in therapy); thirdly, there should be a focus on transferring 'treatment gains to everyday situations' (something already happening when the conversation is itself already an everyday situation).[27] To this extent, aspects of the behaviour Freud records in the *Psychopathologie* accord with recent empirical work on effective forms of therapeutic conversation, without any reference to the theory Freud uses the conversations to bolster. Freud's intuitive and well-mannered decisions about how to conduct his conversations could be made independently of the theoretical edifice he was developing in parallel.

A further aspect of the conversations is also noteworthy when viewed from this new perspective. In the example given by Freud, a work of culture has a special place in the process, as the (mis-)quoting of Virgil allows the conversation to shift from matters of public concern (the anti-Semitic work environment of late nineteenth-century Vienna) to those of a more intimate nature. However, the discussion of Virgil is not itself enough. We don't know where the conversation took place. In the opening example of the *Psychopathologie*, the forgetting of the name 'Signorelli', Freud is talking to a travelling companion. The second example similarly suggests a holiday conversation. The timing of this second conversation has been questioned, and it has even been suggested the slip was made by Freud himself, not an interlocutor.[28] But whether we have the record of an actual example, or a semi-fictionalized account of a further piece of self-analysis by Freud, the upshot is much the same: the train compartment, the café conversation, or the notetaking arising from self-observation are social occasions that allow a certain renegotiation of habits of intimacy. The Freudian assumption of a repressed wish or anxiety doesn't explain the mistake under discussion, but it legitimates a change of topic and a certain intensification of the conversation. The irrepressible Freudian unconscious is thus not the answer to a puzzle, or the explanation of a slip, or even of a dream. Rather, it is a tool that was in some circumstances useful *c.* 1900 for initiating a particular sort of conversation, the sort of conversation that, for instance, Arthur Schnitzler, looking back from the 1920s to the last years of the Habsburg monarchy in *Fräulein Else*, has Else complain was particularly lacking.[29]

If we thus give up the model that there is an unconscious wish driving the slip and move instead to the view that Freud helped to create occasions for a certain kind of conversation, then the question arises as to whether this conversation is itself therapeutically effective in the way Lear imagines, allowing the unconscious to speak through the 'membrane' and be integrated in the ongoing process of self-conscious thought: 'before we know any empirical results — how well psychoanalysis treats this or that disease — we can see simply by looking at its structure, that psychoanalysis is a "cure" for inhibition and constriction of self-consciousness. That is how it is organized' (Lear, p. 5). Lear, in this passage, draws a positive conclusion: the very structure of the conversation is therapeutic. However, recent figures suggest grounds for caution: while 50–60 per cent of patients in psychotherapy improve, 10 per cent deteriorate and at least 30 per cent show no great change.[30] Lear's view of the structural efficacy of the 'peculiar conversation' depends on two assumptions. In addition to the spatial topography, and partly because of it, Lear presupposes that the very conversation which attends to the interruptions of the unconscious is itself part of the healing process: 'When it is well done, and at critical moments in the therapy, the efficacy of the mind is immediately and transparently available to the self-conscious awareness of the analysand' (Lear, p. 15). Rosalind D. Cartwright's study of the dreams of individuals suffering from clinical depression suggests an interestingly different picture.

Cartwright studied adults coming to terms with the break-up of a first marriage. The participants fell into three groups, those in whom the failure of the marriage did not cause a bout of clinical depression, who functioned as her control group and, among those in whom it did prompt clinical depression, those who had recovered five months after the initial study and those who had not. The critical difference between the two groups suffering from depression was the nature of their dreams, in particular those about their former spouse: 'Those recovering experienced much longer, more dramatic dreams, with complex plots and changes of scene. They include many more characters.'[31] For the group that did not recover by contrast:

> When no emotion is expressed, and there is no relation of current images to older memories, and when the dreamer's role in the dream story is passive, dreams of the former spouse appear to have no sustained impact on the waking mood disorder.[32]

Cartwright summarizes her model of the dreaming mind as follows:

> I propose that when some disturbing waking experience is reactivated in sleep and carried forward into REM, where it is matched by similarity in feeling to earlier memories, a network of older associations is stimulated and is displayed as a sequence of compound images that we experience as dreams. This melding of new and old memory fragments modifies the network of emotional self-defining memories, and thus updates the organizational picture we hold of 'who I am and what is good for me and what is not.' In this way, dreaming diffuses the emotional charge of the event and so prepares the sleeper to wake ready to see things in a more positive light, to make a fresh start. This does not always happen over a single night; sometimes a big reorganization of the emotional perspective of our self-concept must be made — from wife to widow or married to single, say, and this may take many nights.[33]

In Cartwright's model, the dreaming itself does the work of healing, with a consequent reorganization of the metaphors with which the mind is conceived. Waking consciousness, NREM and REM sleep are all activities of minds that, as James put it, 'inhabit environments which act on them and on which they in turn react' (*Principles*, 1, 6). Processes of learning, adjustment and emotional evaluation are carried out across all three activities. The distinctions between the three are analytic rather than absolute, as is made clear by the blurring of a clear-cut distinction between waking and sleeping in NREM parasomnias like sleepwalking.[34] Nevertheless, the phases of sleep and waking can be seen as 'different, but coordinated, mechanisms'.[35] Cartwright's metaphor for the mind is that of a unified, if differentiated and open-ended process: 'We are always works in progress. Dreams are a window onto the ongoing work of the mind during its essential night-shift.'[36] In this model, it's not yet clear (it is an empirical, open question) what role, if any, paying attention to our dreams plays in the process of healing. The main agent of change is the dream process itself.[37]

The cases cited by Cartwright, and others such as Matthew Walker, make the ongoing cycle of waking and sleeping the agent of change. In Cartwright's study, the subjects of the experiment were not in therapy; non-depressed, depressive recoverers and depressive non-recoverers all alike made three two-night visits to the sleep laboratory to allow their dreams to be sampled across the different cycles of REM sleep; otherwise there was no therapeutic intervention.[38] In Walker's case, there was a pharmaceutical intervention, but this did not itself directly change the symptoms, rather it allowed a better quality of REM sleep.[39] In both cases, the main aim was to allow sleep to do its work. The conversations that accompany this process need not be dismissed as merely epiphenomenal: 'there is substantial evidence for the efficacy of psychodynamic therapy in depressive, anxiety, somatoform, eating, substance-related, and personality disorders'.[40] Nevertheless, the exact mechanisms of transformation are not yet understood. As Leichsenring and Steinert suggest: 'no method of psychotherapy may claim to be the gold standard'.[41]

Freud and Lear both claim that the analytic conversation itself is doing the work. But from an empirical standpoint, the jury is still out. Methodological pluralism is therefore the order of the day, allowing different traditions to learn from what works in each other's methods. It is possible the process of self-consciousness fostered in the analytic conversation itself is doing some work, as Lear suggests. Or perhaps paying attention to one's dreams helps one to dream differently, as Cartwright suggests of one of her patients.[42] Alternatively, fostering a better quantity and quality of sleep might be the main factor, as Walker argues; or a complex, situation-specific combination of these and other factors. Investigations continue apace. We, meanwhile, despite our inevitable sense of first-person involvement in the process (however irrelevant this first-person perspective might finally turn out to be), are left not knowing whether to talk, and if so, what about. For Lear, we should not ignore this sense of first-person involvement:

> If we want to understand how the human psyche develops we also need to know what experience is like for the person whose psyche is developing. We must take the subjective nature of her experience systematically into account. Psychoanalysis aims to give a rigorous account of how the psyche develops on the basis of what experience is like for the subject. (Lear, p. 172)

To conclude my argument, I want briefly to sum up where our discussion of Freud, James and recent developments in the study of sleep and dreaming have left analytic conversations of the sort embodied in Freud's interpretations of slips and blunders in *The Psychopathology of Everyday Life*. Is there a specific role for talking and interpretation?

Conclusion: A Hermeneutics of Concern and Co-creation

Bruno Latour has coined the term 'matters of concern' for issues about which there is not yet sufficient scientific consensus to establish matters of fact, and hopes that the idea will give a new inflection to debates situated on the border line between the natural and the social worlds:

> the mapping of scientific controversies about matters of concern should allow us to renew from top to bottom the very scene of empiricism — and hence the divide between 'natural' and 'social'. A natural world made up of matters of fact does not look quite the same as a world consisting of matters of concern and thus cannot be used so easily as a foil for the 'symbolic-human-intentional' social order.[43]

The relation between mind and brain is just such a 'matter of concern'. Comparing the responses of Freud and James to the state of neuroscientific research in the 1890s, we have seen how James's approach engages with the broad picture of empirical research, whilst at the same time thinking hard about the very conceptual tools used to make sense of the broad picture without lapsing into scepticism: 'Better live on the ragged edge, better gnaw the file forever' (*Principles*, I, 179). James's example allows a critical assessment of Freud's contrasting mind-only-for-the-moment heuristic, and the topography of conscious versus unconscious 'agencies' that accompanies it. It also allows us to imagine alternative accounts of how a slip works that acknowledge the effects of sub-personal processes beyond the individual's conscious control (processes of second language attrition), without having to posit wishes mysteriously situated in the other, spatially imagined 'agency' of the unconscious. The assumption of such a wish turns out, on a charitable, retrospective re-reading, to be a useful device for allowing a slip of the tongue to become the occasion for another sort of conversation about what, to use Schnitzler's appositely impersonal formulation: 'is going on inside me, what's churning and anxious in me' [was in mir vorgeht und was in mir wühlt und Angst hat].[44]

If we follow the lead of current research on sleep and dreaming, the function of such a conversation is likely to be one of acknowledgement, or, to use Winnicott's phrase, of 'holding', rather than of interpretation or solving a puzzle.[45] Ritchie Robertson makes the same point in assessing Freud's positive legacy for patients in psychotherapy:

> It is a plausible surmise that what has helped them has not been the application of a system but the ability of the analyst or therapist to respond sensitively to the patient and to encourage the patient to feel himself or herself an object of interest.[46]

Following this line of thought allows us to derive from the foregoing historical contextualization of Freud's work an attitude strikingly different from the 'hermeneutics of suspicion' of which, according to Ricoeur, Freud, like Nietzsche and Marx, was a master. Ricoeur himself suggested that hermeneutics can have two contrasting modes: 'Hermeneutics seems to me to be animated by this double motivation: willingness to suspect, willingness to listen; vow of rigor, vow of obedience.'[47] Arguing in a theological vein, he casts the listening type of hermeneutics as one of 'restoration'; disclosing the sacred that has always already been articulated. But the emphasis on listening can be taken up without recourse to ideas of the sacred, or indeed to Ricoeur's rhetoric of disclosure, which employs the same spatial imaginary we have seen in Freud, albeit with a recuperative rather than a demystifying intention. In a new model of conversation, the interlocutors do not know in advance what sort of thing they will uncover (dirty secret or sacred revelation). Indeed, they cannot even know whether anything will be discovered, or have any effect. The ethical force of the conversation lies in the open-minded attitude of concern with which it allows two people to appear and be honoured. The people acknowledging need not, indeed should not, deny their own involvement in the process. The acknowledgement is one of collaborative co-creation. The process may itself sometimes be transformative, as Lear suggests. At other times, it may simply be what we do in order not to get in the way of processes unfolding autonomously. In the end, it is likely that, as a complex social process which forms part of a longer tradition and which is situated among a series of related phenomena, from confession to having a heart-to-heart with a good friend, there will be different aspects of the process that, in any particular situation, differently affect the unfolding cycles of sleep and waking in our continuous adaptation to a changing environment.

For scholars in the humanities this might feel at best like winning the consolation prize: cultural conversations can sometimes, perhaps, contribute to human well-being, and at other times, perhaps, stop us from getting too much in the way. But the more important upshot, following on from Bruno Latour's singling out of issues where we don't have access to 'matters of fact' only 'matters of concern', is that the cultural conversation is part of the wider conversation, although the conclusion of the conversation, in the long run, may be that, in some situations, the cultural bit is irrelevant, or even an obstacle: sorting out the sleep hygiene might be enough to be going on with. Nevertheless, even if we don't, with Jonathan Lear, insist on its necessary therapeutic efficacy, the collaborative, concerned, co-creative acknowledgement of other people can itself be viewed as a 'matter of concern': a proposal for ethical living that is part of our ongoing, empirically informed cultural and scientific self-investigation. A hermeneutics of concern foregoes the spatial topography that looks 'behind' the conversation and instead follows James in finding conceptually probing but open-minded ways of grouping different types of evidence and different forms of intervention. This will entail including unfamiliar issues, unfamiliar conversation partners, unfamiliar forms of evidence: for instance, misremembered classical learning and research on language attrition alongside the self-repairing dreams of depressive divorcees. Freud's *Psychopathologie* prefigures this widening of attention: in addition to the hermeneutics of suspicion, the book already recorded the developing practices of a hermeneutics of concern. Recontextualized, and reassessed, it teaches us that we will need to notice new connections, and that we should not assume in advance that the cultural analysis itself is doing the work, but should rather work with an open-minded and humble curiosity as to its possible effects.

Notes to Chapter 7

1. Virgil, *Eclogues, Georgics, Aeneid I–VI*, trans. by H. Rushton Fairclough and G. P. Goold (Cambridge, MA: Harvard University Press, 1999), pp. 264–65. I am grateful to Naomi Rokotnitz and Charlie Louth for their helpful comments on an earlier draft. Many of the ideas in the essay were first developed in conversation with the inspiring participants of 'German 144: Freud and Psychoanalysis', which I taught at Harvard in the Fall of 2020: Thomas Brooks, Jay Carmichael, Phoebe Carter, Jonas Hermann, Catherine Le, Pranav Misra, Sidney Penny, Sarah Rifky, Therese Shire, Molly Silverstein and Alex Watson.
2. For an overview of debates about the *aliquis* slip to 2016, see Henry Zvi Lothane, 'Freud and Minna: Facts and Fictions', *Journal of the American Psychoanalytic Association*, 64 (2016), 1237–54. For a carefully constructed version of the case for Minna Bernays, see Richard A. Skues, 'On the Dating of Freud's Aliquis Slip', *The International Journal of Psychoanalysis* 82 (2001), 1185–1204. For a further step, looking beyond Minna to Freud's relationship with his sister Anna: Edward A. Jones, 'Freud's Paternity Crises', *The International Journal of Psychoanalysis*, 98 (2017), 1025–46.
3. William James, *The Principles of Psychology*, 2 vols (New York: Dover, 1950), I, 224–90. Further references will be given parenthetically in the text.
4. Jonathan Lear, *Freud*, 2nd edn (London: Routledge, 2015), p. 8. Further references will be given parenthetically in the text.
5. Sigmund Freud, *Aus den Anfängen der Psychoanalyse: Briefe an Wilhelm Fliess, Abhandlungen und Notizen aus den Jahren 1887–1902* (Frankfurt a.M.: Fischer, 1975), p. 330.
6. Eric R. Kandel, *The Age of Insight: The Quest to Understand the Unconscious in Art, Mind, and Brain, from Vienna 1900 to the Present* (New York: Random House, 2012), p. 520. See also: Diego Centonze and others, 'The Project for a Scientific Psychology (1895): A Freudian Anticipation of LTP-Memory Connection Theory', *Brain Research Reviews* 46 (2004), 310–14; Geoffrey D. Schott, 'Freud's Project and its Diagram: Anticipating the Hebbian Synapse', *Journal of Neurology, Neurosurgery & Psychiatry*, 82 (2011), 122–25.
7. Sigmund Freud, *Gesammelte Werke, chronologisch geordnet*, 17 vols (Frankfurt a.M.: Fischer, 1991), II/3, 44–45.
8. Ibid., II/3, 51.
9. Ibid., II/3, 283.
10. Ibid., IV, 10–11.
11. Ibid., IV, 89–90.
12. Bruce Fink, *A Clinical Introduction to Freud: Techniques for Everyday Practice* (New York: Norton, 2017), pp. 115–16.
13. Nick Chater, *The Mind is Flat: The Illusion of Mental Depth and the Improvised Mind* (London: Allen Lane, 2018), p. 130.
14. For a collection of recent essays on habit and cognition, see *Habits: Pragmatist Approaches from Cognitive Science, Neuroscience, and Social Theory*, ed. by Fausto Caruana and Italo Testa (Cambridge: Cambridge University Press, 2020).
15. Freud, *Gesammelte Werke, chronologisch geordnet*, XVII, 127.
16. William James, *Writings 1902–1910* (New York: Library of America, 1987), pp. 722–26.
17. Ibid., p. 772.
18. Freud, *Gesammelte Werke, chronologisch geordnet*, IV, 20.
19. Ibid., IV, 13–14.
20. Virgil, *The Aeneid*, trans. by Sarah Ruden (New Haven, CT: Yale University Press, 2008), p. 88 (= 4.625).
21. Freud, *Gesammelte Werke, chronologisch geordnet*, IV, 14.
22. Ibid., IV, 17; ibid., II/3, 110–26.
23. Ibid., IV, 17.
24. See the contributions to Monika S. Schmid and Barbara Köpke, *The Oxford Handbook of Language Attrition* (Oxford: Oxford University Press, 2019). 'To the degree that L2 syntax depends on lexical semantic representations or discourse factors, it appears to be subject to attrition' (p. 375); 'the hypothesis predicts that the actual lexicon that is lost will be essentially random, in keeping with the tenets of a dynamic systems theory' (p. 389).

25. 'The peculiar conversation' is the title of Lear's introductory chapter (Lear, pp. 1–28).
26. Falk Leichsenring and Christiane Steinert, 'Towards an Evidence-Based Unified Psychodynamic Protocol for Emotional Disorders', *Journal of Affective Disorders*, 232 (2018), 400–16.
27. Ibid., p. 406.
28. Skues, 'On the Dating of Freud's Aliquis Slip', p. 1201.
29. Arthur Schnitzler, *Fräulein Else und andere Erzählungen* (Frankfurt a.M.: Fischer, 1987), p. 86.
30. Jeremy Holmes, *The Brain Has a Mind of its Own: Attachment, Neurobiology, and the New Science of Psychotherapy* (London: Confer, 2020), p. 3.
31. Rosalind D. Cartwright, *The Twenty-Four Hour Mind: The Role of Sleep and Dreaming in our Emotional Lives* (Oxford: Oxford University Press, 2010), p. 67.
32. Ibid., p. 70.
33. Ibid., p. 56.
34. Ibid., p. 172.
35. Julie Seibt and Marcos G. Frank, 'Primed to Sleep: The Dynamics of Synaptic Plasticity across Brain States', *Frontiers in Systems Neuroscience*, 13 (2019), article 2 (here p. 1): 'Waking experience triggers short-lived synaptic events that are necessary for transient plastic changes and mark (i.e., "prime") circuits and synapses for further processing in sleep.'
36. Cartwright, *The Twenty-Four Hour Mind*, p. 178.
37. For comparable discussion of the therapeutic effects of REM-sleep, see: Matthew Walker, *Why We Sleep: The New Science of Sleep and Dreams* (London: Allen Lane, 2017), p. 214. Similarly: Andrea N. Goldstein and Matthew P. Walker, 'The Role of Sleep in Emotional Brain Function', *Annual Review of Clinical Psychology*, 10 (2014), 679–708.
38. Cartwright, *The Twenty-Four Hour Mind*, p. 63.
39. Walker, *Why We Sleep*, p. 214.
40. Falk Leichsenring and Christiane Steinert, 'The Efficacy of Psychodynamic Psychotherapy: An Up-to-Date Review', in *Contemporary Psychodynamic Psychotherapy: Evolving Clnical Practice*, ed. by David Kealy and John S. Ogrodniczuk (London: Academic Press, 2019), pp. 49–74 (here p. 65).
41. Ibid., p. 66.
42. Cartwright, *The Twenty-Four Hour Mind*, pp. 132–33.
43. Bruno Latour, *Reassembling the Social: An Introduction to Actor-Network-Theory* (Oxford: Oxford University Press, 2005), pp. 114–15.
44. Schnitzler, *Fräulein Else und andere Erzählungen*, p. 86 (my translation).
45. Donald Winnicott, *Holding and Interpretation: Fragment of an Analysis* (Abingdon: Routledge, 2018).
46. Sigmund Freud, *A Case of Hysteria (Dora)*, trans. by Anthea Bell, ed. by Ritchie Robertson (Oxford: Oxford University Press, 2013), p. lvi.
47. Paul Ricoeur, *Freud and Philosophy: An Essay on Interpretation*, trans. by Denis Savage (New Haven, CT: Yale University Press, 1970), p. 27. Compare Rita Felski, *The Limits of Critique* (Chicago: University of Chicago Press, 2015), p. 32.

CHAPTER 8

Body Politics in Arthur Schnitzler's *Professor Bernhardi*

Judith Beniston

I

In his fragmentary autobiography, *Jugend in Wien*, published posthumously in 1968, Arthur Schnitzler (1862–1931) makes abundantly clear that he was never entirely comfortable with or committed to his medical career: as a student he was supposedly erratic in his attendance at lectures and practical sessions, applying himself to his studies only sporadically and with little enthusiasm. After qualifying in 1885, as a doctor he was no more conscientious than required and never really developed a research career. Furthermore, both practical medicine and his work as an editor (from 1887 on) of the weekly *Internationale klinische Rundschau* exacerbated a tendency to hypochondria. Such shortcomings made him a disappointment to his father, Johann Schnitzler, a well-regarded laryngologist and co-founder in 1872 of the Wiener Allgemeine Poliklinik. Particularly disliking the surgical disciplines, his son asserts that his only substantial interests lay in 'Nerven- und Geisteskrankheiten', for reasons that were no so much scientific as grounded 'im Poetischen oder doch Belletristischen'.[1]

This autobiographical account, largely written during the First World War, was reconfirmed by the publication in 1987 of the earliest volume of Schnitzler's diary, which covers his university career and all but the last few months in which he was a full-time medical practitioner. (He resigned from the Wiener Allgemeine Poliklinik shortly after his father's death in 1893.) After only a few weeks at university he predicts that 'die Wissenschaft wird mir nie das werden, was mir die Kunst schon jetzt ist'; recently qualified, he calls his medical degree 'eine Rieseneselei von mir'; and in the following years he repeatedly records his unhappiness and frustration. In January 1890 he concludes: 'Ich bin mit der Medizin innerlich fertig. [...] Mich ekelt vor den Patienten, vor den Collegen, vor allem, was mich an den Beruf erinnert.'[2] However, Schnitzler's medical writings, published by Horst Thomé just a year after that diary volume, suggest a slightly different picture. He undoubtedly felt mediocre and apathetic in comparison with his dedicated, high-achieving family — in addition to his father's prominence, his younger brother Julius became a respected surgeon and his sister Gisela married

Markus Hajek, who was to hold the University Chair in Laryngology — but, as Thomé points out, Schnitzler was prone to be hypercritical of both his medical and his literary achievements.[3] Viewed objectively, his medical career progressed in exemplary if not stellar fashion. Moreover, he was thoroughly steeped in that milieu until his early thirties and reviewed publications, often textbooks, covering a range of medical specialisms for the *Internationale klinische Rundschau*. Encouraged by these writings, scholarship has increasingly recognized Schnitzler as rather more than merely Freud's literary *Doppelgänger*, exploring the impact on his literary work of other aspects of his medical training and of contemporary medical culture, such as his knowledge of bacteriology, statistical methods in medicine and debates around medically assisted dying.[4]

Alongside his book reviews, Schnitzler's journalistic writings include a number of articles that testify to a critical engagement with the ethics, politics and sociology of medicine. In May 1887, for instance, he wrote an editorial on 'Die Zustände im k. k. allgemeinen Krankenhause in Wien'. The article responded to an intervention in parliament by the leading Social Democrat Engelbert Pernerstorfer, who had complained forcefully about rough, uncaring and impatient nurses, unpalatable hospital food and the poor working conditions of junior doctors. Widely reported in the Viennese press, Pernerstorfer's attack on the city's flagship hospital gave rise to heated public debate. Schnitzler's intervention focuses on underlying socio-economic considerations: he highlights how badly paid the nurses are ('Für zwölf Gulden monatlich engagiert man keine Engel');[5] he chides the government for spending huge amounts on the military but denying hospital patients a nourishing meal; and, without identifying himself as a junior doctor, he endorses Pernerstorfer's view that this group is often overworked, allocated nasty, cramped rooms and paid a derisory amount. He saves his sharpest criticism for the official response: in a cynical pretence of liberalism that Schnitzler unmasks as a ruse to take control of the debate, the authorities instructed hospitals to institute a complaints book, thereby reducing systemic failings to a series of personal grievances and kicking any prospect of real reform into the long grass.

Schnitzler's 'Londoner Briefe', written during a ten-week study visit in May–July 1888, offer a broader commentary on medical ethics, politics and sociology by comparing the organizational structures and clinical practices of public healthcare in the British capital with their Viennese equivalents. He is, for example, uneasy with the existence in London of a dedicated 'Cancer-Hospital' (presumably what is now the Royal Marsden Hospital), whose designation he reads as a byword for despair, and he condemns the use of closed 'Lock Hospitals' for the treatment of venereal diseases as a policy unlikely to find approval 'bei wirklich ethisch denkenden Ärzten'.[6] He blames the stigma associated with these penitentiary-like institutions for the relatively small numbers of infected patients who seek treatment, in contrast to uptake in Vienna. However, in other respects, London compares favourably: having suggested a year earlier that some nurses will always be more diligent and caring than others, Schnitzler praises the standard of patient care he witnesses in London. This superiority can probably be attributed to the fact that the professionalization of nursing in Britain had been instigated by Florence Nightingale in 1860, whereas in Vienna the Rudolfinerhaus, championed by pioneering surgeon Theodor Billroth, admitted its first trainees only in 1882. Although Schnitzler had initially assumed the pre-eminence of the Vienna Medical School, on the basis that many British and American doctors chose to continue their training there, his last dispatch closes with a sweeping criticism of Viennese medicine. New facilities of various kinds are springing up all across London; unimpeded by state control or professional infighting, they testify to a progressive liberalism ('einem freiheitlichen Sinne') that seems worlds away from the obstructive, factionalized atmosphere of Viennese medical politics and, indeed, of Austrian public life as a whole.[7] Schnitzler recalls in *Jugend in Wien* that his father was willing to forgive him a great deal on the basis of that *cri de cœur*.[8]

As 1888 draws to a close, Schnitzler expresses disillusionment with medicine on both sides of the Channel. In an editorial for the *Internationale klinische Rundschau*, published under the rubric 'Silvesterbetrachtungen', he condemns the bitter public recriminations between the British and German laryngologists who had treated the throat cancer of German Emperor Friedrich III as unworthy of the profession and urges his fellow doctors to train their capacity for unprejudiced rational observation on the ethics of their own behaviour. Drawing on evolutionary discourses, he warns against allowing atavistic behaviours, whereby 'eine ganze Klasse von Menschen zuerst nach der Konfession und erst dann, oder auch gar nicht, nach dem inneren Wert ihres Nächsten fragen wird', to impinge on the medical enterprise.[9] Following this thinly veiled critique of antisemitism within medicine, he closes with a gloomy prediction: 'Wir werden auch im nächsten Jahre viele große Ärzte unter uns haben — aber wir fürchten, nur wenig große Menschen.'[10] Scientific progress will not be accompanied by an advancement of humanitarian ethics.

The critical tone of these early writings, which predate Schnitzler's literary breakthrough by several years, continues in his characterization of the many doctors who feature in his literary work. As Walter Müller-Seidel observes, Schnitzler was one of several doctor-writers of his generation to paint an unflattering portrait of the profession. The recurrent failings of Schnitzler's doctors are either that they have become so caught up in conventional patterns of thought that they have lost sight of their ethical and social responsibilities, or that they focus too narrowly on the ills of the body and lack sympathetic insight into those of the mind.[11] The sole exception appears to be the Jewish title figure of Schnitzler's five-act comedy *Professor Bernhardi* (1912), his only full-length play set in a medical milieu.[12] Certainly, one is hard-pressed to find any criticism of Bernhardi either in Schnitzler's correspondence or in what he termed 'Antikritik' — brief, acerbic responses to the journalistic reception of his work that were written to vent his annoyance at perceived misunderstandings and not intended for publication.[13] As late as the year before Schnitzler's death, he eulogizes Bernhardi as

> [d]iesen Mann, der so völlig konsequent seiner Menschlichkeit und seiner Gesinnung nach handelt, der zwei Monate im Gefängnis sitzt und auch sonst allerlei Unannehmlichkeiten durchmacht, die er sich durch die leiseste

> Nachgiebigkeit ohneweiters hätte ersparen können und der am Ende,
> nachdem er seine Strafe schon abgesessen, auf den billigen Triumph einer
> Revisionsverhandlung verzichtet, deren Ausgang zu seinen Gunsten überhaupt
> nicht mehr zweifelhaft sein kann, der nur vor dem Gesindel Ruhe haben will,
> mit dem er es zu tun hat und sich im übrigen durchaus nicht nach Ruhe,
> sondern nach wirklicher *Arbeit* sehnt.[14]

Schnitzler applauds the humanity of the play's title figure, a respected specialist in internal medicine and director of the charitably funded Elisabethinum hospital, in refusing to allow a Roman Catholic priest to administer the last rites to a young woman who has no idea that, following a botched abortion, she is dying of septicaemia. He also admires Bernhardi for standing firm in the ensuing scandal, which includes the resignation of the hospital's trustees, an attempted power grab by his deputy Ebenwald, questions in parliament, a court case and a two-month prison sentence after Bernhardi is found guilty of obstructing religious observance ('Religionsstörung'). The professor's steadfast convictions stand in contrast to the political flip-flops of the Education Minister, his erstwhile friend and medical colleague Flint. In his aversion to political showboating and commitment to medicine as a scientific discipline and a humanitarian practice Bernhardi can be seen to embody liberal, Enlightenment values, to exemplify what in his 'Silvesterbetrachtungen' Schnitzler calls 'das bißchen Edelsinn' amidst 'die Masse Erbärmlichkeit, die das Wesen des Menschentums auszumachen scheint'.[15]

Despite the personal integrity of its title figure, this play should not be exempted from Ritchie Robertson's observation that 'Schnitzler's work seethes with problems'.[16] Bernhardi's attempt to stand aloof from politics is wilfully naïve and, although he acts with the best of intentions in denying the priest access and wants only to spare his patient an anguished death, the confrontation between doctor and priest generates a surprising role reversal:

> by a supreme irony, the priest was acting in the spirit of the Enlightenment
> by treating his charge as an autonomous human being; while Bernhardi, in
> leaving her under an illusion, was acting in the paternalistic manner supposed
> by Enlighteners to be characteristic of a clerical elite.[17]

The purpose of this essay is not to revisit the tendentiousness of *Professor Bernhardi*, which has been intensively debated and led to the play being banned from performance in Austria until 1918,[18] but to seek out a few more of its 'problems' and in so doing explore Schnitzler's continued engagement with medical politics, ethics and sociology. His interrogation of humanitarianism will be shown to bear comparison with that of fellow doctor's son Michel Foucault, while the work of feminist philosopher Moira Gatens helps to shed critical light on the corporeal metaphors through which Schnitzler's characters conceptualize the genealogy and institutional structure of the Elisabethinum. My reading of the published text of *Professor Bernhardi* will be supplemented by insights drawn from archival materials that are part of the forthcoming digital critical edition.

II

The first act of *Professor Bernhardi* depicts the everyday workings of a hospital around 1900. It presents doctor-centred medicine of the kind addressed by Foucault in *The Birth of the Clinic* (1963): the dialogue foregrounds the management and bureaucratic regulation of the medical institution, together with the practice of medicine as a scientific discipline. The play begins with the medical student Hochroitzpointner and the nurse Sister Ludmilla, the two characters whose false testimony will lead to Bernhardi's incarceration, discussing offstage events: a dissection taking place in a basement mortuary and the aforementioned abortion victim, who is dying in an adjoining room. They give palliative care and simultaneously place her in administrative and scientific frames of reference, as a death certificate to be prepared and a future dissection. As Foucault explains in a chapter headed 'Open Up a Few Corpses', pathological anatomy became the bedrock of nineteenth-century medicine, the cardinal source of knowledge and therefore power.[19] By contrast, technologies for internal investigation of the living body remained rudimentary, leaving doctors to rely on what Foucault calls 'a fine sensibility'[20] or, as Bernhardi's antagonist Ebenwald grudgingly concedes: 'Intuition heißt man das! Diagnostischen Scharfblick!'.[21] Schnitzler's aptly named pathologist Adler indeed dismisses internal medicine as a process of 'im Dunkeln herumtappen' (BER, 35), anticipating Foucault's contention that, from a clinical perspective, 'the living night is dissipated in the brightness of death'.[22]

At the start of *Professor Bernhardi* the staff of the Elisabethinum are completely 'in the dark' about the backstory of the young woman who is dying following an abortion. She remains unnamed until the press callously 'out' her as Philomena Beier in the third act and is repeatedly referred to as 'die Sepsis' (BER, 9, 12, 13). She has had no visitors in three days, is apparently without family and has volunteered no information about her circumstances. In Schnitzler's first typescript draft, she is quoted as saying 'dass sie die alleinig Schuldige ist., [sic] dass sie niemanden mit hinein ziehen will' (BER_K5_T1_0037),[23] but the published text contains no such admission, and Bernhardi takes it upon himself to guard the secrets of the living body, first from the state and its juridical power and then from the Catholic Church. His power struggle with the first of these institutions has received far less critical attention than his stand-off with the second.

When Hochroitzpointner asks what will be recorded as the cause of death, Bernhardi refuses to go beyond 'Sepsis' (BER, 14). Even though septicaemia is by definition a wound infection, he insists that, as there is no visible wound on the living body, the cause of infection can only be conjectured. In the early twentieth century, abortion was illegal in Austria as in many other countries — and indeed remained so until 1975. Bernhardi's actions potentially contravene §359 of the Austrian penal code (the *Strafgesetz* of 1852), which required doctors to report suspicious deaths, with non-compliance attracting a fine of between 10 and 100 guilders.[24] The criminal status of abortion probably explains why, when Bernhardi asks whether the young woman's lover has visited, his assistant Kurt Pflugfelder replies: 'Der wird sich hüten' (BER, 21). Again under the Austrian penal code,

§145 states that a failed abortion is punishable with between six and twelve months' imprisonment; if the intervention achieves its objective, the woman can expect between one and five years of 'schwerer Kerker', and §146 specifies that, if the father of the child is complicit in procuring the abortion, the same punishment is liable to be meted out to him, 'jedoch mit Verschärfung'. Given that, in bodily terms, the patient is paying the ultimate price for her actions, whatever they were, one might be tempted to applaud Bernhardi's kindness in not making the medical case into a legal one.

That Bernhardi exerts agency within juridical structures intended to bind the medical profession to the state anticipates, and is no less ambiguous than, his more dramatic confrontation with the priest. Although the priest explicitly distances himself from the state's sovereign power to punish the body, remarking that he has come to offer the solace of faith, not to pronounce a death sentence (BER, 44), the news of his arrival does cause the patient anguish and hastens her end. Viewed in Foucauldian terms, the priest's quip is anachronistic: contrary to what he suggests, the modern penal system addresses itself not primarily to the body but to what, in *Discipline and Punish* (1975), Foucault terms the 'soul', the 'effect and instrument of a political anatomy'.[25] Correctional systems of punishment focus not merely on the crime but also on the impulses that led to it and attempt to foster a capacity for reflection and remorse potentially akin to that invoked by the priest: 'Sie können nicht wissen, ob nicht irgendwo in der Tiefe ihrer Seele, die Gott allein sieht, gerade in diesen letzten Augenblicken, die ihr noch vergönnt sind, die Sehnsucht wach ist, durch eine letzte Beichte aller Sünden sich zu entlasten' (BER, 46). In addition to the ironic role reversal highlighted by Robertson, one might suggest that, in quizzing the young woman about the causes of her illness, the medical staff, and especially Bernhardi, have taken on the priestly role and are attempting to extract a secular sexual confession.[26] Indeed Bernhardi responds to the priest's insistence that the patient may wish to make confession in terms that suggest she already has: 'Sie ist heiter, glücklich und — reuelos' (BER, 46). What he arguably fails to take into consideration is that she may be withholding information from him because she fears collusion between doctor and state.

In the light of Bernhardi's apparent kindness in refusing to cite abortion as the cause of death, his first words once the priest has left the stage are unexpectedly callous. Turning to the pathologist, he says: 'Also morgen früh, lieber Doktor Adler, die Sektion' (BER, 49). If he has already decided that septicaemia will be given as the cause of death, then why dissect? Must the dead body reveal to the pathologist's eagle eyes the truths that have been withheld from state and Church? On this reading, Bernhardi would be flaunting the hospital's independence from state power by acquiring greater knowledge and refusing to share it. This suspicion is supported by his apparently solicitous question whether the young woman has had any visitors. As Tatjana Buklijas explains in a fascinating if at times grisly doctoral thesis, Habsburg law had stipulated since the reign of Maria Theresa that unclaimed bodies of persons who died in public hospitals could be used for research and teaching purposes, as so-called *Studienleichen*.[27] Applying this regulation to a charitably funded policlinic, Schnitzler's play makes the juxtaposition of caring physician and cold dissectionist all the more shocking by putting aside the forty-eight hours within which families were required to claim the body and pay church taxes (*Stolgebühren*, literally surplice fees). That the bodies of executed criminals were dissected was customary in many countries; in Schnitzler's play dissection appears to be a punishment for poverty and social isolation, as well as being the price of Bernhardi's solicitude towards the living body.

In the first act of *Professor Bernhardi*, Schnitzler pays considerable attention to the bureaucratic regulation of the medical institution, the fragmentation of modern state power and the ambiguous ways in which Bernhardi exerts agency within those frameworks. Furthermore, the entanglement of medical institutions in the power mechanisms of the state leaves only limited room for empathy on the part of the individual practitioner, a restriction that is compounded by the competing demands of humanitarianism and scientific research.

III

With the introduction in Act II of the clinician-turned-politician Flint, who as Education Minister first defends Bernhardi against clerical opprobrium and then abandons him to what Foucault terms the 'carceral' power of the state, attention shifts from individual to collective bodies as sites of care and control. At their first meeting, Flint endeavours to win Bernhardi's practical and moral support for a catalogue of academic and bio-political reforms 'auf dem Gebiete des medizinischen Unterrichtes, der sozialen Hygiene, der allgemeinen Volksbildung'. Although he immediately trivializes this list by adding 'na, und so weiter' (BER, 94), it is worth examining these policy areas in their original socio-historical context, as their inclusion generates unresolved complexities in the body politics of the published text, and particularly the first item on the ministerial agenda — reform of the medical curriculum — is elaborated more fully in Schnitzler's first draft, in a manner that unmistakably builds on his earlier concern with the politics and sociology of Viennese medicine.

In the later nineteenth century, the curriculum of the Vienna Medical School, and in particular the balance between scientific research training and practical medicine, was much discussed. The curriculum was overhauled in 1872, when 'Doktor der gesamten Heilkunde' became the sole medical degree. However, as a rapidly expanding list of specialisms competed for teaching time, the value of pre-clinical studies in the natural sciences was increasingly questioned, while rising student numbers meant that ever more teaching was delivered in the lecture hall rather than at the bedside.[28] Consequently, as Schnitzler observes in his 1887 commentary on patient care and working conditions at the Allgemeines Krankenhaus, 'die Mehrzahl der promovierten Doktoren sieht am Ende ihrer vorgeschriebenen Studien weise ein, daß sie für die Praxis eigentlich blutwenig gelernt haben; daß sie zu ihrer weiteren Ausbildung noch im Krankenhause verweilen müssen, um hier praktische Dienste zu tun'.[29] Only a minority go directly into general practice, often out of financial necessity. In 1896 a curricular review recommended that newly qualified doctors should be obliged to spend at least one year working in public hospitals and receive appropriate remuneration.[30] Although welcomed by professional bodies, this recommendation was not enacted along with other measures in 1900 but continued to be publicly discussed, especially after a similar policy took effect in Hungary in 1902.[31]

In *Professor Bernhardi*, Schnitzler links Flint's plans for curricular reform to the figure of Dr Feuermann, an old friend of Bernhardi's son and assistant, Oskar. Feuermann, who is identified as Jewish, appears in Acts II and V of the play. Oskar recalls that, as a student, Feuermann subsisted on fifteen or twenty guilders a month (little more than Schnitzler quotes as the salary of a nurse in the 1880s), earned by working part-time alongside his studies, and had no choice but to go into general practice immediately after qualification. He is now facing a charge of medical incompetence after a patient in his care died in childbirth and, if found guilty, will be struck off. Feuermann is ultimately acquitted thanks to the vanity of the play's gynaecologist, Professor Filitz, who chooses (for self-serving reasons) to parade a lack of racial prejudice by defending him, 'trotzdem er Jude ist' (BER, 67). Whereas in the published text of *Professor Bernhardi* Flint announces without further explanation that Feuermann's 'geringfügige Angelegenheit' is inspiring 'eine gründliche Reform der medizinischen Studienordnung' (BER, 217–18), in the typescript draft Schnitzler makes a more explicit connection to contemporary medical politics. He has Filitz recommend in his report on Feuermann's case that newly qualified doctors should spend *two* years in hospital medicine before embarking on general practice. This recommendation is endorsed by Flint, who makes 'Lex Feuermann' (BER_K5_T1_0723) his key proposal for curricular reform.

That Schnitzler's inexperienced country doctor is Jewish adds further complexities to this plot strand. Feuermann's misfortunes can be read in the light of views expressed by Theodor Billroth in *Über das Lehren und Lernen der medicinischen Wissenschaften an den Universitäten der Deutschen Nation, nebst allgemeinen Bemerkungen über Universitäten* (1875), a hotly debated treatise on medical education. Billroth, who held one of Vienna's two Chairs of Surgery, was outspoken in his criticism of the many impoverished Jewish students from the Habsburg Empire's eastern territories who, in the years following emancipation, embarked on a medical degree at the University of Vienna. Too many of them, in his view, had a poor command of German and were academically ill-prepared, problems that were exacerbated by the need to do paid work alongside their studies. While some commentators have read Billroth's stance as antisemitic, others view it as evidence of his social and economic elitism, of a resistance to diversity of any kind within the medical profession.[32] Schnitzler has Feuermann tell Filitz, 'ich habe alle meine Prüfungen mit Auszeichnung bestanden, sogar in Geburtshilfe' (BER, 59), and presents his predicament unequivocally as a result of inexperience and economic constraints rather than incompetence. If Flint institutes '[d]ie obligaten zwei Spitalsjahre' (BER_K5_T1_0721), or indeed any other toughening of requirements, without improving the remuneration of junior doctors, the likes of Feuermann will find a medical degree beyond their reach, and the profession will become even more socially — and racially — exclusive.

In stepping back from this explicitly political stance in the published text of *Professor Bernhardi*, Schnitzler considerably reduces the role of Feuermann, making Flint's plans seem all the more devoid of substance and leaving a number of ominous but tantalizingly underdeveloped parallels and contrasts between Feuermann and Bernhardi. Most obviously, both are at the mercy of disciplinary and judicial systems warped by antisemitism. Paradoxically, Feuermann, who bears at least some responsibility for the death of a patient, is acquitted, while Bernhardi, who does not, is imprisoned. Feuermann's initial hope that Bernhardi might use his case to draw public attention to 'die unglückseligen materiellen Verhältnisse der jungen Ärzte, [...] die Schwierigkeiten in der Landpraxis' (BER, 57), is sadly misplaced and his plight in the final act, boycotted by patients despite his acquittal and pleading to be transferred elsewhere in the Empire, is an indictment of both individual and systemic failings.

In the absence of further contextualization, what Flint's references to 'soziale Hygiene' and 'allgemeine Volksbildung' most readily call to mind are anatomo-political strategies targeting major issues in public health — for example, improvements to insanitary housing, the provision of clean water, or measures to combat tuberculosis (long known as the *Wiener Krankheit*), alcoholism and sexually transmitted diseases.[33] While the water supply is the key concern in Ibsen's *A Public Enemy* (1882), with which *Professor Bernhardi* has often been compared, not least by Ritchie Robertson,[34] the play's many allusions to syphilis (which would have been more obvious in 1912 than they are nowadays) suggest that, as explored in Foucault's introduction to the first volume of his *History of Sexuality* (1976), the mechanisms of state power are to be brought to bear on the life of the sexualized body, while 'allgemeine Volksbildung' evokes a 'biopolitics of the population', promoting forms of self-discipline conducive to the preservation of health.[35]

Professor Bernhardi incorporates numerous references to syphilis. The staff of the Elisabethinum includes Tugendvetter as 'Professor für Hautkrankheiten', a specialism that in the early twentieth century included the treatment of venereal diseases (which often have a rash or skin lesions as primary symptoms); when he is called out 'zu einem ang'steckten Fürsten' (BER, 18), he is replaced in the lecture hall by his assistant Wenger, whose 'Serumarbeit' (BER, 28) is most obviously concerned with the treatment of syphilis, the causative bacteria of which were identified in 1905. The disease also impacts on other specialisms: Adler mentions autopsying a patient with 'Tabes' (BER, 31; *tabes dorsalis* is a symptom of tertiary syphilis); the neurologist Cyprian refers to a 'Paralytiker' (BER, 37), suggesting paresis due, again, to late-stage syphilis; and Bernhardi reminds Flint that the life of a patient called Engelbert Wagner might have been extended, had he advocated for 'eine andere (antiluetische) Behandlung' (BER, 98). On the basis of this evidence, sexually transmitted diseases account for a significant fraction of the hospital's work. Although frequent, the references are surprisingly low-key; the doctors treat the symptoms without moralizing or philosophizing and, as I have argued elsewhere, Schnitzler resists the temptation to use the disease, or indeed the septicaemia case, as an explicit metaphor for wider social or political ills, an approach that would have made the play tendentious in ways that he was at pains to avoid.[36]

The connection between Flint's public health agenda and the many allusions to syphilis in *Professor Bernhardi* can therefore only be conjectured. Müller-Seidel hypothesizes on the basis of a comparable lack of respect for the individual life that Flint's approach to 'soziale Hygiene' is no less ominous than that of the eugenicist Berthold Stauber in *Der Weg ins Freie* (1908).[37] Schnitzler's only tentative elaboration of the motif comes in the first typescript draft, where he has Flint propose to institute covert 'hygienisch-sanitäre Inspektionsreisen' (BER_K5_T1_0249), comparing them to Harun al-Rashid's incognito wanderings through Baghdad in *One Thousand and One Nights*. In the Austrian context this glimpse of an oppressive surveillance culture also brings to mind the enlightened despotism of Joseph II, who restlessly toured his Empire, inspecting political, military and social conditions. At the point when Flint canvasses Bernhardi's support for his plans, Schnitzler's title figure has much else on his mind, and he is understandably reluctant to engage with any part of the minister's reform agenda, which at the very least would further entangle the medical profession and him personally in the power mechanisms of the state. In this he is more cautious than his normally clear-sighted ally Cyprian, who seems flattered by Flint's remark that he prefers to work with 'Menschen, nicht Beamte' (BER, 80). It is indeed implicit in Flint's insistence to Bernhardi that their skills and personalities are complementary that he hopes to use his former friend as the caring medical face of state control.

IV

Schnitzler does not implicate Bernhardi in Flint's ominous body politics. However, Bernhardi's use of corporeal metaphors to conceptualize and negotiate the interpersonal dynamics of the Elisabethinum is considerably more problematic, revealing some of the weaknesses of the humanitarian project and by extension also of liberal Enlightenment. As any doctor knows, and as Moira Gatens points out, images of 'the human body', such as those in anatomical textbooks, are not gender-neutral; they are of men's or women's bodies. By extension, metaphorical bodies are inescapably gendered and conventionally gendered male.[38] A classic example of this gendering is the passage in Thomas Hobbes's *Leviathan* (1651) which glosses the book's famous frontispiece:

> by art is created that great *leviathan* called a *commonwealth*, or *state*, in Latin *civitas*, which is but an artificial man; though of greater stature and strength than the natural, for whose protection and defence it was intended; and in which the *sovereignty* is an artificial *soul*, as giving life and motion to the whole body; the *magistrates*, and other *officers* of judicature and execution, artificial *joints*; *reward* and *punishment*, by which fastened to the seat of sovereignty every joint and member is moved to perform his duty, are the *nerves*, that do the same in the body natural; and *wealth* and *riches* of all the particular members are the *strength*; *salus populi*, the people's safety, its *business*; *counsellors*, by whom all things needful for it to know are suggested unto it, are the *memory*; *equity* and *laws*, an artificial *reason* and *will*; *concord*, *health*; *sedition*, *sickness*; and *civil war*, *death*. Lastly the *pacts* and *covenants*, by which the parts of this body politic were at first made, set together, and united, resemble that *fiat*, or the *let us make man*, pronounced by God in the creation.[39]

In Foucauldian terms the 'artificial man' is a form of bio-power, a means of prolonging, safeguarding and improving lives that would otherwise be 'solitary, poor, nasty, brutish and short'.[40]

According to Gatens, the Hobbesian body politic is called into being by 'the pacts and covenants made by men and between men' and is 'based on an image of a *masculine* body which reflects fantasies about the value and capacities of that body'.[41] These include a capacity for reason and for self-sacrifice in defence of the commonwealth. In *Professor Bernhardi*, the genealogy of the Elisabethinum, established fifteen years previously, is repeatedly recalled by its founding trio of Bernhardi, Cyprian and Tugendvetter, especially when its survival is threatened. Tugendvetter remembers it as a youthful masculinist adventure, quoting the opening line of the folksong, 'Es ritten drei Reiter zum Tore hinaus … wie?' (BER, 29). Cyprian, by contrast, foregrounds Bernhardi's progenitive power, likening the hospital to Bernhardi's son Oskar:

> Überlege doch nur! Würdest du nur einen Moment zögern, ein so kleines Opfer deiner Eitelkeit zu bringen, wenn es sich zum Beispiel um die Zukunft deines Oskar handelte? Und so ein Werk wie das Elisabethinum ist am Ende auch nicht viel Geringeres als ein Kind. Es ist doch hauptsächlich dein Werk, wenn ich auch an deiner Seite gestanden bin. (BER, 79)

Just as the Leviathan was created by an act of will, so the Elisabethinum was Bernhardi's brainchild. I use that term deliberately because, for Gatens, the absence of a female contribution to the genesis of the body politic recalls the myth of Zeus swallowing Metis and giving birth to Athena out of his own head.[42] Somewhat ironically, the Roman version of this masculinist fantasy is cited in the typescript draft of *Professor Bernhardi* as an example of an atavistic belief that should not be accorded respect in a scientific age (BER_K5_T1_0609-0611).

Gendered metaphorical bodies abound in references to the institutional structures of the Elisabethinum. The teaching staff ('Lehrkörper' [BER, 137]) is exclusively male, as is the board of trustees, another 'artificial man' that melds together two princes, a bishop, a banker and a senior civil servant to form a committee that acts and ultimately resigns '*in corpore*' (BER, 71). Whereas in the typescript draft the board of trustees is chaired by the hospital's chief fundraiser, Princess Stixenstein, handwritten corrections reassign that role to her husband, leaving her merely to preside over the hospital ball (BER_K5_T1_0163). Nonetheless, as Evelyne Polt-Heinzl points out, the Princess is the first of the hospital's supporters to resign in protest at Bernhardi's actions, an example of a woman participating by whatever means are open to her in the life of the body politic.[43] Convinced that the Elisabethinum can only face down its opponents if its staff behave as a 'Körperschaft' (BER, 136), Bernhardi signals his commitment to that ideal in performative terms, through his preference for the egalitarian address form 'Herr Kollega' rather than the plethora of hierarchical academic titles favoured by other figures in the play.[44]

In contrast to the Hobbesian 'natural man', who generates a supersized version of himself for protection, Bernhardi creates in the Elisabethinum a child-woman to be protected and nurtured, aptly naming his brainchild in honour of Empress

Elisabeth, the troubled spouse of Emperor Franz Joseph I, who was assassinated in 1898. The hospital's newest appointment, Wenger, is quick to embrace this gendered perspective, declaring that, despite the parliamentary question, 'das Elisabethinum steht fleckenlos und rein da' (BER, 133). Institutional honour is conceptualized in terms of sexual purity. While the folksong quoted by Tugendvetter (above) goes on to tell of parting from a sweetheart ('Feinsliebchen das schaute zum Fenster hinaus, ade!'), the fondly recalled act of medical secession can be viewed in Oedipal terms, as allowing a group of ambitious young doctors to liberate themselves from the Vienna Medical School and seek intellectual nourishment elsewhere. Feuermann, by contrast, attributes his professional failings to not having had the opportunity 'sich im Spital weiter ausbilden zu können, an den Brüsten der *alma mater* Kurse zu hören — ' (BER, 55).

Gatens's observation that the metaphor of the unified body politic 'belongs to a dream of equity, based on corporeal interchangeability, that was developed to the full in nineteenth-century liberalism' is highly relevant for *Professor Bernhardi*, in as far as the play sheds light on the failure of that dream and some of its aporias.[45] As in the Hobbesian body politic, any voice that speaks from a position of bodily difference is logically excluded. Hence, women are either animalized or reduced to their sex. Despite the hospital's reliance on her fundraising skills, Bernhardi mocks Princess Stixenstein as a 'durchlauchtigste[] Gans' (BER, 70) and responds petulantly to the news that Sister Ludmilla, whose false testimony helped to convict him, has admitted her perjury in the confessional and been urged by the priest to make amends. While Bernhardi failed to extract a secular confession from his dying patient, somewhat ironically, this more traditional 'confessing animal' opens the way for a retrial.[46] Rather than respecting the honest self-examination that has been fostered by the discipline of confession, his response is to shift from accused to expert witness, wanting to disqualify the nurse's testimony on the grounds that she is 'schwer hysterisch und unzurechnungsfähig' (BER, 246).

The masculinist dream of equity and collegiality that for Bernhardi underpins the medical enterprise — one body, one voice, one reason — takes for granted exclusion on the basis of biological gender but fails to acknowledge its vulnerability to racial difference. To quote Judith Butler, '[t]he body politic is posited as a unity it can never be'.[47] Bernhardi's antagonist Ebenwald attacks him with his own weapons when he argues that Tugendvetter's Jewish assistant Wenger is unsuited to succeed him as head of dermatology because 'in einer Korporation' (BER, 90) the talents of the individual are not the only concern. Elsewhere Ebenwald draws attention to the 'Jargon der Seele' (BER, 19) that supposedly marks out the Jewish voice as different and therefore inappropriate to this univocal institutional body. However, bodily semiotics in *Professor Bernhardi* are more ambiguous than Ebenwald admits: for example, the list of doctors with duelling scars includes Adler, the son of a Jewish father and non-Jewish mother, and Ebenwald's protégé Schreimann, a Catholic convert and former regimental doctor whose 'voice' oscillates between Yiddish-inflected German and what the stage direction terms '[a]uffallend tiefes, biederes Bierdeutsch' (BER, 116).

In the figure of the Jewish paediatrician Löwenstein, who by Schnitzler's own admission is 'beinahe karikaturistisch gesehen', the discourses of race and gender come together to striking effect.[48] One of Bernhardi's most fervent admirers, Löwenstein displays a number of traits and behaviours that Sander Gilman in *The Jew's Body* (1991) associates with male hysteria.[49] An excitable figure, and prone to over-dramatization, he appears in the second, third and fourth acts of the play, and on each occasion rushes breathlessly onto the stage: first with news that Princess Stixenstein has resigned as patroness of the hospital ball; then to update colleagues on events in parliament; and finally running after Professor Pflugfelder to find out the court's verdict on Bernhardi. Schnitzler's revisions to the play heighten the sense that Löwenstein is a body that is never in the right place and that he is perpetually struggling to keep up with the pace of events. In both of the surviving typescript drafts, news of Flint's parliamentary volte-face is delivered not by Löwenstein (as in the published text) but by Bernhardi's non-Jewish assistant Kurt Pflugfelder, who has taken detailed shorthand notes. Consequently he gives a far more orderly report than the breathless Löwenstein, who is admonished: 'Lieber Kollega Löwenstein, versuchen Sie doch möglichst im Zusammenhang — ' (BER, 147). In Act IV a wonderfully comic exchange with the hypermasculine Kurt Pflugfelder further underscores Löwenstein's feminized status. When he discovers that Kurt has been fined for calling Hochroitzpointner a liar in court and may even duel with him, he is delighted:

> LÖWENSTEIN: Lieber Doktor Pflugfelder, darf ich Ihnen auch einen Kuß geben?
> KURT: Danke bestens, Herr Dozent, ich betrachte ihn als genossen. (BER, 172)

In a play that is punctuated by firm manly handshakes, Kurt has just been the recipient of its most effusive gesture of affection — a hug from his father — and politely declines further intimacies. Within the masculinist institution, Löwenstein unmistakably represents the feminized Jewish Other.

While Bernhardi and his supporters are accepting of this unthreatening diversity, Bernhardi's response to any serious opposition is to hark back to the discourse of masculinity that underpinned the founding of the Elisabethinum, for example challenging Ebenwald to reveal his scheming with the words: 'Wenn Sie ein Mann sind, Herr Professor Ebenwald, so werden Sie antworten' (BER, 154). A similar tactic is employed by Professor Pflugfelder in the emotional plea to his colleagues that forms the rhetorical highpoint of Act III. For him, Bernhardi is not a hero but simply a man: 'Und von Ihnen, meine Herren, verlange ich nichts anderes, als daß Sie dieses bescheidenen Ruhmestitels gleichfalls würdig wären' (BER, 165). To restore institutional solidarity is to reaffirm the masculinist principle of corporeal interchangeability.

Schnitzler appears to have had considerable sympathy with Pflugfelder's sentiments. In January 1913, he defends Bernhardi in the following terms:

> [Bernhardi] hat in einem bestimmten Fall einfach seine ärztliche Pflicht getan, ohne die Spur einer demonstrativen Nebenabsicht, lehnt es konsequent ab sich

in irgend eine politische Rolle drängen zu lassen; benimmt sich jedoch, ohne ein Kämpfer zu sein, jederzeit als Mann; und ohne jemals seiner Würde zu vergeben strebt er dem seiner Natur gemäßen Ziele zu, so bald als möglich wieder als Arzt und Gelehrter leben und wirken zu dürfen.⁵⁰

What Schnitzler presents as the protagonist's virtues might equally well be seen as contributing to the complexities and ambiguities of *Professor Bernhardi*. In doing what he regards as his professional duty, Bernhardi challenges the power not only of the Church but also of the state. However, confession is not rendered obsolete but secularized, and Bernhardi's immediate appropriation of the dead body in the name of medical research sits uncomfortably with his earlier solicitude. In his first typescript draft, Schnitzler's depiction of the hapless Feuermann testifies to a continuing critical engagement with the politics, sociology and economics of Viennese medicine. But the published play, like Bernhardi himself, steps back from activism, leaving both that sub-plot and the nature of Flint's biopolitical aspirations tantalizingly underdeveloped. In endorsing the professor's planned return to academic and practical medicine and commending Bernhardi for comporting himself 'als Mann', Schnitzler tacitly acknowledges that his protagonist's retreat from the political fray could be viewed in less flattering terms, but at the same time keeps faith with a liberal ideal that was always exclusionary in terms of gender and in the early twentieth century was becoming ever more untenable.

Notes to Chapter 8

1. Arthur Schnitzler, *Jugend in Wien: Eine Autobiographie* (Vienna: Molden, 1968), p. 190.
2. Arthur Schnitzler, *Tagebuch 1879–1931*, ed. by Werner Welzig with Peter Michael Braunwarth and others for the Kommission für literarische Gebrauchsformen der Österreichischen Akademie der Wissenschaften, 10 vols (Vienna: Verlag der Österreichischen Akademie der Wissenschaften, 1981–2000). Entries for 27 October 1879, 9 May 1886 and 17 January 1890.
3. Horst Thomé, 'Vorwort', in Arthur Schnitzler, *Medizinische Schriften*, ed. by Thomé (Vienna: Zsolnay, 1988), pp. 11–59 (pp. 11–13).
4. See, for example, Laura Otis, 'The Language of Infection: Disease and Identity in Schnitzler's *Reigen*', *Germanic Review*, 70 (1995), 65–75; Caroline Welsh, 'Euthanasie, Lebenswille, Patiententäuschung: Arthur Schnitzlers literarische Reflexionen im Kontext zeitgenössischer Medizin und Literatur', *Jahrbuch der deutschen Schillergesellschaft*, 55 (2011), 275–306; Marie Kolkenbrock, 'Gothic Infections: Arthur Schnitzler and the Haunted Culture of Modernism', *Modern Language Review*, 113 (2018), 147–67; Christiane Arndt, 'Calculating Death in Arthur Schnitzler's Novella *Sterben*', *Germanic Review*, 94 (2019), 299–325. Wide-ranging but more conventional in its medical emphases is Dirk von Boetticher, *Meine Werke sind lauter Diagnosen: Über die ärztliche Dimension im Werk Arthur Schnitzlers* (Heidelberg: Winter, 1999).
5. A. S. [Arthur Schnitzler], 'Die Zustände im k. k. allgemeinen Krankenhause in Wien', in Schnitzler, *Medizinische Schriften*, pp. 103–11 (p. 105).
6. Arthur Schnitzler, 'Londoner Briefe (Original-Korrespondenz der "Internationalen Klinischen Rundschau")', in Schnitzler, *Medizinische Schriften*, pp. 149–64 (p. 160).
7. Ibid., p. 164.
8. Schnitzler, *Jugend in Wien*, p. 300.
9. A. S. [Arthur Schnitzler], 'Sylvesterbetrachtungen', in Schnitzler, *Medizinische Schriften*, pp. 173–76 (p. 175).
10. Ibid., p. 176.
11. Walter Müller-Seidel, 'Arztbilder im Wandel: Zum literarischen Werk Arthur Schnitzlers.

Vorgetragen am 3. November 1995', *Bayerische Akademie der Wissenschaften: Philosophisch-historische Klasse. Sitzungsberichte* (1997), no. 6, 3–82 (pp. 21–32).
12. Ibid., p. 60.
13. Schnitzler's 'anticritical' reflections on *Professor Bernhardi* are included in the forthcoming digital critical edition of the play. Arthur Schnitzler, *Professor Bernhardi*, ed. by Judith Beniston with Gregor Babelotzky and others, in *Arthur Schnitzler digital. Digitale historisch-kritische Edition (Werke 1905–1931)*, ed. by Wolfgang Lukas, Michael Scheffel, Andrew Webber and Judith Beniston, in collaboration with Thomas Burch, 2018– (https://www.cam.ac.uk/Schnitzler-Edition). References to archival materials follow the model of this edition. Schnitzler defends Bernhardi in the documents BER_K5_P^{T}10, BER_K5_P^{T}13, BER_K5_P^{T}14 and BER_K5_P^{T}16.
14. Arthur Schnitzler, *Briefe 1913–1931*, ed. by Peter Michael Braunwarth and others (Frankfurt a.M.: Fischer, 1984), letter to Heinz Salfner, 20 March 1930, p. 668 (emphasis in original). Schnitzler's most detailed reflection on *Professor Bernhardi* is a letter to Richard Charmatz, 4 January 1913, ibid., pp. 1–6.
15. A. S., 'Sylvesterbetrachtungen', p. 173.
16. Ritchie Robertson, *The 'Jewish Question' in German Literature 1749–1939: Emancipation and its Discontents* (Oxford: Oxford University Press, 1999), p. 94.
17. Ibid., p. 109. For Robertson's critical reading of *Professor Bernhardi*, see pp. 105–12.
18. See Judith Beniston, 'Schnitzler and the Place of Tendentious Drama: *Professor Bernhardi*', *Austrian Studies*, 27 (2019): *Placing Schnitzler*, ed. by Judith Beniston and Andrew Webber, 195–209.
19. Michel Foucault, *The Birth of the Clinic: An Archaeology of Medical Perception*, trans. by A. M. Sheridan (London: Tavistock Publications, 1973; repr. London: Routledge Classics, 2003), ch. 8.
20. Ibid., p. 149.
21. Arthur Schnitzler, *Professor Bernhardi*, in *Arthur Schnitzler digital*, reading text, p. 17. References to this edition, which is based on the first print (Berlin: Fischer, 1912), are henceforth given as 'BER' followed by the page number.
22. Foucault, *The Birth of the Clinic*, p. 180.
23. On the play's genesis, see *Professor Bernhardi*, 'Entstehungsgeschichte' and 'Chronologie', in *Arthur Schnitzler digital*. Two typescript drafts (K5_T1 and K5_T2) survive, the second in fragmentary form.
24. *Das österreichische Strafgesetz über Vergehen, Verbrechen und Übertretungen* (1852). The authoritative text is available from the Österreichische Nationalbibliothek (http://alex.onb.ac.at/), Kaiserliches Patent vom 27. Mai 1852 (wirksam ab 1. September 1852), *Allgemeines Reichs- Gesetz- und Regierungsblatt für das Kaiserthum Oesterreich* (1852), pp. 493–591. References are identified by paragraph number.
25. Michel Foucault, *Discipline and Punish: The Birth of the Prison*, trans. by Alan Sheridan (London: Allen Lane, 1977), p. 30.
26. On the proliferation of secular confessional discourses and the power relations within which they operate, see Michel Foucault, *The History of Sexuality*, trans. by Robert Hurley, 3 vols (New York: Pantheon Books, 1978–86), I: *The Will to Knowledge*, especially Part III: 'Scientia Sexualis', pp. 55–76.
27. Tatjana Buklijas, 'Dissection, Discipline and Urban Transformation: Anatomy at the University of Vienna, 1845–1914' (unpublished doctoral thesis, University of Cambridge, 2006), especially Chapter 2.
28. See Erna Lesky, *Die Wiener Medizinische Schule im 19. Jahrhundert* (Graz: Böhlau, 1965), pp. 299–306.
29. A. S., 'Die Zustände im k. k. allgemeinen Krankenhause in Wien', pp. 106–07.
30. See *Gutachten und Anträge zur Reform der medicinischen Studien- und Rigorosen-Ordnung*. Erstattet von den medicinischen Facultäten der österreichischen Universitäten (Vienna: K. K. Universitäts-Buchdruckerei Karl Gorischek, 1894), pp. 25–28. The review's recommendations were summarized in the Viennese press. See, for example, *Wiener Zeitung*, 23 January 1896, pp. 1–2.
31. See Anon., 'Die obligatorische Spitalspraxis', *Neue Freie Presse*, 28 March 1902, Abendblatt, p. 1.
32. For contrasting readings, see Tatjana Buklijas, 'Surgery and National Identity in Late

Nineteenth-Century Vienna', *Studies in History and Philosophy of Biological and Biomedical Sciences*, 38 (2007), 756–74 (pp. 763–69) and Felicitas Seebacher, *Das Fremde im 'deutschen' Tempel der Wissenschaften: Brüche in der Wissenschaftskultur der Medizinischen Fakultät der Universität Wien* (Vienna: Verlag der Österreichischen Akademie der Wissenschaften, 2011), pp. 97–124.

33. On the contemporary understanding of 'soziale Hygiene', see the account of the Allgemeine Hygienische Ausstellung, held in Vienna in 1906, in Alys X. George, *The Naked Truth: Viennese Modernism and the Body* (Chicago and London: University of Chicago Press, 2020), pp. 44–49.
34. Robertson, pp. 106–07. For an early comparison, see B. Z. [Berta Zuckerkandl], 'Professor Bernardi' [sic], *Wiener Allgemeine Zeitung*, 2 December 1912, pp. 4–6 (p. 4). Zuckerkandl is reviewing the public reading of *Professor Bernhardi* given in Vienna on 28 November 1912, simultaneously with the play's Berlin premiere.
35. Foucault, *The History of Sexuality*, I, 142.
36. See Beniston, 'Schnitzler and the Place of Tendentious Drama', especially pp. 204–07.
37. Müller-Seidel, pp. 53–58.
38. Moira Gatens, 'Corporeal Representation in/and the Body Politic', in Gatens, *Imaginary Bodies: Ethics, Power and Corporeality* (London and New York: Routledge, 1996), pp. 21–28.
39. Thomas Hobbes, *Leviathan* (Harmondsworth: Penguin Books, 1968), pp. 81–82. Quoted in Gatens, pp. 21–22 (emphases in original).
40. Hobbes, p. 186.
41. Gatens, pp. 22 and 25 (emphases in original).
42. Ibid., pp. 22–23.
43. Evelyne Polt-Heinzl, 'Liebesrede und Machtfragen', in Konstanze Fliedl, Evelyne Polt-Heinzl and Reinhard Urbach, *Schnitzlers Sprachen der Liebe*, Wiener Vorlesungen im Rathaus, 147 (Vienna: Picus Verlag, 2010), pp. 39–54 (pp. 43–45).
44. On the significance of forms of address in *Professor Bernhardi*, see Judith Beniston, 'Doctors talking to Doctors in Arthur Schnitzler's *Professor Bernhardi*', in *Adapting Translation for the Stage*, ed. by Geraldine Brodie and Emma Cole (Abingdon: Routledge, 2017), pp. 39–55 (pp. 42–44).
45. Gatens, p. 26.
46. Foucault, *The History of Sexuality*, I, 62.
47. Judith Butler, *Notes towards a Performative Theory of Assembly* (Cambridge, MA: Harvard University Press, 2015), p. 4.
48. Schnitzler, *Briefe 1913–1931*, letter to Richard Charmatz, 4 January 1913, p. 3.
49. Sander Gilman, *The Jew's Body* (New York: Routledge, 1991), ch. 3, pp. 60–103.
50. Schnitzler, *Briefe 1913–1931*, letter to Richard Charmatz, 4 January 1913, p. 1.

CHAPTER 9

'Glocalism': Local and Global in Richard Beer-Hofmann's *Der Tod Georgs*

Leena Eilittä

Fremd und sie nie erfassend, war er in die Welt geworfen, in der er im Wachen lebte; wovon er nicht wußte, rührte an ihn, und was er tat, wirkte ins Unbekannte. Aber aus ihm geboren war die Welt, in der er träumte; von ihm gesteckt, waren die Grenzen ihrer Himmel und ihrer Erden.[1]

In recent decades, an overarching concept of 'world literature' has emerged, in which global concerns are incorporated into the purview of literary studies. The representatives of this expanding academic field have put forward ideas and concepts that are able to shed light on the manifold aspects that the study of literature, and of the other arts and their specific situations, faces in the contemporary world of global processes and uncertainties.

In order to contextualize literature beyond its milieu of origins, scholars of World Literature have recently reflected on how both the local circumstances depicted in literary works and their wider, global dimension could be conceptually addressed in literary studies. David Damrosch has introduced the term 'glocalism' — a concept meant to map traffic and transfers which cross national and cultural borders in literary works. In his words, glocalism

> takes two primary forms: writers can treat local matters for a global audience — working outward from their particular location — or they can emphasize a movement from the outside world in, presenting their locality as a microcosm of global exchange.[2]

Damrosch's idea of glocalism allows me to approach the local and global dimensions depicted in Richard Beer-Hofmann's novel *Der Tod Georgs* (1900), written at a time when the situation of Jews in Vienna and across Europe was growing increasingly sombre.[3] In 1917, the German Jewish philosopher Hermann Cohen drew attention to the Jews' predicament in his essay 'Der Jude in der christlichen Kultur', where he explores what living in, and assimilating into, a predominantly Christian culture meant for the Jewish people. As he argues, it was not only the churches but the entirety of Christian culture — beginning with education — that expected Jewish people to adopt a Christian way of understanding the world and its history. The effect of this Christianization, he argues, was to take over Jewish culture and infuse it with ideas and beliefs that were (supposedly) originating from Christian tradition which, as Cohen points out, caused in the person of Jewish origins a feeling of dislocation or *Weltfremdheit*. As Cohen recalls, this conflict between the pressures of living within a predominantly Christian culture and an internalized Jewish world-view and tradition meant that a person of Jewish origins was faced with two alternatives:

> entweder die Welt zu bejahen und als dann dem Geiste der Weltkultur sich schlechterdings unterzuordnen und einzugliedern, wie sehr dagegen auch sein religiöses Gewissen und sein soziales Milieugefühl sich sträuben mag — , oder aber dieser ganzen Kulturwelt mit allen ihren Machtzaubern innerlich zu entsagen und sich auf das Paradies seiner religiösen Einsamkeit zurückzuziehen, welche die Gefahr einer nationalen Isolierung einzuschließen droht.[4]

Although Jewish people had the option of assimilating into liberal Austrian culture, their everyday lives were nonetheless affected by the Viennese political climate, which became increasingly hostile towards the Jews in the latter part of the nineteenth century, a development which, as Robert S. Wistrich argues, remained hidden and largely undiscussed even in Jewish publications of the time.[5] As Steven Beller points out, it is important to analyse 'the special experience of the Jews as assimilants in an antisemitic environment'.[6] For their situation, which included multiple but hidden pressures from outside and often repressed internalized demands, it is relevant 'to show how this complex culminated in certain common attitudes, which came to be reflected in their work'.[7] In their works, the Jewish writers of Viennese modernism experimented with innovative forms 'not by imposing law, but by revealing the hidden forms in which the parts of life are bound to each other'.[8] Such interconnections between political, personal and mental developments can be observed in Beer-Hofmann's *Der Tod Georgs*, which exemplifies the multiple external and internal pressures facing Jewish people at the turn-of-the century Vienna. In his novel Beer-Hofmann thematizes the mental transformation of a Jewish person in which Semitic cultural traditions and other global and universal influences play a crucial role.

Der Tod Georgs

Der Tod Georgs is centred on the sudden death of Georg — a young man who has just been appointed as a professor of medicine at the University of Heidelberg — and its consequences, narrated from the point of view of his friend Paul. The novel's time frame spans approximately three months, which are depicted in four chapters. The first chapter describes an evening in August in Bad Ischl, when Georg has come to visit Paul, the second Georg's death the following night; the third depicts Paul's train journey with Georg's body back to Vienna and the final chapter takes place some months later in the Schönbrunn park. These four chapters contain Paul's reflections, memories and dreams; the novel has little action and its narration largely takes the form of *erlebte Rede*.[9]

The novel begins *in medias res* in Bad Ischl, a popular spa town in Salzgammergut during the last decades of the Austrian Empire, where many cultural personalities, especially musicians, came during the summer months in order to entertain the summer residents staying in the area. Very little of this cultural glamour transpires in the novel, whose action starts in the rural estate which had previously belonged to Paul's grandparents. The opening scene depicts Paul's discussion with a passing neighbour whom Paul tells about Georg's recent arrival for a two-week visit, after which his friend would start his professorship at the University of Heidelberg. Already in the first chapter of the novel, the author introduces a contrast between the different life situations and personalities of Paul and Georg. Esther N. Elstun has pointed out that 'the decadent Paul sees his friend as everything that he himself is not and would like to be: strong of will and sound in mind and body — in short, entirely fit for life'.[10] Ritchie Robertson has identified Paul as 'a skeptical Western Jew who [...] lives under the shadow of Christian society' and Georg, who has enjoyed rapid professional success in his early adulthood, as a gentile.[11] Jacques Le Rider, too, points to the opposition between George and Paul in this novel, for which Beer-Hofmann had used the working title *Der Götterliebling*.[12] As Elstun notes, this title is an obvious reference to the myth about brothers from Argos, Kleobis and Biton, which praises those who served the goddess Hera and died young.[13]

Whereas George appears as somebody favoured by the gods, who succeeds in everything he does, Paul is an uncertain person who largely lives in the world of his subjective perceptions. Stefan Scherer argues that, echoing a *fin-de-siècle* aesthetic, Paul considers external reality to be nothing but the projection of his inner life.[14] His inner world comes into being through his interpretation of natural images ('Naturbilder') and abstract concepts, and conversely, nearly everything from the outer world can become a symbol of the inner life of the subject. Beer-Hofmann's way of exploring perception and subjectivity is typical of the style of *fin-de-siècle* literature, in which an emphasis on subjective perception and decorative ornamentalism dominate:

> Mit dem 'neuen Schauen' realisiert Paul also, was die Zeitgenossen als die Fähigkeit des Künstlers zum Sehen des 'Wunderbaren' diskutiert haben. Neben Mach und Bahr ist es vor allem Hofmannsthal gewesen, der im Struckessay von 1893 den Künstler als jemanden bestimmte, der wie ein Kind 'naiv zu sehen' vermag, wodurch das 'Lebendige ornamental und das Ornament lebendig' wurde.[15]

Childhood

Paul thus represents the *fin-de-siècle* aesthete whose often dreamy reflections depicted in an ornamental style point to an inner conflict and its circumstances. As Elstun notes, Paul is a young man with conflicting desires 'for aloofness from life and for involvement in it'.[16] Even as a child, he seemed to be living in two separate worlds: in his home in Austria and in the world of his phantasies and dreamy ambitions. From early on, his interests went beyond the narrow limits of

Bad Ischl where he spent time alone with books even before knowing how to read them. As the narrator recalls, 'Abseits von andern Kindern war er aufgewachsen, zwischen hohen und vornehmen Büchern, die er liebte, bevor er in ihnen zu lesen verstand' (BH, 536). Paul's isolation is a symptom of his mental distance from Bad Ischl's inhabitants, who come from various, for him often unknown, parts of this heterogenous nation: 'Nichts wußte er von ihnen; von vielen und vielen nur einen Namen, der sie als Volk zusammenfaßte, der bedeutungsleer an sein Ohr schlug, und auch das nicht von allen' (BH, 537). In Paul's later reflections on the Austrian people who are working in the fields, these appear like a collective of people who have lost their individuality: 'wie ein einziges vielmaschiges gleichgeknüptes Netz, schien dasselbe Los über sie alle geworfen; in stumpfem Gleichmut oder mit verdrossenen Worten schwächlich sich auflehnend, lebten sie gefangen unter ihm dahin' (BH, 573).

In his youth Paul thus chooses a state of solitary isolation in which he focuses on subjective concerns. Instead of becoming involved with the life around him, he is fascinated by stories from books that allow him to use his imagination. Through stories he learns to access a world which takes place in the ancient past and in distant cultures:

> Ihr Schicksal kannte er. Aus Zeiten, wo lächelnde Götter herabstiegen und aus Menschentöchtern sich Söhne zeugten, klangen ihre Namen: Helden, in Rätseln empfangen und in Wundern geboren; und andere wieder, die, aus ahnenlosem Dunkel gelassen emporsteigend, mit leichtem Wink sich olympische Tore sprengten. (BH, 537)

These stories about mythical figures and gods from ancient times do not only provide escapism or entertainment for Paul, but they contribute to his growing awareness about another world consisting of heroic personalities and deeds. These stories even teach him a new concept of time. As Scherer argues, the young Paul does not want to accept conventional forms of knowledge or perception.[17] In contrast to an ordinary understanding of time as consisting of the past and the present, Paul is fascinated with a concept of time involving several dimensions. This multi-dimensionality of time contributes to his understanding of a more encompassing Being involving a cosmic dimension which early on makes him dismiss time in terms of simple chronology: 'Er faßte es nicht, daß es gewesen, und er haßte alle, die in selbstverständlichem Begreifen, unerschauernd, an dem Wunder vorüberschritten, das sie Zeit nannten' (BH, 538). Apart from stories about ancient eras and personalities, during his early years Paul is fascinated by a puppet theatre which teaches him about life and death. In the third chapter of the novel, the adult Paul recalls a childhood scene where he was observing the puppets in the window of a toy shop. The memory of these puppets, which are hanging by ropes, is the beginning of his reflections about life, which resemble those depicted in Goethe's *Wilhelm Meisters theatralische Sendung* (1777–85). For Wilhelm the puppet theatre provides access 'in eine mystische Welt der Kunst',[18] and in Paul's perception the puppet also goes beyond 'mere imitative motions'.[19] In Goethe's novel a curtain separates Wilhelm from the puppets, but in Beer-Hofmann's description there exists a transparent glass between Paul and the puppets, which appear to him as living beings. Unlike Wilhelm Paul does not become an artist, and yet the theatre offers him an imaginative access to an exotic world beyond his familiar circumstances in which 'An dünnen Drähten hingen aus gemalten Wolken Könige, Henker, und Prinzessinnen herab, und berührten kaum den Boden' (BH, 592).

These puppets also give Paul an early awareness of the transience of life. Those masks which represent dead people convey old age to him as a state in which everything has been taken away and 'nichts war ihnen geblieben' (BH, 597). As Scherer notes, the marionettes, which are being moved by a thread, recall the classical myth of Parcae, three female figures of destiny who directed the lives of human beings and gods.[20] The marionettes instil in young Paul an awareness of the 'Faden des Lebens' — of life as a thin thread which can be cut at any time: 'Am Faden des Lebens selbst schienen sie zu spinnen, der unzerreißbar — von andern kommend zu anderen — durch ihre schweren Hände glitt; Spinner und — wie sich ihr Leben mit hineinverflocht — Gespinst zugleich für die nach ihnen' (BH, 591). Like the stories in which he is immersed during his childhood years, the puppets in the window contribute to Paul's view of the universal laws which are not man-made. He realizes early on that in the ordinary world the individual will of human beings is decisive, but that other forces rule life, nature and the universe:

> Nicht der Wille eines einzelnen formte die Regel für ihr Tun, und das Gelingen hing nicht an Laune und Gunst von Menschen. Aus Ungemessenem kam zu ihnen, was ihnen befahl. Der Lauf der Sonne, der Wandel des Mondes und das Kreisen von Gestirnen gebot ihren Geschäften; aus Gewitterschauern und sanft träufelndem Regen floß Segen herab oder fiel Unheil über sie. (BH, 591)

Dreams

Paul's early concept of a more universal world, which does not acknowledge limits but oscillates between different eras or places, is sketched out further in the second chapter of the novel, which largely consists of his dreams. As he recollects, dreams played a similar role in his inner development to his early interest in ancient stories: 'Nicht wie ein Wissen von Geschehenem empfand er es; es war sein Eigen wie seine Träume und, wie diese, mehr sein wahres Leben als das, das er lebte' (BH, 538). During Richard Beer-Hofmann's lifetime, dreams and their role in the mental life were theorized by Sigmund Freud,[21] and somewhat later by Carl Gustav Jung. In Freud's dream theory repression plays an important role in the dream work which allows a libido to get rid of unfulfilled desires and wishes. However, Jung who by 1902 had read *Die Traumdeutung,* did not believe that dreams were only about wish fulfilment and even if they were, these were certainly not related to infancy.[22] According to Jung, dreams are a symbolic expression of complexes and come into being as spontaneous self-description of the unconsciousness in a certain situation. Sonu Shamdasani stresses that Jung 'valorized the prophetic and mysterious powers of the dream, to a greater extent than any other modern psychologist'.[23]

In *Der Tod Georgs*, Paul has two dreams during the night when Georg is staying at his house in Bad Ischl and suddenly dies in his sleep. Rather than being related to Georg's tragic death, Paul's first dream features the death of a woman whom he had in reality noticed earlier that evening in the park. In the narrative, the two women whom he had passed when walking in the park in the evening have little individuality and appear, as Elstun remarks, like extensions of Paul's inner life projected onto outside reality.[24] In Paul perception, the woman of his dream is not actually beautiful but evokes in him 'Gedanken an Dinge [...], die ihm lieb waren' (BH, 526), reminding him of holy figures which he knows from the works of visual arts: 'In verstaubten Winkeln eines Antiquitäten-Ladens standen Statuetten von Heiligen, die ihr glichen; ihre Wangen schienen den matten Glanz von lichtem Holz zu haben' (BH, 525).

In Paul's dream, the shift from one person to another points to a psychoanalytically understood shift (*Verschiebung*) in his inner life which, as Robertson has pointed out, suggests that his relationship to Georg had been homoerotic.[25] As Scherer has identified, in the dream scene Paul aesthetizes the woman with whom he had been married for seven years, to a mere surface and ornamental figure.[26] In contrast to Georg's sudden death during that night, the woman in the dream suffers from illness a long time before she dies. In his devastated state, Paul, who knows he will be a widower soon, gets consolation and, as Elstun notes, derives strength from the stories in *Tausend und eine Nacht*.[27] While reading these stories, he becomes familiar with figures who are not melancholic and ambivalent, lacking a clear sense of direction in life, but with characters whose confidence in life remained unshaken: 'Mit klaren ungequälten Augen sahen die Menschen dieses Buches. [...] In gewundenen labyrinthischen Wegen lief ihr Leben, mit dem anderer seltsam verkettet. Was einem Irrweg glich, führte ans Ziel' (BH, 532).

Paul recalls feeling guilty during his wife's illness while remembering episodes from their marriage. As he recollects, he had alienated her from her own inner integrity in his attempt to introduce her to his intellectual world, which, in the last days of her life, appears like a mask she is gradually losing: 'Langsam schien sie seiner Herrschaft zu entgleiten. Wie sie schlafend dalag, war aus ihren Zügen alles gelöscht, was nicht ihr eigen gewesen. Wie eine Maske war es von ihr gefallen, und nur ein blasses Kindergesicht blieb da' (BH, 564).

Whereas Paul's first dream depicts a woman whose own personality had been subordinated to his will and intellectual world, his second dream of the night tells a different story about his attitude towards femininity.[28] This dream depicts the ancient temple of Hierapolis in Syria, which was dedicated to Astarte, the goddess of fruitfulness and sexuality. The narrative recounts the long process of the construction of the temple and its frescos, and the work of the men who sacrificed their lives while working on the site. They projected onto the temple images of their own memories about their mothers and their dreams about women.[29] As the narrator recollects, the temple was meant to become greater than the others dedicated to poorer gods that were made from wood. The golden interior of the temple was financed by the money that had been offered as sacrifice by the young women and boys who were prostitutes: 'Mit Gold waren seine Säulen umkleidet, und trugen ein Dach von purem Gold — die Spende vieler Jungfrauen und Knaben, die in den heiligen Hainen der Künste, fromm der Göttin dienend, fremden ans Land gestiegenen Männern Lust gegeben' (BH, 540–41).

The myth of Astarte, which is presented in the dream scene, allows us to draw a more general link between a myth and a dream. As Herbert Silberer has explained, both myth and dream express hopes which belong either to an individual person or to the collective. While seeking the connection between individual and ethnopsychology in the analogy between myth and dream, Silberer concludes: 'Myth is the dream of the people — the dream is the myth of the individual'.[30] According to Le Rider, Beer-Hofmann's description of the Semitic goddess Astarte benefits from such studies of antiquity as Lucian of Samosata's *De Dea Syria* (second century AD) and Jakob Burckhardt's *Die Zeit des Constantin des Großen* (1853).[31] The goddess Astarte, who was seen as a personification of the planet Venus, appears as the celebration of a powerfully reigning goddess whose decorations were able to illuminate the darkness of the temple:

> Wenn nachts der Glanz der wasserblauen und feuerfarbenen Juwelen ihres Schmucks schlummernd erlosch, gab ein nichtgekannter Stein ihrer Krone dem Tempel Helle. Die offenen Augen der Göttin sahen in die Augen dessen, der ihr nahen durfte, und folgten ihm unverwandt durch den Raum, wohin er sich auch wandte. (BH, 542)

In contrast to the woman in Paul's first dream, who represents a *femme fragile* figure typical of the *fin-de-siècle* era, this scene introduces another female type of that era, the *femme fatale*. As Robertson has pointed out, the goddess who is 'insistently associated with the hardness of stone and an ineluctable gaze' resembles mother figures who were being worshipped in the matriarchal cultures and who expressed fears of the feminine which appeared in the modern world.[32] Instead of being a caring, loving mother, this figure appears as a 'terrifying, phallic mother' who both suppresses the sexuality of her eunuch priests and licenses that of her worshippers. In his dream, Paul, too, takes part in the orgy on the meadow of the temple where the worshippers of Astarte are gathered, acting no longer as individuals but as a collectivity:

> Wissender und ahnender als die einzelnen war die Menge. [...] Fühlen wollten sie — endlich ihr Leben fühlen; den Kreis gleichverrinnender Tage, in den es gebannt, sprengen, und — wie sie die eingeborenen tiefen Schauer vor dem Tode kannten — die schlummernde Lust des Lebendigseins jubelnd wecken. (BH, 547–48)

Le Rider notes that Paul's dream about the goddess Astarte introduces the Dionysian principle of life which enjoyed great popularity among the *fin-de-siècle* generation.[33] The goddess depicted in the novel resembles the female figures featured in Gustave Moreau's *Judith*, in Gustav Klimt's *Judith und Holofernes*, and in Dante Gabriel Rossetti's *Astarte Syriaca*.

Paul's dream about the goddess of Astarte is thus immensely different from his first dream, which depicts a very subjective personal relation to a woman. In contrast, his dream about Astarte is linked to a large array of cultural history values, which gives this dream a prominent place in his mental landscape. Paul's involvement with the goddess Astarte comes close to C. G. Jung's theory in which, as Shamdasani writes, 'dreams revealed not only personal but also cultural memories. The dream could be considered as *via regia* into cultural history'.³⁴ According to Jung, then, dreams are not only about individual but also about collective experiences which he identifies as archetypes.³⁵

Vergänglichkeit

Whereas the dream scenes address Paul's instincts as far as femininity is concerned, the third chapter tells more about Paul's relationship with Georg. Even more than in the earlier part of the narration, the perspectives of both Paul and Georg are so close to each other that they at times appear to contribute to the same point of focalization. In this part of the novel — which takes place while Paul is travelling by train to Vienna with Georg's coffin — the narrator recollects four episodes from Georg's life which highlight the analogy between the cycle of the day and that of life. Whereas the scenes from Georg's childhood and early youth take place in the morning, those from his adulthood take place in the evening. These four scenes may be identified as phases of Georg's changing awareness towards death, which in his early adulthood seems to him distant, even fascinating. In the later scenes, his attitude towards death is depicted as an unjust rival of life. This idea comes up particularly in the scene in which Georg finds himself in the graveyard with a statue which has been built on his mother's memory. Georg's imagination animates this statue, which overlooks the scene, and associates it with a living woman, who is able to see the landscape below her and even to express herself with the words:

> Dann sah er auf sie, denn er fühlte, daß sie sprechen würde. Fest geschlossen schien noch ihr Mund; wie die Schalen einer Muschel fügten sich ihre Lippen ineinander. Schwer sich voneinander trennend, öffneten sie sich, und Worte, deren Sinn er vergessen, hingen einen Augenblick lang in der Form der Lippen, dann lösten sie sich von ihnen, zitterten und starben in die Abendstille. (BH, 579)

Beer-Hofmann's description of this scene bears some similarities to Clemens Brentano's *Godwi oder Das steinerne Bild der Mutter* (1801). In the novel, Godwi, who had lost his mother in an accident in which he was himself present, is confronted again with this traumatic event in the garden where his father had built a statue for her memory. While the statue is brought to life in his imagination, his sorrow at his mother's death only increases. As Kenneth Gross notes, animated images can embody a person's inner fears and desires emerging 'as the foci, the troubled bearers of an interior life', which disrupt conceptual categories and can result in the violation, rather than the healing, of the person's inner world.³⁶ The sudden confrontation with the animated image contributes to Godwi's restless state, which dominates his life from then onwards. Georg, too, is led into a state of agony which is depicted as his isolation from mankind and from the natural world:

> Und ein anderer Abend, [...] Da wußte er [...] — daß er allein war; er und alles. Keine Brücken führten von ihm zum Duft der Pflanzen, zum stummen Blick der Tiere, und zur Flamme, die nach oben lechzte, und zum Wasser, das zur Tiefe wollte, und zur Erde, immer bereit alles zu verschlingen und alles

wieder von sich zu speien. Und Blicke und Worte und erratene Gedanken der Menschen waren lügnerische Brücken, die nicht trugen. Hilflos und niemandem helfend, einsam nebeneinander, lebte sich ein jedes, unverstanden, stumm, zu Tode. (BH, 579–80)

In his emphasis on death, Beer-Hofmann connects to *fin-de-siècle* writers who explored death in their writings. As Oberholzer notes, his depiction of death is particularly similar to Hugo von Hofmannsthal's, for whom death was a gateway into a new life and reveals the truth about a person's soul.[37] In the four scenes about Georg's past life, the narration assumes an omniscient perspective and style which benefits from repetitions related to morning — 'ein Morgen' (BH, 577); 'einen andern Morgen' (BH, 577) — and to evening — 'Und ein Abend' (BH, 578); 'Und ein anderer Abend' (BH, 579). The omniscient perspective combined with these repetitions recalls the biblical style in which the repetitions stress the importance of what is being told and provide the reader with different angles and perspectives.[38] The four scenes depict a change in Georg's consciousness from his childhood innocence, in which he felt bound to his mother, to the insights he gains during his adult life, which is characterized by solitude and an awareness of death.

As Scherer has argued, Paul's reflections upon Georg's death sometimes come so close to Paul's own perspective that two perspectives appear as one. Paul's newly found omniscient perspective allows him to take distance from his own narrow views and to understand the differences between his subjective perceptions and the world.[39] This knowledge teaches him that he can no longer endlessly project his own subjectivity onto the world and its phenomena, but that instead he must find other vital sources for his life. While reflecting upon the end of Georg's life, which also includes imaginative passages from his never realized future, Paul's thoughts eventually turn to his own life situation. Whereas his earlier mood was dominated by sorrow and agony following Georg's death, he had to acknowledge, as Elstun argues, that his grief remains self-centred.[40] Simultaneously he begins to find in himself new energies which lead him to appreciate his own life: 'und er fühlte, daß unter aller Trauer, tief in ihm, geweckt durch Georgs Tod, die Freude am eigenen Lebendigsein schamlos aufjubelte' (BH, 585).

Ecology

Paul's new orientation towards life also bears upon his approach towards nature and natural world. This is indicated particularly in the novel's final chapter, which takes place in the park of Schönbrunn, where Paul is walking one evening, a few months after Georg's death. While observing the late autumn landscape in which the trees were beginning to lose their leaves, he reflects upon another understanding of life in which individuality plays no longer such an important role:

> Was ihn umgab, begriff er so, als übersähe er es aus der Ferne. Das Einzelne bestach nicht mehr. Gerechter als vorher, vermochte er im stillen klärenden Licht des Herbstes den stummen Willen der Landschaft zu erfassen, durch die er schritt, und ihr Gesetz. (BH, 600)

Here Paul begins to envision a concept of life in which life has its own integrity and laws in which justice (*Gerechtigkeit*) prevails, in contrast to his earlier reflections in which life, eventually conquered by death, had appeared unjust. Paul derives a new understanding of justice from the laws of nature, which exhibit a natural rhythm from one season to another, and from blooming to decaying.[41] While showing deep connections between the human situation and the natural world, Beer-Hofmann's description may be understood in terms of contemporary ecocriticism which stresses the involvement of human history in natural history.[42] In ecocriticism, environment is no longer understood merely as a constant or as a given, but as a process which keeps on changing and in which all things and beings, including humans, are participating. Paul's participation in the natural world takes place during his walk in the park, and this appears to be as if he was reflecting upon his own situation in dialogue with nature. As his own situation, the nature depicted in this chapter finds itself at a turning-point. In late autumn, the park is moving towards another season, as nature begins its winter rest. Paul, too, is at the crossroads, where he must find another perspective on his life, which he had so far largely spent in the midst of subjective and somewhat egoistical projections of his inner life. In this final scene of the novel, Paul's involvement with nature changes from decorative ornamentalism, which has largely dominated his earlier relation to nature, to a rather different understanding of the natural world, which shows that nature has its own laws, integrity and righteousness:

> Und es geschah nicht Unrecht. Nicht dem Strom, dem Felsen den Weg versperrten, und den Felsen nicht, gegen die, rastlos sie zernagend, Fluten sich warfen. Unaufhaltsam, nach eigeborenen Gesetzten, entrollten sich ihre Lose, und was Unrecht schien, war nur der Knoten, zu dem gerechte Lose, das Leben flechtend, sich verschlangen. (BH, 617)

Paul's very personal involvement with nature depicted in the last chapter of *Der Tod Georgs* contributes to our understanding about possibilities which literature may have for ecological thought. As Roman Bartosch has argued, literature with its imaginative qualities may be important for our understanding of man's being-in-the-world from an ecological point of view.[43] Bartosch conceptualizes this relation using the notion of 'environMentality', which draws attention to a person's capacity to become less self-centred and more mentally involved with the 'other' of nature: 'EnvironMentality is concerned with this challenge of reading alterity and the question of how an engagement with nature in literature can be described as a way of dealing with 'otherness'.[44]

During his walk, Paul's renewed engagement with life comes up in his reflections which depict important people who are part of his life as organic parts of nature. In his imagination he is able to address the Georg of the past who emerges as a part of natural world in which Paul himself is walking. After having evoked a question about Georg's death he reappears in Paul's imagination as a young vital being resembling the trees growing in the park: 'Als der Georg, den er zuletzt gekannt? [...] Dem noch sein eigener Leib gehörte, schwellend in seinem Saft, wie ein junger Baum an Wasserbächen gepflanzt' (BH, 608). While thinking about the women of his life, Paul depicts their lives in terms of organic processes while making a comparison between the fruits that are ripening and the women's maturing:

> Die Sonne vieler Tage und die dunkle Ruhe vieler Nächte hatten sie gereift. Und in jeder Nacht waren Erinnerungen und sehnsüchtige Wünsche aufgestanden und als Träume durch ihr Leben gezogen, und mit ihnen waren alle Stunden aller Tage am Werk gewesen, ihre Seele zu formen. (BH, 612)

Similarly, he now depicts the relation between real life and the life of dreams in terms of an organic and symbiotic process. He finds that the dreams, which had dominated and perplexed him throughout, are a relevant part of day's circle:

> Und über dem Leben seiner Tage war ein zweites — das seiner Nächte — gewölbt. Aus allen Früchten des wachen Lebens war der Saft in Träume so gepreßt und gedichtet, wie die Taten vieler Jahre in ein Lied, das man zu singen anhebt, wenn es dämmert, und das zu Ende ist, ehe es Nacht geworden. (BH, 619)

Elstun notes that Paul's encounter in the park with two women sets in motion the process of recollection which is related to his earlier dream about the dying woman.[45] This allows him eventually to understand his fascination with dreams. He realizes that this passionate interest expresses his desire to satisfy the need to 'exercise the creative power, omniscience and the control' which he did not have over his life as an aesthete who in fact feared life.[46]

Some core parts of Paul's reflections take place at the fountain of the park. The element of water is important here, providing a reflective surface which encourages Paul's critical reflections about his situation. As Scherer argues, already in the second chapter of the novel, the description of water reflects Paul's conception of aestheticism.[47] While observing the water from the window of the house where his wife is ill, Paul projects upon the still, 'dead' surface of the lake his own aestheticism. It is only after his realization of the seriousness of his wife's situation, and after his dream about the goddess Astarte, that Paul admits to the life inside the lake, in which water is moving. Regarding the park's fountain, Paul's position is similar to that of Narcissus, who sees his own reflection in a pool of water. Unlike Narcissus, however, who is fascinated by the beauty of his own reflection, Paul recognizes his own weaknesses and his failures in life. He acknowledges that instead of being involved with life and other people, he had been interested only in himself:

> Paul trat näher an den Rand des Beckens; aus dem gesunkenen unbewegten Wasserspiegel sah sein eigenes Gesicht deutlich, nur dunkler und trauriger als in Wirklichkeit, ihn an. Sich selbst nur hatte er in allen gesucht, die ihm begegnet waren, und von dem ganzen Reichtum ihres eigenen Lebens, den Frauen ihm entgegentrugen, hatte er nichts wissen wollen. (BH, 613–14)

In confronting his weaknesses, Paul is faced with a shadow, which in Jungian vocabulary characterizes that part of the self which a human being has difficulty in recognizing and acknowledging. As Susan Rowland points out:

> The shadow is that aspect of individuation that is opposition, defeat, darkness, even evil. Like all archetypes, it is a process as much as a 'thing', yet Jung

liked to discuss it as a figure, [...] as an equal and opposite person to the ego personality. In one sense the shadow is that which we repress in ourselves.[48]

Paul's 'shadow' also relates to the *fin-de-siécle* idea that life is a piece of theatre.[49] In his somewhat egoistic focus on himself Paul had assumed to be the main actor in the play which he now realizes is directed by life itself: 'Hochmütig hatte er sich von den andern geschieden, die für ihn spielten, und nie gedacht, daß das Leben — ein starker Gebieter — hinter ihn treten und ihn fassen und drohend ihm zuherrschen konnte: "Spiel mit!"' (BH, 614).

Paul's moment of self-realization, in which he understands that he is only an actor in the life's drama, is depicted by analogy with a late autumn landscape in which the evening is about to turn into a night. In the falling darkness, the branches of the trees come to resemble the hair of a mad person: 'dahinter war das erlöschende kalte Grau des herbstlichen Abendhimmels. Schwarz und trostlos schienen die Zweige darüber hinzutreiben, wie wirres schwarzes Stirnhaar einer Wahnsinnigen, vom Wind erfaßt, über fahle verstörte Wangen und Schläfen treibt' (BH, 614–15).

The moment of self-realization in which he is confronted with his own disturbed state, allows Paul to separate his earlier life, which he sees sinking into the past, from the future, which he envisages as a space which bears similarities to his early exotic dreams:

> Denn vor ihm tauchte aus Dunklem und Verworrenem ein neues Leben, leuchtend, wie in Märchen, im Morgenlicht, die große ersehnte Stadt erstrahlt, zu der man durch Wunder und Gefahren gewandert ist, weil in ihr alle Rätsel sich lösen und Langverheißenes sich erfüllt. Und hinter sich sah er das Leben, das er bis jetzt gelebt, versinken: immer rascher und tiefer. (BH, 615)

Paul recognizes that his life is part of a natural and cosmic order which has eternal and just rules. For this reason, life cannot be unjust, and this realization gives him confidence about earthly life more generally: 'Gerechte Wege ging alles; [...] Und Unrecht konnte nicht geschehen; dann Irdischem war nicht die Macht gegeben, Gesetze zu beugen, die in der buntverworrenen Vielfalt des Geschehens, herrlich, klar, einfältig, geboten' (BH, 616). Scherer has argued that it is the notion of justice that Paul had gained during his walk which transforms the meaning of loneliness, transience and death for Paul who is able to continue his life and feel protected.[50] Simultaneously with this development, the narration goes beyond the timelessness which had dominated the earlier part of the text. This narrative transformation allows one to localize objects, persons and nature in their own context of space and time, which gives them a more independent existence and liberates them from the role within an 'ornamental tapestry'.[51]

Several scholars note that the idea of justice, which Paul is able to experience in the final chapter of the novel, shows that he is able to connect to his Jewish roots and see himself as part of a chain of generations of Jewish people and their history. For instance, Elstun has identified that 'in the final pages of the novel, the theme of a just and purposeful universal order is given a new and unexpected dimension: Paul's experience of it is linked to the Jewish tradition'.[52] Paul's preoccupation with Oriental stories and myths show that his Semitic background is a relevant part of his maturing process, in which he grows to understand life and his place within the universe. As a result, he is able to go through deep, archetypical experiences related to his Jewishness:

> Aber, was diese Abendstunde ihm gegeben, blieb: immer in ihm und nur in ihm; dem Blut in seinen Adern nicht bloß vergleichbar — sein Blut selbst, das zu ihm geredet hatte; und darauf zu horchen, hatte diese Stunde gelehrt. Denn über dem Leben derer, deren Blut in ihm floß, war Gerechtigkeit wie eine Sonne gestanden. (BH, 621)

Paul identifies not only with his own ancestors but with the entire Jewish race, a fact which is explicitly thematized at the end of his walk in the Schönbrunn park. Like Hermann Cohen, who in his 1917 essay emphasized the isolated position of the Jews within Christian culture, Paul identifies their tragic position throughout history when he reflects on his

> Vorfahren, die irrend, den Staub aller Heerstraßen in Haar und Bart, zerfetzt, bespieen mit aller Schmach, wanderten; alle gegen sie, von den Niedrigsten noch verworfen — aber nie sich selbst verwerfend; nicht, in bettelhaftem Sinn, ihren Gott ehrend nach dem Maß seiner Gaben, in Leiden nicht zum barmherzigen Gott — zu Gott dem Gerechten rufend. (BH, 621)

Returning to the city after his walk Paul has undergone a total transformation from a disoriented existence to an existence in which he has confidence in life. But it is most of all in himself that he has learnt to trust during his walk, which has taught him to distance himself from his earlier aestheticism, to find the rhythm of life in nature, and to rediscover a connection to his Jewish background:

> Wie dicht der Nebel war und wie weit die Stadt lag! Aber durch alle Müdigkeit hindurch empfand Paul Ruhe und Sicherheit. Als läge eine starke Hand beruhigend und ihn leitend auf seiner Rechten; als fühle er ihren starken Pulsschlag. Aber was er fühlte, war nur das Schlagen seines eigenen Bluts. (BH, 624)

Conclusion

This analysis has shown that Richard Beer-Hofmann's *Der Tod Georgs* depicts Paul's development from an aesthete to a mature person through several stages in which both local circumstances and global issues have an important role to play. In his youth Paul sought to escape from his local milieu, which was not interesting enough for the growth of his mind which was inspired by the stories, myths and figures about exotic personalities and distant cultures. His life as an aesthete focusing upon his inner concerns is terminated by Georg's death, which forces him to reflect upon his relations with the actual world and its demands upon his own life. Paul's relation to the female gender is depicted not in actual confrontations with women but in the dreams which allow him to elaborate his relation to femininity. These dreams introduce two archetypical figures of the *fin-de-siècle* era: *femme fragile* who corresponds to a dying female figure, and *femme fatale*, who makes an appearance in the form of Semitic myth about Astarte. Exotic, global myths, stories and figures strengthen Paul's growing awareness of a more universal world for which he longed already in his youth. This awareness culminates during his walk in Schönbrunn park, which teaches him a lesson about nature, its laws and justice. In this process Paul's perception of outer world transforms from a mere ornamentalism to an ecological understanding of nature in which the lives of human beings and nature are no longer separated but contribute to same ecological processes. In the crucial part of his maturing process Paul is able to relate to his own background in which he becomes aware of Jewish traditions and his debt to them. In the aftermath of Georg's death Paul thus succeeds in liberating himself from the fatal dualities of his earlier life and finds a vital connection to his body, to his Jewish background and to the cosmic universe which had spoken to him through nature.

Notes to Chapter 9

1. Richard Beer-Hofmann, 'Der Tod Georgs', in *Gesammelte Werke* (Frankfurt a.M.: Fischer, 1963), p. 607. Henceforth cited as BH.
2. David Damrosch, *How to Read World Literature* (Oxford: Wiley-Blackwell, 2009), p. 109.
3. The situation of Jews in the last decades of the Austro-Hungarian empire has been explored, for instance, in the studies of Carl E. Schorske, *Fin-de-Siècle Vienna: Politics and Culture* (New York: Vintage Books, 1981), Robert S. Wistrich, *The Jews of Vienna in the Age of Franz Joseph* (Oxford: Oxford University Press, 1989), Steven Beller, *Vienna and the Jews, 1867–1938: A Cultural History* (Cambridge: Cambridge University Press, 1989), Jacques le Rider, *Modernity and Crises of Identity: Culture and Society in Fin-de-Siècle Vienna* (Oxford: Blackwell Publishers, 1993) and Ritchie Robertson, *The 'Jewish Question' in German Literature 1749–1939* (Oxford: Oxford University Press, 1999).
4. Hermann Cohen, 'Der Jude in der Christlichen Kultur', in *Werke 17: Kleinere Schriften VI* (1916–18), ed. by H. Wiedebach (Hildesheim: Georg Olms Verlag, 2002), pp. 417–47 (p. 418).
5. Wistrich, *The Jews of Vienna*, pp. 159–60.
6. Beller, *Vienna and the Jews*, p. 83.
7. Ibid.
8. Schorske, *Fin-de-Siècle Vienna*, p. 19.
9. On the narration in the novel see Esther N. Elstun, *Richard Beer-Hofmann: His Life and Work* (University Park and London: Pennsylvania State University Press, 1983), pp. 66–77.
10. Ibid., p. 40.
11. Robertson, *The 'Jewish Question'*, p. 456.
12. Le Rider, *Modernity and Crises of Identity*, p. 141.
13. Elstun, *Beer-Hofmann*, p. 57.
14. Stefan Scherer, *Richard Beer-Hofmann und die Wiener Moderne* (Tübingen: Niemeyer, 1983), p. 211.
15. Scherer, *Beer-Hofmann*, p. 212.
16. Elstun, *Beer-Hofmann*, p. 43.
17. Scherer, *Beer-Hofmann*, p. 211.
18. Matthias Pirholt, *Grenzerfahrungen: Studien zu Goethes Ästhetik* (Heidelberg: Winter, 2018), p. 24.
19. Elstun, *Beer-Hofmann*, p. 56.
20. Scherer, *Beer-Hofmann*, p. 234.
21. *Die Traumdeutung* was published in 1899.
22. Sonu Shamdasani, *Jung and the Making of Modern Psychology: The Dream of a Science* (Cambridge: Cambridge University Press, 2003), p. 133.
23. Ibid., pp. 100–01.
24. Elstun, *Beer-Hofmann*, pp. 40–41.
25. Robertson, *The 'Jewish Question'*, p. 456.
26. Scherer, *Beer-Hofmann*, p. 225.

27. Elstun, *Beer-Hofmann*, pp. 51–52.
28. Otto Oberholzer has argued that in these dreams 'die verdrängte Gegenseite von Pauls Persönlichkeit in Erschienung tritt'. Otto Oberholzer, *Richard Beer-Hofmann: Werk und Weltbild des Dichters* (Bern: Francke, 1947), p. 49.
29. Elstun has pointed out that the temple represents the work of the artist. Elstun, *Beer-Hofmann*, p. 51.
30. Shamdasani, *Jung*, pp. 139–40.
31. Le Rider, *Modernity and Crises of Identity*, p. 142.
32. Robertson, *The 'Jewish Question'*, p. 456.
33. Le Rider, *Modernity and Crises of Identity*, p. 141.
34. Shamdasani, *Jung*, p. 139.
35. According to Oberholzer in the Astarte dream 'der in seinem äußern Leben von den Mitmenschen ichbefangen sich abschließende junge Mann schafft sich aus der uneingestandenen Sehnsucht nach Liebe und erotischer Partnerschaft diesen Wunschtraum, wobei sich ihm die Erfüllung in *Mutter-Göttin* gibt.' Oberholzer, *Beer-Hofmann*, p. 54.
36. Kenneth Gross, *The Dream of the Moving Statue* (Ithaca, NY: Cornell University Press, 1992), p. 10.
37. Oberholzer, *Beer-Hofmann*, p. 73.
38. About literary features of the Bible see: John B. Gabel and Charles B. Wheeler, *The Bible as Literature: An Introduction* (New York and Oxford: Oxford University Press, 1986).
39. Scherer, *Beer-Hofmann*, p. 213.
40. Elstun, *Beer-Hofmann*, p. 53.
41. Scherer has also pointed out that 'der behauptete Wandel von der ornamentalen Verschlingung zur "gerechten" Gliederung begründet sich vor allem durch die jahreszeitliche Wandlung'. Scherer, *Beer-Hofmann*, p. 228.
42. See, for instance, Roman Bartosch, *EvironMentality: Ecocriticism and the Event of Postcolonial Fiction* (Amsterdam and New York: Rodopi, 2013).
43. Ibid., p. 58
44. Ibid., p. 81.
45. Elstun, *Beer-Hofmann*, p. 58.
46. Ibid., p. 45.
47. Scherer, *Beer-Hofmann*, pp. 223–25. Also, Oberholzer has argued that water is in Beer-Hofmann's novel 'ein Symbol für die tellurischen Kräfte', Oberholzer, *Beer-Hofmann*, p. 51.
48. Susan Rowland, *Jungian Literary Criticism: The Essential Guide* (London and New York: Routledge, 2019), p. 93.
49. About the relation of theatre and life in literary works, see Elstun, *Beer-Hofmann*.
50. Scherer, *Beer-Hofmann*, p. 233.
51. Ibid., p. 227.
52. Elstun, *Beer-Hofmann*, p. 59.

CHAPTER 10

Churchill versus Bermann — Memory Politics and the Mahdi Uprising: Arnold Höllriegel's *Die Derwischtrommel/The Mahdi of Allah*

Florian Krobb

Die Derwischtrommel, published in Britain and America in the same translation but with different subtitles as *The Mahdi of Allah*,[1] is a German book about British colonial expansionism's most formidable adversary in Africa before the Second Boer War: the Mahdist movement that established a caliphate in the Sudan after the capture of Khartoum in 1885. Fusing, as it does, reportage, literary biography and exoticist adventure story, the German version can be read as a model example of *Neue Sachlichkeit* and, in spite of a subject matter related more to British colonial history, as a contribution to the post-imperial debates surrounding German colonial legacies and revanchist polemics. In the book, Richard Arnold Bermann, who published in Germany under his journalist's *nom de plume* Arnold Höllriegel, uses an incident tangentially related to German colonial history to debunk colonial mythologies and to drag colonial memory into the Weimar Republic's present.[2] The English publications differ from the original in that they are illustrated and carry a foreword by Winston Churchill, participant in the war to overthrow the Mahdist empire. In contrast to the German original, the English versions thus straddle two distinct national memory discourses and the attendant memory cultures. This situation creates an illustrative clash between text and paratext, indicative of contradictions in the appropriation of colonial memory that remain unreconciled in the book.

The reasons for Bermann and Churchill to engage with this subject matter are as diverse as the (post-)imperial cultures of Britain and Germany around 1930. The events surrounding the Mahdi uprising in Sudan, the establishment of a caliphate and the fate of the European actors caught up in the turmoil captured the German collective imagination, not only because this took place in a region that the German scholarly community had long adopted as a destination for their attempts at unlocking Africa's secrets, but also because the only three reports from inside the Mahdist state originated from German captives and found a huge readership throughout Europe. Another German played a different, but equally important, role in forging a collective German self-image as predestined rulers of Africa — the medical doctor Eduard Schnitzer, who achieved European fame as Emin Pasha, governor of Sudan's equatorial province from 1878. Before the German Reich acquired a colonial empire, Emin's governance of the province was lauded as evidence of the German ability, indeed vocation, to govern colonial populations effectively, implementing the aims of stability, security and the rule of law, and creating a system guided by a benevolent approach and scientific principles. This assessment was mainly based on his alleged success in repressing the slave trade, succeeding where others, most notably the British emissary Samuel Baker, had failed. Emin's stand-off with Henry Morton Stanley fuelled the emerging rivalry between Germany and Britain for dominance in Africa.

Bermann's decision to devote a book to the most formidable foe of European expansionism is significant. International interest is evidenced by the fact that the volume, the only one of Bermann's many books, was immediately translated into English. The most prominent surviving participant in the historical events, Winston Churchill, agreed to contribute a foreword.[3] As a young Lieutenant, he had joined Horatio Herbert Kitchener's campaign against the Mahdist empire in 1898 and written about his experiences in the book *The River War* (1898), which gained this rising star of imperial politics a public, and popular, reputation.

German writing on colonial motifs in the aftermath of Germany's loss of her overseas empire espouses for the most part revanchist ambition and nostalgic sentiment. The political agenda and cultural priority of the old elites was indeed focused on attempts to reverse the stipulations of Versailles and to protect from its detractors the memory of Germany's achievement in her overseas possessions. Bermann's publication sits within this set of coordinates. While presenting itself as a literary biography based on factual research and exhibiting traits of travel reportage, it reads like an epic of elemental magnitude about seismic occurrences on the stage of world history, yet it also fundamentally contradicts the imperialist narrative of European destiny in Africa. Bermann chooses as his subject an episode in African history that determined the fate of the continent and of European expansion therein like no other single historical event. This episode galvanized German public attention on Africa more acutely than any other occasion until the Second Boer War of 1899–1902, including even the German acquisition of colonies in 1884/85 and the exploits of Germany's colonial pioneers. In narrating the life of Muhammad Ahmad (1844–85), the self-proclaimed redeemer of Islam whose movement defeated Egyptian and British rule in Sudan and established in its stead a theocratic empire that lasted for almost a decade and a half, Bermann investigates the cultural and personal determinants that propelled this momentous surge, and the factors that produced its ferocity. He attempts to provide insights into the anatomy of the Mahdist movement, its socio-cultural coordinates and the mechanisms by which the appearance of an inspired and inspirational leader galvanized religious sentiment into anti-colonial military action.

The English version, in spite of Robin John's faithful translation, inserts itself into markedly different contexts. The addition of Churchill's foreword and of illustrations from the skewed archives of ethnography and military history give the English publication a distinctly imperialist flavour. Not only is the tension played out within the English publication by way of an intricate dialogue between foreword and text, but also the two conflicting dominant voices of the very same book highlight fundamental differences between German and British approaches in framing coloniality.

Historical Significance and Cultural Memory

On 2 September 1898, Kitchener's army of some 8,000 elite British soldiers and 17,000 well-trained Egyptian troops defeated a 50,000-strong army of followers of the prophet Muhammad Ahmad under the command of the Mahdi's successor as ruler of the theocratic state, the Khalifa Abdullahi. The foremost imperial power of the age had overcome the most formidable 'indigenous' challenge to colonial supremacy. Just over a fortnight later and some 400 miles to the south, a stand-off between the rivals for dominance in northern Africa, the French Republic and the British Empire, ended in a settlement. The so-called Fashoda Incident can be regarded as the climax of the process of partitioning Africa between the European powers. It is directly linked, causally, chronologically and geographically, to the Mahdiyya, the last and most ferocious obstacle on Europe's march towards complete subjugation of Africa. The pre-history to this defining moment supplies the subject of Bermann's book — but as his account is devoted to the enemy, it provides a counterweight to the master-narrative of unstoppable, inevitable, morally justified European advance. In this way, it also intervenes in the discourse that framed the conflict between an Islamist theocracy and the mightiest military power of the age as a conflict of cultures, a contest between belief systems and ways of life, between what the Europeans claimed as progress and what they castigated as fanaticism, anarchy and barbarity, between Europe and the European 'other' — savage Africa and the Islamic Orient rolled into one.

   Kitchener's victory ended a chapter which, it could be argued, was the single most significant episode of anti-colonial resistance in Africa during the imperial era, an episode which sent shockwaves through Europe and rattled its sense of mission and entitlement. The early successes of the Islamist insurrection, culminating in the defeat of an Anglo-Egyptian army under General William Hicks in 1883, occurred at a time when the European scramble for Africa was reaching its peak. This resulted in the almost complete partition of the continent among European powers by 1885, the year when Khartoum succumbed to the siege of the Mahdists and Charles Gordon, Scottish-born, Egyptian-employed Governor-General of the Sudan, was defeated and beheaded. The complete wipe-out of Hicks's army, the brutality of the onslaught on the capital, the apparently frenzied behaviour and sheer size of the Mahdist force, along with their unity — unusual in colonial scenarios when European powers were used to playing different African actors off against one another — struck unprecedented fear into the hearts of European elites. The Mahdist uprising was perceived and feared as something uncontainable that had been unleashed by incomprehensible forces. The movement was thus stigmatized as one of religious fanatics and fundamentalists intent on eradicating any Western and Christian interference in African affairs and on reinstituting ways of life, central among them the practice of acquiring and keeping slaves, that the European 'civilizing mission' had undertaken to eradicate. The success of the Mahdist insurgence and the establishment of a Mahdist state were seen as a complete reversal and obliteration of any supposed 'civilisatory' progress achieved by the European campaign spearheaded by Charles Gordon and his European aides.

To this day, British collective memory remains dominated by the powerful 'myth' of Charles Gordon as martyr[4] and of Kitchener as shining hero, as well as by debates surrounding the status of the Sudanese events in the context of British imperial history as a whole.[5] In German public discourse and analysis, on the other hand, we find hardly any reference at all to the holy war waged by Muhammad Ahmad al-Mahdi against Egyptian rule, and by extension against the most powerful colonial empire of the time. German and Austrian actors such as Emin Pasha and Rudolf Slatin, celebrities in their time, are today almost completely forgotten. Only one German publication of recent years deals comprehensively with the establishment and anatomy of the Mahdist state, but does so in a deeply flawed way, unaffected by any postcolonial sensitivities, instead rehashing a narrative that was shaped by polemical contemporary accounts.[6] Written over seven decades before this latest German treatment of the Mahdiyya, Bermann's engagement with the subject matter displays far more subtlety. Rather than subjecting the Mahdi's mission to disparaging European criteria that would inevitably result in condemnation, he attempts to treat this historical movement with respect, a good portion of exoticist fascination, and an empathy based on his curiosity for the humanity rather than the alleged bestiality of the movement. The result is a version of history that challenges the colonialist master-narrative of the victorious.

The reason why the Sudanese Mahdi obtained a presence (albeit small) in German consciousness that lasted well into the Weimar period (though not beyond it) might lie in the fact that the German language's best-selling author of that period, travel and adventure writer Karl May (1842–1912) (on whose tales at least three generations of Germans were raised) authored a trilogy of novels originally entitled *Im Lande des Mahdi* (1891–93). Even though the eponymous historical character only appears in a short episode in the second volume — where he speaks as apologist for the slave hunters pursued by the fictitious hero[7] — this was enough to bed down the name of the messiah of Islam into German collective consciousness. Furthermore, all three European eye-witness accounts of the Mahdist uprising and conditions inside the Mahdist state under the rule of his successor Abdullahi were published by German speakers (although the three books in question concurrently appeared in English).[8] The most influential was authored by Rudolf Slatin, a young Austrian officer who had been appointed by Governor-General Charles Gordon as district governor in newly conquered Dar Fur in 1879. Slatin's story was to exert considerable influence on his countryman, the young Bermann, because according to Berman it was Slatin who showed Austrian youth 'daß es eine große Welt gab':

Daß ein Österreicher Sklave des barbarischen Khalifá gewesen war: daß er, auf romantische Weise quer durch die Wüste entkommen, dann mit Kitcheners Heer in den Sudan zurückkehrte — das war so wichtig, daß selbst die 'Neue Freie Presse' in ihren sonst mehr dem Sprachenzwist in Böhmen und dem ungarischen 'Ausgleich' gewidmeten Spalten Platz für Berichte fand, die mich, einen romantisch veranlagten Knaben, tief erregten.[9]

By 1919 Rudolf Slatin had become a European celebrity, knighted by Queen Victoria, ennobled by Emperor Franz Joseph and honoured by several other European courts. His name stood for a pan-European colonial past and a shared consensus regarding Europe's destiny of shaping the entire world in its image.

Travel Report and History Lesson

The Austrian-Jewish born journalist Richard Arnold Bermann (1883–1939) moved to Berlin after completing his studies in Romance languages and literatures at Vienna University, and started to write reportage sketches for the renowned liberal *Berliner Tageblatt* around 1908. In the 1920s, he made a name for himself as a travel writer; his trips took him to Egypt and Palestine (1923), the Amazon (1924), the South Pacific (1925/26), the United States (1926) and elsewhere. In 1933 he accompanied Count Ladislaus Almásy, now better known as the 'English Patient' of the eponymous novel and film, into the Libyan desert. He also befriended Charlie Chaplin, Sigmund Freud and other contemporary luminaries. The Nazi seizure of power necessitated his return to Vienna; the annexation of Austria in 1938 forced him into exile in America. In academic scholarship, Bermann has enjoyed a modest renaissance in the context of exile studies, as well as for his reporting on 1920s and 1930s Hollywood.[10] His book about the Mahdi's life and times, resulting from a visit to Khartoum thirty years after Kitchener's victory, has however been virtually forgotten.[11] In the early 1930s, before Bermann's books were banned in Germany, this volume enjoyed some success. As the prophet had died only a few months after the conquest of Khartoum, Bermann's book is not a history of the Mahdist caliphate, but rather an investigation of Muhammad Ahmad's and his movement's appeal.

In German, Bermann's Mahdi epic is entitled *Die Derwischtrommel: Das Leben des erwarteten Mahdi*. It came out in a series of collector's volumes produced by the Volksverband der Bücherfreunde in 1931.[12] The symbol of the drum, depicted alongside spears and a banner in Josef Bató's sleeve design, plays a central role in the text. Bermann narrates not only the life of a significant individual but illuminates the time and place that made him and that he, in turn, shaped so decisively. In March 1929, shortly after his visit to Khartoum, Bermann wrote to Rudolf Slatin of his plan, 'das Leben des Mahdi in der jetzt modern gewordenen Weise isoliert als psychologisches Problem [zu] schildern'.[13] When Bermann undertakes to treat Muhammad Ahmad in an 'isolated' way, he means to liberate him from a discourse that viewed him exclusively as an adversary and the embodiment of the quintessential cultural 'other'. However, Bermann most certainly does not construct his protagonist as socially or culturally 'isolated'. On the contrary, he portrays the prophet as a product of specific conditions and dispositions, and his success as a result of particular circumstances which explain his appeal and the success of his mission.

For this very reason Bermann refrains from representing the thoughts and feelings of his protagonist and instead describes the Mahdi's habits of mystic immersion, of trances and intoxication induced by rhythmical chanting and repetitive reciting of Quran verses. He also draws on the accounts of eyewitnesses to capture the effect of his voice, appearance and extraordinary charisma. On the whole, though, Bermann's Mahdi remains an enigma, and the explanations the author offers — for example, for the ascetic's rapid weight gain and for his erratic bouts of punishment and reward — remain purely speculative. This technique allows Bermann to explain the religious fervour both as an individual trait of the person and at the same time as a social and cultural phenomenon born out of a unique combination of circumstances. The emphasis of his account is on the elucidation of the interplay and mutual enabling of psychological and historical factors that made this devout and purist student of Islam into a charismatic leader and that turned a religious sect into a surging movement. Bermann conducts two kinds of psychological investigations: the first into the individual's sense of godliness and mystical oneness with destiny, the other into mass frenzy and devotion to an embodied cause.

The appeal of this charismatic leader's message is explained by the social circumstances in Egyptian Sudan. These involved the exploitation by a corrupt and selfish colonial administration that drove the diverse population into the arms of the one power that promised unity and resistance. It also promised a return to alleged conditions before the Egyptian regime under European influence took on the duplicitous character of preaching good government and restraint from slave-trading on the one hand, while at the same time imposing itself on the remote province in an oppressive manner. If, as is appropriate and legitimate from the perspective of the disgruntled victims, one considers the Egyptian regime as a lackey for European interests, then it is not only a localized conflict that is played out here but a clash of cultures on a global scale. Bermann and his British preface-writer are in agreement on this matter. With respect to the underlying significance and the inevitability of its outcome, however, the tension in the English edition between the foreword and the text itself is irreconcilable.

Churchill maintains that this development is in accordance with a universal logic of history that vindicates those in possession of superior morality, technology, resolve and the means to pursue their goals. He posits an essential, irreconcilable difference between the two parties and between conditions before and after the episode that started with the emergence of a prophet on the Nile, climaxed with Gordon's death and the capture of Khartoum, and was brought to a conclusion by Kitchener's victory over the Mahdist empire in 1898. Bermann counters by proposing that African history follows the same rules as history everywhere, that assumptions held by the likes of Churchill of Europe as a superior historical and moral force are spurious, and that history unfolds according to inscrutable rules anyway — refuting the supposition of teleological determinism.

The book uses a variety of paratexts, lending the publication its hybrid character. These include an editorial note on available sources, maps and a short bibliography listing all the familiar volumes by Slatin, Ohrwalder, Wingate, etc., as well as background reading such as Richard Buchta's *The Sudan under Egyptian Rule* (1889) and notably some sources by Egyptian witnesses published in the German periodical *Der Islam*. The photographs in the English editions — the Mahdist warriors, the shelled dome over his grave after the re-capture of Omdurman, etc. — lend visual concreteness and strengthen the documentary character of the text. However, they also relegate the events in question to an archived past. The vividness of the text and the use of the present tense in action scenes and some representations of the protagonists' audiences allow for an immediate relationship with the events described, whereas the visual evidence freezes time and calcifies the historical moment of the past. The images emphasize the passage of time in that they document conditions as they existed *then* — before being swept away by British military resolve. The illustrations from the military and colonial archives thus strengthen Churchill's presence in the text. They speak the language of the victors.

The main paratextual device, however, comprises three chapters, one at the beginning, one at the end and one in the very middle of the book, placed immediately before the climax of the Mahdist campaign and the capture of Khartoum. These chapters are presented as excerpts from the author's actual travel diary. But they are actually so carefully composed that they must represent much more than contemporaneous notations. In them Bermann accommodates his threefold message: (a) that the forces of history are unpredictable and any historical dynamic arises from a coincidental combination of forces and circumstances which, occasionally, fuse in an exceptional individual; (b) that beyond all outward difference, a fundamental sameness prevails in the dynamics of communities and the motivations of individuals to take a certain course of action or adopt a certain cause; and (c) that the reading of history postulated by the dominant school of commentary is only superficial. History, argues Bermann, does not unfold in decisive qualitative leaps but, under different conditions and with different players, re-enacts similar scenarios over and over again. Change can thus never be fundamental or categorical, as Churchill alleges, but only ever relative and provisional. The sketches from Bermann's visit to Khartoum contradict the claim implicit in Churchill's declaration that the victory of 1898 fundamentally altered, and at the same time fulfilled, history's destiny. The Africa of the late 1920s, Bermann claims, is a hybrid. It is tempered but not tamed, bereft of its specificity and distinctness, of what had originally made it Europe's 'other', an intriguing amalgamation of Africa and Orient, yet decidedly distinct from the stage of 'development' that the advocates of Western 'progress' propagated.

The author's stated aim — if indeed the diarist of the framing paratext is to be read as the author's mouthpiece — is to treat the Mahdi's story with empathy and understanding: 'I want to be fair to the Mahdi' (p. 22). The opportunity to put this narrative programme into practice is provided by the traveller's observation of a young man immersed in prayer at the site of the Mahdi's tomb. His demeanour is suggestive of unfulfilled desire, and it exudes an earnestness and integrity that must not be belittled as superstition. The observation triggers the following remarks:

> I want to tell the truth — and not to offend this inspired young worshipper. [...] I hear him pray, and I know what he is saying. Even an unbeliever will know this prayer, which is the Fatt'ha, the opening sura of the Koran. [...] I am speaking this sura under my breath, in my unbelieving language. The sun is blazing over Mohammed Ahmed's tomb; my roving eye sees the African town, hot, yellowish, like the desert, and the boundless desert on the horizon. (p. 22)

This episode is placed at the very end of the introductory section of the excerpts from the traveller's notes and thus serves as a touchstone for the entire text. The evocation of the barren landscape suggests a strangeness that cannot be overcome, an environmental cause for the vehemence of feeling that erupts and then lingers on, a feeling from which the European visitor is excluded. Of all the strategies employed by Bermann in pursuit of this programme, the relativization of the Mahdiyya's alleged uniqueness and the demonstration of similarities elsewhere are most prominent, fundamentally undermining the construction of simplistic binaries.

Accusations levelled at the Mahdist regime included those of brutality and 'barbarism', evident in the practice of pinning the heads of slaughtered enemies and executed offenders on lances and displaying them publicly. Bermann turns this argument around at the very outset when he describes certain British actions after victory. After 'the tomb [was] reduced to its present ruined condition',

> the Mahdi's body was first disinterred, and then destroyed. All this was done publicly, in order to show the people that no miracle had occurred, that the Mahdi, whom they had venerated like a divinity, [...] had after all been a mere human. But the Mahdi's head, which was found to be perfectly preserved and with recognizable features, was not destroyed with the body; it was sent, packed in a kerosene tin, as a trophy to Egypt. (p. 20)

Here, the English translation deviates from the German original in a way that obscures Bermann's intention. While the English uses a passive construction ('was disinterred'), thus evading naming the perpetrators of these acts, the German calls the British soldiers who opened the tomb 'Leichenschänder' (*Derwischtrommel*, p. 25) — desecraters, profaners of the dignity and sanctity of death. The measure ordered by Kitchener to demonstrate the finality of his victory, to eradicate the memory of the Mahdi that had spurred on the Sudanese warriors and to prevent the preservation of any future memory site, are exposed by Bermann as equal to the 'barbarity' of the enemy's rituals, revealing any claim to moral or civilizatory superiority as hypocrisy.

Whenever Bermann shifts his narrative focus to Charles Gordon, his aim is to identify similarities between the two antagonists, to portray the devout Scotsman as driven by a higher calling to undertake deeds which, in many respects, resemble those of Muhammad Ahmad. Antagonistic though their aims might have been, both were steeped in their religious convictions, and these, in turn, were similar in nature and intensity. Bermann portrays Gordon as interpreting the words of the Bible as direct and personal prophecies, as messages from a higher authority. The omens enable Gordon to accept his fate, bestowing on him a certain sanctity not unlike the impressions of radiance reported by the Mahdi's followers. While Bermann's description of the Mahdi's mesmerizing effect on others relies on third parties' reports, the availability of very personal confessions from Gordon (in the private letters to his sister, for example)[14] enables Bermann to present the general's innermost thoughts in the form of interior monologues:

> Those storks last night ... He has such presentiments. Of course, he is trusting in God. [The German original has: 'Sein Gottvertrauen ist freilich groß' (*Derwischtrommel*, p. 75), probably better rendered as 'His trust in God is indeed abundant', conveys considerably more laconic cynicism than the English translation.] He is a believer, is Charles Gordon. Now it seems clear enough to him that no hazard, not [Prime Minister] Nubar Pasha, but God himself has chosen him to redeem Africa, to wipe out the disgrace of the slave trade from the face of the earth. [...]
> Since he has been travelling in Egypt, Gordon has been using the Bible as a guide book. [...]
> How many times since yesterday night had he read that passage? Jeremiah viii. 7: 'Yea, the stork in the heavens knows her appointed time ...' (pp. 63, 67 and 66)

Strength of conviction makes for a sense of invincibility; this, too, is a trait shared by both men. Bermann explains that the success of Gordon's initial actions against the insurgents during his first tenure as governor-general (1876–80) — when he single-handedly stared into submission the slave trader and war lord who controlled most of the province of Dar Fur — was due to his determination and charisma. A further common feature of their charismatic leadership is the fact that their work comes undone almost as soon as they leave the scene.

The striking symbol of blurred boundaries between self and other, between fanaticisms of various descriptions, is one of the emblems of the Islamist movement shown to the author upon his visit to Muhammad Ahmad's posthumous son, Sir Abderrahman El-Mahdi, as related in the second of the chapters 'from the traveller's notes'. The sword carried by the Mahdist armies into battle was a weapon acquired by the prophet as part of the dowry of a Dar Fur princess betrothed to him in a bid to align him with royal houses of Muslim northern Africa. It bears an inscription identifying it as having once belonged to a crusader fighting in one of Holy Roman Emperor Charles V's campaigns against the Saracens in the Mediterranean or against the Ottomans on the Balkans: 'VIVAT CAROLUS V. ROEMISCHE KAISER' (p. 154) (thus also in the German version; *Derwischtrommel*, p. 182).

The breaking down of binary oppositions profoundly undermines the validity of the colonialist narrative not only of dominance and assertion, but most fundamentally of 'progress' as defined by European imperialism and its proponent, Churchill.

Conflicting Narratives

At first sight, Bermann and Churchill seem to be in agreement in their assessment of the rise and fall of the Mahdist empire. The latter's remark that the 'rebellion of the Sudan was the last great outburst of the blood-red flower of Sudan' is echoed in Bermann's formulation that the Sudanese uprising was 'perhaps the last epic assault of Islam against Western civilization' (p. 3). This impression, however, is erroneous. For Churchill, the victory over the Mahdist insurgence follows a historical logic and inevitability. Taking his cue from the text itself, he marvels at the fact that the sons of the British empire's main foes, Soliman El-Khalifa Abdullahi and Sir Abderrahman El-Mahdi, now serve their colonial masters in prominent positions, the former as Aide-de-Camp to the governor-general with the rank of an army captain and the latter, a knight of the realm, as land owner and community leader. Even more than the might of weapons, for Churchill this demonstrates the sheer irresistibility of England's dominion. When he compares the capture of Khartoum and the struggle between Gordon and Muhammad Ahmad to a Greek tragedy (p. xiii), Churchill relegates the events of the 1880s and 1890s to an irretrievable mythical past. In this respect, his opening remarks fulfil a function similar to that of the images. In his exclamatory hyperbole, however, he entangles himself in contradictions: claiming on the one hand that Bermann's book depicts a bygone world, a world superseded by the forces that Churchill represents, while on the other hand opining that 'it is too close for the final word'; only 'one day will a Gibbon summarize England's work in Egypt and discover splendid material for a ruthless and unrestricted pen' (p. xiii). This reference to the author of *The Decline and Fall of the Roman Empire* places British empire-building on a par with the rise of the Roman empire of old (the decline in this analogy is that of the Ottomans, whose ability to maintain their empire had been exposed). Victory is so complete that even the most megalomaniac of imperialist dreams has come true. After the defeat of Mahdism, the truce with France and the seizure of power over former German East Africa in 1919, Cecil Rhodes's ambition of an uninterrupted continental connection between the Cape and Cairo over British territory had become a reality.

Bermann takes issue with the very foundational assumptions of colonialism that inform Churchill's assessment of the essential conflict of cultures, as well as with the euphoria regarding its outcome. The introduction to the revised one-volume edition of *The River War* contains a succinct summary of this colonialist master-narrative, couched in highly suggestive rhetorical questions:

> What enterprise that an enlightened community may attempt is more noble and more profitable than the reclamation from barbarism of fertile regions and large populations? To give peace to warring tribes, to administer justice where all was violence, to strike the chains off the slave, to draw the richness from the soil, to plant the earliest seeds of commerce and learning, to increase in whole peoples their capacities for pleasure and diminish their chances of pain — what more valuable reward can inspire human effort.[15]

Any obstacles in the way of this grandiose scheme, in the shape of challengers, disparaged as a parade of 'odd and bizarre potentates against whom the British are continually turned' and the latest of whom was indeed the Khalifa Abdullahi, are ridiculed as 'a pantomime scene from Drury Lane'.[16] With respect to the apparent arrangement of the Mahdiyya's leaders' two sons with the new rulers, the imperial politician Churchill hymns the providential quality of British colonial rule: 'Wonderful are the ways of England!' (p. xiv). The Austrian journalist, with reference to Sir Abderrahman's address in Gordon Avenue, Khartoum, proposes a less confident reading of the course of history: 'These are the jokes of history' (p. 150).

Bermann's analysis of Muhammad Ahmad's success is intended to shed light on the mechanics pertaining to *any* historical upheaval. His take on the events suggests a fundamental randomness of history, since any combination of factors, any social or political circumstances are beyond anyone's control. This sentiment also serves to modify the claim of uniqueness and the identification of Islam as the crucial antagonistic force — since other religious and, indeed, political persuasions possess equal potential to influence the course of history. After deciphering the inscription on the crusader's sword, Bermann's diarist exclaims: 'Allah!' (The German original adds: 'lobpreise ich' (*Derwischtrommel*, p. 182) — 'I give praise') 'What an enthralling romantic adventure is Thy world's history!' (p. 154) In contrast to Churchill's analogy of the dynamics and protagonists of the Mahdist movement with the plot and characters of Greek tragedy, burlesque farce and Enlightenment historiography, Bermann's use of 'romantic' and 'adventure' retains a dimension of unpredictability, openness and residual otherness. The course and outcome of history, this indicates, are not pre-ordained, calculable, or in the gift of any mover and shaker. Like everything else, imperial world dominance is not an inevitability but a fluke.

Bermann, like Winston Churchill, firmly believed that this specific brand of African-Oriental fanaticism had had its day, and that the military might of the West, the inevitable economic and social absorption into worldwide coloniality and European determination to shape Africa in its image would prevail. He nevertheless acknowledges that passions, strong beliefs, the search for salvation and the quest for self-determination are integral to human nature, regardless of the location, skin colour and cultural background of its adherents. The aforementioned sketch of the young worshipper includes the recognition that 'the unrealized promises of prophets only give nourishment to desire, and faith is born of desire' (p. 22). It was this sentiment, rather than Churchill's and the author's own assessment that the Mahdist movement represented the very last surge of African and Islamist resistance against the Westernization of the world, that would eventually prove true. This, then, is Bermann's contention: while the specifics of the content and circumstance of human passions may change, the impulse as such, what the author calls 'desire', and the combination of conditions that provide an outlet, will probably always remain beyond containment: desire, unruliness and passion cannot be pacified, either by ideologies of superiority such as those espoused by Churchill, or by the military, technological and political means at the West's disposal.

Reverberations

Meanwhile, the debates on the long-term effects of the defeat of Mahdism continue. Churchill claimed that the victory of Omdurman offered a unique opportunity to impose order on African chaos: 'The Soudan, tortured for so many years, appeals to its conquerors for rest and peace. [...] The strong hand of civilized government can prevent the warring of tribe with tribe and the strife of classes or individuals.'[17] This validation of the defeat of Mahdism as a decisive leap that made way for a new beginning is echoed in modern commentary which maintains that Kitchener's vision of nation building heralded an entirely new era. The language used by the general himself and by one of his modern biographers betrays the ultimate aim of pacification, of eradicating any unruly and disturbing 'Africanness'. Citing Kitchener's aims as contained in a directive to his administration to 'increase their [the people of the colony's] prosperity', 'develop their resources, and to raise them to a higher level', promote their 'moral and industrial regeneration', 'revenue and production' by practising a 'paternal spirit of correction', John Pollock rehashes the imperialist narrative of achieving progress by eliminating adversity and using the position of strength to implement one's own policies in the region. In the South, Pollock claims, 'animist tribes welcomed [Kitchener] as a liberator from Muslim tyranny and slave-trading'. British governors' 'firm paternal hand for the benefit of the ruled, not the rulers', would demonstrate to all Sudanese that 'an era of justice and kindly treatment had begun, in contrast to the dervish rule that plundered and enslaved': Kitchener 'thus stamped his ideals and personality on the new nation. Long after he had left, and indeed for all the fifty-five years of the Anglo-Egyptian Sudan, until independence, this directive was the inspiration of those who governed.'[18] The colonialist gesture of speaking on behalf of the subaltern is present here in its crudest form. 'Progress' and 'improvement' are posited as universal concepts, the European notion of nationhood under tutelage as the most suitable form of political organization, and British military heroes lauded as the chosen instrument bringing to fulfilment the destiny of the world.

In the epilogue to his study *Armies of God*, Dominic Green suggests continuities between the Mahdiyya of the 1880s and 1890s and more recent troubles in Sudan, quite openly arguing that only European intervention had the capacity to pacify the area, and thereby retrospectively vindicating Churchill's praise for the campaign as necessary and just. Rhetorically condensing the argument into a statement on the most powerful case against the Mahdist state, its embrace of slavery as one of the mainstays of society and economy, Green pronounces that under British rule, the slave trade had been eradicated 'for the first time in Sudanese history', whereas today, when the Mahdists' successors in spirit had regained power, 'the price of a child slave in Sudan is $35'. The argument proposes a causal link between the rebuilding of the Khalifa's house and the Mahdi's shrine as national monuments after independence, and the regime that harboured Osama bin Laden in the 1980s. It also attributes all initiatives to bring a settlement to the divisions of this 'failed state' to Western intervention — even the proposal to partition the Sudan, realized in 2011, is declared as 'revisiting Gordon's proposal of 1884'.[19]

Voices arguing that such interventionist policies failed to bring peace to the region represent but a small minority. Robin Neillands holds that the

> Kalifa Abdulla ruled firmly but fairly according to his rights and the Sudanese people were perfectly content under his rule, certainly far happier than they had been under the Egyptians, and but for the return of the British army in the 1890s, the Mahdist state would in all likelihood have continued and prospered.[20]

Yet, even such a dissenting voice gives credit for a possible peaceful and self-determined development to the stance of a metropolitan agent, Gladstone, and his reluctance to interfere in the affairs of sovereign foreign states, however weak, rogue or defiant of Western principles they might be.

And so the master-narrative remains unchallenged to this day, most obviously in British public memory, of course, with its worship of military heroes and residual enchantment with Empire, but also in German-speaking Europe, where the editor of the first ever German translation of Churchill's *River War* draws parallels between the Mahdist reign and present-day military dictatorships, and confirms Kitchener's assessment that the threat posed by an unruly Sudan to the international order (meaning the cosy cartel of the great powers) demanded action ('angesichts deren Untätigkeit inakzeptabel ist').[21] Continuities are postulated in both directions: on the one hand 'The Mahdist regime was a precursor of the Modern Islamic state'; on the other hand, modern Islamic states are said to replicate structures first witnessed in 1880s Sudan: 'an Islamic state has been reconstructed [in modern Sudan] with many of the features of the Mahdist state a century ago: idealism, pragmatism, vulnerability and repression'.[22]

Almost a century ago, Bermann warned against enthroning the European narrative as the only viable and enduring interpretation of events. He argued that the stirrings of otherness that so mightily provoked the drivers of Westernization were but manifestations of a shared humanity. He further dismissed as folly the assumption championed by the propagandists of 'progress', imperialists and their historiographers, that decisive action conducted by morally and technologically 'superior' parties had the capacity to bring about lasting and decisive qualitative change. The way in which he sympathetically dissects the workings of enthused communities roused by a common cause and incited by an inspiring leader renders his book uncannily prophetic. His subsequent attempt to relativize the alleged uniqueness of this circumstance displays a profound, and decidedly modern, scepticism of master-narratives. The character of the English version of the book as battleground over the meaning of history makes this Weimar text as topical now as it was then.

Notes to Chapter 10

1. Richard A. Bermann, *The Mahdi of Allah: The Story of the Dervish Mohammed Ahmed*, trans. by Robin John (London: Putnam, 1931); Richard A. Bermann, *The Mahdi of Allah: A Drama of the Sudan* (New York: Macmillan, 1932; repr. New York: Cosimo, 2006). Subsequent page references in the main text are to this edition.

2. For a more detailed introduction to the work, see in Florian Krobb, 'Exotik, Geschichtsrelativismus, Kolonialismuskritik: Arnold Höllriegels Epos *Die Derwischtrommel*', *Wirkendes Wort*, 67 (2017), 247–67.
3. Charlie Chaplin, a friend of both, might have been the link between the two unlikely collaborators. The paths of all three crossed at the London premiere of Chaplin's film *City Lights* in January 1931, which Bermann attended by invitation, and on the eve of which Chaplin visited Churchill at Chartwell.
4. Alice Moore-Harell, *Gordon and the Sudan: Prologue to the Mahdiyya 1877–1880* (London: Cass, 2001), p. 3.
5. Publications of recent decades, often somewhat sensationalist in style, include Robin Neillands, *The Dervish Wars: Gordon and Kitchener in the Sudan 1880–1898* (London: Murray, 1996); Michael Asher, *Khartoum: The Ultimate Imperial Adventure* (London: Viking, 2005); Fergus Nicholl, *The Mahdi of Sudan and the Death of General Gordon* (Stroud: Sutton, 2004); Dominic Green, *Armies of God: Islam and Empire on the Nile, 1869–1899* (London: Century, 2007).
6. Erhard Oeser, *Das Reich des Mahdi: Aufstieg und Untergang des ersten islamischen Gottesstaates, 1885–1897* (Darmstadt: Wissenschaftliche Buchgesellschaft, 2012); cf. my review in *Journal of African History*, 55 (2014), 505–07.
7. Florian Krobb, '"den Sudan erobern". Zu diskursiven Kontexten und kolonialistischen Implikationen von Karl Mays Sudan-Erzählungen: Das Beispiel der Großwildjagd', *Jahrbuch der Karl-May-Gesellschaft* (2013), 251–73.
8. Joseph Ohrwalder, *Aufstand und Reich des Mahdi und meine zehnjährige Gefangenschaft dortselbst* (Innsbruck: Rauch, 1892); idem, *Ten Years' Captivity in the Mahdi's Camp 1882–1892*, trans. by F. R. Wingate (London: Sampson Low, Marston & Cie, 1893); Rudolf Slatin, *Feuer und Schwert im Sudan: Meine Kämpfe mit den Derwischen, meine Gefangenschaft und Flucht, 1879–1895* (Leipzig: Brockhaus, 1895); idem, *Fire and Sword in Sudan: A Personal Narrative of Fighting and Serving the Dervishes*, trans. by F. R. Wingate (London and New York: Edward Arnold, 1896); Karl Neufeld, *In Ketten des Kalifen: 12 Jahre Gefangenschaft in Omdurman* (Berlin and Stuttgart: Spemann, [1899]); idem, *A Prisoner of the Khaleefa* (London: Chapman & Hall, 1899). On the lasting impact of these works in framing a specific image of Islam as political force, see Florian Krobb, 'Framing Muslim fanaticism at the end of the 19th century: German accounts of the Mahdist uprising in the Sudan', in *Christian-Muslim Relations: A Bibliographical History*, ed. by David Thomas and John Chesworth, XVIII: *The Ottoman Empire (1800–1914)* (Leiden: Brill, 2021), pp. 63–79.
9. Richard A. Bermann alias Arnold Höllriegel, *Die Fahrt auf dem Katarakt: Eine Autobiographie ohne einen Helden*, ed. by Hans-Harald Müller (Vienna: Picus, 1998), p. 24; cf. also p. 246.
10. A synopsis of Bermann's life and works, with bibliography, is available in Florian Krobb, '"ein Kodak mit einer wilden Phantasie": Richard Arnold Bermann / Arnold Höllriegel', in *Österreichische Kultur und Literatur der 20er Jahre — transdisziplinär. Epochenprofil zu Aspekten der Literatur, Kunst und (Alltags)Kultur der österreichischen Zwischenkriegszeit* <httm://litkult1920er.aau.at/2q=portraits/ arnold-hoellriegel> (2018).
11. As I believe that this work deserves renewed recognition, particularly in post-colonial contexts, I have produced an annotated new edition (Berlin: Die Andere Bibliothek, 2019).
12. Arnold Höllriegel, *Die Derwischtrommel: Das Leben des erwarteten Mahdi* (Berlin: Volksverband der Bücherfreunde; Wegweiser-Verlag, 1931).
13. Quoted in Hans-Harald Müller, 'England, Ägypten, Westafrika, Kanada, Brasilien — Reiseberichte und Literatur (1929–1932)', in *Richard A. Bermann alias Arnold Höllriegel: Österreicher — Demokrat — Weltbürger. Eine Ausstellung des Deutschen Exilarchivs 1933–1945* (Frankfurt a.M.: Die deutsche Bibliothek; Munich: Saur, 1995), pp. 234–68 (here pp. 238–39).
14. *Letters of C. G. Gordon to his sister M. A. Gordon* (London: Macmillan, 1888).
15. Winston Spencer Churchill, *The River War: An Historical Account of the Reconquest of the Soudan*, new and revised edn (London: Longmans, Green, 1902), p. 9.
16. Winston Spencer Churchill, *The River War: An Historical Account of the Reconquest of the Soudan*, 2 vols. (London: Longmans, Green and co., 1899), II, 217–18.
17. Ibid., 399.
18. John Pollock, *Kitchener: The Road to Omdurman* (London: Constable, 1998), pp. 160–64.

19. Green, pp. 309–11.
20. Neillands, p. 155.
21. Georg Brunold, 'Winston S. Churchill und die Geburtsstunde des modernen politischen Islam', in Winston S. Churchill, *Kreuzzug gegen das Reich des Mahdi*, ed. and trans. by Georg Brunold (Frankfurt a.M.: Eichborn, 2008), pp. 7–30 (here p. 30).
22. Peter Clark, 'The Battle of Omdurman in the Context of Sudanese History', in *Sudan: The Reconquest Reappraised*, ed. by Edward M. Speirs (London: Cass, 1998), pp. 202–22 (here pp. 203 and 219).

CHAPTER 11

The Emancipated Woman on the Margins of German Modernism

Charlotte Woodford

As the nineteenth century drew to a close, many artists and writers heralded modernity as a site of possibilities for experimentation and reform. The social changes of modernity disturbed established social systems; at the same time, they created productive (and potentially also destabilizing) ambiguity with regard to the order of gender in society. The emancipated woman disrupts a system of clearly defined bourgeois social identities. 'Für das Herdenweib ist die Ehe gut genug', suggests one of the emancipated women satirized by Ernst von Wolzogen in his novel, *Das dritte Geschlecht* (1899), before concluding: 'Aber ich sehe nicht ein, warum ein Weib immer einen Mann lieben muss. Lieben Sie doch die Wissenschaft, [...] der zu dienen ist eine Ehre!'[1] Literature in the *fin de siècle* provided a space to explore the new sensibilities of a modern age and the related 'gender anxiety', to use a phrase from an essay by Ritchie Robertson.[2] This chapter seeks to add to the rich literature on gender in modernist writing by investigating some socially marginal examples of emancipated women in literature and reflecting on the relationship between contemporary models of masculinity and the literary system of modernism.

In modernist fiction, imaginative critiques of society's gender order help produce new sensibilities; they confront social taboos by engaging with the unsayable. They also deal with the prohibitions, inscribed within the self, that are the legacy of narratives through which we make sense of ourselves and which shape our responses to modernity. Literature helps produce a community of readers, informing their tastes, shaping their expectations. The stories we read cast light on the relations of power in society and the control of dominant groups over knowledge. For different reasons, not only conservative educators of young people, but also the participants in progressive new women's movements recognized the important role of reading in processes of socialization and sought to shape the next generation through the books they read.[3]

Not everyone participates equally in structuring knowledge of the social world.[4] Self-understanding is made more difficult when an individual's own feelings or experiences are not intelligible within the social norms. In Marie von Ebner-Eschenbach's short story 'Ein Original' (1898), a mother is dismayed when her daughter, Gabriele, takes after her engineer father, prefers to play with trains rather than dolls, and starts to make a name for herself through technical innovation.[5] The story positively affirms Gabriele's difference from conventional feminine norms and undermines the mother's reservations with humour. Gabriele's brilliance is supported by generous mentoring from her father, who in turn undergoes his own emotional transformation through her influence. The story makes clear that the workshop has the very latest technology and that, under the guidance of her father, Gabriele is capable of shaping the development of the modern world, solving urgent technical problems.[6] Gabriele designs an electromagnetic motor that is on the point of being sent to London to a trade exhibition. But the story takes a tragic turn before her motor can be dispatched. Agitated by worries about displaying her work, Gabriele visits the workshop alone before the household is awake and suffers a sudden and avoidable death from electrocution. With this abrupt end to the story, Ebner-Eschenbach draws attention to the social pressures faced by a young woman entering a male-dominated field of knowledge, as Linda Dietrick has argued.[7] The rigid enforcement of gender norms has been discredited, but the story seems to imply that an unconscious fear of punishment accompanies such a clear transgression of society's power structures. The technology, of course, lives on: Ebner-Eschenbach also hints at the invisible and unacknowledged contributions women make to modernity.

The moral order and bourgeois ideology of mid-nineteenth-century fiction has been highlighted by Theodor Adorno, among others.[8] However, notwithstanding the 'tone of melancholy resignation and introverted passivity' of some realist fiction, it offers a compelling account of the social structures which shape individuals and how they understand (or fail to understand) their social world.[9] Such fiction casts light importantly on a contradiction in social identity which Hegel acknowledged at the start of the nineteenth century, in his *Vorlesungen über die Ästhetik*: 'Jedes vereinzelte Lebendige bleibt in dem Widerspruch stehen, sich für sich selbst als dieses abgeschlossene Eins zu sein, doch ebensosehr von anderem abzuhängen.'[10] Judith Butler also problematizes the 'self-sufficiency of the subject', drawing a link between the German Idealist thought of Hegel and contemporary theories of gender.[11] Elsewhere Butler argues that 'at the heart of the masculinist idea of the body' is a 'disavowed dependency' which corresponds to 'certain ideals of independence' — again, 'masculinist' ideals.[12] Butler is careful to say 'masculinist', rather than in any way essentially masculine, and it is an observation which it is helpful to keep in mind when considering the strategies through which authors of the modern period in German shaped their performative emancipation from their nineteenth-century literary predecessors and the literary system to which they belonged.

Butler's social theories emphasize the condition of dependency as an inherent part of being human. She calls for a concept of agency that takes into account the vulnerability of the human body and its profound connection to the conditions which shape social existence,[13] arguing that a body 'is defined by the relations that make its own life and action possible'.[14] A challenge for writers of modernity, as Ritchie Robertson points out, was to find 'ways of connecting inward experience with social and political realities'.[15] Achieving the masculinist ideal of 'detachment' was associated with a disavowal of such social conditions, achieving the critical distance of becoming a mere spectator to them.[16] A cultural norm of masculinity was 'to present an impassive face to the world, avoiding the expressions of emotion that were felt to be the characteristic of the female sex' and facilitated, according to Richard Evans, by the late nineteenth-century fashion for beards and prominent moustaches.[17] As Elizabeth Boa points out, it was an 'ascetic masculinity necessitated by the pursuit of social and imperial ambition'.[18]

Russell A. Berman argues that modern authors in Germany from the 1880s onwards sought the 'establishment of a [...] new social relationship or new community within literature, between authors and readers, that would at the same time extend beyond literature and generate a new social community'.[19] Inherent in the programmatic statements of the new literary movements was a clear distance from the conservative *mores* of bourgeois society. This strategy had a gendered dimension. The values of the mass market and of mainstream family literature were polemically associated with women. Andreas Huyssen points out that in debates about mass culture, 'woman [...] is positioned as reader of inferior literature — subjective, emotional and passive — while man [...] emerges as writer of genuine, authentic literature — objective, ironic, and in control of his aesthetic means'.[20] Programmatic statements refer scathingly to the popular book market as dominated by feminine values. The literary periodical *Die Gesellschaft* called for the emancipation of literature 'von der Tyrannei der "höheren Töchter" und der "alten Weiber beiderlei Geschlechts"'.[21] To rescue 'arg gefährdete Mannhaftigkeit' from this feminization demanded masculinist virtues.[22] Independence, detachment and critical distance (codified as masculine) are privileged, while women are associated variously with bourgeois morality or dangerous sexuality, both potentially threatening, and on an aesthetic level with popular fiction and sentiment.

A masculinist concept of emancipation comes through at the end of Frank Wedekind's drama *Frühlings Erwachen* (1891). The Masked Man helps the adolescent protagonist, Melchior, emphatically reject his bourgeois mother and overcome his guilt at the ruin of his former lover, Wendla, with the promise of utopian (sexual) emancipation in the city. Emotional ties to women represent the threat of the bourgeois milieu and its stifling of individuality, and male freedom arises by a masculinist rejection of these ties and the dependency which they represent.[23] Melchior is freed by Wendla's death to adopt a position of symbolic self-sufficiency (just as Georg von Wergenthin-Recco in Schnitzler's *Der Weg ins Freie* (1908) is freed from obligation by a domestic tragedy). In *Frühlings Erwachen*, Ilse, an artist's model, seeks pleasure in an alternative lifestyle beyond the bourgeois norm but in doing so makes herself into a commodity and is unable to escape objectification, as well as potential dependency on others for her future material needs.[24] She cannot achieve the freedom through agency and detachment promised to Melchior.

According to Sigmund Freud, a desire in women to attend lectures and study might equate to symptoms of hysteria. Freud drew attention in 1905 to the malaise of his patient, Ida Bauer (known as 'Dora'):

> Das Hauptzeichen ihres Krankseins war Verstimmung und Charakterveränderung geworden. Sie [...] vertrug sich gar nicht mehr mit ihrer Mutter, die

sie durchaus zur Teilnahme an der Wirtschaft heranziehen wollte. Verkehr suchte sie zu vermeiden; soweit die Müdigkeit und Zerstreutheit, über die sie klagte, es zuließen, beschäftigte sie sich mit dem Anhören von Vorträgen für Damen und trieb ernstere Studien.[25]

Freud did not distance himself from the ambivalence of his patient's family towards her behaviour.[26] The cultural representation of the transgressive woman became emblematic for the destabilizing changes of modernity.[27] Intellectual woman and sexually emancipated women complicate the traditional notion of (maternal) femininity as the other to powerful masculinity.[28] Marianne DeKoven argues that ambivalence towards 'the figure of the empowered feminine' was a way of expressing a fundamental contradiction of modernity: many longed for the emancipation inherent in 'revolutionary cultural and political change', but it was also a source of fear and anxiety.[29]

Socially marginal figures carry taboos. The social anthropologist Mary Douglas argues in *Purity and Danger* that marginal figures are people who are 'somehow left out of the patterning of society'.[30] Since 'their status is indefinable' they are commonly associated with power and danger.[31] Although Freud tended to see taboos as ancient or irrational prohibitions which had no place in modernity, modernist writing engages with the continued power of social prohibitions, expressed through the desire to violate them and the unconscious fear of the punishment which might follow and which was often self-imposed. Elizabeth Boa argues that in modernism the emancipated woman breaks a taboo by aiming to appropriate the power of the phallus, a taboo object, restricted to a limited group, forbidden from general use.[32] Reflecting on the initiation rituals connected to achieving adult masculinity in certain tribes, Mary Douglas notes how young men 'go out of the formal structure and enter the margins' in order to be exposed to 'power that is enough to kill them or make their manhood'.[33] Making manhood, the achievement of heterosexual masculinity through acts of power over women, is a theme which recurs in male-authored modernism, and which is critically interrogated, as we shall see, by Lou Andreas-Salomé in her story *Ruth* (1895).

The representation of emancipated or sexually active women in male-authored writings is therefore culturally overdetermined: women represent a threat to male social power, and to masculinist detachment and self-control. They stand for sensuality and the unruly nature of the body *per se*. Ritchie Robertson points out that in Kafka's novel *Der Verschollene* (1912–14), 'sexually active women are domineering, repulsive, and sometimes violent'.[34] Gregor's sister Greta in Kafka's 'Die Verwandlung' (1915) appropriates phallic power when she raises her fist at her brother ('"Du, Gregor!" rief die Schwester mit erhobener Faust und eindringlichen Blicken'), symbolically linking her to the power held by her father.[35] In *Der Process*, Josef K. unconsciously seeks to exercise control over the independent Fräulein Bürstner, entering her private space and, on parting from her, asserting his power through uninvited kisses. But at the same time he loses control of himself, his own unruly body escaping the discipline associated with masculinity as he kisses her face, 'wie ein durstiges Tier mit der Zunge über das endlich gefundene Quellwasser hinjagt'.[36] Fear of the erosion of male power is viscerally expressed in the misogyny of Otto Weininger's *Geschlecht und Charakter* (1903), in which the author attacks women's emancipation in terms which reserve logic, reason and duty for men alone: 'Das vollkommen weibliche Wesen kennt weder den logischen noch den moralischen Imperativ, und das Wort Gesetz, das Wort Pflicht, Pflicht gegen sich selbst, ist das Wort, das ihm am fremdesten klingt.'[37] Narratives of masculinist emancipation remain indebted to the gender roles and power relations of bourgeois society. They stand in uneasy conflict with women's changing social identity and the ambitions of women as writers to be considered part of the (prestigious, masculinist) system of modernism as opposed to the feminized domain of mass market fiction.

Making Intelligible Women's Experience of Modernity

The act of writing, as a form of communication, offers the writer some possibility of accounting for him or herself, or to reflect on the difficulty of doing so. Modernist literary fiction sees a renewed attention to conflict within the self and to the exploration of taboo experiences and emotions. These are often not fully intelligible to the self, and the narratives they shape are not always fully legible to society. Writers seek ways to explore the powerful hold over the unconscious self of the norms which have shaped individuals' upbringing. Their attempts to understand and articulate their experience of the social world testify to growing scepticism towards many of the overarching interpretations which had previously organized ways of making sense of society. Religious ways of interpreting the world, philosophical idealism and ideas of bourgeois self-assertion are all assumptions which were undermined in artistic and intellectual movements at the end of the nineteenth century. Those commonly held interpretations of the world offered patterns and structures to help situate individuals within their communities. In modernist literature, the reader is more likely to be confronted with aesthetic strategies that work against readers' automatic perception and comprehension of the world, inviting them to see it through fresh eyes, using literary techniques such as defamiliarization devices and conveying a sense that meaning-making is no longer necessarily a shared experience but left to the individual reader.

At the end of the nineteenth century, the women's movement provided a space for the public articulation of private experiences by women, politicizing women's inequality and lack of power. Alongside a mainstream modernist desire for emancipation came a growing recognition that norms and moral codes affected women differently from men. It goes without saying that different women's situated experiences gave rise to different communicative strategies, reaching out to varied readerships. However, the women's movement played a role in shaping a broader context which allowed writers to articulate previously taboo subjects, to challenge moral double standards with regard to sexuality and confront the ways in which women were affected by the unequal distribution of power in society. Such writings formed an important part of the modernist literary landscape.[38] Women writers challenged mainstream norms with oppositional narratives whose core readership consisted of those who shared the expectation that the new century, the twentieth century, would bring with it a positive transformation of society and its values.

The Austrian writer Maria Janitschek (1859–1927), published by Fischer, unsentimentally exposes power relations in stories which use irony and defamiliarization devices, such as in her collection *Vom Weibe: Charakterzeichnungen* (1896). Her short story, 'In Weiß', treats the sexual assault of an adolescent girl in a manner which exposes the silencing of victims of sexual abuse and the emotional impact of not being believed.[39] Janitschek opens the narrative with phrases that make it sound like a form of testimony, a response to the problematic notion that women should share some of the blame for their aggressors' behaviour: 'Es war richtig, daß sie mit ihm geschäkert hatte. So wie junge Mädchen schäkern. Einen am Ohr zupfen, ein bischen [sic] in den April schicken, u. s. w. Aber dabei hatte sie gar nichts gedacht.'[40] The third-person narrator, focused on Treska's attempt to make sense of her experience, shows that she has a clear understanding of the difference between flirting and harassment, even though the dominant voices around her offer an interpretation which conflates these experiences. Treska's encounter with the older man takes place when she is alone, working on the land, and she is never given the opportunity to give full testimony to her experience. Her mother denies the credibility of her story; she dismisses the reported behaviour, trivializing it and sending Treska abruptly to get some rest.[41] Treska is silenced. The narrative conveys the emotional effect of this double victimization and injustice by suggesting that her growth is stunted as a result of her suffering, while her eyes grow wider as she sees the world in a different light; they are a repository of secret knowledge:

> Sie wuchs nicht in die Höhe, sondern blieb klein und unscheinbar. Nur ihre Augen wuchsen, die wurden immer größer und tiefer, und glänzten wie dunkle Geheimnisse in die Welt. Ohne jene Mittagsstunde am Acker wären sie klein geblieben, kleine Instinktaugen eines Bauernmädchens. Der Schrecken hatte sie geweitet, und ihre Seele die dichte Haut des geistigen Schlafes, die sonst wohl nie gesprengt worden wäre, durchbrechen gemacht.[42]

Through this detailed and defamiliarizing description of Treska's eyes, Janitschek articulates how Treska is awakened to the violence of patriarchal power but lacks any means of expressing her new knowledge. Treska's experience is subject to such a powerful social taboo that it cannot be voiced, robbing her of the resources to survive it. But Janitschek's story invites readers to share in Treska's new understanding of society's inequalities.

Janitschek's story shows that it is difficult to articulate the psychological impact of society's power structures without the resources to understand them. Women's writing draws attention to the problem and helps offer readers the resources to interpret their own experiences. Acts of resistance, which might lead to emancipation, are complicated by a recognition that the self has been shaped by the very structures which generate inequalities. The writings of Lou Andreas-Salomé (1861–1937) highlight women's struggles to understand themselves when the available resources no longer seem to offer an adequate basis to interpret lived experience. Andreas-Salomé was a writer of theoretical essays as well as fiction, including essays such as *Die Erotik* (1908), on the psychology of sexual love. In her early twenties she had been a close friend of Friedrich Nietzsche, and she later trained with Sigmund Freud as a psychoanalyst. Andreas-Salomé notes in an essay of 1931 how selfhood is shaped by social conditions not of our making: 'Wir sind nicht *unser* Kunstwerk.'[43] She uses the metaphor of *Dichtung* to suggest that the unconscious self is shaped in ways that are opaque to the individual: 'Leben überhaupt — *ist* Dichtung. Uns selber unbewusst leben *wir* es, Tag um Tag wie Stück um Stück, in seiner unantastbaren Ganzheit aber lebt es, dichtet es *uns*.'[44] While individuals learn to understand their own feelings and experiences through the narratives available to them, the collective narratives which shape the self are by no means fixed. They are shaped by and within society. Literature plays a role in reinstituting them and in creatively reimagining them for the purposes of emancipation, as women's modernist narratives do when they expose their social power.

In Andreas-Salomé's story *Ruth. Erzählung* (1895), the author re-visits autobiographical experience to explore the inner life of an adolescent girl whose path to emancipation is complicated by an emotional relationship to her teacher.[45] The process of *Bildung* involves a journey towards intellectual autonomy, but education also plays a role in instilling social and gendered norms. The novel shows how the education of the eponymous protagonist provides the emotional and intellectual resources for emancipation, but the tutor–pupil relationship casts light on the way gender norms are reproduced and work against women's drive for freedom. Strong bonds of attachment create the potential for a dependency which is in tension with a desire for self-actualization. The novel draws on Andreas-Salomé's experiences of being tutored in St Petersburg by the married religious minister, Hendrik Gillot (1836–1916). The author had sought out the charismatic preacher in 1878 aged seventeen to further her education in the philosophical tradition and religious ideas.[46] By all accounts, Gillot's teaching made a powerful impression on her and according to one biographer, 'sie arbeitete angespannt und intensiv, bis zur Erschöpfung, so daß sie eines Tages auf Gillots Schoß ohnmächtig wurde'.[47] The novel pays particular attention to the dynamics of power between Ruth and her teacher to show that the education Ruth receives is also an unconscious training in subordination ('Ohnmacht'), until it is the teacher's own words which shape the break for freedom.

The novel draws attention to the structures of inequality in which masculine identity is shored up by power over women, but which is at the same time therefore revealed to be contingent on women's acceptance of a subordinate role. An element of dependency is therefore present on both sides. The protagonist, Erik Matthieux, who teaches in a girls' school, unconsciously sexualizes his pupils, suggesting that he sees their education only through the lens of their role in an economy of (male) desire where women's development prepares them for marriage. As he reflects on essays by the girls entitled 'Über das Glück', his remark to a colleague betrays that he thinks of them in a sexual way: 'Arme Mädels, die da in schönem Deutsch beschreiben sollen, was sie doch noch gar nicht genossen haben.'[48] Though he is not directly conscious of it, the youth and inexperience of the girls offer an opportunity for him to assert his masculinity over them. Writings by Ruth leave a powerful impression on him: 'man wurde auch vom ungeduldig drängenden Wunsche überfallen, dem, der hier träumte und stammelte, mit Gewalt die Zunge zu lösen, daß er Aufschluß gäbe über seine Seele' (p. 25). The word 'Gewalt' casts light on the structures of Erik's sexuality. An encounter with a female friend leads to his kissing her in a manner described as 'rasch, heftig, fast gewalttätig' (p. 41) and he associates with love a 'spezifisch männliches Glück' which encompasses feelings of ownership and mastery ('herrschen dürfen') (p. 123). His power over others is located nevertheless almost exclusively in the private sphere. His wife, Klare-Bel, suffers from chronic illness. The doubling of her name emphasizes the associations of conventional femininity with a passive role; her weakness seems exacerbated by Erik's care.

As Ruth undergoes private lessons with Erik, the novel depicts a battle of wills and the discipline of education plays a role in shaping Ruth's gendered identity. At school, Ruth had 'etwas sonderbar Knabenhaftes' about her (p. 28) and was said to be almost like a 'Bacchusknabe' (p. 29), a description suggestive of youthful androgyny. Her gendered development in Erik's company offers the temptation of learning to find pleasure in subordination. Erik describes his role towards her as like a gardener who has found a small, unusual plant to nurture:

> wenn ein guter Gärtner an diesem Bäumchen unablässig seine Dienste tat, und wenn das Bäumchen sich willig behandeln und biegen, pfropfen und beschneiden ließ, — dann, — ja, dann konnte es am Ende seltnere Früchte tragen, als irgend etwas, was sonst auf dem Feldwinkel wuchs. (p. 102)

Ruth articulates some emotional resistance to the passive role of rare plant to be nurtured: '"Noch lieber möchte ich der Gärtner werden," sagte sie unerwartet, "aber es ist vielleicht fast dassselbe"' (p. 103). The discipline of Erik's teaching shapes an attachment based on pleasure in submission:

> 'Ich weiß, daß es manchmal ein harter Zwang war', sagte [Erik], 'und du dein eigenes Wesen unterdrücken mußtest; es tat weh, nicht wahr? Aber es mußte sein. Und nun, — nun bekomme ich dich allmählich gerade so, wie ich dich haben will, Mädel. Ist es nicht schön?'
> 'Wunderschön ist es!' rief sie, mit leuchtenden Augen sich nach ihm zurückwendend, 'das denke ich ja immer dabei, wenn es mir schwer fällt! Ich such's zu vergessen und denke mich nur hinein: wie wunderschön muß es sein, jemand, der ganz anders ist, gerade so zurecht zu kriegen, wie man ihn haben will!' (p. 106)

The discussion here is about education, not sex, but the same social structures inflect both with a degree of masochism. The unconcealed expression of such gender norms by the protagonists exposes them uncomfortably to readers. Ruth is invested emotionally in Erik's power over her. But is there also a glimmer of Ruth imagining the opposite pleasure — the pleasure that comes from wielding power?

The novel engages critically with a society where the process of women's education and self-actualization is connected to male-authored narratives of women's social roles. While Ruth as protagonist lacks the resources fully to make sense of her experience and its emotional consequences, the novel offers 'half-formed understandings' of the workings of power and some possibility for resistance.[49]

In *Ruth*, attachment produces dependency, but the strength of will to resist it and make a break for freedom is sharpened by Ruth's education. She hears the tutor's words: 'Den eigenen Willen festhalten! Haltung! Sich selbst gehorchen, — hörst du?' (p. 263). Although Erik wants to leave his wife for Ruth, the novel implies that marriage would compromise women's path to emancipation.

Andreas-Salomé's short story, 'Mädchenreigen', from the collection *Menschenkinder*, also engages with the way the emancipated woman disrupts the conventional gender order. It was first published in 1898 in the international monthly, *Cosmopolis*, which appeared in Paris, Berlin and London from 1896 to 1898, with sections in three languages.[50] The journal attests to the important cosmopolitan impetus in modernist culture, in which emancipation from old restrictions was being achieved through cultural exchange, furthered by increasingly rapid travel (on the new railways) and easy access to new ideas and books from across Europe. Andreas-Salomé published a well-received study on women in Henrik Ibsen's dramas, for example.[51] Her story 'Mädchenreigen' is set in the bohemian context of a Munich hotel, where the protagonists belong to a progressive milieu of students and artists. When conversation turns to their origins, the group of three men are described as, 'ein Däne, ein Belgier, ein Balte' (p. 77), and the female protagonist as half-Belgian: 'Meine Mutter war Südländerin' (p. 78). This cosmopolitanism offers the possibility through art of forming an alternative community, which transcends German political nationalism. The story is narrated by a voice closely linked to the male protagonist and offers a resolution which appears to restore order after the disruption caused by a woman whose behaviour is coded as masculine.[52] However, the exaggerated reversion to gender normativity at the end of this story leaves the reader questioning the structures which organize gender.

'Mädchenreigen' begins by offering a view of a hotel room through the eyes of a worker, whose gaze lights on smoking accessories, a riding crop, photographs of pretty girls, and a simple comb. Assuming this to be a 'Herrenzimmer', he is surprised to encounter a girl as the occupant, wearing 'Radfahrtracht' and 'Pumphosen' (p. 68), since it would have appeared that the woman's room was the neighbouring one, furnished with 'Dosen, Krystallflacons, Bürsten und Handspiegel' (the accoutrements of vanity), and accompanied by a few sweet-smelling roses (ibid.). But that room belongs to Baron Alexander Vresenhof. The observer

> wäre doch nun wirklich dafür gewesen, daß diese beiden Hotelgäste ihre Stuben und auch ihre Sachen tauschten! Wenn das so weiter ging, dann konnte man in dieser verkehrten Welt bald die Wohnungen der Frauenzimmer wie die der Mannsleute einrichten, und auch umgekehrt. (p. 69)

This introduction to the protagonists indicates that neither figure conforms to conventional gender norms. In the woman's case, gender disruption is overt and intended: 'Ein schlankes, dunkles Mädchen im knabenhaften Kostüm', she is listed in the guest book as 'Hans Holtema'. She also smokes and replicates male courtship rituals when attracting the attention of girls. Hans intends to study law and put it to use in the cause of women's rights. The male occupant of the femininized room, Alex, has travelled to be with his close friends, Ferdinand and Knut. He identifies

Hans initially as a potential rival in his pursuit of an adolescent, but this girl, like a widow he met recently, quickly leaves him indifferent, and close narrative attention is paid instead to his relationship with his friend Ferdinand, a nervous and sickly figure. Ferdinand wants to reassure himself that Alex is not in serious pursuit of the widow (p. 72), flatters Alex repeatedly, and comments 'ich bliebe am liebsten mit Ihnen die ganze Nacht auf' (p. 74) when illness requires Ferdinand to take to his bed early. Their homosocial community does not initially appear to admit women to its number.

The narrative takes up the point of view of Alex, whose curiosity toward Hans is awakened when Hans secretively makes eye contact with a blushing girl; Alex pathologizes Hans's sexuality, regarding her as 'das Problem "Hans"' (p. 77). He does not initially realize, as he seeks out her company, that Hans awakens some inchoate desire in him, as well as calling into question the foundations of his power. Travelling alone, Hans has a desk surrounded by books, and is happy to receive Alex there, treating him as an equal, by offering a cigarette, and outlining why society's sexual relations are in need of reform (pp. 80–81). Alex expresses to his friend Ferdinand his intention to make Hans think again. Ferdinand, blinking at Alex 'hinter halb geschlossenen Lidern', is glad that this enterprise will keep his friend at his side for a few more days (p. 84). By moving directly between Alex's interest in Hans and Ferdinand's friendship for Alex, the narrative suggests both relationships are in some way sexualized and all protagonists capable (whether they acknowledge it or not) of desiring in ways which go beyond the conventional norm. As Marti Lybeck points out, Alex's 'desire for Hans grows as they interact with each other as two men'.[53]

Hans's relationships with women are also subject to a 'double taboo'.[54] Hans describes them to Alex as 'ein Geheimnis' and explains: 'Das sagt man keinem Fremden' (p. 79). So in the first instance they are taboo because they are something of which Hans cannot speak. They also cannot be represented within a mainstream publishing context as a result of continued censorship and homophobia. But the double taboo here arises from the taboo on women's sexuality per se. Heike Bauer argues that the discourse of 'rational female masculinity' failed to address this taboo, shaping an emancipatory *social* identity for women, without addressing women's *sexual* identity.[55] Contemporary sexology associated female masculinity with sexual inversion. However, Bauer suggests that 'notions of inversion served primarily as a strategic tool for challenging the existing gender order'.[56] While they were an 'affirmative feminist project', Bauer argues that they continued to marginalize women's same-sex desire.[57] There are parallels to this marginalization in Andreas-Salomé's story, which Lybeck suggests 'deals with sex obliquely through romantic love'.[58] Hans explains to Alex that relationships between women offer an emancipatory alternative to the structural inequality of heterosexual love. Hans represents her view of love between women as 'eine ganz zusammenhängende Theorie' (p. 82). She rejects the power dynamics of heterosexuality and argues: 'Die Mädchen, die den Mann lieben lernen, kennen ihn gar nicht, sie gestalten ihn sich aus einem eigenen, herrlichen Traum' (p. 81). Hans describes love between women in contrast as 'ein Geheimnis des vollkommenen Miterlebens dessen, was im anderen vorgeht', with an emphasis on emotional intimacy: 'Man geht wie in Hypnose, wie mit ihm selber vertauscht und verwechselt, seinen leisesten Seelenregungen nach, genießt sie, erlebt sie, in ihm' (p. 82). Female same-sex sexuality and sexual acts remain taboo.[59]

However, exploring the power of the sexual drives was an important impetus in modernism; it was a frequent theme of naturalist writing, not least by Émile Zola. In Andreas-Salomé's study of the work of Friedrich Nietzsche, which drew on close personal friendship with him, she reflects on his ideas of the complexity of subjectivity and the inner conflict which derives from the effect of competing drives: 'die Persönlichkeit selbst löst sich gewissermassen in eine Unsumme von eigenmächtigen Triebpersönlichkeiten auf, in eine Subject-Vielheit'.[60] In *Die Geburt der Tragödie* (1872), Nietzsche associated the power of the inner drives with the Dionysian and 'Rausch', as juxtaposed to Apollonian formal control. In 'Mädchenreigen', such 'Rausch' is experienced by Hans in the emergence of mutual desire between Hans and Alex (p. 88). Could this be a strategy to correct disorder and reinforce for readers some moral order of gender normativity? Or does it throw a spotlight on the prevailing gender order? Desire emerges when Alex and Hans, as equals, gaze 'in vollkommener Selbstvergessenheit' at the landscape, 'als seien sie Geschwister' (p. 88). If Alex's attraction to Hans arises from Hans's boyish presentation and behaviour, then perhaps their mutual attraction is less straightforward than it might at first appear. Karl Heinrich Ulrichs, a campaigner against German laws on homosexuality, saw a possibility of opposing binary gender with the idea of the 'third sex'.[61] Robert Tobin argues that in some of Mann's stories 'boyish women and sexually uncertain men' bear traits of the third sex and their desire allows for an engagement with queer sexuality through a model of gender inversion.[62] Lybeck emphasizes the 'gender ambiguity' and 'queer possibilities' of the erotic attraction between Hans and Alex.[63] It can be compared to the queer possibilities of the emancipated woman in some of Thomas Mann's early fiction, explored by Robert Tobin.[64] Tobin suggests a queer possibility in Mann's story 'Gerächt' (1899), for example, in the narrator's desire for the emancipated and comradely protagonist, Dunja Stegemann.[65] It is striking that like many of the protagonists in Mann's fiction, Hans in 'Mädchenreigen' is also an intermediate figure as a mixture of 'southern' and northern European heritage.[66] The narrator describes Hans's desire for Alex as the power of 'dies südländisch heiße Blut' (p. 88).

Lou Andreas-Salomé's story 'Mädchenreigen' draws attention not only to the social construction of gender but also to the power of social norms in women's experience of their body and its desires. The awakening of desire between Hans and Alex is used as an opportunity to critique the social structures of the gender binary, which reassert themselves powerfully and disrupt the utopian 'sibling' equality which had characterized their attraction. Alex's interest in Hans is unconsciously shaped by her appearance as a 'studentischer Bub' (p. 90). But now he explains that he will teach her what it means to be a woman and asks her to grow her hair: 'O sieh, wie schade, daß du dir solchen Bubenkopf gemacht hast und ich nun nicht damit spielen kann' (p. 90). The emancipated Hans had sought gender equality through education. Now she tells Alex:

> 'Du mußt nicht etwa denken, daß ich für mich ehrgeizig bin! Nein! Was das anbelangt, so kann ich gern alle meine Bücher verbrennen. Ich werde nur auf dich stolz sein — aber unbändig stolz. Nicht wahr, dann fühle ich mich doch erst wie eine wirkliche Königin? Nur weil ich in deinem Streben aufgeh!' (p. 91)

The resolution of the story keeps queer sexuality closeted but draws attention in an exaggerated way to the structural inequality of heterosexual relationships; it also calls to mind the issue, raised by Hans earlier in the story, of whether in the light of such inequality, lovers fall in love with someone as they really are, or with an invented image of them (p. 81). When the couple look at each other, they seem to ask each other, 'Bist du es denn, den ich liebe — ?' (p. 94). The story also suggests that society's repression of women's sexuality shapes their response to desire, leading to the experience of sexuality as something that stigmatizes and needs to be brought under control, a source of shame. Bonnie Mann argues that 'shame is the affective power that drives the heterosexualization of women'.[67] As a psychoanalyst, Andreas-Salomé would later reflect on the problem of shame, linking it to coping strategies, including protestations of fidelity: 'vielleicht könnte man sogar argwöhnen, daß eine Frau die allzuviel Voraussetzungen von Treue, Ethik, Ehe und Aehnlichem dazutun muß um sich *nicht* zu schämen, schon in einem etwas zwiespältigen Gutmachenwollen ihres eignen Trieblebens drinsteckt.'[68] Through Hans's exaggerated affective response, the narrative exposes the redemptive strategies needed to alleviate the shame and confusion linked to women's desire. It is hardly an endorsement of gender normativity if women can only experience sexuality through masochistic subordination and a renunciation of their ambition for emancipation. 'Mädchenreigen' casts light on the way social discourses about sexuality shape individuals' attempts to make sense of their own experiences and highlights the confusion which is the result of the ambivalent position of women in a male economy of desire.

The emancipated woman was by no means a peripheral figure in the *fin de siècle*, but one whose disruptive power captured the imagination of readers and who drew attention to the instability of society's gender order. In the cultural programme of modernism, *Die freie Bühne* was described by contributors using masculinist language as 'ein Kampfplatz',[69] at the forefront of a campaign fought under the banner of truth: 'Der Bannerspruch der neuen Kunst, mit goldenen Lettern von den führenden Geistern aufgezeichnet, ist das eine Wort: Wahrheit.'[70] Similarly, at the end of Lou Andreas-Salomé's 'Mädchenreigen', Alex associates with the masculine 'das wirkliche Leben, der Kampf und die Resignation', juxtaposed with 'einen ganzen zarten, lieblichen Mädchenreigen' — within which group he counts Hans, safely the other of the dominant masculine subject (p. 95). Amid fears connected to the feminization of culture and the unstable contours of masculinity, the emancipated woman complicates the gender binary. Her representation in literary texts by women emphasizes the power of the structures which shape conventional gender identity and raises the possibility of creating a new social narrative about gender.

Notes to Chapter 11

1. Ernst von Wolzogen, *Das dritte Geschlecht* (Berlin: Richard Eckstein Nachf., 1899), p. 27. See also Marti M. Lybeck, *Desiring Emancipation: New Women and Homosexuality in Germany, 1880–1933* (Albany, NY: New York Press, 2014), pp. 17–48 and Robert Deam Tobin, *Peripheral Desires: The German Discovery of Sex* (Philadelphia: University of Pennsylvania Press, 2015), pp. 169–84.
2. Ritchie Robertson, 'Gender Anxiety and the Shaping of the Self in Some Modernist Writers: Musil, Hesse, Hofmannsthal, Jahnn', in *The Cambridge Companion to the Modern German Novel*, ed. by Graham Bartram (Cambridge: Cambridge University Press, 2004), pp. 46–61. On the intersection of gender and race, see also Ritchie Robertson, *Kafka: Judaism, Politics, and Literature* (Oxford: Oxford University Press, 1987), and Tobin, p. 176.
3. As Jennifer Drake Askey has analysed in her study of reading and its impact in *Good Girls, Good Germans: Girls' Education and Emotional Nationalism in Wilhelminian Germany* (Rochester, NY: Boydell & Brewer, 2013).
4. See Miranda Fricker, *Epistemic Injustice: Power and the Ethics of Knowing* (Oxford: Oxford University Press, 2007), p. 152, and Sarah Colvin, 'Talking Back: Sharon Dodua Otoo's *Herr Gröttrup setzt sich hin* and the Epistemology of Resistance', *German Life and Letters*, 73 (2020), 659–79 (pp. 661–64).
5. Marie von Ebner-Eschenbach, 'Ein Original', *Erzählungen: Autobiographische Schriften*, ed. by Johannes Klein (Munich: Winkler, 1958), pp. 573–80.
6. See Linda Dietrick 'Gender and Technology in Marie von Ebner-Eschenbach's "Ein Original"', *Women in German Yearbook*, 17 (2001), pp. 141–56 (p. 141).
7. Ibid., p. 151.
8. Theodor W. Adorno, 'Standort des Erzählers im zeitgenössischen Roman' [1958], in *Gesammelte Schriften*, 20 vols, ed. by Rolf Tiedemann and others (Frankfurt a.M.: Suhrkamp, 1974), XI, 41–48.
9. Jeffrey L. Sammons, 'The Nineteenth-Century German Novel', in *German Literature of the Nineteenth Century, 1832–1899*, ed. by Clayton Koelb and Eric Downing (Rochester, NY: Camden House, 2005), pp. 183–206 (p. 192). See for example Michael Minden, 'Grillparzer, *Der arme Spielmann*', in *Landmarks in German Short Prose*, ed. by Peter Hutchinson (Oxford: Peter Lang, 2003), pp. 95–110.
10. G. W. F. Hegel, *Werke*, 21 vols, ed. by Eva Moldenhauer and Karl Markus Michel (Frankfurt a.M.: Suhrkamp, 1970–99), XIII (1986), 199. I am grateful to Johanna-Charlotte Horst for the productive discussion of Hegel's thought.
11. Judith Butler, *Undoing Gender* (New York: Routledge, 2004), p. 150; see also pp. 147–51 and Judith Butler, 'Rethinking Vulnerability and Resistance', in *Vulnerability in Resistance*, ed. by Judith Butler, Zeynep Gambetti and Leticia Sabsay (Durham, NC: Duke University Press, 2016), pp. 12–27 (p. 21).
12. Butler, 'Rethinking Vulnerability', p. 21.
13. Ibid., p. 19.
14. Ibid., p. 16.
15. Robertson, 'Gender Anxiety', p. 47.
16. Ibid., p. 49.
17. Richard Evans, *The Pursuit of Power: Europe 1815–1914* (London: Allen Lane, 2016), pp. 501–02.
18. Elizabeth Boa, 'The Double Taboo: Male Bodies in Kafka's *Der Proceß*', in *Taboos in German Literature*, ed. by David Jackson (Oxford: Berghahn, 1996), pp. 97–118 (p. 111).
19. Russell A. Berman, *The Rise of the Modern German Novel: Crisis and Charisma* (Cambridge, MA: Harvard University Press, 1986), p. 52.
20. Andreas Huyssen, 'Mass Culture as Woman: Modernism's Other', in *After the Great Divide: Modernism, Mass Culture, Postmodernism* (Bloomington: Indiana University Press, 1986), pp. 44–64 (p. 46).
21. M. G. Conrad, 'Zur Einführung', *Die Gesellschaft*, 1 (1885), issue 1: 1–3 (p. 1). See also Charlotte Woodford, *Women, Emancipation and the German Novel* (Oxford: MHRA, 2014), pp. 61–62.
22. Conrad, p. 1, and see Huyssen, p. 50.

23. Elizabeth Boa, *The Sexual Circus: Wedekind's Theatre of Subversion* (Oxford: Blackwell, 1987), p. 46.
24. See ibid., p. 46.
25. Sigmund Freud, *Gesammelte Werke*, 18 vols, ed. by Anna Freud (London: Imago, 1942), v, 181. See also Kirsten Leng, *Sexual Politics and Feminist Science: Women Sexologists in Germany, 1900–1933* (Ithaca, NY: Cornell University Press, 2018), who argues sexologists saw women as 'objects to be studied, managed, and contained', p. 3.
26. See Hannah S. Decker, *Freud, Dora, and Vienna 1900* (New York: The Free Press, 1992), pp. 56–58.
27. Geoff Eley, 'What was German Modernity and When?', in *German Modernities from Wilhelm to Weimar: A Contest of Futures*, ed. by Geoff Eley, Jennifer L. Jenkins and Tracie Matysik (London: Bloomsbury, 2016), pp. 59–82 (p. 70).
28. Sander Gilman, *Freud, Race and Gender* (Princeton, NJ: Princeton University Press, 1993), pp. 8–9.
29. See Marianne DeKoven, 'Modernism and Gender', in *The Cambridge Companion to Modernism*, ed. by Michael Harry Levenson (Cambridge: Cambridge University Press, 1999), pp 174–93 (p. 174 and p. 183).
30. Mary Douglas, *Collected Works*, 12 vols (London: Routledge, 2003), II: *Purity and Danger*, p. 96. First published in 1966.
31. Ibid.
32. Elizabeth Boa, *Kafka: Gender, Class and Race in the Letters and Fictions* (Oxford: Oxford University Press, 1996), p. 107.
33. Douglas, p. 97.
34. Robertson, *Kafka*, p. 72.
35. Franz Kafka, *Drucke zu Lebzeiten,* ed. by Wolf Kittler, Hans-Gerd Koch and Gerhard Neumann (Frankfurt a.M.: Fischer, 1996), pp. 115–200 (p. 166).
36. Franz Kafka, *Der Proceß*, ed. by Malcolm Pasley (Frankfurt a.M.: Fischer, 1990), p. 48. See also Robertson, *Kafka*, p. 109.
37. Otto Weininger, *Geschlecht und Charakter: Eine prinzipielle Untersuchung* (Munich: Matthes & Seitz, 1980), p. 239. See also Ritchie Robertson, *The 'Jewish Question' in German Literature 1749–1939: Emancipation and its Discontents* (Oxford: Oxford University Press, 1999), pp. 296–302.
38. See Helmut Kiesel, *Geschichte der literarischen Moderne: Sprache, Ästhetik, Dichtung im zwanzigsten Jahrhundert* (Munich: C. H. Beck, 2004), pp. 85–92.
39. Maria Janitschek, 'In Weiß', in *Vom Weibe: Charakterzeichnungen* (Berlin: S. Fischer, 1896), pp. 55–66.
40. Janitschek, 'In Weiß', p. 57.
41. See Fricker, pp. 155, who analyses the negative effect on individuals' self-understanding of difficulties in rendering experiences such as sexual harassment intelligible to others.
42. Janitschek, 'In Weiß', p. 60.
43. Lou Andreas-Salomé, 'Mein Dank an Freud', in *"Mein Dank an Freud": Aufsätze und Essays, 4: Psychoanalyse*, ed. by Brigitte Rempp and Inge Weber (Taching am See: MedienEdition Welsch, 2012), pp. 169–266 (p. 178).
44. Ibid.
45. Lou Andreas-Salomé, *Ruth: Erzählung*, ed. by Michaela Wiesner-Bangard (Taching am See: MedienEdition Welsch, 2017). All further page references are drawn from this edition.
46. See Michaela Wiesner-Bangard, 'Zäsur und Neuorientierung: Die Erzählung "Ruth" als Wendepunkt im Leben von Lou Andreas-Salomé', in Andreas-Salomé, *Ruth*, pp. 292–99 (p. 293).
47. Michaela Wiesner-Bangard and Ursula Welsch, *Lou Andreas-Salomé. '…wie ich Dich liebe Rätselleben'. Eine Biographie* (Stuttgart: Reclam, 2008), p. 28.
48. Andreas-Salomé, *Ruth*, p. 23.
49. Fricker, p. 148.
50. Lou Andreas-Salome, 'Mädchenreigen', in *Menschenkinder: Novellencyclus*, ed. by Iris Schäfer (Taching am See: MedienEdition Welsch, 2017), pp. 67–96. All page references given in brackets

refer to this edition. First published in *Cosmopolis: An International Monthly Review*, 11.33 (1898), 803–28.
51. Lou Andreas-Salomé, *Henrik Ibsens Frauen-Gestalten: Psychologische Bilder nach seinen sechs Familiendramen*, ed. by Cornelia Pechota (Taching am See: MedienEdition Welsch, 2012). First published in 1892.
52. On 'female masculinity' in the *fin de siècle*, see Lybeck, pp. 49–82.
53. Ibid., p. 74.
54. See Elizabeth Boa, 'The Double Taboo'.
55. See Heike Bauer, 'Theorizing Female Inversion: Sexology, Discipline and Gender at the Fin de Siècle', *Journal of the History of Sexuality*, 18 (2009), 84–102 (p. 86).
56. Ibid., p. 86.
57. Ibid., p. 102.
58. Lybeck, p. 72.
59. See Bauer, pp. 92 and 102.
60. Lou Andreas-Salomé, *Friedrich Nietzsche in seinen Werken* (Dresden: Carl Reißner Verlag, 1924), p. 29. First published in 1894.
61. Robert Tobin, 'Making Way for the Third Sex: Liberal and Antiliberal Impulses in Mann's Portrayal of Male-Male Desire in His Early Short Fiction', in *A Companion to German Realism*, ed. by Todd Kontje (Rochester, NY: Boydell & Brewer, 2002), pp. 307–38 (p. 308–09).
62. Ibid., p. 314.
63. Lybeck, p. 74.
64. Tobin, 'Making Way for the Third Sex', pp. 312–14.
65. Ibid., p. 313.
66. Ibid., p. 315.
67. Bonnie Mann, 'Femininity, Shame, and Redemption', in *Gender and the Politics of Shame*, ed. by Clara Fischer, *Hypatia: A Journal of Feminist Philosophy*, 33 (2018), 402–17 (p. 402).
68. Lou Andreas-Salomé, *In der Schule bei Freud: Tagebuch eines Jahres 1912/13*, ed. by Manfred Klemann (Taching am See: MedienEdition Welsch, 2017), p. 62. Bonnie Mann also argues for moments of 'redemption' which alleviate women's shame in a 'masculinist economy of desire', in which she includes the marriage proposal and the wedding day (p. 413).
69. Ludwig Fulda, 'Moral und Kunst', *Freie Bühne für modernes Leben*, 1 (1890), 5–9 (p. 9).
70. [Otto Brahm], 'Zum Beginn', *Freie Bühne für modernes Leben*, 1 (1890), 1–2 (p. 1).

CHAPTER 12

Bloch, Benjamin, Brecht and *Bilderrätsel*: Reading the Signs in Weimar

Anthony Phelan

It may have been Detective Chief Inspector Endeavour Morse's alma mater, but neither he nor Lewis and Hathaway have often been seen around St John's. In his own way, however, Ritchie Robertson has proved another sort of literary sleuth, running to earth conspiracies and conspiracy theorists.[1] And in the case of Kafka, he has reminded us that everyday objects tend to become symbolic, both because in Kafka's 'simple' and 'bare' fictional world only the essentials are left to convey meaning, and because repeated mention 'causes these objects to take on more than literal significance'. In consequence, the reader becomes 'adept in reading clues', though 'without a conscious grasp of the system that makes our readings possible'. *Der Process* confronts the reader with the task of 'understanding the various semiotic systems deployed in the novel'.[2]

I

Such a reading of clues and deciphering of signs, within the semiotic systems of modernity, becomes urgently necessary amid the political tensions of the Weimar Republic. In *Erbschaft dieser Zeit* (1935), Ernst Bloch sets out to identify the emergent and declining formations — social, psychological, economic and political — that frame a conflicted consciousness in the interwar years. Like so many others in the period from before the First World War to the collapse of the Republic and beyond, Bloch engages with the rapid expansion of visual culture in print media, in cinema and photography. The book is constructed as a patchwork of texts, ranging from the briefest gloss to extended essays and reviews, some written much earlier and others composed when Bloch was already in exile from Nazi Germany. Scanning the culture of the Weimar Republic and its most characteristic patterns of experience, Bloch seeks out moments of 'nonsimultaneity': 'Nicht alle sind im selben Jetzt da'.[3] Progressive or emancipatory aspects of contemporary experience may turn out to be caught up with nostalgic or retrogressive impulses in the complex dynamic of social change. This reading of the historical process articulated Bloch's unorthodox Marxism as he negotiated the rigid categories of the Second and Third International.[4] Close scrutiny in Bloch's writing reveals the signs and symptoms of emergent forms of awareness alongside and co-mixed with earlier patterns now in decline. When Bloch examines the changing meanings of urban spaces and cultures in post-war Berlin, these indices of change and resistance appear, in a famous phrase, as the enigmatic 'Bilderrätsel eines gesprungenen Bewußtseins', the rebus of a fractured consciousness (*EdZ*, p. 228). The essays and glosses setting out this divided state of mind stand at the very centre of his account of the Weimar Republic and the Nazi ascendancy.

Bloch's book had been in circulation well before its official publication date at the beginning of 1935, and Walter Benjamin had been anxious to discover how his own work had fared in the reviews that were included in *Erbschaft*.[5] When he did finally get sight of the book, Benjamin's letter to Siegfried Kracauer caught the importance of a particular sequence of texts headed 'Übergang: Berlin, Funktionen im Hohlraum', in which Bloch sets out the intellectual framework for his analysis. In his letter on 15 January 1935, Benjamin notes:

> Der Gegenstand lag auf der Hand und ist in den Kapiteln über die Ungleichzeitigkeit gelegentlich sehr genau formuliert. Leider machen sie einen 'Übergang' statt jenes methodische Zentrum abzugeben, von dem allein aus auch der Partner dieser Rede unzweideutig aufzurufen gewesen wäre: ich meine das Kulturbüro der K.P. [Kommunistischen Partei] (GB v, 28)

However much Bloch may read the signs of the times, for Benjamin his account lacks solid forensic proof ('die forensischen Beweismittel'), and the letter drifts on to Benjamin's other recent reading, books by Georges Simenon and Agatha Christie. This casual connection between the forensic power that Benjamin misses in Bloch's account and Benjamin's enthusiasm for murder mysteries returns us to the need to be adept at reading the clues. Crime-scenes re-emerge later in the year in Benjamin's remarks on the photographic work of Eugène Atget. This text appeared in the first draft of 'Das Kunstwerk im Zeitalter seiner technischen Reproduzierbarkeit', which was probably begun in September:

> Sehr mit Recht hat man von ihm gesagt, dass er [die pariser Straßen um 1900] aufnahm wie einen Tatort. Auch der Tatort ist menschenleer. Seine Aufnahme geschieht der Indizien wegen. Die photographischen Aufnahmen beginnen bei Atget Beweisstücke im historischen Prozeß zu werden.[6]

Like Kafka's objects that take on more than literal significance, the photographic image can provide the clues to solve a crime, precisely the forensic evidence of the hidden historical process, or — in a different register — to resolve an enigma.

Bloch too turns to photography and visual effects, but in his case the riddling and complex images of contemporaneity are focused on the cultural and political meanings of *montage*.[7] Montage, he suggests, provides a principle with which to unlock the phenomena of Weimar life. This works in two forms: the first, which he calls unmediated montage ('Montage, unmittelbar'), can be modelled as collage, 'das geschnittene, neu *geklebte* Lichtbild' — recalling both the agit-prop practices of John Heartfield or the Dada collages of Raoul Haussmann and Hannah Höch. Bloch suspects that montage, understood in this literal sense, proves in reality to be 'Schloßrestaurierung des Hintergrunds' (*EdZ*, p. 222). — Behind its two-dimensional surface the old order is being reinstated; as revue, jazz, or any of the kaleidoscopic forms of combinatory art, unmediated montage represents the slackening and fragmentation of order quite directly. Its aesthetic disturbance is part of the very social order it appears to resist. In this, its action is compared to that of 'Sachlichkeit', the principle associated with the New Sobriety of the 1920s. For Bloch, this 'Neue Sachlichkeit' can only present directly the complex and contradictory impulses and desires of a bourgeois past that has nowhere to go. In its attention to shining surfaces, 'Sachlichkeit' only seems to bring renewal to the façades of Wilhelminian culture, society and architecture. Yet it remains a façade, and in both cases the surface conceals mechanisms that are conservative or restorationist, resistant to the very modernity they seem to promote.

What is combined in techniques of collage may hence be no more than what remains of a fragmented social formation. However, Bloch gives a more positive account of 'Bilderrätsel' in a passage outlining the usefulness of a second form of montage. If collage continues to emphasize a totality in the artwork or in the surface of the reconstituted image, montage can also stress a disruptive energy in the force of interruption and a separation of elements. The positive model of this second form is Brecht, whose dramaturgy ruptures the supposed continuities of character and action. The counter-example is provided, as so often on the left, by James Joyce and *Ulysses*. In such a case, 'Bilderrätsel und Vexierbilder', disturbing though they may seem, can be effectively exploited as the '"interessanten" Glanz einer geistigen Produktion, die regulär hier gar nicht mehr möglich wäre' (*EdZ*, p. 226). The disturbance created by some puzzling ambiguity may challenge the status quo, but the risk remains that it merely adds piquancy to the cultural spectacle without changing its fundamental orientation. Such is Bloch's version of the widespread critique of Joyce on the cultural left. Nevertheless, fragments of the shattered surface of a past society can be recombined as 'Partikeln einer anderen Sprache' (*EdZ*, p. 227). Max Ernst and other Surrealists are supposed to have attempted this unknown language, but the outstanding examples cited are Brecht's theatre practice, as a model of 'Umfunktionierung', along with Benjamin's own philosophical investigations, which stress the significance of emphatic interruption (as against mere disturbance). Tacitly, Bloch's own methods of writing in a combinatory assemblage of aphoristic and essayistic texts are implied by the general rubric of philosophical montage. Bloch's allusive summary of montage deployed as radical discontinuity includes the vocabulary of Brecht's dramaturgy alongside many themes of Benjamin's own work. Echoing his essay on Surrealism and its relation to the social and political *locus standi* of French writers, for instance, Bloch sketches the structural force of Surrealist innovation. The two critics even share the sense of a revolutionary reappropriation of fragments whose former coherence has been lost. (One might think of Otto Dix's Dresden paintings immediately after the First World War, or of John Heartfield's or Hannah Höch's collages in this context.) Any unitary recasting of these fragments will only become possible in some post-revolutionary future for which they cry out. Yet, as Bloch says, the process of recasting is inclined to absorb the 'bankruptcy assets' of the dying bourgeois society: 'Doch ist der Guß geneigt, manche Konkursmasse in sich aufzunehmen, vor allem eben Bilderrätsel eines gesprungenen Bewußtseins, so wunderlich und neu "den Menschen" meinend' (*EdZ*, p. 228).

Bloch thus understands the hieroglyphic riddles of Weimar modernity in a specifically historical way. Initially these riddling images are enjoined on the critical spectator by a flawed and fractured consciousness, split between its historic investments and the future possibilities it nurtures — but they do not appear to exceed it. Through the reappropriation and recasting of inherited cultural paradoxes and aporia, however, a necessary critique of the capitalist class in its late self-expression is made possible; the flaws in its self-consciousness give the reader of signs access to the complex political truth that such a class cannot in itself attain to — and these are the 'Bilderrätsel eines gesprungenen Bewußtseins'.

Bloch's use of this strong visual metaphor to capture the complexity of a particular historical and social conjuncture exemplifies his intellectual methods as well as the interrelation of politics and aesthetics in his book;[8] but the immediate emphasis of his analysis is less on any particular enigma and much more on the structural procedures of montage itself. Because, in one version, montage allows for the survival or continuance, in fragmentary form, of an older culture (and the class that sustained it), the recasting ('Guß') that can also be achieved by montage as a practice is interpreted as the site of productive ambiguity. Berlin and its diverse forms of art and architecture are the locus of this politically and historically labile activity:

> Das ebenso abstrakte wie variable Berlin ist diesen Formen, zwischen Proletariat und Bourgeoisie, der immerhin vorgeschrittenste, der lehrreichste Ort. Lehrreich in der Zerstreuung und Lockerung nicht nur, auch in den Vexierbildern geformter Lockerung oder des Experiments, dem ein *spezifisch* 'Irrationales' nicht fehlt. (*EdZ*, p. 215)

In a gloss headed 'Das Schiffshaus', Bloch registers the maritime look of modernist architecture. He is probably thinking of such features as the external steel balustrades of the balconies and the external curves of buildings such as the Dessau Bauhaus, and even its central staircase, made famous by Oskar Schlemmer's 'Bauhaustreppe' of 1932.[9] Bloch's text, following the account of montage in its mediated forms, gives a more concrete instance of the productive ambiguity he seeks: in a discussion that recalls Benjamin's conversations with Brecht on the question of 'dwelling' or 'inhabiting' ('Das Wohnen'), Bloch sees the New Architecture as open to a new kind of mobility that counters the apparent fixity of steel:[10]

> Jazz klingt vortrefflich zu Stahl, und die Weisen Weills zeigen, daß der Stahl nicht stimmt. Das Haus als Schiff verneint den Platz, worauf er steht; denn Schiffe haben Lust, zu verschwinden. Die Ordre, wohin sie bestimmt sind, wird nicht geöffnet, solange man noch kreuzt; erst später. Doch einige Stücke daraus (ein lumpiger oder böiger Wind pfeift durch) sind jetzt schon bekannt. (*EdZ*, p. 229)

The modernist building needs to move, and its mobility towards a different time is perceived here as a riddle whenever the utopian breeze blows through its portholes.

Bloch characteristically identifies the presence of the riddle by the disturbance it causes in its current social and historical position: the modernist moment upsets the broad securities of the Wilhelmine past.

II

This theory of the ambiguity of the image, the 'Bilderrätsel' modelled in photomontage, comes relatively late in a reception of the photographic image that began, perhaps, with Baudelaire's attack on photography in the *Salon of 1859*, and Heine's sometimes quizzical endorsement of the Daguerreotype, in *Lutezia* for instance, as a guarantee of authenticity.[11] In the early twentieth century, there is another current in the turn towards the visual. Before the First World War the visual image had taken a central, though often unacknowledged role in the lyric of the early Expressionists. Technical innovation in the visual sphere, beyond photography, is wittily and alarmingly registered in Jakob van Hoddis's poem 'Kinematograph' (1911), right down to the headless Herr Piefke, decapitated by a jumping projector frame; Alfred Lichtenstein too captures some of the phenomena of early film entertainment in 'Kientoppbildchen' (1912);[12] but it was Ferdinand Hardekopf — according to Kurt Hiller the (unwilling) presiding genius of Expressionism — who self-consciously recognized the force of the image.[13] Lichtenstein already displays the *frame* as a constitutive element in the imagistic *Reihungsstil* of 'Die Dämmerung' (1913: 'An einem Fenster klebt ein fetter Mann'), while at the end of 'Kientoppbildchen' an old woman appears in the frame of a window. Hardekopf's poem 'Bar' in *Lesestücke* (1916) recognizes the spectacle of the apache dancers and the fiddlers who accompany them as a *tableau* –'welch Effekt im Bild'[14] — but more radically, in his poem 'Abneigung' in the same collection, Hardekopf rejects three-dimensional space altogether in favour of the two-dimensional *surface*: 'Ich hasse den Raum, ich vergöttre die Fläche, | Die Fläche ist heilig, der Raum ist profan'. Here the remnants of Jugendstil aesthetics are combined with Hardekopf's early interest in the new medium of film: in a 1912 letter to René Schickele he even suggested the name 'cinema' as an alternative to the current 'Kientopp'.[15] The sinuous lines and abnegation of depth in *art nouveau* open up for Hardekopf a further set of possibilities:

> Ich werde mich listig der Plastik entwinden
> Und laß euch gebläht im gedunsenen Raum.
> Ich denke die lieblichsten Schatten zu finden
> Im gefälligen Teppich, im flächigen Traum.[16]

The 'darling shadows' to be found, once free of plasticity, are projections on the surface of dream. The poem appeared in *Die Aktion* in 1916; and the origin of this insight is apparent in a text from one year earlier, 'Morgen-Arbeit' of 1915: 'Und nahm, der Geistestötung neuster Technik schon verpflichtet, | den Stacheltrieb zur Form erneut in Kauf'.[17] Although for Hardekopf film technology is a kind of distraction, it makes inescapable aesthetic demands. The *Traumfabrik* of cinema production yields a new imaginative technology ('nur flächig sei hinfort geträumt'), which in turn sets the standard for a new literary registration of complex experience.

In the genealogy of the visual hermeneutic traced here and expounded by Ernst Bloch as 'Bilderrätsel', Hardekopf reflects very directly on the imagistic styles of his younger contemporaries; in addition to the cinematic model of the visual imagination, the shadows to be found within the dream surface begin to indicate a psychological dimension of unconscious meanings in and under the imagery.

Such a strain of thought is also at work in Bloch's account of disruptive imagery as a visual riddle. It is surely no accident that in his introduction to the dreamwork in *Die Traumdeutung*, Freud tells us that the dream-content is given as a kind of hieroglyphic communication ('Bilderschrift'), and illustrates the process by reference to 'ein Bilderrätsel (Rebus)'.[18] Freud goes on to establish four dream-functions:

> One is condensation, in which different dream elements are fused. Different people may be identified; different ideas may be linked by a pun [...]. At the same time, the dream-work practices displacement, transferring emotional intensity from the centre of the dream thought to its marginal components.[19]

The well-known quadrilateral is completed by the requirement of adequate and appropriate representation within the dream world, and finally by secondary revision and partial rationalization in the way the dreamer accounts for their dream to themselves or to the psychoanalyst. Bloch's complex reading of the visual as the 'Bilderrätsel' and 'Vexierbilder' of the modernist city clearly adopts some of the hermeneutic techniques that Freud had pioneered. But the meanings of the photographic image in particular had been, and continued to be, examined by other contemporaries, who had also seen the urgent need for political decipherment in a modern world increasingly saturated with imagery.

Throughout the 1920s there were other practitioners and theorists in the field. The photographic elements of Kurt Tucholsky's collaboration with John Heartfield in *Deutschland, Deutschland über alles* (1929), for instance, exemplify some of Bloch's sense of social and political ambiguities rendered visible in the images the book presents. This is often achieved through extensive commentary but sometimes with no more than the laconic legend of a cartoon. Arranged in a loose revue-form, the book impersonates a popular magazine — and even includes a picture puzzle ('Vexierbild') of its own: this page reproduces as a photograph a handwritten letter from Hindenburg in defence of the Kaiser and ending with the words 'Es ist leicht, dem todten Löwen einen Fußtritt zu versetzen!' Treating the letter itself as the 'Vexierbild', Tucholsky's text asks 'Wo ist der Löwe?', and adds in an italicized commentary, 'Der Löwe hat eine Rente von monatlich ungefähr 50 000 Mark'.[20] The riddle of the puzzle-picture deployed here is in fact part of Tucholsky's satire on the exiled Kaiser and his continuing 'presence' in the Weimar Republic that runs through the whole book. The photograph with the title 'S[eine]. M[ajestät]. in Zivil' shows Wilhelm II posing in a suit, wearing a homburg hat, wing-collar, and cravat with a very noticeable jewelled tie-pin. The photograph illustrates a text entitled 'Schädlichkeit des Zivils' which purports to explain the unpopularity of Ludendorff, after his humiliating defeat at the election of 1925, in a society that has set aside the uniforms that had previously guaranteed his authority: 'eine Phantasieuniform, die ja heute nicht mehr vorhanden ist, die es nicht mehr gibt, die zum historischen Maskenkostüm geworden ist'.[21] The implication is that Kaiser Wilhelm II has also forfeited any standing or plausibility, once he has been subjected to the 'Schädlichkeit des Zivils': the fading authority of the pre-republican order, even as it continues to make its presence felt throughout the Weimar years, is dialectically exposed in the tension between the examples of Ludendorff and his Kaiser, and held in the respectable civilian, middle-class dress of 'His Majesty'. The implication of such images begins to have the kind of symptomatic force that Bloch would ascribe to his 'Bilderrätsel eines gesprungenen Bewußtseins'. The textual element associated with a photograph can be minimal, as a kind of *inscriptio*, yet the combined text and image can nevertheless convey social and political fissures as part of the everyday reality of the Republic. Thus an image headed 'Demokratie' shows, in close-up, the elaborately ornamental front door of a grand-bourgeois house and on the wall above the door-bell three small enamel plaques reading, in ascending order: 'Aufgang nur für Herrschaften'; 'Eingang um die Ecke'; 'Nebeneingang für Boten und Dienstpersonal'. The instructions to messenger deliveries and servants in the Republican context of Weimar needs no further commentary: the image speaks for itself. Its contradictory presence, like the riddles set by late capitalism in Bloch's theory, lays bare the class divisions of society.

These images hold together the here-and-now of their empirical representation with a larger meaning, which allegorically underlies the immediate and local. Tucholsky is well aware of this different kind of structural tension:

> im Augenblick, wo man eine Photographie, die einen Bürger, einen Arbeiter, irgendjemand darstellt, der nicht im öffentlichen Leben steht, so textiert, daß diese Figur das ausspricht, was aus der Gesinnung ihrer Gruppe kommt, dann gibt es ein Malheur.[22]

Between the personal, at any rate, and the socio-political there is still a disturbing gap. Walter Benjamin registers a similar anxiety in relation to the validity of photographic images which must be regarded as 'historical' in his 'Kleine Geschichte der Photographie' (1931): the temporality of the image provided by early photography irresistibly invites the modern viewer to seek 'das winzige Fünkchen Zufall, Hier und Jetzt' where 'im Sosein jener längstvergangenen Minute das Künftige heut noch und so beredt nistet, daß wir, rückblickend, es entdecken können'.[23] Benjamin's point of reference is the studio portrait of the photographer Karl Dauthendey and his fiancée: as she gazes past him, beyond the frame of the image, Benjamin seeks the reality of her subsequent suicide, which, he believes, seems to burn through the surface of the photograph ('den Bildcharakter durchsengt hat'). Beyond and within the present moment captured by the photograph, in the temporality of an historical image viewed with hindsight, a larger truth is compacted and concentrated: not only the death of Frau Dauthendey, but the difference in the spectator's relation to and expectations of photography in the changing conditions of its reception, application, and instrumentalization. The full meaning of the image includes, then, at several levels, what has accrued in the passage of time.²⁴ The connection to his next example seems to be this expansion of what is invisibly 'present' in an image or a series of images through slow-motion (in film) or through photographic enlargement to yield insight into an 'optical unconscious'. The technical development of modern photography inclines to the scientific registration of 'Strukturbeschaffenheiten, Zellgewebe', and yet it also gives access to what Benjamin calls 'die physiognomischen Aspekte, Bildwelten, welche im Kleinsten wohnen, deutbar und verborgen' (GS II.I, 371). This allusion to a physiognomic dimension of the image, rendered accessible by contemporary photographic techniques, points towards the kind of resolution that these enigmatic details have in common with other 'Rätselbilder', 'deutbar und verborgen' in another way. In section IV of the 1935 *Exposé* of the *Passagen-Werk*, the physiognomic method is identified both with Edgar Allan Poe as the inventor of the detective mystery (GS V.I, 54), but also, in the case of the collector (at [H2, 7 / H2a, 1]), with a prophetic reading of objects for their historical and future meanings (GS V.I, 274–75).

This reading — not necessarily of images proper, but of certain visual effects, as indices of political meaning — can also be found in the note of a conversation with his friend Ernst Joël in October, 1928. Benjamin is commenting on a problem of representation, or more precisely of 'Veranschaulichung' — of illustration and rendering perceptible. How, he asks, might the items on exhibit in a museum be deployed in such a way that they achieve 'nicht Abbildung sondern Aktualisierung des Raumes oder der Zeit, in der das Ding funktioniert' (GS VI, 416)? In his next note, two days later, he returns to 'Veranschaulichung' via the historical example of Lenin's significance as a political figure. The example chosen by Benjamin to illustrate his thinking is not literally an image but rather a short memoir published in French in June 1928, under the title 'Découverte de Lénine', in the journal *Europe*, in which the Russian author Yefim Zozulia reflects on Lenin's body language and posture at the fifth, seventh, and eighth Congresses of the Soviets (1918–20).²⁵ At the first two congresses Zozulia, observing Lenin's demeanour, registers ennui, contempt ('mépris') and impatience, as if Lenin is preoccupied with other, more pressing matters. It is not until the eighth Congress that Zozulia comes to understand this puzzling behaviour. As if in birthday mood, Lenin seems to be looking to a time beyond the political rhetoric and strategic struggles of the Party. At the eighth Congress, although Lenin may in reality be speaking of grain distribution and biologically derived non-fossil fuels, Zozulia reinterprets the solution of economic problems as metaphors of an ultimate human fulfilment — liberation from forced (i.e. unavoidable) labour ('travail de forçat'). In his note of 28 October 1928, Benjamin cites Zozulia's account of Lenin's speech, on the technical and agricultural development of a future society, as demonstrating a technique of presentation or illustration:

> Die Technik der Veranschaulichung als *wissenschaftliches* Experiment, als heuristisches Prinzip. Ferner: die demonstratio ad hominem: ein politisches Prinzip. Die Metapher aus den Dingen entbinden heißt, ihren anthropologischen Kern entdecken und das ist wiederum identisch mit der Darstellung ihrer politischen Bedeutung. Die politische Bedeutung betrifft die Masse als den

Beschenkten. Und diese Betroffenheit ist gebunden an die überraschende Bindung der gerade in Frage stehenden, entdeckten Metapher an die gerade gegebene Ausdrucksform (Bild, Sprache und so in immer engeren Kategorien); die Metapher wird schließlich, genau gesehen, die einzig mögliche Erscheinungsform des Dinges. (GS VI, 417)

The process in which such visual data are interpreted, along the lines of Zozulia's description of Lenin, progressively narrows the distance between the thing and that for which its stands as a metaphor. Benjamin's sense of the scientific nature of this project recalls his interest in the effects of scientific photography in the Weimar photographer Karl Bloßfeldt's blow-ups of plants, cited in the 'Kleine Geschichte der Photographie' (GS II.1, 372). Commenting on these famous photographs, Benjamin insists that what is primarily the concern of technology or medicine in their enlarged detail is 'der Kamera ursprünglich verwandter als die stimmungsvolle Landschaft oder das seelenvolle Porträt' (GS II.1, 371). The heuristic principle mentioned in Benjamin's meditation on Zozulia's image of Lenin parallels in turn what is thought of as 'physiognomic' in his discussion of Bloßfeldt. The plant photographs seem to reveal archaic forms — a crozier or Gothic tracery — in the detail of botanical specimens, much as the collector in the *Passagen-Werk* can find in each of the objects of his collection a whole history of provenance, ownership, price, which opens out as a 'magische Enzyklopädie, eine Weltordnung' (GS V.1, 274). Like the photographic imagination conjuring historic and archaic objects in botanical enlargements, the objective material of Lenin's speech yields a metaphor which becomes the manifestation of what is implied in the image. Both in its temporal or historical transparency and in its verbalized form, this understanding of 'Veranschaulichung', in the relation of a thing, its image, and the metaphor of which it is a part, is organized in ways that parallel Bloch's consideration of the latent meanings of montage in its various forms. As Miriam Bratu Hansen pointed out, 'the optical unconscious marks a spot that readmits dimensions of temporality and memory via, and into, the very technologies capable of eliminating them':[26] the technical 'coolness' of the image, in becoming transparent to an associative mode of perception and to its temporal implications, mobilizes the metaphorical order with a kind of revelatory force.

III

In Bloch and Benjamin, but also in Tucholsky working with Heartfield, the combinatory montage of the photographic image and even, in the case of Zozulia's Lenin, personal reportage of posture and gesture can be understood as giving access to an unconscious dimension, identified as the political dialectic suspended and concealed in an image, but clearly present and interpretable under certain kinds of interrogation. Siegfried Kracauer's subtle essay on the photographic image ('Die Photographie', 1927) begins from a sense of unease, not unlike the paradox of the personal and the representative to which Tucholsky refers in the preface to *Deutschland*. Kracauer notes that when looking at photographic images of their grandmothers, a younger generation encounters, simultaneously, a representation of time itself: 'Zwar ist die Zeit nicht mit photographiert wie das Lächeln oder die Chignons, aber die Photographie selber, so dünkt ihnen, ist eine Darstellung der Zeit'.[27] Kracauer's critical attack in the piece is aimed, however, at contemporary uses of the photographic image as an exploitative immobilization of rational engagement with the real world. In this respect, Kracauer's essay is ultimately much less optimistic than the work of many contemporaries. As Andrew Benjamin has outlined in a suggestive argument, he may indeed allude to 'the creation of a surface as nature — naturalizing the surface — then the destruction of that surface' because 'the destruction of "coherence" is, for Kracauer, the creation of meaning'.[28] In Kracauer's own formulation from 'Das Ornament der Masse', 'Wo die Vernunft den organischen Zusammenhang zerfällt und die wie immer kultivierte natürliche Oberfäche aufreißt, dort redet sie [...]'.[29] But this possibility of a photographic emancipation remains precariously dependent on the vulnerability of the very society, in its capitalist formation, that offers a possible glimpse of critical consciousness. Kracauer writes of the society that the capitalist production process has created: 'Hat sie aber nicht Bestand, so ist dem freigesetzten Bewußtsein eine unvergleichliche Chance gegeben.'[30] This prospect of fully liberated consciousness remains, however, 'das *Vabanque-Spiel* der Geschichte', History's final desperate throw in the trajectory of human freedom.

This penultimate part of Kracauer's photography essay scans the history of 'bildliche Darstellungen' from a primordial natural community, summarized by a quotation from Johann Jakob Bachofen, in which human consciousness is entirely held by nature, to the critical moment when history has a chance to break with the embrace of nature even if it can only do so by 'going for broke' (the 'Va banque' of chemin de fer). The operative distinction at the centre of this part of Kracauer's essay is the one between symbol and allegory: Kracauer understands symbol in terms of a dependency where humanity is still 'in einer praktischen Abhängigkeit von den Naturverhältnissen'.[31] As critical consciousness frees itself from this natural bond, the relation to the image changes to the more distanced form of allegory.

The term is introduced with a quotation from Friedrich Creuzer's *Symbolik und Mythologie der alten Völker, besonders der Griechen* (1812): 'Diese [Allegorie] bedeutet bloß einen allgemeinen Begriff oder eine Idee, die von ihr selbst verschieden ist, jene [Symbol] ist die versinnlichte, verkörperte Idee selbst.'[32] This quotation is taken from a longer passage in Creuzer's *Symbolik* that also appears in Benjamin's *Ursprung des deutschen Trauerspiels* (GS I.I, 341). Benjamin had known Kracauer since 1923, and it seems clear that Kracauer drew on Benjamin's work: Creuzer's study is relatively obscure. Given that on 20 October 1926 Benjamin complained in a letter to Kracauer (GB III, 205) that Rowohlt had still not published his two books, *Ursprung des deutschen Trauerspiels*, in which Creuzer is expounded, and *Einbahnstraße*, it seems more than likely that Kracauer's discussion of the meaning of photography was at least informed by Benjamin's thinking in his *Habilitationsschrift*, which Kracauer eventually reviewed along with *Einbahnstraße* when they appeared in 1928.[33]

It is in the account of the Baroque origins of modernity that the hermeneutic and semiotic principles that have been considered here across the range of left cultural theory in the Weimar Republic probably find their most sophisticated exposition. Because the Baroque dramas addressed by Benjamin rely on allegory as their most characteristic form of representation, like Kracauer he also needs to trace a cultural history of allegory parallel to the account he gives of the history of drama from the Baroque to Expressionism. The need for a revisionist reading is perhaps even more pressing in the case of allegory, given that the canonical authority of Goethe was so much on the side of the organic unity and harmony of the symbol, as against the supposedly 'mechanical' apparatus of allegory. After the core exposition of his understanding of allegory, in a famous passage of the *Trauerspiel* book Benjamin therefore provides an account of the varying fate of allegorical expression in German culture.

It is clearly significant, for Benjamin, that Creuzer seems to think allegory went hand in hand with a Reformation hostility to symbols. Benjamin quotes Creuzer: '"Mit den Fortschritten der Reformation mußte das Symbolische als Ausdruck der Religionsgeheimnisse mehr und mehr verschwinden"' (GS 1.1, 344–45). This process is echoed, according to Benjamin's account, in the historical position of the *Trauerspiel*. The point would be that the undissolved unity of signified and signifier, in the sacramental bread and wine of the Mass, was rejected by the reformed understanding of the Eucharistic action as memorial or recollection, rather than re-enactment.

In following the efforts of Creuzer to grasp the meaning of allegory as a form of expression, Benjamin draws on Karl Giehlow's more recent historical research on hieroglyphs and their reception in the renaissance (*Hieroglyphenkunde des Humanismus*, 1915). This enables Benjamin to focus on two particular forms of representation. First, the *rebus* is derived from the renaissance humanist view of hieroglyphs not as a form of writing capable of phonetic realization, but as an 'immediate' writing-with-things (Latin: *rebus*). In the aesthetic practice of the Baroque, Benjamin sees a process in which nature is reduced to a mode of signification. In turn, nature suppresses history, which is reduced to a series of exempla: 'Geschichte galt in den moralischen Exempeln und Katastrophen nur als ein stoffliches Element der Emblematik. Es siegt das starre Antlitz der bedeutenden Natur und ein für allemal soll die Geschichte verschlossen bleiben in dem Requisit' (GS 1.1, 347).

History is relegated to the status of a stage-prop in which it is enclosed and locked away. This 'Requisit' yields a second and more flexible term for the fixing of meaning in Benjamin's exposition. The emblematic objects provided by history as *exempla* freeze the world at the very point when they bring it to a stage. In this respect, engagement with the allegorical meaning of the image, in the various forms in which it has been encountered in Weimar cultural thought, involves a theatricalization. As allegory spreads to more and more fields of human knowledge and endeavour, in Benjamin's view, its stock of stage-props becomes effectively limitless (GS 1.1, 349).

In the Trauerspiel the subjection, in this way, of the human world and natural objects to futility, as they are seen to serve no purpose or meaning of their own, is apparent in the indifference with which anything at all can be made to bear an allegorical reading. This is 'eine Welt, in der es aufs Detail so streng nicht ankommt'

(GS I.I, 350), but by the same token such physical objects gain in power merely because they share in some realm of elevated significance. In a return to mystical conceptions of language, Benjamin goes on to rework this dimension of allegorical signification as the conflict between what he imagines as the free use of a revealed language and its inscription in writing. The free use of a revealed language allows for seamless transmission — or rather the undivided unity in expression of word and thing. Inscription in writing, through the very randomness of its possible signifying elements in allegory, is made from 'amorphous fragments' ('dies amorphe Bruchstück') which are able to disclose the 'Unfreiheit, Unvollendung, und Gebrochenheit der sinnlichen Physis' (GS I.I, 351–52) in ways that were unthinkable to the world of late eighteenth-century classicism, but which some Romantics were able to embrace in order to challenge the nature of art itself.

Benjamin's term *rebus* used in this sense, and in the combinatory context we have seen in other Weimar theorists, appears in the earliest material of the *Passagen-Werk*. In 'Pariser Passagen II' Benjamin describes the assorted items offered for sale in the arcades:

> Diese Auslagen sind ein Rebus: es liegt einem auf der Zunge, wie hier das Vogelfutter in der Fixierschale einer Dunkelkammer verwahrt wird, Blumensamen neben dem Feldstecher, die abgebrochene Schraube auf dem Notenheft und der Revolver überm Goldfischglas zu lesen sind. (GS v.2, 670)[34]

In the *Passagen-Werk* the enigmatic arrangement of apparently random objects yields a series of possible narratives. The goldfish are survivors of some long-forgotten ornamental pool ('Bassin'); the revolver is evidence from a crime scene; and the woman who had owned the sheet music starved to death after her last piano pupil left. Such a reading would involve the enunciation and parsing of the combinatory possibilities on display. Benjamin's autobiographical writing too explores vignettes of childhood opening into commentary in *Berliner Kindheit um neunzehnhundert* (1933–38), where 'Der Strumpf' (GS VII.1, 416) seems to model emblematic structures, while the postcards of 'Zwei Rätselbilder' (GS VII.1, 400) appear to moralize the discovery of time and mortality.[35] In the rebus of the arcades these interpretative possibilities together can unlock a historical moment — we seem to have stumbled into a Chekhovian scenario; but for Benjamin these narratives are the collective dream, dreamt by a collapsing economic order, which he finds further reflected in Karl Kraus's description, from a gloss in *Nachts* (1924), of the Castans Panoptikum, a wax museum located between 1873 and 1888 in the Berlin Kaisergalerie and displaying both historical figures, contemporary celebrities, and bizarre and gruesome anatomical models.[36]

The very survival of allegorical patterns reveals a critical moment in the historical process. What began as the emptying out of higher meaning from the allegorical objects of a post-Reformation and secular world makes of the fading commodities offered in the Paris arcades the silent witnesses to the fading society that dealt in them. If, according to a basic Marxian theorem, the commodity enters into regular relations, governed by price and exchange value, the assembled goods on display here enter into the most unregulated patterns of association. But through these 'regellosesten Verbindungen' the combined elements live on to tell a tale. They can be evoked as memoir, thriller, or melodrama, but they reveal the historical process of terminal economic decline ('Untergang einer Wirtschaftsepoche'), perceived by 'the dreaming collective' of its former beneficiaries as the end of the world itself (GS v.2, 670).

Ernst Bloch had seen in Brecht a practitioner of montage who avoided the superficiality of what he called revue-culture. In his diary notes of conversations with Brecht in Svendborg, Benjamin gives an insight into his own early interest in the poet and playwright. The diary recalls an exchange in which Benjamin described the moment when the significance of an allegorical object first occurred to him.

> *29 Juni* Brecht spricht vom epischen Theater; er erwähnt das Kindertheater, in dem die Fehler der Darstellung, als Verfremdungseffekte fungierend, der Vorstellung epische Züge geben. Bei der Schmiere könne Ähnliches sich ereignen. Mir fällt die genfer Aufführung des Cid ein, in der mir beim Anblick der schief sitzenden Krone des Königs der erste Gedanke an das kam, was ich neun Jahre später im Trauerspielbuch niederlegte. Brecht seinerseits zitiert hier den Augenblick, in dem die Idee des epischen Theaters verankert ist. Es war eine Probe zur münchener Aufführung von 'Eduard II'. (GS VI, 534–35)

Effects of derealization can be encountered in school drama or in any provincial fleapit. Benjamin, in response, recalls how the precarious angle of the crown in a production of Corneille's play *Le Cid* (1636) was enough to suggest the precarious nature of sovereignty itself, presented in German Baroque drama through the decrepitude of its allegorical emblems; in return, Brecht evokes the inception of his practice of epic theatre in early rehearsals of *Leben Eduards des Zweiten von England* (1924) — a play which, in its own terms, investigates the same problematic of sovereignty. The allusion at the beginning of this entry to the origins of a notion of epic theatre in 'errors in presentation' in children's theatre may well refer to Asja Lacis' interest in youth theatre. Benjamin had written the 'Programm eines proletarischen Kindertheaters' (1929) for her; she had also been the source of his acquaintanceship with Brecht, and Benjamin probably first heard about the rehearsals for *Eduard II* from Lacis, who had already worked with Brecht when Benjamin met her in Capri. On her account, as Brecht's assistant director she suggested the soldiers in the play should have white make-up.[37] Brecht was fond of the story which recounted how, having difficulty directing a long battle scene in the play, he finally asked the Munich cabaret artist and clown Karl Valentin, who was performing in the same theatre, for his advice about soldiers in a battle. His reply, that they are pale and afraid ('Bleich sans — Furcht hams'), combined with their heavy white make-up, yields the gesture of the scene.[38] In each case, the crown in *Le Cid* and Brecht's white-faced soldiers in *Eduard II*, a complex set of relations can be held by the focal visual element.

Such intense visual moments come to be central to the form of this theatre. Benjamin approaches the question of Brecht's epic theatre with the slogan 'Das epische Theater ist gestisch' (GS II.2, 521): the characteristics of this fundamental action of Brecht's theatre, as Benjamin understands it, are well known. It is 'nur in gewissem Grade verfälschbar': such a theatre achieves a degree of authenticity, of truth to its own methods that is beyond imitation — rather in the way that, as Benjamin will later claim, the concepts introduced in 'Das Kunstwerk im Zeitalter seiner technischen Reproduzierbarkeit' are useless for the purposes of fascism (GS I.2, 473). Epic theatre is strictly delimited by its beginning and end; its enframed potential is derived from and constitutes interruption: Benjamin recognizes that the main function of the text in Brecht's theatre is to interrupt an action — not to expound or 'develop' it. And through this kind of focalizing gesture Brecht's theatre gives access to (social or economic) conditions — 'Zustand'. Benjamin notes that Brecht's coinage of the term (and its plural *Zustände*) has attracted more attention than any other of his formulations: 'Und während fast alle Losungen seiner Dramaturgie unbeachtet verhallten, hat diese letzte es immerhin bis zum Mißverständnis gebracht' (GS II.2, 521). The stance or standing-towards ('Zu-stand') invoked in the 'Gestus' defines and delimits more than just its own terrain, which is perhaps why the 'Zustände' are reached at the end of a play: 'und am Ende, nicht am Anfang dieses Versuchs stehen die Zustände' (GS II.2, 522). In that moment the distance of understanding becomes available. Epic theatre, as Benjamin says, does not represent conditions ('Zustände'), it dis-covers ('entdeckt') them: it is part of the cunning of Benjamin's analysis to have pointed out that the existing theatre apparatus had sought rather to cover up ('verdecken') the situation of its own practice. At one significant level, that is, Brecht's stage is designed to force into the open the postures that the existing apparatus of the theatre is keen to cover up, though without obliterating them.

This returns us to the question of allegory as a description of the figurative force of gesture as Brecht deploys it. The whole mode of Brecht's theatre gives access in its particular forms of representation to 'Zustände'. As Brigid Doherty has pointed out, the list of attitudes given by Brecht that can be understood as 'gestisch' are socially embedded:

> the *Haltung* of the language of the military drill does not simply simulate the soldier's bodily posture (with all its connotations); it manifests the social exchange between soldiers, an exchange that brings instruction and domination together in the name of training. 'The realm of attitudes [*Haltungen*] adopted by the characters towards one another is what we call the realm of the Gestus.'[39]

The structure of 'Gestus' is explored in the terms of a 'literarisiertes Theater' (GS II.2, 524). In the case Benjamin considers, such a theatre is realized through Caspar Neher's designs. Benjamin takes up Brecht's suggestion that the actor selecting the appropriate wooden leg for his performance as a beggar in *Die Dreigroschenoper* (1928) will be as much a crowd-puller as a particular variety item in a cabaret: Neher's designs ('Dekorationen') for *Mahagonny* (1930) are, says Benjamin, more like posters for such numbers than stage-sets proper. In the account from Brecht cited by Benjamin, such visualizations capture the moment of performance — what Brecht calls 'das Durchsetzen des "Gestalteten" mit "Formuliertem"'.[40] The effect is what Rainer Nägele calls a curious doubling 'when Jakob der Vielfraß sits in front of another Jakob der Vielfraß drawn by Caspar Neher'.[41] Brecht locates the reality of Jakob's 'Gestus' in the actor, whose posture is as it were held and grasped by the image in the backdrop that represents him. As Nägele points out, Benjamin then goes a step further. For him a greater reality can be located in the painted image: 'Unter den Spielern erscheinen manche als Mandatare der größeren Mächte, die im Hintergrunde verbleiben' (GS II.2, 525). The visibility of the actor's performance is evidently available in a heightened form through the presence of the visual representation of Neher's drawing. The powers — of societal order, public authority, or economic constraint — infuse the stage presence of actor and set — not as a tautology or repetition, but as an allegory that displays itself. As Benjamin concludes at this point, Neher's designs are the *projections* (the word Brecht himself uses of Neher's work) or material forms of ideas: 'So wären die Neherschen Projektionen materialistischer Ideen, Ideen von echten "Zuständen"' (GS II.2, 525). Once again the constituent elements of the emblem are in place: motto, picture, and epigram (*subscriptio*), as current in the traditional emblem books.[42] In this case, the recognition of real conditions that comes with the act of decipherment does not simply entail the reception of moral or even political instruction; it is already in itself a thoroughly political action, a scene of instruction that requires active engagement. Benjamin's essay 'Was ist das epische Theater?' (?1931) can quote Brecht's own claim that this political activation of the visual in relation to the discursive on his stage opens up new possibilities for the theatre, making connections to other 'Institute für geistige Tätigkeit', as the notes on *Die Dreigroschenoper* cited by Benjamin suggest. As Benjamin understands it, such a theatre demands engagement with the material ideas it inescapably presents.

From the early days of the Expressionist lyric and with increased currency during the Weimar years, the visual technologies of modern culture in photography and film seemed to provide clues to the mysteries of modernity. Through the growth of the illustrated press, from the turn of the century, and as collage and montage of imagery became part of the creative repertoire of political artists, the meanings of visual culture take on central significance in critical theory. The language of things, in the rebus and deciphered with enormous ingenuity and persistence by critics on the political left, yields in Brecht's version a theatre-practice beyond the arcana of utopian divination. In a structural parallel to the rich readings of visual phenomena considered here, Brecht's deployment of the emblematics of gesture and a consequent transformation of the theatre itself might well successfully invoke those institutional forces which Bloch, according to Benjamin's letter to Kracauer, had signally failed to engage.

Notes to Chapter 12

1. See for example Ritchie Robertson, 'Schiller and the Jesuits', in *Schiller: National Poet — Poet of Nations*, ed. by Nicholas Martin (Amsterdam: Rodopi, 2006), pp. 179–200; 'Hoffmann's Elixiere and the Lasting Appeal of Conspiracy Theories', in *Die Aktualität der Romantik/The Actuality of Romanticism*, ed. by Franz-Josef Deiters and others, Limbus, 5 (Freiburg: Rombach, 2012), pp. 11–31.
2. Ritchie Robertson, 'Reading the Clues: Kafka, "Der Proceß"', in *The German Novel in the Twentieth Century: Beyond Realism*, ed. by David Midgley (Edinburgh: Edinburgh University Press, 1993), pp. 59–79 (pp. 64, 71).

3. Ernst Bloch, *Erbschaft dieser Zeit* (Frankfurt a.M.: Suhrkamp, 1962), p. 104. Further references given in the text are to this edition, as *EdZ* with page number.
4. Frederic J. Schwartz identifies striking parallels in the discourse of art history in the Weimar Republic: 'Ernst Bloch and Wilhelm Pinder: Out of Sync', *Grey Room*, 3 (2001), 54–89.
5. See letter of 26 December 1934 to Gershom Scholem: Walter Benjamin, *Gesammelte Briefe*, ed. by Christoph Gödde and Henri Lonitz, 6 vols (Frankfurt a.M.: Suhrkamp, 1995–2000), IV (1998), p. 550. Further references are cited in the text as GB with volume and page number.
6. Walter Benjamin, *Werke und Nachlaß: Kritische Gesamtausgabe*, 21 vols (Berlin: Suhrkamp Verlag, 2008–), XVI: *Das Kunstwerk im Zeitalter seiner technischen Reproduzierbarkeit*, ed. by Burkhardt Lindner (2013), pp. 24, 320.
7. See Andreas Huyssen, 'The Voids of Berlin', *Critical Inquiry*, 24 (1997), 57–81 (pp. 62–63).
8. See Wilfried Korngiebel, *Bloch und die Zeichen: Symboltheorie, kulturelle Gegenhegemonie und philosophischer Interdiskurs* (Würzburg: Königshausen und Neumann, 1999), p. 276.
9. See for example Kirsten Baumgarten, *Bauhaus Dessau* (Berlin: jovis, 2007).
10. See Erdmut Wizisla, *Walter Benjamin and Bertolt Brecht: — The Story of a Friendship* (London: Libris, 2009), pp. 39–40; *Brecht und Benjamin: Geschichte einer Freundschaft* (Frankfurt a.M.: Suhrkamp, 2004), pp. 74–76.
11. See Heinrich Heine, *Sämtliche Schriften*, ed. by Klaus Briegleb and others, 6 vols in 7 (Munich: Hanser, 1968–76), V (1974), p. 239; but compare his more critical remarks in *Geständnisse*, VI.1 (1975), p. 486.
12. See *Die Lyrik des Expressionismus*, ed. by Silvio Vietta (Munich: dtv, 1976), pp. 58–59.
13. Kurt Hiller, *Die Weisheit der Langenweile: Eine Zeit- und Streitschrift*, 2 vols (Leipzig: Kurt Wolff, 1913), I, 207–08. Ritchie Robertson provided an occasion for my exploration of 'Ferdinand Hardekopf and the Origins of German Expressionism', *Oxford German Studies*, 41 (2012), 274–94, a brief portion of which reappears here.
14. See *Die Lyrik des Expressionismus*, ed. by Vietta, p. 210; Ferdinand Hardekopf, *Wir Gespenster*, ed. by Wilfried F. Schoeller (Zürich and Hamburg: Die Arche, 2004), p. 40.
15. See Franco Buono, *Stemma di Berlino: poesia tedesca della metropoli* (Bari: Dedalo, 2000), p. 101.
16. *Wir Gespenster*, p. 51.
17. Ibid., p. 45.
18. Sigmund Freud, *Studienausgabe*, ed. by Alexander Mitscherlich and others, 10 vols and Ergänzungsband (Frankfurt a.M.: Fischer, 2000), II: *Die Traumdeutung*, pp. 280–81. Winfried Menninghaus sketches the function of Freud's term in Benjamin's work on fashion in 'On the Vital Significance of Kitsch: Walter Benjamin's Politics of "Bad Taste"', in *Walter Benjamin and the Architecture of Modernity*, ed. by Andrew Benjamin and Charles Rice (Melbourne: re.press, 2009), pp. 39–58 (pp. 49–50).
19. From Robertson's 'Introduction' to Sigmund Freud, *The Interpretation of Dreams*, trans. by Joyce Crick (Oxford: Oxford University Press, 1999), p. xiv.
20. See Kurt Tucholsky and John Heartfield, *Deutschland, Deutschland über Alles* (Berlin: Neuer Deutscher Verlag, 1929; repr. Reinbek bei Hamburg: Rowohlt, 1980), p. 112.
21. Ibid., pp. 15–16.
22. Ibid., p. 11.
23. Walter Benjamin, 'Kleine Geschichte der Photographie', in *Gesammelte Schriften*, ed. by Rolf Tiedemann and Hermann Schweppenhäuser, 6 vols (Frankfurt a.M.: Suhrkamp, 1991), II.1, 368–85 (p. 371). Further references to this edition appear as GS with volume and page numbers.
24. Oleg Gelikman, 'After Aura', *Angelaki*, 8 (2003), 40–63, especially pp. 50–56, gives a nuanced account of Benjamin's analysis of the ascendancy of the image.
25. Éphime Zozoulia, 'Découverte de Lénine', *Europe: Revue mensuelle*, 66 (1928), 178–87.
26. Miriam Bratu Hansen, 'Benjamin and Cinema', *Critical Enquiry*, 25 (1999), 306–43 (p. 338).
27. Siegfried Kracauer, 'Die Photographie', in *Das Ornament der Masse* (Frankfurt a.M.: Suhrkamp, 1977), pp. 21–39 (p. 23).
28. Andrew Benjamin, 'What, in Truth, is Photography? Notes after Kracauer', *Oxford Literary Review*, 32 (2010), 89–201 (pp. 190–93), comments on the complex functionality of the photographic image.

29. Siegfried Kracauer, 'Das Ornament der Masse', in *Das Ornament der Masse*, pp. 50–63 (p. 60).
30. Ibid., p. 37.
31. Ibid., p. 36.
32. Ibid.
33. Siegfried Kracauer, 'Zu den Schriften Walter Benjamins', in *Das Ornament der Masse*, pp. 249–55.
34. The earlier version appears at a°, 3, GS v.2, 1045–46.
35. See also Carol Jacobs, 'Walter Benjamin, Topographically Speaking', in *Walter Benjamin: Theoretical Questions*, ed. by David S. Ferris (Stanford: Stanford University Press, 1996), pp. 94–117 (p. 97), in relation to Benjamin's own practice in *Berliner Chronik* (GS VI, 465) and n. 10 for an exposition of the same combinatory structure in *Berliner Kindheit*, including a kind of pun.
36. Karl Kraus, *Beim Wort genommen* (Vienna: Kösel, 1955), p. 428–29.
37. Asja Lacis, *Revolutionär im Beruf* (Munich: Rogner & Bernhard, 1976), p. 41.
38. Bertolt Brecht, *Große kommentierte Berliner und Frankfurter Ausgabe*, ed. by Werner Hecht and others, 30 vols in 32 (Frankfurt a.M.: Suhrkamp, 1988–2000), XXII.2: *Schriften 2* (1993), p. 722 and note, p. 1127.
39. Brigid Doherty, 'Test and Gestus in Brecht and Benjamin', *Modern Language Notes*, 115 (2000), 442–81 (p. 457), quoting Brecht, *Grosse Berliner und Frankfurter Ausgabe*, XXVIII: *Briefe I*, 89.
40. Benjamin quotes Brechts's notes (1930) on *Die Dreigroschenoper*: *Grosse Berliner und Frankfurter Ausgabe*, XXIV: *Schriften 4* (1991), 58.
41. Rainer Nägele, 'Trembling Contours: Kierkegaard — Benjamin — Brecht', in *Benjamin and History*, ed. by Andrew Benjamin, (London: Continuum, 2005), pp. 102–17 (p. 113).
42. See Albrecht Schöne, *Emblematik und Drama im Zeitalter des Barock* (Munich: Beck, 1993), p. 19.

CHAPTER 13

The Romantic Affiliations of Benjamin's 'Die Aufgabe des Übersetzers'

Charlie Louth

> Kommentar und Übersetzung verhalten sich zum Text wie Stil und Mimesis zur Natur: dasselbe Phänomen unter verschiedenen Betrachtungsweisen. Am Baum des heiligen Textes sind beide nur die ewig rauschenden Blätter, am Baume des profanen die rechtzeitig fallenden Früchte.[1]

I

Benjamin first began translating Baudelaire, including some of the poems which would later be included in his bilingual edition of the *Tableaux parisiens*, in 1914 or 1915. This book, not published until autumn 1923, had a preface which has since become one of Benjamin's best-known works: 'Die Aufgabe des Übersetzers'. It is not Benjamin's only reflection on the subject of translation, but by far the most extensive. It has been much read for the ideas it puts forward on language, and Benjamin himself referred to it in 1940 as 'den ersten Niederschlag meiner sprachtheoretischen Reflexionen'.[2] But it is important not to let that obscure the fact that it is an essay on translation.[3] Translation as a 'ganz eigentümlicher Darstellungsmodus' (*GS* IV, 12; *TP*, p. 14), which entails but goes beyond a particular view of language.[4] The preface was first mentioned by Benjamin, as a project, in late 1920, and he announced its completion in a letter to Gershom Scholem of 26 May 1921. As can be gleaned from later letters to the publisher of the Baudelaire translations, Richard Weißbach, some small corrections and one larger addition were made before publication.[5]

Within the period outlined above falls a shorter period during which Benjamin worked on, wrote and published *Der Begriff der Kunstkritik in der deutschen Romantik*, his doctoral dissertation. Most of the work on this took place in 1918 and 1919, and it was published in 1920. It seeks to uncover the philosophical premises of the Romantic concept of criticism, and then goes on to analyse *Kritik* itself on the basis of the theoretical writings of Novalis and Friedrich Schlegel. This concept has the closest bearing on the understanding of translation articulated in the preface. The still current practice of distinguishing the German Romantics 'proper' from other writers of the period who in a larger European context appear to belong to the Romantic movement is one that Benjamin both accepts and puts in question. Notably, he suggests that Hölderlin is central to the concerns of Novalis and Schlegel even though he belongs to a quite different realm. When Hölderlin is introduced into the argument of *Der Begriff der Kunstkritik* it is in a peculiar tone which combines drama and sobriety:

> Unter jenem Gesichtspunkt [that of understanding poetry and philosophy to be intimately related in Romanticism] rückt in diesen weiteren [romantischen] Kreis, um nicht zu sagen in seine Mitte, ein Geist, der durch seine bloße Einschätzung als Dichter im modernen Sinne des Wortes (so hoch dieser auch gegriffen werden muß) nicht erfaßt werden kann, und dessen ideengeschichtliches Verhältnis zur romantischen Schule im Unklaren verharrt, wenn seine besondere philosophische Einheit mit ihr unbeachtet bleibt. Dieser Geist ist Hölderlin [...]. (*GS* 1.1, 103)

Hölderlin's works were only partially available during the nineteenth century and only made their full impact in the edition of Norbert von Hellingrath, which came out from 1913 to 1923. The key volumes, containing the translations of Pindar and Sophocles and the later poems (decently edited for the first time), appeared in 1913 and 1916. Hölderlin was the subject of one of Benjamin's first essays in 1914,[6] and there are other scattered but deep traces of the importance he attributed to Hölderlin to be found in his earlier writings and letters. In late 1916 he wrote to Herbert Belmore: 'Seit Jahren strahlt mir aus dieser Nacht das Licht Hölderlins.'[7] And 'Die Aufgabe des Übersetzers' itself shows clear signs of having been written under the immediate influence of Hölderlin's translations and their strikingly odd language.

'Die Aufgabe des Übersetzers' thus draws on three main sources: Benjamin's own experience of translating, especially of Baudelaire; his reading of Hölderlin's translations; his work on the German Romantics. More precisely, it derives from the conjunction of these three activities. A lesser source is Goethe's remarks on translation in the *West-östlicher Divan*, to which Benjamin turns at the end of the essay.[8] In the present essay Romanticism is used in a wide sense, to fetch in Hölderlin, Goethe and Schiller as well as the Schlegels and Novalis.

II

As a preface to a translation 'Die Aufgabe des Übersetzers' is clearly unusual in that it makes not even a passing reference to Baudelaire or to Benjamin's own practice as a translator. There seems to be a considerable 'hiatus'[9] between the arguments about the significance of translation in the preface and the Baudelaire translations themselves which, since they can only fail to live up to the expectations of translation that the preface excites, are in danger of appearing less significant than they really are. They are idiosyncratic but do not, cannot, turn their idiosyncrasy into the purely convincing form that inhabits the translations Benjamin refers to as touchstones — Hölderlin's and Voß's. But at the same time this hiatus, the discrepancy between essay and translations, adds to the point of the essay, which itself makes clear that the conception of translation and of the translator's task it arrives at is utopian, an ideal that reinvigorates the potential of translation without being able or really even seeking to describe, let alone prescribe, a particular method.

There is a similar gap within the essay itself, because that part of it which does attempt to define a course for an actual practice of translation is curiously unattached to the theory of translation, which is also a theory of language, elaborated earlier in the essay. The indications of a particular practice are given in the form of a quotation from Rudolf Pannwitz towards the end. The main point of this quotation is to shift the emphasis between the two poles of translation from which even Benjamin does not quite manage to release it. By the two poles I mean the pull of the original text and the language it is written in and the pull of the language of the translation itself. If a translation can always be placed somewhere along that continuum, what Pannwitz proposes is pushing it towards the source so that a German translation, instead of aiming to make a foreign text appear as if it had been written in German, should aim to make the German bear the marks of its encounter with the foreign tongue, thus almost inverting the conventional direction of translation. When an English text is to be translated into German the German used should in Pannwitz's terms be 'Englished' ('zu [...] verenglischen', *GS* IV.1, 20; *TP*, p. 23) rather than the other way round.

This urging of a particular course of translation stands oddly next to the glittering abstractions in which Benjamin argues that a 'pure language' may be sensed in the language of a translation, and it isn't surprising that intimations of a practice are given through the medium of a quotation. Benjamin's thoughts lead to a new way of *conceiving of* translation; they are a sort of retrospective reflection on (mainly, as I will argue) what Hölderlin did with Pindar and Sophocles. Translations such as Hölderlin's or Voß's could never be prescribed or specified, and similarly the essay cannot put forward a particular technique. This is then borne out by the translations from the *Tableaux parisiens* that accompanied the original publication: they do not obviously grow out of the reflections of the essay, but the essay may allow them to be viewed in a particular, and new, light. Above all, it demands that the reader approach the Baudelaire versions with quite different expectations from the conventional ones, and in that sense the essay's role as a preface is after all discernible.

As if aware of the discrepancy between the preface and the translations, Benjamin's presentation in the blurb he wrote for the book suggests, with what may be a sleight of hand, that they are of a piece. In it he says: 'Was dieser Übertragung ihren Platz sichern wird, ist, daß in ihr einerseits das Gebot der Treue, welches der Übersetzer in seiner Vorrede unwiderleglich begründet, gewissenhaft erfüllt, andrerseits aber das Poetische überzeugend erfaßt wird' (*GS* IV.2, 893; *TP*, pp. 404–05). The 'requirement of fidelity' Benjamin mentions here without any further clarification undergoes in the essay itself a thorough revision. The two terms that always seem to circumscribe discussion of translation, fidelity (closeness) and freedom, to and from the text, are each redefined so that they no longer bear any resemblance to the way they are conventionally understood. *Fidelity*, for Benjamin, means to the intimations of 'pure language' contained in the original work. '[E]ben das [ist] die Bedeutung der Treue [...], daß die große Sehnsucht nach Sprachergänzung aus dem Werke spreche' (*GS* IV.1, 18; *TP*, p. 21). That is, the translation should bring out a certain tendency already contained in the work. This is one of Benjamin's definitions of the 'task': 'in der Übersetzung den Samen reiner Sprache zur Reife zu bringen' (*GS* IV.1, 17; *TP*, p. 20).

The idea of *freedom* is just as radically detached from its usual meaning with regard to translation: it is inverted, no longer meaning freedom from the text of the original, but freedom from the conventions of the language of the translation, which is the freedom to abandon the usage of one's own language and to adopt the forms and turns of the foreign one.

> Freiheit [...] bewährt sich um der reinen Sprache willen an der eigenen. Jene reine Sprache, die in fremde gebannt ist, in der eigenen zu erlösen, die im Werk gefangene in der Umdichtung zu befreien, ist die Aufgabe des Übersetzers. (*GS* IV.1, 19; *TP*, p. 23)

It is a kind of fidelity to the original, to an aspect of the original of which it is perhaps itself unaware; except that freedom also allows the possibility of *not* being faithful. This notion of freedom is a good characterization of Hölderlin's practice as a translator of Sophocles — most of the time he keeps very close to the Greek, but on a few occasions he diverges from it absolutely to create something which has no obvious source in the Greek but which is also without precedent in German. That Benjamin, by inverting the concept of freedom, arrives at a concept of fidelity not in the end unlike the conventional one, that is, to the source text, alerts one to the possibility that his concept of fidelity might be construable as something like the conventional concept of freedom, but this is not the case, since fidelity to 'pure language' is maintained by 'literalness' ('Wörtlichkeit'), by adhering to the individual words of the original. It is in his precise consideration of the complexity of 'Wörtlichkeit' that Benjamin approaches the core of the mystery of translation. Even as it redefines the understanding of freedom and fidelity so that they both become answerable to the idea of 'pure language', exact attention to the texture of the text to be translated is still paramount. The paradoxical nature of such attention is brought out, transcending the notions of fidelity and freedom as they are traditionally understood. For to stick closely to the letter of the original, to take, as Benjamin says, the word and not the sentence as the translator's 'Urelement' (*GS* IV.1, 18; *TP*, p. 22), is to enter into a strange region of difference within sameness, where proximity is also distance. To cleave close is, because of the difference between languages, to point out that difference. But because of the sameness of languages, their relatedness, what Benjamin calls 'eine eigentümliche Konvergenz' (*GS* IV.1, 12; *TP*, p. 14), it can also be to join, to double, to illumine. 'Denn der Satz ist die Mauer vor der Sprache des Originals, Wörtlichkeit die Arkade' (*GS* IV.1, 18; *TP*, p. 22).

To espouse literalness doesn't mean that the 'Sinn', the sense, the message or prose content, will necessarily be painstakingly rendered. On the contrary, a quasi-religious regard for the form of the original, an attentiveness to the traces of 'pure language' concealed there, may lead to distortion or neglect of what is usually thought of as the 'literal' meaning. Benjamin says that the translation touches on this aspect of the original only as a tangent touches a circle, 'um nach dem Gesetze der Treue in der Freiheit der Sprachbewegung ihre eigenste Bahn zu verfolgen' (GS IV.1, 20; *TP*, p. 23).

Although it is hard to discern how the Baudelaire versions might correspond to such statements, there does seem to be a sense in which Benjamin's reflections emerge from within the knowledgeableness of a practice, and in an autobiographical note of 1925 he claimed that the 'Schwerpunkt' of his translation of Baudelaire was to be found in the preface (GS VI.1, 215). This applies above all to the dialectic of contact and distance to which Benjamin returns again and again. His is a close translation in that its literalness also tends to pertain to the 'Sinn' or prose content, and the language produced has a quality of oddness and extreme compression partly forced by the retention of Baudelaire's rhyme-schemes and increased by the fact that Benjamin is very sparing with punctuation, using commas not according to the rules of German grammar but as a rhythmic device (even more markedly so than in his prose). The sum of these effects then is a kind of density of language in which German is often estranged from itself or at least, as German is possessed of special faculties of compression, is in the process of becoming so. To give a brief example, this is how Benjamin renders the lines 'Fugitive beauté | Dont le regard m'a fait soudainement renaître' from 'A une passante': 'Die Flüchtige, nicht leiht | Sie sich dem Werdenden an ihrem Schimmer' (GS IV.1, 41; *TP*, p. 57). The language owes something to George; in fact, it is more like him than George's own version of the same lines: 'o schöne wesenheit | Die mich mit EINEM blicke neu geboren'.[10] The density of Benjamin's translation, which is sometimes more of a clottedness, foregrounds language as such, gives an impression of language *at work*, and so a kind of detachment from the specifics of a particular tongue takes place, giving access, or appearing to, to language itself. This is something *like* or approaching Benjamin's notion of pure or true language which, he says, is 'intensiv in den Übersetzungen verborgen' (GS IV.1, 16; *TP*, p. 19). That is, it inhabits them more intensively than it does original works, without for all that being evident. This intensity is peculiar to translations, and Benjamin's insistence on the special status of translation, its uniqueness as a linguistic activity and form, deriving from his own experience, reaches its clearest definition in an image distinguishing the translation from an original work in its attitude to language:

> Die Übersetzung [...] sieht sich nicht wie die Dichtung gleichsam im innern Bergwald der Sprache selbst, sondern außerhalb desselben, ihm gegenüber und ohne ihn zu betreten ruft sie das Original hinein, an demjenigen einzigen Orte hinein, wo jeweils das Echo in der eigenen den Widerhall eines Werkes der fremden Sprache zu geben vermag. (GS IV.1, 16; *TP*, p. 19)

This process of calling and echoing at the heart of translation, where language acts on language, is represented in Benjamin's edition of the *Tableaux parisiens* in which, for the first time, the French is printed *en face* so that the texts can interact. The topography outlined in the quotation is considerably more complex than this though, and hard to convert into a clear picture. The translation doesn't just stand outside the language of the original, but outside or at least on the edge of language itself, and it calls the original in to a 'place' in itself where, within the language it is nevertheless made of and in some sense inhabits — though in a different way from the original's habitation of language — it creates an echo which is the echo of the foreign work. Benjamin uses two words for 'echo', 'Echo' and 'Widerhall', leaving the possibility that the echo in the language of the translation is not quite the same as the echo (or perhaps then resonance) of the original. The translation, marginalized by nature, echoes with an echo, suggesting several removes and a lack of groundedness that look forward to the end of the essay and the characterization of the language of Hölderlin's translations as 'so erweitert und durchwaltet' that 'der Sinn [stürzt] von Abgrund zu Abgrund' (GS IV.1, 21; TP, p. 24). Remote from what we have to imagine as the primal mountain forest, it is more refined, more abstract, for better or worse. Benjamin's initial statement of this idea, at the beginning of the paragraph, speaks not of a 'place' but of finding 'diejenige Intention auf die Sprache, in die übersetzt wird', from where the echo of the original can be 'ignited' ('erweckt': GS IV.1, 15; TP, p. 19). In Benjamin's usage, the shared etymology of 'Intention', 'intensiv' and 'Intensität' is not forgotten.

III

The quotation about the 'Bergwald der Sprache' continues in a vein which like many other points in the essay is close to preoccupations of Novalis and Friedrich Schlegel, whose writings Benjamin knew intimately, having just published what in a letter to Ernst Schoen (7 April 1919) he called 'ein Hinweis auf die durchaus in der Literatur unbekannte wahre Natur der Romantik' (quoted, GS I.3, 800). Of translation the essay goes on to say that:

> Ihre Intention geht nicht allein auf etwas anderes als die der Dichtung, nämlich auf eine Sprache im ganzen von einem einzelnen Kunstwerk in einer fremden aus, sondern sie ist auch selbst eine andere: die des Dichters ist naive, erste, anschauliche, die des Übersetzers abgeleitete, letzte, ideenhafte Intention. Denn das große Motiv einer Integration der vielen Sprachen zur einen wahren erfüllt seine Arbeit. (GS IV.1, 16; TP, p. 19)

Clearly this formulation more or less depends on Schiller's 'Über naïve und sentimentalische Dichtung', and it is similar too in its implication that the translator, like the modern poet, is in the end, despite appearances, engaged on a 'higher' course. Schiller's essay is also fundamental to Romanticism, and the distinction is in fact perhaps even more closely related to what Schlegel and Novalis call 'Romantisieren', romanticization, the process in which a thing is extended and metamorphosed and at the same time clarified and brought into relation with other things. For the Romantics, poetry should perform this action on the world, and criticism on poetry; and translation too stands in this relation to works. For both the Romantics and Benjamin, the translation acts upon the original, leads it out beyond itself, and that process makes it begin to lose its specificity, its circumscribed form, to a more general 'idea' of itself which for Benjamin corresponds to the element of 'pure language' within it. The 'integration of the many tongues into one true language' is an aspiration towards the Absolute which Benjamin sees as intrinsic to translation and is a large part of its fascination for him; this aspiration is also a crucial element of Romantic thought, an element Benjamin isolates and focuses on in his dissertation, where it effects the distinction between the Romantics and Fichte: 'Das Interesse an der Unmittelbarkeit der obersten Erkenntnis teilte Fichte mit den Frühromantikern. Ihr Kultus des Unendlichen, wie sie ihn auch in der Erkenntnistheorie ausprägen, trennte sie von ihm und gab ihrem Denken seine höchst eigentümliche Richtung' (*GS* I.1, 25). It is this direction that Benjamin then pursues in his investigation of *Kritik*. The Romantic project, *Romantisieren*, involves the turning towards the Absolute. Benjamin quotes to this effect from Novalis: 'Absolutierung, Universalisierung, Klassifikation des individuellen Moments ... ist das eigentliche Wesen des Romantisierens.' 'Indem ich ... dem Endlichen einen unendlichen Schein gebe, so romantisiere ich es' (*GS* I.1, 67–68).

In the essay on translation the Absolute or Infinite appears as 'pure language', a language that doesn't exist as such but comprehends all languages, being a sum of their differences, a total language, the process and fount of language itself. Benjamin also refers to this as 'das Symbolisierte'. The 'symbolized' is to be found not in any one language, not in any particular work, but 'im Werden der Sprachen selbst'. In individual works there is only 'Symbolisierendes', a gesturing towards the 'symbolized'. But 'was im Werden der Sprachen sich darzustellen, ja herzustellen sucht, das ist jener Kern der reinen Sprache selbst' (*GS* IV.1, 19; *TP*, p. 22).[11] In works this core, this trace of the Absolute, is distorted and subdued or as Benjamin puts it, 'behaftet mit dem schweren und fremden Sinn' of a particular story etc. 'Fremd' here means 'strange' in the sense of inappropriate, underlining the fact that 'pure language' has nothing to do with any particular meaning, that it is on the contrary meaningless:

> In dieser reinen Sprache, die nichts mehr meint und nichts mehr ausdrückt, sondern als ausdrucksloses und schöpferisches Wort das in allen Sprachen Gemeinte ist, trifft endlich alle Mitteilung, aller Sinn und alle Intention auf eine Schicht, in der sie zu erlöschen bestimmt sind. (*GS* IV.1, 19; *TP*, p. 22)

'Pure' is thus meant exactly; this 'stratum' is touched by nothing; it is absolute because free of specificity. Translation, focusing on language and not on meaning, derives its special importance from its ability to extricate 'pure language' from the meshes of particulars, to make it appear in a less mitigated, less distorted form. At the same time its own language, affected by what it is rendering, is also deflected away from its specific nature, from its Germanness say, towards a new idiom. Specifics of language fall away, allowing the medium to point through more clearly to the lineaments of pure language itself.

This process bears strong resemblances to Romantic trains of thought, especially as these are understood and expounded by Benjamin. The two notions of language — particular language and pure language — his theory of translation depends on are mirrored by the 'double concept of form' he introduces to explain the workings of irony in Romantic works. Irony has a similar function to translation:

> Die bestimmte Form des einzelnen Werkes, die man als Darstellungsform bezeichnen möge, wird das Opfer ironischer Zersetzung. Über ihr aber reißt die Ironie einen Himmel ewiger Form, die Idee der Formen, auf, die man die absolute Form nennen mag, und sie erweist das Überleben des Werkes, das aus dieser Sphäre sein unzerstörbares Bestehen schöpft, nachdem die empirische Form, der Ausdruck seiner isolierten Reflexion, von ihr verzehrt wurde. Die Ironisierung der Darstellungsform ist gleichsam der Sturm, der den Vorhang vor der transzendentalen Ordnung der Kunst aufhebt und diese und in ihr das unmittelbare Bestehen des Werkes als eines Mysteriums enthüllt. (*GS* I.1, 86)

Translation too discloses the work as a mystery by bringing out its relation to a 'higher sphere' (*GS* IV.1, 11; *TP*, p. 14), and this process, in both cases, assures its life, its survival, its continuance as a work of art, by extending it into infinity. The connection is a 'vital' one ('ein Zusammenhang des Lebens'); translation, like irony, looks to the survival of works in the sense that it reveals their value, which for Benjamin is as transcendental artefacts, as carriers of 'den Samen reiner Sprache' (*GS* IV.1, 17; *TP*, p. 20). 'Fortleben' (*GS* IV.1, 11; *TP*, p. 15), the term Benjamin prefers in the essay as against 'Überleben' in the dissertation (though he uses both), is intrinsic to the significance of translations. 'In ihnen erreicht das Leben des Originals seine stets erneute späteste und umfassendste Entfaltung' (*GS* IV.1, 11; *TP*, p. 14). 'Unfolding' is a Romantic concept, and it refers to that projecting of the work towards the Absolute which gives it life, far more than to the way translation keeps a work alive in the banal sense of 'current', though the two are interconnected.

This pattern of thought, in which something is taken up and extended in a reflective process, is explored and defined most thoroughly by the Romantics in the activity and theory of criticism, and it is to this, of course, to *Kritik*, that Benjamin devotes his attention in his dissertation. There he refers to the 'fruchtbare Entfaltung, die Kritik heißt' (*GS* I.1, 79). The process is most developed and best expressed, by both the Romantics themselves and by Benjamin, with regard to criticism, but at bottom the refinement and subtlety it gains there apply also to other variations. Benjamin remarks on 'eine auffallende Verwandtschaft' between the 'Ironisierung der Form' and criticism (*GS* I.1, 84), and we can extend this, as in the essay he also hints, to *their* understanding of translation.

Translation has an important place, though it is scantly occupied, in Romantic thinking. There is an imbalance between the scarcity of comments on translation in the Romantics' writings and the weight and reach several of these comments seem to carry — especially once the relation between translation and the Romantic project as a whole has been understood. Though it seems odd to say so, translation is central to the Romantics' preoccupations, but in their writings they are only dimly aware of it.[12] This is largely because the real practitioner among them, A. W. Schlegel, distrusted theory, though he also made the revealing observation that if anyone suggested translation was impossible the proper response was that 'der menschliche Geist könne eigentlich nichts als übersetzen, alle seine Tätigkeit bestehe darin'.[13] This was particularly true of the German Romantic mind. The centrality of translation can be suggested by juxtaposing Friedrich Schlegel's conclusion at the end of *Athenaeum* Fragment 116 that all poetry is or should be Romantic ('in einem gewissen Sinn ist oder soll alle Poesie romantisch sein') and Novalis's claim in a letter to A. W. Schlegel (30 November 1797) that all poetry is translation ('Am Ende ist alle Poesie Übersetzung').[14] Likewise Novalis's statement that the world must be romanticized ('die Welt muß romantisirt werden') corresponds to Friedrich Schlegel's imagining of a translation of the universe ('eine Uebersetzung des Universums').[15] Schlegel's requirement that 'Transzendentalpoesie' should be 'zugleich Poesie und Poesie der Poesie' (*Athenaeum* Fragment 238)[16] is eminently satisfied by a translation, which is at once a work in itself and the work *of* a work.

'Die Aufgabe des Übersetzers' is saturated with the characteristic patterns, processes, dynamics and aspirations of Romantic thinking. Even its basic premise, that translation derives its significance from the fact that all languages are related, is anticipated by Friedrich Schlegel: 'Der Imperativ d[es] Uebersetzens beruht wohl auf d[em] Postulat d[er] Spracheinheit'.[17] The preface understands translation in a way that makes it clear why the Romantics obscurely bestowed so much importance on it.[18] At many points it reads like the precipitation of ideas that hung in the air of Romantic thought, and it can really be seen as a direct continuation of the investigation begun in *Der Begriff der Kunstkritik*, this being only partly disguised by the different context: a literary (though also theoretical) preface rather than a carefully footnoted academic work. Benjamin's dissertation on *Kritik* delineates precisely those aspects of Romantic thought which are operative in his essay. And in the essay Benjamin acknowledges the kinship of his reflections with the Romantics, drawing the link between irony, criticism and translation:

> Übersetzung verpflanzt also das Original in einen wenigstens insofern — ironisch — endgültigeren Sprachbereich, als es aus diesem durch keinerlei Übertragung mehr zu versetzen ist, sondern in ihn nur immer von neuem und an andern Teilen erhoben zu werden vermag. Nicht umsonst mag hier das Wort 'ironisch' an Gedankengänge der Romantiker erinnern. Diese haben vor andern Einsicht in das Leben der Werke besessen, von welchem die Übersetzung eine höchste Bezeugung ist. Freilich haben sie diese als solche kaum erkannt, vielmehr ihre ganze Aufmerksamkeit der Kritik zugewendet, die ebenfalls ein wenn auch geringeres Moment im Fortleben der Werke darstellt. Doch wenn auch ihre Theorie auf Übersetzung kaum sich richten mochte, so ging doch ihr großes Übersetzungswerk selbst mit einem Gefühl von dem Wesen und der Würde dieser Form zusammen. (*GS* IV.1, 15; *TP*, p. 18)

In indicating that the concept of *Kritik* drew to it, magnet-like, a degree of Romantic reflection which could as well, or even better, have been given over to translation, Benjamin acknowledges the link between the two, and his reference to irony points to the nature of the relation. The understanding of translation that Benjamin develops is already a Romantic one. In giving it expression he is also elucidating its importance for the Romantics. One important reason for his being able to do so is that he, unlike Schlegel and Novalis, knows Hölderlin's translations. Their peculiar quality allows him to make claims about and to conceive of translation in ways that the Romantics were prevented from doing because they had no such compelling examples of the language of translation, and so a slighter sense of its special status. Hölderlin's translations are in this process a sort of catalyst.

That Benjamin's thoughts on translation are an extension of the Romantics' on criticism, and that it is his concentration on *Kritik* that furnishes him with the elements of his meditation, emerges clearly from the exact equivalence of two terms more or less invented by Benjamin and introduced at key points in dissertation and essay: 'Kritisierbarkeit' ('criticizability') and 'Übersetzbarkeit' ('translatability'). These parallel terms both relate to the value of the original. Benjamin talks about the 'Unkritisierbarkeit des Schlechten' (*GS* I.1, 79): bad works cannot be the object of criticism. In the same way, according to the preface, they cannot be translated: 'Je weniger Wert und Würde seine [des Originals] Sprache hat, je mehr es Mitteilung ist, desto weniger ist für die Übersetzung dabei zu gewinnen'. And, conversely, 'je höher ein Werk geartet ist, desto mehr bleibt es selbst in flüchtigster Berührung seines Sinnes noch übersetzbar' (*GS* IV.1, 20; *TP*, p. 24). What is meant by value, and so by translatability and criticizability? The answer to this in *Der Begriff der Kunstkritik* is very clear:

> der Wert des Werkes hängt einzig und allein davon ab, ob es seine immanente Kritik überhaupt möglich macht oder nicht. Ist diese möglich, liegt also im Werke eine Reflexion vor, welche sich entfalten, absolutieren und im Medium der Kunst auflösen läßt, so ist es ein Kunstwerk. Die bloße Kritisierbarkeit eines Werkes stellt das positive Werturteil über dasselbe dar. (*GS* I.1, 78–79)

Likewise, the question of the translatability of a work asks 'ob es seinem Wesen nach Übersetzung zulasse und demnach — der Bedeutung dieser Form gemäß — auch verlange' (*GS* IV.1, 10; *TP*, p. 12). Only certain works are translatable: 'Übersetzbarkeit eignet gewissen Werken wesentlich — das [...] will besagen, daß eine bestimmte Bedeutung, die den Originalen innewohnt, sich in ihrer Übersetzbarkeit äußere' (*GS* IV.1, 10; *TP*, p. 12). Only particular works are susceptible to criticism and translation, and they are the same works, or the same kind of works. What Benjamin calls the 'specific significance' a translation elicits is also what he calls a 'reflection', that criticism can unfold. It is that trace or glint of the Absolute, which thus becomes a criterion of a 'good' work, though the task of both translation and criticism is not to assert that quality but to change it, to 'potentiate' it. 'Für die Romantiker ist Kritik viel weniger die Beurteilung eines Werkes als die Methode seiner Vollendung' (*GS* I.1, 69). That this goes also for translation emerges from a quotation from Friedrich Schlegel which Benjamin supplies: 'Jene poetische Kritik ... wird die Darstellung von Neuem darstellen, das schon Gebildete noch einmal bilden wollen ... wird das Werk ergänzen, verjüngen, neu gestalten' (*GS* I.1, 69). The terms here, and others like them, recur in relation to translation. 'Jede Uebersetzung ist *Verpflanzung* oder *Verwandlung* oder beides [...] Jede wahre Ueb[ersetzung] muß eine Verjüngung sein' (Friedrich Schlegel).[19] And Benjamin too talks of transplanting (*GS* IV.1, 15; *TP*, p. 18), of 'Wandlung und Erneuerung des Lebendigen' (*GS* IV.1, 12; *TP*, p. 15).

Der Begriff der Kunstkritik, like 'Die Aufgabe des Übersetzers', has its own point where the relation between translation and criticism (in Romanticism) is enunciated. It comes in the form of a quotation from Novalis. Speaking of what he calls 'mythical' translations (a particular, 'higher' kind) Novalis says:

> Sie stellen den reinen, vollendeten Charakter des individuellen Kunstwerks dar. Sie geben uns nicht das wirkliche Kunstwerk, sondern das Ideal desselben. Noch existiert, wie ich glaube, kein ganzes Muster derselben. Im Geist mancher Kritiken und Beschreibungen von Kunstwerken trifft man aber helle Spuren. (*GS* I.1, 70)

The perfection or completion of originals Novalis suggests such translations can achieve clearly resembles, or is in fact the same as, the process in which the 'experiment' of criticism brings the work of art 'zum Bewußtsein und zur Erkenntnis seiner selbst' (*GS* I.1, 65). It should by now be evident that this passage from Novalis is the seed that germinates and develops in the 'Aufgabe des Übersetzers'. Just as Romantic poetry should act upon itself, and criticism can act upon a work of art, so translation can take up and transform originals, pointing them into infinity. For both the Romantics and Benjamin, translation brings out something already inherent in the original, and for both of them this has nothing to do with content. The Romantics entertained the idea that a translation was therefore better than the original — in his letter to A. W. Schlegel of 30 November 1797 Novalis pronounced himself 'überzeugt, daß der deutsche Shakespeare jezt besser als der Englische ist', in exactly the same spirit as Friedrich Schlegel could call his review of Goethe's novel *Wilhelm Meisters Lehrjahre* an 'Übermeister' (see *GS* I.1, 67), almost by definition.[20] By contrast Benjamin appears to delimit this unfettered conception of translation, saying that a translation can never mean anything for the original ('niemals [...] etwas für das Original zu bedeuten vermag'; *GS* IV.1, 10; *TP*, p. 12). The Romantics came close to seeing translation as a kind of operation that can be performed on an original, shifting it into a different sphere. In principle at least, this operation could be repeated in an endless series. Benjamin tempers this, suggesting that only a motion towards another sphere is made:

> In [der Übersetzung] wächst das Original in einen gleichsam höheren und reineren Luftkreis der Sprache hinauf, in welchem es freilich nicht auf die Dauer zu leben vermag, wie es ihn auch bei weitem nicht in allen Teilen seiner Gestalt erreicht, auf den es aber dennoch in einer wunderbar eindringlichen Weise wenigstens hindeutet als auf den vorbestimmten, versagten Versöhnungs- und Erfüllungsbereich der Sprachen. (*GS* IV.1, 14–15; *TP*, p. 17)

Language in this state cannot be taken further. As Benjamin says in a passage quoted earlier, the new realm the translation inhabits or points towards can be thought of as final, as ultimate, in the sense that the translation cannot then be translated out of it. It is therefore interesting to observe that the versions Benjamin cites as exemplary in this respect, Hölderlin's, are among the very few translations which *have* themselves undergone further translation.[21]

IV

Benjamin names Luther, Voß, Hölderlin and George as the translators who have 'extended the boundaries of the German language' ('die Grenzen des Deutschen erweitert'; *GS* IV.1, 19; *TP*, p. 23), but Hölderlin is the only one of these to be mentioned other than in passing. In the last paragraph of the essay Benjamin turns especially to him:

> Übersetzungen [...] erweisen sich unübersetzbar nicht wegen der Schwere, sondern wegen der allzu großen Flüchtigkeit, mit welcher der Sinn an ihnen haftet. Hierfür wie in jeder andern wesentlichen Hinsicht stellen sich Hölderlins Übertragungen, besonders die der beiden Sophokleischen Tragödien, bestätigend dar. In ihnen ist die Harmonie der Sprachen so tief, daß der Sinn nur noch wie eine Äolsharfe vom Winde von der Sprache berührt wird. Hölderlins Übersetzungen sind Urbilder ihrer Form; sie verhalten sich auch zu den vollkommensten Übertragungen ihrer Texte als das Urbild zum Vorbild, wie es der Vergleich der Hölderlinschen und Borchardtschen Übersetzung der dritten pythischen Ode von Pindar zeigt. Eben darum wohnt in ihnen vor andern die ungeheure und ursprüngliche Gefahr aller Übersetzung: daß die Tore einer so erweiterten und durchwalteten Sprache zufallen und den Übersetzer ins Schweigen schließen. Die Sophokles-Übersetzungen waren Hölderlins letztes Werk. In ihnen stürzt der Sinn von Abgrund zu Abgrund, bis er droht in bodenlosen Sprachtiefen sich zu verlieren. (GS IV.I, 20–21; TP, p. 24)

Here Hölderlin's translations are seen as both exemplary and extreme, and as somehow on the very edge of language itself. From them Benjamin moves on seamlessly to speak of Scripture. The status he accords them could hardly be higher, and the effect of placing this passage at the end of the essay is to suggest that it has all along primarily been a meditation on Hölderlin's translations, or on translation as it is revealed in them. Hölderlin translated *Antigone* and *King Oedipus* and the greater part of Pindar's Olympian and Pythian odes. The distinguishing feature the translations have is a perplexing literality — in the Pindar versions Hölderlin transposes word for word, retaining the Greek word order and line breaks, and this results in a language distant from both Greek and German, often confused and turbulent and almost unreadable but occasionally combining into moments of strange beauty. And even outside these moments the translation is animated by a rhythm which the manuscripts show Hölderlin worked to achieve. The Sophocles versions are more various, but essentially derive from the same word-for-word technique, from the attempt to drive the languages together rather than to translate, to carry the sense across. The normal structures of language are undermined and a quality appears which, perhaps only metaphorically, we can think of as suggesting the pre-lingual, as pertaining to the movements of consciousness itself. Hölderlin's translations make many of the assertions in the essay easier to credit, such as the point that sense only needs to be touched as if by a tangent. Benjamin mentions the translation of Pindar's third Pythian ode, and a segment from that will perhaps convey something of the quality that Benjamin is at least tempted to ascribe to the language of translation:

> Nicht, liebe Seele, Leben unsterbliches
> Suche; die thunliche erschöpfe die Kunst.
> Wenn aber der weise die Grotte bewohnt
> Noch Chiron, und einigen
> Liebestrank ihm ins Gemüthe die süßgestimmten Hymnen
> Die unsern haben gebracht: einen

> Arzt würd ich ihn bitten
> Auch jezt den treflichen beizu-
> Geben den Männern in heißen Seuchen,
> Entweder einen vom Latoiden
> Genennet oder vom Vater.
> Und in Schiffen gieng ich das
>   Ionische theilend das Meer
> Zu Arethusa
> Der Quelle [...]²²

As part of a critique of Scholem's translation of the Song of Songs, which he saw as 'apologetic' because it placed Hebrew above German and so not in the same 'sphere', Benjamin went on (in a letter to Scholem of 17 July 1917) to consider the possibility of two languages occupying the same sphere:

> Es wäre nun prinzipiell nicht unmöglich daß zwei Sprachen in eine Sphäre eingehen: im Gegenteil das konstituiert alle große Übersetzung und bildet die Grundlage der ganz wenigen großen Übersetzungswerke die wir haben. Im Geiste Pindars erschloß sich Hölderlin die gleiche Sphäre der deutschen und der griechischen Sprache: seine Liebe zu beiden wurde *eine*.²³

Two languages in one sphere, or two languages having the same sphere, would seem to imply that it is possible to work in a domain where two languages coalesce. One way of understanding what Benjamin means by 'pure language' is as a metaphoric attempt to account for the quality of language in Hölderlin's translations and the sense we have from them, at a few points at least, of a language free of the specificity of either Greek or German and so in some sense 'pure'. By loosening the syntactical bonds and detaching itself from the familiar articulation of meaning, language begins to act as such, or at least to appear to. It is no longer, or not to the same extent, in service of a given sense, but operates in a mode where meaning seems to be flickering in and out of view. Benjamin is speaking of something real when he has recourse to the idea of 'pure language', a disembodiedness of language which does not make it any less concrete. If we turn a few pages back in the essay, to a passage that has in part already been quoted, we can see that it already seems to have been written with Hölderlin's translations in mind:

> Übersetzung also, wiewohl sie auf Dauer ihrer Gebilde nicht Anspruch erheben kann und hierin unähnlich der Kunst, verleugnet nicht ihre Richtung auf ein letztes, endgültiges und entscheidendes Stadium aller Sprachfügung. In ihr wächst das Original in einen gleichsam höheren und reineren Luftkreis der Sprache hinauf, in welchem es freilich nicht auf die Dauer zu leben vermag, wie es ihn auch bei weitem nicht in allen Teilen seiner Gestalt erreicht, auf den es aber dennoch in einer wunderbar eindringlichen Weise wenigstens hindeutet als auf den vorbestimmten, versagten Versöhnungs- und Erfüllungsbereich der Sprachen. (*GS* IV.1, 14–15; *TP*, p. 17)

This catches something of the way language in Hölderlin's translations is fragile and provisional, almost put beyond normal working, hardly functioning, on the one hand, and full of purpose, penetrating into its own creative core, on the other. The translations reveal something essential about their originals, and it has to do with the nature of language itself, its capacity as a 'reine Sprache' beyond the specifics of any one tongue. This making of a pure language — something that can only ever be pointed towards — is contained in Hölderlin's Pindar and Sophocles in its most palpable, if still always imaginary, form, but it also seems to belong to translation itself. This is as much as to say that Hölderlin's translations are the main impulse behind the reflections of the 'Aufgabe', though this can only be stated, not proven.

V

A last source drawn on in the essay is Goethe's discussion of translation in the 'Noten und Abhandlungen' to the *West-östlicher Divan*, which Benjamin fleetingly mentions as (among) the best when introducing a long quotation from Rudolf Pannwitz's *Die Krisis der europaeischen Kultur* (1917). In its final paragraph Benjamin's text becomes particularly gnomic, and having moved from Hölderlin to the Bible, having made the famous statement that 'all great writings' contain their potential ('virtuelle') translation 'between the lines', he closes with the words: 'Die Interlinearversion des heiligen Textes ist das Urbild oder Ideal aller Übersetzung' (*GS* IV.1, 21; *TP*, p. 25).

With this final cadence Benjamin is following Goethe's *Divan* note, which also closes by gravitating towards the interlinear version as a kind of end point of translation. When defining what he calls the 'höchste und letzte' phase of translation, Goethe makes a distinction which points in the same direction as Benjamin's thoughts about two languages sharing the same sphere. It is a phase 'wo man die Übersetzung dem Original identisch machen möchte, so daß eins nicht anstatt des andern, sondern an der Stelle des andern gelten solle'.[24] Benjamin offers a gloss on this when earlier in the essay he says that '[d]ie wahre Übersetzung ist durchscheinend, sie verdeckt nicht das Original, steht ihm nicht im Licht, sondern läßt die reine Sprache, wie verstärkt durch ihr eigenes Medium, nur um so voller aufs Original fallen' (*GS* IV.1, 18; *TP*, p. 21). A good translation does not replace the original, but occupies the same place as it. It is in that sense 'identical'. An interlinear works similarly in that instead of displacing the original it operates together with it; and Goethe says that any translation that seeks to 'identify itself' with the original 'nähert sich zuletzt der Interlinearversion'.[25]

To point to these sources is to put the essay in a broadly speaking Romantic tradition. This tradition is in many ways, and in parts, esoteric. In a letter to Ernst Schoen (8 November 1918) Benjamin writes that the Romantics had several 'esoteric concepts', one of which was their concept of criticism.[26] In translation he uncovered another, maintaining the Romantics' esotericism in his exposition of it. There are many hidden correspondences between *Der Begriff der Kunstkritik* and 'Die Aufgabe des Übersetzers'. One is between the notion of prose as the idea of poetry ('Die Idee der Poesie ist die Prosa': *GS* I.1, 100–01), central to the dissertation, and the notion of 'pure language' in relation to all languages. At the very end of the *Begriff*, in the section titled 'Die frühromantische Kunsttheorie und Goethe', which he added to the dissertation proper and called in another letter to Schoen 'ein esoterisches Nachwort' written for those 'denen ich sie als *meine* Arbeit mitzuteilen hätte' (May

1919[27]), Benjamin finishes on the word 'Idee' and links it back by a composite and cryptic quotation ('das nüchterne Licht') to earlier references to Hölderlin. If in the *Begriff* and the 'Aufgabe' he was writing esoterically, for an inner circle, then it may have included — for *and* against it — the circle around Stefan George in which Hölderlin was rediscovered and with whose peripheries Benjamin was in contact. Certainly Hölderlin is an iceberg-like presence in both pieces of work.

Notes to Chapter 13

1. Walter Benjamin, *Einbahnstraße* (Frankfurt a.M.: Suhrkamp, 1977), p. 20. There have been at least two fairly recent publications which make a return to 'Die Aufgabe des Übersetzers' timely: Antoine Berman's posthumous *L'Âge de la traduction: 'La tâche du traducteur' de Walter Benjamin, un commentaire*, ed. by Isabelle Berman and Valentina Sommella (Saint-Denis: Presses Universitaires de Vincennes, 2008), based on a seminar given in 1984–85; and vol. VII of the new Kritische Gesamtausgabe of Benjamin's *Werke und Nachlaß*, ed. by Christoph Gödde and Henri Lonitz (2008–): Walter Benjamin, *Tableaux Parisiens*, ed. by Antonia Birnbaum and Michel Métayer (Berlin: Suhrkamp, 2017) [henceforth: *TP*].
2. Note quoted in: Walter Benjamin, *Gesammelte Schriften*, ed. by Rolf Tiedemann and Hermann Schweppenhäuser, 7 vols (Frankfurt a.M.: Suhrkamp, 1972–89), IV.2, 891 [henceforth: *GS*].
3. For Berman, the preface is not an essay, 'car Benjamin entend énoncer des vérités qui n'ont pas le caractère hypothétique et provisoire des pensées d'un essai' (*L'Âge de la traduction*, p. 35), but it seems to me that the word catches very well Benjamin's speculative intent and the way he is trying out or venturing an idea.
4. References to 'Die Aufgabe des Übersetzers' are given in both *GS* IV.1, 9–21 and *TP*, pp. 11–25.
5. It is not known what these were. See *TP*, pp. 217–18.
6. 'Zwei Gedichte von Friedrich Hölderlin' (*GS* II.1, 105–26).
7. Walter Benjamin, *Briefe*, ed. by Gershom Scholem and Theodor W. Adorno, 2 vols (Frankfurt a.M.: Suhrkamp, 1966), I, 131.
8. Not that there are no other influences: the Kabbala is almost certainly one, and this is at least part of what Benjamin may mean by writing to Scholem (26 March 1921) that the essay on translation is 'Ihres größten Anteils sicher' (*Briefe*, I, 259). George Steiner says that the essay 'derives from the gnostic tradition': *After Babel: Aspects of Language and Translation*, 2nd edn (Oxford: Oxford University Press, 1992), p. 66.
9. Berman, *L'Âge de la traduction*, p. 35.
10. Stefan George, *Werke*, 2 vols (Munich: dtv, 2000), II, 310. Scholem, in *Walter Benjamin — die Geschichte einer Freundschaft* (Frankfurt a.M.: Suhrkamp, 1975), remembers that when Benjamin read out four of his and George's translations together he always took Benjamin's to be George's (p. 23).
11. There is a parallel with Hölderlin here, the appearing of an absolute amid a process: 'die Welt aller Welten, das Alles in Allen, welches immer *ist*, stellt sich nur in aller Zeit — oder im Untergange oder [...] im Werden des Moments und Anfang von Zeit und Welt dar' (Friedrich Hölderlin, *Sämtliche Werke*, ed. by Friedrich Beissner und Adolf Beck, 8 vols (Stuttgart: Kohlhammer, 1943–85), IV, 282).
12. See Antoine Berman, *L'épreuve de l'étranger: Culture et traduction dans l'Allemagne romantique* (Paris: Gallimard, 1984), who stresses 'la place structurelle qu'occupe la traduction généralisée dans la pensée romantique' and adds: 'On pourrait parler d'un concept opératoire qui, comme tel, n'est pas thématisé, mais ordonne le déploiement de cette pensée' (p. 136).
13. *Kritische Schriften und Briefe*, ed. by Edgar Lohner, 7 vols (Stuttgart: Kohlhammer, 1962–74), IV, 35.
14. Friedrich Schlegel, *Kritische Ausgabe*, ed. by Hans Eichner et al., 35 vols (Paderborn: Schöningh, 1958–), II, 183; Novalis, *Schriften*, ed. by Paul Kluckhohn and Richard Samuel, 5 vols (Stuttgart: Kohlhammer, 1977–88), IV, 237.

15. Novalis, II, 545; Schlegel, XVIII, 235.
16. Schlegel, II, 204.
17. Schlegel, XVIII, 288.
18. Berman says: 'on peut presque lire "La tâche du traducteur" comme la conceptualisation des intuitions romantiques concernant la traduction' (*L'Âge de la traduction*, p. 147).
19. Schlegel, XVIII, 204.
20. Novalis, IV, 237.
21. By, for example, David Constantine into English (*Hölderlin's Sophocles: Oedipus and Antigone* (Tarset: Bloodaxe, 2001)) and Philippe Lacoue-Labarthe into French (Hölderlin, *Antigone de Sophocle* (Paris: Bourgeois, 1978) and *Œdipe le tyran de Sophocle* (Paris: Bourgeois, 1998)).
22. Hölderlin, V, 79–80.
23. Benjamin, *Briefe*, I, 142.
24. Johann Wolfgang von Goethe, *Werke*, ed. by Erich Trunz, 14 vols (Munich: Beck, 1988), II, 256.
25. Ibid., p. 258.
26. Benjamin, *Briefe*, I, 203.
27. Ibid., p. 210.

CHAPTER 14

❖

Verantwortung: Paradoxes of Responsibility in Kafka's *Landarzt* Collection and Beyond

Carolin Duttlinger

In 'Die Losung', his preface to the first issue of the journal *Der Jude*, which appeared in April 1916, Martin Buber describes the war as a unique opportunity for Jewish people across Europe. While the letters and reports of Jewish soldiers had revealed a great yearning to partake in a 'großen und lebensvollen Gemeinschaft' based on 'Mannhaftigkeit und Bewährung, Gemeinschaft und Hingabe', he argues that the communities forged in the battlefield are flawed, a distraction. As political crisis does indeed spark a reorientation towards collective aims and values, this impulse must be channelled towards a different goal. Buber calls on Jews from Eastern and Western Europe to come together, for every individual to follow the 'Ruf der tiefen Gemeinschaft seines Blutes'.[1] As he declares with considerable pathos: 'Wer überhaupt mit seinem Dasein auf der Erde Ernst machen will, muß mit seinem Verhältnis zur Gemeinschaft Ernst machen: indem er sich *verantwortlich fühlt*'.[2] To live properly, then, is to commit to the community; this commitment involves concrete engagement but also, more importantly, an underlying sentiment. At the crucial point in his argument, Buber shifts from 'Ernst *machen*' to 'sich *verantwortlich fühl[en]*'; how exactly this feeling might translate into action, however, is left unspecified.

When Buber first invited Kafka to contribute to *Der Jude* in 1915, Kafka politely declined. In April 1917, however, he responded to Buber's renewed invitation by sending him twelve of the short prose texts he had just produced in his writing retreat in the Alchimistengasse.[3] In his accompanying letter, Kafka echoes the terms of Buber's 'Losung', for it is here that he mentions — for the first and only time in his surviving texts — his intention of publishing these pieces under the joint title *Verantwortung*.[4] This plan never came to fruition. In the end, the collection of short stories, which was published in 1920 by the Kurt Wolff Verlag, was called *Ein Landarzt*.

In a letter to the Kafka scholar Robert Kauf, Gershom Scholem argues that Kafka's suggested title was intended as a homage to Buber, a deliberate reference to his 'Losung', which Buber would immediately have recognized — but that

Kafka never actually intended to use this title. Even though Buber's argument 'war ihm [Kafka] aus der Seele gesprochen', his own conception of *Verantwortung* was 'himmelweit von der Bubers entfernt, denn bei Kafka zeigt eben jeder Versuch, Verantwortung zu praktizieren, das Hoffnungslose darin auf'.[5] Scholem, to be sure, was no unbiased commentator on Buber,[6] and his claim regarding Kafka's intentions cannot be verified. That said, his letter does raise various important questions about the relationship between Kafka's stories, his proposed title and Buber's journal, where Kafka ended up publishing only 'Schakale und Araber' and 'Ein Bericht für eine Akademie'.[7] Even if Kafka's allusion to Buber's preface was a calculated strategy designed to underline the affinities of his stories with the agenda of *Der Jude*, the opportunity to publish in the journal would have also brought Buber's 'Losung' back to his mind, and may have made Kafka aware of an underlying thread connecting the pieces he had written in the preceding months.

So is Kafka's understanding of responsibility as diametrically opposed to Buber's as Scholem suggests? In 'Die Losung', responsibility is cast as the response to a collective crisis, as a sentiment which can reunite a dispersed community, but which is rooted in the individual. Aspects of Buber's argument do, as we shall see, chime with Kafka's stories, several of which are set in times of crisis, whether this crisis stems from exploitation, from regime change, invasion, or from more personal forms of conflict. More difficult to determine is the relationship between community and individual. Buber contrasts two forms of community and the associated mode of personal commitment: the nation-state and the associated war effort versus the Jewish people as an entity which transcends national boundaries. His argument assumes that this Jewish community can be reawakened through the actions, the responsibility, of the individual.

Kafka's texts expand, and thereby complicate, Buber's argument and assumptions. In his writings up to *Der Process*, people live and work alongside each other but without much sense of a shared purpose. In his writings from 1916 onwards, this indifference gives way to a much keener awareness of communal life, and yet the relationship between collective and individual is by no means straightforward, rooted in mutual commitment, but is shown to be tense and precarious. While the word *Verantwortung* only features once in the *Landarzt* collection, it acts as a concept which underpins the stories as a problem and challenge rather than a solution. Contrary to what Scholem claims, however, Kafka does not simply cast responsibility as hopeless; on the contrary, this concept retains a particular appeal, and is depicted, in the *Landarzt* stories and subsequent texts, as a profound human impulse, but one which resists being mobilized for a particular purpose.

In the following, I will first map out the different facets of the term *Verantwortung* before tracing its resonances in Kafka's writings. Unlike existing studies, I will not confine myself to the *Landarzt* collection,[8] but will also draw on preceding and succeeding texts, including diary entries and prose fragments. My aim is not to deduce from these texts one coherent model of responsibility; rather, I am interested in tracing the shifts and continuities, as well as the internal tensions, which inform Kafka's engagement with this issue in his prose fiction, his personal and his philosophical writings. One focal point will be the dynamic between individual(s) and collective as it is described, and also enacted, in these narratives, which use impersonal as well as personal, first-person singular and plural narrative modes, together with the second-person or 'you' perspective, to explore responsibility as an individual and an interpersonal challenge.

* * * * *

Jacob and Wilhelm Grimm's *Deutsches Wörterbuch* gives three definitions of *Verantwortung*. The oldest reference, a late-fifteenth century source, casts responsibility as a '*vorschlag, entwurf zu einer antwort an den kaiser*'. I will return to this definition in due course. More immediately relevant are definitions two and three. From this early and specific use of *Verantwortung* emerges its more general meaning: '*die handlung des sich verantwortens: apologia [...], defensio*'. This act can involve '*rechtfertigung vor gericht*', '*vor gottes richterstuhl*', or indeed '*rechtfertigung überhaupt. wie* verantworten *zunächst eine mündliche rechtfertigung in sich schlieszt, so ist* verantwortung *meist persönliche rechtfertigung in eigener sache oder in einer, die ich zur meinigen gemacht*'.

Third, responsibility can be used in a more general, virtual sense: '*neben dieser concreten bedeutung hat das wort die abstractere "zustand der verantwortlichkeit", wo die handlung der verantwortung nur als möglichkeit besteht*'.[9] As these latter two definitions show, *Verantwortung* has both a passive, defensive, and an active, voluntary, dimension. On the one hand, it implies culpability, having to defend one's actions in front of some authority; on the other, it refers to a more general 'Zustand der Verantwortlichkeit', which underpins any specific action or encounter. But there is another important difference between the two. In the first instance, *Verantwortung* is described as '*persönliche rechtfertigung in eigener sache*', and therefore as a self-reflexive concept — responsibility as something I assume for myself, regarding my own actions and affairs. In the second definition, self-reflexivity is possible but not essential. In its more abstract, virtual dimension, *Verantwortung* is opened up towards the other (the individual or the group), and it is in this sense that the term is used by Buber.[10]

Both of these facets of *Verantwortung* can be identified in Kafka's writings, where they sometimes feature individually, sometimes in combination. Broadly speaking, responsibility as *apologia* or *defensio* is more immediately relevant for Kafka's texts up to and including *Der Process*, with their plot lines of accusation, trial and punishment, although this meaning still underpins later texts such as 'Eine kleine Frau', whose narrative is one long, only moderately convincing, *defensio*. In these texts, responsibility adheres to, inheres within, the individual, and often Kafka's characters respond to this situation by trying to shrug off and shift this responsibility onto others. Immediately following his arrest by the guard, Josef K. thinks aloud as he jumps out of bed, '"Ich will doch sehen, was für Leute im Nebenzimmer sind und wie Frau Grubach diese Störung mir gegenüber verantworten wird"', and a similar impulse informs his later conversation with his landlady: '"Das Fräulein [Bürstner] kommt oft spät nach Hause", sagte K. und sah Frau Grubach an, als trage sie die Verantwortung dafür.'[11]

So where *Verantwortung* is used in the sense of *sich verantworten müssen*, it sparks a defensive reaction in Kafka's characters, who refuse to accept personal liability when confronted with an authority figure or institution. This defensive impulse is still present in some of the texts written in the Alchimistengasse, but there are also some notable differences. While Kafka's earlier texts are centred on the experiences of sons and bachelors and involve scenarios of trial and accusation, the stories from the *Landarzt* period often focus on the complementary role and perspective — that of the fathers, rulers or superiors. These characters embody the definition of responsibility as an ongoing, virtual state, a '*zustand der verantwortlichkeit*', where '*die handlung der verantwortung nur als möglichkeit besteht*', yet Scholem certainly has a point when he underlines the aporia attached to this responsibility. Kafka's *Landarzt* stories subtly redefine *Möglichkeit* as *Unmöglichkeit* while transforming action, *Handlung*, into inaction. Rather than actively trying to shift their responsibility onto others, many of these authority figures are shown to fail at their task, or do not attempt it in the first place. In some of the stories from the *Landarzt* period, a failure of responsibility is the outcome of the narrative, whereas in others this failure stands at the beginning of the narrative and sets in train a whole host of consequences.

★ ★ ★ ★ ★

The only text featuring the term *Verantwortung* is the story 'Ein Besuch im Bergwerk'. Like 'Elf Söhne', it has no plot to speak of but describes a succession of people — the ten engineers visiting the mine, who are seen through the eyes of the miners:

> Ein Fünfter, vielleicht der oberste im Rang, duldet keine Begleitung; ist bald vorn, bald hinten; die Gesellschaft richtet ihren Schritt nach ihm; er ist bleich und schwach; die Verantwortung hat seine Augen ausgehöhlt; oft drückt er im Nachdenken die Hand an die Stirn.[12]

The story both echoes and questions the argument of Buber's 'Losung'. The characterization of the fifth engineer is partially based on his distance from the rest of the group, and yet his detachment is at odds with Buber's definition of responsibility, which is adopted by the individual on behalf of the community. What is more, his posture and appearance suggest that he may not be up to this task, whether or not he has ever attempted it. Here and elsewhere in Kafka's texts, responsibility is depicted as the mental and physical burden associated with a position of authority. It appears to have taken its toll on the engineer's health and manifests itself in a contemplative mindset. As so often in Kafka's texts, the link between appearance and interpretation is far from straightforward. The engineer's position as 'der oberste im Rang' is not backed up by any concrete evidence but is based solely on conjecture — on his *Gestus* of responsibility.

Indeed, it remains unclear what he carries responsibility *for*, just as the narrators never spell out the reason for the engineers' visit. Within their group, a more tangible, practical responsibility attaches to the ninth engineer, who is in charge of the 'Meßapparate' — fragile devices that are wrapped in cotton wool and are being wheeled around in 'eine Art Kinderwagen'. Despite these precautions, the ninth engineer cannot be trusted with these tools, for he is accompanied by a tenth, whose task is to stop him from bumping the pram against the mine walls. This absurd duo, parodying the responsibility of parenthood, concludes the group, in which *Verantwortung* oscillates between an empty gesture and a display of incompetence but is ultimate shouldered by no-one, for these young men seem unequal to the challenge either individually or as a group. By describing this situation from the perspective of an amorphous 'we', the text highlights the gulf which separates the engineers from the miners, while raising the possibility that personal responsibility may be a mere projection on the part of the 'we', the group, who are not expected to carry this burden.

While 'Ein Besuch im Bergwerk' ironizes the concept of personal responsibility, a more blatant failure to act responsibly is depicted in the story 'Ein Brudermord'. Stylistically, this violent yet strangely theatrical (or cinematic) text harks back to Kafka's early, Expressionist stories, while thematically it echoes the emphasis on guilt and culpability in 'Das Urteil' and *Der Process*. Here, the issue of responsibility arises less with regard to the murderer (whose guilt is never in doubt even if his motivation remains unclear) than to the witness or bystander. This individual, who is tellingly characterized as 'der Private Pallas', observes the murder from his window — even leaning out to get a better view — but does nothing to prevent it. The text presents his passivity as a riddle:

> Warum duldete das alles der Private Pallas, der in der Nähe aus seinem Fenster im zweiten Stockwerk alles beobachtete? Ergründe die Menschennatur! Mit hochgeschlagenem Kragen, den Schlafrock um den weiten Leib gegürtet, kopfschüttelnd, blickte er hinab. (*DL* 293)

As in 'Ein Besuch im Bergwerk', the narrative's focus is on appearances. Pallas's gesture is hopelessly inadequate as a response to this graphic murder, while his girth and 'Schlafrock', with its upturned collar, spell inertia and passivity. Pallas is the successor of the (male) window gazers of the *Betrachtung* collection, who can often be found standing at the window, watching the events below from a safe distance and in a state of inner detachment. In 'Zerstreutes Hinausschaun', a girl is being followed, potentially stalked, by a man; the observer at the window above does nothing, and eventually the tension dissipates. In 'Die Vorüberlaufenden', the situation is more tense and dynamic, as the spectacle of a nocturnal chase gives rise to different interpretations: 'vielleicht will der zweite morden, und wir würden Mitschuldige des Mordes, vielleicht wissen die zwei nichts voneinander, und es läuft jeder nur auf eigene Verantwortung in sein Bett' (*DL* 26). The text's underlying premise, however, spelled out at the start, is non-interference, as the ambiguity of the scene is used by the (collective) narrative voice to justify their inaction: 'Und endlich, dürfen wir nicht müde sein, haben wir nicht soviel Wein getrunken? Wir sind froh, daß wir auch den zweiten nicht mehr sehn' (*DL* 27).

On the face of it, the story 'Auf der Galerie' offers a welcome counterpoint, an antidote to this failure or abnegation of responsibility. Here, the spectacle of the circus rider's exploitation at the hands of the ringmaster sparks the young Galeriebesucher's heroic intervention. But then this impulse is dismantled, as its cause is revealed to be a mere illusion ('Da es aber nicht so ist ...'; *DL* 262). Realizing that his actions are not needed, the observer buries his face in the balustrade, a gesture which echoes the fifth engineer's bowed head.

Several of the *Landarzt* stories revolve around the slippery distinction between reality and illusion or deception, most memorably the title story, 'Ein Landarzt'. Its protagonist is an archetypal figure of responsibility, for although he follows in the line of Kafka's bachelors the country doctor is no idle observer. The ringing of the 'Nachtglocke' is the acoustic signal which transforms his virtual 'Zustand der Verantwortlichkeit' into urgent action, although his efforts to answer the call are stalled by a series of surreal events and, most notably, by the patient's family and the wider community, whom he is trying to serve. These events are framed by a more general, institutional crisis of responsibility embodied by the priest tearing up his vestments. As in 'Auf der Galerie', moreover, the cause of his calling — his patient's wound — oscillates between illusion and reality.

Ultimately, the doctor's attempt to enact his responsibility calls into question the validity not only of this specific call but of his more general *Berufung*. The ringing of the night bell turns out to be a 'Fehlläuten' with existential and irreversible consequences: 'Betrogen! Betrogen! Einmal dem Fehlläuten der Nachtglocke gefolgt — es ist niemals gutzumachen' (*DL* 261). Even where responsibility is embraced rather than rejected, the text suggests, it is not a position 'owned' by the individual, as the doctor's role is tested and potentially challenged with every call.

As the collection's titular story, 'Ein Landarzt' is metonymically connected to the problem of *Verantwortung*, which is here framed as a crisis of authority, of vocation and communication. In addition to the definitions given in the *Deutsches Wörterbuch*, the term is here invested with another meaning. In German, the prefix *ver-* often implies a sense of slippage or failure: *verstimmen, verspielen, sich verlaufen, sich versprechen*. By analogy, *Verantwortung* implies a failed *Antwort* or response, that is, a scenario of miscommunication. This is borne out in 'Ein Landarzt'. If the call which summons us to take responsibility is faulty or misleading then the very foundation of *Verantwortung* is thrown into crisis. Responsibility in the *Landarzt* collection is a calling which is both inescapable and impossible to fulfil — precisely because its fulfilment is not up to the individual alone, but is dependent on the other, the community.

The failure of communication and its impact on responsibility are also central to the story 'Eine kaiserliche Botschaft', which depicts the interaction between three parties. The importance which the dying emperor places on this message and its correct transmission is at odds with its complete obscurity in the narrative; a similar dissonance is again apparent in the contrast between the messenger's strength and unwavering commitment and the infinite distance separating him from the addressee: 'Niemand dringt hier durch und gar mit der Botschaft eines Toten. — Du aber sitzt an Deinem Fenster und erträumst sie Dir, wenn der Abend kommt' (*DL* 282). This ending adds another twist to the theme of calling and responsibility, suggesting the emperor's message may not originate from the centre but from within the individual, as the response to a (perhaps equally fictitious) vacuum of authority. Read in this way, the ending chimes with the sentiment of Buber's 'Losung': that in times of political crisis, the individual needs to take personal responsibility rather than rely on top-down structures and authorities. That said, the individual's response is far from decisive; the verb *sich erträumen* does not indicate that he or she will step up to this challenge in an active, practical way and instead recalls the resigned response of the young Galeriebesucher, who likewise withdraws from reality into a dream.

'Eine kaiserliche Botschaft' recalls the first and earliest definition of *Verantwortung* in the Grimms' *Deutsches Wörterbuch* — '*vorschlag, entwurf zu einer antwort an den kaiser*'. Responsibility is here cast as the response to a calling, a summons, or perhaps an interpellation, by the highest authority, and yet the *Antwort* this solicits is a mere draft or suggestion whose tentativeness leads to hesitation rather than an affirmative response. As in Kafka's story, it remains unclear whether this *Antwort* will ever be given.

A similar yet differently weighted breakdown in the communication between emperor and subjects is thematized in the second text associated with the unfinished longer narrative of 'Beim Bau der chinesischen Mauer'. This is 'Ein altes Blatt', a text which in Octavio Notebook C directly succeeds the 'China' complex as a postscript or, rather, a pre-script, for it describes an historical invasion of the country's capital by the dreaded nomads from the north. On the face of it, it serves as a warning example of what happens if a wall is not in place, but on a deeper level this crisis stems from a lack, or abnegation, of personal leadership and responsibility: 'Es ist, als wäre viel vernachlässigt worden in der Verteidigung unseres Vaterlandes. Wir haben uns bisher nicht darum gekümmert und sind unserer Arbeit nachgegangen; die Ereignisse der letzten Zeit machen uns aber Sorgen' (*DL* 263). This opening sentence describes a twofold failure of responsibility, as the failure to defend the *Vaterland* (we are not yet told by whom) is mirrored and exacerbated by the failure of the collective, the narrative 'we', to notice this situation until it was too late.

In the course of the story, the focus then turns to the emperor who bears the blame for this situation. Unlike his counterparts in the rest of the 'China' complex, he is no faceless, quasi-mythical figure, but dwells in the palace at the centre of the capital. His lack of leadership is made all the more conspicuous by his single appearance on the palace balcony, prompted by the horrific spectacle of the nomads' horses devouring a live ox:

> Gerade damals glaubte ich den Kaiser selbst in einem Fenster des Palastes gesehen zu haben; niemals sonst kommt er in die äußeren Gemächer, immer nur lebt er in dem innersten Garten; diesmal aber stand er, so schien es mir wenigstens, an einem der Fenster und blickte mit gesenktem Kopf auf das Treiben vor seinem Schloß. (*DL* 266)

The emperor's bowed head recalls the fifth engineer in 'Ein Besuch im Bergwerk'. Once again, responsibility manifests itself not as inner resolve or concrete action but merely as the bodily expression of an unbearable burden. More explicitly than in the 'Bergwerk' story, this sighting is cast as uncertain and subjective, potentially the product of projection. For in fact, the narrator is clear about who is to blame for this crisis:

> Der kaiserliche Palast hat die Nomaden angelockt, versteht es aber nicht, sie wieder zu vertreiben. Das Tor bleibt verschlossen; die Wache, früher immer festlich ein- und ausmarschierend, hält sich hinter vergitterten Fenstern. Uns

> Handwerkern und Geschäftsleuten ist die Rettung des Vaterlandes anvertraut;
> wir sind aber einer solchen Aufgabe nicht gewachsen; haben uns doch auch nie
> gerühmt, dessen fähig zu sein. Ein Mißverständnis ist es, und wir gehen daran
> zugrunde.

What at the start of the story was presented as the possible result of negligence is here revised, as the narrator spells out that 'the palace' has actively attracted this invasion. The resulting shutdown of the palace, its insulation against the outside world, places all the onus on the collective 'we', a pronoun which is initially used in an unspecified sense to include all subjects, but is then narrowed down to designate a specific (male) group of merchants and tradesmen. While the collective narrative voice of the 'Bergwerk' story speaks of responsibility as a matter for the other, the individual, here the political crisis forces the community to make up for the vacuum of authority at the top.[13] Faced with this situation, the 'we' does not spring into action but is left powerless and confused. In the interplay between individual and collective, neither side is able to assume responsibility.

Even more clearly than in the other *Landarzt* stories, 'Ein altes Blatt' shows responsibility to be impossible, the product of a failure of leadership which cannot be remedied by individuals. In an oblique way, this situation mirrors the contemporary political situation across Europe, and in the Habsburg Empire in particular, where the political crisis was exacerbated by the death of Emperor Franz Joseph I on 21 November 1916; shortly afterwards, Kafka started writing in the Alchimistengasse.[14]

★ ★ ★ ★ ★

In the final year of the war, Kafka returned to the question of *Verantwortung* from a more abstract, philosophical perspective. The texts which make up the Octavio Notebooks H and G date from the winter of 1917–18, which Kafka, having been diagnosed with tuberculosis, spent with his sister Ottla in the village of Zürau. In these notebooks, brief diary-style entries — about personal experiences as well as world politics (the ceasefire and subsequent peace with Russia) — alternate with short literary sketches and philosophical reflections on issues of religion, anthropology and morality. Although Kafka draws no explicit link between the diary entries and the reflective passages, it is clear that the latter are written against the background of political developments as they penetrated even his secluded rural existence.

Even a cursory glance at the manuscript shows that Kafka's method is one of starting and stopping, of short, often paradoxical musings, which do not come to any conclusion but try to illuminate an issue from different, contrasting angles. This method is also applied to the issue of responsibility, which is the subject of three successive passages recorded in Notebook G, begun in January 1918. The first of these was subsequently included, with some changes, in the so-called Zürau 'aphorisms', first published by Max Brod in 1931.[15] As in the *Landarzt* volume, *Verantwortung* seems to require a variety of different perspectives to attempt to capture its multiple meanings and implications. In the first and longest passage, it is at the centre of an anthropological narrative about the history of religion:

> Die erste Götzenanbetung war gewiß Angst vor den Dingen, aber damit zusammenhängend auch Angst vor der Notwendigkeit der Dinge und damit zusammenhängend Angst vor der Verantwortung für die Dinge. So ungeheuer erschien diese Verantwortung daß man sie nicht einmal einem einzigen außermenschlichen Wesen aufzuerlegen wagte, denn auch durch Vermittlung bloß eines Wesens wäre die menschliche Verantwortung noch nicht genug erleichtert worden, der Verkehr mit diesem Wesen wäre allzu sehr von Verantwortung befleckt gewesen, deshalb gab man möglichst jedem Ding die Verantwortung für sich selbst, mehr noch, man gab diesen Dingen auch eine gewisse Verantwortung für den Menschen. Man konnte sich nicht genug tun in der Schaffung von Gegengewichten, diese naive Welt war die komplicierteste die es jemals gab, ihre Naivität lebte sich ausschließlich in der brutalen Konsequenz aus.[16]

In contrast to its treatment in his prose fiction, *Verantwortung* is here not discussed in the context of human relations, but describes people's relationship with the material world. 'Die Dinge' is a vague term which could designate any form of material reality, but the reference to idolatry makes it clear that Kafka is thinking of inanimate (including natural) objects and their mute existence, which can induce fear but also, interestingly, the burden of responsibility. This argumentative chain is held together by the term 'zusammenhängend', which designates no temporal or a causal link but a looser kind of association. What emerges is not a logical syllogism or an anthropological theory about the origins of idolatry, but an argument which circles around the link between fear and responsibility. Kafka's musings echo Kierkegaard's *Fear and Trembling*, which he was reading at the time and where fear is described as a primary human state with no external cause, which is retrospectively projected onto particular objects.[17]

If idolatry shifts the burden of responsibility onto the objects themselves, this entails a potentially unsettling reversal of agency, whereby the things take responsibility for, and thereby charge of, people. Some of Kafka's stories echo this idea. Texts such as 'Die Sorge des Hausvaters' and the earlier 'Blumfeld, ein älterer Junggeselle' depict a *Dingwelt* that has once again come alive, harking back to a pre-Enlightenment age in thrall to mythology. Kafka hints at this outcome in his anthropological sketch, when he speaks of the complications arising from idolatry, and the 'brutality' of its consequences. The (re)turn to animism provides neither reassurance nor relief from the burden of responsibility, but rather results in a deeply unsettling world in which the hierarchy between individual and object has been thrown into disarray.

To make matters even more complicated, the above passage is prefaced by a personal remark, addressed, as so often in Kafka's writings in this period, to an unspecified, perhaps dialogical, perhaps self-reflexive 'you': 'Durch Auferlegung einer allzu großen oder vielmehr aller Verantwortung erdrückst Du Dich.' It remains unclear whether this responsibility is self-imposed or whether its *Auferlegung* is the act of another. Likewise, the remark oscillates between a subjective experience and the description of a general law or principle. In any case, the characterization of responsibility as excessive, perhaps all-encompassing, frames the ensuing reflections about the causes of idolatry, while suggesting that this strategy is closed off to modern, rational man.

This notion of *Verantwortung* as a crushing burden is picked up again in the following, much shorter passage, which is once again addressed to an unspecified 'you': 'Wird Dir alle Verantwortung auferlegt, so kannst Du den Augenblick benützen und der Verantwortung erliegen wollen, versuche es aber, dann merkst Du, daß Dir nichts auferlegt wurde, sondern daß Du diese Verantwortung selbst bist.'[18] Here, Kafka shifts back from an anthropological to a psychological perspective. Idolatry and animism are illusory ways of abnegating one's responsibility, and the impulse simply to collapse under this burden is equally futile. This passage thus provides an implicit answer to the question posed by the impersonal construction of 'Durch Auferlegung einer [...] Verantwortung erdrückst Du Dich'. As it turns out, responsibility is not only self-imposed but self-reflexive, for it is first and foremost responsibility for oneself. It cannot be shifted by either projection or surrender, for it is not external to the subject but an inherent, intrinsic part of human identity (what Freud would call the Super-Ego).

This point is reiterated in the third passage, which takes the form of a short aphoristic parable: 'Atlas konnte die Meinung haben, er dürfe, wenn er wolle, die Erde fallen lassen und sich wegschleichen; mehr als diese Meinung aber war ihm nicht erlaubt.'[19] The figure of Atlas visualizes and personifies the recurrent notion of responsibility as a burden that is imposed, 'auferlegt', on the individual. As the carrier of the world, he echoes what the preceding two passages describe as the absolute, all-encompassing nature of responsibility. The passage once again plays with the idea of simply throwing off this burden, but as in the case of idolatry, this idea is nothing but a comforting illusion, a psychological crutch rather than an actual *Ausweg* or solution.

In these three interlinked reflections, Kafka draws on anthropology, psychology and mythology to make the same essential point. Responsibility is an inherent part of human existence, and while it may appear to be imposed by some external authority, it cannot be shrugged off except in the (literary) imagination. The narratives of religion, idolatry and myth serve to lessen this burden, by associating *Verantwortung* with the realm of the extra-, the non- or the superhuman. Kafka's prose fiction offers a different, more paradoxical take on this issue. With their lowered heads and hunched shoulders, his characters are the heirs of Atlas, but their true burden is not responsibility for the *Dingwelt* or the other but for themselves. The stories Kafka writes during the war depict *Verantwortung* as a calling which defines the subject and yet which cannot be owned or fulfilled. This dilemma continues to occupy him into the 1920s, but here, the scope of his exploration is widened once again to include others, the community.

★ ★ ★ ★ ★

In a revealing chiasmus, Kafka's prose narratives from the *Landarzt* period use the first-person singular or plural narrative voice to explore responsibility, while his reflections in the diaries and notebooks are either addressed to an unspecified 'you' or formulated in general, impersonal terms. This latter mode is again used in a diary entry of January 1920:

> Er lebt in der Zerstreuung. Seine Elemente, eine frei lebende Horde, umschweifen die Welt. Und nur weil auch sein Zimmer zur Welt gehört sieht er sie manchmal in der Ferne. Wie soll er für sie die Verantwortung tragen? Heißt das noch Verantwortung?[20]

In other diary entries, Kafka laments his own distracted state of mind as anathema to creative writing. In this passage, *Zerstreuung* is depicted not as a passing affliction but as an existential state, one which the text visualizes as the physical dispersal of the self into a roaming horde of 'elements'. Recalling the window-gazers from *Betrachtung*, the subject occasionally spots them in the distance but is unable to relate to or control them. This situation raises the question of responsibility, cast once again as a burden to be carried. As the scene underlines, not only are these dispersed elements beyond the subject's control, but this situation throws the very concept of responsibility into question.

On the face of it, this diary entry frames responsibility as a psychological matter; in a state of mental dispersal, it suggests, we are unable to be responsible for ourselves, for our thoughts and actions. A look at the manuscript, however, reveals some telling corrections. Kafka subsequently revised the first sentence, 'Er lebt in der Zerstreuung', to read 'Er ist in der Diaspora'.[21] This is the only instance in Kafka's entire writings where the word 'diaspora' is used. The term transforms *Zerstreuung* from an inner disposition into a collective state of dispersal. The concept also features in Buber's 'Losung', which speaks of the need to secure and stabilize ('sichern and festigen') the Jewish diaspora by giving the Jewish people a 'zentrale Stätte, einen organischen Mittelpunkt' in a new Jewish homeland in Palestine.[22] Kafka would also have come across this political argument in the journals *Der Jude* and *Selbstwehr*, while his friends Max Brod and Hugo Bergmann instead favoured a cultural model of Zionism.[23]

As the manuscript shows, Kafka subsequently reversed these changes, while at the same time retaining the words 'ist' and 'Diaspora'. Both versions of the sentence thus stand alongside each other as two alternative ways of formulating the same problem. Living in a state of *Zerstreuung* and/or diaspora prevents the individual from assuming responsibility and indeed puts the meaning of this very concept into question. Kafka's diary entry both echoes and undermines Buber's argument that by assuming responsibility for others, the individual can facilitate a renewed sense of (Jewish) community in an age of dispersal.[24]

Elsewhere in his writings, however, Kafka presents a more positive, affirmative take on responsibility, most emphatically perhaps in this short diary entry recorded on 8 August 1917: 'Hoch die Lampe gehalten, Du vorn! Ihr andern leise hinter mir! Alle in einer Reihe. Und still. Das war nichts. Keine Angst. Ich trage die Verantwortung. Ich führe Euch hinaus.'[25] The setting vaguely echoes 'Ein Besuch im Bergwerk', but the mood is very different. Here, responsibility is neither impossible nor an empty gesture, but manifests itself in decisive speech and action.

The passage evokes a dangerous mission — an expedition perhaps, or the flight from captivity. Responsibility is not distributed across the group but assumed by the speaker, the decisive leader, who reassures the others while telling them what to do; importantly, s/he is part of the group, leading from the centre, rather than being physically detached from them.

A subtler but equally profound sense of personal responsibility for the collective is expressed in another prose fragment dating from August 1920:

> Versunken in die Nacht. So wie man manchmal den Kopf senkt, um nachzudenken, so ganz versunken sein in die Nacht. Ringsum schlafen die Menschen. Eine kleine Schauspielerei, eine unschuldige Selbsttäuschung daß sie in Häusern schlafen, in festen Betten unter festem Dach ausgestreckt oder geduckt auf Matratzen, in Tüchern, unter Decken, in Wirklichkeit haben sie sich zusammengefunden wie damals einmal und wie später einmal in wüster Gegend, ein Lager im Freien, eine unübersehbare Zahl Menschen, ein Heer, ein Volk, unter kaltem Himmel auf kalter Erde, hingeworfen wo man früher stand, die Stirn auf den Arm gedrückt, das Gesicht gegen den Boden hin, ruhig atmend. Und Du wachst, bist einer der Wächter, findest den nächsten durch Schwenken des brennenden Holzes aus dem Reisighaufen neben Dir. Warum wachst Du? Einer muß wachen, heißt es. Einer muß dasein[.][26]

The night-time scene opens with the contrast between the wakeful (but immersed) individual and 'die Menschen' sleeping all around. But then the notion of people sleeping in their homes is revealed to be an illusion — a 'kleine Schauspielerei' and 'unschuldige Selbsttäuschung'. The text can be read as a narrative elaboration on the concept of diaspora: the settled, sheltered lives of (European) Jews conceal an underlying, existential sense of homelessness and dispersal. For in reality, they are not asleep in their beds but in the wilderness, having made their beds 'unter kaltem Himmel auf kalter Erde'. The reference to a 'Lager' and the description of the group as 'ein Heer, ein Volk' lends this scenario biblical overtones, evoking Israel's flight from Egypt as it is recounted in the Book of Exodus. In contrast to the above-cited diary passage of 1917, however, this exodus narrative is not related by the leader who is guiding his or her people out of captivity, but is centred on a more inconspicuous figure: that of the guard keeping watch at night. All responsibility for the safety of the community rests on his or her shoulders, a situation which resonates with the lowered head described in the second sentence. Over the course of the text, the narrative perspective shifts from the impersonal 'man' to a 'Du', which lends these reflections the character of an address, a calling. This lone 'Wächter' will in turn wake the next person; responsibility is a deeply personal commitment, but at the same time shared between individuals. It does not derive from a personal impulse but is inscribed in collective tradition: 'Einer muß wachen, *heißt es*. Einer muß dasein' (my emphasis).

This narrative is perhaps the purest and most emphatic echo of Buber's 'Losung' and its conception of individual responsibility on behalf of others. And yet the passage also has a more specific, self-reflexive dimension. The opening sentences, which set the narrative in motion, echo diary entries where Kafka describes his nocturnal literary production as lonely but immersive and sometimes elating.

Responsibility can be explored through narratives of Jewish diaspora, but for Kafka this state, or vocation, is inextricably linked to his role as a writer.

The writer's role is thematized in a text recorded in the 'blaues Schulheft' in the spring of 1923, which addresses the ambivalent relationship between individual and collective:

> Es sind viele hier, die warten. Eine unübersehbare Menge, die sich im Dunkel verliert. Was will sie? Es sind offenbar bestimmte Forderungen, die sie stellt. Ich werde die Forderungen abhören und dann antworten. Auf den Balkon hinausgehn werde ich aber nicht; ich könnte es gar nicht, auch wenn ich wollte. Im Winter wird die Balkontür abgesperrt und der Schlüssel ist nicht zur Hand. Aber auch an das Fenster werde ich nicht treten.[27]

The set-up echoes 'Ein altes Blatt'; indeed, its first sentences could be written from the perspective of the emperor barricaded in his palace. This first-person narrator is faced by a vast crowd who want to make their demands heard. As in earlier texts, however, the communication between the ruler and the people is precarious; although the narrator is resolved to respond to their demands, he or she does not want to face them in person: 'Ich werde die Forderungen abhören und dann antworten'. '*Ab*hören', rather than '*an*hören', is an interesting choice of verb, which implies a time lag and suggests that these demands will not be put to the narrator directly but may be recorded — perhaps on one of Felice Bauer's *Parlographen*?[28] — and listened to afterwards. As it turns out, the narrator could not face the crowds even if he wanted to. The fact that the balcony door is locked — we are not told by whom — exempts him from any direct response. So is this narrator a prisoner rather than a mighty ruler, or do the two roles go hand in hand? While the 'unübersehbare Menge' gathered outside echoes the sleeping army of 'Versunken in die Nacht', the individual facing them does not embrace his or her responsibility. S/he does not pick up the torch, but remains at the desk, in a state of defiant seclusion: 'Ich will niemanden sehn, ich will mich durch keinen Anblick verwirren lassen, beim Schreibtisch, das ist mein Platz, den Kopf in meinen Händen, das ist meine Haltung.'[29] Here, we once again encounter the lowered head as the outward sign of responsibility. But here, this posture is associated with the 'Schreibtisch', suggesting that it is no sign of weakness or defeat, but a stance actively and deliberately adopted to shield the writer from the *Verwirrung* and *Zerstreuung* engendered by the more immediate demands of responsibility.

★ ★ ★ ★ ★

As this survey has shown, Kafka's writings explore the challenges of responsibility from contrasting but interconnected perspectives. While Scholem rightly points to the 'hopelessness' which attaches to this concept in some of Kafka's short fiction, their stance, or 'message', cannot be reduced to this interpretation. *Verantwortung* retains a deep, albeit ambivalent, fascination in Kafka's literary and philosophical writings after 1916, where the issue gains a particular urgency against the backdrop of war, dispersal and diaspora. It is no coincidence that the most emphatic treatments of responsibility have remained fragments, arguably reflecting Kafka's deep-seated ambivalence towards this concept in its more straightforward, political or personal, sense. While several of his texts are recognizably rooted in Jewish narratives about individual and collective, his dialectical and persistently self-questioning treatment of this issue retains a universal appeal in the way it resists affirmative conclusions.

Notes to Chapter 14

1. Martin Buber, 'Die Losung', *Der Jude*, 1 (April 1916), 1–3 (p. 2).
2. Buber, 'Die Losung', p. 2. As Ritchie Robertson notes, 'the estrangement of the individual from society, which Buber takes for granted, assumes much more concrete form as the estrangement of the Western Jew from Gentile society': Ritchie Robertson, *Kafka: Judaism, Literature, and Politics* (Oxford: Oxford University Press, 1987), p. 144.
3. On the circumstances surrounding this writing retreat, which yielded a strikingly rich and varied output of short prose texts, see Reiner Stach, *Kafka: The Years of Insight*, trans. by Shelley Frisch (Princeton: Princeton University Press, 2013), pp. 142–43.
4. 'Alle diese Stücke und noch andere sollen später einmal als Buch erscheinen unter dem gemeinsamen Titel: "Verantwortung"' (22 April 1917): Franz Kafka, *Schriften, Tagebücher, Briefe*, ed. by Hans-Gerd Koch (Frankfurt a.M.: Fischer, 1982–), *Briefe III: April 1914–1917*, ed. by Hans-Gerd Koch (2005), p. 297. Kafka made only minor changes to the line-up sent to Buber, adding 'Ein Besuch im Bergwerk', 'Das nächste Dorf' and 'Die Sorge des Hausvaters', while excluding 'Die kurze Zeit'. See Franz Kafka, *Schriften, Tagebücher, Briefe*, ed. by Hans-Gerd Koch (Frankfurt a.M.: Fischer, 1982–), *Drucke zu Lebzeiten: Apparatband*, ed. by Wolf Kittler, Hans-Gerd Koch and Gerhard Neumann (1996), p. 290.
5. Letter of 10 May 1973: Gershom Scholem, *Briefe*, 3 vols (Munich: C. H. Beck, 1994–99), III, 74. Robert Kauf's article in fact anticipates Scholem's argument, for it stresses Kafka's awareness 'of the problematic nature of responsibility': Robert Kauf, '*Verantwortung*: The Theme of Kafka's *Landarzt* Cycle', *Modern Language Quarterly*, 33 (1972), 420–32 (p. 423).
6. Scholem criticized the style and substance of Buber's presentation of Hasidism, in his collections of Hasidic tales *Die Geschichten des Rabbi Nachman* (1906) and *Die Legende des Baalschem* (1908) and in later works, as misleading: Gershom Scholem, 'Martin Buber's Interpretation of Hasidism', in Gershom Scholem, *The Messianic Idea in Judaism and Other Essays on Jewish Spirituality* (London: Allen and Unwin, 1971), pp. 228–50. See also Robertson, *Kafka*, pp. 150–51.
7. The two texts appeared under the title *Zwei Tiergeschichten* in the October 1917 issue of *Der Jude*.
8. The most prominent studies are Robert Kauf's 1972 article, which prompted Scholem's letter, and Ritchie Robertson's lucid chapter on *Ein Landarzt* in his *Kafka: Judaism, Literature, and Politics*. While Kafka's letter to Buber is well known and the proposed title routinely recited in scholarship on the *Landarzt* texts, it has not been the subject of any more recent explorations.
9. Jacob and Wilhelm Grimm, *Deutsches Wörterbuch*, 16 vols (Leipzig: Hirzel, 1854–1961), <http://www.woerterbuchnetz.de/DWB?lemma=verantwortung> [accessed 13 October 2020].
10. Malcolm Pasley makes a similar point, noting that *Verantwortung* can mean either accountability 'for personal inadequacy and failing', the centre of Kafka's earlier fiction, or a responsibility, 'which a man is called upon to carry': Malcolm Pasley, 'Kafka and the Theme of "Berufung"', *Oxford German Studies*, 9 (1978), 139–49 (p. 141).
11. Franz Kafka, *Schriften, Tagebücher, Briefe*, ed. by Hans-Gerd Koch (Frankfurt a.M.: Fischer, 1982–), *Der Proceß*, ed. by Malcolm Pasley (1990), pp. 8, 36. Of course, such accusatory gestures only highlight K.'s own precarious status; asked by the painter Titorelli whether he is indeed innocent, K. answers in the affirmative, yet the narrative immediately adds a caveat: 'Die Beantwortung dieser Frage machte ihm geradezu Freude, besonders da sie gegenüber einem Privatmann, also ohne jede Verantwortung erfolgte' (p. 200).
12. Franz Kafka, *Schriften, Tagebücher, Briefe*, ed. by Hans-Gerd Koch (Frankfurt a.M.: Fischer, 1982–), *Drucke zu Lebzeiten*, ed. by Wolf Kittler, Hans-Gerd Koch and Gerhard Neumann (1996), p. 276. Henceforth cited as *DL*.
13. Unlike in 'Ein Besuch im Bergwerk', this 'we' contains an 'I', namely the narrative voice of a cobbler, whose shop is right opposite the palace and who reports the sighting of the emperor.

14. Franz Josef's death occurred one month after the violent death of his prime minister, exacerbating the prevailing sense of crisis. Kafka's texts of this period reflect this experience, most obviously in his drama fragment *Der Gruftwächter*, in which a new regime is haunted by the remnants of the old.
15. Franz Kafka, 'Betrachtungen über Sünde, Leid, Hoffnung und den wahren Weg', in *Beim Bau der chinesischen Mauer*, ed. by Max Brod and Hans-Joachim Schoeps (Berlin: Kiepenheuer, 1931), pp. 225–49.
16. Franz Kafka, *Schriften, Tagebücher, Briefe*, ed. by Hans-Gerd Koch (Frankfurt a.M.: Fischer, 1982–), *Nachgelassene Schriften und Fragmente II*, ed. by Jost Schillemeit (1992), p. 79.
17. Zachary Sng, 'Das Fehlläuten der Nachtglocke: Zu Kafkas Erzählung *Ein Landarzt*', in *Kafkas Institutionen*, ed. by Arne Höcker and Oliver Simons (Bielefeld: transcript, 2007), pp. 213–34 (p. 221). On Kafka's reception of Kierkegaard, see also Ben Morgan, 'Philosophy', in *Franz Kafka in Context*, ed. by Carolin Duttlinger (Cambridge: Cambridge University Press, 2017), pp. 191–99.
18. Kafka, *Nachgelassene Schriften und Fragmente II*, pp. 79–80.
19. Ibid., p. 80.
20. 14 January 1920; Franz Kafka, *Schriften, Tagebücher, Briefe*, ed. by Hans-Gerd Koch (Frankfurt a.M.: Fischer, 1982–), *Tagebücher*, ed. by Hans-Gerd Koch, Michael Müller and Malcolm Pasley (1990), p. 850.
21. Franz Kafka, *Schriften, Tagebücher, Briefe*, ed. by Hans-Gerd Koch (Frankfurt a.M.: Fischer, 1982–), *Tagebücher: Apparatband*, ed. by Hans-Gerd Koch, Michael Müller and Malcolm Pasley (1990), pp. 397, 925.
22. Buber, 'Losung', p. 3.
23. Articles in *Der Jude* and *Selbstwehr* offered a 'scathing critique of Jewish life in the diaspora', but Brod and Bergmann instead emphasized the importance of a cultural form of Zionism, echoing the thought of Ahad Ha'am, the main proponent of this approach. See Iris Bruce, *Kafka and Cultural Zionism: Dates in Palestine* (Madison, WI: University of Wisconsin Press, 2007), pp. 113–15; 156; and Robertson, *Kafka*, p. 142. Kafka's stories 'Schakale und Araber' and 'Ein Bericht für eine Akademie', contained in *Ein Landarzt* but first published in *Der Jude*, have often been read as Zionist satires of Jewish life in the diaspora. See for instance Robertson, *Kafka*, p. 164 and Bruce, *Kafka*, p. 154.
24. Paul North reads the passage in a positive light, its third-person perspective creating a form of 'grammatical distanciation', which releases the writer, the individual, from (social) responsibility; the passage thus spells a radical type of freedom, the freedom 'to be abandoned by your constituent parts': Paul North, *The Problem of Distraction* (Stanford, CA: Stanford University Press, 2012), p. 75.
25. Kafka, *Tagebücher*, p. 825.
26. Kafka, *Nachgelassene Schriften und Fragmente II*, pp. 260–61.
27. Ibid., p. 16; on the date of the entry, see Franz Kafka, *Schriften, Tagebücher, Briefe*, ed. by Hans-Gerd Koch (Frankfurt a.M.: Fischer, 1982–), *Nachgelassene Schriften und Fragmente II: Apparatband*, ed. by Jost Schillemeit (1992), p. 39.
28. On the recording device of the *Parlograph* and its role in Kafka's literary imagination, see Carolin Duttlinger, *Kafka and Photography* (Oxford: Oxford University Press, 2007), pp. 157–61.
29. Kafka, *Nachgelassene Schriften und Fragmente II*, p. 16.

CHAPTER 15

Quixotic Doubles: Kafka reads Cervantes

Barry Murnane

As Ritchie Robertson tells us, reading for Franz Kafka was 'an existentially urgent activity involving exploration and self-discovery'.[1] Widely read in what we would now call the canon of 'world literature'[2] — from Homer to Goethe, Cervantes to Kleist, Dickens to Chekhov, and Flaubert to Strindberg — some authors were more important to Kafka than others. He called Kleist, Grillparzer, Dostoevsky and Flaubert his 'Blutsverwandte',[3] identifying thematic, stylistic and biographical affinities with his own literary life; other writers, like Dickens and Strindberg, provided inspiration for literary works such as *Der Verschollene* and *Das Schloss* respectively, without necessarily offering the same intense affective connection. Notwithstanding the four fragments and several references in letters to Cervantes's novel *Don Quixote* in Kafka's *Nachlass,* there appears on first inspection to be little basis for a comparison of both writers. *Don Quixote* (1605/15) is a narrative that has come to signify the qualities of a heroic foolishness, lofty idealism and imaginative flights, written by a patriotic war veteran in his prison cell. Kafka's works, on the other hand, are most often associated with protagonists who find their routine lives turned upside down or challenged by extraordinary interventions or events, and are narrated in a darkly comic and even fantastic manner, written by a German-speaking Jewish lawyer from Prague. Nevertheless, Don Quixote is one of the many figures from literature, mythology, the Bible and history, from Odysseus to Poseidon, Abraham to Prometheus, and Alexander the Great to Napoleon to which Kafka turned in later years, sometimes to reflect on his own works, sometimes to engage with broader questions of literary tradition and representation.

In contrast to some of these other intertextual relations, Kafka's comments on Cervantes's novel never amounted to a stand-alone prose text (although Max Brod's edition suggested otherwise), meaning that they have received less critical attention. Walter Benjamin already referred to Brod's version 'Die Wahrheit über Sancho Pansa' in his 1934 essay 'Franz Kafka. Zur zehnten Wiederkehr seines Todestages', but other than suggesting that this is Kafka's most complete achievement, says little else about it.[4] Hartmut Binder's *Kafka-Handbuch* documents the handful of interpretations in Benjamin's wake, noting a tendency starting in the mid-1960s to read the fragments as theoretical or aesthetical reflections on the nature of art and the artist.⁵ Some of these focused on the biographical context of Kafka's identity as a writer engaged in a 'Teufelsdienst'⁶; others took a more abstract approach to the epistemological⁷ and theological⁸ status of literary representation; yet others looked at the socio-historical context of the First World War.⁹ The most substantial responses to Kafka and Cervantes are those by Marthe Robert, Stanley Corngold and Ritchie Robertson, all of whom are concerned with the epistemological and narratological dimensions of Kafka's fragments.¹⁰ The former two are more 'macroscopic' in their approach (addressing the fate of the epic in modernity and the anthropological moment of Kafka's fiction, respectively) and only loosely interested in the Cervantes-fragments in the narrower sense. Robertson's approach is more 'microscopic' (locating the four fragments alongside Kafka's various writings around 1917 and 1922, especially the so-called Zürau 'aphorisms'), but the conceptual depth of his argument extends to matters of fundamental poetological importance to Kafka's literary production from *Der Process* onwards.

In the following essay, I will discuss these intersections of Cervantes and Kafka to argue that the various fragments concerning *Don Quixote* in Kafka's *Nachlass* constitute an idiosyncratic but by no means inaccurate reading of the novel centred on the question of Quixote's project of errant, heroic masculinity. I will suggest that the complex metaliterary reflexivity and critical engagement with Quixote's self-fashioning as chivalrous hero and their frequent association with multiple alter egos and doubles in Cervantes's novel motivate and explain Kafka's various references to *Don Quixote* between 1917 and 1922. Focusing on a surprisingly stable catalogue of shared imagery and thematic concerns — responsibility, sexuality, questionable (male) leadership and the integrity of aesthetic activity — I will argue that Kafka's engagement with Cervantes is shaped by his other fictional texts in the period, from 'Der Kübelreiter' to 'Ein Landarzt', from the notes in Zürau to *Das Schloss*. This engagement enables a wide-reaching account of Kafka's self-conceptualization as an author in the latter part of his literary career and provides the basis for a more critical reading of the Landvermesser K. in *Das Schloss*, whose heroic resistance is revealed as a performance of self-destructive, 'quixotic' leadership.

★ ★ ★ ★ ★

As the story of the country nobleman Alonso Quexana, who reads too many chivalric romances and decides to become the idealistic knight errant Don Quixote, battling windmills and giants, serving damsels and trying in vain to restore the current fallen 'iron age' to the 'golden age' of chivalric romance, Miguel de Cervantes Saavedra's *Ingenious Gentleman Don Quixote of La Mancha* seems to be at a vast historical and thematic remove from the works of Franz Kafka.¹¹ Following Romantic interpretations of the novel that celebrated Quixote's imaginative visions over the impoverished reality of his fellow Spaniards (including his pragmatic sidekick, Sancho Panza), *Don Quixote* is often reduced to a story of either nostalgia for, or insane belief in, the lost unity of chivalric romance and life in a post-chivalric world.¹² Quexana's/Quixote's seemingly mad belief in the power and status of literature, fancying himself an errant questing knight rather than seeing the world for the cruel and violent place it is, shows where Kafka's interest in the novel may have lain. As Corngold writes, Kafka's literary career was the 'project of one who had to live his life as literature',[13] linking the Prague writer with the fictional Spanish nobleman across the centuries, although far from simplistically, as we shall see.

It is indeed possible to read *Don Quixote* as this story of how bibliomaniacal misinterpretations of the world come farcically into conflict with a violent reality principle. The narrative follows Quixote's adventures around La Mancha where he mistakes inns for castles, friars for enchanters, peasant girls for noble love objects and windmills for giant knights, before being brought back home as a confused, insane man. However, with its self-consciousness and metaliterary reflections both on its own fictionality and literary history more broadly, the novel is vastly more complex. The First Part is highly complicated, with the seemingly straightforward depiction of Quexana's deluded self-fashioning as the knight-errant Quixote constantly interrupted by metaliterary reflexions such as the commentary in chapter 9 on the dubious status of the Arabic manuscript from which the narrator is translating and, in actual fact, constructing his story. The novel subsequently descends into increasingly episodic, independent interludes in multiple generic modes and it is notable that Quixote's own 'pursuit' of Dulcinea — already imitating Amadís of Gaul's devotion to Oriana — increasingly mimics these interludes, especially Cardenio's tale of unrequited love for Lucinda. This metaliterary doubling obviously reflects and repeats Quexana's adoption of a fictional alter ego in his original act of self-fashioning as the chivalric Quixote.

Notwithstanding the author's claim in the prologue to the Second Part that the sequel will be more orderly ('a somewhat expanded Don Quixote who is, at the end, dead and buried, so that no one will dare tell more tales about him', DQ, 458), the metaliterary nature of the plot continues, indeed intensifies. Quixote and Sancho are conscious of their *own* literary status, and the figures they meet recognize them as the protagonists of the First Part, adapting their behaviour accordingly. Thus the scholar Sansón Carrasco — a friend of the Priest and Barber in the First Part who first appears as a literary critic in chapters 12–14, discussing the repeated digressions, and who later takes on the roles of the Knight of the Mirrors and the Knight of the White Moon — manages to defeat Don Quixote because he knows how to anticipate his behaviour and actions.[14] Such self-awareness points more towards the status of the novel as mock-heroic rather than as a proto-Romantic celebration of a 'fallen' literary age (ibid., p. 64).

It is this self-awareness, coupled with constellations of doubling, that will be at the heart of Kafka's engagement with the novel in 1917. *Don Quixote* contains, and is partly structured by, multiple constellations of doubles and doubling. To begin with, the novel's narrator appears to be split in two: in the persona of the Second Author we are confronted with a self-conscious framing narrative voice who has an alter ego of his own in Cide Hamete Bengali, whose 'found manuscript' the Second Author claims to be translating and re-narrating.[15] Quixote consciously mimics the behaviour of figures like Cardenio in the First Part, while his and

Sancho's repeated collisions with their 'literary' identities in the Second Part build on this confusion of fiction and reality. Also in the Second Part, Carrasco — as a literary critic — is the nemesis of the Second Author, but he too invents multiple alter egos, firstly the Knight of the Mirrors and finally the Knight of the White Moon. Carrasco also operates as a double of Quixote where he experiences an *amour courtois* which exactly mirrors Quixote's pursuit of Dulcinea (DQ, 538),[16] something which is encapsulated in his alternative identity as the Knight in whose costume made of mirrors Quixote sees himself reflected.[17] The most obvious double constellation is that between Quixote and Sancho, of course: Sancho appears as the pragmatic, realist side-kick to the idealist Quixote's flights of imagination/ madness, a point articulated in the etymology of his name (Panza = belly).[18] There are multiple moments in the plot where Quixote and Sancho swap roles, however, such as in the Second Part where Sancho employs peasant girls to play the role of the supposedly enchanted Dulcinea and her ladies in waiting in chapters 10 and 32, deploying their *real* garlic-breath as a sign of her enchanted *fictional* (but in actual fact *real*) low status.

Don Quixote may have begun as a humorous novel, but its deliberate literariness becomes increasingly palpable. Perhaps the most famous instance of this self-reflexivity is Quixote's descent into the Cave of Montesinos in chapters 22–23, a powerful *mise en abyme*, confronting Quixote literally and figuratively with the groundlessness of his chivalric pursuit of Dulcinea, and thus his self-image as a knight, seeing a supposedly enchanted vision of her as a peasant girl, which of course Dulcinea *actually* is.[19] This is the literal nadir of Quixote's fictions of selfhood and chivalric love, laying the ground for his final, disillusioned return home. This confrontation with a reality principle also points towards a much darker reading of the metaliterary acts of bibliomania, self-fashioning and idealized love in the novel. From the outset, Dulcinea was central to Quixote's act of 'authoring' himself as a knight from the words of his beloved romances, something James A. Parr has termed the quixotic project of 'self-causation'.[20] Michael Pyper identifies this pursuit of the 'mythical, idealized and ethereal femininity of Dulcinea' as a paradoxical and fragile flight from real female bodies described by Sancho as 'brawny', 'sturdy' and 'coarse' (DQ, 199–200).[21] Quixote's dual process of self-imagination and desexualization of women is profoundly masochistic, leading throughout to multiple acts of violence and repeated challenges to his idealized vision of Dulcinea. The dual process of 'illusionment' and disillusionment in his flight from the feminine, and the performance of a self-defined chivalric masculinity, culminates in a painful acknowledgement of the mundane reality of his chivalric project in the Cave.

Following this sobering experience, Quixote rejects the reading of romances entirely and returns home, begging the question whether he ever genuinely believed in his own project. As we will see, the questions around sexuality, fictionality, doubling and the ability of literature to represent reality that are central to *Don Quixote* also run to the heart of Kafka's reading of the novel.

★ ★ ★ ★ ★

Kafka's engagement with Cervantes consists of three short texts in the Oktavheft G (written in October 1917), one further text composed during work on *Das Schloss* (written in the summer of 1922), and several letters, including one to Robert Klopstock of June 1921 in which he compares Don Quixote with Abraham of the Old Testament.[22] Although it is not the first reference,[23] the most famous articulation is a fragment of 21 October 1917 for which Max Brod coined the title 'Die Wahrheit über Sancho Pansa' in his edition (1931):

> Sancho Pansa, der sich übrigens dessen nie gerühmt hat, gelang es im Laufe der Jahre, in den Abend- und Nachtstunden, durch Beistellung einer Menge Ritter- und Räuberromane seinen Teufel, dem er später den Namen Don Quichote gab, derart von sich abzulenken, daß dieser dann haltlos die verrücktesten Taten ausführte, die aber mangels ihres vorbestimmten Gegenstandes, der eben Sancho Pansa hätte sein sollen, niemandem schadeten. Sancho Pansa, ein freier Mann, folgte gleichmütig, vielleicht aus einem gewissen Verantwortlichkeitsgefühl dem Don Quichote auf seinen Zügen und hatte davon eine große und nützliche Unterhaltung bis an sein Ende. (NSII, 38)

Shifting the focus onto his squire Sancho, Kafka reduces Quixote to little more than a subsidiary figure in this fragment. In fact, Quichote is here presented as a demonic part of Sancho's identity, which the erstwhile squire and now main protagonist has cast out from himself as an uncanny double. As idiosyncratic a reading of Cervantes's novel as this seems, Kafka proves himself to be astute reader of his Spanish predecessor. As already outlined, *Don Quixote* contains, and is partly structured by, multiple constellations of doubles and doubling, meaning that in his 'Sancho Pansa' fragment, Kafka was building on an established feature of the novel.

Nevertheless, Kafka's version is a deeply personal reading of *Don Quixote*. His image of Quichote and Sancho as a *doppelgänger* constellation revisits an image he had developed in his penultimate letter to Felice Bauer, written only several weeks earlier: 'Daß zwei in mir kämpfen, weißt Du. Daß der bessere der zwei Dir gehört, daran zweifle ich gerade in den letzten Tagen am wenigsten.'[24] Kafka deploys this image to illustrate his personal conflict between writing and marriage, but he also discusses questions of literary creativity more generally. Perhaps most notable in the letter is the manner in which this opposition is cast in the same antagonistic terms of 'Gut' and 'Böse' present in the juxtaposition of Quichote's 'demonic' groundless imaginary flights and Sancho's groundedness: 'Das Blut, das der Gute (jetzt heißt er uns Guter) vergießt, um Dich zu gewinnen, nützt dem Bösen' (ibid., p. 334). As Robertson has argued, this reflects an increased engagement with ethical, religious and philosophical questions (including Hassidic Judaism and later, in early 1918, Kierkegaard), coupled with an interrogation of literature's ability to represent and even transcend reality in this period, culminating in the so called Zürau 'aphorisms', which include the Cervantes fragments. Indeed, Manfred Engel reads this second Cervantes fragment as an optimistic assessment of these interlinked aesthetic and ethical questions: rather than formulating a clear opposition, as in the first fragment ('Das Unglück Don Quichotes *ist* [...] Sancho Pansa', my emphasis), we now have a symbiotic balance.[25] Quichote gets to live entirely in the literary sphere of the imagination, and rather than freezing in horror, Sancho accepts a sense of responsibility by accompanying him on his errant path.

In a third fragment written only a few hours after the second, longer passage of 21 October 1917, this positive symbiosis is called into question. Now Quichote's status as Sancho's double seems more self-destructive, with Quichote proceeding to divide himself into two warring undead doubles fighting to the death:

> Eine der wichtigsten Don Quichotischen Taten, aufdringlicher als der Kampf mit der Windmühle, ist der Selbstmord. Der tote Don Quichote will den toten Don Quichote töten; um zu töten braucht er aber eine lebendige Stelle, diese sucht er nun mit seinem Schwert ebenso unaufhörlich wie vergeblich. Unter dieser Beschäftigung rollen die zwei Toten als unauflöslicher und förmlich springlebendiger Purzelbaum durch die Zeiten. (NSII, 38–39)

The image of Quixote emerging from a lifeless state for the sole — and senseless — purpose of killing himself is darkly humorous and recalls the episode in chapter 25 of the First Part of Cervantes's novel where Quixote does two tumbles, naked, in front of Sancho (DQ, 204).[26] Bereft of Sancho as his *doppelgänger*, Kafka's text seems to claim that the essence of quixotism is a masochistic death wish.[27] Whereas in the second fragment Sancho could ward off the threat of quixotism both by learning from experience and exercising agency, even finding entertainment in Quichote's actions, the latter's fight to the death with himself reveals a self-obsession that is entirely self-destructive. This recalls chapters 25 and 71 of the Second Part of *Don Quixote* where Sancho pretends to receive 3,300 self-inflicted lashes on his bare buttocks while actually accepting Quixote's compensatory payment, whereas Quixote holds on to the chivalric vision of himself despite the constant self-induced suffering and beatings this role brings him. If the focalization through Sancho's perspective in Kafka's second fragment raises questions over the seriousness of the 'gewisse[] Verantwortlichkeitsgefühl' that he takes on, this third fragment seems to tip the balance towards a critique of Quichote's self-destructive flights of fancy and an appreciation of Sancho's engagement in the world.[28]

This third fragment also reflects the broader concerns with the nature of fiction both in Cervantes's novel and in Kafka's own thinking. On the one hand, the image of the lifeless Quichote emphasizes the groundlessness of his precursor's chivalric ambitions and performative self-causation, recognizing that Cervantes's Quixote is a knight on paper only. This is offset by his *'Springlebendig'-Werden* as a canonical figure of world literature, on the other hand. Here one is reminded of the penultimate letter to Felice Bauer from 30 September 1917 and the link it suggests between the outbreak of Kafka's tuberculosis and an unending fight within himself between his literary ambitions and his 'worldly' aims. Where Kafka writes that the 'Blut stammt nicht aus der Lunge, sondern aus dem oder aus einem entscheidenden Stich eines Kämpfers',[29] this prefigures the image of Quichote as his own daemonic, self-destructive double stabbing at himself. While the motifs of imagination, errantry and deception are shared by both writers, it is clear that Kafka has moved beyond the tighter framework of Cervantes's novel to address a series of aesthetic and personal concerns relating to his own writing here.

Robertson invites us to locate Kafka's reading of *Don Quixote* alongside other fictional texts in the period of 1917–18, the various fragments, 'aphorisms' and short texts written in Zürau, but also the *Landarzt* collection and its focus on questions of individual responsibility. This is clearly important, but the various figurations of spectres and doubles in the Cervantes fragments have not yet been commented on in relation to Kafka's concerted use of such figures in the preceding months. The image of Quichote as a ghostly embodiment of daemonic self-obsession correlates closely with multiple thematic and figurative constellations in this period, notably in the 'Gruftwächter' fragments, 'Der Kübelreiter' and the 'Jäger Gracchus' fragments, while stories such as 'Ein Landarzt' most obviously develop narratives of quixotic split identities in the mould of Sancho and Quichote. I suggest that we need to take such resonances seriously in order to contextualize Kafka's reception of *Don Quixote* more fully.

Written at the start of 1917, and thus predating the Cervantes fragments by almost nine months, 'Der Kübelreiter' documents a complex case of narration and the ability to narrate. The comic image of a man riding on a coal-bucket prefigures Kafka's engagement with Quixote as the prototypical mock-heroic rider on horseback, and the story parallels the *doppelgänger* constellations in the later fragments. In the story, a nameless, disembodied speaker finds his narrative voice through an imaginative act of riding on his coal-bucket while simultaneously proceeding to disappear 'auf Nimmerwiedersehn'.[30] In this dual process we see a progressive split between the Kübelreiter's material presence and his disembodied narrative voice: the 'ich' that 'außergewöhnlich hoch schweb[t]' cannot logically be the same figure watching events unfolding 'tief unten an seinem Tischchen' (D, 445).[31] Stanley Corngold identifies this self-immolating vision as central to what he views as Kafka's long-term 'ascetic' or 'gnostic' poetics.[32] Moreover, his emergence as narrator depends on his demise as an 'empirical' figure with worldly ('Kälte' and 'Hunger'; D, 444) and bodily, sexual concerns (the symbolic 'Frauenschürze' of the coal-dealer's wife; D, 447). In its use of ghostly split-identities to articulate unresolved conflicts between aesthetic and worldly concerns, 'Der Kübelreiter' anticipates the split between Sancho and Quichote as his groundless, spectral double in the fragments some months later.

Written parallel to 'Der Kübelreiter', the undead Jäger Gracchus is more clearly a ghostly apparition, although his dirty corporeality — 'mit wild durcheinandergewachsenem Haar und Bart, gebräunter Haut' — seems distinctly of this world.[33] The figure of the undead Jäger combines multiple intertextual references of biblical, Jewish, mystical and private provenance such as the Eternal Jew, the Flying Dutchman, Rudolf Steiner's theosophy and Kafka's own biography (*graculus*, the jackdaw, is called *kavka* in Czech).[34] Despite these broad frames of reference, the shared uncanny imagery and thematic concerns with literary creativity and the competing responsibilities of the writer provide continuity to the Cervantes-fragments. Thus, Gracchus's simultaneously 'worldly' and 'unworldly' status generates the precise constellation later occupied by Sancho and Quichote respectively, while the image of the bushman, 'der mit einem Speer nach mir zielt' (NSI, 312), recalls the grotesque fight between the two spectral Quichotes in the second fragment. Whereas Kafka interprets *Don Quixote* in terms of an opposition between worldly responsibility and the pursuit of a higher, but groundless, state of visionary ideals, this higher state is cast here in more obviously metaphysical terms. In the first extended Gracchus-fragment, 'Zwei Knaben saßen auf der Quaimauer', Gracchus describes his liminal state to the mayor of Riva as an opposition between a material world ('in irgendeinem irdischen Gewässer') and a celestial 'Jenseits' (NSI, 309) and his monologues return repeatedly to an obscure 'Schuld' (ibid.) that caused this liminal existence, giving an ethical or moral component to his story of responsibility. This is the most obvious correlation with the Cervantes fragments, for although he skirts over the exact misdemeanour, Gracchus's dirty, hirsute corporeality and his repeated references to material goods anchor his paradoxical existence within an opposition of idealistic and materialistic concerns.[35] This merging of the themes of responsibility, and self-obsessed, self-destructive ambition reveals an intimate relationship between this group of texts and Kafka's reading of Cervantes several months later.

The story that has most often been read in terms of uncanny figures and *doppelgänger* constellations is 'Ein Landarzt', most likely because the constellation of split identities outlined in his letter to Felice Bauer ('Daß zwei in mir kämpfen') is the starting point of a reading of the story which Kafka develops himself. Since 'Das Urteil', he had imagined there to be a division between his mundane pursuit of a married life and an idealized literary persona. In a letter to Max Brod, Kafka suggests that his recently identified tuberculosis is actually a result of this division: 'Auch ich habe es selbst vorausgesagt. Erinnerst Du Dich an die Blutwunde im "Landarzt"?'[36] Even without this highly personal reading of the story, 'Ein Landarzt' is indeed dominated by uncanny correlations between characters. There is critical consensus that the dreamlike topography of the texts is underpinned by a close connection between each of the story's central figures — the Landarzt, the Dienstmädchen Rosa, the Pferdeknecht and the Junge, perhaps even as manifestations of different layers of the doctor's personality.[37] This doubling resembles the alter ego constellation and thematic concern with responsibility in the Cervantes fragments, where Sancho accompanies his master on his errant path of imagination out of a sense of duty.

At issue in 'Ein Landarzt' are the competing responsibilities of the physician in his role as 'soziales Identifikationsmuster im zweideutigen Spannungsfeld von Macht und Lust', with the doctor needing to balance his responsibility for the patient and his own household, including Rosa.[38] This sense of responsibility is clear from the first sentence; 'Ich war in großer Verlegenheit: eine dringende Reise stand mir bevor; ein Schwerkranker wartete auf mich in einem zehn Meilen entfernten Dorfe' (D, 253); later we learn that he fulfils 'seine Pflicht bis zum Rand' (D, 256). The doctor's official life is governed by asceticism leading even to a sense of martyrdom (D, 257), with the doctor neglecting the demands of his *oikos*, the 'familial' economy at home ('Man weiß nicht, was für Dinge man im eigenen Hause vorrätig hat', D, 253), including apparently sexual affairs.[39] When the Pferdeknecht suddenly appears to molest the doctor's 'williges Mädchen' Rosa (D, 254) as a projection of his repressed libidinal compulsions,[40] this reinforces his previous 'familial' — that is sexual — abstinence. Later the sick boy is introduced as 'meines Kranken' (D, 255) and the description of his wound as 'Rosa', orthographically identical to the Dienstmädchen's name, suggests a resurfaced sexual desire here too.[41] The flipside of this act of repression is the idealization of his 'higher' calling as doctor, a sense of a spiritual responsibility that is captured through the ritualistic, ceremonial nature of his duties in the latter half of the story. While the family is happy to see the doctor engaging in his duties, his mind wanders to Rosa, to the Pferdeknecht, and finally to his own 'Rettung' (D, 260). His vision of jumping 'gewissermaßen aus diesem Bett in meines' (D, 260) sets his bodily and higher callings in conflict, substituting the family's belief in him with his attraction to Rosa. The doctor finds himself caught between two contradictory responsibilities and fails to fulfil either, underlining the tension between his sense of a physical and a 'higher' calling.[42] His contradictory impulses to heal the boy *and* to secure his 'Rettung' with Rosa mirror Quixote's insertion of an imagined chivalric purity in place of actual physical sexuality and it is precisely this tension between worldly and otherworldly concerns — be they aesthetic, ethical or religious in nature — which the second and third Cervantes fragments continue to address.

Robertson has suggested that Kafka's readings of Hassidic fairy tales and legends in this period are a key to understanding the 'Landarzt' in this respect, articulating as they do a discrepancy between the sexual and spiritual that needs to be reconciled.[43] He is particularly concerned with Kafka's preoccupation with the nature and limits of an individual's sense of calling ('Berufung'), in relation both to his literary activities and to his sceptical response to Hassidic asceticism (ibid., pp. 21–22).[44] In this respect it is notable that the various texts that flank the Cervantes fragments underline this concurrent preoccupation with what Brod called 'd[en] letzten Dingen'.[45] A cursory reading of some of the self-contradictory passages themselves undermines Brod's uncritical narrative of a religious 'turn' in Kafka's thinking, however:

> Es gibt nur eine geistige Welt, was wir sinnliche Welt nennen, ist das Böse in der geistigen. (NSII, 59)
> Nicht eigentlich die sinnliche Welt ist Schein, sondern ihr Böses, das allerdings für unsere Augen die sinnliche Welt bildet. (NSII, 74)

These notes develop an anthropological reflection on the mind–body dualism ('sinnliche' and 'geistige') and related problems of cognition and epistemology ('Schein'). Despite the apparent clarity, any distinction between the *sinnliche* and *geistige* worlds is deconstructed, with both spheres linked and neither afforded primacy. The difficulties generated by this condition are captured in narrative texts such as 'Ein alltäglicher Vorfall; sein Ertragen ein alltäglicher Heroismus' (NSII, 35) — where an important meeting between A. and B. fails to materialize because of A.'s preoccupied and blinded mental state — or 'Wir sind, mit dem irdisch befleckten Auge gesehn, in der Situation von Eisenbahnreisenden' (NSII, 33), where man's status betwixt and between the sensual and spiritual, the mundane and the idealized is described from the position of crash victims hallucinating in a dark tunnel. Indeed even the veracity of this observation is questioned from the start as a product of an 'irdisch befleckten Auge', reproducing the split between Quichote and Sancho as fanciful and earthly, respectively, but also that within the self-harming Quichote himself in the Cervantes fragments.

This anthropological uncertainty is heavily inflected by references to the *Sündenfall* myth, as other texts make explicit:

> Wir sind nicht nur deshalb sündig, weil wir vom Baum der Erkenntnis gegessen haben, sondern auch deshalb, weil wir vom Baum des Lebens noch nicht gegessen haben. [...] Sündig ist der Stand, in dem wir uns befinden, unabhängig von Schuld. (NSII, 72)

There is, indeed, even a clear sexual dimension to the 'sinnliche Welt' familiar from the stories in the *Oktavheften* where Kafka refers to the 'Verführungsmittel des Bösen' being like 'der Kampf mit Frauen, der im Bett endet' (NSII, 34–35). It is unsurprising that Kafka subsequently turns his attention to Odysseus's temptation by the sirens in one of the most famous narrative texts in this period, 'Beweis dessen, daß auch unzulängliche, ja kindische Mittel zur Rettung dienen können', where Odysseus's victory in tricking the sirens by stuffing his ears with wax is exposed either as hubristic ('Überhebung') or as a clever performance ('Scheinvorgang') or fiction (NSII, 40–42). These references allow us to identify a condensed version of the competing responsibilities and concerns between the worldly and otherworldly, the mundane and aesthetic in the Zürau texts that were also central to figures like Gracchus, the Landarzt or Sancho Pansa. The shared catalogue of topoi such as battle, temptation, distraction, responsibility and *Schein*/fiction also point towards the themes developed in the three Cervantes fragments, as seen above. Unlike the Hassidic traditions to which Robertson refers and which are recorded in letters, journals and the fragments written in Zürau, there is no further evidence of Kafka actually having read *Don Quixote*. Nevertheless the shared constellation of themes and figures suggests an idiosyncratic, but prescient, engagement with Cervantes's novel on Kafka's behalf.

My purpose in tracing the various spectral figures and *doppelgänger* constellations in the preceding months was not to negate this constellation, but rather to trace a line of development that helps to explain why Kafka chose *Don Quixote* to illustrate these preoccupations and why he invokes such fantastic imagery in doing so. There are more of the non-narrative texts and fragments from Zürau which share this store of images. Thus the image of the 'Kampf mit den Frauen' is 'Eine der wirksamsten Verführungen des Teuflischen' (NSII, 34), recalling both the description of Quichote as Sancho's 'Teufel' and his 'Kampf mit der Windmühle', but also the alter ego constellations in 'Der Kübelreiter' and 'Ein Landarzt'. Kafka also deploys figures of split personality particularly around the issue of introspection. Thus on the one hand, self-examination is central to the anthropological questions, but we also read that, 'Beobachte Dich ist das Wort der Schlange' and thus 'etwas Böses', culminating in the type of masochistic violence visible in Quichote's suicidal battle with his own double: 'Das Wort bedeutet also: Verkenne Dich! Zerstöre Dich!' (NSII, 42). Other iconic notes such as 'Das Wort "sein" bedeutet im Deutschen beides: Da-sein und Ihm-gehören' (NSII, 123) or 'Das Tier entwindet dem Herrn die Peitsche und peitscht sich selbst um Herr zu werden' (NSII, 119) maintain this use of alter ego constellations and even make it into the separate fair copy of the *Zürauer Zettelkonvolut*.

Whether the tensions that we find in the private correspondence, fragments and published works from the period are shaped by Kafka's reading of *Don Quixote*, or whether his literary texts provide a lens through which he reads Cervantes, can no longer be determined. At the very least we can identify an original and highly productive cross-pollination of texts and contexts in this period, a process that comes to a head during Kafka's stay in Zürau and tensions surrounding his own sense of a higher calling as a writer to generate some of his most iconic interactions with world literature, from Odysseus and Prometheus to Don Quixote.

In light of these discussions, it is notable that Kafka returned to *Don Quixote* in a fragment composed some time towards the end of June 1922, during his work on *Das Schloss* while staying with his sister Ottla in Plána:

> Don Quichote mußte auswandern, ganz Spanien lachte über ihn, er war dort unmöglich geworden. Er reiste durch Südfrankreich, wo er hier und da liebe Leute traf, mit denen er sich anfreundete, überstieg mitten im Winter unter den größten Mühen und Entbehrungen die Alpen, zog dann durch die oberitalienische Tiefebene, wo er sich aber nicht wohlfühlte, und kam endlich nach Mailand. (NSII, 418)

This particular comment is clearly related to Frieda's suggestion to K. that if he wants to hang on to her, 'müssen wir auswandern, irgendwohin, nach Südfrankreich, nach Spanien'.[46] In many ways this incarnation of Quichote appears as an avatar for K. in the contemporaneous novel project, and indeed the 'plot' of struggling through the cold winter, encountering strangers and the opposition between companionship and feeling uneasy here provides a (very) basic summary of K.'s story in the novel. The comments about the Alps, relocating to Italy and settling in Milan remain underdeveloped and have little immediate relation either to Cervantes's or to Kafka's novels, although the idea that life in Spain has become impossible recalls the self-reflexivity of the Second Part of Cervantes's novel where Quixote's reputation as a fool precedes him. Kafka focuses on Quichote's internal struggle here, meaning that we can identify the continuing theme of self-indulgent imagination and the ensuing conflict with the social environment that was already present in his responses to the novel three years earlier.

The lack of reference to this particular fragment in Marthe Robert's parallel reading of *Don Quixote* and *Das Schloss* in her landmark study *The Old and the New* is surprising, given that it would have provided textual support to her frequently brilliant commentary on the degradation of the epic world into the prosaic pragmatism of modernity,[47] something that reaches its peak of expression in K.'s longing for acceptance into the seemingly arcane world of the castle.[48] For her, K. is an unquestionably heroic figure whose visionary task is made impossible by the presence of an actively hostile castle bureaucracy.[49] She views the castle authority's treatment of K. as violent and adversarial, but *Das Schloss* — and indeed Kafka's final Cervantes fragment — is more ambivalent, as I will now suggest.

The fragment's depiction of Quichote as a fool points towards the issues of questionable leadership and the fragile relationship between the individual and the community that Kafka was exploring around 1917. In the case of *Das Schloss* we must ask to what extent K.'s attempt to embody a traditional, epic, sense of agency is compromised by similar 'quixotic' expressions of self-indulgent leadership and self-destructive performances as in the earlier Cervantes fragments. Comparing this final fragment to Kafka's intense questioning of leadership more generally — and messianism in particular — around 1921–22, Robertson shows how the image of Quichote as the alpine pioneer recalls Kafka's use of the figure of a 'Feldherr' in this period: 'Du führst die Massen, großer langer Feldherr, führe die Verzweifelten durch die unter dem Schnee für niemanden sonst auffindbaren Paßstraßen des Gebirges', T 904).[50] *Das Schloss* features a would-be Feldherr K., who aspires to leadership qualities despite his questionable origins and profession. He is aggressive ('Kampf' and 'Sieg' are among his favourite words[51]) and ruthlessly ambitious in his desire to have his status as a Landvermesser officially recognized; the Brückenhofwirtin and Frieda accuse him of being singularly 'zielbewußt' and 'bereit alles zu tun' (S, 246). This obviously revisits an idea that was already central to Kafka's thinking in the *Oktavheften* and in the Cervantes fragments from 1917–18, with K. and the Landarzt both finding themselves caught between the competing aims of a higher calling and physical, worldly compulsion. Such comments identify K. as a potential trickster figure very much in keeping with the quixotic project of performative chivalric questing and the 'project' of self-causation that Parr and Pyper have identified in Cervantes's novel.

As Robertson suggests, one possible reading of K.'s 'quest' in the novel is that he finds himself torn between accepting a place within a community and striving towards the more imaginative goal of reaching his own personal vision of the castle. In the final Cervantes fragment we can see this vacillation between integration in a community and a more imaginative, socially isolating process of striving in phrases such 'hier und da liebe Leute traf, mit denen er sich anfreundete' and 'sich aber nicht wohlfühlte'. The fragment doesn't actually arrive at a conclusion — nor does K.'s journey in *Das Schloss* for that matter — but the fact that Quichote's life in Spain and in Upper Italy seems equally 'unmöglich' by no means bodes well. Unlike Quixote at the end of the Second Part of Cervantes's novel, Kafka's quixotic hero apparently cannot find a simple homecoming.

★ ★ ★ ★ ★

As this essay has shown, Kafka's engagement with Cervantes moves far beyond the tighter framework of *Don Quixote* to address a series of aesthetic and personal concerns relating to his own writing and to literature more generally. As such, this intertextual relationship is an ideal case study for the mode of reception favoured by Walter Benjamin in his — fittingly borrowed — phrase 'Was nie geschrieben wurde, lesen'.[52] Kafka's readings of Cervantes are not simply direct reproductions of a canonical pre-text; rather, they constitute an interpretative act of reframing and re-enacting, which nevertheless maintains a shared stock of themes and motifs relating to imagination, errantry and performative deceptions. Quixote's self-fashioning as a chivalric hero in Cervantes's novel already relied on complex instances of metaliterary reflexivity that frequently depended on alter egos and doubling, in terms of both plotting and characterization. These are features that recur in Kafka's fictional texts in the period around 1917–18, helping us to better understand the idiosyncratic interpretation of the relationship between Sancho Pansa and Don Quichote in his Cervantes fragments.

While such comparisons may initially seem 'microscopic', these instances of close comparison actually enable a wide-reaching account of Kafka's self-conceptualization as an author in his later years, focusing on a highly personal interrogation of the responsibility and integrity surrounding aesthetic activity. Drawing on the 'groundedness' of Sancho and the destructive self-fashioning of Quixote in Cervantes, Kafka develops a reading of the novel that questions the status of literary creativity and casts doubt on the ability of literature to represent and even transcend reality in the manner he had previously believed, as his correspondences with Felice Bauer and Max Brod in this period document. Kafka revisits this opposition between groundedness and errantry, responsibility and performance, around the time of writing *Das Schloss*, using it as a springboard for a broader enquiry into sociability. In the final 1922 fragment, the comparative reading raises serious questions about the heroic status of K. in the novel. Unlike Cervantes's novel, where Quixote returns home to die as Quexana, *Das Schloss* — like the final Cervantes fragment — breaks off in mid-flow and reaches no conclusion as to K.'s heroism or otherwise.

If we take Kafka's comparison seriously, K.'s acts of resistance against what he considers a malevolent castle bureaucracy would be another instance of quixotic, self-destructive performance that comes at the cost of a responsible and grounded relationship with his community. But that is a reading of *Das Schloss* that Ritchie Robertson has made his own: if Kafka's aim in this final novel 'was to confront the world of falsehood, denounced in the Zürau aphorisms', then this is a falsehood that is captured in the self-assumed and suspect '"Vermessenheit" (boldness) with which K. challenges the castle', discarding Frieda and his connection with the other villagers in pursuit of an ideal which he can barely define.[53] If *Das Schloss* is a critique of messianism, as Robertson argues powerfully, then its primary medium is K.'s quixotic self-destructive flights of fancy.

Notes to Chapter 15

1. Ritchie Robertson, 'Kafka's Reading', in *Franz Kafka in Context*, ed. by Carolin Duttlinger (Cambridge: Cambridge University Press, 2018), pp. 82–90 (p. 82).
2. Monika Schmitz-Emans provides an incisive and wide-ranging overview of Kafka's writing in this perspective in her essay 'Kafka und die Weltliteratur', in *Kafka-Handbuch: Leben — Werk-Wirkung*, ed. by Oliver Jahraus (Göttingen: Vandenhoeck & Ruprecht, 2008), pp. 273–92.
3. Franz Kafka, Letter to Felice Bauer, in Franz Kafka, *Schriften, Tagebücher, Briefe*, ed. by Hans-Gerd Koch and others (Frankfurt a.M.: Fischer, 1982–), *Briefe II: 1913–März 1914*, ed. by Hans-Gerd Koch (2001), p. 275 (2 September 1913).
4. Walter Benjamin, 'Franz Kafka. Zur zehnten Wiederkehr seines Todestages', in Walter

Benjamin, *Gesammelte Schriften*, ed. by Rolf Tiedemann and Hermann Schweppenhäuser, 7 vols (Frankfurt a.M.: Fischer, 1972–99), II: *Aufsätze, Essays, Vorträge*, ed. by Rolf Tiedemann and Hermann Schweppenhäuser (1991), pp. 409–37 (p. 438).

5. *Kafka-Handbuch*, ed. by Hartmut Binder, 2 vols (Stuttgart: Alfred Kröner, 1979), I, 357–58; Gabriele Eckart and Meg Brown, *Shifting Viewpoints: Cervantes in Twentieth-Century and Twenty-First Century Literature written in German* (Newcastle: Cambridge Scholars Publishing, 2013), pp. 178–82 provides a summary of scholarship since 1980.

6. Franz Kafka, Letter to Max Brod, in *Briefe 1902–1924*, ed. by Max Brod (Frankfurt a.M.: Fischer, 1975), p. 384 (5 July 1922). See more widely: Heinz Hillmann, *Franz Kafka: Dichtungstheorie und Dichtungsgestalt* (Bonn: Bouvier, 1964), pp. 31–34; Walter Sokel, *Franz Kafka: Tragik und Ironie* (Munich, Vienna: Albert Langen 1964), p. 42.

7. See e.g. Jörgen Kobs, *Franz Kafka* (Bad Homburg: Athenäum, 1970), pp. 539–42.

8. See e.g. Winfried Kudzus, 'Kafka's Cage and Circus', in *Kafka and the Contemporary Performance*, ed. by Alan Udoff (Bloomington: Indiana University Press, 1987), pp. 158–64 (pp. 159–60) and Gert Mattenklott, 'Gewinnen, nicht siegen', *Merkur* 39 (1985), 961–68.

9. Arno Dusini, 'Sancho Pansa Kafka Don Quichote', in *Transkulturelle Beziehungen: Spanien und Österreich im 19. und 20. Jahrhundert,* ed. by Marisa Siguán and Karl Wagner (Amsterdam: Rodopi, 2004), pp. 47–62.

10. Marthe Robert, *The Old and the New: From Don Quixote to Kafka* (Berkeley, CA: University of California Press, 1977 [1963]); Stanley Corngold, *Kafka: The Necessity of Form* (New York: Cornell University Press, 1988), pp. 165–202; Ritchie Robertson, 'Kafka und Don Quixote', *Neophilologicus*, 69 (1985), 17–24.

11. Miguel de Cervantes, *Don Quixote*, trans. by Edith Grossman (London: Vintage, 2004), p. 142. All further references are to this addition and will appear abbreviated as DQ and relevant page numbers in the main body of the essay.

12. See Anthony Close, *The Romantic Approach to Don Quijote* (Cambridge: Cambridge University Press, 1978), pp. 29–30.

13. Corngold, *Kafka*, p. xi.

14. See Anthony J. Cascardi, 'Don Quixote and the Invention of the Novel', in *The Cambridge Companion to Cervantes*, ed. by Anthony J. Cascardi (Cambridge: University Press, 2006), pp. 58–79: 'It immediately becomes clear that Part II establishes possibilities for novel-writing that build reflectively, relentlessly, even incestuously upon the history of Part I' (p. 76).

15. Corngold, *Kafka*, p. 184.

16. See Howard Mancing, *The Cervantes Encyclopedia*, 2 vols (Westport, CT: Greenwood, 2004), II, 654.

17. Michael Pyper, 'Modern Fools: An Errant Journey from the Quixotic to the Kafkaesque' (unpublished doctoral thesis, Trinity College Dublin, 2013), p. 252; see also Carroll B. Johnson, *Don Quixote and the Quest for Modern Fiction* (Prospect Heights, IL: Waveland Press, 2000), pp. 71–88.

18. Rachel Schmidt, *Critical Images: The Canonization of Don Quixote through Illustrated Editions of the Eighteenth Century* (Montreal: McGill-Queen's University Press, 1999), pp 147–49.

19. The Cave thus represents 'an underworld where the characters are distortions of their previously heroic selves' and a Quixote who is 'deeply troubled by his role in life and in history and especially worried about Dulcinea' (Manuel Durán and Fay R. Rogg, 'Constructing Don Quixote', in *Miguel De Cervantes' Don Quixote*, ed. by Harold Bloom (New York: Blooms Literary Criticism, 2010), pp. 91–108 (p. 100)).

20. James A. Parr, 'Cervantes Foreshadows Freud: On Don Quijote's Flight from the Feminine and the Physical', *Bulletin of the Cervantes Society of America* 15.2 (1995), 16–25.

21. Pyper, 'Modern Fools', p. 37. Pyper builds on the work of Susan Bordo, *The Flight to Objectivity: Essays on Cartesianism and Culture* (Albany, NY: SUNY Press, 1987). In this respect see also Sherry Velasco, 'Marimachos, hombrunas, barbudas: The Masculine Woman in Cervantes', *Bulletin of the Cervantes Society of America* 20.1 (2000), 69–78.

22. Franz Kafka, Letter to Robert Klopstock, in *Briefe 1902–1924*, ed. by Brod, p. 333 (June 1921).

23. There is an earlier one-liner from 19 October 1917 in which Kafka emphasizes the virtues

of imagination and spirituality over the blindness and impatience of a worldly materialism: 'Das Unglück Don Quichotes ist nicht seine Phantasie, sondern Sancho Pansa' (Franz Kafka, *Schriften, Tagebücher, Briefe*, ed. by Hans-Gerd Koch and others (Frankfurt a.M.: Fischer, 1982–), *Nachgelassene Schriften und Fragmente II*, ed. by Jost Schillemeit (1992), p. 32). All further references are to this edition and will appear in the main body of the text with the abbreviation NSII and the relevant page number. I will refer to the established English translation 'Quixote' rather than Kafka's 'Quichote' when discussing the literary figure more generally.

24. Franz Kafka, Letter to Felice Bauer, in Franz Kafka, *Schriften, Tagebücher, Briefe*, ed. by Hans-Gerd Koch and others (Frankfurt a.M.: Fischer, 1982–), *Briefe III: April 1914–1917*, ed. by Hans-Gerd Koch (2005), p. 332 (30 September 1917).
25. Manfred Engel, 'Kleine Nachgelassene Schriften und Fragmente 3', in *Kafka-Handbuch. Leben — Werk — Wirkung*, ed. by Bernd Auerochs and Manfred Engel (Stuttgart: Metzler, 2010), pp. 343–70 (pp. 355–56).
26. See Dusini, 'Sancho Pansa', p. 61.
27. See Pyper, 'Modern Fools', pp. 120, 253–54.
28. Reading the fragment against the background of the Zürau aphorisms, however, Robertson, 'Kafka und Don Quixote' (pp. 19–20) argues strongly that Sancho's pragmatism and 'worldliness' mean that he is incapable of seeing a potential truth in Don Quichote's imaginative visions.
29. Kafka, *Briefe III: April 1914–1917*, ed. by Koch, p. 334.
30. Franz Kafka, *Schriften, Tagebücher, Briefe*, ed. by Hans-Gerd Koch and others (Frankfurt a.M.: Fischer, 1982–), *Drucke zu Lebzeiten* ed. by Wolf Kittler, Hans-Gerd Koch and Gerhard Neumann (1994), p. 477. All subsequent references to this edition will appear in the main body of the essay with the abbreviation D and the relevant page number.
31. See Sonja Dierks, *'Es gibt Gespenster': Zu Kafkas Erzählung* (Würzburg: Königshausen & Neumann, 2003), pp. 73–83.
32. Stanley Corngold, *Lambent Traces: Franz Kafka* (Princeton, NJ: Princeton University Press, 2004), p. 123; see also pp. 9–12. This is a much broader model that Corngold explains with reference to comments by Kafka such as the need, 'alle Fähigkeiten leer stehn [zu lassen], die sich auf die Freuden des Geschlechts, des Essens, des Trinkens [...] richteten' in order to focus on writing (Franz Kafka, *Schriften, Tagebücher, Briefe*, ed. by Hans-Gerd Koch and others (Frankfurt a.M.: Fischer, 1982–), *Tagebücher* ed. by Hans-Gerd Koch, Michael Müller and Malcolm Pasley (1990), pp. 341–42).
33. Franz Kafka, *Schriften, Tagebücher, Briefe*, ed. by Hans-Gerd Koch and others (Frankfurt a.M.: Fischer, 1982–), *Nachgelassene Schriften und Fragmente*, I, ed. by Malcolm Pasley (1993), p. 307. All subsequent references to this edition will appear in the main body of the essay with the abbreviation NSI and the relevant page number.
34. See Gerhard Neumann, 'Die Arbeit im Alchimistengäßchen (1916–1917)', in *Kafka-Handbuch*, ed. by Binder, II, 313–50 (pp. 336–38) and Frank Möbus, *Sündenfälle: Die Geschlechtlichkeit in Erzählungen Franz Kafkas* (Göttingen: Wallstein, 1994), pp. 10–16, 39–45.
35. Möbus, *Sündenfälle*, p. 16.
36. Franz Kafka, Letter to Max Brod, in *Briefe III: April 1914–1917*, ed. by Koch, p. 314 (5 September 1917).
37. See e.g. Hans H. Hiebel, *Die Zeichen des Gesetzes: Recht und Macht bei Franz Kafka* (Munich: Fink, 1983), p. 155; noticing the frequency of personal pronouns ('ich' appears twenty-eight times, 'mein' twenty-nine times) Möbus has called the text 'im ganz buchstäblichen Sinne, ein[en] egozentrische[n]' (p. 125).
38. Neumann, 'Alchimistengäßchen', pp. 334–35.
39. Henry Sussman, 'Double Medicine: The Text that was Never a Story', in *Kafka-Studien*, ed. by Barbara Elling (New York, Bern, Frankfurt a.M.: Lang, 1985), pp. 183–96 (p. 185).
40. Hiebel, *Zeichen*, p. 155.
41. In *Orte der Gewalt: Kafkas literarische Ethik* (Munich: Diaphanes, 1990), Joseph Vogl argues that 'die Begegnung mit dem Jungen [...] eine Begegnung des erzählenden Ichs mit sich selbst [ist]' (p. 124).
42. Sokel, *Franz Kafka*, p. 261.

43. Ritchie Robertson, *Kafka: Judaism, Politics, and Literature* (Oxford: Clarendon, 1985), pp. 179–80.
44. Robertson, 'Kafka und Don Quixote', pp. 21–22.
45. Max Brod, 'Der Dichter Franz Kafka', in *Juden in der deutschen Literatur*, ed. by Gustav Krojanker (Berlin: Welt Verlag, 1922), pp. 55–62 (p. 57).
46. Franz Kafka, *Schriften, Tagebücher, Briefe*, ed. by Hans-Gerd Koch and others (Frankfurt a.M.: Fischer, 1982–), *Das Schloß* ed. by Malcolm Pasley (1982), p. 215. All further references are to this edition and will appear in the main body of the essay with the abbreviation S and the relevant page number
47. Robert, *The Old*, pp. 32–33.
48. Ibid., pp. 194, 222.
49. Ibid., pp. 187, 251
50. Robertson, 'Kafka and Don Quixote', p. 23.
51. See Betiel Wasihun, *Gewollt — nicht-gewollt: Wettkampf bei Kafka. Mit Blick auf Robert Walser und Samuel Beckett* (Heidelberg: Winter, 2010).
52. Walter Benjamin, 'Über das mimetische Vermögen', in Walter Benjamin, *Gesammelte Schriften*, ed. by Rolf Tiedemann and Hermann Schweppenhäuser, 7 vols (Frankfurt a.M.: Fischer, 1972–99), II: *Aufsätze, Essays, Vorträge*, ed. by Rolf Tiedemann and Hermann Schweppenhäuser (1991), pp. 210–13 (p. 213). Benjamin is quoting from Hugo von Hofmannsthal's *Der Tor und der Tod*. In his Kafka essay, Benjamin actually illustrates this associative mode of reading by quoting from the 'Sancho Pansa' fragment; see ibid., p. 438. Samuel Weber discusses this point, see: 'Going along for the Ride: Violence and Gesture. Agamben Reading Benjamin Reading Kafka Reading Cervantes', *The Germanic Review: Literature, Culture, Theory*, 81.1 (2006), 65–83.
53. Robertson, *Kafka*, pp. 218, 228.

CHAPTER 16

Uncertainty, Realism and the Self in Kafka

Jennifer Anna Gosetti-Ferencei

If Kafka aims, as Ritchie Robertson has argued, 'to confront the world of falsehood [...] by opposing it to a fictional world which, just because it is fictional, rises above the deceits of the physical world and approaches truth',[1] within Kafka's fictional worlds the striving for truth or knowledge proves either fruitless or disastrous for his protagonists. Their plight is reflected at the level of form. Insofar as realism implies a faithful representation of reality or an innocence of seeing, Kafka's works exploit or parody its pretensions, to Sisyphean effect. This essay will examine the theme of epistemic uncertainty in Kafka's narratives within the context of a counter-epistemic tradition that extends from ironic Socratic ignorance to Nietzschean perspectivism. It will be suggested that in absorbing these diverse influences Kafka's writing reflects diverging approaches to reality. These include a metaphysical dualism hinting that this world may exist in the shadow of a higher but inaccessible one, and a radical perspectivism according to which reality, in contrast to our fixed cognition of it, is subject to incessant change. In light of these alternatives Kafka both plays with and departs from realism, with repercussions for the stability of the self.

Epistemic Uncertainty and its Implications

Epistemic uncertainty involves a state of unknowing or a frustration of knowledge such that truth is inaccessible, and Kafka's fiction explores this problem in both subjective and objective aspects. *Der Process* (1914–15) challenges the knowing subject when the priest instructs Josef K. that: 'Richtiges Auffassen einer Sache und Mißverstehn der gleichen Sache schließen einander nicht vollständig aus.'[2] In this novel the 'characteristic mode' of which is ambiguity,[3] K.'s every undertaking to uncover the truth of his predicament seems to bring him further from it. Like a modern Augustine,[4] K. considers writing a confession of all significant actions ever undertaken and his reasons for them. Attempting to impose logic upon the trial's inscrutable proceedings, his personality gradually breaks down, his eventual execution effecting only an 'anti-revelation'.[5] At the same time, the procedures of the trial itself appear unknowable. They manifest not judicial objectivity but what may be a drama of the mind. It may be 'even uncertain how far the court exists independently of K.'.[6] In response to the priest's comment regarding the necessity of accepting the doorkeeper's word in the parable, K. almost paraphrases Nietzsche's view that untruth is a condition of life, surmising dejectedly: 'Die Lüge wird zur Weltordnung gemacht.'[7]

Competing claims to truth situate the fatal conflict of Kafka's story 'Das Urteil' (1912). A dispute arises between Georg and his father about Georg's friend in Russia to whom he has been writing a letter, which marks the narrative's foray into fantasy. In the same exchange the father both demands to know whether the friend in Russia exists, and proclaims that he himself has been in correspondence with the friend. In the course of this conflict, the fragile, childlike father arises monstrously, so large that his hand touches the ceiling, and sentences Georg to death by drowning. When, like K. of *Der Process*, Georg dutifully submits to his execution, he succumbs to a judgement based not on facts or evidence but on the power to define reality.[8]

Kafka's novella *Die Verwandlung* (1912) also contains a pivotal epistemic issue, reflecting Gregor Samsa's knowledge of his own situation. Despite the unreality of Gregor's transformation, his anxiety about getting to work on time and supporting his indebted family is all too real in psychological terms. So too is the abuse by his father who fatally injures Gregor by throwing apples at him, 'der überraschende unglaubliche Schmerz' caused by one particular apple nailing him to the spot and confusing his senses before he crawls helplessly back to his room.[9] Everyday objects in Kafka's writings 'tend to become symbolic', such that 'the repeated mention of these objects causes them, by accumulation, to take on a more than literal significance',[10] and here the apple takes on a fairly obvious yet nuanced symbolism. In the description of the attack on Gregor, 'Apfel' appears five times (including once in the plural), illustrating the persistence of the attack while evoking biblical imagery that links the attainment of knowledge with the origin of mortality. While Gregor's devolution has reduced his human sensibilities, he has progressed from a state of ignorance that his family's debts had long been paid to knowledge of what has been in effect his servitude. His real status in the family exposed, Gregor is banished to his room to die alone.

In *Der Process* a rupture of this ancient symbolic connection is poignant. In the first chapter K. eats an apple in lieu both of his breakfast the arresting guards have taken for themselves and of any answers to his questions about his arrest. That the apple brings no knowledge to the one identified as guilty anticipates the year-long trial K. is about to undergo. While K., breakfasting on his apple, is apparently at ease and confident, he considers the prospect of suicide.

> [W]enigstens aus dem Gedankengang der Wächter wunderte es ihn, daß sie ihn in das Zimmer getrieben und ihn hier allein gelassen hatten, wo er doch zehnfache Möglichkeit hatte sich umzubringen. Gleichzeitig allerdings fragte er sich, mal aus seinem Gedankengang, was für einen Grund er haben könnte, es zu tun. Etwa weil die zwei nebenan saßen und sein Frühstück abgefangen hatten?[11]

A year later, K. assumes the point of view of the guards, having learned nothing except his duty to die: 'K. wußte jetzt genau, daß es seine Pflicht gewesen wäre, das Messer [...] selbst zu fassen und sich einzubohren.'[12]

Walter Benjamin described Kafka's fictional world as one 'designed to reduce to insignificance the person who experiences it, to render him invisible by concealing him at the heart of banality'.[13] Yet if 'the sole topic of his work' concerns 'almost incomprehensible distortions of existence',[14] this presents difficulties in Kafka's worlds for the individual self. An unknowable world with ever shifting or inaccessible points of orientation will prove existentially challenging for what existentialists call being-in-the-world, and in light of this, existential readings of Kafka, like political ones, 'cannot be set aside'.[15]

Kafka explores the elusiveness of any fixed point of reference for his protagonists' searches or researches, and elaborates through their fates its repercussions. In this light Blanchot identifies in Kafka a kind of existential scepticism. With his figure of the land surveyor, for example, Kafka has transformed 'wayfaring without any goal into the certitude of the goal without any way there'.[16] Accordingly the self in Kafka becomes a 'region of error' in which 'one does nothing but stray without end'.[17]

Perspectivism, Ironic Ignorance and Mystical Unknowing

Kafka's renderings of epistemic uncertainty reflect his interest in Nietzsche,[18] whose hermeneutics of suspicion[19] characterized the commitment to truth and knowledge as a vain desire to fix the world in stable concepts. Truth where it is recognized by Nietzsche could only ever be grasped partially, subjectively, and manifested in proliferating perspectives. Yet the recognition of epistemic uncertainty need not necessitate abandonment of truth or its pursuit. In his diary Kafka himself described the aim of his writings, to elevate 'die Welt ins Reine, Wahre, Unveränderliche'.[20] In light of this Max Brod may have been right to point to a difference, if not the polarity he claims to identify, between Kafka and Nietzsche, whose inversion of Platonism discredits exactly such elevation.[21] There are moments in Nietzsche where truth is at stake — the veil of Maya torn away in Die Geburt der Tragödie (1872) — but exposure would not reveal a pure, unchanging truth but an unpresentable chaos, a Heraclitean becoming. Kafka's experiments with Nietzschean perspectivism are best understood in a wider context.

Forms of uncertainty have been promoted as indirect modes of access to truth, beginning with the ironic claim to ignorance by Socrates. Kafka would have grasped the force of Nietzsche's critique of Socratic ignorance as a diversion from a truth too unbearable to admit.[22] Yet Kafka would also have been informed by Kierkegaard's praise for Socratic ignorance, extolled as a realization at 'which the point becomes to understand more and more that there is something which cannot be understood'.[23] Kafka was a reader both of Plato's depictions of Socrates and of Kierkegaard,[24] the latter of whom he regarded intimately — 'Er bestätigt mich wie ein Freund'[25] — even if his relation to Kierkegaard was 'deeply ambiguous'.[26] Kierkegaard promoted the 'supreme paradox of all thought' he found expressed in the Socratic stance, namely the 'attempt to discover something that thought cannot think'.[27] Such ignorance may itself be ironized when K. of *Das Schloss* (1922) admits and even affirms his own unknowing:

> Freilich unwissend bin ich, die Wahrheit bleibt jedenfalls bestehn und das ist sehr traurig für mich, aber es hat doch auch den Vorteil, daß der Unwissende mehr wagt und deshalb will ich die Unwissenheit und ihre gewiß schlimmen Folgen gerne noch ein Weilchen tragen, solange die Kräfte reichen.[28]

If he is attempting to discover in the castle 'something that thought cannot think', *Unwissenheit* only perpetuates K.'s fruitless pursuit.

Yet K. hints at some advantage in unknowing. Kierkegaard equates Socratic unknowing to a freedom from mental capture by phenomena, an ironic understanding of the 'nothingness of the determinate content of the world as it is' in deference to a higher unknown, because infinite truth.[29] This would resonate with Kafka insofar as he identified an ethical task in freedom from sensuous entanglements in the physical world.[30] While Socratic inwardness involves a negation of the finite, however, Kierkegaard's philosophy proposes, further, faith in an infinite God. Such faith would require an embrace of paradox achieved through the radical uncertainty illustrated by the story Abraham and Isaac reconsidered in *Fear and Trembling* (1843). In critical dialogue with Kierkegaard, Kafka constructed alternative scenarios for Abraham's dilemma.[31]

Irony in Kafka's writings has been interpreted in light of the indirect communication offered by Socratic-Kierkegaardian irony, while reflecting an 'unrelenting dualism of hope and despair' that will not be resolved through the dialectical movements Kierkegaard's thought prescribes.[32] While Kierkegaard indicates faith in an unfathomable infinite, Kafka evokes an otherworldly truth inaccessible for the human subject. In this light, the castle of *Das Schloss* appears otherworldly for the land surveyor: 'Das Schloß, dessen Umrisse sich schon aufzulösen begannen, lag still wie immer [...]. [J]e länger er hinsah, desto weniger erkannte er, desto tiefer sank alles in Dämmerung.'[33] The division between the world of the castle and that of the village in which K. awaits his recognition is never overcome. In *Der Process*, the doorkeeper closes the door on the law as the man from the country faces death, his vision dimmed by old age and fruitless waiting. Indeed 'beyond the semiotics of realism K. has occasional glimpses of another world with its own system of meaning, different from and in some ways antithetical to his everyday reality'.[34] Both novels may suggest a truth beyond human reach.

Constraint on the ambitions of knowledge-seeking was promoted by another of Kafka's influences, the medieval German mystic Meister Eckhart.[35] Modernist writers, Kafka among them, revived interest in such mysticism in 'a search for forms of experience that slipped through the iron grid of scientific materialism'.[36] While he likened Kierkegaard to a friend, for Kafka Meister Eckhart's were among those books that illuminate inner recesses of thought, 'wie ein Schlüssel zu fremden Sälen des eigenen Schlosses'.[37] Eckhart repudiated definitively knowable truth in favour of a special state of intellectual emptiness. In his first sermon Eckart praises knowledge in non-knowledge:

> Wenn es schon ein Unwissen heisst und eine Unerkanntheit, so hat es doch mehr in sich drinnen als alles Wissen und Erkennen von aussen: denn dies Unwissendes Äussern reizt und zieht dich von allen Wissensdingen und auch von dir selbst.[38]

Unknowing alienates one from all worldly understanding, and prepares the soul as it were for an experience of God. For Eckhart, a state of unknowing prepares the barrenness in one's inward and outward comportment necessary to foster a reception of the divine.

Of particular relevance to Kafka is the relation Eckhart draws between unknowing and justice. Eckart argues that the just man acts without knowledge and reason, just as God acts 'ohne Warum'.[39] In the same way as God acts, so the just man acts without why. Justice is equated with action in accordance only with itself, lacking any further motive. Yet Eckhart's formulation could invite another reading: if justice pertains without why, it requires no knowledge or justification outside itself.

This theme is ironically explored in several of Kafka's texts. In *Der Process* K. is arrested without why. Knowledge of the accusation against him, of the procedures by which he might be brought to justice, and of the law itself, remains inaccessible. Benjamin argued that ignorance of the law all but guarantees its transgression, a conflict casting K. into 'fated ambiguity'.[40] In 'In der Strafkolonie' ambiguity yields to absolutism: justice amounts to the equivalence of verdict and sentence, since guilt is always to be assumed: 'Die Schuld ist immer zweifellos'.[41] Again no reasons need be given, for guilt is 'without why'. Justice is exercised by the apparatus via lethal inscription — a self-reflexive 'Sei gerecht!'[42] is to be carved on the body of one condemned, an inscription contradicting the very command it bears.[43] Cut off from any higher divinity, justice 'without why' in Kafka's worlds effects a catastrophic tautology.

The stabilizing ontology of dualism — stabilizing since another world, however inaccessible to us, could hold the key to this one — may be challenged of course by a perspectivist view of an ever-changing reality, which Kafka's work also intermittently evokes. In *Die fröhliche Wissenschaft* (1882) Nietzsche challenges both Platonic idealism — the aim to grasp essences or ideas beyond their appearance in reality — and realism — any assumption that the world is as it appears, without cognitive and psychological interference from our subjective standpoint. As Nietzsche argues, 'Es gibt für uns keine "Wirklichkeit"' if that means a view from nowhere.[44] The castle's dissolving contours may be attributed not only to the waning light but to the unstable ontology of the castle itself, and its world.

In *Das Schloss* ontological contingency is also suggested in a report about the changing appearance of castle officials. Olga reports to K. of the elusive Klamm that a picture of his appearance has been built up 'aus Gerüchten und auch manchen fälschenden Nebenabsichten'.[45] Yet if distortion may presuppose correct rendering of certain basic features, this picture is variable, though not so much so as Klamm's real appearance: 'Sonst ist es veränderlich und vielleicht nicht einmal so veränderlich wie Klamms wirkliches Aussehn.' Klamm is said to look different when coming or going from the village, when awake or asleep, alone or in conversation, in the castle or within the village. Olga goes on to say that: 'alle diese Unterschiede [...] entstehen durch die augenblickliche Stimmung, den Grad der Aufregung, die unzähligen Abstufungen der Hoffnung oder Verzweiflung, in welcher sich der Zuschauer [...] befindet'.[46] It seems both appearances and their underlying reality are changing, in respect to both their contexts and their observer.

Other worlds in Kafka's works shift unpredictably. In 'Ein Landarzt' (1917) travel to the village of the patient is instantaneous, but the return home said to be so slow that the doctor will never arrive. A rendering of Paris in an early version of 'Beschreibung eines Kampfes' (1903–07) is similarly unstable: it is pondered whether its people consist only of ornate clothing, its houses only of portals, the clouds only glued like paper onto its blue sky. Such a world 'appears as mere surface — without any deeper foundation, without any (metaphysical) truth' that would ground it as a permanent reality.[47] Like the settings for a number of his works, it 'has no intrinsic truth-content'.[48]

The metaphysical dualism of a worldly realm and an inaccessibly higher one may compete with a more Heraclitean view of reality in 'Beim Bau der chinesischen Mauer' (1917). The ancient construction serves to unify the Chinese culture, drawing from the population architectural expertise and historical knowledge, training and scholarship. The narrator himself is a researcher seeking an explanation for the wall's piecemeal construction, and the narrative describes how its discontinuities are to be bridged by further construction. If the wall itself is fragmentary, so too are the people's grasp of the project and communication from the imperial centre. The latter must traverse such great distances that accounts of battles waged long ago may arrive as fresh news. In the fable enfolded within the story, published as 'Eine kaiserliche Botschaft' (1917), the messenger bearing the message of a dying emperor must push through the innumerable throng, traverse the vast complex of palaces and the courts, and cross the imperial city, such that the delivery of the message is impossibly obstructed. The fable ends with the suggestion that the message itself is but a fiction of imagination: 'Du aber sitzt an Deinem Fenster und erträumst sie Dir, wenn der Abend kommt.'[49]

This inaccessible imperial centre, like the otherworldly castle for which K. searches, evokes the 'finite-infinite dualism'[50] that may motivate ironic or indirect stances towards knowledge or truth. Yet here too there are hints of a more radical instability than such dualism would admit. Meditation on imperial decrees is discouraged with the parable of the river which when rising too high overflows its banks, damages the surrounding landscape and dries up. The metaphor of an overflowing river echoes the allegory of Heraclitus, who describes a moving river as never self-identical since, stepping into it a second time, other waters would be flowing there. Like the overflowing river, Kafka's parable admonishes, knowledge-seeking breaks boundaries; inquiry must be restrained. While the narrator dismisses the parable as irrelevant to his own researches into the building of the wall, he absorbs its central image in describing the difficulty of his task: 'Die Grenzen, die meine Denkfähigkeit mir setzt, sind ja eng genug, das Gebiet aber, das hier zu durchlaufen wäre, ist das Endlose.'[51]

Between the finite–infinite dualism and the perspectivist view of a more shifting reality in Kafka's works there also resonates the Jewish mysticism Gershom Scholem identified in Kafka's thinking. In such mysticism 'the material world is reduced, in relation to the infinity of divine Being [...] to a mere game of appearances'. From such a perspective 'the world is no longer conceived of as an objective reality, but as a chance combination of shadows and reflections'.[52] The inaccessibility of the infinite commits the earthly world to a proliferation of mere appearances in which any moment could be seen, as Kafka's investigating dog says, as 'die einzige wenn auch nur scheinbare Wirklichkeit'.[53] In lieu of an otherworldly infinite, Kafka's works may allude to a worldly multiplicity. They echo Nietzsche's perspectivist suggestion that 'die Welt ist uns vielmehr noch einmal "unendlich" geworden: insofern wir die Möglichkeit nicht abweisen können, daß sie unendliche Interpretationen in sich schließt'.[54]

Yet Scholem also saw in Kafka a prospect in which revelation is void of its other-worldly content. In a letter to Benjamin he described of Kafka's works a state 'in which revelation appears to be without meaning, in which it still asserts itself, in which it has validity but no significance'.[55] As the narrator of 'Beim Bau der chinesischen Mauer' reveals: 'Wenn man aus solchen Erscheinungen folgern wollte, daß wir im Grunde gar keinen Kaiser haben, wäre man von der Wahrheit nicht weit entfernt.'[56] Whether Kafka's works signal to the higher but elusive reality or whether the existence of any higher reality is to be doubted leaves epistemic uncertainty as an existential problem for Kafka's protagonists and an interpretative one for his readers.

Realism, Perspectival Truth and the Myth of Innocence

The perspectivism that comes through in Kafka's works invites consideration of his relation to literary realism and its commitment to truth. Realism has been associated with innocent perspective, even a cognitive naivety. George Eliot famously championed realism in these terms in a review of a work by John Ruskin. The eminent Victorian art critic promoted 'the innocence of the eye', a form of 'childish perception' or seeing in a way that a blind person suddenly gifted with sight might see.[57] The artist should break free from the signification human perception has come to assume and restore 'consciousness of the real aspect of the signs we have learned to interpret'.[58] Only pre-interpretatively can the artist see 'the colours of nature exactly as they are' and reproduce them on the canvas accordingly.[59] For the realist artist, truth and innocence are equivalent; interpretation obstructs. Eliot draws a direct analogy between the realist visual artist and the realist writer, who should undertake a 'faithful study of nature' by refusing to substitute 'vague forms, bred by imagination on the mists of feeling, in place of definite, substantial reality'.[60] Beyond representational fidelity, the achievement of realism is a moral one, offering, Eliot argues, a 'truth of infinite value'.[61]

Of course, literary realism in a broader sense can also perform a critical task, concerned as it is not only with nature but with the social world. Realism could expose how societies failed to 'embody a meaning adequate to the needs of their members'.[62] As such nineteenth-century realism was able to depict the 'transcendental homelessness' of the subject in the modern world.[63] Beyond naive realism, writers may register the divergence between reality and its representation. Theodor Fontane, for example, distinguished between the real and the true, supporting a more expansive realism that included 'alle[] wahren Kräfte und Interessen im Elemente der Kunst'.[64] Kafka's fiction may parody a naive model of realism, disrupting both the faithful study of reality and any innocent perception on which it would be based.

Such realism would be challenged equally by a metaphysical dualism that posits a higher but inaccessible key to reality, as it would by a radical perspectivism that denies any stable basis for reality at all. Yet Kafka's works do not simply displace realism but engage it in multiple ways, hovering ambiguously between realism and modernism.[65] Kafka presents both the monotony of the ordinary and the breakdown of the presumptions which uphold its perception. An admirer of realist fiction himself, Kafka ventures beyond it, challenging with his distortions the presumptive continuity between realism and truth.[66]

Realism is evoked in *Der Process* in a number of ways, including the depiction of K.'s concrete concerns. For example, the morning of the arrest, K. helps himself to a glass of schnapps in addition to the apple, drinking a second glass 'ihm Mut zu machen [...] nur aus Vorsicht für den unwahrscheinlichen Fall, daß es nötig sein sollte'.[67] Anticipating a meeting with a foreign client of the bank, K. stays up late reviewing an Italian grammar book. Yet realism breaks down intermittently: in déjà vu when K. opens the lumber closet and finds the thrasher beating the guards exactly as he had the day before, surreally when Leni's fingers are revealed to be webbed, and uncannily in the shifting location and procedures of the court. Moments of unreality are interwoven into a situation that, for all its ambiguity, is sometimes misleadingly familiar.

Die Verwandlung too relies on some aspects of a realist presentation. Despite 'the initial shock of the unreal' the narrative 'exhibits many of the attributes of a particularly trenchant kind of realism'.[68] When the narrative opens, Gregor's extraordinary transformation is embedded in 'a commonplace, even a trite, situation'. The economic entanglements of family life, and the concrete detail of Gregor's predicament, form the core of the story's allegorical meaning.[69] The narrative presentation, moreover, remains straightforward, even instructive, as when the narrator indicates at the outset that it was not a dream. Conventional realism is exploited rather than abandoned, exposing 'behind the seeming transparency of representational language, a baffling opacity'.[70]

In *Die Verwandlung* even cognitive confusions are realistically portrayed. Gregor's inward transformation is narratively traced through sensory details, as when Gregor loses human tastes and his primitive senses are amplified. With the shallowing of Gregor's sight, the reader can follow 'the horizons of visibility closing'.[71] Liminal perceptions — attempts to see in vague and murky atmospheres, or with compromised sight — are implicitly contrasted to a stable perception. In this way cognitive dissonance may be 'still framed by an accepted empirical reality'.[72]

Das Schloss begins with an ostensibly realist narrative, a traveller identified only by his initial arrival in the dark at an unfamiliar village. Almost immediately, however, perceptual ambiguity is introduced: 'Vom Schloßberg war nichts zu sehn, Nebel und Finsternis umgaben ihn, auch nicht der schwächste Lichtschein deutete das große Schloß an.'[73] Contrast is drawn between a concrete reality presumably known to the narrator and its imperception by the protagonist. The castle's invisibility resonates metaphorically when K. stands for a long while gazing 'in die scheinbare Leere empor'.[74]

If the appearance of the castle is in question at the novel's outset, in subsequent depictions its ontological status is uncertain. Upon closer approach K. finds it a ramshackle collection of dilapidated houses 'nur dadurch, daß vielleicht alles aus Stein gebaut war, aber der Anstrich war längst abgefallen, und der Stein schien abzubröckeln'.[75] The boundary between the castle and the town itself is obscure. That the tower's battlements are childishly rendered — 'unsicher, unregelmäßig, brüchig wie von ängstlicher oder nachlässiger Kinderhand gezeichnet' — suggests the possibility, ever in play throughout the novel, that the reality of the castle is not only subject to imaginative interpretation but may itself be imaginary.[76] A similar motif can be found in *Der Process*, where K. in search of the court offices comes upon a sign indicating them 'in einer kindlichen, ungeübten Schrift'.[77] Obviously, the childish rendering of the castle or of the court would differ from the innocent perception Ruskin attributes to the realist artist, for Kafka's narrative invokes imaginative rather than naive seeing. Yet there are further narrative invocations of childishness in Kafka's works,[78] apart from the childish assistants in *The Castle* and descriptions of K. himself as childish.[79] When K. reaches the castle by telephone he hears in the receiver murmur of 'zahlloser kindlicher Stimmen'.[80] The narrative seems to toy with what a naive imagination might not only perceive, but produce.

Kafka's depiction of shifting perception may reflect a realism of another kind, though one wrought with the tension of instability for the perceiver. In 'Über Wahrheit und Lüge im aussermoralischen Sinne' (1873) Nietzsche argued that the original state of cognition for a living, embodied human subject is shifting and heterogeneous rather than the fixed stasis shaped by our conceptual constructs. In contrast to the definite, substantial reality described by Eliot's literary realism, Nietzsche conceives of pre-cognitive, original access to a shifting world of particulars. Before the imposition of linguistic constructions, human perception would be fluid, receptive of particularity and difference arising 'aus dem Urvermögen menschlicher Phantasie'.[81] On this view the ontological ambiguity of the castle in Kafka's narrative would preserve the 'change and potentiality' of the real that essentialist cognition suppresses.[82] Its ambiguous rendering may echo the perspectival instability of pre-cognitive, imaginative perception. As such it would challenge, as fiction, the stable constructs of rational thought.

If we think of truth, to paraphrase Eliot, as the factual grasp of 'definite, substantial reality' — an epistemic concern — or as its 'faithful' portrayal — a moral one — both reality and faithfulness are at issue for the protagonist of 'Das Urteil'. By realist standards it is impossible to tell whether the friend on whom the dispute pivots actually exists. Kafka himself admitted that the friend was a shifting figure and perhaps only 'der perspektivische Wechsel der Beziehung zwischen Vater und Sohn'.[83] Their confrontation also reflects the existential implications of the narrative break with realism enacted in the story itself. Given this shifting and pivoting figure, Kafka found the titular judgement inexplicable: 'Das "Urteil" ist nicht zu erklären.'[84]

Accompanying Georg's sentence to death by drowning is the father's claim that Georg, once the innocent child, has become a devilish human being. If Georg's innocence meant that he saw the world through a child's eyes, in overtaking his father in the family business and household he has left such innocence behind. As Georg considers whether or not to divulge to the friend in Russia the news of his impending marriage, he is in effect toying with the representation of reality. Given Georg's status as a letter-writer, which may be taken as 'self-reflective of literal writing' on Kafka's part,[85] Georg's alleged loss of innocence parallels a shift away from realist depiction.

Georg's transgression may lie not in the engagement but in his unfaithful representation of it. Instead of a childish perception as Ruskin promotes in his artists, Georg now sees the world through the possibilities of its interpretative rendering. Imaginative variations would be incompatible with Eliot's realist or 'faithful' attitude to the facts. Georg may be guilty now of straying from 'the definite and the substantial' and indulging what are yet 'vague forms, bred by imagination on the mists of feeling', or in other words of irrealism. The portrayal of reality is not merely an aesthetic choice, however, as the condemnation by the father shows. In the absence of any objective grasp of reality, and in the context of proliferating perspectives on it, its representation will provoke a contest of power in which, to quote Adorno's view of Kafka, 'life and death are at stake'.[86]

While Kafka's narratives may obliquely parody the naive realism advocated by Eliot and Ruskin, realism goes beyond the portrayal of the world in perceptual or cognitive innocence. Henry James pointed out that while the realist novelist is 'no less occupied with the truth' than the historian,[87] reality has 'myriad forms' in the 'very atmosphere of the mind' that conducts experience.[88] The realist writer's task necessitates no commitment to uninterpreted nature, for there is also the reality of human thought and feeling. The latter, moreover, may conflict with social forms of representation.[89] In promoting realism, Fontane defended a more expansive sense of what it could include. Realism would mean presenting not merely 'das nackte Wiedergeben alltäglichen Lebens',[90] but what is true for 'the social, political, and cultural experience of the age.'[91] Realism is not merely the grasp of what is palpable but must involve transfiguration in order for it to achieve what Fontane calls 'die Widerspiegelung alles wirklichen Lebens'.[92]

Of course, Nietzsche criticized the very idea of innocent perception, which would amount to mistaking one's own partial perspective for a god's-eye view. Any perception is 'von unsrer Ecke aus' and thus ought not be upheld as truth as such.[93] For Nietzsche of the 'Über Wahrheit und Lüge' essay, the most original perception would be inseparable from imagination. Echoing Nietzsche, Ernst Gombrich wrote that 'the innocent eye is a myth'.[94]

The partiality of perception and knowledge is explored in Kafka's story 'Der Dorfschullehrer (Der Riesenmaulwurf)' (1914–15). The narrator, a businessman from the city, comments on the appearance of a giant mole in a country village, evidence for which is obsessively pursued by the village schoolmaster. Empirical investigation, evidence-seeking, witness statements, academic journals, scholarly advisers and scientific methods are enlisted to explain the phenomenon. Academic debate is parodied through competing pamphlets which are confused for one another by the editors of a scholarly agricultural journal. Sceptical of the sincerity of the schoolmaster's account, the narrator insists on scientific evidence-gathering and objective analysis.

Yet in the absence of any direct empirical evidence for the mole, acceptance of reportage comes down to the credibility of the conveyor, and all perspectives are revealed to be partial. The schoolmaster exaggerated the size of the mole in his exasperated effort to enlist help from an anonymous scholar, and his covetousness of an original discovery and resources to support his large family put his objectivity in doubt. At the same time the narrator's motives for insisting upon scholarly verification, and the imposition of a hierarchical structure of inquiry, may reflect the interests of the urban scientific community in suppressing pre-scientific claims to knowledge from the provinces. This may amount to an indirect taming of nature; in one variation of the story the narrator explains that 'erst in der Stadt' would the discovery receive its real legitimation.[95]

'Der Dorfschullehrer' also echoes Nietzsche's identification of knowledge as the elimination of strangeness, the assimilation and thus suppression of the unknown. Like the mole in question allegedly appearing and disappearing, a novel discovery is said to disappear into the whole total of knowledge. But here even the validity of the scientific undertaking appears to be questionable, for it is admitted that the absorption of facts into scientific understanding may lead to inscrutable abstraction. The narrator of 'Der Dorfschullehrer' explains:

> Jede Entdeckung wird gleich in die Gesamtheit der Wissenschaften geleitet und hört damit gewissermaßen auf Entdeckung zu sein, sie geht im Ganzen auf und verschwindet, man muß schon einen wissenschaftlich geschulten Blick haben, um sie dann noch zu erkennen. Sie wird gleich an Leitsätze geknüpft von deren Dasein wir gar nicht gehört haben, und im wissenschaftlichen Streit wird sie an diesen Leitsätzen bis in die Wolken hinaufgerissen.[96]

The newness of the unfamiliar and the uniqueness of its recognition are threatened by assimilation into a knowledge system which recedes from the discoverer's grasp. Defending the novelty of his discovery, the schoolmaster may stand for the prospect of wonder, of belief in unique, perhaps irrational phenomena. In contrast, the narrator would legitimate phenomena only within a rationally ordered system, one that extends, however, to otherworldly heights of abstraction — and thus beyond our grasp.

These opposing viewpoints may express competing cognitive attitudes that may compete not only within a culture but within the same self. The narrator despairs at the story's conclusion that he may never be rid of the visiting schoolmaster: 'es werde überhaupt nicht möglich sein, ihn aus dem Zimmer hinauszubefördern'.[97] It has been argued that Kafka offers a bifurcated image of the self, an interior of the depths that strives for transcendence and an outward self that must engage through insufficient language a social world.[98] Similarly, the opposing figures in 'Der Dorfschullehrer' seem to suggest not the struggle for and against knowledge, but conflicting epistemologies of uncertainty.

Conclusion

While realist writers may take as their goal the faithful representation of a definite, substantial reality, Kafka's play with realism, and with its implicit sense that the real is graspable, reflects competing, if equally challenging, visions of the prospects for knowledge or truth. Kafka's works are suggestive, on the one hand, of a metaphysical dualism in which the world appears in the shadow of a higher reality we can never know, and on the other hand, of a perspectival view of reality as essentially unknowable because ever in flux, despite all our efforts to fix it in stable concepts. These alternatives reflect Kafka's absorption of a counter-epistemic tradition in which uncertainty or unknowing may be extolled as liberating the individual from the seductions of a lesser reality or as enabling a higher state of being. Yet just as Kafka toys with realism and treats with irony the pretensions of innocent perception, so too he renders difficult any celebration of epistemic uncertainty that would convey indirect access to a higher truth. Glimpses of an inherently unstable reality are persistent enough to trouble faith in a higher realm, even if the spectre of the latter cannot be vanquished. It seems that Kafka's Socratic unknowing, his Kierkegaard and his Eckhart, must contend with Kafka's Nietzsche.

The existential implications of epistemic uncertainty are both thematically and stylistically explored in Kafka's works, and are manifest in their resistance to interpretative closure. In light of this hermeneutic evasiveness, Benjamin advised the reader of Kafka's texts 'to find one's way in them circumspectly, cautiously, and warily',[99] while Adorno famously identified an interpretative prohibition, paradoxical in that the texts demand interpretation whilst prohibiting the same.[100] While the general problem of interpretability in Kafka is a long-celebrated theme in Kafka scholarship,[101] Ritchie Robertson has criticized the 'despairing agnosticism [...] in which Kafka's texts were alleged to have no discoverable meaning and to exhibit merely the operations in which meaning was offered and withdrawn'.[102] Such agnosticism characterizes Blanchot's view of the fundamental errancy in Kafka, an errancy pushed to the limit. In this reading Kafka's land surveyor becomes a figure of exile, performing for Blanchot a movement outside truth itself:

> The tragic difficulty of the undertaking is that in this world of exclusion and radical separation, everything is false and inauthentic as soon as one examines it, everything lacks as soon as one seeks support from it, but nevertheless the depth of this absence is always given anew as an indubitable, absolute presence.[103]

Blanchot's identification of the 'absolute presence' of the absence of truth may be challenged by a reading of Kafka that recognizes competing visions. Uncertainty may be irresolvable not because in reading Kafka we face the void, but because through Kafka we are poised between some transcendent truth we cannot reach and a world of flux upon which, in all our fragility, we project stabilities that fail us.

For Kafka's readers, epistemic uncertainty may entail not a total refusal of meaning, but rather an invitation to consider the forms of our striving and the need for it. Kafka seems to invite us to consider our susceptibility to hope. As Ernst Bloch pointed out, even deception must work with hope if it is to be effective, however corruptly it is aroused.[104] Kafka effects an ironic reversal of the innocent gaze which destroys hope for any definite and substantial grasp of reality and exposes the power abused in its representation. If the striving for and the suspicion of truth are equally characteristic of modernity,[105] Kafka stages this conflict in his works. Yet the epistemic uncertainty manifest in this conflict does not only deny access to truth but also implicitly challenges any presentation of truth as unrevisable. This may paradoxically leave Kafka's reader with the sense of reality that is, while potentially despairing, also invigilated by possibility. Kafka's works can be understood to manifest the 'open dimension of indeterminacy', which is so pronounced in modern literature and supports plurivocity in its interpretation.[106] Perhaps it can be said that Kafka, in the very texts that demonstrate the unreachability of truth, 'affirms the freedom of the reader'[107] — both by inviting multiple interpretations and by exposing the instability of any fixed vision of the world.

Notes to Chapter 16

1. Ritchie Robertson, *Kafka: Judaism, Politics, and Literature* (Oxford: Oxford University Press, 1985), p. 218.
2. Franz Kafka, *Schriften, Tagebücher, Briefe*, ed. by Hans-Gerd Koch (Frankfurt a.M.: Fischer, 1982–), *Der Proceß*, ed. by Malcolm Pasley (1990), p. 297.
3. Ritchie Robertson, 'Introduction', in Franz Kafka, *The Trial*, trans. by Mike Mitchell (Oxford: Oxford University Press, 2009), p. xxiii.
4. On Kafka's interest in Augustine's *Confessions*, see Ben Morgan, 'Philosophy', in *Kafka in Context*, ed. by Carolin Duttlinger (Cambridge: Cambridge University Press, 2018), pp. 191–99 (p. 191).
5. Jean-Michel Rabaté, 'Kafka's Anti-Epiphanies', in *Kafka and the Universal*, ed. by Arthur Cools and Vivien Liska (Boston: De Gruyter, 2016), pp. 215–37 (p. 232).
6. Robertson, 'Introduction', p. xvi.
7. Kafka, *Der Proceß*, p. 303.
8. Ritchie Robertson's lecture at Johns Hopkins University on 30 September 2020, '"Really, but more really": What is "real" in Kafka's "The Judgement"?' helpfully illuminated the question of the real in Kafka's story.
9. Franz Kafka, *Schriften, Tagebücher, Briefe*, ed. by Hans-Gerd Koch (Frankfurt a.M.: Fischer, 1982–), *Drucke zu Lebzeiten*, ed. by Wolf Kittler, Hans-Gerd Koch and Gerhard Neumann (1996), p. 171.
10. Ritchie Robertson, 'Reading the Clues: Kafka, *Der Proceß*', in *The German Novel in the Twentieth Century: Beyond Realism*, ed. by David Midgley (Edinburgh: Edinburgh University Press, 1993), pp. 59–79.
11. Kafka, *Der Proceß*, p. 17.
12. Ibid., p. 311.
13. Walter Benjamin, 'Franz Kafka: Beim Bau der chinesischen Mauer', in *Selected Writings*, II: *1927–1934*, trans. by Rodney Livingstone, ed. by Michael W. Jennings, Howard Eiland and Gary Smith (Cambridge, MA: Harvard University Press), pp. 494–500 (p. 495).

14. Ibid., p. 496.
15. Ritchie Robertson, 'Biographical Preface', in Franz Kafka, *The Castle*, trans. by Anthea Bell (Oxford: Oxford University Press, 2009), pp. ix–x. See also Jennifer Anna Gosetti-Ferencei, *On Being and Becoming: An Existentialist Approach to Life* (New York and Oxford: Oxford University Press, 2020), pp. 100–01, 207–08.
16. Maurice Blanchot, *The Space of Literature*, trans. by Ann Smock (Lincoln, NE: University of Nebraska Press, 1982), p. 76.
17. Ibid., p. 76.
18. See Walter H. Sokel, 'Nietzsche and Kafka: The Dionysian Connection', in *Kafka for the Twenty-First Century*, ed. by Stanley Corngold and Ruth V. Gross (Rochester, NY: Camden House, 2011), pp. 64–74; Benno Wagner, 'Insuring Nietzsche: Kafka's Files', *New German Critique*, 99 (2006), 83–119; Patrick Bridgwater, *Kafka and Nietzsche* (Bonn: Bouvier, 1976).
19. The 'hermeneutics of suspicion' is a term associated with Paul Ricoeur, who writes of Marx, Nietzsche, and Freud as 'masters of suspicion' in the context of 'hermeneutics', in *Freud and Philosophy: An Essay on Interpretation*, trans. by Denis Savage (New Haven and London: Yale University Press, 1970), pp. 33, 35. Hans-Georg Gadamer regards the 'hermeneutics of suspicion' as 'inaugurated by Nietzsche' in 'The Hermeneutics of Suspicion', *Man and World*, 17 (1984), 313–24 (p. 313).
20. Diary entry 25 September 1917. Franz Kafka, *Schriften, Tagebücher, Briefe: Kritische Ausgabe*, ed. by Hans-Gerd Koch, Michael Müller and Malcolm Pasley (Frankfurt a.M.: Fischer, 1982–), *Tagebücher 1883–1924*, ed. by Hans-Gerd Koch (1990), p. 838.
21. Max Brod, *Über Franz Kafka* (Frankfurt a.M.: Fischer, 1966), p. 259. On Nietzsche's inverted Platonism, see Friedrich Nietzsche, *Kritische Studienausgabe 7: Nachgelassene Fragmente, 1869–1872*, ed. by Giorgio Colli and Mazzino Montinari (Berlin: DTV, 1988), p. 199.
22. Cf. Rainer Nägele, in 'I don't want to know that I know: The Inversion of Socratic Ignorance in the Knowledge of the Dogs', *Philosophy and Kafka*, ed. by Brendan Moran and Carlo Salzani (Lanham, MD: Lexington Books, 2013), pp. 19–32.
23. Søren Kierkegaard, *The Journals of Søren Kierkegaard*, trans. by Alexander Dru (New York: Harper, 1959), p. 172.
24. On Kafka's relation to Kierkegaard, see Max Brod, 'Nachwort', in Franz Kafka, *Das Schloss* (Munich: Kurt Wolff, 1926), 500–01; Jorge-Louis Borges, 'Kafka and his Precursors', in *Labyrinths* (New York: New Directions, 1964), pp. 363–65 (p. 364). See also Leena Elittä, 'Art as Religious Commitment: Kafka's Debt to Kierkegaardian Ideas and their Impact on his Late Stories', *German Life and Letters*, 53.4 (2000), 499–510; Morgan, 'Philosophy', pp. 195–98; and Richard Shepard, 'Kafka, Kierkegaard, and the K.'s: Theology, Psychology, and Fiction', *Literature and Theology*, 5.3 (1991), 277–96. Ritchie Robertson outlines Kafka's express objections to Kierkegaard in 'Kafka's Reading', in *Kafka in Context,* ed. by Carolin Duttlinger (Cambridge: Cambridge University Press, 2018), pp. 82–90 (pp. 87–88).
25. Diary Entry 21 August 1913. Franz Kafka, *Tagebücher 1883–1924*, p. 578.
26. Shepard, 'Kafka, Kierkegaard, and K.'s Theology', p. 280.
27. Søren Kierkegaard, *Philosophical Fragments*, trans. by David Swenson, 2nd edn, rev. Howard V. Hong (Princeton: Princeton University Press, 1962), p. 46. See also Harold Sarf, 'Reflections on Kierkegaard's Socrates', *Journal of the History of Ideas*, 44.2 (1983), 255–76.
28. Franz Kafka, *Schriften, Tagebücher, Briefe*, ed. by Hans-Gerd Koch (Frankfurt a.M.: Fischer, 1982–), *Das Schloß*, ed. by Malcolm Pasley (1982), p. 91.
29. Søren Kierkegaard, *The Concept of Irony*, trans. by Lee M. Capel (Bloomington: University of Indiana Press, 1971), p. 199.
30. See Ritchie Robertson, 'Kafka als religiöser Denker', in *Franz Kafka: Zur ethischen und Aesthetischen Rechtfertigung*, ed. by Jakob Lorhe and Beatrice Sandberg (Freiburg: Rombach, 2002), pp. 142–49.
31. Franz Kafka, *Schriften, Tagebücher, Briefe* ed. by Hans-Gerd Koch (Frankfurt a.M.: Fischer, 1982–), *Nachgelassene Schriften und Fragmente II*, ed. by Jost Schillemeit (1992), p. 103.
32. Reed Merrill, '"Infinite Absolute Negativity": Irony in Socrates, Kierkegaard and Kafka', *Comparative Literature Studies*, 16.3 (1979), 222–36 (p. 225).

33. Kafka, *Das Schloß*, pp. 156–57.
34. Robertson, 'Reading the Clues'.
35. See Morgan, 'Philosophy', pp. 192–93. See Ritchie Robertson, 'Everyday Transcendence? Robert Musil, William James, and Mysticism', *History of European Ideas*, 43.3 (2017), 262–72 (p. 262).
36. Robertson, 'Everyday Transcendence?', p. 262.
37. Franz Kafka, *Schriften, Tagebücher, Briefe*, ed. by Hans-Gerd Koch (Frankfurt a.M.: Fischer, 1982–), *Briefe 1900–1912*, ed. by Hans-Gerd Koch (1999), p. 29.
38. Meister Eckhart, *Meister Eckharts mystische Schriften*, trans. by Gustav Landauer (Berlin: Karl Schnabel, 1903), pp. 21–22.
39. Ibid., p. 63.
40. Walter Benjamin, 'Franz Kafka: On the Tenth Anniversary of his Death', in *Selected Writings*, II: *1927–1934*, trans. by Harry Zohn, ed. by Michael W. Jennings, Howard Eiland and Gary Smith (Cambridge, MA: Harvard University Press), pp. 794–818 (p. 797).
41. Kafka, *Drucke zu Lebzeiten*, p. 212.
42. Ibid., p. 238.
43. See Willi Goetschel, 'Franz Kafka: "In the Penal Colony"', *The Germanic Review*, 90.2 (2015), 81–86 (p. 83).
44. Friedrich Nietzsche, *Kritische Studienausgabe 3: Idyllen aus Messina, Die Fröhliche Wissenschaft, Nachgelassene Fragmente*, ed. by Giorgio Colli and Mazzino Montinari (Berlin: De Gruyter, 1980), p. 422.
45. Kafka, *Das Schloß*, p. 277.
46. Ibid., p. 278.
47. Mark M. Anderson, *Kafka's Clothes: Ornament and Aestheticism in the Habsburg Fin de Siècle* (Oxford: Clarendon Press, 1992), p. 43.
48. Rolf J. Goebel, 'Paris, Capital of Modernity: Kafka and Benjamin', *Monatshefte*, 90.4 (1998), 445–64 (p. 453).
49. Kafka, *Drucke zu Lebzeiten*, p. 282.
50. Merrill, '"Infinite Absolute Negativity"', p. 226.
51. Franz Kafka, *Schriften, Tagebücher, Briefe*, ed. by Hans-Gerd Koch (Frankfurt a.M.: Fischer, 1982–), *Nachgelassene Schriften und Fragmente I*, ed. by Malcolm Pasley (1993), p. 346.
52. Stéphane Moses and Ora Wiskind-Elper, 'Gershom Scholem's Reading of Kafka: Literary Criticism and Kabbalah', *New German Critique*, 77 (1999), 149–67 (p. 58).
53. Kafka, *Nachgelassene Schriften und Fragmente II*, p. 479.
54. Nietzsche, *Kritische Studienausgabe 3*, p. 627.
55. Gershom Scholem, Letter to Walter Benjamin (1934), in *The Correspondence of Walter Benjamin and Gershom Scholem 1933–1940*, ed. by Gershom Scholem, trans. by Gary Smith and Andre Lefevre (New York: Schocken, 1989), p. 142.
56. Franz Kafka, *Nachgelassene Schriften und Fragmente I*, p. 354.
57. John Ruskin, *The Elements of Drawing, in Three Letters to Beginners* (New York: Wiley and Halstead, 1858), p. 22.
58. Ibid., p. 22.
59. Ibid., p. 23.
60. George Eliot, 'Art and Belles Lettres', *The Westminster Review* (April 1856), 625–33 (pp. 626–27).
61. Ibid., p. 627.
62. John Walker, *The Truth of Realism: A Reassessment of the German Novel 1830–1900* (Oxford: Legenda, 2011), p. 3.
63. Georg Lukács, *The Theory of the Novel*, trans. by Anna Bostock (London: Merlin, 1971), p. 40.
64. Theodor Fontane, 'Unsere lyrische und epische Poesie seit 1848', in *Sämtliche Werke, vol. 21: Literarische Essays und Studien. Erster Teil*, ed. by Kurt Schreinert. (München: Nymphenburger Verlagshandlung, 1963), pp. 7–15 (p. 13).
65. See Ritchie Robertson, 'Reading the Clues' and 'Style', in *Kafka in Context*, ed. by Carolin Duttlinger (Cambridge: Cambridge University Press, 2018), pp. 62–72 (pp. 65–66).
66. See Judith Ryan, 'Literary Modernism,' in *Kafka in Context*, ed. by Carolin Duttlinger

(Cambridge: Cambridge University Press, 2018), pp. 73–81. See also Stanley Corngold, *Franz Kafka: The Necessity of Form* (Ithaca: Cornell University Press, 1988), pp. 250–87.
67. Kafka, *Der Proceß*, p. 18.
68. William J. Dodd, *Kafka and Dostoyevsky: The Shaping of Influence* (New York: Palgrave Macmillan, 1992), p. 52.
69. Norman N. Holland, 'Realism and Unrealism in Kafka's Metamorphosis', *Modern Fiction Studies*, 4.2 (1958), 143–50 (p. 144).
70. Jesse Cohn, '"Don't Trust Anybody, Not Even Us": Kafka's Realism as Anarchist Modernism', *Studies in 20th and 21st Century Literature*, 35.2 (2011), 295–315 (p. 307).
71. Michael G. Levine, '"A Place so Insanely Enchanting": Kafka and the Poetics of Suspension', *Modern Language Notes*, 123.5 (2008), 1039–67 (p. 1044).
72. Joel Morris, 'Josef K.'s (A + x) Problem: Kafka on the Moment of Awakening', *The German Quarterly*, 82.4 (2009), 469–82 (p. 473).
73. Kafka, *Das Schloß*, p. 7.
74. Ibid., p. 7.
75. Ibid., p. 17.
76. Ibid., p. 18.
77. Kafka, *Der Proceß*, p. 88.
78. On childhood in Kafka's works see Ritchie Robertson, 'Kafka, Childhood, and History', *Nexus: Essays in German Jewish Studies*, 4 (2018), 5–22; idem, 'Children and Childhood in Kafka's Work', in *Kafkas 'Betrachtung': Neue Lektüren*, ed. by Carolin Duttlinger (Freiburg im Breisgau: Rombach, 2014), pp. 179–99; and idem, 'Das Bild des Kindes bei Kafka im Lichte von Ellen Keys Das Jahrhundert des Kindes', in *Influx: Der deutsch-skandinavische Kulturaustausch um 1900*, ed. by Søren Fauth and Gísli Magnússon (Würzburg: Königshausen & Neumann, 2014), pp. 217–30.
79. See Kafka, *Das Schloß*, pp. 216, 84, 243.
80. Ibid., p. 36.
81. Friedrich Nietzsche, *Kritische Studienausgabe 1: Die Geburt der Tragödie Unzeitgemäße Betrachtungen I–IV Nachgelassene Schriften 1870–1873*, ed. by Giorgio Colli and Mazzino Montinari (Munich: DTV and Berlin: De Gruyter, 1988), p. 883.
82. Cohn, '"Don't Trust Anybody, Not Even Us"', p. 302.
83. Franz Kafka, *Schriften, Tagebücher, Briefe*, ed. by Hans-Gerd Koch (Frankfurt a.M.: Fischer, 1982–), *Briefe 1913–März 1914*, ed. by Hans-Gerd Koch (2001), p. 205.
84. Ibid., p. 205.
85. Corngold, *Franz Kafka*, p. 295.
86. Theodor W. Adorno, *Prisms*, trans. by Samuel and Shierry Weber (Cambridge, MA: MIT Press edition, 1981), p. 213.
87. Henry James, *Selected Literary Criticism*, ed. by Frank Raymond Leavis (Cambridge: Cambridge University Press, 1963).
88. Ibid., pp. 85–86.
89. See Walker, *The Truth of Realism*, pp. 26–27.
90. Fontane, 'Unsere lyrische und epische Poesie seit 1848', p. 12.
91. Walker, *The Truth of Realism*, p. 3.
92. Fontane, 'Unsere lyrische und epische Poesie seit 1848', p. 13.
93. Friedrich Nietzsche, *Kritische Studienausgabe 3*, p. 626.
94. Ernst Gombrich, *Art and Illusion* (Princeton, NJ: Princeton University Press, 1956), p. 298.
95. Franz Kafka, *Schriften, Tagebücher, Briefe*, ed. by Hans-Gerd Koch (Frankfurt a.M.: Fischer, 1982–), *Nachgelassene Schriften und Fragmente I: Apparatband*, ed. by Malcolm Pasley (1993), p. 196.
96. Ibid., pp. 214–15.
97. Ibid., p. 216.
98. Walter H. Sokel, *The Myth and Power of the Self: Essays on Franz Kafka* (Detroit: Wayne State University Press, 2002), pp. 65–80.
99. Benjamin, 'Franz Kafka: On the Tenth Anniversary of his Death', p. 804.
100. Adorno, *Prisms*, p. 245.

101. See for example Stanley Corngold, *The Commentator's Despair: The Interpretation of Kafka's Metamorphosis* (Port Washington, NY: Kennikat Press, 1974); Horst Steinmetz, *Suspensive Interpretation: Am Beispiel Franz Kafkas* (Göttingen: Vandenhoeck & Ruprecht, 1977).
102. Ritchie Robertson, 'In Search of the Historical Kafka: A Selective Review of Research, 1980–92', *The Modern Language Review*, 89.1 (1994), 107–37 (p. 107).
103. Blanchot, *The Space of Literature*, p. 76.
104. Ernst Bloch, *The Principle of Hope*, I (Cambridge, MA: MIT Press, 1996), pp. 4–5.
105. Bernard Williams, *Truth and Truthfulness* (Princeton: Princeton University Press, 2002), p. 1.
106. Gadamer, *The Relevance of the Beautiful*, ed. by Robert Bernasconi (Cambridge: Cambridge University Press, 1986), pp. 70–71.
107. Robertson, 'Introduction', p. xxv.

CHAPTER 17

Kafka and his Recursors: The Process of Post-Holocaust Authors

Kirstin Gwyer

'Someone must have been spreading rumours about Franz Kafka, for without having done anything wrong, he was proclaimed one fine morning the prophet of the Holocaust.'[1] Lawrence Langer's fittingly intertextual rebuke of an enduring tendency, not only in extra-academic circles, to respond to Kafka's works as if, 'possessed of a fearful premonition', he had, 'to the point of exact detail', seen 'the horror gathering',[2] is irrefutable not least on the grounds that Kafka presumably 'did not have extra-sensory perception' to 'see into the future', a future which, in any case, is mutable and always 'still undecided'.[3] What such responses testify to, as Ritchie Robertson has shown, is that, 'if Kafka seemed so prescient' about the atrocities of the mid-twentieth century, 'the reason lay not in Kafka's prevision of the future but in his perception of his present': 'He had an extraordinary insight into the mechanisms of power, authority, and violence, mechanisms that are in some measure common to a wide variety of social systems.'[4] 'Reinterpreting Kafka in the light of later experience' may thus be a 'perfectly legitimate response', and perhaps it is also simply an inevitable one, but 'appropriating' him by reading 'his imaginative world as an anticipation of the deathcamp universe' at once 'risks distorting Kafka's achievement and obscuring the challenge facing the Holocaust writer in search of [their] own authentic inspiration'.[5] And yet, it is striking not just how many post-Holocaust readers have regarded Kafka as someone 'who proleptically internalized the disaster', but also how many Holocaust writers and, within that category, how many German-Jewish authors who survived the Holocaust, have looked to Kafka's writing in their struggle to develop the 'own authentic inspiration' cited by Langer.[6] Little has been written about such intertextual resort to Kafka by first-generation post-Holocaust authors writing in German, as indeed little has been written about this collective at all.[7] Where recourse to the (generally not closely specified) 'Kafkaesque' in the writing of Holocaust survivors more broadly is discussed, it is attributed to thematic correspondences such as those accounted for by Robertson. Yet however evocative Kafka's ability 'to disclose patterns of oppression and subservience, ultimately underpinned by violence' or his 'visions of persecution and accusation and unexplainable feelings of anxiety' may be to post-

Holocaust writers attempting to give, and post-Holocaust readers attempting to gain, access to a reality that 'turned out to be more grotesque and more surrealistic than even [Kafka's] fictional nightmares', it remains that he was not faced with conveying 'the concrete threat of dehumanized extermination'.[8] Through an outsider's post-Holocaust lens, we might read Kafka's works for their illustrations of 'a sinister proliferation of bureaucratic institutions, both private and governmental, with their burgeoning technological apparatuses', or even as 'literal expressions of the way human life, or perhaps better, "bare life", can, in certain conditions, only be expressed as some form of animal life'.[9] Yet any thematic resemblance can ultimately only ever be on the surface, and passing allusions to Kafkaesque themes or a Kafkaesque style do not seem satisfactorily able to account for the significance he apparently holds for the first generation of Jewish authors attempting to write after and about the Holocaust. My contention here will be that these authors did not primarily look to Kafka's writing for its thematic resonance at all. What they encountered in their engagement with his texts is more structural than thematic or, more precisely, it dissolves the divide between the two. Historian Otto Dov Kulka writes in his Holocaust memoir *Landscapes of the Metropolis of Death* how reading literary or documentary works about the Holocaust makes him feel nothing but 'alienation' because 'I cannot find in them what they seek to convey': 'Between the description of a world' and 'the presence of the past that is perpetually part of my present' there lie 'rivers that cannot be crossed'.[10] Failing to find a gateway to the past in descriptive representations of the concentrationary universe, Kulka turns to Kafka, and specifically to Kafka's parable 'Vor dem Gesetz' from *Der Process* (1914–15), not as a way in but, on the contrary, 'as a way of coming to understand how he [Kulka] can arrive at the "gate" of comprehension but not pass through it'.[11] Kulka was emphatically not alone in this. The range of first-generation post-Holocaust authors who draw on Kafka, and especially on *Der Process*, in a non-thematic, or secondarily thematic, mode in their effort to capture experiences that seem to defy description is striking. A reading of the structural workings of *Der Process* alongside texts by three German-language Jewish authors who survived National Socialist persecution, H. G. Adler (1910–88), Jenny Aloni (1917–93) and Erich Fried (1921–88), will illustrate this and suggest that what speaks to these authors in Kafka's writing is not his imaginative worlds or nightmarish vision as such but the aporias in which his protagonists are caught that make these worlds or visions feel inescapable.[12] These aporias are replicated and perpetuated by the structure of Kafka's writing, much of which, analogous to the model of 'Vor dem Gesetz', takes the form of the irresolvably parabolic and, rather than culminating in conclusive resolution, is shaped by a 'near-nauseating ability to describe infinite regress'.[13] Thus, while the claim that 'Kafka's novels are uncanny premonitions of Auschwitz' is readily refuted at a thematic level, it will be proposed that J. Hillis Miller may be closer to the truth in his suggestion that 'Kafka's work preprograms the form fiction about Auschwitz took'.[14]

Franz Kafka's *Der Process* (1914–1915)

Franz Kafka's *Der Process* starts after an unreconstructable event, a presumed 'Verleumdung', in the aftermath of which the text's protagonist, Josef K., finds himself 'verhaftet'.[15] Though K. feels 'als ob durch die Vorfälle [...] eine große Unordnung [...] verursacht worden sei', he also believes that he will be able to restore order and resume the thread of his existence: 'War aber einmal diese Ordnung hergestellt, dann war jede Spur jener Vorfälle ausgelöscht und alles nahm seinen alten Gang wieder auf' (22). Yet K.'s assumption that he can restore 'Ordnung' is based on a misapprehension of the 'Process' in which he is caught up. His reading of his situation is informed by the belief that he is on trial in a court of law, where the proceedings will establish his guilt or his innocence and he will be handed down a verdict, either an acquittal or a conviction followed by a sentence. In this case, linear progression would be possible, seeing him first admitted to the court, then trialled by the court, and finally dismissed by the court. However, *Der Process* hinges on the ambiguity between K.'s reading and its opposite, in which K. is on trial in some far less linear and concrete sense. In his trial, without due process, the 'Verhandlung' dissolves into endless 'Verhandlungen', in the course of which any 'Urteil' remains provisional opinion, rather than solidifying into a conclusive verdict, leading at best to the illusionary reprieve of a 'scheinbare Freisprechung', which, over time, will simply trigger the next arrest and cause the process to repeat itself, or to the indefinite deferral of a verdict in a 'Verschleppung' (139; 145; 207).

The ambiguity of K.'s 'Process' that turns his trial into inescapable tribulation thematically is reproduced structurally by the text, which also fails to advance as a linear narrative with a beginning, middle and end and 'ultimately undoes the concept of linearity altogether'.[16] Its beginning is a non-beginning not only in the sense that it seems to place us *in medias res*, without any clear indication of what the *res* are, but above all because the 'Verleumdung' that is presumed to have led to K.'s 'Verhaftung' is, in fact, indistinguishable from the 'Process' that follows it. Since the court operates on the presumption of guilt and, once a person is 'angeklagt', is 'von der Schuld des Angeklagten überzeugt', thus paradoxically reducing 'wirkliche Freisprechungen' to the improbable stuff of legends, the untraceable 'Verleumdung' merges seamlessly into the indefinitely deferred 'Verurteilung' (136; 141). Indeed, inasmuch as the terms 'Verleumdung' and 'Verhör' have shared etymological roots in the Indo-European word for 'hören', it could be argued that, through the dual lens of ambiguity, *Der Process* suggests even linguistically that K. has always already been on trial: the distorted perception of 'verleumden' or 'sich verhören' is indistinguishable from the desire to be more clearly informed that nominally underpins a 'Verhör'. This would make K.'s 'Verleumdung' not so much a precipitating event as an ongoing state: a 'Verhaftetsein' as an existential condition that pre-exists the text but also outlasts it, and a life sentence that even death cannot fully remedy. As with the 'Fliegen' that K. pictures in the run-up to his execution 'die mit zerreißenden Beinchen von der Leimrute webstreben', this is not a clean exit: once 'verhaftet', always 'verhaftet', he leaves a sticky residue of 'Scham' behind after he is gone (207). Resolution is deferred, as in a 'Verschleppung'.

Yet the undoing of structural linearity does not stop there. The text's inconclusive ending also enacts the structural approximation of a 'scheinbare Freisprechung' followed by the resumption of the 'Process', by causing the text to loop back on itself to two prior passages in its reference to 'Scham' and its invocation of the 'Hund'. Though there might arguably have been plenty of occasion for K. to experience shame, the only prior reference to it in the text occurs in 'Advokat, Fabrikant, Maler' when he, in a miniature replica of his trial and the novel as a whole, tries but fails to write the definitive petition to submit to the court that might ensure his acquittal, a petition designed to give a conclusive and comprehensive account of his entire life viewed from all aspects. Here, we are told how, even just a week earlier, the thought of submitting such a petition had filled K. with shame, but today, fully immersed in his trial, 'wußte K. nichts mehr von Scham' (115–16).[17] Not only does this textual doubling back on itself mark K.'s death out as a mere 'scheinbare Freisprechung', but it also connects to another prior passage, in 'Kaufmann Block, Kündigung des Advokaten'. K.'s observation in his final moments that he is dying like a dog develops his earlier observation of Block pleading with the lawyer in the presence of Leni. In this passage, Block, apparently more fully entangled in the 'Process' than K. himself at this stage, had, in K.'s eyes, humiliated himself so much that he had become the dog of the court in a way that 'fast den Zuseher entwürdigte' (178). The simple realization that K. is here the next dog in sequence but, through the looping back of the text, also that he was deceiving himself in his earlier belief that he was any less faithfully subservient to the court than Block obviously disrupts the horizontal linear plot progression of the narrative. However, the novel goes further in its undoing of linearity by at the same time extending the sense of having no traceable origin and no reachable end to the text's vertical plane. The use of non-specific masculine nouns and pronouns in the section just cited already points to a confusion of identities that culminates, at least provisionally, at the end of the text in our observation of K.'s canine debasement in death, a debasement which, by analogy to the Block passage, contaminates us, K.'s 'Zuseher' at the close, suggesting that we, too, are in fact always already immersed too deeply to extricate ourselves, even as we hold on to the illusion (as K. does in his use of the term 'fast') that we are still safely separate from the 'Process' of the text.[18] This not only telescopes the text horizontally but vertically, by deconstructing the diegetic ceiling to suggest that, in witnessing K.'s fate, we are already implicated 'wie ein Hund' (and raising the spectre of who, then, may be observing us). The 'Scham' apparently does indeed outlive K. (211). Like him, we find ourselves traduced and arrested.

To the text's rooflessness corresponds a bottomless pit at its heart. Nested at the point where K. feels (and so we feel) he may be on the verge of gaining an insight into his predicament we find not a hearing and verdict but a miniature replica of the text as a whole: the parable 'Vor dem Gesetz'. Reproducing the encounter between K. seeking admittance and the 'Geistlicher' deferring admittance to the court, the parable gives us the 'Mann vom Lande' seeking admittance and the 'unterster Türhüter' deferring it (196–98). As if in an infinity mirror, the doorkeeper is merely the first in a series of receding doorkeepers, while the man from the country is in turn just one of countless supplicants. Neither has access to the scripture of the law. There will always be another supplicant, and there will always be another gate, and the process of seeking admittance in between that non-beginning and that non-end is one of endless deferral, with the object of deferral inaccessible both to the uninitiated, who do not know this, and to the somewhat initiated, who do.

The *mise en abyme* in the text of its own bottomless structure at once illustrates and perpetuates the indefinitely deferred and recursive structure of the 'Process', and of the text that seeks to capture it. As well as reproducing this structure, the stand-off between supplicant and gatekeeper at its abysmal heart is also a replica of the perspectival struggle within the text, and perhaps even, on some unacknowledged level, within K. himself. The encounter between the man who does not know that his admittance to the law is indefinitely deferred and the man who knows this throws into conflict (literally parabolizes) two irreconcilably opposed readings that inform *Der Process* and K.'s more or less conscious understanding of his 'Process'. From the subjunctive of its first line ('ohne daß er etwas Böses getan hätte' (7)) to the subjunctive of its last ('es war, als sollte die Scham ihn überleben' (211)), and from the ambiguity of the titular 'Process' to the 'not-yet'/'nevermore' stand-off at its heart, the novel remains suspended between conflicting perspectives and irreconcilable narrative structures.

In *Der Process*, it is hard to decide to what extent K. allows himself to become aware of the self-deception and suspension of disbelief required of him to read his story as a linear progression towards the restoration of order, even if this restoration of order comes at the cost of removing himself from it. Shortly after the chaplain has recounted the parable, K. senses that 'die einfache Geschichte war unförmlich geworden', though like the 'Schein des Silbers' reflected off the statue of a saint in the cathedral, flashing up fleetingly in the dark without an external source of light to cause this, it is unclear whether this is a glimmer of genuine insight or merely the illusion of illumination (204). In any case, K. immediately experiences the urge to leave these 'ungewohnte Gedankengänge' behind and to 'von sich abschütteln' the disorderly narrative, and moments before his execution, he still wonders where the 'hohes Gericht' must be to which he never penetrated (204; 210–11).

The 'ungewohnte Gedankengänge' into which the parable has led K. reflect, and are reflected in, his labyrinthine surroundings, which in turn act as both emblem and perpetuation of the internal-external confusion produced by the labyrinthine court as a whole and by the text that conveys it (204). They are a model of his world and mind and a blueprint for the text. As with the parable, the key (or non-key) is not in the absent content but in the present structure.

For the first-generation post-Holocaust authors looking to Kafka for a template it is precisely the irremediability of the disruption of an 'einfache Geschichte' by an 'unförmliche' one that appears to have resonated, for its ability to take us to the gate of comprehension but refuse to admit us.

H. G. Adler, *Die unsichtbare Wand* (1954–1961)

H. G. Adler's *Die unsichtbare Wand* starts after an unreconstructable event, an unspecified 'Verfolgung' and 'Unglück', in the aftermath of which the text's protagonist, Artur Landau, finds himself 'verworfen' and his life put on hold.[19] After emigrating from his hometown of Prague to London, Landau believes that he will be able to resume the thread of his existence and take it forward into a better future: 'Fast untergegangen war ich; das galt es wettzumachen. Nun wollte ich mich entfalten' (196; 10). In order to do this, he tells himself that the death blow dealt him by the 'Unglück' is surmountable: 'Die Todeswunde, von der ich nicht genesen war, verleugnete ich oder hielt sie für geheilt' (10). However, something unbroachable and unbreachable lies interspersed 'zwischen der Zeit, da ich war, und der Zeit, da dies nicht mehr zutrifft', and it 'sträubt sich, ein Sagbares zu bilden, verwehrt sich, setzt Grenzen, die nicht überfahren werden dürfen' (54). When the unspeakable 'es' manifests itself in Landau's existence, it is not as past memory but as present-day re-experience, in the form of arbitrarily surfacing, uncontrollable flashes of traumatic reliving that assault Landau out of the blue: 'Ich weiß, daß ich die Verfolgung nicht los werde. Das Ungeheuer springt einem immer auf den Nacken. Aber diese Erfahrung und die Erinnerung sind nicht dasselbe' (196). Because such 'Erfahrung' is inaccessible to willed, conscious recall, Landau is left feeling as if he faces an invisible wall that prevents him from accessing his past and resists any effort to breach it 'bis ich vor ihr ermatte und geschlagen von meinem Vordringen ablasse' (45). Unable to access what lies beyond the wall, Landau cannot restore his past to the order of narrative, which leaves him lastingly unable to overcome the interruption of his existence and restore a sense of linear progression to his life story. Built just for him, the 'unsichtbare Wand' precludes him from having 'Teil an einem Kontinuum', including that of human community, leaving him on his own before his wall: 'Die Wand ist nicht mein Eigentum, aber mir allein ist sie zugehörig, für keinen anderen ist sie erschaffen' (45). The wording points to Kafka's 'Vor dem Gesetz', and like the 'Mann vom Lande', Landau, who even resembles him in appellation, cannot move beyond the wall but nor can he walk away from it.

The intertextual connection to Kafka is also signalled by other thematic means, most notably in the fact that, repeatedly over the course of the text, two men arrive with a coffin and orders to take Landau away to a crematorium for his dead remains to be 'verbrannt' while onlookers from the building opposite are watching the protagonist from their windows (129; 131). On another occasion, the protagonist tries to escape his 'menschliche Gestalt' with its 'leidgeschundenes Dasein, das nicht zu ertragen war' by means of a 'Verwandlung in eine Raupe', only to find that he cannot ever shed his human existence entirely, however depleted it has become (30–31).

At least as much as the thematic analogies, however, it is the structural correspondences in which these are embedded that recall Kafka. Like *Der Process*, *Die unsichtbare Wand* ends on the structural approximation of a 'scheinbare Freisprechung', in a direct address to the protagonist's children, expressing the hope that 'euer Dasein [wird] euch zu einem gewaltigen Fund' (644). It is a hope deferred, projected into the future, and its wording implies that Landau's own 'Dasein', by contrast, has become one of 'Verlust', at once filled with loss and a thing of which he has been deprived, suggesting that his 'Todeswunde' remains unhealed at the close. This impression is further underscored by the fact that the projected hope is framed by the — in a post-Holocaust context inevitably suggestive — image of a 'schwarze Rauchfahne' rising skywards, which is also the image on which the text began (644; 7). As with the 'scheinbare Freisprechung' in Kafka, the lack of true acquittal triggers repetition and causes the narrative to double back on itself.

The same tension between a narrative attempting to establish teleological progression and a counter-narrative working against this and undoing linearity manifests itself repeatedly throughout the text. Whenever Landau is most acutely aware of the wall, when flashbacks to his unreconstitutable past stop him in his tracks and subvert his attempts to write a linear narrative, the text's narrative progression is also arrested. As in Kafka, this disrupts linearity on a vertical, as well as a horizontal, plane. One striking example of this, which, analogous to Kafka's 'Vor dem Gesetz', reads like a miniature replica of Landau's 'Dasein' since the 'Unglück', and of the text's structure as a whole, nested within it, unfolds over a good fifteen pages near the start of the novel (15–32). At the beginning of the passage we are with Landau in his garden in London when the (personified) past catches up with him, reminding him, in direct address, that he has not escaped its clutches, and threatening fresh persecution. This triggers the memory of an earlier incident when Landau, already in exile, had received a summons to report to the immigration authorities. About this memory we are then told the following: on receiving the summons, Landau is terrified that the past is repeating itself and decides to flee the country to return to Prague. On his arrival there, in a sequence of events again reminiscent of Kafka, Landau is denounced, arrested, interrogated and imprisoned, though as in K.'s trial, this is no linear due process, and in response to Landau's question 'Bin ich angeklagt?', he is told: 'Noch nicht. Erst müssen Sie gestehen' (27). He is imprisoned and, as the cell walls begin to close in on him, there follows the sequence where Landau tries to dig his way out, of the cell in the past and the memory flashback in the present, by metamorphosing into a caterpillar. Just as his captors come for him, he abruptly finds himself, covered in soil, back in his garden in London. The entire sequence, which was presented as reminiscence, is retroactively revealed to have been a nightmare. Yet on reading the next sentence, we realize that the garden in which Landau has 'woken up' is not the garden he had left in his flashback or nightmare: 'Mit Entsetzen merkte ich, daß ich zu bald triumphiert hatte, Haus und Garten waren von Polizei umstellt, Gewehre im Anschlag gegen mich gerichtet. Da schrie ich unmenschlich auf, und Johanna schüttelte mich aus dem Traum' (32). At this point, at the very latest, we expect the narrative to pick up back where it left off when it slid into the flashback/nightmare sequence. However, instead of returning to what we assumed was the primary diegetic level of the first garden scene, the narrative returns only to the beginning of the flashback/nightmare sequence. In consequence, we not only lose sight of where recollection ends and nightmare begins, especially since, in terms of their content, the two are indistinguishable, but we lose track of the main diegetic level entirely and, having ended up a level 'down' from where we began, find ourselves drawn into the vortex of the past, and of narrative self-reflexivity, rather than safely separate from it. We cannot be certain if what we have just read was a nightmare within a flashback within the 'reality' of exile, or whether what we read as nightmare is 'reality', which would make the initial escape to the idyll of the garden no less a dream than the second one. As in Kafka, the slippage between diegetic levels causes us to lose our bearings and feel 'verhaftet' too.

Jenny Aloni, *Korridore oder das Gebäude mit der weißen Maus* (1966–1969)

Jenny Aloni's novel *Korridore oder das Gebäude mit der weißen Maus* starts after an unreconstructable event, a 'Vorher' described as a 'verbotenes Gelände' and 'mit Minen besätes Feld', in the aftermath of which the text's protagonist, X., finds himself 'verwundbarer', with his life put on hold.[20] Having believed himself to have left his native country behind, X. is recalled to his former hometown to carry out a cryptic 'Auftrag' that requires him to gain access to a labyrinthine building with the purpose of achieving an unspecified goal in the interest of avenging the past. On his aimless roaming through the many nonsensical and mutable corridors and rooms that constitute the building, X. comes across a court room, where he stops off to observe a trial and what he perceives as a miscarriage of justice, and he has destabilizing encounters with, among others, a woman and an artist. Only ever advancing 'vorläufig zum Ziel', X. loses faith in the objective and achievability of his mission and decides to leave without having accomplished it, but the unsettlingly protean nature of the building draws him further in instead of releasing him (30).

As in *Der Process* and *Die unsichtbare Wand*, the structure of *Korridore* reflects its content. It, too, is modelled on, and incorporates in miniature, structural approximations of both 'scheinbare Freisprechung' and 'Verschleppung', continually doubling back on itself and indefinitely deferring any resolution. In addition to this horizontal disruption of linearity, we find nested within the narrative miniature replicas of the textual edifice as a whole, which in turn recall the structure of X.'s building, and that of the 'Gedankengänge' of his mind. Where Kafka's K. comes up against the gate of the Law and Adler's Landau against his wall, X. encounters, at the abyssal heart of the building and of the novel, a room with a 'Leinwand' (70). Like Landau's 'Wand', X.'s 'Leinwand' turns out to be a gateway to the past, marking at once the closest possible proximity to it and a barrier precluding access. As X. enters the room, a film sequence unfolds on the screen showing the inside of a man's head and, within that, another man who resembles the first one, clad in a black-and-white striped uniform. We are then told that 'he' must have fallen asleep, but what we take to be a reference to X. turns out to be to a boy about whom we cannot initially be sure if he is X. himself as a child, and so it is unclear whether the next section of the text, a sequence of recollections, unfolds on the 'Leinwand' or in X.'s mind, or if there even is a distinction between the two. As in the other novels, we are drawn into the recollective sequence by the blurring of diegetic levels that prevents us from knowing where we as observers are positioned and whether we are separate from the action, seeing what X. is seeing on the 'Leinwand', or whether a slippage has occurred and we have adopted X.'s initial position relative to the man on screen and are seeing directly into the man's mind, as X. was at the outset of the screen sequence. Embedded in this sequence is a further memory strand. This one, belonging to a friend of the boy's, takes us right up to the impenetrable wall within the 'Leinwand', with a recollection set in a concentration camp. It refers to a 'Vollzugskommando', reportedly made up of 'Juden, deren Aufgabe darin besteht, andere Juden nach Vergasung zu verbrennen', before abruptly drawing back out and ending on the idea of seeking vengeance for the past (88). At this point, the initial film sequence terminates, but the projection cuts to a different film sequence, this one of an encounter between a man and a woman, and an instance of failed revenge that reflects X.'s own aborted mission. The 'Leinwand' section finally breaks off in a synopsis of its structure that doubles up as a summary of the text as a whole: 'Hier endete der Film. Nicht endete, brach ab. Er hatte auch den Titel dieses Filmes verpaßt' (91). Unable to gain access to a past known fully only to 'andere Juden', who have not lived to tell the tale, X. is also left without any sense of purpose or direction, unable to progress into the future: 'Er hatte sein Ziel vergessen. Nicht vergessen. Es gab kein Ziel mehr. Es war sinnlos geworden, noch weiterzugehen. Er hätte genauso gut stehen bleiben können' (102). At this moment, the building seemingly releases him, albeit through an 'illegaler Ausgang' (105), and he finds himself outside again. However, the release turns out to be a 'scheinbare Freisprechung' only, and the text ends on another encounter between X. and the woman whom he had met earlier. This repeat encounter causes the narrative to double back to the plotline inside the building, and to drop down its own rabbit hole by also recalling the encounter between a man and a woman that had concluded the film sequence at its abyssal heart, and so calling into question whether the protagonist has left, or can ever really leave, the 'Gebäude' of his 'Gedankengänge' at all (116).

Erich Fried, *Ein Soldat und ein Mädchen* (1946–1960)

Erich Fried's *Ein Soldat und ein Mädchen* starts after an unreconstructable event, an 'Urteilsverkündung' without an 'Urteilsvollstreckung', in the aftermath of which the text's protagonist, the 'Soldat', finds himself 'verloren' and his life put on hold.[21] The titular encounter between the 'girl', a German concentration camp guard on death row after the Belsen trial, and the soldier, a German-Jewish émigré to the United States, who has returned to Germany with the US occupying forces and is one of her guards, ends in a one-night stand between them, followed by the girl's execution the next morning, in the wake of which the soldier suffers a mental breakdown and is admitted to a psychiatric hospital. While at the hospital, the soldier is encouraged to write about what has happened in order to work through it. However, his attempt at narrative processing produces a proliferation of nonsequential and disconnected text fragments that compulsively revolve around aspects of his experiences but fail to come together to form the linear narrative that might enable him to resolve the question posed in the final fragment of how to 'mein Weiterleben berechnen, das nach einer Hinrichtung eine Richtung sucht' (223). Though the text does not spell this out, the implication is that the soldier cannot achieve this calculation and resume the thread of his life story because, in incessantly revisiting his encounter with Helga under the shadow of the 'über ihr hängenden Todesurteil', he is in fact not returning to the true source of his trauma but merely to a screen memory covering the much more pernicious original German–Jewish encounter with a fatal outcome that was the Holocaust (42). Claiming his entire family but sparing him, it is his own death sentence, the pronouncement of which is followed by the indefinite deferral of its execution, that has left him feeling unable to find 'einen neuen *modus vivendi*' (231; 176). But because this original experience of having to navigate a 'Weiterleben nach Eintritt einer Katastrophe' is inaccessible to the soldier's conscious and deliberate recall, it remains unnarrativized and he, like the protagonists of so many of his text fragments, remains 'im Schatten des Urteils' (180; 218). Rather than as an 'unsichtbare Wand', or a 'Leinwand', the gateway taking the soldier close to, but not into, the past is figured as a 'toter Winkel', the blind spot at the parapet of a trench that cannot be seen, or penetrated by one's own projectiles, even as it stands in immediate proximity to the armaments and their deadly fire (e.g. 39). The image illustrates both the soldier's existence under the gaze of death and his inability to access the full truth of what has happened by representing the unbreachable barrier 'wenn einer schon ganz nah is' bei seiner eigenen Wahrheit, aber er will nicht oder er kann nicht und sagt dafür was anderes!' (13).

Like Adler's and Aloni's, Fried's novel contains numerous thematic intertextual references to Kafka, including allusions to the desperate mouse in an impasse of Kafka's 'Kleine Fabel' and a reworking of, among others, his short story 'Die Wahrheit über Sancho Pansa'. However, as the narrator acknowledges with reference to the structure of one of the soldier's narrative fragments, though the comment could just as easily be applied to the text as a whole, it is also the case that: 'Die Form ist sichtlich von Kafka beinflußt' (170). Fried's novel is reported by two voices, the soldier's own and that of a third-person narrator who is tasked with putting the soldier's disjointed fragments into some sort of order and offering a running commentary and exegesis of sorts. Yet from the outset, the narrator not only actively resists imposing narrative order but deliberately paraphrases the soldier's already periphrastic fragments further still to make them more impenetrable, openly acknowledging his inability 'aus einer wirklichen Begebenheit eine wahre Geschichte zu machen' and concluding that there will be 'keinen Weg durch das Geschehene hindurch' and that the soldier is therefore unlikely to be able to 'verwinden' what has happened (7; 64; 231).

The struggle to liberate oneself through narrative is also picked up in the soldier's fragment that offers an intertextual response to Kafka's 'Die Wahrheit über Sancho Pansa' (171–73). In Kafka's version, Sancho Panza is able to banish his demon, Don Quixote, by having his exploits turned into the stuff of fiction and thus neutralized.

In Fried's version, however, the soldier's narrative fragment that counters Kafka with the 'Wahrheit über Don Quijote' sees Don Quixote try to administer the same treatment to his shadow, which follows him around like one of the horsemen of the Apocalypse, but Fried's harbinger of death resists being exorcized, and his Don Quixote's attempt to banish his sidekick through narrative fails to rid him of the pall hanging over him. Like Fried's Don Quixote and his shadow, and like Kafka's 'Mann vom Lande' and his 'Türhüter', the soldier and his narrator remain locked in a stand-off. Unable to gain admittance to the 'toter Winkel' of the past but also unable to move away, they, figuratively speaking, stay at their post like 'zwei Spiegel im Londoner Nebel, einander gegenübergestellt, und eine unendliche Reihe wechselseitiger Bespiegelungen, während sie langsam erblinden' (14).

This stand-off is also enacted structurally across the text, as well as repeatedly reproduced in miniature in its fragments. Perhaps the most striking example of such *mise en abyme* occurs at the heart of the work, at the point where the narrator takes us up to the moment of Helga's execution and breaks off to insert the soldier's own aborted account thereof, in a passage which reads like a further structural approximation of 'Vor dem Gesetz' and an icon of the soldier's suspended existence in the wake of the Holocaust and, by extension, of Fried's novel as a whole (54). Like the narrator's account, the soldier's embedded description of Helga's last morning proceeds in linear fashion up to the point of the execution but then breaks off and is reversed like a 'Film beim Aufspulen' (73). Just as the progressive account that preceded it stopped short of describing the actual execution, the retrogressive sequence stops short of the pronouncement of the death sentence. By failing both to trace its steps back to the original life-suspending trauma and to reach its completion in death, the passage initiates an (in theory) perpetually mobile process of toing and froing like the pendulum of a clock (55). At the same time, the disruption of the text's linear progression is extended to the vertical plane. The diegetic levels of the text are already blurred and rendered seemingly open-ended in an upwardly mobile sense by the serial embedding of the film scene within the soldier's account, within the narrator's account, within a multiply layered authorial frame consisting of a prologue and glossed intertextual epigraph and an annotated double epilogue. Meanwhile, the oscillating film sequence makes the core of the text appear as a bottomless pit, in that where we would expect to encounter the moment of execution, we find instead a reference to an unspecified 'man' observing the scene through binoculars, holding them first the right way round, then in reverse. However, the 'man' is then also used to refer to what the binoculars observe. This use of the impersonal pronoun for both the holder of the binoculars and the object they behold enacts a blurring of diegetic levels at the novel's heart by obscuring whether the reader is the subject or the object of the gaze and suggesting that deeper levels of the text will only ever produce further observers without ever homing in on the object of observation itself. The novel as a whole reads like a 'toter Winkel' that can never be fully accessed and from which there can be no emerging.

H. G. Adler, *Theresienstadt 1941–1945: Das Antlitz einer Zwangsgemeinschaft* (1945–1948)

In each of the post-Holocaust primary texts examined here, we have encountered notably similar structural features that recall crucial recurring elements of Kafka's writing, as modelled by the irresolvably parabolic form of 'Vor dem Gesetz' (and of *Der Process* as a whole). Two contending voices (one implying the possibility of resolution, the other indefinitely deferring it) are placed into conflict and cause the text to be suspended between different readings of its own process: the teleological reading in which resolution and closure would be conceivable, and the non-linear, non-progressive one that, in looping back on itself and sliding up and down diegetic levels, precludes linear progression in any sense and direction and indefinitely defers its conclusion. Yet none of these formal echoes of Kafka lead straightforwardly back to the Kafkaesque qualities conventionally invoked in the context of his purportedly prophetic capacity, his vision of institutions or mechanisms of power and violence contemporary or future. So what do authors in this first generation of Jewish post-Holocaust literature gain from their intertextual recourse to Kafka's writing beyond an overlap in content, however present such thematic resonances may also be? By way of an answer, I shall close with a final example of a text constructed around the same irresolvable structural conflict that informs 'Vor dem Gesetz' and the other post-Holocaust works already discussed. In this concluding analysis of an author cribbing Kafka, I am returning to the beginning of this piece, to H. G. Adler, this time not as a writer of fiction but as the author of what to this day remains the most comprehensive academic study of any single concentration camp: his *Theresienstadt 1941–1945: Das Antlitz einer Zwangsgemeinschaft*, an academic monograph on the history of the Theresienstadt ghetto and a sociological and psychological analysis of the camp.[22]

Theresienstadt 1941–1945 was written in the aftermath of the 'abgründiges Unglück' of the Holocaust (xxi). Its author, Adler, describes himself as 'vorangetrieben im Auftrag' (685), and the explicit aim of the study is, as one would expect of a project of this nature, to offer a 'precise depiction of historical reality', as Adler's son, Jeremy Adler, summarizes in his afterword to the English translation.[23] Adler himself stresses the breadth, depth and comprehensiveness to which his 'weit ausholende Monographie' aspires (xiv). Even just on the first page of his preface for the revised edition, Adler's use of terms such as 'Materialsammlung', 'Übersicht', 'Darstellung', 'geklärt', 'beleuchtet' or 'Dokumentation' clearly gestures towards the potential ideal of a near-encyclopaedic account in which the 'innere Geschichte des Lagers' will become 'in fast mikroskopischer Betrachtung vieler Einzelheiten darstellbar', and Adler's stated intention is for this 'Betrachtung' to be as 'lückenlos' as possible (xi; xiii). For broad stretches of the text, this aim is achieved to a remarkable degree. However, there is a moment in even this most encompassing and scientifically rigorous of reports where the linear progression of the report is disrupted and the entire work briefly hovers on the brink of its own deconstruction. When Adler reaches the indescribable heart of his study, in a chapter titled 'Verfall und Auflösung', which concludes the section detailing the camp's history and attempts to convey the dissolution of all structure and points of reference in the final weeks of Theresienstadt in April of 1945, the attempt to communicate the full extent of the 'Zernichtung' (sic), the 'Ende als Untergang', the 'Nichts' sees Adler's narrative voice split in two as the scientific rigour of his project comes up against the brick wall of its limitations (213, 212):

> Wer [...] durch diese letzte Verzweiflung, durch die Nacht der Nächte, durch den namenlosen Untergang geschritten ist, ihn überdauert hat [...], der soll seine Stimme erheben und sagen, wie es wirklich war. Er soll die Wirklichkeit verkünden [...], jenseits von allem theatralischen Grauen noch lebender Verwesung und toter Knochenberge, die nichts von der inneren Wahrheit enthüllen, da sie nur Schandmäler sind, aber nicht die Wahrheit selbst. Nein, die Wirklichkeit gilt es zu nennen [...], die Wirklichkeit des *Nichts*, die weder denkbar noch nachfühlbar ist, denn nicht zu denken und nicht zu fühlen ist das Nichts, nur ungeschaffen ist es [...] zu leiden. (212–13)

One voice continues to endorse the possibility of emerging from the 'Untergang' to give a full and truthful account of it ('die Wirklichkeit verkünden') (213). The other, always still 'umringt' by the 'unversöhnlicher Abgrund', recognizes what is at stake ('die Wirklichkeit gilt es zu nennen') but dismisses this as a possibility by invoking the essentially unknowable formless void of the 'Nichts' whose inner truth cannot be communicated, conceptualized, or empathetically accessed ('die Wirklichkeit, die weder denkbar noch nachfühlbar ist') but only experienced as raw, unformed suffering ('nur ungeschaffen ist es [...] zu leiden') (212; 213). The contention of narrative voices marks another stand-off akin to that between Kafka's Josef K., seeking access to something that lies beyond an invisible barrier, and his gatekeeper, who obstructs K.'s passage even as he seems to acknowledge his claim. The text's linearity is disrupted and it ceases to progress as it reaches an aporia that cannot be resolved, merely sidestepped, as Adler the historian briefly falls silent and hands over his narrative, in the form of citation, to a third-party eye-witness account, and only resumes his own account in the study's next section (213–14). Though nothing in the excerpt itself points explicitly to a formal correspondence to Kafka, Adler refers to the work as a whole as a 'Kafka Roman mit umgekehrten Vorzeichen', so an account that has been 'der Wirklichkeit nachgeschrieben' and whose facts are worse than fiction, not the other way round, reproducing, rather than anticipating, a reality more unspeakable than anything conjured up by the imagination.[24] Moreover, the monograph's historical section, which concludes with the chapter containing the excerpt, is prefaced with an epigraph drawn from Kafka's 'Ein Landarzt': 'Betrogen! Betrogen! Einmal dem Fehlläuten der Nachtglocke gefolgt — es ist niemals gutzumachen' (1). The use of the Kafka quotation at the outset raises a spectral counterpart to Adler the witness and historian who feels 'vorangetrieben im Auftrag' (685). It seems to acknowledge the otherwise unspoken fear that the part of Adler that hopes for 'Rettung' may just be deluding itself, and that the country doctor's concluding assessment of his own situation, though not cited, may be closer to the truth where Adler himself and his undertaking are concerned also: 'Niemals komme ich so nach Hause [...]. Nackt, dem Froste dieses unglückseligsten Zeitalters ausgesetzt [...], treibe ich mich alter Mann umher.'[25]

Thus the spectre of a survivor adrift, unable to navigate his life or his text in any straightforward sense that would allow him to return to the past to master it and achieve 'Rettung', haunts the historical section of the monograph from before its beginning to beyond its therefore impossible closure in the self-undermining contention between the voice that demands 'Wirklichkeit' and seeks progress and that which disputes its very possibility. In the context of Holocaust representation, these vying voices between them evoke what Raymond Federman has referred to as the simultaneous 'necessity' and 'impossibility' of speaking or writing about the Shoah:

> It is necessary to speak, to write [...] about the Jewish Holocaust during the Nazi period even if words cannot express this monstrous event. It is impossible to speak or write about the Holocaust because words cannot express this monstrous event.[26]

Lawrence Langer has identified this contention between a voice of continuity — which seeks to embed what has happened in a sequence of cause and effect — and a voice of disruption — which undermines any chronology and causality and disputes all rhyme or reason — as a fundamental recurring characteristic of oral Holocaust witness testimonies. However, it is a feature that can affect any attempt in any genre to give a chronological, factual account of the events and effects of the Holocaust.[27] Between them, the vying voices give the impression of the witness inhabiting two worlds at the same time: a life after the abyss, and one in which the 'Abgrund' is still and always all around. Unable to return to the origin of the trauma, and therefore unable to work through and emerge at the other end of it, the narrators in and of the abyss remain caught in a repeated doubling back over old ground with no closure in sight. Without either ingress or egress, there remains only infinite regress.

This, it seems, is the self-deconstructing structure for which Kafka's irresolvable parabolic models, informed by irreconcilably opposed perspectives and composed of interminable 'scheinbare Freisprechungen' and 'Verschleppung', have provided a template. As another of Kafka's recursors, Jacques Derrida, recognized, and demonstrated in his own reading of Kafka's 'Vor dem Gesetz' as a 'living illustration of *différance*', Kafka's parable can be read as an instantiation of the spatial difference and temporal deferral that indicates the unreachability of the signified, which in the case of the authors discussed here is the Holocaust and their own singular experience, or non-experience, of it.[28] As it did for Derrida, the model of 'Vor dem Gesetz' appears to have provided his Jewish post-Holocaust emulators with a way of thinking and performing this unreachability, and so of thinking and performing their own aporia, through indefinite recursion, as the closest possible approach to communicating the abyss of the past without falling in or falling silent. To return to Robert Eaglestone's assessment of Otto Dov Kulka's interest in Kafka, it presents them with a model for how they might 'arrive at the "gate" of comprehension but not pass through it'.[29]

Reading these post-Holocaust authors for the structural correspondences between their work and Kafka's helps unlock a body of writing the key to whose understanding resides not in its anyway only partially speakable content but in its self-deconstructing forms. Yet at the same time, such a reading also illustrates the extent to which, as Jorge Luis Borges playfully proposes, again with reference to Kafka, authors (and readers) create their own precursors.[30] Observing Kafka's post-Holocaust recursors from this perspective, especially when we do so through the lens of gatekeepers preceding us such as Derrida, may therefore also shine a more differentiated light on what makes Kafka feel so 'Kafkaesque' to us in the 'Froste' of an 'unglückseligsten Zeitalters' which he himself only narrowly avoided witnessing. In this post-Holocaust age, perceptions of Kafkaesqueness may have less to do with what he wrote about than with the ways in which he wrote it in more general terms. The sense of coming 'after', but never really after, an irretrievable but therefore also insurmountable breach can be argued to have informed, more or less consciously, every work of cultural theory or critical analysis responding directly or indirectly to the traumatic upheavals of the twentieth and twenty-first centuries, and particularly the Holocaust, from deconstruction to trauma theory to all recent forms of individual or collective memory theory. All seem founded on the perception of a 'common pattern' in which 'a disaster occurs of overwhelming, disorienting magnitude, and yet the world continues', but existing structures of thought and language have been shattered in ways that 'effect their own erasures from memory' and can only be 'reconstructed by means of their traces, remains, survivors, and ghosts: their symptoms'.[31] Even works of cultural theory that appear to deal with epistemological or economic developments rather than social or political trauma may exhibit these features, as James Berger has proposed with regard to 'theories of the modern by Foucault and of the postmodern by Lyotard, Baudrillard, and Jameson', all of which 'take as their starting point some cataclysmic and irrevocable shattering or flattening or decentering that infiltrates and rearticulates all areas of culture', moving them to 'diagnose a post-apocalyptic condition'.[32] Against this backdrop of an in any sense of the word unrecoverable apocalypse, a reading of Kafka as a preprogrammer of form, rather than a predictor of content, appears to have more general validity. To both his post-Holocaust recursors and to their recursors in turn he offers the anti-model of the 'unförmliche Geschichte' as the least inadequate approach to thinking and writing 'after' the 'Nichts' that is 'nur ungeschaffen [...] zu leiden'.[33]

Notes to Chapter 17

It feels entirely appropriate that this essay should engage with the idea of following in others' footsteps. I am indebted to a range of precursors of my own, with Ritchie Robertson chief among them, and while I may not be able to pay back that debt of gratitude, I feel privileged to be carrying some of it forward. The thinking behind this piece is informed by discussions with my own students, in particular this year's takers of the German-Jewish Literature since 1945 Special Subject and of Kafka as a Special Author, and I gratefully acknowledge the input of Katie Baxter (Lincoln), Freddie Cheatle (Merton), Susie Dunn (Jesus), Juliet Gurassa (Lincoln), Jasper Manzini (Oriel), Josh Penollar (Brasenose), and Will Sealy (Wadham).

1. Lawrence L. Langer, *Admitting the Holocaust* (New York, Oxford: Oxford University Press, 1996), p. 109.

2. George Steiner, *Language and Silence: Essays on Language, Literature, and the Inhuman* (1967) (New Haven and London: Yale University Press, 1998), p. 121.
3. Ritchie Robertson, 'Kafka, Goffman, and the Total Institution', in *Kafka for the Twenty-First Century*, ed. by Stanley Corngold and Ruth Gross (Rochester, NY: Camden House, 2015), pp. 136–50 (p. 136).
4. Ibid., p. 137.
5. Langer, *Admitting the Holocaust*, pp. 109, 110.
6. Michael Rothberg, *Traumatic Realism: The Demands of Holocaust Representation* (Minneapolis and London: University of Minnesota Press, 2000), p. 40; Langer, p. 110.
7. Cf. also Kirstin Gwyer, *Encrypting the Past: The German-Jewish Holocaust Novel of the First Generation* (Oxford: Oxford University Press, 2014), pp. 1–56.
8. Robertson, p. 140; Gershon Shaked, *The Shadows Within: Essays on Modern Jewish Writers* (Philadelphia: Jewish Publication Society, 1987), p. 17; Lawrence Langer, *The Holocaust and the Literary Imagination* (New Haven and London: Yale University Press, 1975), p. 21.
9. J. Hillis Miller, *The Conflagration of Community: Fiction before and after Auschwitz* (Chicago, IL and London: University of Chicago Press, 2011), pp. 42, 51.
10. Otto Dov Kulka, *Landscapes of the Metropolis of Death* (London: Penguin, 2020), p. 80. I am grateful to Robert Eaglestone, who comments on this same passage in *The Broken Voice: Reading Post-Holocaust Literature* (Oxford: Oxford University Press, 2017), p. 93, for drawing my attention to Kulka's memoir.
11. Eaglestone, *The Broken Voice*, p. 93.
12. These three examples were chosen because their intertextual connection to Kafka is also evident at a thematic level, but they were drawn from a broad range of first-generation German-Jewish texts with demonstrable ties to Kafka and notably similar narrative strategies, including Ilse Aichinger, Elisabeth Augustin, Wolfgang Hildesheimer and Gertrud Kolmar.
13. Jason Baker, 'Introduction', in Franz Kafka, *The Metamorphosis and Other Stories*, trans. by Donna Freed (New York: Barnes & Noble, 2003), pp. i–xxxi (p. ii). See also Gerhard Neumann, 'Umkehrung und Ablenkung: Franz Kafkas "Gleitendes Paradox"', *Deutsche Vierteljahrsschrift für Literaturwissenschaft und Geistesgeschichte*, 42 (1968), 702–44, for an important earlier assessment of the significance of recursive structures in Kafka.
14. Miller, pp. 50; 39.
15. Franz Kafka, *Der Proceß* (1925) (Stuttgart: Reclam, 2007), p. 7. Further references to this edition will be included in parentheses in the text.
16. Joshua Kavaloski, '*Fabula interrupta*: The Rupture of Narrative and the Arrest of Time in Franz Kafka's *Der Proceß*', *Modern Austrian Literature*, 36 (2003), 39–57 (p. 41).
17. Joshua Kavaloski picks up on this prior invocation of 'Scham' also, though his interpretation from the passage differs from mine. See ibid., pp. 50–51.
18. For instance: 'Das war kein Klient mehr, das war der Hund des Advokaten. Hätte ihm dieser befohlen, unter das Bett wie in eine Hundehütte zu kriechen und von dort aus zu bellen, er hätte es mit Lust getan' (p. 178).
19. H. G. Adler, *Die unsichtbare Wand* (Vienna: Zsolnay, 1989), pp. 54, 268. Further references to this edition will be included in parentheses in the text.
20. Jenny Aloni, *Gesammelte Werke in Einzelausgaben*, ed. by Friedrich Kienecker and Hartmut Steinecke, 10 vols (Paderborn: Schöningh, 1990–97), VIII: *Korridore oder das Gebäude mit der weißen Maus* (1996), pp. 60–61; 13. Further references to this edition will be included in parentheses in the text.
21. Erich Fried, *Ein Soldat und ein Mädchen* (1960) (Düsseldorf: Claassen, 1982), pp. 218; 28. Further references to this edition will be included in parentheses in the text.
22. H. G. Adler, *Theresienstadt 1941–1945: Das Antlitz einer Zwangsgemeinschaft (Geschichte, Soziologie, Psychologie)* (1955; rev. edn, 1960) (Göttingen: Wallstein, 2005). Further references to this edition will be included in parentheses in the text.
23. Jeremy Adler, 'Afterword', in H. G. Adler, *Theresienstadt 1941–45: The Face of a Coerced Community*, trans. by Belinda Cooper (New York: Cambridge University Press, 2017), pp. 803–28 (p. 812).
24. Cited ibid., p. 906.

25. Franz Kafka, 'Ein Landarzt', in Kafka, *Erzählungen* (Stuttgart: Reclam, 1995), pp. 168–74 (p. 174).
26. Raymond Federman, 'The Necessity and Impossibility of Being a Jewish Writer' (2001), <http://www.federman.com/rfsrcro.htm> (para. 1 of 30). [accessed 19 March 2021].
27. See for instance Langer, *Holocaust Testimonies: The Ruins of Memory* (New Haven: Yale University Press, 1991).
28. Geoffrey L. Brackett, 'Franz Kafka's "Before the Law": A Parable', *Pace Law Review*, 35.4 (2015), 1107–23 (1108).
29. Eaglestone, *The Broken Voice*, p. 93.
30. Jorge Luis Borges, *Labyrinths*, trans. by Donald Yates and James Irby (1962) (Harmondsworth: Penguin, 2000), p. 236.
31. James Berger, *After the End: Representations of Post-Apocalypse* (Minneapolis: University of Minnesota Press, 1999), pp. 6, 19. For further compelling explorations of the relationship between the Holocaust and the postmodern, see also Dominick LaCapra, *Writing History, Writing Trauma* (Baltimore: Johns Hopkins University Press, 2001); Robert Eaglestone, *The Holocaust and the Postmodern* (Oxford: Oxford University Press, 2004); Colin Davis, *Haunted Subjects: Deconstruction, Psychoanalysis and the Return of the Dead* (Basingstoke: Palgrave Macmillan, 2007).
32. Berger, p. 31.
33. Kafka, *Der Proceß*, p. 204; Adler, *Theresienstadt*, p. 213.

CHAPTER 18

Stefan Zweig's Translations of French Poetry

Robert Vilain

The editor of Stefan Zweig's translations of French-language poetry in the *Rhythmen* volume of his *Gesammelte Werke in Einzelbänden* asserts, without any supporting detail, 'Kritiker haben befunden, Stefan Zweig habe mit seinen lyrischen Nachdichtungen eine höhere Stufe poetischer Kunst erreicht als mit seinen eigenen Versen.'[1] Walter Benjamin was deeply unimpressed by Zweig as a translator, however, suggesting in a letter to Gershom Scholem of 7 July 1924 that Zweig's 1908 volume of Baudelaire was 'die drittschlechteste deutsche Baudelaire-Übersetzung'.[2] Benjamin had remarked sardonically in an earlier letter that he kept Zweig's translations 'im Giftschrank meiner Bibliothek geborgen'.[3] As one might expect, however, there is greater complexity to be uncovered than is conveyed by these polarized views — and it helps to know that Benjamin was writing in the wake of a savage review by Zweig in the *Frankfurter Zeitung* for 1 June 1924 of his own 1923 translation of Baudelaire's *Tableaux parisiens*. This essay is concerned less with overarching value judgements of that kind, however, than with at least partially making good lacunae in the secondary literature on Zweig by investigating some of the translations themselves and interrogating them for what they reveal about Zweig's implicit poetics of translation.[4] It aims to demonstrate how blind spots in his appreciation of post-Parnassian aesthetics render most of his translations unsatisfactory, and how his misreadings of French poets help explain weaknesses in his own verse.[5] Whilst it relies on detailed comparisons between Zweig's German versions and the French originals, it uses these to reach beyond quibbles about individual features that may or may not have been 'lost in translation' to show how the consistency with which certain choices have been made amounts to unconscious 'policy decisions' that themselves reflect Zweig's understanding of what poetry is and how it works.

Zweig did not expound his understanding of translation in any systematic way; nor did he develop a theory of translation. His views or presuppositions emerge from essays and correspondence and have to be pieced together. Core terminology varies without an obvious rationale: in *Die Welt von Gestern*, Zweig exclusively uses the term 'übertragen', but earlier he often preferred 'nachdichten'; in the foreword to *Gedichte von Paul Verlaine* he uses 'Übersetz[ungen]' and 'Übertragungen' as well as 'Nachdichtungen', and in his correspondence with Verhaeren 'Rekreation' and the phrase 'poetische Transposition' also occur.[6] Some of Zweig's underlying assumptions were articulated very early in his career in a letter to Ludwig Jacobowski in which he wrote of his desire 'dem Volke einen Band Übersetzungen aus allen Sprachen zu bringen'. He saw this as a public service, making it possible for Burns to become a German folksong, for Béranger to be known for more than just his *Sprüche*, or for Ada Negri (an Italian working-class poet) to provide inspiration for the German factory worker.[7] Zweig was thus nothing if not eclectic in his aims for what is, in this vision, a form of cultural appropriation via translation — translation had a function for its target culture. He was ambitious, too, writing of the translator as enabling an 'Ausblick auf ein stärkstes zeitgenössisches Empfinden, Botschaft, die nicht mehr an einzelne, sondern an eine Generation sich wendet'.[8] But he also frequently referred to himself as the humble servant of the authors he translated, and to how mediating their work was an act of homage. In *Die Welt von Gestern* he wrote of his decision to 'serve' Verhaeren via translation, in the expectation that his own literary work would be interrupted for two or three years. His reflection on this decision and its ultimately positive potential for his creativity is intense:

> Aber indem ich mich entschloß, meine ganze Kraft, Zeit und Leidenschaft dem Dienst an einem fremden Werke zu geben, gab ich mir selbst das Beste: eine moralische Aufgabe. Mein ungewisses Suchen und Versuchen hatte jetzt einen Sinn. Und wenn ich heute einen jungen Schriftsteller beraten sollte, der noch seines Weges ungewiß ist, würde ich ihn zu bestimmen suchen, zuerst einem größeren Werke als Darsteller oder Übertragender zu dienen. In allem aufopfernden Dienen ist für einen Beginnenden mehr Sicherheit als im eigenen Schaffen.[9]

The foreword to the 1904 edition of Verhaeren articulates his aims in cognate terms: 'alle Eigenheit Verhaerens in deutscher Sprache bewusst werden zu lassen und sich so unter Preisgebung eigenpersönlicher Gestaltung in dem mächtigen Werke restlos zu lösen'.[10]

Roman Reisinger summarizes this idealistic perspective, quoting Zweig's own essay on German versions of Walt Whitman from 1922:

> Übersetzen erscheint hier als ein Akt der Demut, der Anerkennung des Werks eines anderen Bewunderten, als eine Geste der Würdigung, was nicht heißt, in passiver Bewunderung zu erstarren, sondern den Vorgang, die Herausforderung der Übersetzung, als Berauschung zu erleben: '[S]o scheint einem dies eigen Bewußte in einem panischen Taumel zu entschwinden; man rauscht selbst hinein, weggerissen von den rauschenden Kaskaden dieser Ströme'.[11]

The quotation from Zweig above in fact refers to the experience of *reading* Whitman rather than to *translating* Whitman, but the essay does reflect some of the assumptions that Zweig makes as a translator, for he praises Hans Reisiger because his edition 'stellt nur dar, ohne zu übertreiben, ohne zu umschreiben', and eschews 'modisch[e] Versuche, einen Menschheitsdichter rasch in eine neue Religiosität umzuschwindeln'.[12] Imposing a transient interpretative trend is not the task of the translator any more than exaggeration or paraphrase are appropriate. The familiar idea of 'fidelity' is present here, *ex negativo*, in Zweig's use of the verb 'schwindeln', and *ex positivo* in his use of 'wiedergeben', 'ummodellieren' and 'nachbilden'. In his 1900 review of Otto Hauser's Verlaine translations Zweig had also raised explicitly the issue of how closely one should try to adhere to the formal properties of an original, criticizing Hauser because in making that attempt he loses something more fundamental: '[Hauser] bietet uns sorgfältige, schöne Verse, stimmungsvolle Gedichte, die aber im Grundtone von dem Originale um so mehr abweichen, je sclavischer sie sich an Form und Wort halten'.[13] But 'das Prinzip der getreuen Anpassung an die Form' is one of the criteria he claims were used for selecting the versions in *Gedichte von Paul Verlaine* (p. 21). It is hardly possible to distil from inconsistent references like these anything approaching an 'Übersetzungspoetik', but a strong tendency towards the prioritization of the character and personality of the author is nonetheless discernible, and only scant attention is paid to the role of the very medium of poetry, the language(s) in which it is written.

Zweig began publishing his translations of French-language poetry in 1900 with five poems by the prolific Parnassian Paul-Armand Silvestre.[14] In the same year he attempted a more famous poet, and even though he only translated one of his poems, Arthur Rimbaud came to fascinate Zweig. He must have discussed him with Verhaeren, since his visits to the Belgian poet were commemorated with the gift in 1908 of a very rare copy of the original 1873 edition of *Une Saison en enfer*.[15] Early in 1901, Zweig tried his hand at Verlaine, of whose poems he published eight (or possibly nine) translations: three first appeared in journals,[16] the others in the two selections from Verlaine that Zweig edited in 1902 and 1922.[17] Between these volumes he co-translated an edition of Baudelaire with thirty-eight versions by himself, some of which he also contributed to an anthology two decades later.[18] Zweig's translations of the Belgian poet and dramatist Emile Verhaeren began in the summer of 1902, resulting in the appearance of a selection of his versions in a small luxury edition in 1904 (illustrated by the influential neo-impressionist artist Théo van Rysselberghe); this was expanded significantly for a volume published by Insel in 1910.[19] Another selection under the title *Hymnen an das Leben* appeared in several editions from 1912, with print-runs of tens of thousands of copies. The two became close friends, although their relationship was upset by Verhaeren's decline into outspoken patriotism at the outbreak of the First World War.[20]

These translations of nineteenth- and early twentieth-century French-language poetry are routinely mentioned in accounts of Zweig's life and career but have received little detailed critical attention.[21] They are usually compared with his own early verse, which sat firmly in the shadow of the French nineteenth-century tradition. Zweig began publishing poetry as a very young man, and the editors of his letters surmise that 'Impressions musicales', a poem in German published in *Die Gesellschaft* in 1896 by one 'Ewald Berger', is in fact by the fifteen-year-old Zweig. His first original collection, *Silberne Saiten*, appeared in the spring of 1901 with Schuster & Loeffler in Berlin, a publisher that had acceded to Zweig's demands for an artistically suitable presentation of his carefully crafted aestheticist verse.[22] Critics praised the delicacy of the verse, hearing 'die leisesten Empfindungstöne in ihr anklingen',[23] and reviews regularly singled out how remarkably melodious the verse was, accepting that this was poetry in the vein of the French Symbolists, for whom

Verlaine's dictum from 'Art Poétique' in *Jadis et Naguère* — 'de la musique avant toute chose' — was a defining characteristic.[24] The subject matter, imagery and moods owe much to French Symbolism: longing, isolation, intuition, confession, introversion, transience, the transitional time of dusk, shadows, intimations of death, faded colours, seductive music — all are present throughout the collection. Clusters of images in these poems seem to emerge directly from Verlaine's *Poèmes saturniens* or *Romances sans paroles*, sometimes probably mediated by Hofmannsthal.[25] Zweig himself quickly recognized the shortcomings of the poems, later calling them 'gutes, geschicktes, zum Teil sogar bemerkenswertes Kunsthandwerk, entstanden aus einer ehrgeizigen Spielfreude an der Form, aber unecht in ihrer Sentimentalität' (*WvG*, p. 144). He refused to republish them:

> Wie ich bald selbst über diese frühen Verse dachte, ist durch die einfache Tatsache bezeugt, daß ich nicht nur diese Silberne Saiten [...] nicht mehr neu drucken, sondern kein einziges Gedicht daraus in meine 'Gesammelten Gedichte' aufnehmen ließ. Es waren Verse unbestimmter Vorahnung und unbewußten Nachfühlens, nicht aus eigenem Erlebnis entstanden, sondern aus sprachlicher Leidenschaft. (*WvG*, p. 122)

The reason that Zweig gives in his memoir for consigning this early verse to the past seems like an uncontroversial preference for poetry 'aus eigenem Erlebnis' over poetry motivated by 'sprachliche Leidenschaft', but it masks important presuppositions about the nature of poetry that directly affected his translations. Zweig tried to read French symbolist poetry as directly articulating an 'eigenes Erlebnis' that is surely absent, and almost entirely neglected the linguistic constructedness of whatever experiences the verse conveys or creates. Consideration of Zweig's essays on each writer makes this abundantly clear. In the introduction to a collection of Verlaine's translations, Zweig gives a vigorous defence of great art as 'nicht Abziehen und Entfernen vom Leben, sondern ein Weiterschreiten von eigener Wirklichkeit zu neuen fremden und höheren Wirklichkeiten', and of great poets as those who embed in the various guises that their work takes on 'die Machtformel, durch die sie das Schicksal beherrschen'.[26] The powerful individuality of great writers is what enables them to affect the lives of others, and (perhaps not surprisingly for a man who went on to be one of the century's most prolific biographers) Zweig celebrates the importance of 'Persönlichkeit' in poetry.

This is an odd way to approach Verlaine, however, and Zweig is forced to identify him as an exception, 'ein Dichter der Schwäche und Kraftlosigkeit', in whose works individuality is suppressed in favour of typicality and who conveys to us a kind of 'original' or unformed reality — 'die reinste und klarste Form des realen Lebens' (p. 6), the raw material of experience and identity for us to form. Nonetheless Zweig asserts, 'Wie in einem Spiegel haben sich so in seiner Dichtung die wichtigsten Augenblicke seines Lebens eingefangen', claiming 'Man könnte ohne Mühe mit Zeilen seiner Gedichte jenes traurige Auf und Nieder von Rausch und Ernüchterung, Liebe und Cynismus, Bewusstheit und Ekstase erzählen, das uns das Leben Paul Verlaines bedeutet' (p. 7). Zweig also tended to see German qualities in French poetry and claimed that Verlaine had brought the German 'Lied' to France, despite the fact that the term is 'den Franzosen noch heute so unfassbar und unbegreiflich [...], dass sie sich kein Eigenwort dafür gefunden und es hilflos in Anführungszeichen im Texte stehen lassen' (p. 15). Despite this highly idiosyncratic stance, Zweig writes persuasively of the revolutionary turn that poetry took in this generation and of Verlaine's distancing of himself from cold Parnassian precision:

> hier offenbart sich jene grosse Wendung der französischen Lyrik von der kalten unnahbaren Plastik, vom Architektonischen und Präzisen zur Musik des Verses, zu den gleitenden und verlockenden Intimitäten des Rhythmus, zu jenem innersten Wesen aller lyrischen Dichtung, zur Stimmung, die wie ein sanfter und flüchtiger Hauch über den freibeflügelten Zeilen zittert und sie nicht bedrückt und beängstigt, wie ein pointierender Gedanke.[27]

Zweig concludes that all important aesthetic shifts, including Verlaine's, 'w[erden] immer von einer Persönlichkeit und nie von einer Theorie geschaffen; Verlaine war auch nie Theoretiker und jenes so programmartige Gedicht [= 'Art poétique'] ist nichts anderes, als einer seiner vielen unerschütterlichen Versuche, sich selbst zu erklären und offenbaren' (p. 16).

Zweig's essay on Verlaine articulates a strong desire to identify the biographical sources of poetry and 'explain' it, and this stance is more subtly evident in the translations, particularly in his version of what is almost a paradigm for the Symbolist 'soulscape', Verlaine's famous 'Clair de lune', the opening poem of the Rococo-inspired *Fêtes galantes* (1869).

> So seltsam scheint mir deine Seele, wie
> Ein Park, durch den ein Zug von Masken flimmert,
> Doch Tanz und ihrer Lauten Melodie
> Verbirgt nur Schmerz, der durch die Masken schimmert.
>
> Von Liebe singen sie, bespöttelnd ihr Geschick,
> Doch Mollklang macht das lose Klimpern trüber,
> Es dünkt, sie glauben selbst nicht an ihr Glück,
> Und leise rinnt ihr Lied in Mondschein über,
>
> In Mondschein, der, sanft-traurig, blass und blank,
> Die Vögel träumen lässt hoch in den Bäumen
> Und schluchzen die Fontänen, dass sie schlank
> Und schauernd in die Marmorschalen schäumen.[28]
>
> Votre âme est un paysage choisi
> Que vont charmant masques et bergamasques
> Jouant du luth et dansant et quasi
> Tristes sous leurs déguisements fantasques.
>
> Tout en chantant sur le mode mineur
> L'amour vainqueur et la vie opportune,
> Ils n'ont pas l'air de croire à leur bonheur
> Et leur chanson se mêle au clair de lune,
>
> Au calme clair de lune triste et beau,
> Qui fait rêver les oiseaux dans les arbres
> Et sangloter d'extase les jets d'eau,
> Les grands jets d'eau sveltes parmi les marbres.[29]

Zweig shies away from the indeterminacy of the original in many salient respects. He substitutes the familiar 'du' for the deliberately distancing 'votre'; he spells out the role of the perceiving identity by adding 'mir' in line 1 — its absence in the French signifies a quite different relationship; he makes the 'paysage' into a more precise 'Park', and reduces the simple but allusive identification of self and park (via the verb 'est') to a banal simile ('*wie* | Ein Park'). The original is curious in that after the initial bold statement positing the equivalence of soul and landscape, 'Votre âme est un paysage choisi', it avoids finite verbs almost entirely: 'vont charmant' is an archaic form that stresses the durative nature of the effect of the charm, 'jouant' and 'tout en charmant' are present participles. 'Ils n'ont pas l'air' and 'leur chanson se mêle' include finite verbs in the present tense, but the third stanza has only one finite verb, in a subordinate clause, with two dependent infinitives (it is mostly a continuation of 'se mêle [...] au calme clair de lune [...] qui [...]' — a structure that Zweig imitates effectively). This is a typically Verlainean technique, allowing clauses to snake continually onwards, defining and redefining their subjects and objects such that one easily loses one's grip on the precise grammatical relationships. These effects are undoubtedly extremely hard to reproduce in another language, but Zweig seems not even to have noticed them: it really is not the case, as Rovagnati suggests, '[daß] in ihrer Aufmerksamkeit für alle Strukturen Zweigs Nachdichtung auch die hervorstechenden parataktischen Züge der Syntax nach[bildet]'.[30]

Certain features of Zweig's version undermine the valiant syntactic efforts that he does make in the last stanza: his verbs are almost all finite and in the present tense (although 'läßt' in the third stanza has two dependent infinitives); the participles 'playing' and 'dancing' in the first stanza become nouns ('Melodie' and 'Tanz') and the simple 'sous', beneath, is turned into something more concrete and explanatory by the finite verb 'verbirgt'. 'Doch' and 'nur' both over-emphasize the tension between the landscape or soulscape and the subjacent layer of misery. Leaving out 'quasi' (subtly placed at the end of a line, leaving 'quasi tristes' across the enjambement, and boldly rhyming an adverb with a past participle), fixes too clearly what is an exquisitely elusive emotion in the original, and turning the vague adjective 'tristes' into the more specific noun 'Schmerz' does the same. Finally, in Zweig's version, the highly sexualized image of the fountain jets sobbing in ecstasy as a result of the musical seduction of the 'masques et bergamasques' is overwhelmed by — rather than set in contrast to — the dreaminess of the birds in the trees, and the insertion of 'schauernd' seems to prescribe the reader's emotional response rather than stimulate it. If we are to take seriously Zweig's stated aim as a translator, 'den Übersetzer ganz zu Gunsten des Dichters zurücktreten zu lassen' and to attempt 'möglichst anschließende Übersetzungen',[31] then the very marked divergences of approach here and in other translations suggest strongly that it is his appreciation of the originals that is lacking rather than his skill with language or form, both of which are amply demonstrated here. It may be true that every translation is also an interpretation, but Zweig's is reductive to the point of being dogmatic and robs the poem not only of its charm but of any characteristics that might be called 'Verlainean'.

The approach to French poetry that this translation implies is not unique, and equivalent reductions and explications, *mutatis mutandis*, can be observed in Zweig's translation of Rimbaud's 'Sensation':

> An blauen Abenden geh' ich auf Pfaden,
> Die eng' umsäumt von gold'nen Saaten sind,
> In tiefem Traum. — Mit leisen Wellen baden
> Das bloße Haupt mir Ernteduft und Wind.
>
> Ich spreche nichts. — Ich denke nichts. — Ich träume nur
> Und eine Liebe ist in mir erwacht
> So grenzenlos. — Ich wandle durch die Flur
> So selig, wie in einer Liebesnacht ... [32]

> Par les soirs bleus d'été, j'irai dans les sentiers,
> Picoté par les blés, fouler l'herbe menue:
> Rêveur, j'en sentirai la fraîcheur à mes pieds.
> Je laisserai le vent baigner ma tête nue.
>
> Je ne parlerai pas, je ne penserai rien:
> Mais l'amour infini me montera dans l'âme,
> Et j'irai loin, bien loin, comme un bohémien,
> Par la Nature, — heureux comme avec une femme.[33]

Read on its own, this is an accomplished poem, metrically very polished. Some elegant variation in line 1 yields a four-stressed line with two dactyls, and there is a deliberately retarding effect in line 5 with an extra stressed syllable to establish the reflective importance of the tricolon 'ich spreche', 'ich denke', 'ich träume'. Gentle phonetic effects complement the rhythmic ripples, assonance on 'a' in the first two lines, some play with 'b', 'd' and 't' in the first stanza — and so on. There is perhaps nothing technically remarkable about this, but it produces nonetheless a convincing evocation of the emotional effect of the evening walk, exploiting the contrasts of constriction and exposure ('eng' umsäumt' vs '[d]as bloße Haupt', 'grenzenlos') and subtly generating a comparison of the excursion with a sexual experience.

Closer comparison of the translation with the original nonetheless identifies some curious decisions. Rimbaud writes consistently in the future tense — 'j'irai', 'j'en sentirai', 'je laisserai', 'je ne parlerai pas, je ne penserai rien', 'l'amour [...] montera', 'j'irai loin' — which lends the original a frisson that is absent from the translation. This derives perhaps from the contrast of the anticipation or deferral expressed so clearly in every single finite verb in the poem with the extremely present and immediate force of the sense-impressions with which the first stanza of the poem is packed ('picoter', 'fouler', 'sentir', 'fraîcheur', 'baigner', 'tête nue'). The power of these sensations makes it clear that they do not express a *hope* so much as articulate a certainty and confidence about what will be. This is wholly missing from Zweig's version, however, which suppresses this tension both by using the present tense and by underplaying the very sense-impressions for which the poem is titled. Rimbaud's poem appeals above all to the sense of touch, but Zweig displaces physicality into the world of dream (it may be symptomatic of this shift that he omits all mention of sensations connected with the speaker's feet, preferring to concentrate on the head). Rimbaud's speaking persona does describe himself as 'Rêveur', but that surely implies mental abstraction, day-dreaming, rather than anything truly oneiric, which is what Zweig over-literally suggests ('In *tiefem Traum*'). Maybe this overt allusion to the subconscious is understandable in the immediate post-*Traumdeutung* era in Vienna. Line 5 gives a particularly noticeable example of this shift of emphasis: Zweig omits the 'Steigerung' (from 'parlerai pas' to 'penserai rien') by using 'nichts' with both verbs, and he then adds 'ich träume nur', which disrupts the poem significantly. Where love in Zweig's text emerges from the unconscious, being 'awakened' ('erwacht') from the (deep) dream referred to twice, in Rimbaud's it emerges from silence and absence — or more precisely *will* emerge, '*montera* dans l'âme' (and the hint here of the idiom 'monter à la tête' gives suggestions of intoxication or self-aggrandisement). Interestingly, the sense-impressions cease in the second stanza of Rimbaud's poem. The body has been stimulated; consciousness is, as it were, 'switched off'; and in that empty space — not a psychological hidden depth but a Symbolist arena of purity — infinite love can emerge. The adjective 'infini' is much more than a conventional or sentimental tag for the noun, whereas Zweig's 'grenzenlos' is trivialized by the invocation of the dream-state. Even the punctuation conspires in the same direction. Zweig's dreamy *points de suspension* are not the same as Rimbaud's confident, precise identification of the sensation of infinite expansion with sexual self-loss in what is quite clearly an expression of orgasmic climax not unlike the end of Verlaine's 'Clair de lune'.

Once more, Zweig's essays offer useful perspectives. In an extended reflection on Rimbaud that first appeared in *Zukunft* in 1907, Zweig recognizes the revolutionary effect of Rimbaud's poetry, how he had 'in den wilden, von aller Ästhetik losgeketteten Versen der "Effarés" und anderen konvulsiven Gedichten ein irrlichterndes Land neuer Möglichkeiten eröffnet', but he insists that as a poet Rimbaud was 'achtlos, unwillig fast. [...] Die Poesie war ihm nichts'.[34] He sees the poetry exclusively as one of the many intense impulses of a life and personality wholly unconcerned with achievement and effort, being essentially the sustained expression of anarchic, even paroxysmic energy. Zweig collects personal reminiscences of Rimbaud as a boy 'frühreif, jähzornig, brutal, durchaus männlich, ein Kerl mit großen, derben Fäusten, ein wenig Muskelmensch' (p. 11) to explain the poet. He is casually dismissive of the inner man, claiming 'Die Dékadence — die Verfeinerung, die krankhafte Überreizung, die halluzinative Vision [...] war eine rein seelische und hat nie in sein äußeres Leben gereicht'. And when he writes of Rimbaud's aesthetic or poetic principles, he sees them almost exclusively in terms of the social and personal iconoclasm that he has already analysed: 'In [der] blinden Freiheit des Instinkts wächst seine Dichtung eigenartig auf, uneuropäisch, unkonventionell, urwüchsig und groß' (p. 13) — just like the jungles in which the poet took refuge in later life.

Zweig identifies here, in general terms, some of the aspects of Rimbaud's poetry that this reading of 'Sensation' has foregrounded. '[Er] umfaßt die Außendinge nicht nur gewissermaßen dimensional, sondern läßt sie in sich mit allen ihren Qualitäten einquellen; er sieht sie nicht nur, er hört sie, schmeckt sie, riecht sie, befühlt und durchdringt sie' — but reduces this insight once more to the assertion of the dominance of instinct:

> so tief, so vehement saugt er alle Sinnneseindrücke ein, daß ihre geordneten Stränge zerreißen, die Qualitäten sich verlieren: Duft, Ton, Farbe, Stoß, alles das rinnt ineinander, berührt sich in jener untersten Schicht, wo kein Wissen mehr ist, sondern dumpfes Empfinden einer Betastung von außen, gereizter Instinkt. (p. 14)

At no point does he reflect on the linguistic tools with which Rimbaud articulates these perceptions. His emphases are somewhat different from what Rimbaud himself says in a phrase quoted (in fact slightly misquoted) a few pages later by Zweig: 'J'écrivais les silences, les nuits, je notais l'inexprimable' (p. 17). Rimbaud has '*des* silences, *des* nuits', and Zweig omits the next sentence, 'Je fixais des vertiges', perhaps because the fixing, the capturing of ineffable excitement in poetic form is not the image of Rimbaud that Zweig has in his mind.

This essay contains further examples of Zweig's habit of seeing German influences in the French poetry of this period. He describes Rimbaud's poetry as 'germanisch und barbarisch' (p. 13), brimming with Nietzschean vitalism,[35] and referring specifically to 'Sensation' he describes it as 'das schönste deutsche Gedicht der französischen Sprache' (p. 8), a misreading as fundamental as his claim that Verlaine incarnates the German 'Lied' in French verse, I would suggest, but one that certainly helps explain the approach Zweig took to translating it. Zweig concludes by linking Rimbaud with Goethe's Faust, both of whom he says began with 'Im Anfang war das Wort' only to strike it out and inscribe in the book of life, 'Im Anfang war die Tat' (p. 19). This bizarre comparison encapsulates very neatly Zweig's disregard for the importance of the medium in which poetry is written.

A third French poet whom Zweig translated more often than either Rimbaud or Verlaine was Baudelaire. Zweig saw Baudelaire, with a somewhat different emphasis from what would nowadays be usual, as the prince of French Decadence:

> er repräsentiert das verfeinerte raffinierte Individuum, in dem sich die sensitive Schwäche und Depravation einer kranken Kultur in tausendfachen Nuancierungen widerspiegelt. [...] Er empfindet die verzitterndsten Sinnessensationen [...] zu denen nicht mehr der Intellekt, sondern nur ein geschärfter Instinkt führt, mit fast krankhafter Genauigkeit und reproduziert sie mit rücksichtsloser Schärfe.[36]

Zweig expounds the relationship of poetry and life in Baudelaire's verse in keeping with his usual part-biographical, part-psychoanalytical approach: 'Wie in einem Hohlspiegel gesehen, zieht das Leben vorbei'. Art is a mirror for life, in this case magnifying it and making it grotesque, and Zweig locates the value of Baudelaire's poetry in its capacity to convey the concerns of his life, identifying '[eine] interessante Subjektivität der Lebensspiegelung' in the poems (p. 66). He is fascinated by the eroticism, orientalism and exoticism he finds there and explains it as 'ein Reflex seines [= Baudelaire's] zerrissenen, überreizten Seelenlebens'. He concludes by suggesting that Baudelaire and Verlaine, despite their manifold differences, share '[die] kulturmüde Sehnsucht des Individuums, das sich einer entnervten, dekadenten und kranken Zeit vergebens entringen will, weil es sich als ihr ureigenstes Kind fühlt und als ihr getreues Spiegelbild' (p. 68). It is this fundamental assumption of the detectable presence of a poet's life in every aspect of his verse that allows Zweig to miss the point when he complains about Baudelaire's 'gewaltsame und unkünstlerische Metaphern' (p. 68) when he likens a young dancer to a baby elephant, for example, or about '[das] furchtbar krasse Gedicht' that he twice refers to as 'La carogne'. Zweig naively suggests that Baudelaire must himself have been aware of its 'rücksichtslose Kühnheit', because the poem supposedly ends with one of the few examples in the collection of 'eine optimistisch-transcendentale Weltanschauung' and 'reingestimmte Harmonie'. The modern reader of 'Une charogne' — to give it its proper title — is left speechless. Zweig fails entirely to see the irony of Baudelaire's late and deliberately perfunctory recourse to the conceit of immortality conferred by verse, or the truth that even as early a critic as Sainte-Beuve saw, namely that '*pétrarquisant* sur l'horrible' constitutes a powerful, original aesthetic statement.[37]

Zweig quotes his own translation of Baudelaire's sonnet 'Recueillement' as an exemplar of the French poet's major contribution to the development of the poetic tradition, his 'eminente Technik', thanks to which '[s]eine Form einen Übergang [bedeutet], der von den klassisch-strengen Parnassiens zu den Symbolisten führt' (p. 67).

> Sei weise, du mein Schmerz, und laß dein irres Stöhnen.
> Der Abend war dein Wunsch. Und sieh', er ist schon hier.
> Ein Dunst umhüllt die Stadt mit matten Farbentönen;
> Der Glanz des Friedens und die Trauer wacht in ihr.
>
> Indes die andern feilem Sklavendienste fröhnen
> – Denn ohne Mitleid peitscht sie wilde Sündengier –
> Und bitt're Reuetropfen nur ihr Mühen krönen,
> Gib du mir deine Hand, mein Schmerz, und komm' mit mir.
>
> Im Grund der Fluten wiegt sich lächelnd das Bedauern,
> Und träumend neigen sich von hohen Wolkenmauern
> Die toten Jahre im verblich'nen Kleid herab.
> Fern unter einer Brücke will der Tag vergleiten.
> Und sieh'! Ein dunkler Schleier auf des Toten Grab,
> Naht schon die Nacht, und sacht hörst du ihr Schreiten.[38]
>
> Sois sage, ô ma Douleur, et tiens-toi plus tranquille.
> Tu réclamais le Soir; il descend; le voici:
> Une atmosphère obscure enveloppe la ville,
> Aux uns portant la paix, aux autres le souci.
>
> Pendant que des mortels la multitude vile,
> Sous le fouet du Plaisir, ce bourreau sans merci,
> Va cueillir des remords dans la fête servile,
> Ma Douleur, donne-moi la main; viens par ici,
>
> Loin d'eux. Vois se pencher les défuntes Années,
> Sur les balcons du ciel, en robes surannées;
> Surgir du fond des eaux le Regret souriant;

Le Soleil moribond s'endormir sous une arche,
Et, comme un long linceul traînant à l'Orient,
Entends, ma chère, entends la douce Nuit qui marche.³⁹

In some ways this translation is much more satisfactory than those explored above. Metrically it is fluent and flexible, as usual, imitating Baudelaire's alexandrines closely but not slavishly, although perhaps with less attention to the French poet's very deliberate use of the caesura than is ideal (line 2 observes this, line 4 does not, for example). There is nothing he can do to convey an equivalent of the effect of the initial capitals for 'Douleur', 'Plaisir', 'Années', 'Regret' and 'Soleil', as this is of course the norm for German nouns.⁴⁰ But there are choices made that fit the patterns identified so far in this essay, especially the reduction of suggestion and ambivalence to simpler certainties. The choice of 'Beruhigung' for the title, for example, reflects certain prominent elements of the poem rather than attempting to capture the range of impressions suggested by the original. In French 'recueillement' has a sense of 'meditation', 'withdrawn contemplation', 'self-communing' even, accompanied by a note of reverence. Zweig's German title simplifies this, suggesting (more narrowly than, say, 'Ruhe', which is used by others) a quasi-parental attitude of reassurance. Ironically, the opening line, which most obviously articulates this attitude, is rendered too literally to support that reading: 'Sois sage' and 'tiens-toi plus tranquille' are just what one might say to calm or reassure a child, whereas 'Sei weise' and 'laß dein irres Stöhnen' certainly are not (although 'sage' does undeniably also have the sense of 'weise' as well as 'artig' or 'brav'). But when 'Douleur' is apostrophized once more at the end of the second quatrain, again in a manner that might suit a child, the German picks this up nicely.

The second quatrain sets out the lot of the majority of humanity, tormented by the dictates of Pleasure — which Zweig reads with a religious connotation, absent from the original, as '*Sünden*gier' — and caught up in the 'fête servile' whose bacchanalian dimension Zweig diminishes in his choice of 'Sklavendienst'. The rhetorical impact of the enjambement between octave and sestet in Baudelaire's original (as the phrase 'Loin d'eux' slides into line 9) is also lost — it thwarts the traditional expectation of a 'volta' at this point — as is the fluidity provided by 'vois' followed by three infinitives across both tercets ('se pencher', 'surgir' and 's'endormir'; Zweig puts a full stop at the end of the first tercet necessitating new finite verbs). Baudelaire's use of non-finite forms is a technique shared by Verlaine and Rimbaud; here it prepares the way for another, repeated imperative in the last line, 'entends, ma chère, entends'. Zweig captures something of the grandeur generated by rhetorical delays in the positioning of the subject in these clauses, but collectively these subjects lack the quiet power of their French equivalents (perhaps to some extent because of the choice of 'der Tag' for 'le Soleil', which substitutes the personification of the declining orb with a simple metonymy). Baudelaire is insistent that the comparison of the march of Night and the dragging of a shroud is an auditory phenomenon, but Zweig renders the imperative visually ('sieh'!'), a line earlier and creating a much more crudely theatrical effect than anything in Baudelaire's poem. Again Zweig opts here for a sequence of present tenses. He explicitly inserts the idea of the dream (line 10) where there is none in the original (recalling a similar intervention in Rimbaud's 'Sensation'): the French poets do not overtly identify their unusual image-clusters as oneiric. Spelling out the effects in this way neutralizes them and reduces the challenge of the poetic image that both conveys a form of reality and draws us away from mere mimetic representation.

Zweig's relationship with Verhaeren and his poetry has been studied more extensively than his translations of Baudelaire, Rimbaud and Verlaine, so a few words here should suffice to show how far it fits into the patterns already adumbrated. As noted already, Zweig's admiration for Verhaeren was often expressed passionately and hyperbolically:

> Emile Verhaeren ist seit Victor Hugo und vielleicht seit allem Anbeginn der erste Lyriker grossen Stiles unter den Franzosen. Er hat ihre Dichtung mit so heftigen und aufschwellenden Empfindungen erfüllt, dass ihm das formende Gefäss — die kristallhelle Form des Parnasses — splitternd unter den Händen zerbrach. Aber aus Trümmern schweisste er sich eine neue, wie alle die Starken vor ihm; Baudelaire hatte sich seine kühle und eherne Gestalt der Schönheit aus den biegsamen Werten der Parnassiens geschaffen. Verlaine eine süsse und wundersam tönende Laute gebaut. Mallarmé und Maeterlinck das runde und klare Erz mit dunklen und mystischen Gewalten durchfärbt, die magnetisch der ewigen Gefühle dumpfe Ahnung anlockten. Verhaeren schmiedete eine Waffe, die er wie seiner Blutsgenossen kriegerischer Gott, wie Thor, siegend über die Welt warf.[41]

This quotation is from Zweig's well-known introduction to the volume of his translations of Verhaeren that appeared in 1904. An essay in *Das litterarische Echo* from the same year expands on a theme that has been noted here more than once, Zweig's conviction that the decisive turn in French poetry in the nineteenth century was the product of German influence.[42] 'Wer einmal objektiv die Geschichte der "Symbolistes" und "Décadents" und ihrer erstaunlich schnellen Erfolge darstellen wird, dem kann die eigentliche Ursache dieser Bewegungen — die man in Frankreich unterschlägt — nicht verborgen bleiben' (col. 972), he claims, noting that this has nothing to do with the debate about 'vers libre' as is often assumed: 'Die Grundthatsache ist, daß einfach fremdnationale Elemente in die französische Dichtung einsickerten. [...] die moderne französische Kunst [...] hat das spezifisch Französische abgestreift und dadurch ungleich an Lebendigkeit und Farbe gewonnen' (cols 972–73). Verhaeren is 'ein wie deutscher Dichter in ihrer Mitte', 'schon beinahe ein Deutscher', and Zweig is careful to explain, correctly, that the 'ae' in his name should be pronounced 'aa' (just as in Maeterlinck) rather than *à la française*. The essay is structured to follow Verhaeren's biography and, like those on the other poets, relies heavily on his 'frappante und grandiose Persönlichkeitsentwicklung'.

Of the many poems one might choose to illustrate Zweig's attitude to the translation of Verhaeren, 'Lassitude' from *Les Soirs* (1887), is perhaps appropriate here because of its thematic similarities with texts by others already explored. Zweig's title is 'Müdigkeit':

Endlos die Ebene im Nebelmeer verlischt
Und langsam auch der Eschen herbstlich heller Glanz,
Und weit, oh weit verliert sich in den Wiesen ganz
Das Netz der Bäche und ihr perlenbunter Gischt.

Aus fernen Abendtiefen klagen arme Melodien,
Manch mattes Liederwort von einem müden Mund;
Landstreicher wandern singend durch die Tale und
Ziehn weiter ihren Weg — wer weiß, wer weiß, wohin?

Und Ruderschläge zucken auf und ab, — müd
Hinkend und verklingend — dann noch schwerbeschwingt
Ein Vogelflug, der schwebt und schwebt und fern versinkt
Ins hohe Himmelsgrau, wo fahl der Mond verblüht.[43]

La terre immensément s'efface au fond des brumes
Et lentement aussi les frênes lumineux
D'automne et lentement et longuement les nœuds
Des ruisselets dans l'herbe et leurs bulles d'écumes;

Lointainement encor des sons pauvres et las.
Voix par des voix lasses au fond des soirs hélées;
Et les chansons et les marches, par les vallées,
Des mendiants qui vont, sait-on vers où, là-bas?

Et des rames en désaccord, et l'autre, et l'une.
Et boitantes et tombantes — et, longuement,
Un vol d'oiseaux qui plane et plane et, lourdement,
Chavire en un ciel gris, où se fane la lune.[44]

Despite a familiar tendency towards the explanatory in some places, Zweig has rendered Verhaeren more sensitively than he did the other poets. There is an obvious attempt at an equivalent musicality, with alliteration and assonance very evident (although no more blatantly than in the original), and a markedly fluent use of the alexandrine with more adventurous enjambements than previously (lines 3–4, 7–8 and 9–10). Compare the prominence of 'v' sounds in Verhaeren's second stanza with similarly dense 'w' sounds in Zweig's; 'Hinkend und verklingend' in line 10 of the German corresponds neatly to the phonetic richness of 'boitantes et tombantes' in the French; the opening phrase 'Endlos die Ebene' seeks to some extent to transpose the /e/ sounds and sibilants of 'immensément s'efface'. Once more, however, Zweig seems anxious about the syntactic sinuosities of the French and splits the first five lines into three main clauses where Verhaeren has only one, with the subject of 's'efface' consisting of a sequence of five nouns ('la terre', 'les frênes', 'les nœuds', 'leurs bulles' and 'des sons'). The slight sense of dislocation that Verhaeren achieves by beginning a new sentence in the *second* line of the second stanza is lost (as was the enjambement between octave and sestet in Baudelaire's sonnet), but the challenge of the repetitions and phonetic echoes in '[...] et las. | Voix par des voix lasses au fond des soirs hélées' is nicely met with the alliteration of 'm' and the variation of 'müde' with 'matt'. No-one could reproach a translator for failing to convey the subjacent sense of 'hélas' in 'et las', and one must surely be similarly tolerant of the absence of any rhythmic equivalent in the German of the five ponderous polysyllabic adverbs in French ('immensément', 'lentement', lentement et longuement' and 'Lointainement'). It is a moot point whether the reliance on verbs with the 'ver-' prefix ('verlischt', 'verliert', 'verklingend', 'versinkt' and 'verblüht') constitutes a resurgence of Zweig's familiar habit or whether this is largely unavoidable in German given that the subject-matter matches so closely what the prefix routinely connotes, evanescence and transience. There are certainly compromises made here, but there is more evidence than previously of an awareness of what these are.

Zweig was nearly twenty-three when his Verhaeren versions were made, so it is perhaps no surprise that increased experience in the art of translation generated more sensitive transpositions. A much more powerful commitment to the poet in question will also have played its part: Verhaeren was the only one of the four poets studied here who was still alive and known personally to Zweig, and all four of the essays excerpted above make clear his attachment to real lives as a means of access to poetry, and specifically to personality and character. More significantly, perhaps, none of Zweig's reflections on individual poets makes reference to any aspect of prosody, technique or style at a level any more precise than 'mood', 'musicality' or 'suggestion'. They all show a marked lack of interest in language itself. But these two aspects — identity and language — are intimately linked in this verse, in ways that I suspect Zweig did not fully understand. This is the poetry *par excellence* of the absence or even rejection of the overt contours of identity; it is poetry that mistrusts attempts to pin a firm underlying self to fleeting sense-impressions and prefers instead to deploy language to convey a deep-seated insecurity about identity. Linguistic skill is here a tool for deferring (in the poem itself) an engagement with anything as solid or suspect as personality, and the original poems are frequently so self-conscious about their art, sometimes even (as in 'Recueillement' for example) so ironically self-*referential*, that their poetological dimensions are at least as interesting as the landscapes and soulscapes ostensibly 'depicted'. Zweig seems insufficiently conscious of the distinction between lyric persona and authorial personality.

Zweig's grasp of literary history is sometimes more primitive than it need have been (and certainly more simplistic than that of his near-contemporaries Hofmannsthal and Rilke). He seems most comfortable when identifying all four poets as part of the phenomenon of 'decadence', and although he does occasionally refer to 'symbolism', too, he is not concerned to explore whether there is a meaningful difference between what these labels imply. Decadence is primarily characterized by certain themes and moods, whereas Symbolism is concerned with the transformational effects of form and language — Hermann Bahr made this distinction clear in essays from the 1890s that Zweig must have known.[45] Zweig notes that all four poets leave the plasticity of Parnassianism behind; he is less interested in what they strove *towards*, in formal terms at least. The consequences of this for his own poetry were unsurprisingly far-reaching. Zweig was imitating a generation of poets who worked in a different language, and to the extent that he was influenced by German-language contemporaries' reception of the same poets, he was also imitating their imitators, deriving from what was already in some respects derivative. Hofmannsthal's uncannily acute appreciation of the implications of French Symbolist poetry for his own poetic practice permitted him to be inspired but not overwhelmed by it; he never forgot the lessons of the French stimuli and was perpetually aware of the precariousness and inexpressibility of that identity.[46] But at this point in his life at least, Zweig seems not to have recognized the threat to self-confidence and self-possession that these poets posed, to have been perfectly happy to reduce at every turn the challenges to perception that this poetry continually makes, and to have restricted himself to borrowing their imagery, vocabulary and moods, all of which constitutes a fundamental misreading of their power.

Notes to Chapter 18

1. Stefan Zweig, *Rhythmen: Nachdichtungen ausgewählter Lyrik von Emile Verhaeren, Charles Baudelaire und Paul Verlaine*, ed. by Knut Beck (Frankfurt a.M: Fischer, 1983), p. 232. This is a volume in the (unnumbered) series *Gesammelte Werke in Einzelausgaben* (= *GWE*).
2. Walter Benjamin, *Gesammelte Briefe*, ed. by Christoph Gödde and Henri Lonitz, 6 vols (Frankfurt a.M: Suhrkamp, 1995–2000), II, 474.
3. Ibid., II, 465 (letter to Scholem of 13 June 1924).
4. The gap is specifically identified in 'Forschungsperspektiven' in the *Stefan-Zweig-Handbuch*, ed. by Arturo Larcati, Klemens Renoldner and Martina Wörgötter (Berlin: De Gruyter, 2018), p. 596 (= *SZH*).
5. Notwithstanding periodic protests that the qualities of Zweig's own poetry have been underestimated, e.g. 'Dass Stefan Zweig auch als Lyriker Brillantes schuf, fand zuweilen nicht die gebührende Beachtung', from the back cover of a recent edition: *'Was wir wollen': Gedichte und Nachdichtungen*, ed. by Klaus Gräbner (Krems an der Donau: Roesner, 2019) (= *Www*).
6. *Gedichte von Paul Verlaine: Eine Anthologie*, ed. by Stefan Zweig (Berlin: Schuster & Loeffler, 1902), pp. 19–20. See also Roman Reisinger, 'Stefan Zweig als Übersetzer Verhaerens', in *Österreichische Dichter als Übersetzer*, ed. by Wolfgang Pöckl (Vienna: Verlag der Österreichischen Akademie der Wissenschaften, 1991), pp. 239–66 (pp. 247–48), and Reisinger, 'Übersetzungen', in *SZH*, pp. 588–97 (pp. 589–90).
7. Zweig, *Briefe 1897–1914*, ed. by Knut Beck, Jeffrey B. Berlin and Natascha Weschenbach-Feggeler (Frankfurt a.M: Fischer, 1995), p. 17 (letter of 14 June 1900).
8. Emile Verhaeren, *Hymnen an das Leben*, trans. by Stefan Zweig (Leipzig: Insel, 1911), p. 5.
9. Zweig, *Die Welt von Gestern* (Stockholm: Bermann-Fischer, 1947), p. 150 (= *WvG*).
10. Emile Verhaeren, *Ausgewählte Gedichte in Nachdichtungen von Stefan Zweig* (Berlin: Schuster & Loeffler, 1904), p. 12.
11. Reisinger, 'Übersetzungen', in *SZH*, p. 590, quoting 'Das deutsche Walt Whitman-Werk', *Das Berliner Tageblatt*, 147 (28 March 1922), p. 2 (reprinted in *GWE: Begegnungen mit Büchern*, pp. 214–17 (p. 215)).
12. 'Das deutsche Walt Whitman-Werk', p. 2; *Begegnungen mit Büchern*, p. 215.
13. Zweig, review of Paul Verlaine, *Gedichte*, trans. by Hauser (1900), *Jung-Deutschland*, 1.5 (1900), 94–95 (p. 95).
14. Randolph J. Klawiter's bibliography at zweig.fredonia.edu has detailed information about these and all Zweig's other translations, including the extensive reprints during his lifetime.
15. See Chris Michaelides, 'Stefan Zweig's Copy of Rimbaud, *Une Saison en enfer* (1873)', *British Library Journal*, 14.2 (1988), 199–203.
16. 'Die Unverdorbenen' ['Les ingénus'], *Stimmen der Gegenwart*, 2.11 (1901), p. 333; 'Einst war ich gläubig ...' ['Je fus mystique et je ne le suis plus'], *Deutsche Dichtung*, 32 (1902), p. 178; 'Der Tod' ['Mort!'], *Das Inselschiff*, 1.3 (1920), p. 128. The bibliographies list a fourth, 'Bücherseelen', *Stimmen der Gegenwart*, 3.5 (1902), p. 146 (*Www*, p. 117), but the original of this poem has never been identified and it is probably not by Verlaine.

17. Six in *Gedichte von Paul Verlaine*, and two new poems amongst the seven in *Paul Verlaine's Gesammelte Werke*, ed. by Stefan Zweig, 2 vols: *Gesammelte Gedichte: Eine Auswahl der besten Übertragungen* and *Lebensdokumente* (Leipzig: Insel, 1922). See also *Www*, pp. 116–20 and *Rhythmen*, pp. 215–21.
18. Charles Baudelaire, *Gedichte in Vers und Prosa*, trans. by Camill Hoffmann and Stefan Zweig (Leipzig: Seemann, 1902); Charles Baudelaire, *Die Blumen des Bösen: Eine Anthologie deutscher Übertragungen*, ed. by Erich Oesterheld (Berlin: Oesterheld & Co., 1921).
19. Emile Verhaeren, *Ausgewählte Gedichte* (Leipzig: Insel, 1910; repr. 1913 and 1923).
20. See Harry Zohn, 'Stefan Zweig and Verhaeren. In Memoriam Stefan Zweig, 1881–1942', *Monatshefte*, 43.4–5 (1951), 199–206.
21. SZH lists only the 'Nachbemerkung' in *Rhythmen*, a 2016 MA Thesis submitted to the University of Lisbon, and one journal essay: Norbert Bachleitner, 'Stefan Zweig als Übersetzer symbolistischer französischer Lyrik, insbesondere von Charles Baudelaires *Les Fleurs du Mal*', *Moderne Sprachen*, 57 (2013), 75–91.
22. See Oliver Matuschek, *Drei Leben: Eine Biographie: Stefan Zweig* (Frankfurt a.M: Fischer, 2006), p. 46.
23. Leonhard Adelt, review of Zweig, *Silberne Saiten* (1901), *Die Zeit* (Vienna), 9 November 1901, p. 94, quoted by Matuschek, *Drei Leben*, p. 47.
24. Paul Verlaine, *Œuvres poétiques complètes*, ed. by Y.-G. Le Dantec, revised by Jacques Borel (Paris: Gallimard, 1962), p. 326.
25. It would not be difficult to trace many of Zweig's images and phrases to Hofmannsthal. This is hinted at by Gabriella Rovagnati: *'Umwege auf dem Wege zu mir selbst': Zu Leben und Werk Stefan Zweigs* (Bonn: Bouvier, 1998), Chapter II: 'Auf den Spuren des "Jungen Wien": *Silberne Saiten*', pp. 14–28.
26. Zweig, 'Paul Verlaine', in *Gedichte von Paul Verlaine*, pp. 5–21. The essay and a biographical study were extended and revised to form a book-length work: *Paul Verlaine* (Berlin: Schuster & Loeffler, 1905), p. 5.
27. Zweig, 'Paul Verlaine', p. 15.
28. Zweig, *Rhythmen*, p. 215.
29. Verlaine, *Œuvres poétiques complètes*, p. 107.
30. Rovagnati, *'Umwege'*, p. 32.
31. Zweig, *Briefe 1897–1914*, pp. 41–42 (letter to Richard Dehmel, 3 May 1902).
32. 'Empfindung', *Die Gesellschaft*, 16.4 (1900), 47–48 (*Www*, p. 132).
33. 'Sensation', in *Œuvres de Jean-Arthur Rimbaud*, ed. by Paterne Berrichon and Ernest Delahaye (Paris: Mercure de France, 1898), p. 24.
34. Zweig, 'Artur [sic] Rimbaud', *Die Zukunft*, 15, 58:21 (1907), pp. 300–05; this is nearly identical to his introductory essay, 'Arthur Rimbaud', in *Arthur Rimbaud: Leben und Dichtung*, trans. K. L. Ammer (Leipzig: Insel, 1907), pp. 2–14 (quoted here from the second edition, 1921, pp. 7–19 [p. 8]).
35. See Rémy Colombat, 'Zweig, lecteur enfiévré de Rimbaud', *Magazine Littéraire*, 245 (1987), 24–28.
36. Zweig, 'Charles Baudelaire', *Deutsche Dichtung*, 32.3 (1902), 65–68 (p. 65). Note again the idiosyncratic use of the prefix in 'verzitterndsten'.
37. Charles-Augustin Sainte-Beuve, *Correspondance 1822–1865*, 2 vols (Paris: Calmann Lévy, 1877–78), I, 220 (letter to Baudelaire of 20 November 1856). One need only read the relevant section of Rilke's *Malte* (§ 22) to see that a more sophisticated reading was current amongst Zweig's contemporaries.
38. Zweig, *Rhythmen*, p. 203.
39. Charles Baudelaire, *Œuvres complètes*, ed. by Claude Pichois (Paris: Gallimard, 1975), pp. 140–41. For a comparative analysis of four German versions of this poem (not including Zweig's), see Hermann Krapoth, 'Die Kategorie des "Fremden" und die Frage der Übersetzbarkeit: Am Beispiel von Baudelaires "Recueillement" und einiger Übersetzungen dieses Gedichts ins Deutsche', in *Die literarische Übersetzung als Medium der Fremderfahrung*, ed. by Fred Lönker (Berlin: Schmidt, 1992), pp. 204–20.

40. Incidentally, Stefan George, who alone perhaps had a choice in the matter, opted to maintain his idiosyncratic orthography in his own version of this poem and use a lower-case initial letter for the equivalent German nouns.
41. Stefan Zweig, 'Worte der Einleitung', in Verhaeren, *Ausgewählte Gedichte*, pp. 7–12.
42. Zweig, 'Emile Verhaeren', *Das litterarische Echo*, 6.14 (1904), cols 972–78, reprinted in Stefan Zweig, *Emile Verhaeren*, ed. by Knut Beck (Frankfurt a.M: Fischer, 1984), pp. 7–18.
43. Verhaeren, *Ausgewählte Gedichte*, p. 35.
44. Quoted from Emile Verhaeren, *Poèmes* (Paris: Mercure de France, 1896), pp. 25–26.
45. 'Die Décadence' (1891) and 'Symbolisten' (1892), in particular (available at <https://www.univie.ac.at/bahr/sites/all/ks/4-studien-2.pdf>). I explore in more detail this relationship, and Zweig's contemporaries' understanding of it, in 'Temporary Aesthetes: Decadence and Symbolism in Germany and Austria', in *Symbolism, Decadence and the Fin de Siècle*, ed. by Patrick McGuinness (Exeter: Exeter University Press, 2000), pp. 209–24.
46. This is the thesis of my monograph, *Hugo von Hofmannsthal and French Symbolism* (Oxford: Clarendon Press, 2000).

CHAPTER 19

Stefan Zweig und Frankreich: Sein 'drittes Leben' im Exil 1933–1942

Jacques Le Rider

Wie für unzählige Zeitgenossen bedeutete das Jahr 1933 im Leben Stefan Zweigs eine Wende, ja sogar einen Bruch: durch die Machtübernahme der Nationalsozialisten in Deutschland und das Berufsverbot für jüdische Autoren und Künstler, das bald folgte, wurde es Zweig unmöglich, die Position eines überparteilichen und unpolitischen Intellektuellen weiterhin zu vertreten, die er bis 1932 meistens bezogen hatte.[1]

Im Oktober 1933 beschließt Zweig, eine Wohnung in London zu mieten, die ihm einige Monate später zum Hauptwohnsitz wird, nachdem er sein schönes Salzburger Haus und Österreich endgültig verlassen hat. Die Einrichtung seines Londoner Zweitwohnsitzes im Herbst 1933 hat auch private Gründe, denn das Familienleben in Salzburg mit seiner Frau Friderike und deren Töchtern Alix und Suse von Winternitz war ihm zur Belastung geworden. Doch spielten politische Sorgen um die Zukunft Österreichs bei dieser Entscheidung, nach London zu übersiedeln, eine ebenso große Rolle. In diesem Punkt zeigte sich der so oft als unpolitisch bezeichnete Zweig hellsichtiger als viele politisch engagierte Schriftsteller und Intellektuelle seiner Zeit. Schnell war ihm klar geworden, dass Wien nicht lange der Unterwanderung durch die Nationalsozialisten und der Annektierung durch das Dritte Reich würde widerstehen können. Bereits am 10. April 1933 schreibt er an den französischen Autor Romain Rolland: 'Österreich ist verloren, der *Anschluss* wird bald kommen. Machen wir uns darüber keine Illusion.'[2] Und er fügt in seinem nächsten Brief an Rolland vom 26. April 1933 hinzu: 'Die Dinge gehen in Österreich immer mehr in die Richtung einer nationalsozialistischen Diktatur.'[3] Im März 1933 hat die Regierung Dollfuß mit der Ausschaltung des Nationalrats einen autoritären Kurs eingeschlagen.

Der Entschluss, Salzburg endgültig zu verlassen, wird von Zweig nach der traumatischen Erfahrung der Durchsuchung seines Hauses am 18. Februar 1934 gefasst. Vom 12. bis 16. Februar hat ein blutiger Bürgerkrieg in Österreich gewütet. Auf Grund einer anonymen Denunziation wird Zweigs Haus nach Waffen des sozialdemokratischen *Republikanischen Schutzbundes* durchsucht. Dieser Vorfall zeigt, dass Zweig, dem linke Intellektuelle oft eine gewisse politische Feigheit vorwarfen, von den Behörden als ein zwielichtiger Sympathisant des roten Lagers eingestuft wurde. Von diesem Zwischenfall schockiert, trifft Zweig die lange hinausgezögerte Entscheidung: Von nun an wird er in London leben. Am 20. Februar 1934 verlässt er Salzburg und reist über Paris nach London. An diesem Tag kann er sich noch in der Illusion wiegen, dass er selbst über sein Schicksal entscheidet. Bis zur Annexion Österreich im März 1938 kann er sich einbilden, dass er nicht im Exil lebt, sondern ein Weltbürger ist, der immer viel gereist ist und sich oft auf längere Zeit im Ausland aufgehalten hat.

Obwohl Zweig die Rolle des internationalen berühmten und gefeierten Schriftstellers, der in jeder europäischen Stadt schnell heimisch wird, souverän spielen kann, wird er von Ängsten und Zweifeln verfolgt. Im März 1935 sieht er einen neuerlichen Krieg in Europa voraus, eine Aussicht, die ihm, wie er an Rolland schreibt, unerträglich ist:

> Wenn es einen Krieg gibt, hat man wenigstens den Trost, dass er so schrecklich sein wird, dass wir ihn nicht überleben. Ich werde keine Gasmaske anlegen, um mein Leben zu retten, ich ziehe es vor zu krepieren — immer eingedenk des alten arabischen Philosophen, der mit 60 blind wurde und, wenn man ihn fragte, ob er das Sehvermögen durch eine Operation wiedergewinnen wolle, jedesmal antwortete: Nein, ich will nicht, ich habe von der Welt genug gesehen. Ich habe kein Verlangen, einen zweiten Krieg zu überleben. [...] Die Politik verblödet uns. Sie ist dermaßen widerlich, absurd, dass man sich nur vor ihr rettet, indem man drauf spuckt. [...] Amerika hat mir Mut gemacht. [...] Ich habe große Lust, nächstes Jahr einige Wochen in Südamerika zu verbringen: Man muss eine andere Luft atmen als die europäische — .[4]

Ein solcher Ekel vor 'der Politik' (implizit ist hier gemeint: vor jeder Politik, sowohl der faschistischen als auch der antifaschistischen) geht doch etwas weiter als die großbürgerliche und mondäne unpolitische Einstellung, die Hannah Arendt in ihrem scharfsinnigen, schonungslosen, aber voreingenommenen Essay an Zweig kritisierte.[5] In diesem Fall handelt es sich nicht nur um die in der *Welt von Gestern* immer wieder betonte unpolitische Haltung des zu Ruhm gekommenen assimilierten Juden, sondern um die affektgeladene Verwerfung jeder Parteipolitik.

Zweigs explizit antipolitische Haltung führt ihn keineswegs dazu, sich der 'Forderung der Solidarität' zu entziehen, deren brennende Aktualität er 1934 in seinem Beitrag zur Festschrift zum fünfzigsten Geburtstag von Max Brod betont.[6] Im Band *L'Esprit européen en exil* wurden Zweigs zahlreiche Aufsätze, Vorträge und Interviews gesammelt, die seine Reaktionen und Stellungnahmen zum politischen Geschehen ab 1933 dokumentieren. Hannah Arendts Vorwurf an Zweig, er habe nur ein einziges Mal, und zwar in seiner von *Radio Paris* ausgestrahlte Ansprache vom 24. April 1940 'Pour ceux qui ne peuvent pas parler' (Das große Schweigen), auf die Verbrechen der Nationalsozialisten hingewiesen und selbst an dieser Stelle auf das Schicksal der Juden nicht aufmerksam gemacht, wird von dieser Textsammlung entkräftet.[7]

* * * * *

Warum hat Zweig gerade London und nicht Paris als neuen Wohnort gewählt? Zwei Briefe vom Juni 1933 zeigen, wie tief er von der Angst um die Zukunft aufgewühlt ist, und wie er zwischen diversen Fluchtmöglichkeiten schwankt.

An den jüdisch-österreichischen Schriftsteller Andreas Latzko schreibt er am 9. Juni 1933:

> Hier ist nicht mehr zu leben, man kann kein Wort mehr zu jemandem sprechen, da alles nationalsocialitisch ist, selbst nahe Freunde sind nicht mehr sicher. Das Salz. Volksbl. [*Salzburger Volksblatt*] ist klar und eindeutig Concurrenzblatt des Völk. Beobachters, nein, es geht nicht mehr. [...] Die Schweiz ist offensichtlich animos, die Neue Z. Z. *total* zum neuen Deutschland aus Socialistenangst hingebogen. Paris ist *zu* prononciert Emigrantenstation. Am liebsten wäre mir Rom, das ich sehr liebe oder (lächeln Sie nicht) Antwerpen, für das ich immer ein Faible hatte. Aber wie weit liegt das? [...] Und wann? Die Lawine kann morgen über Salzburg niederrutschen oder in drei Monaten. Ist man zu früh oder zu spät?[8]

Einen Tag später, am 10. Juni 1933, schreibt er an Rolland:

> Jetzt bin ich entschlossen, alles zu verlassen, mein Haus, meine Bücher, meine Sammlungen. [...] Nur weiß ich noch nicht, wo ich mich ansiedeln soll. Ich hätte Rom vorgezogen, aber ach, die Politik! Ich würde mich nicht gern in der Schweiz niederlassen, vor allem nicht in der deutschen Schweiz; und in der Nähe von Paris fürchte ich, in den Jahrmarkt der Eitelkeiten zu sehr verstrickt zu werden.[9]

Im Herbst 1933 entscheidet sich Zweig zunächst für England. Warum kommen Frankreich und Paris für ihn nicht in Frage, wo er dort doch so viele Freunde hat und jedes seiner Bücher in französischer Übersetzung eine breite Leserschaft gewonnen hat? Zweig begründet dies damit, dass er sich in Paris dem 'Jahrmarkt der Eitelkeit' kaum entziehen könnte. In London hofft er, seine Anonymität wahren und sich auf seine Arbeit besser konzentrieren zu können.

Aber es kommt ein anderer Aspekt hinzu: die Entscheidung für London bedeutet für ihn auch die Entscheidung, sich mit der literarischen Arbeit künftig weniger an ein deutsches Publikum zu wenden, sondern für den englisch-amerikanischen Sprachraum zu schreiben. Also wird Zweig ab sofort mit seinen Verlegern und Übersetzern in London und New York Absprachen treffen. Etwas später, nachdem er ab 1936 engere Kontakte zu Argentinien und Brasilien angeknüpft an, wird er ebenfalls mit Übersetzern und Verlegern seines Vertrauens in verschiedenen lateinamerikanischen Ländern eng zusammenarbeiten.[10]

Diese Entscheidung hat unmittelbare Auswirkung auf seine literarischen Projekte: in London vor allem auf seine Maria Stuart-Biographie. Einige Werke seiner Exil-Zeit wie die historischen Essays über Magellan und Amerigo Vespucci wird Zweig an die nord- und südamerikanische Öffentlichkeit richten. Selbst *Die Welt von Gestern*, das Memoirenbuch, das heutzutage als eines seiner Meisterwerke betrachtet wird, wurde nicht für die deutschsprachige Öffentlichkeit konzipiert, sondern für eine internationale, angesichts der historischen Umstände zunächst außereuropäische, wie es Zweig in seinem Brief vom Januar 1942 an den deutschen Schriftsteller Richard Friedenthal andeutete.

> Bei meiner eigenen Arbeit bin ich ziemlich behindert durch das unbewußte Gefühl, daß ich kein richtiges Publikum mehr besitze. Wenn ich bei meiner Autobiographie zum Beispiel über Hofmannsthal oder Beer-Hofmann etwas sagen wollte, so mußte ich mich daran erinnern, daß in dem Sprachbereich, in dem das Buch erscheinen soll, niemand von den beiden etwas weiß. Und so kritzele ich nun an einem Montaigne.[11]

Die Erwähnung des Projekts eines Essays über Michel de Montaigne zeigt, dass Zweigs prekäre Stellung zwischen den Sprach- und Kulturräumen nach 1933 an der Tatsache nichts ändert, dass die französische Kultur in diesem letzten Jahrzehnt seines Lebens die ihm vertrauteste nicht-deutschsprachige Kultur bleibt. Frankreich ist bis zur deutschen Invasion das Land, in dem er als einer der größten deutschsprachigen Schriftsteller gefeiert wird und in dem seine Bücher eifrig übersetzt und außerordentlich gut verkauft werden. Seine historische Biographie *Marie Antoinette* z.B. wird ein Jahr nach ihrem Erscheinen im Insel Verlag Leipzig schon von Alzir Hella übersetzt und erscheint im November 1933 im renommierten Verlag Grasset.

Alzir Hella spielt als Zweigs literarischer Agent in Paris eine wichtige Rolle. Wie Stefan Zweig 1881 geboren, war er an der belgischen Grenze nördlich von Valenciennes in einer Arbeiterfamilie aufgewachsen. Vor dem Ersten Weltkrieg war er eine Figur der anarchistischen und antimilitaristischen Bohème von Montmartre. In den zwanziger Jahren wird er Redakteur der Rubrik 'Lettres allemandes' der Zeitung *L'Humanité*, die 1921 zum Organ der KPF (Kommunistische Partei Frankreichs) wurde. Hella übersetzte im Jahre 1922 die Erzählung *Episode am Genfer See*, eines der deutlichsten Zeugnisse von Zweigs Pazifismus und Internationalismus. Übrigens wurde Alzir Hellas Nähe zu Zweig der Redaktion der kommunistischen Zeitung *L'Humanité* bald zum Problem. Am 22. Januar 1927 polemisierte *L'Humanité* gegen Zweigs bürgerlichen Pazifismus in scharfen Tönen:

> Stefan Zweig ist einer der bemerkenswertesten Vertreter jenes 'europäischen' Geistes, jenes Neochristentums, das wir als die letzte Abirrung der bürgerlichen Intelligenz betrachten, die den Krieg überlebt hat. Wir müssen unsere Genossen gegen die Ideologie solcher Schriftsteller wie Romain Rolland, der das Vorwort zu Zweigs Buch verfasst hat, und Zweig selbst warnen.[12]

In seinen Briefen an Alzir Hella bezeichnet ihn Stefan Zweig als seinen 'Finanzminister'[13] in Paris. Über Hella fließen z.B. Zweigs Geldzuwendungen an Joseph Roth, den Dauergast im Hotel Foyot in der rue de Tournon, oder an Ernst Weiß, der im Hotel Malherbe, rue de Vaugirard, untergebracht ist.[14]

In seinem Nachruf auf Zweig erinnert sich Emil Ludwig in der deutsch-jüdischen New Yorker Exilzeitung *Aufbau* vom 29. Februar 1942 an ein Gespräch mit dem verstorbenen Freund in einem Londoner Café. Seinen verstorbenen Freund ansprechend, schreibt er: 'Da ging es sehr gut ohne Österreich und Salzburg, denn Sie liebten Ihr Leben lang die Franzosen mehr als die Deutschen, und die Engländer noch mehr als die Franzosen. Unsere übernationale Welt vermittelte Ihnen alle denkbaren, ästhetischen Genugtuungen.'[15] Zweig hätte als aufrichtiger Europäer eine solche Hierarchisierung der ihm nahestehenden nicht-deutschsprachigen Kulturen wahrscheinlich vermieden.

In Frankreich und im französischen Kulturraum lebten auch nach 1933 weiterhin viele seiner ausländischen Freunde (es seien hier nur die Namen von Georges Duhamel, Roger Martin du Gard, Frans Masereel, André Maurois, Jules Romains, Paul Valéry erwähnt) und ebenso viele Briefpartner, an erster Stelle Romain Rolland. Nach dem Abschluss der neuen dreibändigen Ausgabe des Briefwechsels zwischen Rolland und Zweig im Pariser Verlag Albin Michel, die zwischen 2014 und 2016 erschienen ist, kann man die überragende kulturhistorische Bedeutung und das außerordentliche literarische Niveau dieser europäischen Korrespondenz besser ermessen als in der alten, 1987 in Berlin (Ost) herausgegebenen Edition.

Obwohl Rolland und Zweig alte Freunde sind, obwohl Rolland seine Popularität in den deutschsprachigen Ländern zu einem wesentlichen Teil den Bemühungen Zweigs verdankt, und obwohl Zweig seinerseits einen großen Wert auf seine Briefpartnerschaft mit Rolland legt, dessen Prestige seit dem Nobelpreis im Jahre 1915 weltweit ständig gewachsen ist, ist in den dreißiger Jahren eine bemerkenswerte Abkühlung der Beziehungen zwischen den beiden Autoren zu spüren. Die Politik ist daran schuld, jene Politik, die Zweig so sehr fürchtet und hasst. Rolland ist ab 1927 schrittweise zu einem Sympathisanten der UdSSR geworden. Zweig ist zwar bereit, alten Freunden treu zu bleiben, die Weggefährten der Kommunisten geworden sind, wie man im Falle von Henri Barbusse deutlich sehen kann, zu dem Zweig bis zuletzt eine freundschaftliche Beziehung aufrechterhielt. Mit Rollands streng prosowjetischer Linie kann er sich jedoch nie anfreunden.

Am 14. Juni 1937 schreibt Zweig aus London an Rolland:

> Alle Länder, die von der Polizei beherrscht werden, sei es die Gestapo oder die Tscheka, sind mir verdächtig und unerträglich [...]. Die Geschichte wiederholt sich und man muss [angesichts Stalins] an Iwan den Schrecklichen denken: wahnsinnig vor Furcht und Angst — jetzt ist die ganze Gruppe Lenins tot und niedergeschlagen.[16]

Rolland antwortet ihm am 23. Juni 1937 in einem frostigen Ton:

> Nach Ihrem letzten Brief fürchten ich, dass wir zueinander den Kontakt verloren haben. [...] Sie sind immer [...] davon ausgegangen, dass die Trotzkisten, die Kamenevs, die Zinovievs, ja sogar die Toukhatchevskis als unschuldig zu betrachten seien. Sie haben die These ihrer Anhänger in Europa akzeptiert, die Stalin beschuldigt, diese Prozesse geschmiedet zu haben, um seine persönliche Herrschaft zu festigen. Meine Ansicht und mein Urteil sind den Ihrigen entgegengesetzt. Und das muss zwischen uns klar sein.[17]

Ein Jahr später, nämlich am 24. Juni 1938, schreibt Rolland aus seinem letzten Wohnort Vézelay wieder freundlicher an Zweig:

> Ich hoffe, dass Sie sich endgültig in England niederlassen werden. Bei allen Nachteilen, sind unsere alten demokratischen Länder unser Nährboden. [...] Ich kann mir nicht vorstellen, dass Sie in Brasilien ansässig werden. Es ist in Ihrem Leben zu spät, um dort tiefe Wurzeln zu schlagen. Und ohne Wurzeln wird man zum Schatten.[18]

Eine weitere französische Persönlichkeit, der Schriftsteller und Journalist Jean-Richard Bloch, spielt bis zuletzt eine wichtige Rolle in Stefan Zweigs Leben. Die

2019 zum ersten Mal veröffentlichte Korrespondenz zwischen Bloch und Zweig beginnt 1912 und setzt sich bis ins Jahr 1940 fort.[19] Beide sind fast gleichaltrig und viel jünger als ihr gemeinsamer berühmter Freund Romain Rolland. Zu Bloch hat Zweig von Anfang eine geradezu kameradschaftliche Beziehung. Er schreibt seinem Freund Bloch in einem entspannteren und vertrauensvolleren Ton als in seinen Briefen an Rolland, in denen er immer die respektvolle Haltung eines jüngeren Verehrers einnimmt. Anders als im Dialog zwischen Zweig und Rolland ist die Politik kein trennendes Element zwischen Zweig und Bloch, obwohl Bloch ein engagierter Kommunist und Antifaschist ist, der am Spanischen Bürgerkrieg auf der Seite der Republikaner teilgenommen hat. Als Jude wurde Bloch verfolgt. Seine Tochter Blanche Bloch wurde 1942 als Widerstandskämpferin verhaftet und 1943 in Hamburg mit dem Fallbeil hingerichtet. Deren Ehemann wurde im berüchtigten Gefängnis am Mont Valérien 1944 ermordet. Jean-Richard Blochs Mutter wurde in Auschwitz ermordet. Bloch selbst überlebte den Krieg und die Shoah in der Sowjetunion. Von Ende 1941 bis Ende 1945 wirkte er an den französischsprachigen Sendungen von Radio Moskau mit.

1932 erscheint die deutsche Übersetzung (durch Paul Amann, eine wichtige Figur im deutsch- und österreichisch-französischen Kulturtransfer) von Blochs Essay-Sammlung *Vom Sinn unseres Jahrhunderts* (*Destin du siècle*) mit einer Einleitung von Stefan Zweig.[20] In seinem Dankesbrief an Zweig schreibt Bloch, er habe 'die Vereinigung unserer beiden Namen auf dem Umschlag des Buchs [...] als Symbol der Allianz, in der sich unsere alten jüdischen Seelen mit einer heimlichen Freude wiederfanden' aufgefasst.[21] Mancher Brief Zweigs an Jean-Richard Bloch enthält aufschlussreiche Bemerkungen zur Zeitpolitik. Im Januar 1932 schreibt Zweig, er habe in Paris Anna de Noailles und Paul Valéry getroffen und macht diesen Kommentar:

> Ich war entsetzt über ihre Gleichgültigkeit und ihre Unwissenheit über die *wahren* Probleme der Zeit entsetzten mich. Wenn sie nach Ordnung verlangen, denken an die alte Ordnung der Dinge, an gute Börse, gute Renten, ruhiges Lebens — sie begreifen nicht, dass diese 'Krise' nur die Oberfläche einer tiefen Veränderung unserer Welt ist.[22]

Im Dezember 1933 erklärt Zweig seinem französischen Briefpartner, warum er zu den nationalsozialistischen antisemitischen Maßnahmen keine öffentliche Erklärung abgibt: 'Man möchte handeln, einem sind aber die Hände gebunden durch die inständige Bitte der Juden in Deutschland, die uns darum anflehen, still zu bleiben, damit wir ihre Lage nicht schlimmer machen.'[23]

In Frankreich war Zweig seit den zwanziger Jahren berühmt und beliebt: Seine neuen Bücher wurden sofort übersetzt, meistens von Alzir Hella, und erreichten hohe Auflagen — eine Popularität, die bis heute nicht nachgelassen hat. Einige der für ihn wichtigsten Themen fand er immer noch in der französischen Kultur- und Literaturgeschichte, von Balzac, dessen Biographie und Werkgeschichte er doch nicht abschließen konnte, bis Montaigne, mit dem er sich in Rio de Janeiro und Petrópolis intensiv beschäftigt.

Eine Dimension der Popularität von Zweig ist die Sympathie, die man in Frankreich den Vertretern der österreichischen kulturellen Identität entgegenbringt, die zugleich entschiedene Gegner des Anschluss-Gedankens sind. In der Zwischenkriegszeit war es ein Anliegen der französischen Außenpolitik (wie auch der französischen Germanisten und Historiker), Österreichs Eigenart hervorzuheben und die Unterschiede zwischen Wien und Berlin zu betonen.

In Zweigs Werken spielt die Darstellung der österreichischen Identität vor 1938 keine wesentliche Rolle. Er verstand sich als deutschsprachiger europäischer Autor von weltweiter Geltung. Nach dem Untergang Österreichs besann er sich aber auf das gefährdete Kulturerbe seiner Heimat und untersuchte seine historische und politische Herkunft. In dem Roman *Ungeduld des Herzens* (1939), im Pariser Vortrag 'Das Wien von Gestern' (1940), in seinen Memoiren *Die Welt von Gestern*, die er Mitte November 1941 beendete, im unvollendeten Roman *Clarissa* und natürlich in seinem letzten Meisterwerk, der *Schachnovelle*, wird Österreich, vor allem das alte Kaiserreich aber auch die Republik Österreich, die bis 1938 bestand, mit Nachdruck thematisiert.

Bis zu seinem letzten Besuch in Paris im April 1940 reiste Zweig sehr oft zu kürzeren oder längeren Aufenthalten nach Frankreich. Lange vor dem Ausbruch des Zweiten Weltkriegs wurde ihm bewusst, dass die europäische Welt von gestern nicht mehr vorhanden war. Im September 1935 fiel ihm in dem Augenblick, in dem er Frankreich verließ und nach England weiterreiste, auf, dass die Grenzkontrollen selbst zwischen demokratischen Ländern erheblich umständlicher geworden waren.

> Noch einmal Passkontrolle, die englische nach der französischen, und noch strenger für die Einreise nach dem milderen für die Ausreise. [...] Warten und Warten und Warten [...]: So hat Europa 1935 gelebt, so voll Misstrauen ein Land gegen das andere! So war unsere herrliche Welt Europa abgeteilt und verriegelt und vergittert mit Grenzen für den frei geborenen Menschen. War jemals dieser Widersinn größer, dieses Absurde absurder? Ich glaube niemals. [...] Schande über Europa, Schande über unser ganzes Geschlecht![24]

Von Ende November 1934 bis Anfang Januar 1935 hielt sich Zweig in Nizza auf. Dort wurde seine Beziehung zu Lotte Altmann durch seine Ehefrau Friderike entdeckt. Am 10. Januar 1935 begann dann seine Reise vom Hafen Villefranche-sur-Mer nach New York auf dem Schiff Conte di Savoia, auf dem auch der Dirigent Arturo Toscanini und der Schriftsteller Scholem Asch mitreisten. Am 29. Januar 1935 hielt er in den Räumen des New Yorker Verlags Viking Press eine Pressekonferenz und machte zur politischen Lage in Europa eine Bemerkung, aus der klar hervorgeht, dass er die innenpolitische Entwicklung Frankreichs kritisch verfolgte: 'Kein einziger der gegenwärtigen Weltdiktatoren hat den geringsten akademischen oder intellektuellen Hintergrund. Die Massen misstrauen dem Intellektuellen. Sie suchen Führung in sich selbst. So ist es mit Mussolini, Hitler, Stalin, dem verstorbenen Dollfuß und jetzt in Frankreich mit Laval.'[25]

Pierre Laval war damals französischer Außenminister. Im Januar 1935 hatte er mit Mussolini das französisch-italienische Abkommen unterzeichnet, das Italien als ein grünes Licht für die Invasion Abessiniens ausnutzen wollte. Zweigs Aussage ist auf den ersten Blick überraschend, da Laval und der von 1933 bis 1934 diktatorisch regierende österreichische Bundeskanzler Engelbert Dollfuß beide ausgebildete Juristen waren. Dennoch ist die ahnungsvolle Scharfsicht, mit der Zweig schon 1935 die katastrophale politische Entwicklung Pierre Lavals bis zu seiner maßgeblichen Beteiligung am Vichy-Regime zu antizipieren schien, beeindruckend.

Zweigs gewöhnliche Unterkunft in Paris war das Hotel Louvois, das ihm wegen seiner Lage gegenüber dem Eingangstor zur Bibliothèque nationale an der rue Richelieu besonders gut passte. Mit Julien Cain, seit 1930 Direktor der französischen Nationalbibliothek, verband ihn eine 1932 geknüpfte, herzliche Freundschaft. Im Salon der Dienstwohnung von Julien Cain an der rue des Petits Champs und in der Patriziervilla von Louveciennes, die Cains Frau Lucienne, eine Übersetzerin vom Russischen und Autorin eines Essays über Paul Valéry, von ihrer Familie geerbt hatte, versammelte sich ein Kreis von Autoren und Intellektuellen, dem Zweig seit 1932 angehörte.

Zweig besuchte Cain und dessen Kreis zum letzten Mal im April 1940 in Paris und in Louveciennes. Nach Frankreichs Besetzung durch die Wehrmacht wurde Cain im Sommer 1940 durch die Regierung von Vichy abgesetzt, im Februar 1941 inhaftiert und im Januar 1944 nach Buchenwald deportiert. 1945 wurde er in sein Amt als *Administrateur général* der Nationalbibliothek neu eingesetzt.

Ein anderer österreichischer Exilant, der am 27. Mai im Pariser Hôpital Necker gestorben war und auf dem städtischen Pariser Friedhof in Thiais beerdigt wurde, war Joseph Roth. Zweig hatte Roths Beerdigung nicht beigewohnt, aber am 22. Juni 1939 verlas er in London einen Nachruf auf Roth.[26] Darin ist von den drei Menschen die Rede, die in Roth lebten: der russische Mensch, der jüdische und der österreichische. Zweig definiert hier den österreichischen Menschentypus, den Roth verkörperte, mit diesen Worten: 'Nobel und ritterlich in jeder Geste, ebenso verbindlich und bezaubernd im täglichen Wesen wie musisch und musikalisch in seiner Kunst.'[27] Den habsburgischen Mythos Joseph Roths verdichtet Zweig in diesen Sätzen:

> In unserem sonderbaren Österreich [waren] die eigentlichen Bekenner und Verteidiger Österreichs niemals in Wien zu finden, in der deutschsprechenden Hauptstadt, sondern immer nur an der äußersten Peripherie des Reiches [...]. In all jenen Randgebieten, wo der Bestand der deutschen Sprache bedroht war, [wurde] die Pflege der deutschen Kultur einzig und allein von Juden aufrechterhalten.[28]

Leider konnte dieser beeindruckende Nachruf auf Roth von Zweigs französischen Zeitgenossen nur auf deutsch gelesen werden. Eine gekürzte Fassung des deutschsprachigen Textes erschien am 1. Juli 1939 in der *Österreichischen Post — Courrier autrichien*, einer in Paris publizierten österreichischen Exilzeitschrift. Die französische Übersetzung des Nachrufs war schon im Vorbereitung und hätte in der Nummer 201 der Zeitschrift *Europe* im September 1939 erscheinen müssen, die als 'Hommage à Joseph Roth' geplant war. Das Erscheinen von *Europe* wurde jedoch nach der Nr. 200 vom August 1939 durch den Kriegsbeginn unterbrochen; die für die 'Hommage à Joseph Roth' intendierten Beiträge sind verschollen und gelten als Kriegsverlust.

Großes Aufsehen erregte dagegen die Rede über 'La Vienne d'hier' (Das Wien von gestern), die Zweig am 26. April 1940 im Pariser Théâtre Marigny gab. Ein Interview mit Zweig, das am Vormittag des 26. April in der Pariser Tageszeitung

L'Intransigeant erschien, nimmt ihren Ton vorweg. Der Redner habe die Absicht, schreibt der Journalist in seiner Einleitung 'den Unterschied hervorzuheben, der die österreichische Mentalität von der deutschen, den Geschmack am Geist von dem Kult der Stärke trennt'.[29] Und Zweig erklärt am Ende des Interviews: 'Kein Verschmelzen ist zwischen diesen so andersartigen Seelen möglich.'[30]

Diese Aussage erscheint zwei Jahre nach dem Anschluss als wirklichkeitsfern, ja als die schlichte Verleugnung der finsteren Realität. Sie wird erst verständlich, wenn man berücksichtigt, dass Zweig seine Apologie Österreichs an die französische Öffentlichkeit richtete und sozusagen für eine im April 1940 noch unabsehbare Nachkriegszeit arbeitete, in der die Zukunft Österreichs davon abhängen würde, dass man im Ausland bereit sei, es nicht mehr mit Deutschland zu verwechseln.

Stefan Zweigs letzter Aufenthalt in Paris vom 11. bis zum 28. April 1940 verdient besondere Aufmerksamkeit. Wenige Wochen vor der deutschen Eroberung der französischen Hauptstadt wurde am 24. April von Radio Paris seine Ansprache 'Pour ceux qui ne peuvent pas parler' (Das grosse Schweigen) ausgesendet.[31]

> Ich glaube, dass die erste Pflicht aller, die die Freiheit des Redens haben, heute die ist, im Namen der Millionen und Abermillionen zu sprechen, die es selber nicht mehr können, weil dieses unentwendbare Recht ihnen entwendet worden ist. Niemals in der Geschichte ist so weithin, so methodisch und systematisch, ähnliche Gewalt geübt worden.[32]

Im schon zitierten Interview der Zeitung *L'Intransigeant* vom 26. April 1940 erklärte Zweig:

> Das Pariser Publikum habe ich den Eindruck schon immer gekannt zu haben! Ich wohne seit sechs Jahren in London. Ich bin englischer Staatsbürger geworden, aber — fassen Sie meine Aussage bitte keineswegs als Schmeichelei auf — ich fühle mich in Frankreich am wohlsten.[33]

In Paris sah er im April 1940 seine erste Ehefrau Friderike Zweig wieder, die sich nach dem Anschluss in Paris niedergelassen hatte, und er traf viele seiner französischen Bekannten und Freunde. Während dieser dicht gefüllten Tage arbeitete er in der Bibliothèque nationale über Balzac. Im Interview vom 26. April kündigte er an: 'Ich hoffe, zwei dicke Bände von jeweils tausend Seiten über Ihr grösstes Genie bald veröffentlichen zu können'.[34]

Und doch wurde Zweigs grosses Balzac-Projekt durch den Krieg verhindert. In einem im *New York Times Book Review* veröffentlichten Interview mit dem Titel 'The Future of Writing in a World at War' erklärte er im Juli 1940:

> Reluctantly I had to abandon this nearly finished volume because the library of Chantilly which contains all of Balzac's manuscripts had been closed for the duration of the war and brought away to an unknown and inaccessible place; on the other hand, I could not take with me the hundreds and thousands of notes because of the censorship.[35]

Damals war nämlich die 1905 von Vicomte Spoelberch de Lovenjoul dem Institut de France vermachte Sammlung, in der 90% der überlieferten Balzac-Manuskripte enthalten sind, in einem historischen Gebäude von Chantilly untergebracht und dem Publikum zugänglich gemacht worden. Vom Herbst 1939 bis Juli 1946 aber wurde die ganze Sammlung heimlich ins Loire-Schloss Lauroy in Clémont ausgelagert und dort versteckt. Zweigs Anspielung auf die Zensurbehörde, die ihm seine Aufzeichnungen zu Balzac weggenommen hatte, wird im Bericht des französischen Romanciers Jules Romains verständlicher. Ihm erzählte Zweig, man habe am Hafen von Liverpool, von wo aus er nach New York ausreiste, sein Gepäck durchsucht und einen Teil des Manuskripts seiner Arbeit über Balzac konfisziert. 'Vermutlich glaubten Sie, es enthalte Militärgeheimnisse', schrieb Zweig an Romains.[36]

★ ★ ★ ★ ★

Am Ende des Vortrags 'Die Geschichte als Dichterin', den Zweig für den Internationalen PEN-Kongress in Stockholm im September 1939 vorbereitet hatte, der schließlich infolge des Kriegsausbruchs nicht stattfinden konnte, macht er diese Bemerkung: 'Selten ist es einer Generation auferlegt gewesen, in einer so gespannten und überspannten Zeit zu leben wie in der unseren.' Er spricht von 'der Überfülle der Geschehnisse' und der 'unablässigen politischen Bestürmung durch die Zeit'.[37]

In einem Essay aus dem Jahre 1940, 'Die Angler an der Seine', der zuerst unter dem Titel 'The Fishermen on the Seine' in *Harper's Magazine* veröffentlicht wurde,[38] beschreibt Zweig eine Episode aus der Französischen Revolution, die für ihn das Aufbäumen des Individuums gegen die Übermacht der kollektiven Geschichte veranschaulicht. Am Tage der Hinrichtung von Ludwig XVI. auf dem Place de la Concorde, der damals Platz der Revolution hieß, am 21. Januar 1793 also, steht eine Reihe von Anglern an den Ufern der Seine, die ihre Rücken zum Schauplatz des historischen Ereignisses zukehren und nur auf ihre Angelruten achten. Über diese unglaubliche Gleichgültigkeit sollte man sich nicht empören, schreibt Zweig. Im vierten Jahr der Revolution hätten die Angler an der Seine erkannt, 'wie sehr sie als kleine, anonyme Menschen machtlos und wertlos waren in ihrer historischen Zeit', und so versuchten sie, sich 'auf ihre stille, private, unscheinbare tägliche Tätigkeit' zurückzuziehen.[39]

Zweig vergleicht sich selbst mit jenen Anglern an der Seine: Um im Sturm der Geschichte nicht unterzugehen, hat er immer wieder versucht, im Elfenbeinturm seiner literarischen Arbeit etwas Geborgenheit zu finden, und diese Haltung wurde ihm von vielen Zeitgenossen zum Vorwurf gemacht. Nicht er, nicht der von der Macht der Geschichte zermalmte Einzelne trägt die Schuld, meint Zweig, sondern die Geschichte selbst: 'Sie, die gleichgültig ist gegen das Leiden ihrer Geschöpfe, trägt die Schuld, wenn wir manchmal gleichgültig scheinen [und], statt unablässig auf die Trümmer der stürzenden Welt zu starren, versuchen, eine neue und bessere zu bauen.'[40]

Als Zweig im November 1941 in Petrópolis damit anfing, einen biographischen Essay über Michel de Montaigne zu schreiben, identifizierte er sich voll und ganz mit einer historischen Figur, an die er sich in *Erasmus von Rotterdam* und in *Castellio gegen Calvin* schon angenähert hatte. In seinem unvollendeten Manuskript über Montaigne vergleicht Zweig seine eigene Flucht nach Brasilien mit dem Rückzug des Humanisten in seinen berühmten Bücherturm. Im Dezember 1941 schreibt er an seinen New Yorker Verleger Ben Huebsch:

> Wir fühlen uns in unserem Winkel, je mehr sich der Horizont verdüstert, umso zufriedener, abgeschieden zu sein. Was meine Vorarbeiten zum Montaigne betrifft, so hat sich ein doppelter Glücksfall ergeben, erstens dass Fortunat Strowski, der fünfundsechzigjährige Altmeister der Montaigne-Kunde, in Rio lebt und mir gemeinsam mit einem brasilianischen Diplomaten [...] ziemlich viele Bücher zur Verfügung stellen konnte.[41]

Vor diesem Hintergrund konnte sich Zweig mit Montaigne identifizieren, 'der in eine ebenso furchtbare Zeit wie die unsere verschlagen war und sich nur um eines bemühte: seine innere Freiheit zu retten'.[42]

Fortunat Strowski, der große Montaigne-Spezialist, der die Epoche machende Edition der *Essais* nach dem Exemplar von Bordeaux (d.h. der Auflage von 1588 mit den handschriftlichen Aufzeichnungen von Montaigne) betreut hatte, lebte als emeritierter Professor der Pariser Sorbonne von 1938 bis 1944 in Rio de Janeiro, wo er an der Universität von Brasilien, der damaligen Bundesuniversität Rio de Janeiro, lehrte.[43] Seinen Gesprächen mit Fortunat Strowski verdankte Zweig entscheidende Impulse zu seinem eigenen Buch über Montaigne. In Strowskis Vorwort zu *Montaigne: Sa vie publique et privée* [Sein öffentliches und sein privates Leben, 1938] konnte Zweig Worte lesen, die seiner eigenen Auffassung von Montaigne durchaus entsprachen:

> In einer Zeit, in der die materielle Organisation der menschlichen Arbeit das Individuum in ein Rädchen der Maschine zu verwandeln droht, dessen Herz, Hirn und Arme ganz in den Dienst eines auferlegten Werks gestellt werden, tut es einem gut, ein Bild von Montaigne als dem freien Menschen anzuschauen.[44]

In Zweigs Augen war die Situation von Montaigne, dessen Mutter einer Familie von spanischen konvertierten Juden entstammte,[45] in der grausamen Zeit der Religionskriege mit seinem eigenen Los im Zweiten Weltkrieg vergleichbar.

> Es gibt keine Sicherheit mehr auf Erden: dieses Grundgefühl wird sich in Montaignes geistiger Anschauung notwendigerweise ins Geistige spiegeln, und man muss darum suchen, sie außerhalb dieser Welt zu finden, abseits seines Vaterlandes und jenseits der Zeit, sofern man sich weigert mitzutoben im Chor des Besessenen und mitzumorden, sein eigenes Vaterland, seine eigene Welt.[46]

Ein anderer Grund für Zweigs Identifizierung mit Montaigne in den letzten Wochen seines Lebens war die eindrucksvolle Rechtfertigung des philosophischen Freitods, die er in den *Essais* gefunden hatte: 'Der willentlichste Tod ist auch der schönste', schreibt Montaigne dort.[47]

Wie in der 1934 veröffentlichten historischen Biographie *Triumph und Tragik des Erasmus von Rotterdam* tendiert Stefan Zweig in seiner unvollendeten Montaigne-Biographie dazu, zwischen den Zeilen eine Selbstbiographie zu entwerfen, in der er sich selbst zugleich heroisiert und rechtfertigt.[48] Dies ist aber nur um den Preis empfindlicher Abweichungen von der historischen Wahrheit möglich. Im Fragment über Montaigne wie im Buch über Erasmus wird z.B. der jeweiligen Titelfigur eine unpolitische, ja eine antipolitische Haltung unterstellt, die den historischen Fakten kaum entspricht. Montaigne war jahrelang Bürgermeister von Bordeaux und bekleidete im französischen Königreich hohe Ämter. Selbst in der Zeit, als Montaigne sich in seinen Bücherturm zurückzog und die *Essais* verfasste, verlor er die zeitgenössische Politik nie aus den Augen. Diese Dimension seiner Identifikationsfigur wird aber in Zweigs biographischem Fragment beharrlich ausgeblendet.

★ ★ ★ ★ ★

Ende Januar oder Anfang 1942 nahmen Stefan und Lotte Zweig den Zug aus Rio, um Georges Bernanos zu besuchen, der mit seinem ersten Meisterwerk *Sous le soleil de Satan* (Die Sonne Satans) aus dem Jahre 1926 zu einem der berühmtesten französischen Autoren der Gegenwart geworden war und in Barbacena, ca. 300 km nördlich von Rio im Süden des brasilianischen Bundesstaats Minas Gerais, im Exil lebte. Der fromme Katholik Bernanos konnte Stefan und Lotte Zweigs Doppelselbstmord in der Nacht vom 22. zum 23. Februar 1942 nicht verstehen. Folgenden strengen Satz kann man in Bernanos' Feuilleton 'Le suicide de Stefan Zweig' (Stefan Zweigs Selbstmord) vom 6. März 1942 lesen:

> Tausende und Abertausende Menschen, die Herrn Zweig für einen Meister hielten und ihn als solchen verehrten, konnten sich sagen, jener Meister habe an ihrer Sache verzweifelt und diese Sache sei verloren. Die bittere Enttäuschung dieser Menschen ist eine noch bedauerlichere Tatsache als Herrn Stefan Zweigs Verscheiden.[49]

Für Bernanos war der Doppelselbstmord Lotte und Stefan Zweigs weit mehr als eine private Tragödie — es war nach seiner Auffassung ein Verrat an der Pflicht des berühmten Schriftstellers, das Weltgewissen nicht zu entwaffnen und die Unglücklichen um ihre Hoffnung nicht zu berauben.[50]

Aus diesem Überblick über Stefan Zweigs Beziehung zur französischen Literatur und zu den französischen Intellektuellen während seines letzten, im Exil verbrachten Lebensjahrzehnts geht hervor, dass für ihn die französische Kultur in dieser Zeit eine intellektuelle und emotionale Ersatzheimat war — wenn auch vielleicht eine illusorische, wie alle alternativen Heimatländer, die er zu finden geglaubt hatte, nachdem er Österreich verlassen hatte.

Notes to Chapter 19

1. Vgl. Klemens Renoldner, 'Stefan Zweig und die Krise der Identität im Exil', Stefan Zweig, *L'Esprit européen en exil: Essais, discours, entretiens 1933–1942*, hrsg. v. Klemens Renoldner und Jacques Le Rider (Paris: Bartillat, 2020), S. 7–31.
2. "L'Autriche est perdue, l'*Anschluss*, question de peu de temps: Aucune illusion là-dessus', in Romain Rolland und Stefan Zweig, *Correspondance 1928–1940*, hrsg. v. Jean-Yves Brancy (Paris: Albin Michel, 2016), S. 334.
3. ''Les choses en Autriche vont de plus en plus vers la dictature nationale-socialiste.' Rolland und Zweig, *Correspondance*, S. 335.
4. 'S'il y avait une guerre, on aura au moins la consolation qu'elle sera si terrible que nous ne survivrons pas. Moi, je ne prendrai pas un masque à gaz pour me sauver la vie, je préférerai crever — toujours en pensant à ce vieux philosophe arabe qui, devenant aveugle à 60 ans,

répondait quand on voulait lui rendre la vue par une opération: 'Non, je ne veux pas, j'ai assez vu le monde'. Je n'ai aucune envie de survivre à une seconde guerre. [...] La politique nous abrutit. Elle est tellement dégoûtante, absurde, qu'on ne se sauve qu'en crachant sur elle. [...] L'Amérique m'a donné du courage [...]. J'ai grande envie de passer l'année prochaine quelques semaines en Amérique du Sud! Il faut respirer un autre air que celui de l'Europe.' (Stefan Zweig, Brief an Romain Rolland, 18. März 1935, *Correspondance*, S. 437) Falls nicht anders angegeben, sind die Übersetzungen aus dem Französischen von mir.
5. Vgl. Hannah Arendt, 'Juden in der Welt von Gestern', in Hannah Arendt, *Sechs Essays* (Heidelberg: Schneider, 1948), S. 112–27.
6. Stefan Zweig, 'Die Forderung der Solidarität', in Stefan Zweig, *Das Geheimnis des künstlerischen Schaffens*, Knut Beck, Gesammelte Werke in Einzelbänden (Frankfurt a.M.: Fischer, 1984), S. 312–15.
7. Stefan Zweig, 'Pour ceux qui ne peuvent pas parler', in Stefan Zweig, *L'Esprit européen en exil*, S. 337–43 ('The Great Silence', übers. v. William G. Phelps, in *The Shreveport Times*, 30. Juni 1940, S. 5).
8. *Andreas Latzko und Stefan Zweig — eine schwierige Freundschaft: Der Briefwechsel*, hrsg. von Hans Weichselbaum (Berlin: Frank & Timme, 2018), S. 131.
9. 'Maintenant je suis décidé de quitter tout, ma maison, mes livres, mes collections. [...] Seulement je ne sais pas encore où m'installer. J'aurais préféré Rome, mais hélas, la politique! Je n'aimerais pas m'installer en Suisse, surtout pas en Suisse allemande; et près de Paris, je crains d'être trop mêlé à la foire sur la place', Rolland und Zweig, *Correspondance*, S. 347 (meine Übersetzung).
10. Renoldner, 'Stefan Zweig und die Krise der Identität im Exil', S. 27.
11. Stefan Zweig, Brief an Richard Friedenthal, undatiert, vermutlich Januar 1942, in Stefan Zweig, *Briefe an Freunde*, hrsg. v. Richard Friedenthal (Frankfurt a.M.: S. Fischer, 1984), S. 340.
12. 'Stefan Zweig est un des plus remarquables représentants de cet esprit 'européen', de ce néo-christianisme que nous considérons comme la dernière aberration de l'intelligence bourgeoise rescapée de la guerre. Nous nous devons de mettre en garde nos camarades contre l'idéologie d'écrivains tels que Romain Rolland, préfacier de Zweig, et Zweig lui-même.' ('Critique de la justice' (Vorwort der Redaktion, von 'P.' unterschrieben, zu einem Auszug aus Zweigs *Virata* [= *Die Augen des ewigen Bruder*], übers. v. Alzir Hella und Olivier Bournac), in *L'Humanité*, 22. Januar 1927, S. 4)
13. Stefan Zweig in einem Brief vom 22. November 1935. Vgl. Anne-Élise Delatte, *Alzir Hella: La voix française de Stefan Zweig* (Paris: Éric Jamet, 2018), S. 310.
14. Am 22. März 1934 bittet Stefan Zweig Alzir Hella darum, Joseph Roth, tausend Francs, 'que je lui dois', zukommen zu lassen; im Juli 1935 bittet Zweig Hella darum, Ernst Weiß 2500 Francs zur Verfügung zu stellen. Vgl. *Alzir Hella: La voix française de Stefan Zweig*, S. 315 und 254.
15. Emil Ludwig, 'Stefan Zweig zum Gedächtnis', *Aufbau* 8.9, 27. Februar 1942, S. 15.
16. 'Tous les pays où la police règne, soit Gestapo soit Tcheka, me sont suspects et intolérables [...]. L'histoire se répète et on est obligé [face à Staline] de penser à Ivan le terrible, fou de terreur, de peur — maintenant toute l'équipe de Lénine est morte et terrassée.' (Rolland und Zweig, *Correspondance 1928–1940*, S. 514)
17. 'Votre dernière lettre me fait craindre que nous n'ayons perdu contact. [...] Vous avez toujours [...] pris la position préalable de considérer comme innocents les trotskistes, les Kamenev et les Zinoviev, voire les Toukhatchevski. Vous avez accepté la thèse de leurs partisans en Europe, accusant Staline d'avoir machiné ces procès, pour établir sa domination personnelle. Ma façon de voir et de juger est opposée à la vôtre. Et il faut que ceci soit clair entre nous.' (ibid., S. 516)
18. 'J'espère que vous vous établirez définitivement en Angleterre. Avec tous leurs défauts, nos vieux pays démocratiques sont notre terre nourricière. [...] Je ne vous vois pas installé au Brésil. Il est trop tard, dans votre vie, pour y prendre racines profondes. Et sans racine, on devient une ombre.' (ibid., S. 552–53: Brief vom 24. Juni 1938)
19. Stefan Zweig und Jean-Richard Bloch, *Correspondance (1912–1940)*, hrsg. v. Claudine Delphis, Collection Écritures (Dijon: Éditions universitaires de Dijon, 2019).
20. Jean-Richard Bloch, *Vom Sinn unseres Jahrhunderts*, übers. v. Paul Amann, Vorwort v. Stefan Zweig (Berlin, Wien, Leipzig: Zsolnay, 1932).

21. 'L'union de nos deux noms sur la couverture [...] comme un symbole d'alliance, où nos vieilles âmes judaïques se retrouvaient avec une joie secrete.' Stefan Zweig und Jean-Richard Bloch, *Correspondance (1912–1940)*, S. 140.
22. 'J'ai été effrayé de leur indifférence et aussi de leur ignorance envers les *vrais* problèmes de l'époque. S'ils désirent l'ordre, ils pensent au *vieil* ordre des choses, bonne bourse, bonnes rentes, vie calme — ils ne comprennent pas que cette 'crise' n'est que la surface d'une profonde mutation de notre monde.' (ibid., S. 133)
23. 'On voudrait agir, mais on a les mains liées par les supplications des Juifs en Allemagne qui nous prient de garder silence pour ne pas aggraver leur situation.' Ibid., S. 156.
24. Stefan Zweig, *Tagebücher*, hrsg. v. Knut Beck, Gesammelte Werke in Einzelbänden (Frankfurt a.M.: S. Fischer, 1984), S. 386 und 390.
25. Stefan Zweig, *'Worte haben keine Macht mehr': Essays zu Politik und Zeitgeschehen 1916–1941*, hrsg. v. Stephan Resch (Wien: Sonderzahl, 2019), S. 232.
26. Am 22. Juni 1939 organisierte der Freie Deutsche Kulturbund (Free German League of Culture) eine Feier zum Gedächtnis an Joseph Roth und Ernst Toller, der sich in New York am 22. Mai 1939 das Leben genommen hatte, in der Conway Hall in London.
27. Stefan Zweig, 'Joseph Roth', in Stefan Zweig, *Zeiten und Schicksale: Aufsätze und Vorträge aus den Jahren 1902–1942*, hrsg. v. Knut Beck, Gesammelte Werke in Einzelbänden (Frankfurt a.M.: S. Fischer, 1990), S. 325–39 (S. 326).
28. Ebd., S. 326–27.
29. 'de marquer la différence qui sépare la mentalité autrichienne et la mentalité allemande, le goût de l'esprit et le culte de la force'. 'Stefan Zweig nous dit: "La victoire de la France sera celle de tous les hommes libres"' (*L'Intransigeant*, 26. April 1940, S. 2), in Stefan Zweig, *L'Esprit européen en exil*, S. 345–48 (S. 345).
30. 'Aucune fusion n'est possible entre ces âmes si dissemblables' Zweig, in *L'Esprit européen en exil*, S. 348.
31. 'Pour ceux qui ne peuvent pas parler' (Rundfunkrede, Radio Paris, 24.4.1940; 'Das große Schweigen', in *Das Neue Tage-Buch*, Paris, 4. Mai 1940, S. 424–26; in *Neue Volkszeitung*, New York, 22. Juni 1940, S. 2; 'The Great Silence', übers. v. William G. Phelps, in *The Shreveport Times*, 30. Juni 1940, S. 5.
32. 'Je crois qu'aujourd'hui, le premier devoir de tous ceux qui ont la liberté de parler est de parler au nom des millions et des millions d'individus qui ne le peuvent plus parce que ce droit inalienable leur a été ravi. Jamais, dans l'histoire, pareil arbitraire n'a été exercé si largement et d'une façon si méthodique et si systématique.' (Stefan Zweig, *L'Esprit européen en exil*, p. 338)
33. 'Le public de Paris, il me semble que je l'ai toujours connu! J'habite à Londres depuis six ans. Je suis devenu citoyen anglais, mais — et ne voyez dans mon propos aucun désir de flatterie — c'est en France que je me sens le plus à mon aise.' (Zweig, *L'Esprit européen en exil*, S. 346)
34. 'J'espère publier bientôt deux gros volumes qui auront chacun mille pages, sur votre plus grand génie.' Ebd., S. 347.
35. Robert Van Gelder, 'The Future of Writing in A World at War: Stefan Zweig Talks on the Plight of the European Artist and the Probable Form of the Literature of the Coming Years', *New York Times Book Review*, 28. Juli 1940, S. 2.
36. 'Il me conta qu'il avait eu toutes sortes de difficultés à la sortie d'Angleterre. 'La police a fouillé mes bagages comme ceux d'un suspect. Ils ont confisqué le manuscrit d'un Balzac que j'étais sur le point d'achever. Ils devaient croire qu'il y avait là-dedans des secrets militaires... Cela va me gêner terriblement.' (Jules Romains, 'Derniers mois et dernières lettres de Stefan Zweig',*La Revue de Paris*, 62.2 (1955), 3–23 (S. 4))
37. Stefan Zweig, 'Die Geschichte als Dichterin', in Stefan Zweig, *Die schaflose Welt: Aufsätze und Vorträge aus den Jahren 1909–1941*, hrsg. v. Knut Beck, Gesammelte Werke in Einzelbänden (Frankfurt a.M.: S. Fischer, 1983), S. 249–70, S. 269.
38. Stefan Zweig, 'The Fishermen on the Seine', *Harper's Magazine*, Februar 1941, S. 273–75.
39. Stefan Zweig, 'Die Angler an der Seine', in Stefan Zweig, *'Nur die Lebendigen schaffen die Welt': Politische, kulturelle, soziohistorische Betrachtungen und Essays 1911–1940*, hrsg. v. Klaus Gräbner und Erich Schirhuber (Krems: Edition Roesner, 2016), tranScript Nr. 2, S. 167–73 (S. 173).

40. Ebd., S. 173.
41. Stefan Zweig, Brief an Ben Huebsch, 8.Dezember 1941, in Stefan Zweig, *Briefe 1932–1942*, hrsg. v. Knut Beck und Jeffrey B. Berlin (Frankfurt a.M.: S. Fischer, 2005), S. 331.
42. Ebd.
43. Vgl. Christophe Charle, 'Strowski de Robkowa (Fortunat, Joseph)', in *Les Professeurs de la faculté des lettres de Paris: — Dictionnaire biographique 1909–1939*, hrsg. v. Christophe Charle (Paris: Institut national de recherche pédagogique, 1986), S. 202–04 < https://www.persee.fr/doc/inrp_0298-5632_1986_ant_2_2_2796>.
44. 'Dans une époque où l'organisation matérielle du travail humain menace de transformer l'individu en un ressort de machine, n'ayant ni cœur ni cerveau ni bras que pour une œuvre imposée, une image de Montaigne, homme libre, est bonne à regarder.' (Fortunat Strowski, Vorwort zu *Montaigne: Sa vie publique et privée* (Paris: Éditions de la Nouvelle Revue Critique, 1938); 3. Ausgabe von Fortunat Strowski, *Montaigne* (Paris, Félix Alcan, 1. Ausgabe 1906, 2. Ausgabe 1931) Ein weiteres Buch über Montaigne wird von Stefan Zweig oft zitiert: Marvin Lowenthal, *The Autobiography of Michel de Montaigne* (Boston und New York: Houghton Mifflin, 1935).
45. 'Diese Mutter jüdischen Bluts, mit der Montaigne über ein halbes Jahrhundert im gleichen Hause lebt und die ihren berühmten Sohn sogar noch überlebt' (Stefan Zweig, *Montaigne [Fragment]*, in Stefan Zweig, *Zeiten und Schicksale: Aufsätze und Vorträge aus den Jahren 1902–1942*, hrsg. v. Knut Beck, Gesammelte Werke in Einzelbänden (Frankfurt a.M.: S. Fischer, 1990), S. 468–556 (S. 486).
46. Ebd., S. 475.
47. 'La plus volontaire mort est la plus belle'. Michel de Montaigne, *Essais*, Buch II, Kap. 3, 'Coutume de l'île de Céa'.
48. Philippe Desan, 'Le biographe autobiographé: Sur le Montaigne de Stefan Zweig', *Montaigne Studies*, 27 (2015), S. 217–24.
49. 'Des milliers et des milliers d'hommes qui tenaient M. Zweig pour un maître, l'honoraient comme tel, ont pu se dire que ce maître avait désespéré de leur cause, que cette cause était perdue. La cruelle déception de ces hommes est un fait beaucoup plus regrettable encore que la disparition de M. Stefan Zweig.' (Georges Bernanos, 'Le suicide de Stefan Zweig' (unter dem Titel 'Apologias do suicido' ['Apologien des Selbstmords'] in der Zeitung O *Jornal* vom 6. März 1942 erschienen), in Georges Bernanos, *Scandale de la vérité: Essais, pamphlets, articles et témoignages*, hrsg. v. Romain Debluë (Paris: Robert Laffont, Bouquins, 2019), S. 718–24 (S. 719))
50. 'Qui touche à ce bien sacré [une humble et ardente espérance], qui risque d'en dissiper une parcelle, désarme la conscience du monde, et dépouille les misérables.' Bernanos, 'Le suicide de Stefan Zweig', S. 719.

CHAPTER 20

'Auf der Flucht': The Motif of Flight in the Works of Bertolt Brecht

Tom Kuhn

The discourse of migration was prominent in Brecht's time (as in our own), with vast and enforced population movements in Europe in the years following the First World War, and then again, across the globe, during European Fascism and the Second World War. My initial purpose in this essay was to interrogate Brecht's perspective on the phenomenon but, as you will see, my findings took me somewhere rather different.[1]

Refugees 'in flight' or 'on the run' are a common sight in Brecht's writings of exile. He himself is 'geflüchtet unter das dänische Strohdach', as he says in the motto to the *Svendborger Gedichte*.[2] He several times speaks of his 'Flucht', for example in the poem 'Im zweiten Jahre meiner Flucht' of 1935 (XIV, 289) where he also speaks, more generally, of 'das Los der Geflohenen'. Five years later he is still 'Auf der Flucht vor meinen Landsleuten', in the *Steffinische Sammlung* (XII, 98), and in 'An die dänische Zufluchtsstätte' (XII, 99) and 'Finnische Landschaft' (XII, 110), amongst other places, he explicitly calls himself a 'Flüchtling' — or, more personally and more colourfully, 'der landflüchtige | Stückschreiber' in one of the poems of the *Messingkauf* ('Rede an die dänische Arbeiterschauspieler', XII, 326). There is plenty of room in his work for other exiles too: to name just one example, Dr Waldemar Goldschmidt, whose fate is referred to in the poem 'Klage des Emigranten' of 1939: 'Ob meiner Nase Form, der Farb des Haars | Wurd Dach und Brot mir eines Tags verwehrt' (XIV, 439). I am not going to rehearse so many more examples — the list could go on for some time. Besides, it is not surprising that, in anti-fascist exile, the image of the refugee is frequent and so positively understood.

As far as other writers are concerned, Brecht creates (and he wasn't the only one to do this) a veritable genealogy of banished poets, for example in 'Besuch bei den verbannten Dichtern', where he enlists such diverse figures as Ovid and Du Fu, Villon and Shakespeare, Dante and Heine to his cause, not all of them precisely 'banished', by any means, but all victims to some extent of persecution or legal process and all worthy 'forebears' in what Brecht wants to understand as a tradition of the exiled poet. And he reflects on the semantics in 'Über die Bezeichnung Emigranten':

> Immer fand ich den Namen falsch, den man uns gab: Emigranten.
> Das heisst doch Auswandrer. Aber wir
> Wanderten doch nicht aus, nach freiem Entschluss
> [...]
> Sondern wir flohen. (XII, 81)

He weighs up alternative terminology: *Vertreibung*, *Verbannung*, *Exil*, without, it has to be said, ever arriving in his own writing at a consistent usage. It is more a questioning and, precisely, a weighing up of the implications and associations of alternatives.

He looks at the phenomenon, both of an individual and of a mass exile, from a variety of perspectives and in several different genres. In the *Flüchtlingsgespräche* he has the anti-Nazi refugees speak for themselves, the class differences between them now overshadowed by their far greater common experience and interest. We learn, amongst Ziffel and Kalle's many other exquisite reflections on their own formation and fate and on contemporary politics, that emigration is 'die beste Schul für die Dialektik' (XVIII, 265). In *Die Gesichte der Simone Machard*, in contrast, the French refugees, fleeing before the German invasion in the summer of 1940, hardly get a voice at all — rather we hear how the 'Ströme von Flüchtlingen' (the formulation is reminiscent of current anti-immigration political rhetoric) smell and beg and generally get in the way of the happily collaborationist bourgeoisie and of the war effort: Père Gustave remarks sarcastically, 'Für die Kriegsführung sind solche Flüchtlingsströme ruinös. [...] Entweder man schafft das Volk ab oder den Krieg; beides kann man nicht haben' (VII, 121). Ziffel, a couple of years earlier, had expressed the very same idea in the *Flüchtlingsgespräche*, and in very similar terms, namely that a civilian population only gets in the way of the war (XVIII, 235).

In *Simone Machard* Brecht is speaking of internal exile or, perhaps better, displacement, and if we widen our understanding of refugees to include such other involuntary migrations we discover the theme in yet more works. Galileo Galilei moves from the Republic of Venice to the Duchy of Tuscany as an economic migrant of sorts — not perhaps a good move as things develop — and is subsequently summoned to the capital of the Papal dominions in Rome. Commentators have often remarked on possible parallels with intellectual emigrants in Brecht's own day. Despite the threats, however, he refuses to recognize himself as a victim of persecution and tells the iron founder, Vanni, a representative of a new manufacturing class and new economic interests, 'Ich kann mich nicht als Flüchtling sehen' (V, 265). Intellectually, he is 'ohne Halt und in großer Fahrt' (V, 191), but physically he is hamstrung. His failure to recognize the value, or even the option, of 'flight' is his downfall. In contrast, Grusche, in *Der kaukasische Kreidekreis*, is very evidently a refugee. She may never leave 'Grusinien' (although the geography of this play is far from clear-cut) but she treks around its perimeter borders with her precious bundle, clearly a *Vertriebene*, from Nukha in the East (actually in Azerbaijan) to Janga-Tau in the north (on the border with Kabardino-Balkaria). Scene 2 is called 'Die Flucht in die nördlichen Gebirge'. Amongst the materials that Brecht gathered for this play and collected in a file as he worked are Scandinavian press photographs of refugee mothers with their children, one entitled 'Flyende finsk moder med sitt lilla barn'

–'Fleeing Finnish mother with her little child'.[3] *Mutter Courage und ihre Kinder* is yet another play, set in yet another war, in which traffic and transit of various kinds are a prominent theme. Courage's wagon can be read as a trope of migration, and she and her family are always restlessly on the move, 'auf rastlosen Fahrten' (VI, 50). In her case one might argue that the course is circular, that they are stagnated in frenetic motion — in any case, the possibility of actually settling down, in a pub in Poland, appears impossibly remote.

It is striking, although again perhaps not so surprising, how often the specific lexis of *fliehen* and *Flucht* and their cognates crops up, in these plays as much as in the poems of the 1930s and early 1940s. And it is noticeable how Brecht muddies what is more often assumed to be a simple distinction, namely between 'refugees' on the one hand and 'fugitives' on the other, *Flüchtlinge* and *Flüchtige*. Which label best describes Grusche? Which does Galileo fail to be? Perhaps more significant still, there is also a degree of overlap between the vocabulary and motifs of *Flucht* and of *Flug*. The English word 'flight' serves as the noun from both 'to flee' and 'to fly', whereas modern German can distinguish very clearly, not only between *fliegen* and *fliehen*, but also between *Flug* and *Flucht*. The German words have long and occasionally intertwining etymological paths (back to OHG *fluc* (*fliogan*) and *fluht* (*fliohan*)), and their meanings and usages appear often to cross, perhaps particularly in the early modern period where Brecht so often situates his fables.[4] Interestingly, they are intertwined as motifs in Brecht's own work as well.

In the final scene of *Leben des Galilei* Andrea is held up crossing the border. He is reading the precious *Discorsi* which thus, in plain sight, he will smuggle to freedom. He is a scholar-refugee from repressive papist Italy, at the very moment of escaping to the intellectual and political freedom of Amsterdam. The parallels here to later paths of migration are made explicit by Galileo's famous warning at the end of the previous scene, 'Gib acht auf dich, wenn du durch Deutschland kommst, die Wahrheit unter dem Rock' (V, 285). In this final scene, while the customs men grumblingly inspect his luggage, Andrea engages in conversation with a group of children who are letting their superstitious imaginations run riot. With reference to a local woman, rumoured to be a witch, one of them asks Andrea if it is possible to fly through the air. Andrea answers only after he has already crossed the border, and so successfully fled. These are the final words of the play:

> Auf einem Stock kann man nicht durch die Luft fliegen. Er müßte zumindest eine Maschine dran haben. Aber eine solche Maschine gibt es noch nicht. Vielleicht wird es sie nie geben, da der Mensch zu schwer ist. Aber natürlich, man kann es nicht wissen. Wir wissen bei weitem nicht genug, Giuseppe. Wir stehen wirklich erst am Beginn.[5]

We are standing at the beginning of flight: of *Flucht* and of *Flug* — all these things are possible and hold promise for the future. More precisely: we speculate that Andrea's *Flucht* will initiate a science that will lead eventually to *Flug*.

I am not going to delve much in the semantic field of *fliegen*, which clearly also has a separate life as a motif with its own symbolic force and associations in Brecht's work. Nonetheless, the two are related and they interconnect. To invoke one contrasting example: in *Der gute Mensch von Sezuan* there is no explicit talk of *Flucht*, but a great deal about *Flug* and *Flieger*. Sun's aspiration to be a pilot has all sorts of symbolic associations, but in one sense it very clearly represents a flight, an escape from the misery of working-class poverty. As Shen Te explains, 'der Hoffnungslose soll fliegen, Frau Yang. Einer wenigstens soll über all dies Elend, einer soll über uns alle sich erheben können!' (VI, 219). It is also symbolic of the escape from superstition and the social values of the past into the technological world of modernity, a *Flucht nach vorn* if you like. Sezuan is a developing economy, characterized by Blochian *Ungleichzeitigkeiten*, where there are, in Brecht's own words, 'schon Flieger und noch Götter' (*Journal*, 2 July 1940, XXVI, 397). In the event, however, flight here is not the positive symbol of the future that it appears to be in *Leben des Galilei*. Rather, it turns out to be horribly and inextricably entangled in the corrupt economy of capitalism. Sun can only hope to fly if he can bribe one of the ground crew to get one of the other pilots sacked. So we are dragged, metaphorically, back down to earth. This is not the flight Andrea had in mind, and it represents no sort of viable escape from material misery. All the same, *Flug* and *Flucht* evidently offer a rich cluster of motifs in Brecht's work.

What is also striking is the extent to which and how frequently flight is understood not only as a positive escape, but also as a very individual choice and fate. This is not universal. The refugees of *Die Gesichte der Simone Machard* are a 'mass', and Kalle and Ziffel are to some extent representatives as well as very distinct individuals. But these, although they provided one of my starting points, turn out to be exceptions. Given the great mass migrations of Brecht's own youth, and the renewed mass flow of refugees of which he was himself a part, one might have expected him to address migration as a large-scale social issue. For the most part, that does not seem to be his interest. Also, we hear of the privations of the life of a refugee in some detail in the *Flüchtlingsgespräche*; the misery of Dr Waldemar Goldschmidt's fate is plain enough, and Grusche most certainly struggles, yet the emphasis is not on the social misery of exile, but rather — even in some of these examples — on the good fortune of escape from a far more awful fate. This is particularly striking in the more or less autobiographical poems, where Brecht speaks of the isolation and worry, but also clearly tries to realize his 'Flucht' as an opportunity: to stylize himself as a fugitive, to identify with a tradition of grand exiles, and to find a new voice as a poet. It is also the case with those other exiles with whom Brecht identifies, like Laotse perhaps before all others, whose happy escape from a country in which 'die Bosheit nahm an Kräften wieder einmal zu' (XII, 32) is the occasion for the creation of his great work. This is another encounter with a customs official which has a positive outcome, like Andrea's, without even the necessity of concealing the truth beneath his tunic.

With these thoughts of flight as individual and positive in mind, let us turn now to works written before 1933 and before Brecht's own flight from Nazi Germany. Perhaps surprisingly, although obviously not as prominent as in the exile period, the motif of *Flucht* is widespread in Brecht's earlier work too.

Macheath, for example, in *Die Dreigroschenoper* finds himself, albeit for very different reasons, in an analogous position to Galileo, where flight would have been the sensible option, but his pride, perhaps his blind folly, perhaps his 'sexuelle Hörigkeit' (II, 269), do not permit it. At the beginning of Act 2 Polly tries to persuade him to flee, and we have the strangely ironic parting scene of the lovers. We soon encounter him again, however, with the 'Huren von Turnbridge', whence, it transpires, when the police do eventually come, he cannot escape because the establishment has only one door (remember that door!). Subsequently there is another botched flight from prison. In keeping with the argot of the opera, there is little talk of *fliehen*, but rather of 'abhauen' or 'auf den Bummel gehen' (II, 282), but Mackie Messer is, throughout, a fugitive on a long elastic leash, always dragged back into the action by his own desires and his inability to live differently.

Around the same time the troupe of ne'er-do-wells who found Mahagonny are introduced as already fugitive from another world, and pursued by the *Konstablern*, although we never discover quite why.[6] For Begbick, Fatty and Dreieinigkeitsmoses, flight is not only escape, it becomes also an opportunity to attempt the foundation of a new city, a new world even, and a new social order. Of course, that all goes horribly wrong, but the starting point is nonetheless striking — as if it were only possible to imagine this experiment 'on the run'. It is not, moreover, only social and economic adventures that are, in this work, predicated on flight. Jenny and Jim's illustration of 'Lieben' in Scene 14, the tentatively, possibly positive counterpart to the thoroughly commodified prostitution that we see first, also builds from a premise of flight. The famous love tercets, delivered as a duet in the opera, introduce, as an image for the lovers, a crane (or cranes) and a cloud (or clouds) in flight (both *Flug* and *Flucht*): 'sie entflogen | Aus einem Leben in ein andres Leben' (Basisbibliothek, p. 37; or BFA II, 364). Even such a precarious happiness, founded on illusion, is only achievable for these *Vertriebenen* after a flight from normality, 'Wo Regen drohen oder Schüsse schallen' (Basisbibliothek, p. 38). Later in the opera, Jim, Bill and Jenny make yet another half-hearted attempt at flight — this time *from* Mahagonny, rather than *to* Mahagonny, when, in Scene 16, Jim proposes the pantomime of the billiard-table ship:

> Am besten ist es, wir flieh'n
> Es ist ganz gleichgültig, wohin!
> (Basisbibliothek, p. 43; or BFA II, 370)

Here, it seems clear in each of these cases, albeit in different ways, the flight is from society, from its corruption, and from its constraints or repressions. The opera is overall thoroughly cynical of course, but it is striking that all three enterprises that we perhaps glimpse here — revolutionary social experiment, authentic love, and personal freedom — are only even vaguely conceivable in flight and further flight.[7]

Even before these texts from the late 1920s we encounter characters in Brecht who are in some sense fugitive. The most prominent is Baal.[8] Already in the 1919 version, Baal seems, like the *Mahagonny* trio, to be in flight from society, from its constraints and from normal decency — and, more mundanely, from the police. As he himself puts it in a drastic formulation to the priest in the prison scene, 'Ich fliehe vor dem Tod ins Leben' (I, 54). Indeed, it is that flight which may be the only guarantor of the authenticity of his lifestyle and of his poetry. Throughout the play, he blunders on, 'torkelt über den Planeten' (19), 'schreitet' or 'stolpert' or 'läuft hinaus' (26, 80, 72), 'läuft wie ein Narr', 'über die Felder her' or 'querfeldein' (63, 66, 80) in constant flight from authority, and from experience to experience. Even in death he is on the point of leaving (albeit now reduced to crawling, rather than running). Elsewhere, the agitated movement is again associated with flight in the other sense: 'Wenn man nachts im Gras liegt, ausgebreitet, merkt man, daß die Erde eine Kugel ist, und daß wir fliegen', says Baal to Johannes (27). The condition of this humanity, emancipated from the shackles of convention, is perpetual flight. Also prominent in the earlier years is François Villon, 'durch Wind und Regen lang geflohn' (XI, 56 and XIII, 115), Brecht's first model of the fugitive poet, who provided some of the inspiration both for Baal and for Mackie Messer too. It is, much later, in the 1930s, a raggedy Villon who asks the 'Ankömmling' in 'Besuch bei den verbannten Dichtern', '"Wie viele | Türen hat das Haus, wo du wohnst?"' (XII, 35), recalling both how Mackie is cornered in Turnbridge and how Brecht describes his own 'Zufluchtsstätte' as a refugee: 'Das Haus hat vier Türen, daraus zu fliehn' (XII, 83). Flight itself is the underlying condition, but the potential for further flight may be no less crucial.[9]

So we begin to discover a distinct kinship between the figures of the pre-Nazi era and those of the anti-Nazi exile. And looking forward through this long lens from Brecht's youth, the developments of the writings of exile, although they are of course motivated by the personal experience of persecution and overlaid by the concerns of anti-fascist exile, appear also as the reprise and development of deep-seated ideas and inclinations in Brecht's thinking: that flight is the first step on the road to some sort of authentic or positive engagement with life, possibly even a necessity for the creative writer. Indeed the force of the literary motif of exile in Brecht's own writings of the anti-fascist exile suddenly seems strangely apolitical. The persona of the 'verbannter Dichter' and 'landflüchtiger Stückschreiber' is not simply a response to the exigencies of political exile, nor yet to the comforts of discovering a tradition of exiled poets, but also a part of the long-nurtured self-image of a vagabond poet who inclined to see himself as 'on the run' from bourgeois society, convention and authority — even in their pre-fascist forms.

There is something slightly smug about this, in the midst of all the misery and deprivation of the real refugees of the 1930s and 1940s. The self-stylization is of one who has the chutzpah to reject the comforts of bourgeois life, or, to put it more critically, who has the privilege to spurn his privilege. Brecht may not have wished to go into exile, but he finds himself relatively happy to cast aside the advantages of his birth and of his financial success (ironically brought to him by the failed fugitive Mackie Messer, who reintegrates into bourgeois society with such gusto). In the otherwise rather wonderful poem 'Zeit meines Reichtums' (*c.* 1934) Brecht laments the fact that he never got to experience the change of the seasons in his recently acquired house in Utting am Ammersee:

> [...] denn
> Nach sieben Wochen echten Reichtums verließen wir das Besitztum, bald
> Flohen wir über die Grenze.

> Die Lust des Besitzes fühlte ich tief und ich bin froh
> Sie gefühlt zu haben. [... | ...] Doch scheinen mir sieben Wochen genug.
> Ich ging ohne Bedauern, oder mit geringem Bedauern.   (xiv, 279)

Nevertheless, what seems most important about Brecht's *Flucht*, in all of these examples, is that it is a perpetual and restless movement, not a static condition. The difference between the implications of finding oneself merely 'im Exil' and being 'auf der Flucht' is considerable. The dynamic verb 'flohen' is emphasized in the poem above by its position at the beginning of the line. And it is worth for a moment looking back again to 'Über die Bezeichnung Emigranten' (xii, 81), where Brecht rejects the potentially lackadaisical 'wandern aus', and insists, 'sondern wir *flohen*': this is no 'wandern' — the nature of the movement is abrupt and again emphasized by the rhythm of the line and the caesura that follows. To reprise the language of the intellectual journey of *Leben des Galilei*, we are whisked along 'ohne Halt und in großer Fahrt' (v, 191). And the flight is never-ending. The tenuous happy ending of *Der kaukasische Kreidekreis*, for example, turns out to be not a proper ending at all, but a prelude (yet again) to further flight, as Grusche recognizes: 'Da gehen wir besser heut nacht noch aus der Stadt, was, Michel?' (viii, 91). We recall that Brechtian *Verfremdung* itself is also a restless process, not a state. Like Brecht's whole creative endeavour, it is a journey into perpetually changing and ever more unfamiliar territories: flight and always the capacity for further and more remote flight — even as far as Santa Monica and beyond! It is true, there may perhaps be an obverse or a corollary to this restlessness: not stasis, but also a positive possibility, albeit only intermittently glimpsed, of *Ruhe* or stillness. This is a state that may contain the dangers of complacency, rigidity, even death, but it may also be necessary: for reflection and considered critique, for reading Hegel, for writing the *Discorsi*, or for writing the poems of the *Buckower Elegien*.[10] It would take another essay to pursue that. In the meantime, it is flight that emerges as the key motif — theme even — which winds its way throughout Brecht's oeuvre and, undergoing all sorts of modulations through the social, political and cultural, appears at times an almost existential necessity.

Let me end with at least the hint that one of the roots of this restlessness is far from the intellectual or political, and not to be found in the material circumstances of biography, but — almost taboo in Brecht commentaries — in the more deep-seatedly psychological. Here is an unpolished sketch of a poem from early in Brecht's career, around 1924, 'Stunde des großen Kotzens':

> Denn mir gefällt nicht mehr
> Diese Welt.
> Vor allem aber blick ich fremd
> Auf dies Geschöpf mit Namen Mensch, dem ich
> Gleichen soll, besonders dies Geschöpf
> Mißfällt mir sehr. Doch auch ich selbst, daß ich's
> Gestehe nur, mißfalle mir und drum und
> Auch aus Gründen, die ich nicht weiß
> Hab ich seit einiger Zeit vor, zu entfliehen dieser Welt und mir
> Und hätte gern

> Den Absprung! In hellrer Stund, in kältrer Heiter-
> keit, ohne Mißgunst, weil ich
> Geschlagen bin, mich, ohne daß ich's merke
> Zu entfernen! (XIII, 294)

Brecht, not as a political migrant after all, nor, on this occasion, as a commentator on the social misery of his times, but 'auf der Flucht' from the fellowship of humanity and even, 'aus Gründen, die ich nicht weiß', from himself.

Notes to Chapter 20

1. This essay originated in a paper for the Leipzig symposium of the International Brecht Society (2019). I am grateful to my one-time Masters student, Jana Luck, for first drawing my attention to some of the instances of *Flucht* in Brecht's writings, and to contributors at the symposium for thought-provoking additions: in particular, Rob Kaufman, Dorothee Ostermeier, Freddie Rokem, Melanie Selfe and Marc Silberman.
2. Quotations from Brecht's work are, unless otherwise mentioned, from the *Große kommentierte Berliner und Frankfurter Ausgabe*, ed. by Werner Hecht, Jan Knopf, Werner Mittenzwei and others, 30 vols (Berlin and Weimar: Aufbau, and Frankfurt a.M.: Suhrkamp, 1987–2000), henceforth BFA. This poem is at BFA XII, 7. Further short references to this edition are given parenthetically in the text by volume and page number only.
3. The file is in the Bertolt Brecht-Archiv of the Akademie der Künste, Berlin (BBA 28/10).
4. Compare Hermann Paul, *Deutsches Wörterbuch*, 9th edition, edited by Helmut Henne, Georg Objartel and Heidrun Kämper (Halle-Saale, 1992); and *Deutsches Wörterbuch von Jacob und Wilhelm Grimm*, 16 vols (Leipzig 1854–1961, Quellenverzeichnis Leipzig 1971), in *Wörterbuchnetz* <http://woerterbuchnetz.de/> [accessed 5 November 2020].
5. We are reminded of the Bishop of Ulm in the children's poem of 1934: 'Es wird nie ein Mensch fliegen | Sagte der Bischof den Leuten' ('Ulm 1592', XII, 20). The year 1592 is the 100th anniversary of Columbus' expedition to the 'New World' and the year, possibly purely coincidentally, in which Galileo discovered the thermometer. Brecht is possibly alluding to these expeditions and discoveries, and in any case clearly ironizing the bishop's scoff.
6. I am citing here the Universal Edition first publication of the libretto (Vienna, 1929), now available as Suhrkamp Basisbibliothek 63: Bertolt Brecht, Kurt Weill, *Aufstieg und Fall der Stadt Mahagonny: Oper in drei Akten*, ed. by Joachim Lucchesi (Berlin, 2013), in which a headnote explains, 'alle drei sind flüchtig' (p. 9).
7. The critic of the Vienna *Arbeiterzeitung*, D. J. Bach, picked up on this tendency of the opera on the occasion of the Vienna production, commenting on 'Die Liebenden': 'Der Dichter Bert Brecht ist ein Lyriker und fast möchte man sagen ein Romantiker. [...] In Wahrheit bedeutet, wenn man will, auch dieses wunderschöne Gedicht eine Flucht. Zwar nicht mehr in das eigene Ich, aber in den Glauben an eine bessere Menschheit, in der es auch wieder Liebe geben wird, nicht bloß Hurerei für Geld und um des augenblicklichen Genusses willen' (*Arbeiterzeitung*, Vienna, 4 April 1932), BFA XIV, 474.
8. Other contrasting examples include Eduard II, who is forced to flee (II, 51), Tanhäuser in 'Herbststimmung aus "Tanhäuser"' (XIII, 36), and the project 'Flucht Karls des Kühnen nach der Schlacht bei Murten' which remained a sketch (XVII, 409–19).
9. All this is not to say that words for 'flight' are exclusively positively freighted, either in the writings before 1933 or in those after. We should note the ambivalence of the plays and poems feting the feats of early aviators; and for the gods, fleeing may be an *Entfliehen* (or *Entfliegen*) too, an abandonment of their responsibilities: in both *Die drei Soldaten* (XIV, 85) in 1930 and *Der gute Mensch von Sezuan* (VI, 277–78) in 1940.
10. Cf. Melanie Selfe, 'Reading Hegel with Brecht', *Brecht Yearbook*, 35 (2010), 182–202 (p. 183). In Brecht's own itinerary the stations of this restfulness are the houses in Utting am Ammersee, Skovsbostrand on Fyn, Marlebäk in Finland (see XXVII, 71), and the final years at Buckow in the Märkische Schweiz.

CHAPTER 21

The Impossibility of Homosexual Exile: Klaus Mann's *Der Vulkan*

Peter Morgan

Introduction: Where to From Here?

Exile can be imagined as leaving but not arriving. Cafes, hotels, train stations and airports mark stages in journeys that had a beginning but have no end. Emigrants can leave without being existentially endangered, and can, in principle, return freely. But exile means loss of home and of the sense of belonging, stability and safety that home signifies. Yet exile is far from a coherent category. Communists could have a home in Weimar Germany, as could Jews, socialists and the other groups later targeted by the Nazis. Members of these groups enjoyed a social identity and could participate in a symbolic imaginary linking them with each other and with intersecting group identities. But what did exile mean for those without a social identity?

In this chapter I explore the concept of exile as it could apply for homosexual men during the Nazi period.[1] With reference to Klaus Mann's novels of exile I put forward the argument that the concept of homosexual exile was a conceptual impossibility given the particular situation of homosexual men in Germany at this time. For the concept entails a sense of 'home' that remained denied to homosexual men, as Klaus Mann would come to realize in the writing of his final novel, *Der Vulkan*. The irony of this situation was that homosexuals in Germany were the most emancipated and accepted anywhere in Europe, at least until the late 1920s, as a result of particular developments in German social and cultural conditions over the previous decades. However, they had scarcely begun to envision the possibility of an end to their existential homelessness before it was torn away from them. Homosexual exile operated in an environment where 'home' had only just begun to appear on the socio-cultural horizon. But it did not gain concrete reality, least of all as a place of refuge to remember and to seek safety, stability and continuance in, before it was revoked. If neither home nor refuge existed, can we speak of 'homosexual exile' in the case of writers such as Klaus Mann or Bruno Vogel, or even of 'inner exile' in reference to others such as Erich Ebermayer or Ernst Glaeser?

The Changing Face of Exile Studies

In the immediate aftermath of the war, refugees such as Walter A. Berendsohn, Alfred Kantorowicz, Stefan Hermlin and Hans Mayer sought to retain the memory and significance of the exile experience in German literary studies.[2] An early theme of these discussions was the diversity of individual experiences hidden by the term 'exile'. At the 1971 Wisconsin conference, 'Exile and Inner Emigration', Jost Hermand and Hans Mayer focused on the diverse array of left-wing, 'un-German', Jewish or other groups that were terrorized and forced into exile. Far from forming a humanist or anti-fascist front, this was a period of isolation, fragmentation and chaos among refugees.[3] The refugees may have been identified by Nazi authorities in one way or another as undesirables in the new body politic (i.e. as Jews, communist, socialist or left-leaning, as 'asozial', etc.), but among themselves in exile they recognized their differences more perhaps than their similarities. For Mayer the consequence of this was that the literature of exile itself remained caught up in a false perception of the exile experience as a uniting factor. Manfred Durzak takes up this point, writing that the experience was far from a unifying 'Damascus moment' for these writers. The refugees may have discussed their conflicting understandings of the exile situation 'mit Härte und ohne Illusionen', but did not necessarily come to understand and support each other; on the contrary they remained divided in exile.[4]

Up until the 1990s, write Doerte Bischoff and Susanne Komfort-Hein, the consensus was that the study of exile-literature should occupy itself with the writings of those authors who were forced into exile after the Nazi takeover. While the politically engaged, anti-fascist literature of the years 1933–45 was the main focus of research in both the FRG and the GDR, research has moved in different directions since the 1990s, especially in terms of the definition of 'literature of exile' and of its causes and consequences.[5] In an important contribution in 1995, Wolfgang Frühwald formulated exile as 'der meist durch religiöse, politische oder rassische Verfolgung bedingte, auf Rückkehr in die Heimat angelegte Aufenthalt im Ausland [...] nach Flucht, Verbannung, Verfolgung oder Ausbürgerung'.[6] Paul Michael Lützeler revisited Frühwald's redefinition in 2013 to compare the Nazi experience of the polarities of belonging and expulsion, home and exile with those of exiles in the broader literary tradition since Ovid, thus stressing the universal theme of belonging (home) and expulsion (exile) vis-à-vis political, racial or other determinants under Nazism, and relinking the German experience to wider literary and philosophical precedents and traditions.[7] For Lützeler, the category of exile literature has been linked to 'Außenseitertum' since the beginnings of European history, and can be understood as a metaphor of the universal themes of belonging and expulsion in the writer's existence.[8] For Zimmermann too, writing around the same time, in 2012, the diversity of individual experiences needs to be addressed in exile studies, not merely of the categories of emigration, exile, and 'inner emigration'.[9] Much remains to be understood regarding this phenomenon, particularly in terms of how the homosexual experience relates to the categories of the exile experience, such as *Heimat*, home and nation, exile and homelessness, 'inner emigration' and closeted self-denial. Nevertheless, this reconsideration of the exile experience recognizes that homosexuals such as Klaus Mann can be counted among German refugees.[10]

Homelessness, Exile and 'Inner Exile' for Homosexuals

Exile, indeed, homelessness, had long been a trope of homosexual identity in Germany — at least since Winckelmann and Platen, both of whom sought refuge in an Italy that corresponded more closely to their imagined homoerotic homeland than did Germany. For others who remained in their everyday lifeworlds, 'inner exile' was the *de facto* state of existential normality. But the inner Germany of the typical middle-class homosexual was defined largely in terms of classical references and the Mediterranean south.[11] Homosexuality as existential homelessness had been a literary theme since the late 1890s in the work of John Henry Mackay. But by the late 1920s, homosexuals had begun to move from the 'inner exile' of private dreams and internalized fantasies, typified in Hans von Hülsen's novelistic recreation of the life of mid nineteenth-century poet August von Platen-Hallermünde in *Den alten Göttern zu* (1918), to a newly liberated, valorized and socially validated sense of self.

By the 1920s, Germany had become the first European nation in which it was becoming possible to imagine that homosexuals could feel 'at home' — in some environments at least. Over the years since the early voices of homosexual emancipation had been heard in the 1860's, gay men had begun to take control of the term 'homosexual', transforming it from its status as a forensic, legal or clinical label into a legitimate self-appellation. German writers of fiction openly experimented with models of identity, legitimizing homosexuality as something more than a sexual act. It became integral to and even definitive of character, with a nascent but increasingly compelling social aspect. Since the late 1990s, figures representing a range of social groups from Hirschfeld's *Wissenschaftlich-humanitäres Komitee* to the sexually radicalized components of the *Wandervogel* movement had advocated increased social acceptance of homosexuals. At the same time writers and poets, above all Stefan George, created an explicit homosexual imaginary of radical masculinism, and homosexual men began to find a social identity in a variety of settings from the congregations of 'warme Brüder' in small-town bars to the notorious nightclubs and meeting-spots of Berlin. Amid the confusion and crises of the post-war years and the early Weimar Republic homosexual men had begun to discover the possibility of a *homosexual life*, not merely an anonymous sexual act.[12] Homosexual milieus existed in the German cities and even smaller towns, characterized by identifiable forms of *Habitus* and no longer completely hidden from view. Homosexual men began to sense what it would be like to belong in social environments; to have a sense of 'wir-Gefühl' (or 'feeling of belonging together') in Elias's sense, rather than living in self-denial or finding refuge in an inner realm of safe, but solitary fantasy.

Just as this sense of social self was coming to awareness, however, it was brutally rescinded as Nazism claimed the political centre. Already by the late 1920s it was becoming dangerous to be identified as homosexual; by 1933 all hope of Germany becoming a place of safety and belonging for male homosexuals was gone. By the late 1920s the promise of homosexual trust, social capital and emerging group identity was revoked. Homosexuals who had felt increasingly 'at home' in the Weimar Republic found themselves exiled without even having to make a move. The nation moved from under them, exiling them, and forcing them into forms of 'inner emigration' that many chose only as a last resort as they realized how dangerous their lives had become. This included prominent figures such as Erich Ebermayer, Max René Hesse, Albert Rausch (Henry Benson), even Stefan George and Thomas Mann.

This enforced return to existential homelessness as a means of survival was not new. Nazism represented a return to older forms of inner exile, to the particular existential homelessness of homosexuals determined by the exclusion from family and nation alike and by the absence of an alternative place of refuge other than in their imaginations. However, this change created panic and despair among men who had begun to identify themselves through their new sense of community. Hans Siemsen's story of the suicide of the young homosexual Nazi and lover of Baldur von Schirach, Heinz Holk, in *Die Geschichte des Hitlerjungen Adolf Goers* exemplifies this situation. Yet the term 'exile' remains ambiguous when applied to Germany's homosexuals. Categorical distinctions between exile, inner exile, home and return are by no means as clear for a homosexual writer such as Klaus Mann as they are for a heterosexual writer such as Bertolt Brecht, regardless of their shared socialist politics and their sympathies on so many other topics.

Communists such as Brecht could watch the political situation over the border for signs of change and of possible return to the homeland. Lion Feuchtwanger coined the term 'waiting room' for this exile situation. But homosexuals in Germany had had their own 'waiting room' for the past fifty years, watching as the social situation changed and beginning to see signs of a possible 'coming home' in the sense of finding belonging and community. Of course, 'exile' used in this sense is metaphorical, but under the conditions of the early 1930s onward, with the threat of Nazi persecution or even the death penalty, the term is not misused when applied to known homosexuals from the Weimar period who were under direct physical threat from Nazism. The term 'inner exile' can be applied to those hitherto known homosexuals who covered their tracks and merged back into the normality of German life under the Nazis from the early 1930s onward, as their new-found freedoms were taken from under their feet, figures such as Erich Ebermayer, Albert Rausch or Ernst Glaeser. But this 'inner exile' was different in many ways from that of figures such as Frank Thiess, who coined the term in 1933 with those non-homosexual writers such as himself in mind who rejected Nazism in order to turn away and inward, but whose sense of isolation and exclusion was of a very different order.

Known homosexual men found themselves in a unique situation. They were forced into exile from the new *Vaterland* but had nowhere to go other than into 'inner exile' again. But at the same time, there *was* no place of social origin to which they could return. Their families, whether bourgeois or working class, rarely accepted them. Both left and right rejected homosexuality in the strongest terms.[13] The assassination of Ernst Röhm in 1934 signalled the end of the era of measured tolerance of homosexuality on the political right. Emigration to the Soviet Union or to the United States or elsewhere such as Britain *as a homosexual* was impossible. For those whose homosexuality was no longer tolerated in Germany, refuge could be sought on the basis of political allegiance (as members of the left) or racial identification (as Jews), but not sexuality (as homosexuals). Unless they were also communists or Jews, they had little option other than to 'return' to Nazi Germany under cover as 'inner exiles', to a Germany that had terminated the homosexual civil society and social imaginary that was emerging during the Weimar period.

The typical experience is that of Richard Plant, who fled Germany in 1933 at the age of twenty-two. Born in 1911 and brought up by socialist parents, Plant like many German and Austrian Jews, did not identify as 'Jewish'. He fled Germany out of fear of Nazi persecution as a homosexual, but in the United States he was faced with the question of how to identify himself as a refugee.

> I realized that my identity, if I wanted to have one, had to be Jewish [...] This was Hitler-time. If you were not Jewish, what were you doing in America? [The gay movement in America] was terrible. It was all secret, secret, secret. It was all closets. [...] In Germany it was much more open. Then the Nazis came and everything disappeared.[14]

There was no place of origin or identity in which homosexuals could find refuge *qua homosexuals* at this time. The only option for most was to remain in Nazi Germany and hide behind a façade of 'normality'.

Klaus Mann's Exile

Restlessly on the move, yet always seeking a sense of belonging, Klaus Mann was a figure of the Weimar transition, traversing and documenting the male homosexual experience from the early days of the youth movements to the exile experience under Nazism. Homosexual figures appear in the early novels, *Der fromme Tanz* (1925) and *Treffpunkt im Unendlichen* (1932). But *Treffpunkt* signals the end of the Weimar experiment for Mann. In *Flucht in den Norden* (1934) and *Mephisto* (1936), homosexuality is disguised behind various heterosexual alibis in order to enable political themes to dominate. As early as 1929 Mann expressed the incompatibilities between life and politics, aestheticism and engagement, homosexual affection and political necessity in *Alexander*, his tale of the Macedonian king and homosexual legend, Alexander the Great. And in *Symphonie Pathétique* (1935) the homosexual theme is similarly present but historically distanced in order to explore the psychology of homelessness and lack of belonging in the composer Pyotr Ilyich Tchaikovsky, which corresponded so closely to his own as 'ein Emigrant, ein Exilierter, nicht aus politischen Gründen, sondern weil er sich nirgends zu Hause fühlte, nirgends zu Hause war'.[15]

Exile from Nazism was to prove an ambiguous experience for Mann, since as a homosexual he had never felt 'at home' in Germany in any case. 'Inner exile' signified a loneliness and despair that Mann had fought against all his life, identified already by the precocious seventeen-year-old leaving his Odenwald School: 'Überall werde ich — Fremdling sein. Ein Mensch meiner Art ist stets und allüberall einsam.'[16] Exile from Nazism, then, seemed not so different from German normality. The reality was that Nazism had forced him to flee. He was a known anti-fascist, since his journal, *Die Sammlung,* published by Querido in Amsterdam, had come to the attention of the Nazi authorities, but like other homosexual men seeking refuge in other lands, he would remain in inner exile wherever he went, whether in France, the Soviet Union or the United States. The old realities of inner exile were again the new normal.

On 13 March 1933 Klaus left Germany and would not return as a German citizen. His presence had become dangerous and untenable by late 1933. In November that year prominent Nazi writer Hanns Johst suggested in a letter to Heinrich Himmler that Thomas Mann be interned as a hostage in the newly created Dachau concentration camp as a warning to his son, Klaus, and others like him, of what was awaiting them in Germany should they return.[17] With his sister Erika, Mann at first assumed the mask of the political exile. However, after Stalin's recriminalization of homosexuality in the Soviet Union in 1934, Mann could no longer identify with Soviet communism. He penned the essay 'Die Linke und das Laster', arguing that homosexuality was not a bourgeois deviance, but it was too late.[18] The possibility of being a homosexual communist exile was over. He would eventually seek refuge in the United States, but here too, any hint of homosexuality had to be carefully disguised.

Only in one novel, *Der Vulkan: Roman unter Emigranten*, his last and best, did Mann take the male homosexual exile as his explicit theme in the figure of the fictive writer and authorial alter ego, Martin Kurella.–*Der Vulkan* documents his realization that leaving Hitler's Germany in order to seek exile along with like-minded refugees in foreign environments did not bring about a sense of liberation, purpose or fulfilment for him as a homosexual man. On the contrary, the identity, support and togetherness that communists, Jews, socialists or anti-fascist artists discovered in their social identifications in exile only brought home to the homosexual the impossibility of his situation. Martin Kurella's suicide is the endpoint of his recognition that existential homelessness remained the fate of the homosexual in the exile milieu as well.

Exile in *Flucht in den Norden*

Klaus Mann wrote two — very different — novels of exile. In the development of his representation of the exile situation from the early *Flucht in den Norden* (1933–34) to *Der Vulkan* (1937–39), Mann grasped the particularities and the uniqueness of the homosexual in exile, mirroring his own experiences of politics and life during the first half of the twentieth century as inner exile came to exist alongside anti-fascist exile as a defining element of his experience.

In *Flucht in den Norden* Mann's own personal homosexual experiences are translated into heterosexual fiction, but in the process Mann creates an unconvincing and skewed perception of the exile experience. The heroine, Johanna, committed to communism mainly through the influence of her brother Georg, is on the run from Germany. Her political affiliations are known to the Gestapo and she must flee. On the way to joining Georg in Paris, she joins up with a friend, Karin, for a brief sojourn on the latter's family estate in rural Finland. There the 'boyish' Johanna meets the unpredictable, moody loner, Ragnar, Karin's brother. Johanna and Ragnar fall in love. During a long and aimless road journey northwards that symbolizes the loss of social context for both, she learns of the death of one of her communist friends at the hands of the Gestapo and faces the choice between a love without direction or clarity on the one hand, and her political and ethical duty as a German communist on the other. At the last minute she rejects Ragnar in order to devote herself to the communist underground and continue her journey to Paris.

The novel is based on Mann's trip by car with sister Erika and mutual friend Annamarie Schwarzenbach to Finland in early 1932, where Klaus caught up again with Hans Aminoff, whom he had met earlier that year in Paris and whom he would later refer to as the love of his life. The Aminoffs were members of the Finnish-Swedish gentry. Their estate, Pekkala, described in the novel, lies beside lake Näsijärvi, in the far east of the country, less than 150 km from the Russian border. Klaus becomes Johanna, Hans becomes Ragnar. Shortly after Klaus's departure, Hans Aminoff submitted to family pressure to marry a wealthy Swedish countess and found a family, although he appears to have continued to have homosexual affairs. While Klaus was heartbroken, he accepted the situation with his characteristic clear-sightedness regarding the difficulties of homosexual love and commitment at that time.[19]

Flucht is an orthodox novel of political exile. Johanna is intended to be a committed communist and the ending is about her choice between love and politics, self-fulfilment and ethical duty. However, Mann's own interests and concerns during these years, in particular the love affair with Hans Aminoff, undermine the political cues throughout the novel. Not only does Johanna's commitment to the communist underground seem too weak to support her decision to leave Ragnar, but the attraction between Ragnar and Johanna, though powerful, lacks conviction and there are intimations of lesbianism in Karin's relationship with Johanna. Altogether these and other factors render the plot unconvincing. Sex and sexuality play a much more powerful role than politics, but remain largely unspoken in this work. Ragnar is a Finnish Heathcliff whose anarchic sexual power overpowers Johanna's pallid communism: their first night together is described from her perspective with a power that betrays the real motive of this novel.

A key scene occurs during the car journey in the far north of Lapland. A wild horse almost collides with the car, an image at once of magnificent natural beauty in the moonlight and of confusion on the road in the glare of the car lights.[20] For Johanna it is a moment of revelation. The possible car crash suggests death as the only alternative to the choice between love and duty. But the accident doesn't happen. The wild horse springs back in time and canters away into the night, and Johanna, robbed of her *Liebestod*, must continue her existential journey towards

Paris. It would take Klaus Mann a further five years before he would recognize his exile to be something other than that to which Johanna commits herself, in a desperate attempt to maintain her sense of reality and of her known world.

Handsome and masculine, socially inept but good-hearted, and angrily rejecting his brother's fascism for a rugged, if vulnerable, individualism, Ragnar is a problematic figure. He veers from merriment to anger in a moment and spends long periods in brooding bitterness. In both him and Johanna a sense of inauthenticity is palpable. Neither appears to be able to negotiate the existential questions around their love for each other. Only in the desolate overnight hotels of their road-journey without friends, family or company are they able to be together; neither home (Ragnar) nor exile (Johanna) seems able to offer a viable life for the implied narrative presence of Mann himself. Home is a heterosexual family environment in Finland that hides all sorts of family secrets (including a hidden senile grandmother in an attic), and exile is foreshadowed as a life of unfulfilled loneliness in foreign hotels for the sake of duty. The hidden truth of *Flucht in den Norden* is that it is a novel of homosexual exile in disguise, a work in which the true motive forces remain unspoken. The story of political exile functions as a palimpsest for a homosexual exile that could not speak its name.

Homosexual Exile in *Der Vulkan*

Mann began *Der Vulkan* in New York in 1939 and finished it two years later. This novel follows the stories of a group of German intellectuals in exile in Paris and other parts of Europe: the writer Martin Kurella, his female friend the actress Marion Kammer (who shares traits with Klaus' sister Erika), the sociologist David Deutsch and the literary historian Professor Abel. Around them are grouped various individuals, most importantly Marion's friend and later husband, the French writer Marcel Poiret and Martin's Brazilian lover, Kikjou. The action takes place from April 1933 in the prologue until 1 January 1939 in the epilogue, in the exile hubs of Paris, Zurich, Prague, Amsterdam, the United States and Spain.

The work was intended as a social novel of emigration. In his *Tagebuch* Mann wrote on August 20 1936:

> Mein nächster Roman. Grosse Komposition aus Emigranten-Schicksalen: 'Die Verfolgten' oder so. Laufen nebeneinander her, jedoch durch irgendeine Klammer miteinander verbunden. In vielen Städten: Paris, London, Prag, New York, Hollywood, Zürich, Amsterdam, Palma, Florenz, Nice, Sanary u.s.w. Salzburg. Wolfgang. E. [Erika Mann] Treuberg, Sundheimer. Junger Prolet. Brentano. Regler. F. Ferdinand Lion. Kommunisten. Katholiken. Gründung einer neuen Partei. Pass-Schwierigkeiten. Geldnot. Sexualnot. Der Hass. Die Hoffnung. Das Heimweh. Kriegsangst (und Hoffnung ...) Politik: Saar, Spanien, Olympiade. Verbindung zu illegalen im Reich. Melancholie. Les sans-patrie ... Das werde ich können.[21]

He hoped and intended to put his individual problems behind him for the sake of the general and the political.[22] But the hope proved illusory. At the centre of the novel is the exile and authorial alter ego, the homosexual Martin Kurella who leaves Germany not out of political conviction, but rather to accompany his friend, Marion. While he shares Marion's disgust and hatred of the Nazis, he is not a political exile.[23] Just over half way through the novel Martin dies not as the result of political activity but rather from his drug addiction.

Early in the novel, homosexual Helmut Kündinger whispers to Martin the story of his lover's suicide.

> Während die Stimmen immer lauter wurden, rückte der junge Helmut Kündinger näher an Martin heran. 'Mein Freund und ich', sagte er leise, — und die Worte 'Mein Freund' sprach er mit einer innig getragenen Betonung aus —, 'haben in Göttingen so wundervolle Zeiten verlebt. In einem kleinen Zirkel, der sich nur aus wertvollen Menschen zusammensetzte, lasen wir gemeinsam Hölderlin und George, auch Rilke, aber den liebten wir weniger, er war uns zu weich, George hat die ganze herrliche Härte des Deutschtums, Hölderlin seine ganze unauslotbare Tiefe — : das pflegte mein Freund zu sagen. Ihm fielen immer so schöne Dinge ein. Sie können sich gar nicht vorstellen, wie er an Deutschland hing; wie ... wie an einer Geliebten', sagte Helmut Kündinger und sah Martin hilflos an. 'Er liebte den Begriff "Deutschland", deutsche Dichter und deutsche Landschaft viel mehr, als er irgend einen einzelnen Menschen geliebt hat'. Dabei gab es eine kleine Flamme, wie von Eifersucht, in Helmut Kündingers Blick... . 'Ja, er liebte es von ganzem Herzen', bestätigte Helmut Kündinger ernst. (*Vulkan* 44–45)

Helmut Kündinger's lover represents a group of which Klaus Mann had been contemptuously aware since the Weimar years, namely the men who had valorized their homosexuality through the heightened masculine ethos of the right-wing men's organizations or *Männerbund*. The evocation of German hardness, the idealization of Stefan George's poetry, and the close bonding in the all-male environment are common to this group. Kündinger's lover commits suicide after he is discovered to be of part-Jewish ancestry and therefore no longer able to participate in the national *Heimat*, or homeland, and homosocial *Gemeinschaft*. The loss of his lover destroys Helmut Kündinger's sense of *Heimat*, sending him into exile from a land that cannot accept difference. Kündinger is the most openly homosexual refugee *and* exile in this novel. It is this homosexual experience that alienates him from his homeland. As he tells Martin, Germany seems defiled: 'Die Heimat war mir verleidet. Ich mußte weg — ich mußte einfach weg' (*Vulkan* 45).

Helmut Kündinger's tale of exclusion finds a deep echo in Martin's own experience of sexual alienation. 'Wo ist die Gemeinschaft, an die ich mich wenden könnte?' (*Vulkan* 191), he writes in mid-1934, the year in which Paragraph 175 (the provision of the German Criminal Code rendering male homosexual acts a crime) was revised to include the death penalty for homosexuality. In the absence of such a community, Martin sets out to write 'den großen Roman der Ruhelosen und Heimatlosen' (*Vulkan* 191), but it remains uncompleted. His failure to make progress is representative of his failure to find community through meaningful relationships, even to those around him whose experiences of exile he shares, such as Helmut Kündinger. Where the others find community in their political beliefs, Martin dies alone, accompanied only by the syringe that symbolizes his withdrawal into the inner realm, beyond the reach, even, of Kikjou. Morphine provides the sense of the oceanic, of immolation into a totality that is otherwise missing from Martin's life, and which is not redeemed through his intimate relationship. Against Martin, the French writer Marcel Poiret uses the Spanish Civil War as his means of participating in a morally justified social action and thereby of becoming part of a group, losing his intellectual isolation and redeeming his humanity. Poiret also dies, but is remembered as a martyr and political hero of the left.

Helmut Kündinger's story is of exclusion from one of the new forms of community naively believed by some to offer a promise of emancipation, namely the homosocial fatherland of the *Männerbund*.[24] Martin's story represents the deeper, truer story for Klaus Mann of the core experience of homosexuality as the sense of exile from the bonds of community. The programmatic introduction to his planned novel, addressing those who resurface after the apocalypse, reveals itself to be a last fragment of hope for a world otherwise lost: 'Für wen schreibe ich? — [...] Für die Kommenden! Nicht euch, den Zeitgenossen, gehört unser Wort; es gehört der Zukunft, den noch ungeborenen Geschlechtern' (*Vulkan* 191). That the novel is never finished confirms the loneliness of Martin's exile experience. Martin finds no sense of community, whether real or unreal, supportive or otherwise in friends or family. At the funeral, Martin's parents disapprove of his friends and condemn and disown the homosexuality that they could no longer ignore. Only in the inner realm of addiction can Martin alleviate the sense of existential homelessness felt from not belonging to a broader group-identity. After writing these words he succumbs to his addiction, losing even the last vestiges of hope that this appeal represents. Death provides relief where, for the others, a sense of identity provides support.

Martin's despair in exile is not merely, or even primarily, the consequence of his political rejection of Nazism. Even the existence of his lover Kikjou does not assuage Martin's loneliness, since they are both exiles, both lacking any sense of wider human community. Refusing to identify in terms of the political categories of left and right, both of which reject him on account of his sexuality, Martin is left with little option other than the withdrawal into the inner realm of a narcissistic subjectivity symbolized by his drug addiction and contrasted with Kikjou's internalized, personalized religiosity. The memory of the hope for a homosexual social imaginary as it existed in Germany fleetingly from around 1910 and 1930 was dead. Had homosexual men in Germany not experienced the beginnings of a social imaginary during the first three decades of the century, they would not, perhaps, have felt so keenly its absence. Reminded of the inner exile they had begun to leave behind, they found themselves thrown back into existential homelessness by 1934.

After Martin's death the other refugees spread to the four corners of the earth, each experiencing his or her exile differently, becoming more and more separate from one another. The lingering homelessness which had accompanied Martin throughout his life is felt by all, even as life is re-established. They gradually lose each other but find new roles and identities, buoyed by the social conventions that exclude the homosexual. Even those whose lives take a tragic turn have a social identity: Marcel

Poiret abandons his wife, Marion dies a hero and martyr to the Spanish cause; Helmut Kündinger will forget his Göttingen lover and the homosexual poetry of Stefan George in order to become a successful foreign correspondent (*Vulkan* 473). Working from China with neither home nor social identity he embraces homelessness beyond exile as a way of life. Marion finds happiness in marriage to Professor Abel after both of them reconnect by coincidence in the United States. David Deutsch, the only one to have been with Martin at the end, undergoes a crisis of conviction in his role as a German sociologist and intellectual, and resolves to join a Danish organization retraining Jews as tradesmen to build a future Israel. Hans Schütte finds purpose in Marcel's death and joins the Party:

> Nun ist er hin. Ist ein Sinn dabei? ... Natürlich ist ein Sinn dabei. Der hat schon gewußt, warum er hergekommen ist, und hier mit uns gekämpft hat, und sich hat totschießen lassen von den verfluchten Faschisten. [...] Ich habe das satt — so als interessanter Einzelgänger herum zu laufen. Ich trete in die Partei ein ...
> (*Vulkan* 355)

Kikjou seems destined to take up a role for which he must abandon the 'tierische Geilheit' (*Vulkan* 348) of his past and suppress his homosexual identity. After the death of his father he will return to a role as older brother-and paternal substitute for his orphaned sisters in Brazil, a life that means nothing to him. Even if it proves illusory, the exile experience of the non-homosexual characters finds resolution, tragic or otherwise, in the resumption of a social identity, whether it be in the Spanish civil war, the fight against Nazism or the dedication to a new sense of Jewish identity. For Martin and Kikjou, however, there is no social component with which to find an identity.

Der Vulkan is not a novel about homosexual exile. It is a novel in which a homosexual perspective is brought to bear on the broader refugee experience. Martin's refugee experience is superimposed over a deeper existential sense of exile from family and community that is determined by his homosexuality. Homosexual existence is revealed to be a persisting form of exile from heterosexual society in the sense of not having a home. But homosexual exile does not include the expectation of eventual return home. The homosexual's homelessness predates and continues throughout the refugee experience and is determined by the absence of the sense of community or 'wir-Gefühl' that his heterosexual comrades take for granted before exile and which continues to maintain their expectations of return after exile.

Conclusion: 'Homosexual' Exile as an Impossibility

For Hans Mayer writing in the early 1970s and himself both a refugee and a homosexual, *Der Vulkan* is at its most impressive in describing the decline of a morphine addict, but has nothing to do with the exile situation.[25] More recently, Arwed Schmidt similarly dismissed Martin's homosexuality as peripheral to and a distraction from the theme of exile. For Schmidt, Martin's life in exile is just irresponsible 'migrantische[r] Freiheitstaumel' as opposed to the 'Courage derer, die konsequent und zielgerichtet damit begonnen haben, den mühsamen Weg des selbstbewußten Widerständlers zu wählen'.[26] Schmidt fails to see Mann's point: namely that Martin's life is not considered worthy even of refugee status.[27] As a homosexual he has no status at all.

The dismissal of homosexuality as a phenomenon of Weimar flippancy or indulged *jeunesse dorée* is indicative of the failure to take the theme of *Der Vulkan* seriously, namely the specific situation of the homosexual in exile. Martin's anguish finds no echo in the stories of political and racial exclusion and endangerment of the others. His homosexuality is a defining aspect of his existence, deeper seated and more fundamental than a political position or ethno-cultural identification, and therefore certainly no less significant in existential terms. It is a part of Martin's existence which finds acceptance neither in his homeland nor in exile, and not even among the refugees with whom he shares so much in other respects. Martin is truly alone in this novel. Mann reveals the effects of the destruction of an emerging modern collective identity in the political environments of the 1930s when the political communities of both left and right refused entry to the homosexual individual. Homosexuality did not come to sit alongside race and politics as categories of exile experience and validation. The brief period of hope for a social existence and a symbolic imaginary that had emerged by the Weimar years, in which the homosexual could exist as a social being, was over, leaving no trace in the exile experience.

In *Der Vulkan* homosexuality emerges for the first time as a theme in the novel of exile. In *Flucht in den Norden*, by comparison, homosexual love still has to masquerade as heterosexuality in order to fit the contours of the novel of exile. The linkage of homosexuality with drug-abuse in the later novel and the downward spiral of depression is symptomatic of the inability of the homosexual refugee to find a place of exile other than in himself, in a turn inward that ultimately alienates him from everything and everyone around him, ending in death. *Der Vulkan* exemplifies Hans Mayer's identification of the incommensurability of the exile experience.[28]

In order to conceptualize homosexual exile as a problematic category in the context of *Exilliteratur*, we must recognize that the homosexual experience itself was one of exile from the childhood safe haven of family and community at an early age for a life of dissembling or of exclusion. Moreover, the end-point, namely arrival in a new country where safety and security are possible, is problematic. For homosexuals from Germany, the destination was by no means safe in the way that the Soviet Union was for communists, France was for anti-fascists of various political colours, or some countries were for Jews.

Klaus Mann remained in exile as an anti-fascist. This, however, was a temporary solution. By 1949 his alibi had disappeared and his life spiralled downward into the abyss that Martin Kurella had faced. Mann's suicide in that year was a gesture of despair. The end of Nazism signalled the end of the anti-Nazi, leaving the individual homosexual in all his existential isolation. Homosexual liberation would have to wait until the 1970s before it even began to be imagined again in Germany.

Notes to Chapter 21

1. I use the neutral term 'homosexual', rather than terms such as 'gay' or 'queer' which carry associations inappropriate for the period under consideration. While some aspects of the following article apply also to homosexual women, the main argument applies to homosexual men, given historical conditions and the focus on the life and literary works of Klaus Mann.
2. Walter A. Berendsohn, *Die humanistische Front: Einführung in die deutsche Emigranten-Literatur* (Zurich: Europa Verlag, 1946); Alfred Kantorowicz and Richard Drews, *Verboten und verbrannt: Deutsche Literatur 12 Jahre unterdrückt* (Berlin: Ullstein-Kindler, 1947): pp. 42–51; Hans Mayer, 'Die Literatur der deutschen Emigration', in *Ansichten über einige neue Schriftsteller und Bücher*, ed. by Stephan Hermlin and Hans Mayer (Wiesbaden: Limes Verlag, 1947), pp. 20–25; Franz Carl Weiskopf, *Unter fremden Himmeln: Ein Abriß der deutschen Literatur im Exil 1933–1947* (Berlin: Dietz, 1948).
3. Jost Hermand, 'Schreiben in der Fremde: Gedanken zur deutschen Exilliteratur seit 1789', in *Exil und innere Emigration: Third Wisconsin Workshop*, ed. by Reinhold Grimm and Jost Hermand (Frankfurt a.M.: Athenäum, 1972), pp. 7–30 (p. 15); Hans Mayer, 'Konfrontation der inneren und der äußeren Emigration: Erinnerung und Deutung', in *Exil und innere Emigration: Third Wisconsin Workshop*, ed. by Reinhold Grimm and Jost Hermand (Frankfurt a.M.: Athenäum, 1972), pp. 75–88 (p. 79).
4. Manfred Durzak, 'Deutschsprachige Exilliteratur: Vom moralischen Zeugnis zum literarischen Dokument', in *Die deutsche Exilliteratur 1933–1945*, ed. by Manfred Durzak (Stuttgart: Reclam, 1973), pp. 9–26 (pp. 10–15).
5. Doerte Bischoff and Susanne Komfort-Hein, 'Literatur und Exil: Neue Perspektiven auf eine (historische und aktuelle) Konstellation', in *Literatur und Exil: Neue Perspektiven*, ed. by Doerte Bischoff and Susanne Komfort-Hein (Berlin: de Gruyter, 2013), pp. 1–19 (pp. 1–2).
6. Wolfgang Frühwald, 'Die "gekannt sein wollen": Prolegomena zu einer Theorie des Exils', in *Innen-Leben: Ansichten aus dem Exil. Ein Berliner Symposium*, ed. by Hermann Haarmann (Berlin: Fannei & Walz, 1995), pp. 59–69 (p. 56).
7. Paul-Michael Lützeler, 'Migration und Exil in Geschichte, Mythos und Literatur', in *Handbuch der deutschsprachigen Exilliteratur: Von Heinrich Heine bis Herta Müller*, ed. by Bettina Bannasch und Gerhild Rochus (Berlin: de Gruyter, 2013), pp. 3–26 (p. 8).
8. Ibid., p. 7.
9. Hans-Dieter Zimmermann, '"Innere Emigration": Ein historischer Begriff und seine Problematik', in *Schriftsteller und Widerstand: Facetten und Probleme der 'Inneren Emigration'*, ed. by Frank-Lothar Kroll and Rüdiger von Voss (Göttingen: Wallstein 2012), pp. 45–62 (pp. 47–48, 57).
10. See, for example, Susanne Wolfram, *Die tödliche Wunde: Über die Untrennbarkeit von Tod und Eros im Werk von Klaus Mann* (Frankfurt a.M.: Peter Lang, 1986), and Arwed Schmidt, *Exilwelten der 30er Jahre: Untersuchungen zu Klaus Manns Emigrationsromanen* Flucht in den Norden *und* Der Vulkan, Roman unter Emigranten (Würzburg: Königshausen & Neumann, 2003).
11. See Robert Aldrich, *The Seduction of the Mediterranean: Writing, Art and Homosexual Fantasy* (London: Routledge, 1993).
12. The literature covering the emergence of homosexuality as a modern sexual orientation and of its social manifestations is now comprehensive. See, for example, Robert Beachy, 'The German Invention of Homosexuality', *Journal of Modern History*, 82.4 (2010), 801–38; Laurie Marhoffer, *Sex and the Weimar Republic: German Homosexual Emancipation and the Rise of the Nazis* (Toronto: University of Toronto Press, 2015); Robert Beachy, *Gay Berlin: Birthplace of a Modern Identity* (London: Vintage, 2015); Clayton J. Whisnant, *Queer Identities and Politics in Germany: A History, 1880–1945* (New York: Harrington Park Press, 2016).
13. Ironically the Soviet Union promulgated a new anti-sodomy statute in 1934, in the same year as Nazi Germany increased the punishment under Paragraph 175 to the death penalty for homosexual offences. See Gert Hekma, Harry Oosterhuis and James Steakley, 'Leftist Sexual Politics and Homosexuality: A Historical Overview', in *Gay Men and the Sexual History of the Political Left*, ed. by Gert Hekma, Harry Oosterhuis and James Steakley (New York: Harrington Park Press, 1995), pp. 1–40 (p. 30).

14. Richard Plant, 'Being Gay, Becoming Jewish' in *Hitler's Exiles: Personal Stories of the Flight from Nazi Germany to America*, ed. by Mark M. Anderson (New York: The New Press, 1998), pp. 311–16 (pp. 313–15).
15. Klaus Mann, *Der Wendepunkt: Ein Lebensbericht* (Reinbek bei Hamburg: Rowohlt, 2006), p. 458.
16. Klaus Mann, *Briefe und Antworten 1922–1949*, ed. by Martin Gregor-Dellin (Reinbek bei Hamburg: Rowohlt, 1991), p. 15.
17. Kurt Pätzold, 'Zur politischen Biografie Thomas Manns (1933)', *Weimarer Beiträge*, 9 (1975), 178–81 (p. 181). (My thanks to Dr. Claudia Hein of *Weimarer Beiträge* for making this article available to me during the COVID pandemic.)
18. Klaus Mann, 'Homosexualität und Faschismus' (first published under the title 'Die Linke und das Laster'), in *Zahnärzte und Künstler: Aufsätze, Reden, Kritiken 1933–1936* (Reinbek bei Hamburg: Rowohlt, 1993), pp. 235–42.
19. See Frederic Spotts, *Cursed Legacy: The Tragic Life of Klaus Mann* (New Haven: Yale University Press, 2016), pp. 75, 86.
20. Klaus Mann, *Flucht in den Norden* (Reinbek bei Hamburg: Rowohlt, 2003), pp. 255–56.
21. Klaus Mann, *Tagebücher 1936–37* (Reinbek bei Hamburg: Rowohlt, 1995), pp. 69–70.
22. See Lutz Winkler, 'Ästhetizismus und Engagement in den Exilromanen Klaus Manns', in *Schreiben im Exil: Zur Ästhetik der deutschen Exilliteratur 1933–1945*, ed. by Alexander Stephan and Hans Wagener (Bonn: Bouvier, 1985), pp. 196–211 (p. 196), from original documentation in the Klaus-Mann-Archiv, Munich, KM560, p. 2.
23. Klaus Mann, *Der Vulkan: Roman unter Emigranten* (Reinbek bei Hamburg: Rowohlt, 2006), p. 19. All further citations are given in brackets in the text.
24. On the *Männerbund* as an environment of homosocial companionship and more or less covert homosexuality, see Peter Morgan, 'Coming out in Weimar: Crisis and Homosexuality in the Weimar Republic', *Thesis Eleven*, 111/1 (2012), 48–65 (pp. 50–53).
25. Mayer, p. 78.
26. Schmidt, p. 32.
27. Ibid., pp. 224–25.
28. Mayer, p. 79.

CHAPTER 22

Exile and Reality in Erich Auerbach's *Mimesis*

Steffan Davies

Möge meine Untersuchung ihre Leser erreichen; sowohl meine überlebenden Freunde von einst wie auch alle anderen, für die sie bestimmt ist; und dazu beitragen, diejenigen wieder zusammenzuführen, die die Liebe zu unserer abendländischen Geschichte ohne Trübung bewahrt haben.[1]

Erich Auerbach's *Mimesis*, written in Istanbul from 1942 to 1945, is — in Edward Said's words — 'an exile's book'.[2] Auerbach had been dismissed in October 1935, as a Jew, from his chair in Romance philology in Marburg; he moved to Istanbul the following year to chair the university's faculty for Western languages and literatures, a post that was part of its drive to Westernize its curriculum. *Mimesis* starts and ends with Odysseus, across a span from Homer's *Odyssey* to Joyce's *Ulysses*. Begun in May 1942, as information about the Holocaust was beginning to emerge, the study opens by immediately juxtaposing Jewish victimhood, the sacrifice of Isaac in Genesis 22, with Odysseus' return.[3] Its epilogue claims a direct connection with exile: that Auerbach's being in Turkey, without access to a well-stocked library for European studies (*M*, p. 497; *ME*, p. 557), had been decisive to the book's existence, as it released him from the weight of specialized scholarship that might otherwise have killed off the project from the start. That stark claim is not borne out entirely by the evidence of the library holdings in Istanbul, and it is a rhetorical gesture as much as a statement of fact: the tropes of the 'empty' Orient, and of exile as a uniquely productive state, combined to explain the book's unconventional method.[4]

Much has been made of the circumstances in which *Mimesis* was written, and of the traces of Auerbach's exile in the first chapter, which contrasts the modes of representation in the *Odyssey* and the Bible. I want to ask, however, how exile influenced *Mimesis* in other ways. In her analysis of the final chapter, 'Der braune Strumpf', on Marcel Proust and Virginia Woolf, Kader Konuk finds that 'tropes of detachment are central not only to literary modernism but also to Auerbach's own methodology', an insight I wish to develop here for the rest of *Mimesis* too.[5] Thematically, exile is present throughout, including, as Konuk shows, in the way in which Marie, the Swiss maid in *To the Lighthouse*, gazes into space as she mourns her dying father at home.[6] Methodologically, Auerbach's account relies on distance and separation, because he sees 'the representation of reality' in the same terms as his hope for his own time: a task of re-collecting the dispersed. *Mimesis* extends more broadly than the high canon of Western literature: Homer and the Old Testament are not followed by Virgil, say, whose *Aeneid* is the story 'of arms and of the exile' as the founder of Rome,[7] but by Petronius's *Satyricon*, whose wandering characters Encolpius and Giton can be seen as parodies of Odysseus.[8]

This essay will first set out the argument of *Mimesis*, to trace how Auerbach gave such variety a coherent purpose. It then looks for nuances in his contrasting accounts of nineteenth-century Realism in Germany and France. *Mimesis* is notoriously dismissive of German literature; its admiration for German *Historismus*, however, is equally clearly stated but less well known.[9] Tracing Auerbach's commitment to historicism, which he derived from his studies of Giambattista Vico, reveals the essence of his own scholarly approach, and his conviction that the writing of history and of literature are interdependent: that literature should fundamentally be historiographical, a 'representation of reality'. Starting from his remarks on Germany, the essay also identifies a significant tension in Auerbach's attitude to nationhood, oscillating between affirming the value of singular national identities and desiring their end. In conclusion, the essay suggests that the figure who sums up Auerbach's key concerns in *Mimesis* is Michel de Montaigne.

'Reality' for Auerbach is the life of ordinary individuals, which is contingent and unpredictable. His recurring question is how literary representation has made random lives universally meaningful so that, in turn, all individuals can relate to them. *Mimesis* starts in the twin worlds of legend — ancient epic — and history, the Old Testament. Whilst the *Odyssey* describes a scene meticulously, the Bible gives its readers only the few details they need to follow the story (*M*, pp. 7 and 15; *ME*, pp. 3 and 10–11), so legend is 'comparatively simple' despite the detail, because history allows for complexity beyond what is immediately described. Scripture is historical not because it is all factually true, but because it admits of human complexity and is written to make sense of it. In the Bible's case, that sense is the text's claim to unique, universal authority, which fits all events to a divine plan. Homer, by contrast, can be fully appreciated without being believed (*M*, p. 19; *ME*, p. 14).

Auerbach knew that modernity's distance from the Old Testament, both chronological and spiritual, stretched so far that the biblical stories were now themselves ancient legends (*M*, p. 21; *ME*, p. 16). Scripture's truth-claim made it 'tyrannical' (*M*, p. 19; *ME*, p. 14). What is important, however, is his idea that reality is agelessly complex:

> Man denke an die Geschichte, welcher wir selbst beiwohnen; wer etwa das Verhalten der einzelnen Menschen und Menschengruppen beim Aufkommen des Nationalsozialismus in Deutschland, oder das Verhalten der einzelnen Völker und Staaten vor und während des gegenwärtigen (1942) Krieges erwägt, der wird fühlen, wie schwer darstellbar geschichtliche Gegenstände überhaupt, und wie unbrauchbar sie für die Sage sind; das Geschichtliche enthält eine Fülle widersprechender Motive in jedem Einzelnen [...]; nur selten kommt (wie jetzt durch den Krieg) eine allenfalls eindeutige, vergleichsweise einfach beschreibbare Lage zustande, und auch diese ist unterirdisch vielfach abgestuft,

ja sogar fast dauernd in ihrer Eindeutigkeit gefährdet [...]. (*M*, p. 25; *ME*, pp. 19–20)

Yet although history is many-sided and 'unfit for legend', the historian is forced, paradoxically, to make concessions to legend's techniques, for legend offers the clarity which history lacks. This reads like an observation of historical writing as narrative, a precursor of the 'linguistic turn' advanced by Hayden White, but it is an unsatisfactory conclusion.[10] Simplicity is the mode not of understanding, but of propaganda (*M*, p. 25; *ME*, p. 20). As James Porter has shown, this first chapter practises a polemical 'counter-philology', with 'everything that Auerbach rues about the current political situation in Germany [...] abundantly attested in Homer: superficiality, simplification, the technique of legend, the absence of depth, [...] of any sense of reality or of ethical calling'; all their opposites are in the Old Testament.[11] C. S. Lewis, in his chapter 'On Realisms' — which Ritchie Robertson recommended to his tutees to challenge our thinking — points out that 'realism of content', plausible truth-to-life, is far abler to deceive the reader than clear fantasy, 'which never deceives at all'.[12]

At the end of *Mimesis*, another passage addresses this paradox again (*M*, p. 493; *ME*, pp. 552–53). Because life's complexity cannot be fully explained, Auerbach instead, in conclusion to 'Der braune Strumpf', claims the political and moral potential of 'randomness' over synthesis:

> gerade der beliebige Augenblick ist vergleichsweise unabhängig von den umstrittenen und wankenden Ordnungen, um welche die Menschen kämpfen und verzweifeln; er verläuft unterhalb derselben, als tägliches Leben. Je mehr man ihn auswertet, desto schärfer tritt das elementar Gemeinsame unseres Lebens zutage [...]. Es muß aus der absichtslosen und vertiefenden Darstellung der gedachten Art zu entnehmen sein, wie sehr sich [...] schon jetzt die Unterschiede zwischen den Lebens- und Denkformen der Menschen verringert haben.

Auerbach suggests here that the differences between nations — the very precondition of modern-day exile — are disappearing. There are two ways to read this. Describing the change as an 'Ausgleichsprozeß' echoes Horkheimer and Adorno's diagnosis of modern, mass society in *Dialektik der Aufklärung*, which was being written at the same time as *Mimesis*, though the echo of their terms — 'nivellieren', for example — is stronger in Willard Trask's translation, 'leveling process'. Auerbach, too, hints at the richness that stands to be lost as the process tends to simplicity. This would be the triumph of 'legend' over 'history', and he suggests that he will be glad not to live to see it. On the other hand, and more immediately too, representing random lives does not point individuals away from each other, but towards a common humanity. That goal was still far from being lived in practice, but it was coming into sight: a different synthesis from the propagandist's, and surely a hopeful prospect. This community, most clearly apparent now 'in der absichtslosen, genauen, inneren und äußeren Darstellung des beliebigen Lebensaugenblicks der verschiedenen Menschen', was the future vision to which 'our western history', beloved of Auerbach's intended readers according to the epilogue, was the counterpart in the past.

Diversity was thus the constant ingredient in the representation of reality and the measure of its success. This faced a barrier in the convention that connected literary style to the social standing of its subjects (high style only depicting socially superior characters, and so on): courtly romance was limited by the fact that it did not distinguish between levels of expression, and thus between its characters (*M*, p. 131; *ME*, pp. 132–33), whereas medieval Christian drama accepted the paradox that its highest truths were — in Jesus's words — revealed not to the wise, but to children.[13] Out of this diversity of style comes the ability to derive meaning from parallel contexts. Auerbach claims that the Bible is read by 'revisional interpretation', 'umdeutende Interpretation', where Adam's sleep at the creation of Eve, say, is given a new layer of meaning by the death-sleep of Christ (*M*, pp. 54–55; *ME*, p. 48). The 'great drama' of the Fall contained, in essence, all the events of world history (*M*, p. 154; *ME*, p. 158). This is a method which Auerbach had set out before: 'figural' interpretation, in which one entirely real thing represents another. Events that are causally and chronologically detached carry each other's meaning, the 'figure', which signifies the other as well as itself, and the 'fulfilment', which 'encompasses' the figure.[14] The elements of figural interpretation can thus be young and old at the same time, they are time-bound but hold universal meaning, such that the conflation of time in medieval Christian narratives is figural, not simplistic (*M*, p. 154; *ME*, p. 158). In exile from anti-Semitism, Auerbach argued that in this reading of the Bible, the Old Testament was not the Gospels' prehistory, but their centre, as it figurally told and retold Christian salvation.[15] Methodologically, detachment — the permanent difference between figure and fulfilment — is also essential here. Both elements are fully historical ('innergeschichtlich'), by comparison, say, with allegory, where an immaterial concept is illustrated in material terms. Allegory fixes meaning: for C. S. Lewis, medieval allegory offered the ancient gods, no longer worshipped as deities, 'new dwellings' as vehicles of poetic imagination.[16] *Figura*, on the other hand, does not settle: it does not permit conclusive interpretation, '[die] naiv[e] wie [die] modern-wissenschaftlich[e] Auffassung von der vollzogenen Tatsache', but remains unfinished and open-ended. It is believed in or hoped for, not understood. Historically, it does not mark progressive development; rather, the events it connects are 'torn apart' from each other, isolated, and kept waiting for a 'third' which is always yet to come.[17]

Auerbach saw *figura* at its most apparent in Dante's *Divine Comedy*, a constant focus of his scholarship. Dante's achievement was to have depicted life as vividly real and, simultaneously, as entirely connected to the divine plan of salvation. His style reflected the content: his language extended to the colloquial and even the vulgar, but was fixed firmly, and for the first time in the vernacular, in an elevated tone. He showed human reality with almost painful immediacy (*M*, p. 194; *ME*, p. 199). But this near-perfect synthesis of earthly reality and divine meaning could not hold, as the figure was so realistic as to surpass the fulfilment. Dante brought the whole historical world to life, but at the price 'daß die Wirkung ins Irdische umschlägt [...]; das Jenseits wird zum Theater des Menschen und seiner Leidenschaften' (*M*, p. 195; *ME*, p. 201). His work both realized *figura* and destroyed it (*M*, p. 196; *ME*, p. 202).

Dante is a central figure in *Mimesis*, but a turning point, too, and the passage from the *Inferno* with which Auerbach starts reminds us that he was an exile: the expulsion of Guelph families from Florence by Farinata degli Uberti, in 1260, had been an earlier episode in the conflict which saw Dante exiled from the city in 1302. In *Dante als Dichter der irdischen Welt* (1929), Auerbach had emphasised exile in the genesis of the *Comedy*, and positioned Dante at a high point not just of style, but of mentality:

> Die Komödie hat die physische, ethische und politische Einheit des scholastisch-christlichen Kosmos dargestellt zu einer Zeit, als sie begann ihre ideologische Unversehrtheit einzubüßen: Dantes gedankliche Haltung ist die eines konservativen Verteidigers, und sein Kampf geht um die Wiedergewinnung des schon Verlorenen; in diesem Kampf wurde er besiegt, und seine Hoffnungen und Prophezeiungen erfüllten sich niemals.[18]

In lectures in Istanbul (1939/40) and at Penn State University (1947), Auerbach again emphasized Dante's exile, a 'political refugee' for his Ghibelline opposition to Italian particularism. Passages in the *Comedy* repeatedly showed the 'bitterness' of exile and his homesickness for Florence.[19] Farinata and Cavalcante de' Cavalcanti are also exiles, of sorts. Dante's Farinata, as Auerbach observes, is unaffected by death and is the same man as he was in his lifetime; he is confined to a Hell from which he cannot return, but which is otherwise a concrete place (*M*, pp. 185–86; *ME*, p. 191). He rises from his tomb as Virgil and Dante pass because he hears the language of home, Dante's Tuscan accent, in a far-off land (*M*, p. 172; *ME*, p. 177). The high tide of *figura* which the *Comedy* achieved rests on this: on real people living on in the afterworld as if they were still on earth, except that only memory connects them to earthly life ('[z]um irdischen Leben stehen sie nur noch in dem Verhältnis der Erinnerung': *M*, p. 185; *ME*, p. 190). Dante's afterworld is a world of earthly people and passions (*M*, p. 194; *ME*, p. 200): arguably death has not changed them, in body or character, but exiled them instead.

Auerbach does not spell out why the study of European literature should be a study of realism, though the call to set reality against Nazi mythography was widespread in exile writing. Two key themes give a more specific answer for *Mimesis*. First, the representation of reality is democratic. Conceptually, *figura* resists dogma, and in modern vocabulary, totalitarianism, as it enables multiple different connections between the realities that interpret each other,[20] though over time it became schematic, with the same connections made repeatedly (*M*, pp. 118–20; *ME*, pp. 118–20). The 'mixing of styles' meant dignifying everyday existence with meaning, an achievement of Shakespeare, and a quality missing from French classical drama, but present in the 'radical realism' of Louis, Duc de Saint-Simon, a man ahead of his time (*M*, p. 365; *ME*, p. 414) whose memoirs explored human nature in its full complexity (*M*, p. 378; *ME*, p. 431). Nineteenth-century Realism picked up the thread from Saint-Simon, promoting a broader range of society as objects of complex representation and embedding the everyday, not just the exceptional, in the general course of history (*M*, p. 437; *ME*, p. 491). In a lecture on 'Literature and War' published in 1941, Auerbach set out how the citizen armies that fought for and against Revolutionary France transformed a popular sense of participation in history; Georg Lukács was making the same argument in *The Historical Novel* at the same time.[21]

Second, Auerbach expects literature to give meaning to a changing world. He sees Boccaccio as Dante's natural successor, yet despite encompassing worldly reality, the *Decameron*'s stories told in flight from the plague lacked the depth of meaning which the *Divine Comedy* had found in salvation. In the story Auerbach excerpts, Frate Alberto, an outcast by his own fault from his native Imola, pretends to be the Angel Gabriel to lure a woman into bed; when he is found out he gets his come-uppance by public humiliation. After Dante, Boccaccio depicted the world, but did not have a footing on which to explain it (*M*, p. 223; *ME*, p. 231). It is in Shakespeare that, after the break with *figura*, a secular drama of human life found a settled centre-point and comprehensive order within itself (*M*, p. 310; *ME*, p. 323). 'Tragedy' and 'tragic', as well as 'sublimity' and 'sublime', here become Auerbach's labels for depth of meaning in modern literature. Shakespeare achieved this, but with the significant flaw that his tragic characters are all of high social rank. Shylock may seem a tragic character, and is often acted thus, but socially, as a Jew, he is a pariah, 'forgotten and abandoned' before the end of a play which is too 'slight' for tragedy (*ME*, pp. 314–15; *M*, p. 300). The tragic aspects of his character are 'doch nur eine Würze […] in dem Triumph einer höheren, edleren, freieren, und auch aristokratischeren Menschlichkeit' (*M*, p. 301; *ME*, p. 315).

Both of these considerations informed Auerbach's account of German literature. Understanding realism as democratic predisposed him, in 1942, to look for its absence in German. In the chapter 'Musikus Miller', Schiller's *Kabale und Liebe* — originally titled *Luise Millerin* — is a first example. This was a love story with revolutionary potential, but from too narrow a base, like the 'slight' *Merchant of Venice*, to have any serious effect; it opposed absolutism, but was itself demagogic (*M*, p. 386; *ME*, p. 440). Auerbach does not comment on Schiller's historical writing, but the method Schiller set out in his inaugural lecture for confronting the fragmentary past is perilously close to 'legend': 'indem [der philosophische Verstand] diese Bruchstücke durch künstliche Bindungsglieder verkettet, erhebt er das Aggregat zum System, zu einem vernunftmäßig zusammenhängenden Ganzen'.[22] The backhanded praise for *Kabale und Liebe* is that it was significant, despite its shortcomings, as the only one of its kind in the better-known literature of its time (*M*, p. 389; *ME*, p. 443). The chapter laments German particularism, which meant that '[d]ie zeitgenössischen Zustände […] boten sich nur schwer für ein großzügige Realistik' (*M*, p. 391; *ME*, p. 445), and it laments that Goethe, despite his talent for grasping life in its fullness, had never loved contemporary, changing society enough to make it the object of that talent. Although Auerbach concedes that it would be absurd ('vollkommen närrisch') to wish Goethe were different from what he was (*M*, p. 398; *ME*, p.452), in reality his analysis at this point proposes a cultural *Sonderweg* with Goethe as the 'turning-point' where Germany 'failed to turn'.[23] According to *Mimesis*, Germany's Realism was weak compared to France (*M*, pp. 459–61; *ME*, pp. 516–19). Tellingly, the only Austrian authors in Auerbach's account, Ludwig Anzengruber and Peter Rosegger, are included as evidence that life in Germany was provincial and old-fashioned (*M*, p. 458; *ME*, p. 516). He does not mention Nestroy, in whose dramas Ritchie Robertson attests 'Dickensian' qualities and a sharp focus on society.[24] Nestroy might have been a better candidate for *Mimesis*, though Auerbach also dismisses Dickens, unfairly, on the grounds that his novels are dense but static depictions of social life, revealing little of history's broader development.[25]

By contrast, Auerbach's admiration for French literature is evident, though it is far from monolithic. Stendhal and Balzac stand out as the founders of modern Realism, because their works captured history's dynamism in their time.[26] But Hugo is largely absent, as the 'strong effects' of his Romantic technique were 'improbable' and 'untrue' in their depiction of human life (*M*, p. 415; *ME*, p. 468). In Flaubert's hands, Realism became 'unparteiisch, unpersönlich und sachlich', and Flaubert — like Goethe — hated the age in which he lived, and thus offered no way out of its crises (*M*, pp. 428 and 433–34; *ME*, pp. 482 and 487–88). The naturalism of the Goncourt brothers was similarly isolated in aesthetics, even if they inspired others to go beyond that limitation (*M*, p. 450; *ME*, p. 505). Zola was 'a critical Realist for his age', like Balzac (*M*, p. 461; *ME*, p. 519), the last of the French Realists, not yet fully appreciated (*M*, p. 457; *ME*, p. 515).

Stendhal wrote about society, argues Auerbach, because he had personally experienced society's continual change. A son of an aristocrat who had a glowing career under Napoleon, he was on the wrong side of the Restoration in 1814–15, and he was exiled from Austrian Milan to Paris in 1821. He wrote 'aus seinem Unbehagen in der nachnapoleonischen Welt, und aus dem Bewußtsein, nicht in sie hineinzugehören und in ihr keinen Ort zu besitzen' (*M*, p. 406; *ME*, p. 461). Balzac was not one of history's victims, but his focus, too, was society in flux. He conceived of his literary work as an all-encompassing 'encyclopaedia of life' from which no part should be omitted and in which the random moment is universally real: '[c]e ne seront pas des faits imaginaires; ce sera ce qui se passe partout', he wrote in 1834 (*M*, pp. 425–26; *ME*, pp. 479–80). Balzac's principle carries forward to the Modernist authors discussed in the last chapter of *Mimesis*: Woolf, Proust and, more briefly, Joyce. Proust himself recorded that Balzac's novels gave 'literary value' to 'a thousand things in life which had previously seemed too contingent'.[27]

With Woolf and Proust, who trust that a random moment extracted from a human life can depict the entirety of the life from which it is extracted (*M*, p. 488; *ME*, p. 547), Auerbach is finding precursors of his own method. The method had contemporary relevance: he disliked *Ulysses* because Joyce, although aiming to represent an Everyman, did not resolve the novel's refractions of human consciousness, such that it was impossible to find any order in its apparent arbitrariness. Bettina Englmann argues that at this point, *Mimesis* shows its limitations: asking authors to make sense of a world in flux is asking too much. Auerbach makes Joyce responsible for the fragmented state of modernity even though that fragmentation is itself reality and, at that, a reality which defies harmonious, rational ('erkenntnisorientiert') representation.[28] Joyce thus joins Goethe in the 'should have ...' category. Yet Auerbach's insistence is that even in Modernism — witness Proust and Woolf — the same randomness can also produce meaning. He concluded another of his Istanbul lectures, 'Realism in Europe in the Nineteenth Century' (1942), with the remark that realist literature keeps developing in order to 'show forth to the mind our life on earth and its increasing tendency to become a life shared in common'. This has a direct influence, he told his audience, on our response to the political world:

> Those who understand this should not be shaken by the tragic events occurring today. History is manifested through catastrophic events and ruptures. That which is being prepared today, that which has been in preparation for a century, is the tragic realism I have discussed, modern realism, the life shared in common which grants the possibility of life to all people on earth.[29]

Mimesis was one of four *magna opera* from the same publisher, Francke in Berne, to approach literature transnationally as an immediate response to the Second World War: Fritz Strich's *Goethe und die Weltliteratur* (published in 1946, the same year as *Mimesis*), Ernst Robert Curtius's *Europäische Literatur und lateinisches Mittelalter* (1948) and Hugo Friedrich's *Montaigne* (1949), which claimed for the *Essais* the status of a 'Weltbuch'.[30] Curtius presented his study as an attempt to revive appreciation of the West's literary tradition, having warned against the loss of that tradition just before Hitler came to power, in *Deutscher Geist in Gefahr* (1932).[31] Strich, who was Jewish and had moved to a chair in Basle in 1929, noted how his work on 'Weltliteratur' had begun as lectures in London after the First World War and was now urgently timely 'at a moment in history where all can be lost or won'.[32] He saw national literatures as so indelibly intertwined that all literary scholarship has to work beyond borders and approach its subject as world literature: 'Es ist ganz unmöglich, eine Literatur nur isoliert für sich zu behandeln.'[33]

Auerbach echoed Strich in a *Festschrift* for him in 1952. His essay, 'Philologie der Weltliteratur', a foundation text of comparative literature, concludes:

> Jedenfalls aber ist unsere philologische Heimat die Erde; die Nation kann es nicht mehr sein. Gewiß ist noch immer das Kostbarste und Unentbehrlichste, was der Philologe ererbt, Sprache und Bildung seiner Nation; doch erst in der Trennung, in der Überwindung wird es wirksam. Wir müssen, unter veränderten Umständen, zurückkehren zu dem, was die vornationale mittelalterliche Bildung besaß: zu der Erkenntnis, daß der Geist nicht national ist.[34]

The quotable phrase, 'der Geist [ist] nicht national', hides the more complex tension in the passage, which runs through *Mimesis* and 'Philologie der Weltliteratur' alike, between the national and the universal, between the 'levelling process' as gain and as loss. In *Mimesis* Auerbach dismisses the literature of the 'Goethezeit', but by contrast he praises the emergence of *Historismus* in the same period: the understanding of past phenomena on their own terms. In Leopold von Ranke's phrase, 'jede Epoche ist unmittelbar zu Gott'; Auerbach writes of 'Einsicht [...] in die Lebenseinheit der Epochen, so daß jede als ein Ganzes erscheint, dessen Wesen sich in jeder ihrer Erscheinungsformen spiegelt' (*M*, p. 390; *ME*, p. 444).[35] This break with preconceived teleology (*M*, p. 390; *ME*, p. 443) founded the prestige of German historiography in the nineteenth century, and it enabled the writing of national history by understanding modern nations individually. Paradoxically, it resulted in the promotion of nationhood as a *telos* in itself. Friedrich Meinecke, whose *Die Entstehung des Historismus* (1936) Auerbach praises highly (*M*, p. 391; *ME*, p. 444), had observed in *Weltbürgertum und Nationalstaat* (1907) that modern nations have 'a highly singular character' like all historical artefacts.[36] *Weltbürgertum und Nationalstaat* enquired into the place of universal, not just national, developments in the formation of German nationhood. Auerbach's emphasis was different, nonetheless: for him, the value of *Historismus* was that grasping individual phenomena enabled a grasp of the universal. This also meant seeking history's sources not just in politics, but in society, economic life and culture. By placing the emergence of this historical consciousness at the end of the eighteenth century but showing, in the broader sweep of *Mimesis*, how this change was rooted in early modern secularism, Auerbach pre-empted Reinhart Koselleck's mapping of the historical 'paradigm shift'.[37]

Auerbach called *Historismus* the 'Copernican discovery'[38] in historical studies; when he describes it, he is also describing his own approach. An essay on Machiavelli in 1944 begins with the familiar cynicism which made *The Prince* all too relevant in the present day, but by the end shows how its recipients misread it, by reading it morally rather than in context: the work of an émigré from Florence, advocating the mainstream political tactics of the day in the minority cause of Italian unity.[39] Auerbach called his field, Romance philology, a 'minor branch' of the 'tree' of *Historismus*, and he explained that *Mimesis* was 'unthinkable' outside an intellectual tradition rooted in German Romantic philosophy.[40] At first glance, this sits oddly with insisting 'daß der Geist nicht national ist'. For all its ills, the modern nation is an essential category in *Mimesis*. Auerbach observed that 'Romanistik', because it did not work on its own national culture, had not been as susceptible as the 'German' disciplines to the patriotic cause, but where he did study Germany, the tension lingered.[41] Germany's deficiency by comparison with France, in his account, is its lack of a clear national history for its authors to write. The sense of greater participation in history, which began in revolutionary France, also meant universal knowledge of that history: Stendhal's *Le Rouge et le Noir*, subtitled *Chronique de 1830* (and in its first edition, *Chronique du XIXe siècle*), was thus anchored in a shared national past which everyone knew — indeed, the novel would be incomprehensible without it (*M*, p. 401; *ME*, p. 455). In Germany, on the other hand, *Historismus* did not change the prevailing, parochial mentality; it prepared ground on which literature could not build. Justus Möser and Johann Gottfried Herder, its first exponents, did not connect the particularities of the past to the specific potential of the present day (*M*, pp. 391–92; *ME*, p. 445). Goethe, similarly, was not 'historistisch' enough, ignoring those parts of history which he disliked (a point Meinecke also makes at length), painting a quietist picture of an unchanging society in *Wilhelm Meisters Lehrjahre*, and, in 'Literarischer Sansculottismus', rejecting the upheavals which might have united Germany and produced a single centre for its culture.

Despite his praise of Meinecke, Auerbach's *Historismus* makes fuller sense through the lens of his lifelong work on Vico. Auerbach had translated Vico's *Scienza Nova* into German in 1925, and continued to write about him in and after exile. Vico, in Auerbach's account, was another social outsider, unnoticed by scholarship in his own time and since and, like Saint-Simon, more modern than the seventeenth century into which he was born.[42] He had the method of *Historismus*, but not its nationalism; he never used the term 'Volksgeist', which would become so important in German historiography.[43] Whereas Herder looked north, to primitive cultures uninhibited by social structure, Vico's focus on classical antiquity placed him 'weit entfernt vom erdhaften Dunst des Völkischen'.[44] Auerbach reads in him the conviction that history is comprehensible from within itself, by searching its totality, which put him, like Saint-Simon, at odds with the rationalism of their age (*M*, p. 381; *ME*, p. 433). His proposal of a *senso commune*, which Auerbach echoes in the 'life shared in common', meant that modern humanity understands the past because it is a human past. In Auerbach's reading of Vico, the historian's task is 'verstehende Philologie', both in the sense of understanding (and not imposing upon) the traces of past societies, and in the sense that knowledge of history comes entirely from this 'understanding' of the interpreter. *Senso commune* is objectively a given of history and, subjectively, the precondition of historical interpretation.[45] Because all of history can be grasped from within this human community, historical understanding is a narrative process, of 'research and re-evocation'.[46] The work of the historian is less a science than 'an art working with scholarly material': philology, rather than the technique of 'legend', is the acceptable version of the 'linguistic turn'. This notion, that universal truth is only contained in the entirety of history, and that it is only obtainable by understanding history in its entirety, Auerbach declared to be 'Vico's idea of philology which I learned from him'.[47]

'Philologie der Weltliteratur' is another restatement of what Auerbach 'learned' from Vico. Exile starts the essay and ends it: at its start, the division of humanity into separate cultures was a 'happy Fall' from Eden, whilst at the end, Hugh of St Victor's teaching, that Christian perfection is to see the whole world as exile, receives a secular twist: 'Hugo meinte das für den, dessen Ziel Loslösung von der Liebe zur Welt ist. Doch auch für einen, der die rechte Liebe zur Welt gewinnen will, ist es ein guter Weg'.[48] 'Philologie der Weltliteratur' confronts, with greater focus, the 'Ausgleichsprozeß' Auerbach had addressed in *Mimesis*. Modern nations themselves are becoming more alike, and have been doing so since their emergence in the French Revolution (*M*, p. 404; *ME*, p. 459), so the essay's declaration that the nation cannot be 'our philological home' is not a wish, but an inevitability. At the same time, the multiplicity of vision needed for the scholar's task of 'integrating' human diversity is endangered, because history has reached the point of fullest development at which it could still be fully understood, 'eine[n] Kairos der verstehenden Geschichtsschreibung'.[49] The growing volume of literature — especially by contrast with the early societies on which Vico focused — and the specialization of education, notably, of language-learning, meant that Auerbach's generation would be the last which could interpret it 'philologically', in depth and breadth. This was also the generation whose adulthood had been a 'practical seminar in world history': on the pattern of Vico's hermeneutics, they were better able to understand history because they had so intensely experienced historical change themselves.[50]

'Philologie der Weltliteratur' thus again describes and defends Auerbach's method. With its remarks on 'kairos' it adds Auerbach's own time to the turning-points of modern intellectual history: the 'kairos', with Dante, of divine salvation as a means to understand the world; Vico's discovery of an intra-historical equivalent; the spread of historical awareness throughout national societies since the French Revolution, captured by Balzac and Stendhal; now a second, secular high tide of historical understanding at which, as with Dante, the fullness of experience also marks the point at which it is lost. 'Philologie der Weltliteratur' also spells out more fully that the historian's technique is literary. The 'synthesis' of diversity is only possible as a work of art, and the objection that art is fantasy, not fact, does not hold given the sheer range and volume of material with which historical scholarship contends:

> die geschichtlichen Gegenstände, wie sie sich heute darstellen, bieten der Einbildungskraft Freiheit genug in Auswahl, Problemstellung, Kombination und Formung. Ja, man kann sagen, daß die wissenschaftliche Treue eine gute Beschränkung ist: indem, bei so großer Versuchung, sich der Wirklichkeit zu entziehen, sei es durch triviale Glättung, sei es durch gespenstische Verzerrung, die wissenschaftliche Treue im Wirklichen das Wahrscheinliche bewahrt und verbürgt; denn das Wirkliche ist das Maß des Wahrscheinlichen.[51]

Auerbach reverses conventional hierarchies between history and literature here: literature does not lend technique to scholarship, but rather, scholarly fidelity enables the work of the imagination. In place of Aristotle's dictum that 'poetry is at once more like philosophy and more worth while than history' because poetry is concerned not with the particular but with 'the sort of thing that would happen', Auerbach argues that we can only see things as generally probable because they are similar to what is specifically real.[52]

In *Mimesis*, the other figure who unites Auerbach's key themes is Montaigne, whose remarks on the representative quality of his own random life bridged literary and scientific method and stood at another 'kairotic' point in literary history. Chapter 12, on him, comes after the 'failure' of secular realism in Boccaccio (chapter 9) and just before its realization in Shakespeare (chapter 13). Auerbach's 1932 essay 'Der Schriftsteller Montaigne' had emphasized the insecurity of Montaigne's life at the time of the Wars of Religion, the crisis 'die, zum letzten Male, den nationalen Bestand Frankreichs gefährdete'. Montaigne withdrew from public office into private life, to defend his property but also for intellectual seclusion: 'dort ist sein eigentliches Zuhause; dort ist er bei sich'.[53] His part-Jewish ancestry, which was a standard assumption of mid-twentieth-century scholarship, and his secular attitudes, are further components of an outsider figure with whom Auerbach may have felt a personal affinity.[54] His significance for German literary exiles is also evident in Heinrich Mann's *Henri Quatre* novels and in his portrait by Stefan Zweig, who claimed his particular resonance with a generation 'die, wie etwa die unsere, vom Schicksal in einen kataraktischen Aufruhr der Welt geworfen wurde'.[55]

Auerbach does not reiterate Montaigne's political circumstances in *Mimesis*, but instead alludes to them whilst emphasizing the profound intellectual change that was under way at the time:

> Die Loslösung von den christlichen Rahmenvorstellungen versetzte Montaigne […] nicht einfach in die Anschauungen und Verhältnisse zurück, in welchen seinesgleichen zur Zeit Ciceros oder Plutarchs gelebt hatte. Die nun errungene Freiheit war weit erregender, aktueller, mit dem Gefühl der Ungesichertheit verbunden; der verwirrende Überfluß von Erscheinungen, auf die nun erst das Auge gelenkt wurde, schien überwältigend; die Welt, sei es die äußere oder die innere, schien ungeheuer, grenzenlos, unfaßbar; das Bedürfnis, sich in ihr zurechtzufinden, schien schwierig zu befriedigen und doch dringend. […] [V]on all den bedeutenden und zuweilen gleichsam überlebensgroßen Menschen dieses Jahrhunderts [ist] Montaigne der ruhigste […]. (*M*, p. 296; *ME*, p. 310)

At this moment, Montaigne represented the best of the old and the new. He was formed by the emergence, in his own age, of a fashion for broad general knowledge: an inheritor of Renaissance humanism, but one who did not share the specialization, and thus the abstracted thinking, which the humanist rediscovery of all-round education had, paradoxically, brought about (*M*, pp. 292–93; *ME*, pp. 306–07). The *Essais*, which began — like *Mimesis* — as 'eine Sammlung von Lesefrüchten mit begleitenden Bemerkungen' (*M*, p. 280; *ME*, p. 295), are also like *Mimesis* because they were uncertain of finding an audience. Montaigne was the first independent writer, says Auerbach, who did not write for a particular audience, but for a readership that was first created by his book (*M*, p. 293; *ME*, p. 308).

Montaigne's concern, in the essay 'On Repenting' which Auerbach reads in detail, is to 'give an account of Man and sketch a picture of a particular one of them who is very badly formed'.[56] His ambition to make 'a man' represent 'Man' is complicated by his subject's instability, as he is 'not portraying being but becoming', and by the fact that being good is harder in private than in public. The task is to portray the individual in an 'ordinary' state, not at the extremes of goodness and evil, which everybody sees but which are exceptional: 'We must […] judge souls in their settled state, when they are at home with themselves — if they ever are.'[57] For Auerbach, Montaigne's 'essais', 'attempts', are a 'scientific', experimental method to establish the changing 'I', begun from the subject itself rather than an outside premiss. He both quotes and paraphrases Montaigne's declaration that '[a]uthors communicate themselves to the public by some peculiar work foreign to themselves; I — the first ever to do so — by my universal being, not as a grammarian, poet or jurisconsult but as Michel de Montaigne'.[58] Knowing oneself, for Montaigne, was the only way to understand history; his dislike of formal ('schulmäßig') moral philosophy (*M*, pp. 288–89; *ME*, pp. 302–04) is Auerbach's too. Absolute focus on the subject means 'nicht ein Haufen von beziehungslosen Momentaufnahmen, sondern die spontan erfaßte, aus der Vielfalt der Beobachtungen sich zuammenfügende Einheit seiner Person' (*M*, p. 279; *ME*, p. 294).

To conclude: Montaigne's attitude is precisely that which Auerbach would later adapt from Hugh of St Victor, detachment from the world which, in turn, finds the 'right love' of it. It is not only Montaigne's place in intellectual history that lets him see his person at a remove from himself, but his awareness of his mortality. Farinata and Cavalcante, as 'living' characters exiled permanently in the world beyond, are part of Dante's enactment of the divine plan, but Montaigne has a heightened sense of *this* life because he knows that one day he will die. In 'Der Schriftsteller Montaigne' Auerbach asked at greater length how his attitude to death sat with his Roman Catholicism, remarking that the *Essais* have precious little to say about transcendental Christian hope. Rather, Montaigne's awareness of his mortality refocuses him on this life: it 'schweißt ihn zusammen, macht ihn heimisch in sich'.[59] In line with his own sense of standing at a final moment in cultural history, Auerbach claimed that Montaigne had a uniquely high vantage point, but Montaigne, in 'On repenting', is more reserved. Age has given him no superiority over his younger self: '[w]hat we call wisdom is the moroseness of our humours and our distaste for things as they are now'.[60] He is happy to see himself as a pioneer, but he is uninterested in posterity, rejecting the saying of Christ that 'no prophet is accepted in his hometown' as 'the motive of those who hide away when alive and present, so as to enjoy a reputation when they are dead and gone'. He prefers instead '[the reputation] I can enjoy now'.[61] In Auerbach's view he was a writer who had grasped 'das Problem der Selbstorientierung des Menschen [...]; die Aufgabe, sich ohne feste Stützpunkte in der Existenz Wohnlichkeit zu schaffen' (*M*, p. 296; *ME*, p. 311). Metaphorically speaking, Montaigne overcame exile, as 'the first one, perhaps the only one to have taught us how to live on this real earth, without any conditions but those of life'.[62]

Notes to Chapter 20

1. Erich Auerbach, *Mimesis: Dargestellte Wirklichkeit in der abendländischen Literatur* (Berne: Francke, 1946), p. 498. Hereafter: *M*. Page references are also given to the English translation, *Mimesis: The Representation of Reality in Western Literature*, trans. by Willard R. Trask (Princeton, NJ: Princeton University Press, 2003 [first edn 1953]). Hereafter: *ME* (here, p. 557).
2. Edward W. Said, 'Introduction to the Fiftieth-Anniversary Edition', in *ME*, pp. ix–xxxii (p. xvii).
3. Earl Jeffrey Richards, 'Erich Auerbach und Ernst Robert Curtius: Der unterbrochene oder der verpaßte Dialog?', in *Wahrnehmen Lesen Deuten: Erich Auerbachs Lektüre der Moderne*, ed. by Walter Busch and Gerhart Pickerodt (Frankfurt a.M.: Klostermann, 1998), pp. 31–62 (esp. pp. 37–38); see also Ottmar Ette, 'Migration und Konvivenz', in *Literatur und Exil: Neue Perspektiven*, ed. by Doerte Bischoff and Susanne Komfort-Hein (Berlin: de Gruyter, 2013), pp. 297–320 (esp. pp. 309–10).
4. Kader Konuk, *East West Mimesis: Auerbach in Turkey* (Stanford, CA: Stanford University Press, 2010), esp. pp. 138–43. From 1923 to 1929, Auerbach had been a librarian at the exceptional Preußische Staatsbibliothek. The Istanbul University library grew rapidly in the 1930s, but could not have competed with a long-established collection like Berlin's; other libraries he used were dispersed around Istanbul and would not have matched its convenience.
5. Konuk, p. 160.
6. Ibid., pp. 161–62. In addition, the two 'excursuses' in this passage — including Mrs Ramsay's recollection of the conversation with Marie — are compared with the passage from the *Odyssey*

back in chapter 1 (*M*, pp. 479–81; *ME*, pp. 538–40). In Woolf's text Mrs Ramsay, when younger, was 'the happier Helen of our days' (*M*, p. 467; *ME*, p. 525).

7. This is C. S. Lewis's striking translation of Virgil's opening phrase: *C. S. Lewis's Lost Aeneid*, ed. by A. T. Reyes (New Haven, CT: Yale University Press, 2011), p. 37.
8. Ewen Bowie, 'Literary Milieux', in *The Cambridge Companion to the Greek and Roman Novel*, ed. by Tim Whitmarsh (Cambridge: Cambridge University Press, 2008), pp. 17–38 (p. 36).
9. One significant exception, on *Historismus*, is Frank R. Ankersmit, 'Why Realism? Auerbach on the Representation of Reality', *Poetics Today*, 20 (1999), 53–75 (pp. 53–55).
10. White's volume *Figural Realism: Studies in the Mimesis Effect* (Baltimore: Johns Hopkins University Press, 1998), pays tribute to Auerbach's 'great work' (p. vii) and includes his 1996 essay 'Auerbach's Literary History: Figural Causation and Modernist Historicism' (pp. 87–100).
11. James I. Porter, 'Philology in Exile: Adorno, Auerbach, and Klemperer', in *Brill's Companion to the Classics: Fascist Italy and Nazi Germany*, ed. by Helen Roche and Kyriakos N. Demetriou (Leiden: Brill, 2017), pp. 106–29 (p. 120). Auerbach later conceded that his analysis of ancient epic had been too one-sided: Erich Auerbach, 'Epilegomena zu Mimesis', *Romanische Forschungen*, 63 (1953), 1–18 (p. 2); *ME*, p. 560.
12. C. S. Lewis, *An Experiment in Criticism* (Cambridge: Cambridge University Press, 1961), p. 67.
13. *M*, p. 150; *ME*, p. 154; see Matthew 11. 25 and Luke 10. 21.
14. Auerbach, 'Figura' (1938), in *Gesammelte Aufsätze zur romanischen Philologie*, ed. by Gustav Konrad and Fritz Schalk (Berne: Francke, 1967), pp. 55–92 (p. 77).
15. 'Figura', p. 76; see Porter, p. 119.
16. C. S. Lewis, *The Allegory of Love: A Study in Medieval Tradition* (Oxford: Oxford University Press, 1936), p. 76.
17. 'Figura', pp. 80–81.
18. Erich Auerbach, *Dante als Dichter der irdischen Welt*, 2nd edn (Berlin: de Gruyter, 2001), p. 213; see also ibid., pp. 103–04, and Konuk, pp. 29 and 37.
19. Erich Auerbach, 'Dante' and '[Über Dantes Dichtung]', in *Kultur als Politik: Aufsätze aus dem Exil zur Geschichte und Zukunft Europas (1938–1947)*, ed. by Christian Rivoletti (Konstanz: Konstanz University Press, 2014) pp. 95–109 and 111–29.
20. See Ankersmit, p. 63.
21. Auerbach's lectures 'Realism in Europe in the Nineteenth Century' and 'Literature and War' are published, in English translation from Turkish by Victoria Holbrook, in Konuk, pp. 181–93 and 194–204 (here pp. 198–99). *The Historical Novel*, published in Russian in 1937/38, was first published in German in 1955.
22. Friedrich Schiller, *Sämtliche Werke*, ed. by Gerhard Fricke and Herbert G. Göpfert, 5 vols (Munich: Hanser, 1959), IV, 763.
23. This is A. J. P. Taylor's well-known claim, in 1945, about 1848: 'German history reached its turning-point and failed to turn' (Taylor, *The Course of German History* (London: Methuen, 1961), p. 69). See also Auerbach, 'Epilegomena zu Mimesis', p. 14 (*ME*, p. 571).
24. Ritchie Robertson, 'Nestroy's Dickensian Realism', in *Enlightenment and Religion in German and Austrian Literature* (Cambridge: Legenda, 2017), pp. 318–33.
25. *M*, p. 438; *ME*, p. 492. The criticism of Dickens is similar, and more forceful, in 'Realism in Europe in the Nineteenth Century' (1942): Konuk, p. 191.
26. See Wolfgang Asholt, 'Vom *Hôtel de la Mole* zu *Germinie Lacerteux*: Auerbachs *Mimesis* und der moderne Realismus als Krisensymptom', *Romanistische Zeitschrift für Literaturgeschichte*, 38 (2014), 277–91.
27. Marcel Proust, *Contre Sainte-Beuve*, 3rd edn (Paris: Gallimard, 1954), p. 223: 'ils donnent pour nous une sorte de valeur littéraire à mille choses de la vie qui jusque-là nous paraissaient trop contingentes'. See also Scott Lee, 'Balzac's Legacy', in *The Cambridge Companion to Balzac*, ed. by Andrew Watts (Cambridge: Cambridge University Press, 2017), pp. 175–88 (p. 183).
28. Bettina Englmann, *Poetik des Exils: Die Modernität der deutschsprachigen Exilliteratur* (Tübingen: Niemeyer, 2001), p. 72.
29. Konuk, p. 193.
30. Hugo Friedrich, *Montaigne* (Berne: Francke, 1949), p. 10.

31. Ernst Robert Curtius, *Europäische Literatur und lateinisches Mittelalter* (Berne: Francke, 1948), p. [9]. Curtius stated this still more explicitly in the preface to the second edition (1954).
32. Strich, pp. 7–9. On Auerbach, Curtius and Friedrich in the Francke-Verlag: Frank-Rutger Hausmann, 'Michel de Montaigne, Erich Auerbachs "Mimesis" und Erich Auerbachs literaturwissenschaftliche Methode', in *Wahrnehmen Lesen Deuten*, pp. 224–37 (p. 227).
33. Strich, p. 20.
34. Erich Auerbach, 'Philologie der Weltliteratur' (1952), in *Gesammelte Aufsätze*, pp. 301–10 (p. 310).
35. Leopold von Ranke, *Aus Werk und Nachlaß*, ed. by Walther Peter Fuchs and Theodor Schieder (Munich: Oldenbourg, 1964–75), II: *Über die Epochen der neueren Geschichte*, ed. by Theodor Schieder and Helmut Berding (1971), pp. 59–60.
36. Friedrich Meinecke, *Werke*, ed. by Hans Herzfeld and others (Munich: Oldenbourg, 1957–), V: *Weltbürgertum und Nationalstaat*, ed. by Hans Herzfeld (1962), p. 21.
37. Reinhart Koselleck, 'Vergangene Zukunft der frühen Neuzeit', in *Vergangene Zukunft: Zur Semantik geschichtlicher Zeiten* (Frankfurt a.M.: Suhrkamp, 1979), pp. 17–37 (pp. 22–24).
38. Erich Auerbach, 'Vico's Contribution to Literary Criticism', in *Gesammelte Aufsätze*, pp. 259–66 (p. 261).
39. Erich Auerbach, 'Über Machiavelli', in *Kultur als Politik*, pp. 131–35 (p. 135).
40. Erich Auerbach, 'Vico und Herder', in *Gesammelte Aufsätze*, pp. 222–32 (p. 223); 'Epilegomena', p. 15; *ME*, p. 571.
41. Erich Auerbach, *Literatursprache und Publikum in der lateinischen Spätantike und im Mittelalter* (Berne: Francke, 1958), p. 9.
42. *M*, p. 380; *ME*, p. 433; Auerbach, 'Vico und Herder', p. 225; Auerbach, 'Vico und der Volksgeist', in *Gesammelte Aufsätze*, pp. 242–50 (pp. 242–43); Konuk, p. 28. Cf., on Saint-Simon, *M*, p. 365; *ME*, p. 414.
43. Auerbach, 'Vico und Herder', p. 232.
44. Auerbach, 'Vico und der Volksgeist', pp. 243–44 and 247.
45. Erich Auerbach, 'Giambattista Vico und die Idee der Philologie', in *Gesammelte Aufsätze*, pp. 233–41 (pp. 239–40).
46. Erich Auerbach, 'Vico and Aesthetic Historism', in *Gesammelte Aufsätze*, pp. 266–74 (p. 274).
47. Auerbach, 'Vico's Contribution to Literary Criticism', p. 265.
48. Auerbach, 'Philologie', p. 310.
49. Auerbach, 'Philologie', pp. 302–03; see further Ben Hutchinson, 'Late Reading: Erich Auerbach and the *Spätboot* of Comparative Literature', *Comparative Critical Studies*, 14 (2017), 69–85.
50. Auerbach, 'Philologie', p. 306. Similarly, *M*, p. 493; *ME*, p. 553.
51. Auerbach, 'Philologie', p. 307.
52. Aristotle, *Poetics*, 1451^{a-b}: *Classical Literary Criticism*, ed. by D. A. Russell and M. Winterbottom (Oxford: Oxford University Press, 1989), p. 62.
53. Erich Auerbach, 'Der Schriftsteller Montaigne', in *Gesammelte Aufsätze*, pp. 184–95 (pp. 184–85).
54. See Hausmann, pp. 230–32.
55. Stefan Zweig, 'Montaigne', in *Europäisches Erbe*, ed. by Richard Friedenthal (Frankfurt a.M.: Fischer, 1960), pp. 7–81 (p. 7).
56. Michel de Montaigne, *The Complete Essays*. trans. by M. A. Screech (London: Penguin, 1991), p. 907.
57. Ibid., p. 913.
58. Ibid., p. 908; cf. *M*, pp. 271 and 282 (*ME*, pp. 285 and 298).
59. Auerbach, 'Der Schriftsteller Montaigne', pp. 190–91.
60. Montaigne, p. 921.
61. Luke 4:24 (cf. also Matthew 13:57, Mark 6:4 and John 4:44); Montaigne, p. 912.
62. Auerbach, review (1951) of Friedrich's *Montaigne*, in *Gesammelte Aufsätze*, pp. 323–25 (p. 325).

CHAPTER 23

'A second life': Shakespeare-Übersetzungen in der Gegenwartsliteratur

Karen Leeder

> What is your substance, whereof are you made,
> That millions of strange shadows on you tend?
>
> SHAKESPEARE, *Sonnet 53*

Neil Corcorans *Shakespeare and the Modern Poet* (2010) orientiert sich an Harold Bloom, der Shakespeare als Ursprung aller 'influential anxiety' identifiziert und somit nahelegt, dass Shakespeare für DichterInnen, die auf Englisch schreiben, auf vielfältige Art und Weise 'the most anxiety-inducing of all' erscheinen muss.[1] Ähnliches kann über jene gesagt werden, die auf Deutsch schreiben: In der Tat bezeichnet Roger Paulin in seinem *Critical Reception of Shakespeare in Germany* die deutsche Kultur als 'in Harold Bloom's terms, a "Shakespeare-haunted" culture'.[2] Schon im Jahre 1773 beschrieb Christoph Martin Wieland sich und seine zeitgenössischen Dichterkollegen in Deutschland als von Shakespeares Geist heimgesucht, ähnlich wie Hamlet von seinem Vater, in einem Aufsatz, der den bezeichnenden Titel 'Der Geist Shakespears' (1773) trägt.[3] Die Geschichte der deutschen Shakespeare-Rezeption stellt im Vergleich zu der in anderen Ländern ein besonderes Kapitel dar, da sie durch eine bestimmende Aneignung von Seiten der empfangenden Kultur gekennzeichnet ist, die mit den Feierlichkeiten 'Shakespeare is German' 2010 am Globe Theater in London unter der Leitung von Rüdiger Görner einen prägnanten Ausdruck gefunden hat.[4] Vor dem Hintergrund der Themen, die für diesen Beitrag relevant sind — Debatten über kulturelle Autorität, kulturelle Energien, kulturelle Übertragung und die Verfahren, die an Schreibprozesse geknüpft sind — werde ich der Frage nachgehen, welche Anwendung Shakespeares *Sonette* in der zeitgenössischen deutschsprachigen Lyrik finden und inwiefern deutsche AutorInnen den *Sonetten* ein zweites Leben in einem neuen Zusammenhang geben.

Shakespeare hat bekanntlich in Deutschland als Maßstab für die Bildung einer eigenen kulturellen Identität und der damit verwandten Entwicklung des deutsch-nationalen Dramas gedient: 'Shakespeare, for good or ill, is identified with national aspirations, the creation of a national literary canon, and the mythology of a German national literature'.[5] Infolgedessen befanden sich Shakespeares Dramen immer dann im Zentrum der kulturellen Auseinandersetzung, wenn in der deutschen Geschichte nationale Identität in Frage gestellt wurde, ob in der deutschen Revolution von 1918–19, im Nationalsozialismus nach 1933, nach der Teilung Deutschlands in der Nachkriegszeit, zur Zeit der Studentenbewegung nach 1968 oder bei der Wiedervereinigung 1990, kurzum, in Situationen, in welchen 'redefining the meaning of the classical canon was tantamount to changing attitudes and values — an eminently political act'.[6] Eines der aufschlussreichsten Beispiele war Heiner Müllers dreistündige Inszenierung seiner *Hamlet/Maschine* (in der er in seine eigene *Hamlet*-Übersetzung Szenen aus der *Hamletmaschine* einschaltete) während der Ereignisse von 1989/1990 (wobei der Lärm der Demonstration außerhalb des Proberaums zu hören war), die der Forderung nach politischem Handeln eine neue Vehemenz verliehen.

In Analysen der Shakespeare-Rezeption im Ausland war bisher ein Großteil der Aufmerksamkeit eben dieser zentralen Rolle der Dramen gewidmet: z.B. der Art und Weise, wie sie der Franzose Jean-François Ducis nach klassizistischem Muster umgoss, wie sich die Deutschen selbst in Hamlet wiederfanden und wie die Polen sowie andere Nationen Zentral- und Mitteleuropas Shakespeare zu Zeiten des Kommunismus für subversive Zwecke auf die Bühne brachten. Im Mittelpunkt steht natürlich *Hamlet*; spätestens seit Ferdinand Freiligraths emblematischer Aussage 'Deutschland ist Hamlet' im Jahre 1844 avancierte speziell dieses Stück zu einem besonders wichtigen Anhaltspunkt und führte zu einer großen Anzahl an häufig avantgardistischen Adaptierungen und zu einer regen kritischen Auseinandersetzung.[7] In dieser Untersuchung kultureller Transformationen fanden die *Sonette* und die Verserzählungen verhältnismäßig wenig Beachtung. In gewisser Hinsicht handelt es sich hier um eine sonderbare Vernachlässigung, denn im 20. Jahrhundert und insbesondere im letzten Jahrzehnt haben drei Ereignisse den Bekanntheitsgrad der *Sonette* erhöht.

Zunächst gibt es eine derart beträchtliche und steigende Anzahl an DichterInnen, die sich mit den *Sonetten* anhand von Übersetzungen, Adaptierungen und Neufassungen auseinandersetzten, dass die Kritik von einer 'incurable sonnetomania' spricht.[8] In regelmäßigen Abständen bringt Manfred Pfister die anwachsende Zahl der einschlägigen Neuerscheinungen auf den aktuellsten Stand. 2012 waren es einundsiebzig deutsche Übersetzungen des gesamten Zyklus. Hinzu kommt, dass sich viele LyrikerInnen nur mit einer Auswahl der Sonette beschäftigen und somit die Anzahl um ein Vielfaches vermehren (circa hundertfünfzig LyrikerInnen versuchten sich an einer Auswahl, während es gleichzeitig mehr als zweihundert Variationen der berühmtesten Sonette gibt). Für Pfister hat die Übersetzung der *Sonette* mittlerweile den Status eines 'nationalen literarischen Sports' erreicht.[9] Es sollte nicht außer Acht gelassen werden, dass die *Sonette* auf der Bühne und am Bildschirm Einzug gehalten und somit eine neue Präsenz in Deutschland erreicht haben. Christa Jahnson erfasst diese erhöhte Sichtbarkeit in ihrem Beitrag 'Glocal Shakespeare: Shakespeare's Poems in Germany'.[10]

Darüber hinaus zeichnet sich eine Veränderung der kritischen Auseinandersetzung, auch im englischsprachigen Raum, darin ab, dass sie sich immer mehr damit beschäftigt, wie Shakespeare weltweit gesehen und gelesen wird. Ab den 1990er Jahren hat die Übersetzungsforschung einen *cultural turn* erfahren, in dem sich eine Annäherung der Übersetzungstheorie an das Feld der Cultural Studies vollzog. Das Ergebnis war ein waches Interesse für die Art und Weise, in der eine Übersetzung sowohl von der aufnehmenden Kultur konstruiert wird als auch innerhalb dieser Kultur Veränderungen auslösen kann.

> Translation is, of course, a rewriting of an original text. All rewritings, whatever their intention, reflect a certain ideology and a poetics and as such manipulate literature to function in a given society in a given way. [...] Rewritings can introduce new concepts, new genres, new devices and the history of translation is the history also of literary innovation, of the shaping power of one culture upon another.[11]

Damit verbunden ist die Thematisierung der Rolle des Übersetzers. Trotz der anerkannten Position von Übersetzung als Technik des Kulturtransfers, beklagt z.B. Lawrence Venuti die Unsichtbarkeit des Übersetzers als Person, mit besonderem Augenmerk auf den Übersetzer im anglo-amerikanischen Raum. Diese Unsichtbarkeit des Übersetzers konstituiert sich aus zwei sich gegenseitig bestimmenden Phänomenen. Das eine bezeichnet er als einen 'illusionistic effect of discourse', die Manipulation der Zielsprache durch den Übersetzer selbst. Das andere ist die Art, wie Übersetzungen selbst gelesen und bewertet werden, denn ein übersetzter literarischer Text wird eher akzeptiert, wenn die Übersetzung ohne stilistische Eigenheiten auskommt: D. h. 'the appearance [...] that the translation is not in fact a translation, but the "original"'.[12]

Innerhalb dieses Gedankenganges ist die Beziehung zwischen Original und Übersetzung also immer verknüpft mit Fragestellungen zu Autorität und Macht. Diskutiert werden unter anderem auch die Annahme von Übersetzung als etwas Untergeordnetem, dem etwas Ausschlaggebendes aus dem Original fehlt, sowie die Benjaminsche Vorstellung der Übersetzung als Fortleben des Originals, das es dem Text ermöglicht auch in neuerer Zeit zu überleben. Diese literaturkitischen Impulse werfen ein neues Licht auf die Übersetzung als literarisches Feld und öffnen das Feld selbst für neue Impulse. Es ist beispielsweise bezeichnend, dass jüngste Handbücher zu Shakespeare und seinen Gedichten immer ein Kapitel über sein Nachleben in Europa und darüber hinaus beinhalten. Das signalisiert ein grundlegendes Umdenken in Bezug darauf, wie Shakespeare gelesen wird. Hinzu kommt, dass wir in den letzten Jahrzehnten immer besser erkannt haben, dass Übersetzung nicht Verlust, sondern Gewinn, nicht ein Scheitern am Original, sondern dessen Bereicherung bedeuten kann. Durch besonderes Augenmerk auf die zwischensprachliche Kreativität, die Shakespeare erzeugt, lernt man die Energien, aus welchen sich Originaltexte und heutige ästhetische Projekte zusammensetzen, noch besser würdigen. Dieses plurale Nachleben spiegelt nicht geradlinig wider, was Shakespeare gemeint haben könnte, sondern, und hier nehme ich auf Terence Hawkes Bezug, was *wir* meinen, wenn wir von Shakespeare sprechen. D. h. also, dass wir seine Werke dafür verwenden, um unsere eigenen Anliegen zu einem sehr viel späteren Zeitpunkt und/oder an unterschiedlichen geografischen Orten zur Sprache zu bringen, was dazu führt, dass man Übersetzungen und künstlerische Aneignungen als Indiz dafür verwenden kann, wie Shakespeare auf die jeweilige Kultur einwirkt.[13] Noch klarer als in Übersetzungen wird dies in Originalwerken, die sich dichterisch mit Shakespeare auseinandersetzen, wie sie z.B. in Tobias Dörings hervorragender Anthologie *Wie er uns gefällt: Gedichte an und auf William Shakespeare* versammelt sind, die zu besprechen aber den Rahmen dieses Beitrags sprengen würde.[14]

Bei der Rezeption der *Sonette* haben die unterschiedlichsten Erkenntnisinteressen eine Rolle gespielt. Es würde hier zu weit führen, sie alle erfassen zu wollen. Besonders wichtig waren zwei Vorgehensweisen, der biografische und der politische Denkansatz. Die biografische Lesart der *Sonette* ist von der Rezeption Shakespeares in der Romantik inspiriert und sieht sie als Schlüssel, mit dem 'Shakespeare unlocked his heart', wie Wordsworth 1826 in einem Sonett über das Sonett schrieb.[15] Dies hat eine Faszination besonders mit der 'dark lady' und dem 'fair friend' der *Sonette* hervorgerufen, sowie eine folgenreiche Auseinandersetzung im Rahmen der Geschlechterpolitik. In einem Artikel von 2016 und unlängst in *Shakespeare's Literary Lives* geht Paul J. C. M. Franssen dem die Geschlechtergrenzen überschreitenden Entwicklungsverlauf der Sonette Shakespeares nach, einem Aspekt, der besonders dem Interesse Shakespeares als Mann gilt.[16] Um nur ein Beispiel zu nennen, das bezeichnenderweise einen queeren deutschen Shakespeare zelebriert: Die kontroverse Inszenierung der Sonette Shakespeares am Berliner Ensemble aus dem Jahre 2009 unter der Regie von Robert Wilson, in welcher Männer die Rollen der Frauen und Frauen die Rollen der Männer übernahmen. Ein Clip im Internet zeigt drei als Frauen verkleidete und stark geschminkte Männer, von welchen zwei abwechselnd Sonett 29 in der Vertonung des amerikanischen Liedermachers (und Schwulenikone) Rufus Wainwright singen.[17]

Gender ist jedoch nur einer der möglichen Gesichtspunkte, unter welchen der kulturelle Einfluss der *Sonette* gemessen werden kann. Ebenso bedeutsam (wenn auch nicht ganz davon zu trennen) ist der politische Ansatz. Die Übersetzungswissenschaft leistet dabei Hilfe, indem sie uns darüber informiert, wie in der Interaktion von Sprachen auch die Kulturen interagieren, die in die jeweilige Sprache eingebettet sind. So zeigt beispielsweise die Übersetzungs- und Rezeptionsgeschichte von Shakespeares Sonett 66 ('Tired with all these, for restful death I cry', mit der Zeile 'And art made tongue-tied by authority'), dass Übersetzungen dieses Sonetts bis heute beliebter sind, als es jemals das Original war. Besonders im Laufe des zwanzigsten Jahrhunderts wurde dieses Sonett, in dem, hamletartig, sich der Selbstmord als Ausweg aus den Missständen in der Gesellschaft anbietet, in Kontinentaleuropa zu einem Schlüsseltext des Protests gegen Repression, während ihm in Großbritannien vergleichsweise wenig Beachtung geschenkt wurde. Es gibt hierzu eine Publikation von Ulrich Erckenbrecht in mehrfachen Auflagen und Erweiterungen, in welchen die Übersetzungsgeschichte des Sonetts genau beleuchtet wird.[18]

Es gibt zahlreiche Überblicke über die Geschichte der Übersetzungen und Kontrafakturen der *Sonette* in Deutschland.[19] Werner Koppenfels bezeichnet das Projekt einer Komplettübersetzung der Sonette Shakespeares als 'the crown glory on the brow of ambitious German translators'.[20] Und in der Tat haben grosse Namen sich daran versucht. Wichtige Stationen im frühen zwanzigsten Jahrhundert sind sicher die Ausgaben von Stefan George oder Karl Kraus.[21] Eine der ersten bedeutenden Nachkriegsübersetzungen der *Sonette* erfolgte durch Paul Celan, der 1967 *Einundzwanzig Sonette* übersetzte und darin das 105. Sonett durch eine ganz eigene 'Intention auf die Sprache' zu einer 'Poetik der Beständigkeit'[22] fortsetzte, um so die Gedichte markant ins eigene Werk zu integrieren. In ihnen wird durch den Dialog zweier Zeitalter die Dringlichkeit von Shakespeares Konflikt zwischen Schönheit, Liebe, Poesie und Zeit für ein modernes poetisches Bewusstsein aufbereitet. So konnte Celan durch seine individuelle Poetik ein modernes 'skeptisches Gegenbild der Sonette' erzeugen.[23]

Auch im 21. Jahrhundert scheint der Übersetzungseifer nicht abzuflauen. Neben vielen auf radikale Modernisierung abzielenden Versionen erschien 2007 etwa die zwischen Prosa und Vers schwebende Neuübersetzung Klaus Reicherts.[24] Ergänzend dazu möchte ich mich aber auf zwei 'radikale Übersetzungen' von Ulrike Draesner und Franz Josef Czernin konzentrieren. Vor dem hier skizzierten Hintergrund werfen diese von etablierten LyrikerInnen verfassten Versuche interessante Fragen in Bezug auf die Funktion von Übersetzungen und Nachbildungen, sowie das sich verändernde Erscheinungsbild Shakespeares in den Kulturen des deutschsprachigen Raumes auf.

Draesner selbst benutzt den Ausdruck 'Radikalübersetzungen' in dem Aufsatz 'Dolly und Will', der die erste Veröffentlichung von siebzehn Sonetten unter dem Titel 'Twin Spin' (2000) begleitet.[25] Czernins Übersetzungen des Zyklus sind in der Ausgabe der Hanser-Akzente unter dem Titel *Sonnets, Übersetzungen* (1999) ebenfalls mit einem begleitenden Aufsatz gesammelt.[26] In einem Beitrag über Draesner und Czernin zur Thematik der 'Unsichtbarkeit der Übersetzenden' versucht sich Manfred Pfister an einer Typologie poetischer Vorgehensweisen: von 'Übersetzung' bis zu 'Nachdichtung', 'Nachbildung', 'Umdichtung' und 'Adaptierung', die der zunehmenden Sichtbarkeit des/der ÜbersetzerIn entspricht. Seine Sequenz findet ihren Höhepunkt in dem Ausdruck 'Radikalübersetzung'. Obgleich es sich dabei nicht um einen Gattungsbegriff handelt, ist es wohl, auf den Einzelfall bezogen, ein sinnvoller Ansatz, um mit diesen beiden Übersetzungen zu arbeiten.[27]

An dieser Stelle möchte ich ein wenig genauer darauf eingehen, wie diese beiden Dichter sich Shakespeares Sonetten nähern. In diesem Zusammenhang werde ich mich hauptsächlich auf Draesner konzentrieren, jedoch werde ich versuchen, beide im Fazit meines Beitrages zusammenzubringen, um meinen Überlegungen eine breitere Basis zu geben.

'Not marble nor the gilded monuments | Of princes, shall outlive this pow'rful rhyme', lautet die selbstbewusste Botschaft von Shakespeares Sonett 55, das die Dichtkunst zur eigentlichen Überwinderin der Zeit erklärt.[28] Was Dichterworte produzieren, besteht nicht aus vergänglichem Material und kann daher nicht verfallen. Die *Sonette* greifen hier auf einen Topos des Horaz zurück, um sich und ihr dichterisches Medium als ewig junge Zeugnisse wahren Wertes zu feiern und aller Schönheit ('the living record of your memory'), die ansonsten mit der Zeit vergeht, Dauer zu verleihen ('in the eyes of all posterity'). Hier hebt Shakespeares

Sprache ihre eigene Machtvollkommenheit hervor. Doch sind es gerade die *Sonette*, die uns vielfach in Erinnerung rufen, dass kein Dichterwort isoliert existiert und dass kein Gedicht aus eigener Kraft überdauert: 'So long as men can breathe or eyes can see, | So long lives this, and this gives life to thee' heißt es am Schluss von Sonett 18, in Anerkennung dessen, dass Worte Atem und dass Texte LeserInnen brauchen, um fortzubestehen.[29] In Draesners radikaler Version heißt es: 'solange einer atmen kann, solange augen sehn | solange lohnt auch dies und klont dir leben ein'.[30]

Über die Politik und Sexualpolitik dieser Sonette hinaus thematisieren diese Gedichte in erster Linie das Fortbestehen des Selbst in der Kunst und der Nachwelt: die obsessiven 'Träume des Überlebens',[31] die Shakespeares *Sonette* und die Gegenwart heimsuchen. Hier kommt Draesners 'Twin Spin' zum Tragen, welches durch einen Durchbruch der Reproduktionstechnologie, die erfolgreiche Geburt des ersten geklonten Säugetieres, des Schafs Dolly, inspiriert wurde. Draesner erklärt in ihrem Aufsatz 'Dolly und Will', dass als sie die *Sonette* in ihrem Bücherregal inmitten der Berichterstattung über Dolly sah, es ihr in den Sinn kam, dass die semantische Struktur der *Sonette* ('From fairest creatures we desire increase', Sonnet 1) auf dieselbe Art und Weise reproduziert werden könnte, denn '[d]ie Gedichte', beschloss sie, 'sprachen von Klonen'.[32] Ihre Auswahl der siebzehn Sonette ist an sich schon bezeichnend, indem sie jene herausgreift, welche sich mit Fortpflanzung auseinandersetzen, und die sie in das Jetzt der Gentechnologie verlagert. Die Sonnete 1–17 sind als 'Procreation Sonnets' in die Literaturkritik eingegangen. Oder wie es Don Paterson in seiner ausgelassenen Auseinandersetzung mit Shakespeares *Sonetten* auf den Punkt bringt: 'Multiplication. That's the name of the game.'[33] Das trifft Draesners Sicht genau: '"zeugen, zeugen, sich selbst reproduzieren" — nur das flüstert ihr obsessiver Traum'.[34] Fünf der 'Procreation Sonnets' sind in Draesners Auswahl enthalten. Pfister fasst zusammen: 'Shakespeare's neo-platonic discourse of idea and image, original and copy, love and procreation is translated into the current lingo of informatics and bio-technology, proclaiming Love in the Age of Mechanical Reproduction.'[35] Das wäre genauer gesagt Angst im Zeitalter der biotechnischen Reproduktion. Weiter Draesner: 'Traum und Alptraum ist der Klon, dessen Erscheinen das Subjekt grundlegend, fundamental, in allem, wie wir es je verstanden haben, ändert — indem es sich gleichen läßt.'[36]

Draesner greift daher die Natur des Selbst auf, wie sie sich in der Lyrik äußern kann und wie sie verändert werden kann:

> Das Ich-Subjekt der Rede wechselt ständig, ohne jemals das Thema zu wechseln (wie krieg ich dich und wie überleben wir, was ein Teil dessen ist, wie ich dich kriege). Als Spirale gesagt: in der Unwechselbarkeit des Themas wird das Subjekt dann allerdings seinerseits unverwechselbar und somit zu einem Subjekt, das sich nicht unterwirft, indem es sich dem Rondo der Rollen stets unterwirft, um am Ende dadurch, daß es nicht mehr wechselt, sondern sich als Wechselndes fixiert, dem Thema eine weitere Spiraldrehung zuzufügen im Bäumchen-wechsel-dich-Spiel der Rede.[37]

Draesners radikale Versuche überschreiten bewusst die Grenzen der Übersetzung, indem sie sich auf die Suche nach nicht etablierten semantischen Bedeutungen und unkonventionellen Effekten machen, indem sie die vertrauten Gedichte mit dem Wortschatz der zeitgenössischen Naturwissenschaften und der heutigen Gesellschaft samt der digitalen und biologischen Reproduktion durchziehen. Draesner führt das Sprachspiel der *Sonette* selbst mit dem Namen 'Will' und seiner wandelbaren Semantik fort, indem sie ihre eigene Übersetzungsstrategie als ein 'will-ful misunderstanding' versteht;[38] mit diesem 'ge-will-ten Missverständnis' entrichtet die Dichterin Shakespeare nicht nur ihren Tribut, sondern entwickelt auch ihre eigene Kunst im Widerstand gegen seine literarische Autorität. Natürlich ist das Teil des Nachfolgertums: 'strong poets make [poetic] history by misreading one another, to clear imaginative space for themselves' (Bloom).[39]

Des Weiteren fühlt sich Draesner durch die kanonische Geltung der *Sonette* und ihre langjährige Übersetzungserfahrung bestärkt, einen Aspekt der Übersetzung hervorzuheben, der im Allgemeinen eher versteckt bleibt: die Interpretation, welche selbstverständlich einem bestimmten Moment angehört und somit zeitgebunden bleibt. 'Radikalübersetzungen stellen beides, Interpretation und Zeithorizont, sichtbar aus', erklärt Draesner, was aber örtlich gebundene Missverständnisse und Missdeutungen auf verschiedenen Ebenen zur Folge haben kann.[40] Erstens werden einige Texte Shakespeares von Draesner bewusst leicht fehlerhaft wiedergegeben und damit entstellt; zweitens hat Draesner drei schon bestehende Übersetzungen der *Sonette* (einschließlich zwei der radikalsten von Stefan George und Paul Celan) 'trianguliert', so dass eine Art Nachhallraum entstanden ist, in dem Fragen von Autorschaft und Originalität sich überkreuzen.[41] Wie Draesner es formuliert: 'Radikalübersetzungen sind Parasiten und geben zu, daß sie es sind.' Jedoch findet sie hier wieder ihren eigenen Weg, indem sie der Etymologie der Wörter nachgeht oder indem sie durch kunstvoll fließende Übergänge in andere Sprachen rutscht und somit neue Bedeutungen schafft — ein Prozess, den Tobias Döring als 'polyglot poetics' bezeichnet.[42] Draesners Radikalübersetzung mit ihrem bewusstem Einsatz von Druckfehlern, Missverständnissen, Fehlübersetzungen und sprachlichen Sonderlingen hat das Ziel, zum Vorschein zu bringen, was Draesners Ansicht nach das Grund- und Produktionsprinzip *jedes* Textes ist; genauso wie die mögliche Fehlablesung des genetischen Codes, welche mit jeder Zellteilung reproduziert wird, eine Variabilität in den Populationen und infolgedessen die Evolution erst ermöglicht. Replikation ist niemals perfekt, sondern vielmehr beinhalten Fehler buchstäblich Sinn und Bedeutung.

Für Draesner ist das nicht nur Thema — es wird stattdessen buchstäblich in die sprachliche Vorgehensweise übertragen. Das betrifft Form wie Lexis. In 'Dolly und Will' benutzt Draesner den Begriff 'Anklanggedicht'.

> Im Sonett als klassisches Anklanggedicht klingt heute der Reim selbst nurmehr an bzw. wird in (Teil-)Anagramme aufgelöst: in der Welt der reproduzierbaren und damit gesteigerten Einzelheit reimt sich nichts mehr. Es besteht nur mehr aus den gleichen Buchstaben (wie für die Genetiker, wir).[43]

Genau gesehen reimen Draesners Übersetzungen viel mehr als man vielleicht annehmen würde.

Die lexikalische Vorgehensweise ist auch bezeichnend. Übersetzt man beispielsweise 'fair' mit 'hell' (Sonett 1), bringt man neue Themenkomplexe ins Gedicht: z.B. auch die Hölle. Aber 'beguile' wird auch mit 'begeilen' (Sonett 4) übersetzt;

'tyrants' mit 'transplanteure' (Sonett 5), 'print' mit 'klon' (Sonett 11), 'date' mit 'dattel' (Sonett 18), oder 'invention' mit 'muse' (Sonett 38). So ergeben sich 'Fehlübersetzungen', die aus einem rhetorischen Repertoire schöpfen, das sich auf Polysemie, Homophonie, Homonyme, 'figura etymologica', Polyptoton und Volksetymologie stützt und somit eine tiefe Verunsicherung in Bezug auf die Eindeutigkeit sprachlicher Bedeutung aufzeigt. Draesner kommentiert selbst: 'Meine Radikalübersetzungen drehen Shakespeares Worte um, fassen sie bewusst an den "falschen" nämlich nicht-kanonisierten Enden ihrer Polysemantizität, stellen sie von den Füßen auf den Kopf.'[44] Das Ergebnis ist eine radikale Wiederaneignung Shakespeares, die uns jedoch auch die Bedeutungsvielfalt von Wörtern vor Augen führt, sodass wir letztendlich nicht mehr sicher sein können, wo sich nun die Köpfe und Füße befinden. Thomas Döring bemerkt in diesem Zusammenhang: 'This, in effect, turns the interlingual practice of translation into a practice used to explore intralingual ruptures.'[45]

Diese sprachlichen Brüche werden durch das neuerliche Interesse an jenen Prozessen wieder vereint, welche die Reproduktion des Textes unterbrechen und den Vorgang des Lesens, des Erinnerns, des Schreibens und des Übersetzens inszenieren. Die Zeilen aus Sonett 15 — 'And, all in war with Time for love of you, | As he takes from you, I engraft you new' — werden in Draesners Version: 'und ganz und gar überworfen mit zeit, aus liebe zu dir | während sie an dir frisst, dreh ich dich neu, die retorte, von mir'.[46] Das Ziel bei Draesner ist ebenfalls das Überleben (Sonett 68: 'To live a second life on second head').[47] Die Frage, auf die es ankommt, ist aber: Was für ein Leben? Ich glaube, dass Draesner auf ein besseres und freieres Leben anspielt, das durch eine Offenheit gegenüber neuen Sprachen und sprachlichen Möglichkeiten zustande kommen kann; ein Leben, das gerade durch die Übersetzung errungen wird und sich der dabei zum Tragen kommenden Prozesse bewusst ist.

Ähnliche Belange regten auch Czernins Auswahl von einundvierzig Sonetten an, in der er untersucht, was er im begleitenden Aufsatz 'Zur Übersetzung' als die Zwischenräume zwischen Shakespeares und seiner eigenen Sprache und Zeit bezeichnet. Anstelle des Klons als thematischer Ordnungsstruktur, fokussiert Czernin auf 'das Bild des Kampfes' zwischen 'Fremdem' und 'Eigenem', jedoch stets mit dem ausdrücklichen Ziel 'zeitgemäß' zu sein.[48] Auf diese Weise versucht Czernin eine neue Art des Übersetzens zu schaffen: eine, die den traditionellen 'Dienst am Original' zurückweist, und dagegen ausschöpft, was durch die Übersetzung gewonnen wurde und was durch den zeitlichen Abstand zwischen Autor und Übersetzer zum Original hinzugekommen ist:

> Die geglückte Übersetzung würde bestimmte Eigenschaften sowohl beider Sprachen als auch beider Zeitalter tragen und wäre dennoch insofern ein eigenständiges Gedicht, als es diese Eigenschaften so vereint, dass sie als zeitgemäßes Gedicht glückt, zu dessen Form, und das heißt: Bedeutung gehört, dass es eine Übersetzung ist.[49]

Indem Czernin sich selbst und die Gegenwart in das Zentrum dieser Konfiguration rückt, werden Shakespeares Texte zu Hilfsmitteln, um seinen spielerischen Umgang mit den Texten vorzuexerzieren. Wie Draesner behält er die Form der

Sonette bei, jedoch bedient er sich eines Deutsch, das in sich gekehrt ist: mit drastischen syntaktischen Auslassungen, mehrdeutigen Wandlungen von Nomen oder Adjektiven sowie zahlreichen Reflexivpronomen. Für Sonette 62, 128 und 141 bietet er sogar zwei Versionen an: Die erste, die sich nah am Originaltext orientiert, nennt er eine Übersetzung, die zweite, die sich weiter davon entfernt, die 'Übertragung der Übersetzung'.[50]

Den Gesamteindruck, der entsteht, nennt Pfister einen 'energetic gestus'.[51] Sprache in ihrer erhöhten Reflexivität profiliert die Selbstbezogenheit des Sprechers. Dies wird noch radikaler in den zweiten Fassungen der drei Sonette, in welchen die Gedichte durch die Lexik von Sprache und Übersetzung (das Wort 'übertragen' z.B. wird mehrfach verwendet) eindeutig zu metapoetischen Spiegelungen von Übersetzungspraktiken werden. Beachtlich an Czernins fortlaufenden Reproduktionen Shakespeares ist der Fokus auf das übersetzende Subjekt (den/die ÜbersetzerIn), bei dem es sich jedoch um ein Subjekt handelt, das sich im Dialog mit dem Subjekt in Shakespeares Sonetten herstellt, was dazu führt, dass die Anrede des 'du' verkompliziert wird. Hilfreich ist es vielleicht an dieser Stelle ein Gedicht aus Czernins fortlaufender Sonettenreihe mit Shakespeares Sonett zu vergleichen. Shakespeares berühmtes, Horaz aufgreifendes und den Formen des Überlebens gewidmetes Sonett 55 fängt so an:

> Not marble nor the gilded momuments
> Of princes shall outlive this pow'rful rhyme;
> But you shall shine more bright in these contents
> Than unswept stone, besmeared with sluttish time.[52]

Draesner übersetzt mit Blick auf moderne Techniken der Reproduktion:

> marmor nicht noch goldne website-monumente
> werden das alphabet des dichtgepackten überdauern;
> heller wirst in seinen containern du leuchten
> als von hündischer zeit besabberte screens.[53]

Czernin wechselt dagegen auf eine (selbst-)reflexive Ebene:

> sein nicht wird mehr der prunk aus gold, aus stein gehauen,
> wenn mächtig sprechend, dies auf sich reime macht;
> was nicht aus staub, aus sand, ist hiermit fest zu bauen,
> bildend aus feinstem stoff in deinem sinn gebracht.[54]

Was vordergründlich von Draesner als Zubehör des digitalen Fortdauerns ins Bild gesetzt wird ('website', 'containern', 'screens', im weiteren Fortgang auch 'viruskill', 'ins globale netz', 'server', usw.), wird von Czernin als gedichtimmanente Angelegenheit verhandelt: 'auf sich reime macht'. Das zusammenfassende Reimpaar bringt es auf den Punkt.

> So, till the judgement that yourself arise,
> You live in this, and dwell in lovers' eyes.

Draesner:

> hier lebst du, bis du auferstehst im letzten menü,
> — haust in den augen liebender, ein revenue.

Interessant hier ist das Miteinbeziehen der Nachwelt — oder besser gesagt das projizierte Bild des Fortlebens des Du — womit hier sowohl Dichter, Geliebter und Text als Geist in einer digitalen Zukunft (als 'revenue') gemeint sind. Für Czernin wohnt das mögliche Fortleben (wohlgemerkt mit Fragezeichen) in der verdoppelten Beziehung des Ich und des Du, die sich in der Übertragung begegnen.

> bis du, im eigenen namen!, trittst neu selbst zu tage,
> wohnst du in dem, was ich so schön von dir uns sage?

Die 'Liebenden' aus dem englischen Gedicht werden zu den Dichtern, die sich hier im Gedicht treffen, oder, besser gesagt, sie werden zu einem Prozess: zum Geschäft des Übersetzens selbst ('was ich *so schön* von *dir uns* sage?').

Dies wird noch deutlicher im Sonett 62, das die 'self-love' des lyrischen Subjekts im Alter anspricht. Das zusammenfassende Reimpaar bei Shakespeare wendet das Gedicht auf überraschende Weise. Was vorher als Selbstbezogenheit erschien, war eigentlich Selbstlosigkeit: Es ging um die Geliebte und natürlich um die Kunst: 'Tis thee (my self), that for myself I praise, | Painting my age with beauty of thy days.'[55] In Czernins Übersetzung wird daraus: 'wär ich, wie ich mich preise selbst, mich selbst verzückend, | was in mir frisch erglänzt, mein selbst!, wärst du, mich schmückend'.[56] Die darauffolgende 'Übertragung' hat ausnahmsweise einen Titel: 'to ws' und bringt den ödipalen Kampf deutlich ins Bild: 'ach, ins frische, reine übertragen | wärs seine stimme — alleine die meine muss versagen'.[57]

Im Hinblick auf ein Fazit lohnt es sich zu fragen, was den Autor und die Autorin trotz ihrer Unterschiede miteinander verbindet. Jahnson merkt an, dass es einerseits eine Übung in poetischer Ambition für ausländische DichterInnen ist, sich mit den *Sonetten* zu beschäftigen; es zeigt sich aber auch, dass, während die Übersetzung von Shakespeares Dramen von August Wilhelm Schlegel und Ludwig Tieck aus dem frühen neunzehnten Jahrhundert immer noch ein Standardtext im deutschsprachigen Raum ist, das Fehlen einer einzelnen maßgeblichen Übersetzung der *Sonette* für DichterInnen ein Ansporn ist, selbst Hand anzulegen.

Ein ähnliches Muster ist bei einem anderen bedeutenden Dichter zu beobachten, der häufig übersetzt, imitiert und adaptiert wird, aber vom Deutschen ins Englische: Rainer Maria Rilke, der ein in diesem Ausmaß von keinem anderen fremdsprachigen Dichter der Neuzeit erreichtes Nachleben auf Englisch führt. Es gibt zweifellos ein Bedürfnis der Nachgeborenen, 'to measure the achievement' (William Gass zu Rilke), also sich selbst mit einem großartigen Dichter zu messen und auf sein Werk zu reagieren, um hier auch das eigene Zeitalter erfassen zu können.

Die *Sonette* sind, wie oben angedeutet, intrinsisch auf das Verfassen von Lyrik ausgerichtet, was Shakespeare im besten Sinne des Wortes zu einem 'poet's poet' macht. Viele seiner Gedichte bündeln letztlich die transformative und sich erinnernde Energie der Lyrik selbst: als Beispiele von 'P^2', wie es Erich Fried in Hinsicht auf Brecht nannte.[58] Die Nachfolger fühlen sich aufgefordert, die Anforderungen der Dichtung selbst zu kommentieren. Das ist all jenen gemeinsam, die versucht haben, den *Sonetten* eine neue Spracheigentümlichkeit zu geben. Sowohl Draesner als auch Czernin konzentrieren sich zum einen auf die intime Sphäre des Selbst, und zum anderen auf die politischen Implikationen der Individualität an sich in einer radikal zerbrochenen Welt. Das vielleicht Neue an ihrem Ansatz ist, dass sie den Prozess des Lesens, des Schreibens und vor allem den Prozess des Übersetzens in den Vordergrund stellen, während sie sich inmitten all dieser Prozesse befinden. Darüber hinaus heben sie ihre eigene Rolle in einer Rezeptionsgeschichte hervor und animieren uns dazu, die stattfindende Bedeutungstriangulation zu erkennen, sowie die 'will-ful misunderstandings', die Auseinandersetzungen, die sprachlichen Ausrutscher und das Bedürfnis über die und mit der Gegenwart zu sprechen. So regt uns Draesner dazu an, ihre radikalen Übersetzungen als ihre eigenen Klone zu betrachten, als Produkte des Reproduktionsprozesses und somit als 'Fehlkopien', da selbst die präziseste technologische Reproduktion der Kopie oder des Fotos bis hin zum Zellklonen immer ein gewisses Grad an Variation, Abweichung und Mutation mit sich bringt.

'In such a model', behauptet Pfister,

> in which original and translation share the same matrix, the translation refuses to be considered as a second-order derivative version of the original, but claims instead to be of the same order with it and thus calls the distinction between original and translation into question.[59]

Wie bereits angedeutet, sieht Pfister dies ausdrücklich vor dem Hintergrund der Wiederkehr des sichtbaren Übersetzers und der sichtbaren Übersetzerin: 'the radical translations [...] are radical also in staging highly manifest translators performing self-reflectively their own office of translating against the problematic history of translating, its uncertain status and its aporia'.[60] Das ist auf einer bestimmten Ebene sicher richtig, denn die ausdrückliche Distanzierung, mit der sich AutorInnen, die nicht auf Englisch schreiben, von der englischsprachigen Kultur loslösen können, bringt Vorteile mit sich; zum Beispiel scheint die ödipale Angst dem Vorgänger gegenüber aufgrund der Zugehörigkeit zu einer anderen Sprachgemeinschaft weniger erdrückend.[61]

Gewiss thematisieren Draesner und Czernin den Prozess der Übersetzung, jedoch glaube ich, dass ihr Engagement darüber hinausgeht. Sie bringen sich nicht nur als Übersetzerin und Übersetzer ein, sondern auch als Lyrikerin und Lyriker, die fest im eigenen Zeitalter verankert sind (ihre Shakespeare-Übersetzungen sind in vielerlei Hinsicht auch mit dem Rest ihres Werkes vergleichbar) und trotzdem auch innerhalb einer breiteren Tradition schreiben. Hierbei handelt es sich um ein zweischneidiges Schwert, denn die lange Tradition, innerhalb derer sie sich wiederfinden, hebt ihre Stellung als eine des 'afterness' ('Danachkommens') hervor. Beide positionieren sich ausdrücklich in einem 'aftermath of unquestioned belief in genius and original creative afterlife, in an enduring aftermath of understanding Shakespeare as original genius'.[62] Das unterstreichen die ganz bewusst inszenierten Symptome der 'Verspätung',[63] eine Kategorie, die für viele philosophische und poetische Werke aus Deutschland bestimmt ist. Aber gleichzeitig greifen sie auch die kreative Energie Shakespeares wie auch seiner früheren Übersetzer auf, um ihre eigene Sprache zu verfremden und ihr Energie zu verleihen, gerade indem sie diese 'Nachzeitigkeit' thematisieren. Beide haben mit einer Angst, die dieser Status mit sich bringt, zu kämpfen: Czernin im Bild des Kampfes und in den vielen reflexiven Verdoppelungen (Sonett 55) und Draesner im Bild des 'Heimgesuchtwerdens', wie die letzten Verse desselben Sonettes zeigen: 'hier lebst du, bis du auferstehst im letzten menü | — haust in den augen liebender, ein revenue'.

Draesners und Czernins radikales Übersetzen trägt als extreme Form poetischer Hermeneutik zu einer ständigen Erneuerung des Originals bei und garantiert gleichzeitig das Überdauern über die Grenzen der nationalen Literatur hinaus.[64] Solches kreative Übersetzen kann auch einen Einfluss auf das Original ausüben: Im Original ist sozusagen das Potential zu seinen möglichen Übersetzungen schon enthalten, deren Bandbreite sich mit der Zeit immer weiter vergrößert. Durch ein solches Vorgehen wird diese Bandbreite radikal erweitert. Somit 'kann der Einzeltext mit dem Blick auf den formalen, historischen oder metaphorischen Kontext in verändertem Licht erscheinen'.[65]

Überdies erlaubt es ihnen die Auswegslosigkeit der Nachträglichkeit zu dramatisieren und sich aber selbst auch einen Ausweg daraus zu erschreiben wie zuvor vielleicht nur Paul Celan. Um hier auf den Titel von Draesners erster Shakespeare-Publikation zurückzukommen: Es ermöglicht SchriftstellerInnen im wahrsten Sinne des Wortes 'to change the subject'. Aber es erlaubt auch, dass Shakespeares *Sonette* in einer neuen Zeit Wurzel fassen und dort 'ein zweites Leben' geniessen: ein Überleben, das voller ist und radikaler als es die *Sonette* je für sich erträumt hätten.

Notes to Chapter 23

1. Neil Corcoran, *Shakespeare and the Modern Poet* (Cambridge: Cambridge University Press, 2010), S. 2–3.
2. Roger Paulin, *The Critical Reception of Shakespeare in Germany 1682–1914: Native Literature and Foreign Genius* (Hildesheim, Zürich, New York: Olms, 2013), S. 1.
3. Christoph Martin Wieland, 'Der Geist Shakespears', in *Shakespeare-Rezeption: Die Diskussion um Shakespeare in Deutschland I. 1741–1788*, hrsg. v. Hansjürgen Blinn (Berlin: Schmidt, 1982), S. 119–22. Vgl. auch Ernst Stadler, *Wielands Shakespeare* (Straßburg: Trübner, 1910).
4. Vgl. <http://www.shakespearesglobe.com/uploads/ffiles/2011/02/295900.pdf>. Weiter: Jonathan Bate, *The Romantics on Shakespeare* (London: Penguin, 1992); Werner Habicht, *Shakespeare and the German Imagination* (Hertford: International Shakespeare Association, 1994); Ruth Freifrau von Ledebur, *Der Mythos vom deutschen Shakespeare: Die Deutsche Shakespeare-Gesellschaft zwischen Politik und Wissenschaft, 1918–1945* (Köln: Böhlau, 2002); Joep Leerssen,'Making Shakespeare National', in *Shakespeare and European Politics*, hrsg. v. Dirk Delabastita, Jozef De Vos and Paul Franssen (Cranbury: Associated University Presses, 2008); *Shakespeare as German Author: Reception, Translation Theory, and Cultural Transfer,* hrsg. v. John A. McCarthy (Leiden: Brill Rodopi, 2018).
5. Paulin, *The Critical Reception*, S. 4; vgl. Bate, *The Romantics on Shakespeare*, S. 12; Leerssen, 'Making Shakespeare National', S. 42.
6. Wilhelm Hortmann, *Shakespeare on the German Stage: The Twentieth Century* (Cambridge: Cambridge University Press, 1998), S. xviii.
7. Heiner Zimmerman, 'Is Hamlet Germany? On the Political Reception of Hamlet', in *New Essays on 'Hamlet'*, hrsg. v. Mark Thornton Burnett and John Manning (New York: AMS, 1994), S. 293–318; *The Hamlet Zone: Reworking 'Hamlet' for European Cultures*, hrsg. v. Ruth Owen (Newcastle upon Tyne: Cambridge Scholars Publishing, 2012); Harold Bloom, *Hamlet: Poem Unlimited* (Edinburgh: Canongate, 2003).

8. Werner von Koppenfels, '"dressing old words new": William Shakespeare's Sonnets into German', in *Shakespeare's Sonnets for the First Time Globally Reprinted: A Quatercentenary Anthology (with a DVD)*, hrsg. v. Jürgen Gutsch und Manfred Pfister (Dozwil: Edition SIGNAThUR 2009), S. 277–92 (S. 277); einen Überblick bietet 'Shakespeares Sonette in Deutschland': <http://exist.hab.de/apps/projekte/sonettbibliographie/view/display.xql>.
9. Manfred Pfister, 'Made in Germany: Shakespeare's Sonnets', *ANGERMION: Yearbook for Anglo-German Literary Criticism, Intellectual History and Cultural Transfers*, 5.1 (2012), 29–57 (S. 30).
10. Christa Jahnson, 'Glocal Shakespeare: Shakespeare's Poems in Germany', in *The Oxford Handbook of Shakespeare's Poetry*, hrsg. v. Jonathan Post (Oxford: Oxford University Press, 2013), S. 671–88. Vgl. *Shakespeare and the Language of Translation*, hrsg. v. Ton Hoenselaars, 2. erweiterte Ausgabe (London: Bloomsbury, 2012).
11. Susan Bassnett und André Lefevere, 'General Editors' Preface', in André Lefevere, *Translation, Rewriting, and the Manipulation of Literary Fame* (London, New York: Routledge 1992), S. vi–vii (S. vii).
12. Lawrence Venuti, *The Translator's Invisibility: A History of Translation* (London, New York: Routledge 2005), S.1. Dagegen Susan Bassnett, 'When is a Translation not a Translation?', in *Constructing Cultures: Essays on Literary Translation*, hrsg. v. Susan Bassnett und André Lefevere (Clevedon: Multilingual Matters, 1998), S. 25–40.
13. Terence Hawkes, *Meaning by Shakespeare* (London: Routledge, 1992), S. 42.
14. Tobias Döring, *Wie er uns gefällt: Gedichte an und auf William Shakespeare* (Zürich: Manesse, 2014).
15. William Wordsworth, 'Scorn not the Sonnet', in Wordsworth, *Poetry and Prose*, ausgew. v. W. M. Merchant (London: Hart-Davis, 1955), S. 785.
16. Paul J. C. M Franssen, 'The Myth of Shakespeare's Sonnets', *Cahiers Élisabéthains: A Journal of English Renaissance Studies*, 90.1 (2016), 85–100; Paul Franssen, *Shakespeare's Literary Lives: The Author as Character in Fiction and Film* (Cambridge: Cambridge University Press, 2016).
17. 'Shakespeare Sonnets at the Berlin Ensemble (Robert Wilson, Rufus Wainwright)', <http://www.robertwilson.com/shakespeares-sonnets>. Vgl auch Manfred Pfister, 'Will, Wilson und Wainwright: Shakespeares Sonette light?', *Shakespeare Jahrbuch*, 146 (2010), S. 177–82.
18. Ulrich Erckenbrecht, *Shakespeare Sechsundsechzig: Variationen uber ein Sonett* (Gottingen: Muriverlag, 1996; 3. erneuerte, erweiterte Auflage, 2009); Manfred Pfister, 'Route 66: The Political Performance of Shakespeare's Sonnet 66 in Germany and Elsewhere', in *Four Hundred Years of Shakespeare in Europe*, hrsg. v. A. Luis Pujante and Ton Hoenselaars (Newark: University of Delaware Press, 2003), S. 70–88; Jürgen Gutsch, '"Millions of Strange Shadows": Vom Übersetzen der Shakespeare-Sonette in jüngerer Zeit (nicht nur) ins Deutsche', *Shakespeare Jahrbuch*, 139 (2003), 161–89; Raimund Borgmeier, *Shakespeares Sonett 'When forty winters...' und die deutschen Übersetzer: Untersuchungen zu den Problemen der Shakespeare-Übertragung* (München: Wilhelm Fink, 1970).
19. Manfred Mixner, 'Zweimal Shakespeare: Die Übersetzungen von Erich Fried und die Bearbeitungen von Karl Kraus', *Literatur und Kritik: Österreichische Monatsschrift*, 131 (1979), 413–20.
20. Koppenfels, 'dressing old words new', S. 277.
21. Stefan George, *Shakespeare Sonnete: Umdichtung* (Berlin: Georg Bondi, 1909); Eugene Norwood, 'Stefan George's Translation of Shakespeare's Sonnets', *Monatshefte für deutschsprachige Kultur und Literatur*, 44 (1952), 217–24; Ray Ockenden, 'Shakespeare and Stefan George's Circle', *ANGERMION: Yearbook for Anglo-German Literary Criticism, Intellectual History and Cultural Transfers*, 5.1 (2012), 3–28; Karl Kraus, *Shakespeares Sonette: Nachdichtung von Karl Kraus* (München: Kösel 1964). Vgl. auch zu den Kriegsjahren: *Cupido lag im Schlummer einst: Drei neue Übersetzungen von Shakespeares Sonette: Englisch-deutsche Ausgabe*, hrsg. v. Christa Jansohn (Tübingen: Stauffenburg, 2001).
22. Peter Szondi, 'Poetry of Constancy — Poetik der Beständigkeit', in Szondi, *Celan-Studien* (Frankfurt a.M.: Suhrkamp, 1972), S. 13–45.
23. Koppenfels, 'dressing old words new': S. 282; Rainer Lengeler, *Shakespeares Sonette in deutscher Übersetzung: Stefan George und Paul Celan* (Opladen: Westdeutscher Verlag, 1989); Heino Schmull, 'Übersetzung als Sprung: Textgenetische und poetologische Beobachtungen an

Celans Übersetzungen von Shakespeares Sonetten', *arcadia*, 32.1 (1997), 119–47; Ludwig Lehnen, 'George und Celan als Übersetzer Shakespeares', in *Celan-Jahrbuch*, 9 (2003–05), hrsg. v. Hans-Michael Speier (Heidelberg: Winter, 2007), S. 273–300; Leonard Olschner, '"Spiel der Spiegelungen": Celan und Rilke lesen Shakespeare', in Olschner, *Im Abgrund Zeit: Paul Celans Poetiksplitter* (Göttingen: Vandenhoeck & Ruprecht, 2007), S. 125–38; Wolfgang Kaussen, '"Ich verantworte Ich widerstehe Ich verweigere": Celans Shakespeare', in William Shakespeare, *Einundzwanzig Sonette / Deutsch von Paul Celan; erweiterte Neuausgabe* (Frankfurt a.M.: Insel, 2001), S. 49–92. Kaussen ist selbst renommierter Shakespeare-Übersetzer: William Shakespeare, *Die Sonette*, übersetzt von Wolfgang Kaussen (Frankfurt a.M.: Insel, 1998). Nicht zu vergessen: Wolf Biermann, *Das ist die feinste Liebeskunst: 40 Shakespeare-Sonette* (Köln: Kiepenheuer & Witsch, 2004).

24. William Shakespeare, *Die Sonette — The Sonnets. Deutsch von Klaus Reichert* (Frankfurt a.M.: Fischer, 2007). Vgl. Klaus Reichert, *Der fremde Shakespeare* (München, Wien: Hanser, 1998) und *Die unendliche Aufgabe: Zum Übersetzen* (München, Wien: Hanser, 2003).
25. Ulrike Draesner, 'Twin Spin', in Peter Waterhouse, Ulrike Draesner, Barbara Köhler, *:to change the subject* (Göttingen: Wallstein, 2000), S. 11–30 und der dazugehörende Aufsatz 'Dolly und Will', S. 30–33. Vgl. *Twin Spin: 17 Shakespeare Sonnets radically translated by Ulrike Draesner and radically back-translated by Tom Cheesman; with an Exhibition Catalogue for 'Shall I Compare thee: Shakespeare in Translation'* (Oxford: Taylor Institution Library, 2016).
26. William Shakespeare/Franz Josef Czernin, *Sonnets, Übersetzungen* (München: Hanser, 1999).
27. Manfred Pfister, '"Bottom, thou art translated": Recent Radical Translations of Shakespearean Sonnets in Germany', in *Crossing Time and Space: Shakespeare Translations in Present-Day Europe*, hrsg. v. Carla Dente und Sara Soncini (Pisa: Edizione Plus/Pisa University Press, 2008), S. 21–36 (S. 25–26).
28. Die *Sonette* werden nach folgender Ausgabe zitiert: William Shakespeare, *The Oxford Shakespeare: The Complete Sonnets and Poems*, hrsg. v. Colin Burrow (Oxford: Oxford University Press, 2008), S. 491. Weiter: Stephen Booth, *Shakespeare's Sonnets* (New Haven, CT: Yale University Press, 2000); Katherine Duncan-Jones, *The Arden Shakespeare Shakespeare's Sonnets* (London: Methuen Drama, 2010).
29. Shakespeare, *The Complete Sonnets and Poems*, S. 417.
30. Draesner, 'Twin Spin', S. 30.
31. Draesner, 'Dolly und Will', S. 31.
32. Ebd., S. 30.
33. Robert Crosman, 'Making Love Out of Nothing At All: The Issue of Story in Shakespeare's Procreation Sonnets', *Shakespeare Quarterly*, 41.4 (1990), 470–88; Don Paterson, *Reading Shakespeare's Sonnets: A New Commentary* (London: Faber, 2010), p. 7. Weiter zu Shakespeares Sonetten siehe Helen Vendler, *The Art of Shakespeare's Sonnets* (Cambridge, MA: Harvard University Press, 1999).
34. Draesner, 'Dolly und Will', S. 31.
35. Pfister, 'Made in Germany', S. 42.
36. Draesner, 'Dolly und Will', S. 33.
37. Draesner, 'Twin Spin', S. 32. Vgl auch zu der Drehung im Gedicht: Karen Leeder '"Twin Spin": Ulrike Draesner's Poetry of Science', in *Ulrike Draesner: A Companion*, hrsg. v. Karen Leeder und Lyn Marven (Berlin, New York: de Gruyter, 2021), S. 00–00, im Druck.
38. Draesner, 'Twin Spin', S. 32.
39. Bloom, *The Anxiety of Influence: A Theory of Poetry*, 2. Ausg. (Oxford: Oxford University Press, 1997), S. 5.
40. Draesner, 'Twin Spin', S. 31.
41. Persönliches Gespräch mit Ulrike Draesner.
42. Tobias Döring, 'German is a Foreign Anguish: Draesner and the Sprite of Translation', in *Ulrike Draesner: A Companion*, S. 00–00, im Druck.
43. Draesner, 'Dolly und Will', S. 32. Dass die Buchstaben A, C, G und T, 'des vier buchstabenworts (Sonnet 65, 'Twin Spin', S. 27)', die DNA-Grundlagen bilden, wird weitgehend thematisiert: Tom Cheesman, 'Shall I Compare, Vergleichen, Recombine? Reversioning Ulrike Draesner's "Twin Spin"', *In Other Words*, 30 (2007), 6–15 (S. 10).

44. Draesner, 'Dolly und Will', S. 32.
45. Döring, 'German is a Foreign Anguish', S. 00 (im Druck).
46. *The Complete Sonnets and Poems*, S. 411: Draesner, 'Twin Spin', S. 17.
47. Shakespeare, *The Complete Sonnets and Poems*, S. 517.
48. Shakespeare/Czernin, *Sonnets, Übersetzungen*, S. 125.
49. Ebd., S. 126.
50. Shakespeare/Czernin, *Sonnets, Übersetzungen*, S. 126.
51. Pfister, 'Bottom, thou art translated', S. 25.
52. *The Complete Sonnets and Poems*, S. 491.
53. Draesner, 'Twin Spin', S. 25.
54. Czernin, *Sonnets, Übersetzungen*, S. 29.
55. *The Complete Sonnets and Poems*, S. 505.
56. Shakespeare/Czernin, *Sonnets, Übersetzungen*, S. 97.
57. Ebd., S. 98.
58. Fried übernimmt das von Friedrich Schlegel (*Literarische Notizen 1797–1801*, hrsg. v. Hans Eichner (Frankfurt a.M.: Ullstein, 1980), Absatz 518, und S. 250), der p^2 oder π^2 benutzt.
59. Pfister, 'Bottom, thou art translated', S. 43.
60. Ebd., S. 36.
61. Diese Behauptung wird auf interessante Weise durch zwei Anthologien in Frage gestellt: *On Shakespeare's Sonnets: A Poets' Celebration*, hrsg. v. Hannah Crawforth und Elizabeth Scott-Baumann (London: Bloomsbury, 2016); *The Sonnets: Translating and Rewriting Shakespeare*, hrsg. v. Sharmila Cohen und Paul Legault (Brooklyn: Nightboat Books, 2012).
62. Tobias Döring, '"On the wrong track to ourselves": Armin Senser's Shakespeare and the Issue of Artistic Creativity in Contemporary German Poetry', *Shakespeare Survey*, 66 (2013), 145–54 (S. 147).
63. Vgl. *Figuring Lateness in Modern German Culture*, hrsg. v. Karen Leeder (= *New German Critique*, 119 (2015)).
64. *Post-Colonial Shakespeare*, hrsg. v. Ania Loomba und Martin Orkin (London: Routledge, 1998). Vgl. Martin Orkin, *Local Shakespeares: Proximations and Power* (London: Routledge, 2005).
65. Kathrin Volkmann, 'Shakespeares Sonette auf deutsch: Übersetzungsprozesse zwischen Philologie und dichterischer Kreativität', Univ. Diss. Universität Heidelberg 1996, S. 159.

INDEX

Abderrahman El-Mahdi 159–61
Adler, H. G. 263
   Die unsichtbare Wand 267–69, 271
   Theresienstadt 1941–1945: Das Antlitz einer Zwangsgemeinschaft 273–74, 276
Adorno, Theodor 167, 254, 256
   Dialektik der Aufklärung 90, 335
Alexander the Great, King of Macedon 229, 323
Alain de Lille 34
Alighieri, Dante 55, 70, 82, 311, 336–38, 343, 345
Aloni, Jenny 263
   Korridore oder das Gebäude mit der weißen Maus 269–70, 271
Altmann, Lotte 302, 307
Amann, Paul 301
Aminoff, Hans 325
Anaximander 10
Anderson, Benedict 54
Andreas-Salomé, Lou 171–77
   'Mädchenreigen' 174–77
   Ruth 172–74
Anzengruber, Ludwig 93, 98–99, 338
Arendt, Hannah 297
Aristotle 9, 12, 343
Asch, Scholem 302
Astarte 141–42, 148
Atget, Eugène 182
Auerbach, Erich 333–47
   Mimesis 333–47
   'Philologie der Weltliteratur' 340, 342–43
Augustine of Hippo 245, 257 n. 4

Bachofen, Johann Jakob 190
Bacon, Francis 21 n. 42
Bahr, Hermann 87, 138, 292
Ba Jin 66 n. 60
Baker, Samuel 152
Balzac, Honoré de 301, 304–05, 309 n. 36, 339, 343
Barbusse, Henri 300
Bartosch, Roman 145
Baudelaire, Charles 185, 198–200, 202, 279, 281, 287–90, 291
Bauer, Felice 226, 233, 234, 236, 241
Bauer, Heike 175
Baumgarten, Alexander Gottlieb 11
Beer-Hofmann, Richard 136–50, 299
   Der Tod Georgs 137–50

Bellarmin, Roberto Francesco Romolo 26
Beller, Steven 137
Belmore, Herbert 199
Benjamin, Andrew 190, 196–97 n. 28
Benjamin, Walter 80, 181–97, 198–213, 229, 240, 244 n. 52, 247, 249, 251, 256, 279
   Berliner Kindheit um neunzehnhundert 192
   'Das Kunstwerk im Zeitalter seiner technischen Reproduzierbarkeit' 182, 194
   Der Begriff der Kunstkritik in der deutschen Romantik 198–99, 206–07, 211–12
   'Die Aufgabe des Übersetzers' 198–213
   Einbahnstraße 190, 198
   'Franz Kafka: Zur zehnten Wiederkehr seines Todestages' 229, 244 n. 52
   'Kleine Geschichte der Photographie' 187–89
   Passagen-Werk 188–89, 192
   Ursprung des deutschen Trauerspiels 190–92
Béranger, Pierre-Jean de 280
Berendsohn, Walter A. 320
Berengar of Tours 15
Berger, James 276
Bergmann, Hugo 224, 228 n. 23
Berlin, Isaiah 82
Berman, Antoine 121 n. 1, 121 n. 3, 212 n. 12
Berman, Russell A. 168
Bermann, Richard Arnold:
   Die Derwischtrommel / The Mahdi of Allah 151–65
Bernanos, Georges 307
Bernays, Minna 104
Billroth, Theodor 127
Blanchot, Maurice 247, 256
Bloch, Blanche 301
Bloch, Ernst 181–89, 193, 195, 257, 314
   Erbschaft dieser Zeit 181–85
Bloch, Jean-Richard 300–01
Bloom, Harold 348, 354
Bloßfeldt, Karl 189
Blumauer, Aloys 99 n. 4
Boa, Elizabeth 168, 169
Boccaccio, Giovanni 338, 343
Bonaparte, Napoleon 30, 41 n. 104, 48, 52, 54, 83, 229, 339
Borchardt, Rudolf 209
Borges, Jorge Luis 276
Brandt, Susanne Margarethe 44–45
Bratu Hansen, Miriam 189

Brecht, Bertolt 182–84, 193–95, 311–18, 322, 357
  Aufstieg und Fall der Stadt Mahagonny 194, 315
  Das Leben des Galilei 312, 313, 314, 317
  Der gute Mensch von Sezuan 312–13
  Der kaukasische Kreidekreis 312, 313
  Die Dreigroschenoper 194, 195, 314–15, 316
  Leben Eduards des Zweiten von England 193
Breier, Eduard 102 n. 58
Brentano, Clemens:
  Godwi oder Das steinerne Bild der Mutter 143
Brod, Max 221, 224, 228 n. 23, 229, 233, 236–37, 241, 247, 297
Buber, Martin 214–15, 217, 219, 224–25, 227 n. 4, 227 n. 6, 227 n. 8
Büchner, Ludwig 93
Buklijas, Tatjana 125
Buonarotti, Michelangelo di 55
Burckhardt, Jakob 142
Burns, Robert 280
Butler, Judith 131, 167
Byron, George Gordon, Lord 90

Cain, Julien 303
Cain, Lucienne 303
Calvin, John 31
Cardano, Gerolamo 15
Carracciolo, Francesco 56
Cartwright, Rosalind D. 114–15
Celan, Paul 352, 354, 359
Cervantes, Miguel de:
  Don Quixote 229–44
Chaplin, Charlie 155, 164 n. 3
Chater, Nick 108
Chekhov, Anton 192, 229
Christ, *see* Jesus
Christie, Agatha 182
Churchill, Winston 151, 152, 156–57, 159–62, 163
Clemens Wenzeslaus von Sachsen, Elector of Trier 29
Clement XIV 31
Cohen, Hermann 136–37, 148
Constantine, David 213 n. 21
Copernicus 95
Corneille, Pierre:
  Le Cid 193
Corngold, Stanley 230–31, 235, 243 n. 32
Creuzer, Friedrich 190
Curtius, Ernst Robert:
  Europäische Literatur und lateinisches Mittelalter 340
Czernin, Franz Josef 352, 355–59

Damrosch, David 136
Dante, *see* Alighieri, Dante
Darwin, Charles 89
Dauthendey, Karl 187
Davie, Donald 3
DeKoven, Marianne 169

Derrida, Jacques 275, 276
Descartes, René 12
Deubler, Konrad 102 n. 48
Dickens, Charles 229, 339, 346 n. 25
Dirty Harry 79
Dix, Otto 183
Doherty, Brigid 194
Dollfuß, Engelbert 296, 302
Dostoevsky, Fyodor 229
Douglas, Mary:
  Purity and Danger 169
Draesner, Ulrike 352–59
Droste-Hülshoff, Annette von 90
Ducis, Jean-François 349
Du Fu 311
Duhamel, Georges 300

Eberhard, Johann August 11
Ebermayer, Erich 319, 322
Ebner-Eschenbach, Marie von 93–94, 102 n. 48
  Ein Original 166–67
  Glaubenlos 93, 95–96, 98, 99
Eckermann, Johann Peter 76, 83
Eichendorff, Joseph von 90
Elias, Norbert 321
Eliot, George 251, 253–54
Elstun, Esther N. 138, 141, 143, 146, 147, 150 n. 29
Engels, Friedrich 52
Epictetus 20 n. 34
Erasmus, Desiderius 11, 31, 306
Erhard, Johann Benjamin 32
Ernst, Max 183
Eusebius 40 n. 72
Evans, Richard 168

Fechner, Gustav Theodor 106
Federman, Raymond 275
Feuchtwanger, Lion 322
Fichte, Johann Gottlieb 41 n. 99, 204
Flaubert, Gustave 229, 339
Fontane, Theodor 2–3, 252, 254
Forster, Georg 32
Foscolo, Ugo 57
  Last Letters of Jacopo Ortis 53, 54–57, 60, 61, 62, 64
Foucault, Michel 124–25, 126, 128
  The Birth of the Clinic 124
Franklin, Benjamin 27
Franz Joseph I, Emperor of Austria-Hungary 131, 155, 221, 228 n. 14
Freiligrath, Ferdinand 349
Freud, Sigmund 4, 89, 94, 104–07, 109, 110, 111–13, 115, 116, 117, 121, 140, 155, 168–69, 172, 186, 223
  Die Traumdeutung 105–06, 112, 140, 186, 286
Fried, Erich 263, 357
  Ein Soldat und ein Mädchen 270–72
Friedenthal, Richard 298

Friedrich, Hugo:
   Montaigne 340
Fricker, Miranda 179 n. 41
Friedrich III, Emperor of Germany 122
Friedrich Wilhelm III, King of Prussia 36

Gadamer, Hans-Georg 84, 258 n. 19
Galilei, Galileo 55, 318 n. 5
   Discorsi 311, 317
Gard, Roger Martin du 300
Gatens, Moira 123, 129, 130–31
Gecks, Johann Christian 30
Gelikman, Oleg 196 n. 24
George, Stefan 208, 212, 295 n. 40, 321, 322, 327, 329, 352, 354
Gibbon, Edward:
   The Decline and Fall of the Roman Empire 160
Gillot, Hendrik 172
Gilman, Sander 132
Glaeser, Ernst 319, 322
Göchhausen, Louise von 48, 51 n. 1
Goethe, Johann Wolfgang 11, 40 n. 74, 68–85, 191, 199, 211, 229, 338, 339, 341
   Die Leiden des jungen Werthers 52–67
   Faust I 42–51, 287
   Faust 80–81, 82
   Grenzen der Menschheit 78–79
   Italian journey 68–75
   Prometheus 76–78
   West-östlicher Divan 83, 199, 211
   Wilhelm Meisters Lehrjahre 72, 208
   Wilhelm Meisters theatralische Sendung 139–40
Goeze, Johann Melchior 16
Gombrich, Ernst 254
Goncourt, Edmond and Jules de 339
Gordon, Charles 153–54, 156, 158–59, 160
Görner, Rüdiger 348
Gramsci, Antonio 88, 92–93
Grassi, Gaetano 65 n. 18
Green, Dominic 162
Grillparzer, Franz 86, 99 n. 4, 229
Grimm, Jacob and Wilhelm:
   Deutsches Wörterbuch 216, 220
Gross, Kenneth 143
Grün, Anastasius 86
Gundling, Julius 102 n. 58
Guo Moruo 57, 60

Hadot, Ilsetraut 9
Hadot, Pierre 9–11, 14
Haeckel, Ernst 88
Hafiz 83
Hajek, Markus 121
Halm, Friedrich 86
Hamerling, Robert 98
Hardekopf, Ferdinand 185–86

Hartmann, Moritz 102 n. 58
Hauser, Otto 281
Haussmann, Raoul 182
Heartfield, John 182, 183, 186, 189
Hegel, Georg Wilhelm Friedrich 317
   Vorlesungen über die Ästhetik 167
Heine, Heinrich 1, 3, 58, 185, 311
Hella, Alzir 299, 308 n. 14
Hellingrath, Norbert von 199
Helmholtz, Hermann 104
Heraclitus 10, 247, 250
Herder, Johann Gottfried 34, 341, 342
Hermes, Johann Peter Job 29–30, 39 n. 45
Hermlin, Stefan 320
Hesse, Max René 322
Hicks, William 153
Hiller, Kurt 185
Himmler, Heinrich 324
Hindenburg, Paul von 186
Hirschfeld, Magnus 321
Hitler, Adolf 302, 323, 324, 340
Hobbes, Thomas 129–30
Höch, Hannah 182, 183
Hoddis, Jakob van 185
Hoffmann, Ernst Theodor Amadeus 1
Hofmannsthal, Hugo von 87, 138, 144, 244 n. 52, 282, 292–93, 294 n. 25, 299
Hölderlin, Friedrich 64, 199, 200, 201, 203, 206, 208–12, 212 n. 11, 327
Höllriegel, Arnold, *see* Bermann, Richard Arnold
Homer 229
   Odyssey 333, 334
Horace 15, 34, 352, 356
Horkheimer, Max:
   Dialektik der Aufklärung 90, 335
Horn, Christoph 10, 14
Huebsch, Ben 306
Hugh of St Victor 342, 345
Hugo, Victor 339
Hülsen, Hans von:
   Den alten Göttern zu 321
Humboldt, Alexander von 94
Humboldt, Wilhelm von 11
Huyssen, Andreas 168

Ibsen, Henrik 53, 128, 174

Jacobowski, Ludwig 280
Jacobs, Carol 197 n. 35
James, Henry 254
James, William 104, 106, 107–11, 112, 114, 115, 116, 117
Janet, Pierre 104
Janitschek, Maria 171
Jaques, Eliot 73–74
Jean Paul, *see* Richter, Jean Paul
Jesus 32, 336, 345

Jiang Guangci 60, 63, 66 n. 50
   The Young Wanderer 53, 60–63, 64
Joël, Ernst 188
John, Robin 152
Johst, Hanns 324
Joseph II, Emperor of Austria 129
Joyce, James 183, 333, 339
Jung, Carl Gustav 140, 142–43
Justin Martyr 40 n. 69

Kafka, Franz 1, 3, 4–5, 82, 169, 181, 182, 214–28, 229–44, 245–61, 262–78
   'Auf der Galerie' 218–19
   'Beim Bau der chinesischen Mauer' 220, 250–51
   'Beschreibung eines Kampfes' 250
   Betrachtung 218, 224
   Das Schloss 229–30, 233, 239–41, 248–50, 253
   'Das Urteil' 218, 236, 246, 253–54, 264
   'Der Dorfschullehrer' 255–56
   'Der Jäger Gracchus' 235–36, 238
   'Der Kübelreiter' 230, 235, 238
   Der Process 169, 181, 215–16, 218, 227 n. 11, 245–49, 252–53, 263–66
   Der Verschollene 4, 18, 169, 229
   Die Verwandlung 169, 246, 252
   'Die Vorüberlaufenden' 218
   'Die Wahrheit über Sancho Pansa' 233–35, 238, 271
   'Ein altes Blatt' 220–21, 226, 227 n. 13
   'Ein Bericht für eine Akademie' 215
   'Ein Besuch im Bergwerk' 217–18, 220, 224, 227 n. 4, 227 n. 13
   'Ein Brudermord' 218
   'Eine kaiserliche Botschaft' 219, 250
   Ein Landarzt (collection) 214–28, 235
   'Ein Landarzt' (story) 219, 230, 235–38, 240, 250, 274
   'Schakale und Araber' 215
   'Zerstreutes Hinausschaun' 218
   Zürau 'aphorisms' 221–23, 230, 233, 238–39, 241, 243 n. 28
Kandel, Erich 105
Kang Youwei 57
Kant, Immanuel 11, 27, 28–29, 30–31, 32, 36, 38 n. 24, 26, 33, 109, 111
Kantorowicz, Alfred 320
Karl August, Duke of Sachsen-Weimar 70
Kauf, Robert 214, 227 n. 5, 227 n. 8
Kautsky, Minna 89, 102 n. 48
Kent, Clark 68
Kepler, Johannes:
   Astronomia nova 95
Kierkegaard, Søren 222, 228 n. 233, 247–48, 256, 258 n. 24
Kitchener, Horatio Herbert 153–56, 158, 162–63
Kleist, Heinrich von 229
Klimt, Gustav 142

Klopstock, Robert 233
Konuk, Kader 333
Korff, Hermann August 56
Koselleck, Reinhart 341
Kracauer, Siegfried 182, 189–91, 195
   'Das Ornament der Masse' 190
   'Die Photographie' 189–90
Kraus, Karl 192, 352
Kulka, Otto Dov 263, 275

Lacoue-Labarthe, Philippe 213 n. 21
Langer, Lawrence 262, 275
Latour, Bruno 116, 117
Latzko, Andreas 298
Laval, Pierre 302–03
Lear, Jonathan 105, 107, 112, 113–14, 115, 117
Leibniz, Gottfried Wilhelm 12, 31, 33, 34, 79
Leichsenring, Falk 112–13, 115
Lenau, Nikolaus 98
Lenin, Vladimir 188–89
Le Rider, Jacques 138, 142
Lessing, Gotthold Ephraim 4, 7–22, 26
Lewis, C. S. 335, 336
Liang Qichao 57
Lichtenstein, Alfred 185
Louis XVI, King of France 305
Lovenjoul, Vicomte Spoelberch de 304
Lubojatzki, Franz 102 n. 58
Lucian of Samosata 142
Lucretius 34, 94
Luden, Heinrich 51 n. 13
Ludendorff, Erich Friedrich Wilhelm 187
Ludwig, Emil 299
Lukács, Georg 56, 89, 338
Luther, Martin 16, 31, 208
Lybeck, Marti 175, 176

Machiavelli, Niccolò 341
Mackay, John Henry 321
Macron, Emmanuel 64 n. 3
Maior, Georg 34
Mancinelli, Antonio 34
Mann, Bonnie 177, 180 n. 68
Mann, Erika 324, 325, 326
Mann, Heinrich 344
Mann, Klaus 319–32
   Der Vulkan 319, 324, 326–30
   Flucht in den Norden 323, 324–26, 330
Mann, Thomas 82, 322, 324
Marx, Karl 41 n. 108, 116, 258 n. 19
Masereel, Frans 300
Maurois, André 300
May, Karl 154
Mayer, Hans 320, 329, 330
Mazzini, Giuseppe 54
Meier, Georg Friedrich 21 n. 43, 22 n. 54

Meinecke, Friedrich 341, 342
Meissner, Alfred 102 n. 58
Meister Eckhart 248–49, 256
Mendelssohn, Moses 7, 18
Michelangelo, *see* Buonarotti, Michelangelo di
Miller, J. Hillis 263
Mohr, Ludwig Weyprecht 30
Montaigne, Michel 11, 40 n. 83, 82, 299, 301, 305–07, 310 n. 44, 310 n. 45, 334, 343–45
Moreau, Gustave 142
Moritz, Karl Philipp 1
Morton Stanley, Henry 152
Möser, Justus 341
Mozart, Wolfgang Amadeus 92
Muhammad Ahmad al-Mahdi 152–53, 154, 155, 158–61
Müller, Heiner 349
Müller-Seidel, Walter 122, 129
Murnau, Friedrich Wilhelm 81
Mussolini, Benito 302

Nadler, Josef 87
Nägele, Rainer 194–95
Napoleon, *see* Bonaparte, Napoleon
Negri, Ada 280
Neher, Caspar 194–95
Neillands, Robin 163
Nestroy, Johann Nepomuk 339
Neurohr, Johann Anton 31, 33, 36, 39 n. 61
Newton, Isaac 12
 Philosophia naturalis 95
Nicolai, Friedrich 18
Nightingale, Florence 122
Nietzsche, Friedrich 11, 116, 172, 176, 246, 247, 249, 251, 253, 254, 255, 256, 258 n. 19, 258 n. 21
Nisbet, Hugh Barr 22 n. 64
Noailles, Anna de 301
North, Paul 228 n. 24
Novalis 198–99, 203–04, 206–08

Oberholzer, Otto 144, 150 n. 28, 150 n. 35, 150 n. 47
Oeser, Adam Friedrich 73
Osiris 27
Otto, Rudolf 90
Ovid 311, 320

Pannwitz, Rudolf 200, 211
Parmenides 10
Parr, James A. 232, 240
Pasha, Emin 152, 154
Pasley, Malcolm 227 n. 10
Paul, St 32–33, 34
Pecchio, Giuseppe 54
Pernerstorfer, Engelbert 121
Petrarch, Francesco 11, 55
Petronius:
 Satyricon 334

Pez, Bernhard 34
Pfister, Manfred 349, 352, 353, 356, 358
Photius 33
Pindar 199–200
Pius VII 86
Pius IX 95
Plant, Richard 323
Platen, August von 321
Plato 12, 13, 37 n. 2, 247
Plutarch 55, 344
Poe, Edgar Allan 188
Pollock, John 162
Prawer, Siegbert Salomon 3
Proust, Marcel 333, 339, 346 n. 27
Pyper, Michael 232, 240

Rabbow, Paul 9
Ramboux, Johann Anton 23
Ranke, Leopold von 340
Ratschky, Josef Franz 2
Rausch, Albert 322
Reichert, Klaus 352
Reimarus, Elise 7
Reinhold, Karl Leonhard 39 n. 57
Reisiger, Hans 280
Reisinger, Roman 280
Reiss, Timothy J. 54
Rhodes, Cecil 160
Richter, Jean Paul 90
Ricoeur, Paul 116–17, 258 n. 19
Rilke, Rainer Maria 292, 294 n. 37, 327, 357
Rimbaud, Arthur 281, 285–87, 289, 290
Robert, Marthe 230, 239
Robertson, Ritchie 116, 123, 128, 138, 141, 142, 166, 167, 169, 181, 227 n. 2, 227 n. 8, 229, 230, 234, 237, 240–41, 256, 258 n. 24, 335
Röhm, Ernst 323
Roland, Jeanne-Marie 102 n. 48
Rolland, Romain 89, 296, 297, 298, 300, 301
Romains, Jules 300, 305, 309 n. 36
Rosegger, Peter 102 n. 56, 338
 Das ewige Licht 93, 95, 96–98
Rosmäßler, Johann August 25
Rossetti, Dante Gabriel 142
Roth, Joseph 299, 303, 308 n. 14, 309 n. 26
Rousseau, Jean-Jacques 20 n. 38, 27, 31
Rowland, Susan 146–47
Rudigier, Franz Joseph 100 n. 6
Ruskin, John 251, 253–54
Rysselberghe, Théo van 281

Saar, Ferdinand von:
 Innocens 93–94, 95, 96, 98
Sacher-Masoch, Leopold von 102 n. 58
Said, Edward 82, 333
Saint-Simon, Louis Duc de 337, 342

Sainte-Beuve, Charles Augustin 288
Salmusmüller, Georg Wilhelm 35
Scherer, Stefan 138, 139, 140, 141, 143, 146, 147,
    150 n. 41
Schiaparelli, Giovanni 95
Schickele, René 185
Schikaneder, Emanuel 92
Schiller, Friedrich 11, 48, 50, 53, 83, 199, 203
    Kabale und Liebe 338
Schirach, Baldur von 322
Schlegel, August Wilhelm 203, 205–06, 208, 357
Schlegel, Friedrich 198–99, 203, 205–08, 362 n. 58
Schlemmer, Oskar 184
Schlüter, Christoph B. 40 n. 65
Schmid, C. C. E. 41 n. 99
Schmidt, Arwed 329–30
Schmitz-Emans, Monika 241 n. 2
Schneeberger, Franz Julius 102 n. 58
Schnitzer, Eduard, *see* Pasha, Emin
Schnitzler, Arthur 113, 116, 120–35, 168
    Jugend in Wien 120, 122
    'Londoner Briefe' 121–22
    Professor Bernhardi 122–35
Schnitzler, Johann 120
Schnitzler, Julius 121
Schnorr von Carolsfeld, Veit 25
Schoen, Ernst 203, 211
Scholem, Gershom 196 n. 5, 198, 210, 212 n. 8,
    212 n. 10, 214–15, 217, 226, 227 n. 5–6, 251, 279
Schwartz, Frederic J. 196 n. 4
Schwarzenbach, Annemarie 325
Secchi, Angelo 95
Seidel, Gotthold Emanuel Friedrich 39 n. 65
Shaftesbury, Anthony Ashley Cooper, third earl of 11
Shakespeare, William 53, 82, 208, 311, 337, 338, 343,
    348–62
    Hamlet 53, 348, 349
    Sonnets 349, 351–59
Shamdasani, Sonu 140, 142–43
Siemsen, Hans:
    Die Geschichte des Hitlerjungen Adolf Goers 322
Silberer, Herbert 142
Silvestre, Paul-Armand 281
Simenon, Georges 182
Sisyphus 74
Slatin, Rudolf 154–55, 157
Socrates 8–10, 11–13, 16, 18, 19, 22 n. 59, 40 n. 69,
    79, 247
Soliman El-Khalifa Abdullahi 160
Sophocles 199–201, 209, 211
Spinoza, Baruch 31, 95
Staël, Germaine de 53
Stalin, Joseph 300, 302, 324
Steiner, Rudolf 235
Steinert, Christiane 112–13, 115
Stendhal 339, 341, 343

Stifter, Adalbert 90–92, 98
Stobaeus 41 n. 91
Strich, Fritz:
    Goethe und die Weltliteratur 340
Strindberg, August 229
Strowski, Fortunat 306
Sulzer, Johann Georg 11
Sun Yatsen 57
Svoboda, Adalbert 102 n. 56

Tantalus 74
Tasso, Torquato 74
Thales 10
Thiess, Frank 322
Thomasius, Christian 21 n. 44
Thomé, Horst 120–21
Tieck, Ludwig 357
Tischbein, Johann Heinrich Wilhelm 71
Tobin, Robert 176
Toscanini, Arturo 302
Trask, Willard 335
Tucholsky, Kurt:
    Deutschland, Deutschland über alles 186–87, 189

Ulrichs, Karl Heinrich 176

Valéry, Paul 300, 301, 303
Venuti, Lawrence 350
Verhaeren, Émile 280, 281, 290–92
Verlaine, Paul 281, 282–84, 286, 287, 289, 290
Vico, Giambattista 334, 342–43
Villon, François 311, 316
Virgil 337
    Aeneid 104, 111–12, 113, 334
Vogel, Bruno 319
Voß, Johann Heinrich 25, 41 n. 111, 200, 208
Vulpius, Christiane 83

Wagner, Richard 64
Wainwright, Rufus 351
Walker, Matthew 115
Wedekind, Frank:
    Frühlings Erwachen 168
Weininger, Otto:
    Geschlecht und Charakter 169
Weiß, Ernst 299, 308 n. 14
Weißbach, Richard 198
Whitman, Walt 280
White, Hayden 335
Wieland, Christoph Martin 11, 348
Wilhelm II, Emperor of Germany 186–87
Williams, Raymond 87, 89
Wilson, Robert 351
Winckelmann, Johann Joachim 73, 321
Winnicott, Donald 116
Wistrich, Robert S. 137

Wolzogen, Ernst von:
   Das dritte Geschlecht 166
Woolf, Virginia 333, 339
Wordsworth, William 58, 75, 351
Wundt, Wilhelm 104
Wyttenbach, Johann Hugo 23–41

Xi Jinping 52, 63–64

Yu Dafu 60
   Sinking 53, 58–60, 62, 63, 64

Zeus 43, 130
Zola, Émile 176, 339
Zozulia, Yefim 188–89
Zweig, Friderike 296, 302, 304
Zweig, Stefan 279–95, 296–310, 344
   Die Welt von Gestern 279, 280, 297, 298, 302

www.ingramcontent.com/pod-product-compliance
Lightning Source LLC
Chambersburg PA
CBHW080834230426
43665CB00021B/2840